The
WORST-CASE SCENARIO
Survival Handbook:
EXTREME
Junior Edition

The
WORST-CASE SCENARIO
Survival Handbook:
EXTREME
Junior Edition

By David Borgenicht and Justin Heimberg

Illustrated by Chuck Gonzales

chronicle books · san francisco

A WORD OF WARNING: It's always important to keep safety in mind. If you're careless, even the tamest activities can result in injury. As such, all readers are urged to act with caution, ask for adult advice, obey all laws, and respect the rights of others when handling any Worst-Case Scenario.

Copyright © 2008 by Quirk Productions, Inc.

A QUIRK PACKAGING BOOK.
All rights reserved.

Worst-Case Scenario and The Worst-Case Scenario Survival Handbook are trademarks of Quirk Productions, Inc.

Book design by Lynne Yeamans.
Typeset in Adobe Garamond, Blockhead, and Imperfect.
Illustrations by Chuck Gonzales.
Manufactured in China.

Library of Congress Cataloging-in-Publication Data
Borgenicht, David.
  The worst-case scenario survival handbook : extreme junior edition / by David Borgenicht and Justin Heimberg ; Illustrated by Chuck Gonzales.
      p. cm.
  ISBN 978-0-8118-6568-5
  1. Social skills in children—Juvenile literature. 2. Socialization—Juvenile literature. 3. Children—Humor—Juvenile literature. I. Heimberg, Justin. II. Gonzales, Chuck. III. Title.
  HQ783.B663 2008
  613.6'9—dc22
  2008014580

10 9 8 7 6 5 4 3

Chronicle Books LLC
680 Second Street, San Francisco, California 94107

www.chroniclekids.com

The publisher, packager, and authors disclaim any liability from any injury that may result from the use, proper or improper, of the information contained in this book.

CONTENTS

Welcome to Team Extreme

You may have heard the saying "If life hands you lemons, make lemonade." That's great, but what do you do when those lemons are being handed to you by a 400-pound (181-kg) gorilla? This guide will prepare you for just that sort of scenario, and it'll give you hundreds of other tips to help you become the ultimate extreme adventurer.

And when we say extreme, we mean *EXTREME!* In capital letters. And italics. With an exclamation point. Yes, the first day of school is *extremely* uncomfortable, and a wedgie from a bully can be *extremely* painful. But we're talking about a whole different level of *extreme.* We're talking pythons, tarantulas, sandstorms, piranhas, sharks, quicksand, elephant stampedes, mountain lions, tigers, and bears, oh my!

When faced with these kinds of extreme situations, extreme action must be taken. FAST! There's no time to sit down and draw a flow chart. No time to phone a friend or ask your parents for advice. It's all about *you*, and what *you* know, right then, right away.

But don't freak out. The information in this book spans the globe, across the seven continents, from ocean to desert to forest to tundra. No unsafe place is safe from our extreme survival know-how. So whether you're going on an adventure in Africa, the Arctic, or merely in your imagination, you're covered. Just stay calm. Surviving an extreme worst-case scenario is as easy as 1, 2, 3 . . . (OK, sometimes you might need 4, 5, 6.)

But even if you don't have plans to go on safari or explore the tundra any time soon, you'll still find this book packed with interesting (and sometimes surprising!) facts. Did you know, for example, that the most dangerous animal in Africa is actually the mosquito? Or that lightning really *can* strike the same place twice? And did you know that tarantulas can shoot their hairs like tiny darts? You *will* know after you read this guide.

Read, and dare we say, study up. Commit these tips to memory, because a good extreme adventurer is an informed extreme adventurer.

So turn the page and begin your initiation into Team Extreme. When you're done reading, you'll have everything you need to take on the world's worst (not to mention lots of cool information to impress your friends with). Good luck on your journeys.

Be safe. Be smart. Be extreme.

—*David Borgenicht and Justin Heimberg*

CHAPTER 1

How to Survive at Sea

How to Fend Off a Shark

Few images spark as much fear in swimmers as a shark fin slicing through the water. Never mind that deer kill 300 times more people a year than sharks! (See *Oh Deer!*, page 38.) But even though shark attacks are *very* rare, it's good to know what to do if Jaws drops in on your swim.

1 Stay calm.

This is sort of a given. It wouldn't be very good advice to tell you to panic and scream like a baby, would it? The point is, just because you see a shark does not mean it will attack. Signs a shark may be getting just a little deadly include it swimming in increasingly smaller circles and rubbing its belly against the seafloor.

2 Hit it!

If a shark comes at you, you have just one choice: Fight back. Fight dirty. Go for the shark's most sensitive spots: its eyes and gill openings. Punch, poke, and kick. This is a pro-wrestling match, and you're the bad guy.

3 A boxer never quits.

Keep on hitting the shark—jab it over and over in its sensitive spots. If you can convince your toothy opponent you're too much trouble, it may look elsewhere for its lunch. After all, you wouldn't want to eat a peanut butter and jelly sandwich that slapped you across the face, would you?

4 Get away.

Your best bet is to get on dry land, where Jaws can't follow (at least not before another million years of evolution). If you're in too deep (like if you're scuba diving), try hiding in weeds or against the seafloor, where it'll be harder for the shark to get to you.

Real or Ridiculous?

Which of these sharks are real?

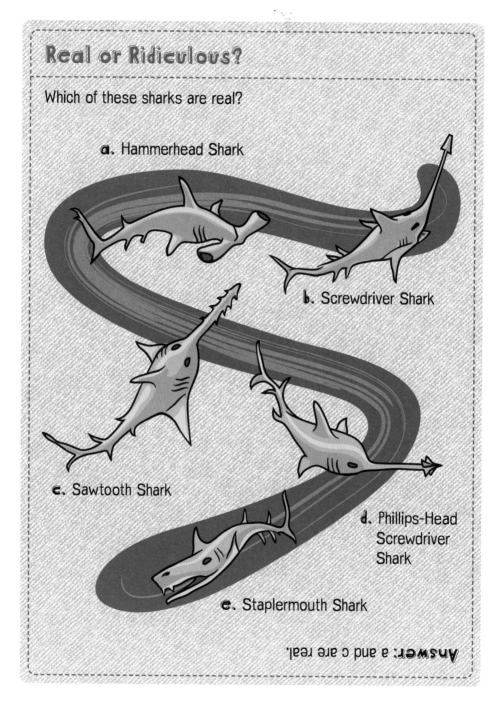

a. Hammerhead Shark

b. Screwdriver Shark

c. Sawtooth Shark

d. Phillips-Head Screwdriver Shark

e. Staplermouth Shark

Answer: a and c are real.

How to Build a Raft After a Shipwreck

At first, the idea of being shipwrecked on a remote island seems pretty cool—endless days frolicking on the beach. Then again, there's no air conditioning or video games. Here's how to get back to the real world.

1 Go logging.

Clear a path into the interior of the island and find two logs about your height and ten logs about twice your height. OK, lumberjack, now lug those babies back toward the shore. Hey, no one said this was going to be easy.

2 Live on the edge.

Place the two short logs at the edge of the water at low tide. This is important: You wouldn't want to build the world's greatest raft, complete with swimming pool and mini golf, only to realize you can't get it in the water. Lay the longer logs on top of and across the shorter ones so they extend a bit past both short logs.

③ The rest is easy—*knot!*

Here's the hard part. You need to tie the logs together. Seaweed or vines are probably your best bet for string substitutes if you don't have actual string. Securely tie the logs together with long lengths of vine wrapped in figure eights and as many knots as you can.

④ Surf's up, ship out.

When the tide comes in, the water will flow under and around the raft. The raft will start to float, and you can push it out into the water. Now all you need to do is survive in the world's biggest wave pool (see *How to Survive When You're Adrift at Sea*, page 18). Good luck!

Island Inventions
(in Decreasing Order of Genius)

Surviving is all about being resourceful and creative. What would *you* make if you were stranded on a deserted island?

Tepee using logs
and parachute

Shiny coin fishing
lure and thorn hook

Palm leaf
water collector

Coconut basketball

Flounder hat

How to Survive When You're Adrift at Sea

If you're ever in a shipwreck, you'll need your wits, your strength, and your nerves of steel. Oh, and a lifeboat would help! Once you're adrift in the great deep blue, use these tips to steer yourself to safety.

1 Collect rainwater.

Supply your boat or raft with things that can function as containers: bottles, hollow coconuts, your World's Greatest Grandkid mug, anything. Let them sit in the rain to collect water. Then put lids on your containers (you can make lids out of whatever is handy) so you can store the water and avoid spills. Drink small sips, not big gulps, so your body can absorb the water.

2 No loose ends.

Tie your water containers to you or the boat to make sure you don't lose them. In fact, you may want to tie *yourself* to the boat so you don't lose *you*.

3 Don't work on your tan.

Act like a vampire at the beach and cover your skin as much as possible to avoid sunburn and sunstroke.

4 Land ho!

If you're in a busy area, you might be found by another ship. If not, keep your eye out for land. Even if you can't see land, there are signs you're nearing it:

- **Birds.** They'll fly back to an island at night, so follow their lead.
- **Driftwood.** If it's floating, land's approaching.
- **Murky water.** Muddy water means a river's mouth may be near—land could be just over the horizon.

5 Shore thing.

Choose a sandy beach over a more dangerous rocky or coral shore. If necessary, drift along the shore until you find the perfect place to land.

What's Your Worst Case?

Being stranded in a sea of snot?

or

Being stranded in a sea of vomit?

How to Avoid a Tsunami

Rearrange the letters in the word *tsunami,* and you can spell "I am nuts," which is what you are if you stay near the ocean when one of these monster waves approaches. Learn the warning signs so you can be far away when the ten-story-high waves come crashing down.

1 Hey, wasn't there an ocean here just now?
If the water level suddenly drops or rises for no clear reason, that's one sign of a coming tsunami. Or maybe a giant sea creature just took a big swallow. Either way, take the water movement as a cue to get your butt out of the water—and away from the beach altogether.

2 Water-quake!
Tsunamis are caused by underwater earthquakes. If you're on the shore and the ground begins to shake or you hear a low continuous roar, it's time to get going. Don't stop to grab your flippers.

3 Up, up, and away.

Get yourself off the beach and up to a high place, like the peak of the local mountain or the top floor of a tall building.

4 Aah—aaah—*tsu*!!

Like sneezes, the waves of a tsunami can keep on coming. Stay high and dry till things calm down. You don't want to end up soaked.

What Would You Do?

You are on a sailboat in a small harbor when you hear a loud roar and the sea level toward the shore seems to have dropped. What should you do?

a. Take your boat far into open water.

b. Stay where you are and lower the sail.

c. Sail near other boats—safety in numbers.

d. Abandon ship and dive to the magical undersea land of Zarnia, where the water nymphs and naiads can protect you.

Answer: a. Take your boat far into open water. Oftentimes, tsunamis are not even felt in deep water.

My Hero!

In 2004, a ten-year-old British girl named Tilly Smith, who had studied tsunamis in geography class, saw the receding ocean on Mai Khao Beach in northern Phuket, Thailand, and became a hero. She and her parents warned others on the beach, which was evacuated safely.

How to Treat a Jellyfish Sting

Imagine a mop made of stingers brushing across your body, and you'll have an idea of what it feels like to get stung by a jellyfish. The good news is that with the right recipe, you can at least lessen the zing of that sting.

1 Please pass the *salt* water.

Freshwater's the way to go when brushing your teeth, shampooing, and just about everything else. But with

a jellyfish sting, freshwater will actually make the sting feel worse, because it washes away salts that help lessen the sting. Rinse the sting with seawater.

2 Break out the vinegar.

White vinegar, to be more specific. Why treat your wound like a salad? Because of *nematocysts*. Nematocysts are tiny structures in the cells of jellyfish that deliver the sting by firing tiny "darts" of venom. The acid in the vinegar deactivates these beasts. Bottom line: The vinegar takes the sting out. (No need to add croutons.)

3 Remove any tentacles.

Lift, don't scrape, any tentacles off using a stick or glove. If you scrape them off, you'll cause more stings to occur. You already have an entire Braille alphabet of stings on you, so there's no need for more.

4 To pee or not to pee? That is the question.

Some say *peeing* on a jellyfish sting will ease the pain. However, an Australian study showed that it actually caused more, not less, firing of nematocysts. So, it's best not to pee on yourself or a friend. What a relief!

How to Navigate by the Stars

Centuries ago, sailors used the stars to keep their ships on course at night. And guess what? Those stars are still twinkling, so you can use them to figure out which way is which, whether you're at sea or on land.

1 Take a dip.

The North Star (also known as Polaris) isn't the brightest star, so we use other stars to locate it, like the stars of the Big Dipper. You can't miss the Big Dipper—it looks like a big ladle that's scooping up some star soup.

2 Use your pointers.

Focus on the two stars that form the far end of the ladle's cup. These stars are called "pointers" because they point to the North Star. Just draw an imaginary line through the pointer stars and out across the sky, as shown on the right. The next star you'll see is the North Star.

3 Catch a falling North Star.

OK, stargazer. You've found the North Star. Now imagine that the North Star fell straight to the ground. Go find that fallen star. That's where North is. Now you can figure out south, east, and west—and head in the direction you want to go!

BE AWARE • If you're in the Southern Hemisphere, you can navigate by finding the Southern Cross, which is in the southern part of the sky. Either that, or just turn this page upside down and hope for the best.

Note: The Big Dipper might look like this, or it could be upside down in the sky. Look for it both ways!

Real or Ridiculous?

Which of these constellations are real?

a. Canes Venatici (Hunting Dogs)
b. Ursa Major (The Great Bear)
c. Pantus Cleanus (The Clean Slacks)
d. Castoris Bloatus (The Bloated Beaver)
e. Piscis Austrinus (The Southern Fish)

Answer: a, b, and e are real. Note: The Big Dipper is actually a part of the constellation Ursa Major. Can you spot it in the tail?

CHAPTER 2

How to Survive in the Mountains

How to Survive an Erupting Volcano

A volcanic eruption is basically a mountain throwing up. Things have been gurgling around inside for a while, and suddenly—SPEW!—a mess of liquid, solids, and gas is vomited out in a fiery mess. And this stuff really burns. Here's how to make sure that spew doesn't get on yew.

1 Look out—it's raining rocks.

When you think of an erupting volcano, you picture red hot lava flows dripping off a mountain like melting ice cream. But along with the rivers of fire, there are rocks being spit high into the air. If you're anywhere near a mountain that's blowing chunks, take cover if you can, and roll into a ball to protect your head.

Cool Volcano Words

aa (ah-ah): That is not a typo. And it's not you screaming either. *Aa* is a Hawaiian word for a type of lava with a rough surface of hard lava fragments.

caldera (call-DARE-uh): The crater formed by a volcanic explosion. (The mouth of the vomiting volcano.)

kipuka (kip-OOK-uh): A Hawaiian word for an area (like a hill) surrounded by lava flow, like an island in a sea of lava.

magma: Molten rock that is underground.

pillow lava: Blob-shaped formations of cooled lava that form when a lava flow enters the water.

② Head for the hills!

Oh wait, the hills are on fire. That's not such a good idea. If the lava is headed your way, get out of its path as fast as you can. If you can put a ditch—or better yet, an entire valley—between you and the flow, so much the better.

③ Get inside.

Boiling lava on the ground, rocks raining from the sky? Time to seek shelter. Get inside—anywhere will do—as fast as you can, and try to get to a high story. Close all doors and windows. Don't open the door, not even if the lava knocks politely.

④ Up, up, and away.

Another nasty thing about a volcanic eruption is the mix of deadly gases that are belched forth. Carbon dioxide gas is the worst of 'em, and because it is denser than air, it will collect near the ground, so start climbing—stairs, furniture, whatever will keep your head above the murk.

How to Survive an Avalanche

Imagine being hit by a snowball as big as an ocean liner. That's what it feels like to be in an avalanche, and it's clearly a fight you want to avoid. But if Mother Nature throws the first snowball, staying on top of it (literally) is your best shot at riding to safety.

1 Brace yourself for impact.

If an avalanche is heading your way, don't let your jaw drop in shock—keep your mouth closed tight so you won't choke on snow. If you have ski poles, drop them (they can be dragged away, pulling you down), and crouch behind a tree or find shelter ASAP.

2 Ride the wave.

As the avalanche starts to close in around you, stay on top of the sliding snow by swimming in a freestyle (crawl) motion, using your arms and legs to keep you on the surface. It's the ultimate in bodysurfing.

> **BE AWARE** • Never hike alone in avalanche country, and always carry an emergency beacon—a signaling device that will help rescuers find you if you are buried under snow.

3 When in doubt, spit.

If you end up in the middle of a snow cone, you need to find the surface. If you can't tell which end is up, dig a hole around you and spit. Your loogie will head downhill and give you an idea which way is up. Cool, huh?

4 Dig up.

Dig toward open air. Dig quickly, or someone may discover you in 2,000 years in the ice and say, "Wow, look at that perfectly preserved expression of panic!"

Avalanches to Imagine

Which kind of avalanche would you *least* like to be in?

- Soccer balls
- Pudding
- Fingernail clippings
- Thumbtacks
- Donuts
- Belly button lint
- Spray cheese
- Marbles
- Worms

How to Avoid a Bear Attack

For the most part, bears just want to live an easy country life. However, in certain situations, they can get testy. Like when they're protecting their cubs, feasting on deer, or when their houses have been broken into and vandalized by little blond girls who eat their porridge. Here's how to show bears the respect they deserve.

1 Sing out loud, sing out strong.

You don't want to freak out a bear by surprising it. As you hike, make noise by talking, singing a little forest karaoke, or by having a fascinating conversation with your echo. You could also fasten bells to your shoes or hat. Any sound will clue the bear in that you're coming, so *it* can choose to avoid *you*. That's the best-case scenario!

2 Keep your distance.

If you spot a bear, hold very still, and wait for the bear to go on its merry way. If you can, back away s-l-o-w-l-y to get more distance from the bear.

3. Know who you're dealing with.

Check if the bear is black or brown. Black bears are the most common in North America, but if you're in western North America, you might encounter a brown bear (like the grizzly or Kodiak). Coat colors can vary, though, so if you hike in a region with both black and brown bears, learn all the ways to tell the difference before you head out.

4. Play tricks.

If the bear is a black bear, and it's starting to charge you from afar, wave your arms and make noise—the bear will think you're bigger than you are and will back off. If it's a brown bear, curl up and lie still—playing dead will hopefully cause the bear to lose interest.

Oh Deer!

The most dangerous animal in America? The deer. That's right. Cute little Bambi is responsible for around 1.5 million car collisions in the Unites States alone every year, according to the Insurance Institute for Highway Safety. A total of 150 of these crashes are fatal for humans, and the horns-meeting-headlights destruction causes more than one billion dollars in property damage annually.

But the road isn't the only place a deer can be dangerous. As our neighborhoods start to take over the deer's homes, deer are losing their natural fear of people. During mating season (November–December), there have been an increasing number of deer attacks on humans by rambunctious bucks. With sharp antlers and club-like hooves, deer can be vicious.

Tell your parents to use the following tips when driving in deer country:

- Pay attention to deer-crossing signs and drive slowly when you see them.
- Be aware that deer are most active between the hours of 6 and 9 p.m.
- Do not attempt to sing a duet with a deer or any other woodland creature.

How to Survive a Lightning Storm on a Mountainside

Have you seen those "storm chasers" on TV? Those crazy folks who drive into the eyes of hurricanes? Do *not* try that at home! But even if you're not chasing storms, sometimes *they'll* chase *you*. Here's how to win this game of tag.

1 Stormwatch.

You love nature—if there are a few black clouds overhead, a little torrential downpour, so what? Lightning, however, is a different story, and you need to be aware of the signs when a storm is so close, you could be stuck:

- **A buzzing sound.** This is the sound of static electricity caused by tiny particles called electrons dancing about.
- **A sudden gravity-defying change in your hairstyle.** Your new 'do is the result of electricity in the air and in your hair!
- **A halo of light around people or trees.** No, you're not seeing things—well, actually you are,

but it's a real phenomenon known as "St. Elmo's Fire." The high voltage in the air reacts with the gas around objects and people to create the glow. Pretty cool.

2 Do the math.

Arithmetic may be the last thing on your mind at a time like this, but a little division can help you figure out how close to you the storm is. When you see lightning, count the number of seconds until you hear thunder. Then divide by five. That's how far away the storm is in miles. Get to a safe place immediately if the thunder snaps,

crackles, or pops less than 30 seconds after the lightning. A storm even 6 miles away is within lightning-strike range. (It doesn't have to be raining on you for lightning to find you!)

3 Heavy metal?
Take off backpacks with metal frames and any jewelry. That navel piercing makes your belly button a bull's-eye. Tall things and metal objects are what lightning likes. That's why telephone poles aren't good hiking buddies.

Real or Ridiculous?

Which of the following are *real* effects of being struck by lightning? Which are *ridiculous*?

- You can turn the lights on and off by blinking.
- Your popcorn starts to pop before you put the bag in the microwave.
- Your hair is dark and curly (but it used to be blond and straight).
- You now sneeze the sound of thunder.
- You have a magnetic personality (literally).

Answer: Of course, *all* of these are ridiculous!

4 Gimme shelter (the right kind).

If you're in the forest and there are trees all around you, choose the shortest one and crouch under it, so you're the shortest thing in the area. If a tree has a lightning scar (usually a vertical patch that's been cut out of the tree or is covered in new, lighter bark), stay away— lightning *can* actually strike the same place twice. Stay away from isolated trees, metal fences, and bodies of water. All of these can attract lightning strikes.

How to Escape from a Mountain Lion

Ah, the peaceful sounds of the mountainside—birds calling, the wind in the trees, the low growl of a mountain lion—uh-oh. Here's how to stay safe in cougar country.

1 Don't be a copycat.

When you're near mountain lions (also called cougars and pumas), don't be a copycat; if you don't do like the big cats do, you'll be less likely to meet one. Don't hike at dusk or dawn (when they're on the prowl). If you see scratch marks on the trees, don't think, "Time to sharpen my fingernails." And definitely don't kill and eat a deer.

2 Run away? Not today.

Not to sound like the annoying lifeguard, but upon sighting a mountain lion, please do not run. If you run, it is likely to chase you. It's got four legs to your two. It's a lot faster than you. Don't find out the hard way.

3 **Grow up.**

You want to appear like a big ferocious animal so the lion doesn't think you're some easy-to-chomp little morsel. Look as big as you can. Stand up straight. Flex those muscles! Wave your arms over your head. Spread out your jacket like a king cobra. Bare your teeth and make some noise, y'all!

④ Back up.

If your tough-guy act doesn't petrify the puma, then you need to make the first move to break up this unhealthy relationship. Standing tall, slowly back away from the mountain lion.

⑤ Throw up.

This lion is not getting the hint; instead of walking away, he's stalking today. He's looking intently at you and crouching. You need to make it clear that you're not defenseless. Pick up some stones and toss them at the lion. Hard.

⑥ Protect your neck.

If the lion pounces, do not curl up to protect yourself. Mountain lions like to bite the back of the neck. Stay upright and maneuver to keep your neck away from the lion—kind of like how you'd avoid turning your back to a bully who likes to give wedgies. And yeah, a mountain lion neck bite is a *little* different from a wedgie, but you get the idea!

How to Go to the Bathroom in the Woods

Mountain lions, avalanches, volcanoes—all formidable foes. But what's the #1 wilderness worry? It's going #2.

1 Find your magic spot.

Pick a potty spot behind a tree or rock for privacy, far from the trail. This isn't a spectator sport. Stay at least 100 feet (30 m) away from any water source.

2 Dig a doo ditch.

Use a stick to dig a hole to bury your treasure. Make the hole deep enough to cover your "deposit."

3 Gather materials.

Find some nice soft leaves (unless you brought toilet paper) as wipes. Some hikers use pine cones, dry pine needles, or even a smooth "wiping stone." (Not something you'd want to keep for your rock garden or pet rock collection.)

BE AWARE • You should always make an informed decision on your brand of toilet foliage. Make sure you know what poison ivy looks like!

Poison Ivy

Cluster of three leaves

Grows as a vine or shrub

4 Bury your treasure.

Bury the leaves along with your poo. If you brought toilet paper, carry it out of the woods with you in a sealed plastic bag.

5 Wash your hands.

Wiping in the woods is an art that is rarely perfectly executed. So be sure to wash up. Wet your hands with water from a canteen or use a hand sanitizer.

MAGIC SPOT

The Circle of Life

Everyone has a favorite technique for fertilizing the soil. What's yours?

- **The Invisible Chair**
  Press your back against a tree so your butt is suspended above the ground, as if you were sitting on an imaginary chair.

- **The Standard Squat**
  Take a wide stance and crouch down over your homemade toilet. Note: This is only for those who have good balance.

- **The Hanging Squat**
  Hold on to a tree in front of you, ideally one that bends (but doesn't break!). Place your feet near the base of the tree, bend your knees, and lean back.

- **The Fallen Log**
  Hang your butt over the edge of a fallen log. There are two theories for the origin of the name of this method.

CHAPTER 3

How to Survive in the Desert

How to Get Along with Tarantulas

Relax. It's just a spider. A big hairy spider. With fangs. Fangs that can inject venom. Actually, you *can* relax. A tarantula is not that dangerous. Its venom causes nothing more than some minor swelling (unless you're allergic to it, which is rare). But why get that far?

The Tarantula Twist

1 Play poker.

If a tarantula makes a pit stop on you, find something like a stick or a rolled-up newspaper and gently poke your furry visitor. Poke at it the way you poke your fork at vegetables you don't want to eat. The big guy should mosey on off. Move along fella, nothing to see here.

2 Shake your booty.

If the poking isn't doing the trick, it's time to bounce up and down like an idiot. Stand up, bounce, and shake. So you look a little goofy. The tarantula is not one to judge. Who knows? The Tarantula Twist may become the next big dance craze.

Cool or Scary?

- The Goliath tarantula from South America has a body as big as a Chihuahua.
- Tarantulas actually run after their prey; they don't wait in a web.
- If forced to defend itself, a tarantula may flick tiny barbed hairs from its abdomen at its enemy.

How to Deal with a Scorpion

The scorpion, a relative of spiders, has eight legs and a stinger right at the end of its tail. But a wagging tail doesn't mean a scorpion is happy to see you. Do not lean over it and say, "Oh, wook at dat widdle guy waggin' his widdle tail!" When that stinger-capped tail uncurls like a party blower, the party's over.

1 Play hide and seek.

Comfy hiding spots, such as inside your shoes, under your bed linens, and under your pile of laundry are four-star accommodations to scorpions. Shake out your boots, bed linens, and clothes before using them. And at night, stuff your empty shoes so the scorpions don't tuck themselves in.

2 Leave stones unturned.

Resist turning over rocks or reaching into crevices. If you surprise a scorpion, the next surprise will be on you.

3 No shoes, you lose.

If you're camping in the desert, and you need to go to the bathroom at night, take the time to shake out and put on your shoes before venturing out. Scorpions are nocturnal (meaning they're active at night), and they will sting bare feet if they come their way.

BE AWARE • On rare occasions, scorpions can be born with two tails. Double the pleasure!

How to Protect Yourself in a Sandstorm

Sandstorms can strike quickly and with little warning. One moment you're strolling along the dunes, enjoying the scenery, and the next, you're being blasted by a blizzard of sand grains. Here's how to ride out the storm.

1 Seal your lips.

The first thing to do is to cover your nose and mouth. Wet a bandanna, and, doing your best bandit imitation, wrap it around your face and nose. Resist the temptation to rob a train.

2 Don't stare.

Ever have something caught in your eye, like a gnat? It's torture. In a sandstorm, it's cool to be a four-eyes. If you have goggles or sunglasses, put them on. Turn your head away from the wind and close your eyes.

3 Back that act up.

Turn away from the wind. If you need to move toward the wind—say, back to your car or shelter—walk backward.

Super Sandstorms

Some of the biggest sandstorms in the world occur in the Sahara Desert of Africa, where they're called *haboobs*—Arabic for "strong wind." And "strong wind" is right! Gusts can create walls of sand 3,000 feet high—*twice* as tall as the Empire State Building!

How to Survive an Encounter with a Rattlesnake

Rattlesnakes, like all snakes, are cold-blooded and prefer hot climates. Not surprisingly, these venomous vipers, along with many other scary slitherers, call the desert home. Here's how to keep your cool if a rattler crosses your path.

1 **Name that tune.**

So, you're hiking a desert trail through the dunes when suddenly you find a large brown snake. You can check your field guide for a snake with a flat triangular head, thick body, and fangs like retractable needles. Or you can take your cue from the rattle at the end of its tail, which will probably start shaking and clacking. It's got a rattle, and it's a snake. Chances are you know what it is already.

> **BE AWARE** • Always stay on clear paths, so you can see what's underfoot!

2 Don't get rattled.

So the rattler is still and coiled up, with a tail that sounds like it's playing the maracas. What does that rattling mean? Rattlesnakes don't come with warning labels, but if they did, this is what they'd say: Warning—if the snake is coiled and head is raised, get out of striking range. Also, if the rattle is a rockin', don't come a knockin'.

3 Freeze!

Don't move. Don't throw stones at the snake or poke it with a stick. Just back away. Give the rattler plenty of room—its striking distance can be half its overall length.

4 Fang you very much.

If you are bitten, stay calm, walk (don't run) to get medical help, and keep the bite above your heart if possible. Do not try to treat the bite yourself by bandaging it or putting anything on it—leave the rescue to the professionals. Though painful, rattler bites are rarely fatal.

Nanny, Nanny Boo-Boo!

Why does a snake stick out its tongue and hiss?

a. It's a warning to would-be attackers.

b. It thinks it's funny to taunt you.

c. It's feeding off particles in the air.

d. It uses its tongue to smell.

Answer: d. The forked tongue picks up odors from the air and touches them to openings in the snake's mouth. This is how a snake smells!

How to Find Water in the Desert

Out in the desert, there's no escaping the sun. Keeping hydrated is the only way to battle the constant thirst. When you've emptied your canteen, here's how to find some new, fresh water.

1 Dry stream? I thought you said ice cream.

Look for a dry creek bed—even if there is no water flowing, there may be some beneath the surface. Use a stick or your hands, and dig into the stream bottom to see if you find moist sand or water pooling. Dirt soup. Yummy.

2 Trust your animal instincts.

Animals need water too. If you follow an animal's tracks or call, you may be heading for the local wildlife water cooler. Of course, before getting a drink, you'll want to scope out the poolside for any predators.

Are Mirages Real?

A mirage is a real phenomenon that can make you think you're seeing a pool of water ahead of you in the desert. The sight you're seeing is absolutely real—you can even take a picture of it! But of course (sadly!), there's no real water there. This kind of mirage happens when the hot ground warms up the air above it, which causes rays of sunlight to bend so much that you actually see an image of the sky on the ground. This image can *look* like water and even *ripple* like water, but don't be fooled—there's not a drop to drink!

3 Show a "can dew" spirit.

Even in the desert, mornings following cold nights result in desert dew. (There's a bad name for a soda, huh?) You can scrape the dew drops off plants into your mouth. Hey, take what you can get.

How to Stop a Runaway Camel

Whether it's got one hump or two, a camel is the perfect desert transport. It can travel long distances with very little water and withstand the scorching desert sun. Though camels are easily trained, they're still prone to getting startled by loud noises and other surprises, so you'd better be prepared in case the one you're riding decides to make a run for it.

HOW TO RIDE A CAMEL

Before you can rein in a runaway, it's important to know how to ride a camel the right way.

1 You scratch its back . . .

It won't break yours. Rake the camel's coat before putting a saddle on. This removes any sticks or burrs that might be a real pain in the hump if stuck under the saddle. Feel free to gossip with the camel as you do its hair.

The Perfect Desert Vehicle

Paint job: A camel's thick coat reflects sunlight and insulates the body from the heat.

Headlights: Long eyelashes and—check this out—*sealable nostrils* help against blowing sand. There are times when we all wish we had sealable nostrils.

Fuel efficiency: A camel's organs and fatty humps allow it to go without water for long periods. Its pee comes out as thick as syrup and its poop is so dry it is used to light fires.

Wheels: Tough feet protect against hot sand.

headlights

paint job

fuel efficiency

wheels

2 "Down, boy!"

It's a bad idea to take a running jump to mount a camel. Instead, trainers have taught camels to learn commands to make them kneel down. The trainer's Secret Word #1 will get the camel to crouch low enough that you can get on the hump.

3 Don't get tossed.

After you utter Secret Word #2 for "up," the camel will stand. But brace yourself! The camel's backside goes up first and fast. Lean back, or you'll get a face full of sand.

4 Gentle reins.

Riders use reins to steer a camel, just like they would with a horse. However, in the camel's case, the reins are attached to a peg in the nose. It's very punk rock. But be gentle. Think of how painful it is to yank a nose hair, and multiply that by ten.

5 Sway with it.

A camel walks differently from a horse—the camel moves both right legs together, then both left legs, causing it to sway side to side. Sway with it, and you won't fall off.

HOW TO STOP A RUNAWAY CAMEL

1 Rein it in (sideways).

At speeds up to 40 miles per hour (64 kph), a runaway camel ride is no pony trot. You need to rein in your dashing dromedary. But don't pull back—that could snap the reins. Instead, pull the reins to one side. This will cause the camel to run in circles. Pull toward the side that the camel seems to prefer, not against it.

2 Hang on for your life.

Pretend you're in a rodeo, and while you may need to hang on for more than 8 seconds, it won't be *too* long. Get low, grip the camel with your legs, and hold onto the horn of the saddle tightly. The camel will eventually get tired of running in circles and realize it isn't really getting anywhere.

3 Make your perfect dismount.

The camel will sit when it gets tired, giving you a perfect chance to hop off. Tell the camel "good boy" for sitting. Give it a treat.

Spit Take

You may have heard that irritable camels will spit on people. Is it true? Yes and no. Camels rarely spit and are generally good-natured. However, if a camel feels threatened, it may spit at whatever is threatening it. Only, it's not really spit. It's worse. It's more like projectile vomit. A camel burps up the semi-digested food in its stomach into its mouth and then uses its lips to sling the goods. The result is a stream of stomach stuff that can cover your entire upper body!

CHAPTER 4

How to Survive in the Jungle

How to Cross Piranha-Infested Waters

What's worse than the worst day you've ever had at school? Spending a day in a school of piranhas. With their super-sharp teeth (which can bite through a steel fishhook!), a school of piranhas can strip the flesh from a fish or small animal in seconds. Here's how to stay off the menu.

1 Choose the non-piranha section of the restaurant, er, river.

The safest section of a river is away from the fishing docks. Docks where fish are cleaned are like fast-food restaurants for piranhas (complete with swim-through service and snappy meals).

> **FAST FACTS** • Piranhas mostly live in South American rivers, like the rivers in the Amazon rain forest. People in the Amazon region have used piranhas' sharp teeth as tools.

② Flee the frenzy.

In a "feeding frenzy," piranhas will snap wildly at anything in reach. Even though you are unlikely to be the main course, don't let any parts of you become a side dish. Piranhas generally eat fish that are smaller than they are, so they'll only bite you if you get in the way.

3 Nighttime is the right time.

If you absolutely must cross a piranha-infested river, do it at night. The fish are less active, and if you awaken them, they're likely to swim away. Dawn is the worst time for a dip, as piranhas are hungriest in the morning.

What Would You Do?

You're bushwhacking in the Amazon in search of an ancient relic rumored to have mystical powers. You machete your way through the underbrush and come upon a river. The water is low since it's the height of the dry season. You're pretty scraped up from fighting through some thorns, and the water will feel good. Great time for a quick dip, right?

Answer: No chance, Crazy Pants. Piranhas can be dangerously hungry during the dry season, especially if they smell the blood from your wounds.

How to Escape the Grip of a Python

The world's largest snake, the python, can grow as long as a fire hose and as wide as a telephone pole. The reptilian giant is also a "constrictor," meaning it squeezes its catch in its coils until the pressure is too much to take. Here's how to avoid the Hug of Doom!

1 Be on the lookout.

Pythons are all about the ambush. If that branch is moving, get your patootie out of there. Pythons can strike suddenly. They can also stay underwater for 30 minutes.

2 Remain still.

If a python manages to give you a squeeze, relaxing your muscles may trick the snake into thinking you've been properly tenderized and are ready for consumption. He may loosen his grip. If so . . .

3 Go for the head.

Take off your reptilian body wrap. Just grab the head and unwrap it. Hey look, you shouldn't have tried it on in the first place.

What's Your Worst Case?

Sharing a sleeping bag with a python?

or

Taking a bath with a school of piranhas?

Who Would Win in a Fight— an Alligator or a Python?

In 2005, a 13-foot (4-m) python and a 6-foot (2-m) alligator were found in an unusual position. The lifeless alligator was discovered sticking out from a tear in the equally lifeless snake's body. The snake probably thought it had won the battle after it swallowed the gator. However, it's not over till it's over, and unfortunately, in the end, it was over for both of them.

How to Escape from Quicksand

How many times have you been walking to school when BAM!, you suddenly stumble into a pit of quicksand? OK, so maybe quicksand isn't as common in daily life as cartoons seem to indicate. But if you're walking around the right (or wrong) riverbank, you just may encounter that rare substance that's created when water mixes with sand but doesn't form clay. Which makes it extra sticky and possible to sink into—like a big bowl of earth pudding!

1 Walk softly and carry a big stick.

If you're in quicksand country, bring a pole. The pole will help you if you get stuck. Try not to step anywhere that looks suspicious, like onto a sand-topped puddle or in the hole by that sign that says "quicksand."

2 If you start to sink, lay the pole on top of the quicksand.

Think of the pole as one of those foam-noodle-floaty things at the pool. Moving slowly, wiggle your back onto the "noodle" and slowly spread your arms and legs. Chill out until you start to float.

> **BE AWARE •** Always move slowly in quicksand. Thrashing around will tire you out and puts you at risk of inhaling sand, which can suffocate you.

3 Float, don't flap.

OK, so you forgot your pole. Don't panic: Your body is less dense than quicksand, so if you can relax, you will eventually begin to float. If you have a heavy backpack, shrug it off—anything that makes you heavy will make you sink.

How to Deal with an Angry Gorilla

There's a reason for the expression "to go ape"—a gorilla will scream, beat his chest, and bare his teeth when upset. Of course, it's all just a big show to look tough and assert the gorilla's rank in the group. To stay safe, you need to learn your role.

1 Let's get ready to humble!

Gorillas are usually pretty peaceful—unless you're threatening them. So swallow your pride and let the gorilla win the staring contest. Stay quiet and keep your arms to your side, so he doesn't think you're testing his dominance.

2 Don't call his bluff.

A gorilla may make a "bluff charge" to intimidate you. Well, be intimidated. If you're nose-to-nose with a 400-pound (181-kg) gorilla, make yourself small and act afraid. If he thinks you got his point, he'll let you off easy.

3 Offer groom service.

So you've just been charged by a giant ape. Caressing the mad monkey's fur probably seems like odd advice. In this case, however, the ape may take the hair care as a nonthreatening gesture, because lower-ranked gorillas will groom the head ape. In other words, if you can't beat 'em, groom 'em.

How to Remove a Leech

In the warm shallows of jungle pools lurks a little blood-sucker that loves to latch onto unsuspecting swimmers like you. Here's how to avoid being a leech's juice box.

1 Don't start in the middle.

When you find a leech stuck on you, resist the urge to just grab the leech in the middle and pull. The leech is lip-locked on your arm in not one, but two places! Playing tug-of-war with your own body is a game no one wins.

Leech Anatomy

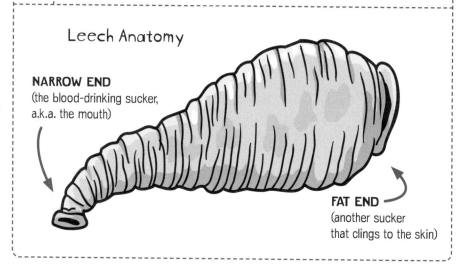

NARROW END
(the blood-drinking sucker, a.k.a. the mouth)

FAT END
(another sucker that clings to the skin)

What Would You Do?

Which of these methods are other ways of getting leeches off you?

- Salt
- Heat
- Insect repellent

BUG OFF

URP

Answer: None of them. These irritants will cause the leech to throw up into the bite, which can spread bacteria and cause infection.

2 Nail the leech.

Look for the small end of the leech—this is the mouth. Put your fingernail on your skin next to the leech, but not directly on it. Push against it sideways to break the seal.

3 So long, sucker!

Now push away the big end, while flicking at the mouth so it doesn't reattach. Fling the leech away, shaking it off your finger like an unwanted booger.

How to Catch Fish Without a Rod

Anybody can catch a fish with a motorboat, a fancy rod, and a state-of-the-art lure. The test of a true fishing master is whether you can catch a fish with nothing but the clothes on your back. Literally.

1 Make the frame for a net.

Find a young plant that splits into two branches, like the one shown on the right. It should be about as long as your leg. Bend the two branches toward each other and tie them together to make a circle.

2 Take the shirt off your back.

And your front. Don't forget your arms. In fact, take the shirt off completely! After you take off your shirt, tie a knot in the shirt below the armpits. Then tie the shirt to the sides of the net frame. Voilà, a net!

③ Stay out of the sun.

This is about catching fish, not rays. Fish like the shadowy places near the edges of the water, so that's your target area. Once you find the right spot, it's time to . . .

④ Net the surf.

When you swipe your homemade net through the pool, water should flow through the shirt, but fish will be caught.

How to Build a Shelter in the Rain Forest

With a name like "rain forest," it's probably going to rain in this forest—a lot. Which means that if you're lost here, you need to find (or make) some cover fast.

1 Location. Location. Location.

High and dry ground is ideal. Look for a clearing. Stay away from any swampy or low-lying spot, a.k.a. the mosquito breeding ground. And don't pick a spot under a coconut tree or a tree with any dead limbs, or else more than raindrops may fall on your head.

2 Lean on me.

Sticks and stones *can* protect your bones. Find a sturdy fallen tree trunk or a rock. Lean some thick branches and sticks at an angle against the fallen tree. This is why this sort of shelter is called a "lean-to." Crawl under it to make sure you have enough room to fit (your lean-to shouldn't be too-lean).

3 Seal it up.

Fill in all the holes with lots of large leaves and moss. Pile it on! You don't want any leaks. Hang a "Do Not Disturb" sign on the side of your shelter, so the jungle critters will leave you alone.

The Rain Forest by the Numbers

- The Amazon rain forest alone produces 20 percent of Earth's oxygen.
- More than 3,000 fruits are found in rain forests.
- Some experts believe we are losing 50,000 plant species a year from the destruction of the rain forest.

Other Shelters

The lean-to is just one easy shelter to make. There are loads of others to choose from depending on your circumstances.

The Dry Inn

If you have a poncho and rope, you can use it, instead of the leaves, as siding.

The Swamp Bunk

If you can't find a site away from the swamp, then you need to elevate your game with a covered, raised bed made from four trees and lots of brush.

The A-Frame

This is like a lean-to with two sides. Take a long log and balance it on a tree stump or rock. Then follow directions for a lean-to on both sides.

The Fantasy Fort

Who says rain forest living can't be posh? Just fly in an architect and some builders and make your abode a tad less humble. Star-gazing deck optional.

CHAPTER 5

How to Survive in the Arctic

How to Avoid a Polar Bear Attack

Here's the problem with polar bears: They have no natural predators, so they have little fear. This means they're not afraid of humans. All the more reason to watch your tushy on the tundra!

1 **If the bear doesn't see you, keep it that way.** Don't try to get a closer look or a better picture. Stay downwind of the bear, so it doesn't catch your funky odor. No offense.

2 **If the bear sees you, show you're only human.**
If you see the bear standing, sniffing, or taking notice of you, let the bear know you're human by talking and waving your arms. If you're in a group, everybody should do this. Make a commotion. Have a dance contest.

Real or Ridiculous?

a. Polar bears have clear hair, not white hair. The hair *looks* white because it reflects light.

b. Some polar bears in Antarctica have black hair.

c. Polar bears have webbed front feet.

d. Polar bears have been known to make snowman-like structures and rub their backs against them.

e. Under their fur, polar bears have spotted skin.

f. Polar bears have taste buds on their toes.

Answer: a and c are real. Choice b was doubly ridiculous—there *are* no polar bears in Antarctica.

3 Stand your ground.

If the bear charges, should you jump in the water? No good. Polar bears are great swimmers. Hit the ice? No dice. Polar bears are quite the speed skaters. And in the snow, forget about it. Your only chance is to pollute the atmosphere and increase global warming, thereby making these beasts extinct. Just kidding. If the bear *does* attack, you and the group all need to attack back. Hopefully the bear will retreat, giving you enough space to then leave the area.

How to Survive Falling Through the Ice

Let's say you're walking on ice. (Which you shouldn't do.) Then let's say you walk onto *very thin* ice. (Which clearly you shouldn't do. *Dude, what the heck is wrong with you?!*) It's too late now. You've fallen in—but the good news is, you *can* get out.

1 Inhale. Exhale. Repeat.

Guess what? The water is going to be cold. As in shockingly, gaspingly cold. Try not to hyperventilate; stay calm. Tread water.

2 Remember where you came from.

Chances are you just walked away from the strongest ice. So turn to face the direction you came from. Look for your foolish footprints or a landmark like a tree or building to locate your point of origin.

3 Elbows out.

Get your elbows on the ice and hoist yourself up but not completely out of the water. You just gained a few pounds

How to Rescue Someone Else Who Fell Through the Ice

If someone else breaks the ice, don't jump in, too. Instead of becoming a second ice cube, coach them out. If they can't do it, throw them a rope, hockey stick, or even a long branch. Just don't reach with your hands, or the panicked person might pull you in!

with your "liquid diet," so let the water weight drain from your clothes before trying to pull yourself up.

4 Go kicking and screaming.

Kick your feet as if you're swimming to propel yourself forward as you pull yourself up onto the ice.

5 Roll on.

When you get out, do not stand up. Instead, roll away. This spreads your weight out over the ice and makes you less likely to fall through for a second time. And since you've already been introduced to the frigid water, there's no need to break the ice again.

How to Deal with a Charging Moose

A moose is a lot like a Ferrari. It's shiny, sleek, and glamorous. OK, maybe not. But like a Ferrari, a moose can go from being completely still to moving very fast in a matter of seconds, bowling over anything in its way. Including you.

1 **Dog-gone it.**

To a moose, your dog looks a lot like a wolf. And a wolf is no friend to a moose. If you and Fido meet up with a moose, a) the dog is going to get upset and bark, b) the moose will think it has to defend itself, and c) the dog will then run back to its master. Which means, d) you are about to come face-to-face with an angry moose. So the moral of the story is: Don't bring your doggy on a hike in moose territory!

2 **Give it an escape route.**

Make sure the moose has a place to run other than over you. Generally a moose isn't looking to butt heads with you, and it will take a clear path if it has one.

Doodie Calls!

The Talkeetna Moose Dropping Festival is an annual celebration that has taken place in Talkeetna, Alaska, for more than 30 years. Varnished, numbered moose turds are dropped onto a target from a helicopter. People are given raffle numbers that correspond to the numbers on the turds. The closest turd to the target wins!

Moose Body Language

ears up

hair up

"Hm, what is that all about?"

"I don't like you. I think I'll knock you over."

"Would you like to join me for tea?" (rare)

3 Speak "Moose."

The moose may look at you with its ears up. If so, you can back away from the merely curious moose. If the moose lowers its head and the hair on the back of its neck stands up, then you need to start worrying.

4 Olé? No way!

If the moose charges, don't act like a matador. The bull of the north has a mighty set of antlers. Get behind something solid and stay as still as a pill until the moose has passed. In fact, stay put until the moose has left the area, resettled, and started a new life as an accountant.

How to Make Emergency Snowshoes

Why get exhausted and risk frostbite slogging through deep snow when you can make a pair of snowshoes and walk right on top of the snow surface? All you need is a pair of tree branches and a little string. Here's how to get your kicks on the snow.

1 Branch out.

You're shopping in Old Man Winter's shoe store, so the selection is limited. Look for two tree branches about 2 feet (.6 m) long. As far as style goes, you want branches with lots of little branches and green needles on them. It's all the rage on the tundra.

2 Step on it.

Time to try on your new shoes. Step on your gathered branches. About a hand's length of branch should stick out in front of your foot. The rest of the bushy part should be around and behind your foot.

③ Tie it up.

You'll need string. Good thing you brought some for that Arctic String Convention. If not, you might be able to use plant roots, or there may be a drawstring on your bag or coat that you can repurpose.

a) Tie one end of the string to the front of the branch.

b) Lace the string through the front holes of your shoe.

c) Tie the other end of the string securely to the branch.

④ Make them yours.

Carve or mark your new shoes with whatever symbols or stripes designate your favorite shoe brand.

Pick Your Kicks!

Which of the styles below is your best bet for snowshoeing?

The Fir Flop

The Pine Pump

The Beaver Boots

Answer: The Fir Flop. You want lots of little branches so your weight is spread out and you don't sink, like you could with a heel.

How to Build a Snow Cave

So you're camping out in the wintry wilderness, when a sudden gust of wind sends your tent off for a solo hang glide. You need a new shelter fast, or you'll soon be a snow angel. Here's how to stay warm and dry even when surrounded by snow and ice.

1 Find the right spot.

Look for a steep-ish slope with a buildup of snow that's soft enough to shovel but hard enough to pack together.

2 Dig it.

Every ice fortress needs a door. Dig an entrance tunnel straight into the slope about 3 feet (1 m) deep. Next, carve the main chamber in and upward from the end of the tunnel. Keep the chamber floor flat and make the ceiling domed. The entrance tunnel must be lower than the main chamber. Otherwise, snow could be blown or fall through the tunnel into the chamber.

3 Make it holy.

When finished with the main chamber, poke a ventilation hole though the roof. This will ensure you have enough air to breathe, and you'll be thanking yourself if your fellow snow-caver lets one rip in the night.

FAST FACT • The Yupik Eskimos have more then 20 words for snow, including *muruaneq* (soft deep snow), *natquik* (drifting snow), and *kanevvluk* (fine snow particles). They do not have a word for snow that isn't deep enough to cancel school, though.

POOT

How to Survive If Stranded on an Iceberg

No matter how you got *on* this floating chunk of ice, here's how to make the best of it—and how to get off.

1 Build on your 'berg.

You need shelter. You can build a trench (a long hole covered by blocks of ice) or, if you see an extended stay in your future, build a snow cave (see page 99)—icebergs are almost always covered in snow.

2 Snow + sun = water.

The surface of an iceberg is made mostly of freshwater, so you can drink to your heart's desire. Put the snow or ice in a container and let the sun beat down on it. Eating snow is not the same as drinking water (eating uses your body's energy, sapping you of much-needed strength), so fully melt the snow first. As a last resort, scrape at the top ice to make your own personal snow cone. Flavor: plain.

3 Go fish.

In general, a human can go three days without water and three weeks without food. That's a theory you don't want to test. End your hunger strike as soon as you can. Make a fishing rod out of anything you can. If necessary, hunt sea birds with ice balls.

4 Catch my drift?

In Anarctica, icebergs drift clockwise around the South Pole. Keep your eye out for ships and weather stations. In the Arctic, the currents flow east to west. You may drift to populated areas near Greenland. Of course, this ride will take a few months, so you'll have time to decorate your mobile home.

Real or Ridiculous?

Nature is a master ice sculptor. Scientists classify icebergs with different names, depending on their shape. All the icebergs in the world are monitored so that another *Titanic* disaster can't occur!

Which of these iceberg shapes are works of nature and which are not?

Tabular

Punch bowl

Dome

Tubular

Wedge

Globe

Answer: Tabular, dome, and wedge are real.

CHAPTER 6

How to Survive on Safari

How to Dress for Success on Safari

When a typical day on safari in East Africa may include meeting with lions, crocodiles, and elephants, looking fashionable may not be a top priority. But pick your clothing carefully: It's worth the effort to sport the right duds for your trip.

1 Be an onion.

This isn't about smelling bad or making people cry—this is about dressing in layers. You might be thinking, "It's gonna be steamin'!" Well, you're half right. It *will* be hot during the day. But night is a different story—believe it or not, it can get pretty cold in the African savannah.

2 Don't forget PJs.

In this case, PJs stand for "pull-over jackets." You'll want a warm jacket if you plan to be out or camp at night. Pack layers so you can control your temperature.

Extreme Makeover: Safari Edition

Before

After

Uncovered

Shady

Bright

Loose

Tight

Layers

Khaki

Zipper

Uncomfortable

Comfortable

③ Hang loose.

Tight clothes are a bad idea. You'll often need to cover your whole body to protect against mosquito bites and sunburn, and loose clothes will keep you cooler in the heat. And cotton has a way of getting wet and staying wet, so wear fabrics that dry quickly next to your skin instead.

④ Accessorize.

Protect your head with a wide-brimmed hat, sunglasses, and some sunblock. Cover your feet in sturdy, comfortable walking shoes. Better yet, wear special hiking boots or lightweight, quick-drying shoes with thick soles.

⑤ Go khaki, not wacky.

Leave the Hawaiian shirt at home. Blending in with your environment is the goal, and khaki is ideal. Bright colors can alarm animals.

> **FAST FACT** • The color blue can attract the tsetse fly, which carries a toxin that can cause the illness sleeping sickness, which causes fever, headaches, and joint pain, in addition to sleepiness.

Safari, So Good

Safari means "journey" in the African language of Swahili. Safaris used to be hunting trips, but these days, going on safari usually means traveling to a nature reserve in eastern or southern Africa, riding around in a car, and taking lots of pictures.

Safari-goers often search for the "Big Five" animals, but there are plenty of other great animals to see beyond these big shots. A short list is below, along with their Swahili names (which are pronounced just like they're spelled, for the most part).

The Big Five		
	Lion	simba
	Elephant	tembo
	Rhino	kifaru
	Leopard	chui (pronounced "chewy")
	Buffalo	nyati
	Giraffe	twiga
	Hippo	kiboko
	Cheetah	duma
	Zebra	punda milia
	Gazelle	swara
	Hyena	fisi

How to Track Animals

Tracking is a crucial wilderness survival skill. Keep your eyes open for the signs an animal leaves, and you'll be able to avoid any predators and find the animals you *do* want to see when you're on safari.

1 Dust for prints.

Look for prints where impressions may be left, such as along streams or in dusty areas. Know the characteristic footprints of the critters you're interested in:

- Four toes per foot suggests dog or cat family.

- Elongated prints may be from the hoofs of a gazelle or giraffe.

- Comma-shaped prints might be a warthog or wild pig.

2 Be a poop-snooper.

Animals leave behind more than just footprints. Keep your eyes peeled for poop along the trail. The scoop on poop: If the animal is an herbivore (a vegetarian), it will leave round pellets. If the animal is a carnivore (meat-eater), its leavings will be long and tapered. It's your doodie, er, duty to track.

③ Watch their diets.

Knowing what comes out of an animal is important, but so is understanding what goes in. You gotta know what your animals like to munch on. Wildebeests eat the tops of grasses, while zebras mow their lawns down to the roots. Skilled trackers can even recognize the patterns of teeth marks on shrubs and bushes!

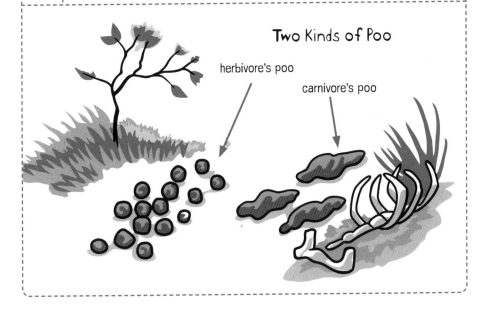

Two Kinds of Poo

herbivore's poo

carnivore's poo

How to Survive the Deadliest Animal in Africa

What do you think is the deadliest African animal? Go ahead, guess. The lion? The rhino? Wrong. The deadliest animal in Africa is no bigger than your fingernail. It's the mosquito. In Africa, mosquitoes can carry malaria, which kills up to two million people a year, so you want to be utterly repulsive to mosquitoes in Africa (or anywhere else where malaria is present). Here's how to get these pests to bug off.

① Be as repulsive as possible.

Get an insect repellent with the chemical DEET. Spray it on your clothes and skin as directed.

FAST FACT • Only female mosquitoes suck blood—they need it for their eggs. Both males and females eat flower nectar and other sweet-smelling foods.

② Don't smell.

Avoid using hairspray, perfume, or other scented items that could smell sweet and attract the pests. If you smell like flowers or fruit, they'll think you're food.

③ Don't show skin.

At night, when mosquitoes are most active, cover your body from head to toe. Sleep in rooms with screened windows or under mosquito nets.

DID YOU KNOW? • A small donation (as little as $10) can help a family in Africa get mosquito nets. If you want to help, just search online for organizations that take donations.

How to Escape from a Crocodile

How do you tell the difference between a crocodile and an alligator? Here's a rule of thumb: A crocodile has a long, narrow, V-shaped snout, while the alligator's snout is wide and U-shaped. Here's another rule of thumb: Never get close enough to be able to tell the difference.

1 Don't go it alone.

Never swim or boat by yourself in waters that are home to crocodiles. To a croc, a solo swimmer looks like a tasty treat, but a group of people just looks like trouble. Stay with your buddies.

2 Surrr-prise! *Not.*

If caught off-guard, a croc may attack on instinct. So if you suspect there could be one nearby, slap the water, shout, do impressions, sing your favorite song, whatever! Just make some noise.

③ Give it some space.

Crocodiles and alligators have been known to jump well out of the water to snag prey that thought it was safe to chill on low-hanging tree branches. If you see one, stay at least 20 feet (6 m) away from the water.

20 feet
(6 m)

4 Do not feed the animals, please.

Feeding crocs can cause them to get over their fear of humans.

5 Get out of the croc-pot.

Both crocs and gators have two sets of eyelids. They have a pair of clear inner lids that function as natural goggles and allow them to see perfectly underwater. Still think you're a match for Old Four-Eyes in the water? Consider this: Crocs have "skin sensors" that can sense vibrations when something enters the water. Bottom line: If you even suspect there's a crocodile around, get out of the water yesterday!

6 Run!

If you spot a croc on land, run. Run fast. Run straight. Run far.

3 Myths About Crocodiles and Gators

Myth #1: They're slow. A large croc can run 10 mph (16 kph), which is probably about the same speed you can run. Do the math. Actually you don't have time. Just run.

Myth #2: You should run in zigzags. This idea stems from the idea that crocs can only see straight ahead, so they'll lose sight of you if you zig and zag all over the place. However, you're better off running away any way you can. The more distance you can put between you and the croc, the better.

Myth #3: Crocs like to chase people. Actually, they're not like lions. They don't like to chase down their prey. They're way too cool for that. They're lurkers. They lie low before attacking.

How to Survive an Elephant Stampede

Sure, elephants may look big, clumsy, and slow, but they can actually run faster than 25 mph (40 kph). Their speed and strength makes elephants the linebackers of the Animal Kingdom. And while a herd of charging pachyderms can be scary, stay calm. Do the wrong thing, and you'll soon be elephant toe-cheese.

1 Take cover.

Running's not an option—the elephants will just catch up. Instead, find a sturdy structure to get into. Of course, there aren't always a whole lot of sturdy structures on the African plains. So . . .

2 Grab a trunk.

Of a tree, not an elephant! If you're a skilled tree-climber, you might be in luck. Elephants, even in a frenzied stampede, will try to avoid trees. Grab a branch and hoist yourself up, staying close to the trunk. If you can't climb a tree, huddle close to the tree trunk. *Be* the tree trunk.

③ Get down.

This might sound crazy, but if all else fails, lie down. Unless it sees you as a threat, an elephant is unlikely to step on you. If you stay standing, you run a higher risk of getting shish-kebab'ed on an elephant's tusk.

Do not grab an elephant trunk.

What's Your Worst Case?

Being sneezed on by an elephant? **or** Falling in a pile of fresh elephant poop?

How to Survive a Charging Rhinoceros

The black rhino has a horn on its face and a chip on his shoulder. If one lowers its horny head and snorts at you, it's got goring you on its mind. You don't want to be on the receiving end of the charge from an animal that weighs more than a ton. Here's how to avoid it entirely.

1 **Tree up, don't tee up.**

At 30 mph (48 kph), a charging rhino is not outrunnable. If one comes at you, climb a tree. Make sure you get higher than the horn can reach, or you're just teeing yourself up for the rhino.

2 **Scrub-a-dub-dub.**

If you can't get to a tree, the next best thing is thick, scrubby brush. Get as far into the bush as you can. Don't worry, your panic will keep you from feeling the pricks of those sharp thorns. Better a thorn than a horn.

③ Opposites don't always attract.

Once you have avoided the charge, run in the opposite direction the rhino is running. These big boys don't like to turn around, so once they get going in one direction they're unlikely to reverse course. It's not a bullfight; you just need to avoid that first charge.

Real or Ridiculous?

The jolly-looking hippopotamus is actually one of the most deadly animals in Africa. Hippos are known for being aggressive when humans enter their territory, and they get particularly riled up when their path to water is blocked, as they spend most of their time underwater (even though they're mammals). Can you tell which of these hippo activities are real and which are ridiculous?

a. Hungry, hungry hippos have been known to tear full-grown crocodiles in half.

b. Hippos eat rocks to help them sink in the water.

c. A hippo is capable of jumping 2 feet (60 cm) in the air.

d. A hippo might fall asleep right in the water—and stay underwater for as long as five minutes before surfacing to breathe, all without waking up.

e. Baby hippos are born underwater, then they swim to the surface for air.

f. Hippos spin their tails to spread their poo, to mark their territory.

Answer: a, d, e, and f are true.

Appendix

HOW TO TELL DIRECTION WITHOUT A COMPASS

The Stick Shadow Method

1. Stand a stick up in the ground.

2. Mark the tip of the shadow of the stick.

3. Mark it again 15 minutes later.

4. Draw an imaginary line from the first line to the second. The line points east.

The Watch and Learn Method

1. Hold your watch so that the hour hand points directly at the sun.

2. Imagine a line halfway between the hour hand and the 12. That line will be pointing south.

OTHER WAYS TO TELL DIRECTION

- Most moss grows on the north side of trees.
- Spiderwebs are often built on the south side.
- Clouds often travel west to east.

Appendix

HOW TO SIGNAL FOR HELP

Third Time's the Charm

A series of three is the universal call for distress. If you have a whistle, blow it three times to call for help. If you have three pieces of bright material (a tent, poncho, tarp, etc.), set them side by side in a clearing so they can be seen by a plane flying by. Three rock piles will work as well.

Steer the Mirror

On sunny days, you can signal for help with a mirror or anything shiny that reflects light.

Appendix

FIELD GUIDE TO EXTREME FOODS

While on your travels, you are likely to encounter some pretty extreme foods. Know what they'll taste like before you take a bite with this handy chart.

Place	Food	What It Tastes Like
Ecuador	Guinea pig	Chicken
China	Turtle shell gelatin	Bitter cola
Tibet	Yak butter tea	Oily, salty tea with sour milk
Shanghai	Duck heads	Chewy chicken
Egypt	Camel	Grainy and fatty beef
Philippines	Sautéed crickets	Crunchy, buttery chewy morsels

Place	Food	What It Tastes Like
Hong Kong	Snake soup	Chicken broth with fish
Cambodia	Deep-fried spider	Crab with gooey black juice
Scandinavia	Lutefisk (air-dried whitefish prepared with lye)	Soapy, fishy gelatin
Morocco	Pigeon pie	Chicken pot pie
Mexico	Corn fungus	Mushrooms on the cob
France	Pâté (spreadable liver)	Wet cat food
Scotland	Haggis (sheep stomach lining stuffed with minced organ meats)	Wet cat food mixed with oatmeal, served in a balloon. (Do not eat the balloon.)
Your House	Fried chicken	Guinea pig, duck heads

Appendix

FOREIGN EMERGENCY PHRASES

Brazil (Portuguese)
Do those fish have teeth?
Aqueles peixes têm dentes?
a-KEH-les PEH-shehs teng DEHN-ch.

Kenya and other parts of Africa (Swahili)
Excuse me, there seems to be a large lion behind me.
Kubwa simba nyuma mimi.
CUB-wuh SIHM-buh NYOO-muh ME-ME.

Norway (Norwegian)
I'm sure that ice is safe to walk on.
Jeg er sikker på at den isen er trygg å gå på.
Yay ehr SEEK-er poh at dehn EE-sen ehr treeg oh goh poh.

Indonesia (Indonesian)
Look out! There's an orangutan behind that tree—maybe he wants your banana!
Awas! Ada orangutan* di belakang pohon itu—mungkin dia mau pisang kamu!
Ah-WAHS! Ah-dah ore-AHNG-oo-tahn dee beh-LAH-kahng
poe-hone EE-too—MOONG-kin DEE-ah mao PEE-song KAH-moo!

* The Indonesian word *orangutan* means "person of the forest" (*orang* = person; *hutan* = forest).

About the Experts

These experts reviewed all the tips in this handbook and offered their extremely good advice. Consider them the coaches of Team Extreme!

"Mountain Mel" Deweese has more than 30 years of worldwide experience teaching survival skills. His work has spanned the globe, from the Arctic to the tropics, and he has dealt with animals of all sorts. He has shared wilderness survival skill knowledge with more than 100,000 students around the world and continues to do so through his Web site, www.youwillsurvive.com.

John Lindner is the director of the "Wilderness Survival School" for The Colorado Mountain Club, and he runs the "Snow Survival School" for Safety-One International, Inc. A former instructor for Denver Public Schools and the Community College of Denver, John has taught mountaineering and survival training for almost 30 years.

Charles Maciejewski has a degree in Adventure Education and has worked at Outward Bound, the Bronx Expeditionary Learning High School, and the Kurt Hahn Expeditionary Learning School. He has planned numerous urban and wilderness expeditions with students and trained teachers on doing work in nature. He loves the natural world, cycling, and snowboarding.

About the Authors

David Borgenicht is a writer, editor, publisher, and the coauthor of all the books in the Worst-Case Scenario Survival Handbook series. He has been known to float on quicksand, overpack while on safari, and employ "the standard squat" (see page 48). He lives in Philadelphia.

Justin Heimberg defines the word *extreme*. He is extremely cautious and wary. He is an extreme sleeper and an extreme television watcher. On the rare occasion when Justin is not being extreme, he writes books and films. He lives in an extreme suburb in Maryland.

About the Illustrator

Chuck Gonzales is a New York City–based illustrator who was raised in South Dakota. He's no stranger to worst cases, having illustrated *The Worst-Case Scenario Survival Handbook: Junior Edition*. Growing up in the Dakotas, he is very familiar with surviving on the tundra.

KNOW
YOUR
RIGHTS

READER'S DIGEST

KNOW YOUR RIGHTS

And How to Make Them Work for You

The Reader's Digest Association, Inc.
Pleasantville, New York ▪ Montreal

A READER'S DIGEST BOOK
PRODUCED BY REBUS, INC.

Executive Editor
PAMELA THOMAS

Consulting Editor
MARYA DALRYMPLE

Editors
JULEE BINDER
HARVEY LOOMIS
NANCY NICHOLAS

Copy Editors
ERIN CLAREMONT
JENNIFER KOONTZ
LAUREN LONG
CATHY PECK
CONNIE STALLINGS

Researcher
TANYA NÁDAS

Fact Checkers
ROBERT CINQUE
SCHELLIE HAGAN
LAURYN HART
ADA PENTZ
JEFFREY SCHAPER

Indexer
MARTY JEZER

Art Director
JUDITH HENRY

Assistant Art Director/Illustrator
TIMOTHY JEFFS

Electronic Production Manager
KARIN MARTIN

Electronic Production Assistant
ANDERSON TEPPER

CONSULTANTS AND
CONTRIBUTORS

Chief Legal Consultant
CYNTHIA L. COOPER

Legal Consultants
TONI-DIANE DONNET
TERRY GILBERT
STUART MILLER
DOUGLAS PETERSON
ELIZABETH SCHROEDER
NORMAN SILBER
BARBARA ZANDER

Tax Consultant
PHILIP MELLON
JAMES WEIKART

WRITERS

Your Money
BARBARA BEDWAY

Your Car, Your Consumer Rights
ELEANOR BERMAN

Your Marriage and Family
STEVEN BESCHLOSS

Your Home and Community
SUSAN COHEN

Your Rights in Action
CYNTHIA COOPER

Your Health Care
ANDREA KOTT

Your Job
TOM WEYR

FOR READER'S DIGEST

Project Editor
INGE N. DOBELIS

Project Art Director
ROBERT M. GRANT

READER'S DIGEST
GENERAL BOOKS

Editor in Chief
JOHN A. POPE, JR.

General Books Editor, U.S.
SUSAN WERNERT LEWIS

Affinity Directors
WILL BRADBURY
JIM DWYER
KAARI WARD

Art Director
EVELYN BAUER

Editorial Director
JANE POLLEY

Research Director
LAUREL A. GILBRIDE

Group Art Editors
ROBERT M. GRANT
JOEL MUSLER

Copy Chief
EDWARD W. ATKINSON

Picture Editor
MARION BODINE

Head Librarian
JO MANNING

Library of Congress Cataloging in Publication Data
Know your rights, and how to make them work for you / Reader's Digest.
        p.   cm.
    Includes index.
    ISBN 0-89577-831-9
        1. Law—United States—Popular works.   I. Reader's Digest Association
KF387.K574   1995
349.73—dc20
[347.3]   95-9561

CONTENTS

 # YOUR MONEY 287

YOUR CAR 373

YOUR CONSUMER RIGHTS 401

YOUR RIGHTS IN ACTION 463

ABOUT THIS BOOK

"I know my rights!"

You've heard these words time and time again. In moments of frustration, fear, or anger, you may well have uttered them yourself. But do you *really* know your rights? And even if you do understand the legalities, do you have the knowledge to use that information to get what you rightfully deserve?

Very likely you have had the experience of believing that you were entitled to something—a refund for a faulty product, a service from a real estate agent or a physician, a response from one of your children's teachers—only to discover that either you were not legally within your rights, or if you were, that you had no idea how to take effective action.

KNOW YOUR RIGHTS was conceived to solve this kind of dilemma. An action-oriented guide, it explains what you need to know about that awesome entity The Law, and then it shows you how to use that legal knowledge to get the best results. Covering hundreds of situations that ordinary citizens encounter every day—from the negligent dry cleaner to the unfair boss to the belligerent policeman—KNOW YOUR RIGHTS tells you how to avoid hassles, negotiate disputes, solve problems, and get a fair shake—all with maximum speed, efficiency, and economy.

Furthermore, this problem-solving book will prevent that numb sensation of helplessness and hopelessness that can strike when you must deal with life's problems, whether small (getting your neighbor's pesky puppy to stop barking) or large (getting the U.S. government to pay your rightful Social Security benefit). In other words, it gives you confidence and power.

KNOW YOUR RIGHTS is organized by topics in seven major areas: your home and community, your marriage and family, health care, job, money, car, and consumer rights. The last chapter, "Your Rights in Action," tells you how to assert yourself and take the decisive steps necessary to ensure corrective action whenever your rights are infringed.

The information is readily accessible: *Easy-to-read boxes* appear on every page, giving you handy checklists of facts you need and steps to take in order to secure your rights. *Detailed charts* help you compare and contrast important options. *Sample letters and forms* show you what to say and how to say it, whether you are complaining to a manufacturer, hiring a nanny, or resigning from a job. *True-to-life scenarios* give you insights into the way real people cope with real problems. At the back of the book, a *directory of resources* lists scores of organizations that offer further information and help.

Although no single book can cover every facet of the law, KNOW YOUR RIGHTS does tell you what your rights are and how to take action to secure them. Because, at times, you may nevertheless need the services of a lawyer, this book also advises you when professional help is necessary and how to work effectively with a lawyer to save both money and time.

"You can't fight city hall!"

This is another expression that you, no doubt, have heard a thousand times. But don't you believe it. The fact is, you *can* fight city hall, and this book gives you the know-how to do just that—and to win.

YOUR HOME AND COMMUNITY

*Owning a house or apartment may be the biggest
financial responsibility you will ever assume,
so secure your home by understanding your rights.*

HUNTING FOR YOUR HOME ■ NEGOTIATING
AND SETTLING ■ PAYING FOR YOUR HOME
■ MANAGING YOUR HOME ■ REPAIRS AND
IMPROVEMENTS ■ NEIGHBOR PROBLEMS
■ ENVIRONMENTAL CONCERNS ■ CONDOS,
CO-OPS AND PLANNED COMMUNITIES ■ RENTING
■ OWNING A SECOND HOME ■ HOME OPTIONS
FOR SENIORS ■ MOBILE HOMES
■ SELLING YOUR HOME ■ MOVING

HUNTING FOR YOUR HOME

Knowing your rights and responsibilities while house hunting could protect you from costly mistakes now and in the future.

123..

KEEPING AN EYE ON THE BROKER

Real estate agents or brokers occasionally resort to shady tactics in their eagerness to make a deal for a seller. As a buyer working with a traditional seller's broker, you should be wary of:

1. A broker who asks you the top price you are willing to pay for a house. It is unethical, and in some states illegal.

2. A broker who creates a sense of urgency or false intimacy by revealing personal information about the seller, such as a pending divorce or financial woes. These claims may be pressure tactics meant to hurry your decision to buy.

3. A broker who tries to exhaust or confuse you. This is done by showing unsuitable properties and saving the best—and highest priced—choice until last.

4. A broker who keeps showing you homes you cannot afford. If you learn from neighbors that houses in the area are available within your price range, question the broker.

5. A broker who insists that your offer is too low. The broker should give you advice, and has a right to disagree about a price, but is legally bound to present your offer to the seller.

Working With Real Estate Brokers

Whether you are a first-time home buyer or back in the housing market after many years, you will need to find out what houses are available in the location you want, at a price you can afford, with the features you desire. While some buyers find suitable properties through word of mouth, classified ads, or "For Sale" signs, most enlist the services of one of three types of real estate professionals: real estate brokers, Realtors, or real estate agents.

Real estate brokers are licensed by the state to negotiate real estate transactions between a buyer and seller for a fee; Realtors are brokers who belong to the National Association of Realtors; real estate agents, who also must be licensed, sell property on behalf of a broker or Realtor but cannot earn fees on their own. Traditionally, someone wanting to sell a house hires a broker or agent to advertise the property and find a buyer willing to pay the asking price. For these services the broker receives a commission from the seller—usually six percent of the sale price.

Because brokers generally advertise properties in a computer listing that other brokers can access, the broker who lists the house may not be the one who brings in the buyer. When this happens, the broker who brings in the buyer takes half the commission from the broker who listed the property. If you are a buyer, note that a broker showing you a house may not necessarily be representing your interests but simply trying to get a commission. Note, too, that you are not legally obligated to a broker just because he spends a lot of time with you: in fact, you are free to change brokers or use several simultaneously. Once you decide to make an offer on a specific house, though, you are obligated to deal through the broker who first showed you the house.

FINDING A BROKER

To protect home buyers from the false impression that a broker is working in their interest, most states have laws requiring brokers to tell buyers whom they represent. However, the majority of states do not require this disclosure until after the first round of house hunting. If you are looking for a house,

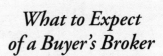

take the time to search for a reputable broker through friends, associates, a mortgage lender, attorney, or the local board of the National Association of Realtors.

While some house hunters may feel comfortable only working with a traditional real estate broker, others may find advantages in using an alternative broker, such as a discount broker or a buyer's broker. These alternatives can provide knowledgeable buyers with savings in money or time—or both.

ALTERNATIVE BROKERS

Discount brokers, like traditional brokers, are hired by the seller, but at a lower commission (three or four percent of the selling price rather than the standard six percent). Because the broker takes a reduced commission, the seller can lower the asking price on the house and thus create savings for the buyer. Discount brokers cost less because they do not show buyers properties or negotiate the final deal. In fact, they do little more than give the buyer a seller's name, address, and telephone number. While you may not mind looking at houses on your own, understand that the discount brokers will not be around to provide the services traditional brokers offer, such as helping to negotiate an impasse in a sale price.

Buyer's brokers are gaining great popularity nationwide. Working as independents or as employees of a traditional real estate company, they differ from traditional brokers and discount brokers in that they are paid by the buyer. For a fee, they try to find exactly what the buyer is looking for and negotiate a favorable purchase price.

Like any other broker who brings a buyer to a seller's broker, a buyer's broker may divide the six percent broker's commission with the seller's broker. This three percent payoff usually serves as the basic fee for a buyer's broker. But a buyer's broker may additionally charge a retainer fee or may ask that her commission be based on an hourly rate or a flat fee. In the end, you could pay hundreds of dollars more to a buyer's broker than you would to a regular (or seller's) broker.

On the positive side, however, buyer's brokers claim to save as much as 20 percent average on selling prices by negotiating hard on a client's behalf and working to get discounts from sellers for such things as defects or potential repairs. Buyer's brokers also save busy clients time by weeding out inappropriate properties, in contrast to traditional brokers who may choose to show unsuitably high priced properties.

YOUR RIGHT TO FAIR HOUSING

In any house-hunting situation, you are protected by the Fair Housing Act, a federal law that prohibits discrimination based on race, national origin, religion, or gender. Under this law, it

What to Expect of a Buyer's Broker

Buyer's brokers are expected to provide clients with specific services and guarantees:

✔ **Exclusivity.** A buyer's broker should work solely for the buyer and should not represent the seller in any way. Some brokers try to do this in order to collect both the listing broker's fee and the buyer's broker fee on the sale of a house. Called fee splitting, this is illegal in some states and is unethical everywhere.

✔ **Contract.** A buyer's broker should provide you with a contract explaining services, fee structure, any bonus provisions, and the time frame of the agreement. Be sure you understand all its elements.

✔ **Basic fee.** A buyer's broker's basic fee may be expressed in terms of a flat fee, an hourly rate, a percentage of the home's list price, or a percentage of the purchase price.

✔ **Retainer fee.** Besides the basic fee, a buyer's broker's contract usually calls for a retainer fee, covering a period varying from 30 days to six months. If the broker fails to find the buyer a suitable home within the time period, the client has the right to an immediate refund of the retainer fee.

YOUR RIGHTS TO INFORMATION FROM A SELLER

As a prospective buyer, you have the right to certain key information from the seller. Some Realtors will not show a property without a detailed written disclosure form from the seller; and some states, like California, require such a form. Still, most Realtors and most states require only verbal disclosure by the seller—and only if he is asked. Be sure to ask questions and get full answers before agreeing to a contract. Some key information to dig out:

1. Does the house have any structural or property defects not obvious to the naked eye?

2. Which appliances and fixtures, such as refrigerators, dishwashers, or light fixtures, are included in the sale price of the house? Make notes of what you expect and add these items to your purchase agreement.

3. Does the house or property have easements (allowance of property use by others), zoning violations, or building-code violations against it?

4. Are there any environmental hazards that may affect the quality of the house or environs? Since a seller may be unaware that the home harbors hazards such as asbestos or radon, take full advantage of your right to a home inspection.

5. What is the full amount of property taxes and other assessments on the home?

is illegal for a broker to discriminate by refusing to negotiate or to falsely deny that there are suitable homes available for sale or inspection. It is also illegal for the seller of a house to discriminate by refusing to negotiate the sale of a house that is on the market, setting different terms or conditions of sale for different people, or falsely denying availability. If you feel you have been discriminated against, contact your local unit of the federal Office of Fair Housing and Equal Opportunity.

If You Find the "Perfect" House

After many days of house hunting, you finally find the house you want to buy. In your enthusiasm, you might eagerly instruct your broker or real estate attorney to start drawing up the purchase agreement. But before making any commitments, you need to get prepurchase information about defects in and around your future home. You can then incorporate this information into the negotiating process or, at worst, cancel the sale.

Although a house may look fine to you, it takes a professional home inspector to make sure that the basic structure is in good shape and that the heating, plumbing, and electrical systems are sound. Many states and most mortgage lenders require a prepurchase home inspection soon after a purchase contract is signed. The state or the mortgage lender may insist on the use of an inspector of its choosing; usually, however, the buyer hires the inspector and pays for the service.

In most states, home inspectors do not have to be licensed engineers or architects; so before you hire an inspector, question him about his professional affiliation (ideally with the American Society of Home Inspectors or another reputable association) and length of experience. The cost of a standard inspection varies from $50 to $500, depending on where you live and the condition of the home. Older houses generally cost more to inspect because they are assumed to have more problems. An inspector should set the fee in advance and provide a written report upon completion.

ADVANTAGES OF A HOME INSPECTION

If you worry about getting your money's worth, ask the inspector if you can join him on his rounds. Most inspectors, as a matter of professional courtesy, encourage buyers to do so. The two- or three-hour examination will probably be well worth your time and money because it can give you a quick education about this major purchase you are about to make, from the way the house is put together overall to its structural peculiarities and unique features. Your guided tour will alert you to major problems, which can be used as leverage in your purchase negotiations (or could make you decide to back out), as well as to minor defects or conditions that could affect you immediately upon moving in, such as a water heater too small to supply your two teenagers. (Small problems can also bolster your position at the bargaining table.) Your prepurchase inspection will help you anticipate the nature and extent of repairs and maintenance in the months and years to come.

Your home inspection may also reveal problems that should be examined more carefully by a specialist. For example, older homes are often subject to termites, and while a general inspection may call your attention to the problem, you should hire a professional termite inspector to determine the full extent of the situation and to estimate how much it will cost to remedy the problem; some states, in fact, require termite inspections by mortgage lenders. Similarly, tests for asbestos, radon, lead in drinking water, and other environmental hazards should be conducted by specialists whom your home inspector can recommend. (Don't forget, however, that you can make your inspections only with the cooperation of the occupant.)

Only after these inspections should you negotiate your deal with the seller. If you have already starting negotiating, be sure your purchase agreement contains a prepurchase home inspection contingency clause, so that if major structural problems are discovered during the inspection—for example, if the foundation of the house sits on sand and is clearly unstable—you can break the purchase contract without penalty.

An expert is someone who knows some of the worst mistakes that can be made in his subject and how to avoid them.

WERNER HEISENBERG
Physics and Beyond

Make Sure Your Home Inspector Does His Job

A professional home inspection is the best way to uncover any flaws in the structure or systems of a house you plan to buy. The following checklist highlights the areas a good inspector must evaluate in his written report to you:

• **Foundation, basement:** Structural stability; moisture, cracks; insects (especially termites); accessibility of crawl spaces.

• **Attic:** Accessibility to attic and to crawl spaces; insulation, ventilation; condition of chimney; infestation by squirrels.

• **Exterior walls, roof, and gutters:** Basic construction. Condition of siding materials, trim. Fans, vents. Roof leaks, condition of shingles, sun damage, sags, skylights. Leaks in gutters, drains.

• **Windows and doors:** Condition of glass, screens, storm windows; caulking, weather stripping; sashes, frames, hardware shutters, insects.

• **Interior:** Condition of walls, floors, stairways, ceilings, insulation. Presence of leaks, cracks, moisture, squeaks, sagging, insects.

• **Electric, plumbing, heating systems:** Capacity and condition of grounding; fuses; circuit breakers; outlets. Capacity and distribution of heating and cooling systems throughout the house; effectiveness of thermostats. State of septic system, pipes, faucets, water heater, kitchen, laundry room; water pressure.

• **Outdoor structures, grounds:** Condition of garage, barn, and other structures; pool, pool surround; fences, walls; drainage, septic-tank location, troublesome trees.

Check Out the Neighborhood

Your own investigation of the area around your potential new home is as important as an inspection of the house itself. Before buying check:

✔ *The neighborhood.* Consider the quality of the house- and lawn-care of homes on your street, space between lots, street lighting, traffic.

✔ *The overall community.* To determine the quality of a community, get information from the chamber of commerce, real estate brokers, and local residents. Find out who your neighbors will be and what they think about crime, police, and fire protection and the quality of hospitals and schools in the area.

✔ *Development plans.* Ask the seller and other local people about any upcoming development plans for the community. An unsightly fast-food restaurant or shopping mall could affect the enjoyment or value of your property.

✔ *Zoning laws.* Do restrictions prohibit building a deck or other sorts of remodeling? Are noisy businesses allowed next door? Can you have a home office on the property? If your home is in a planned community, is it subject to zoning restrictions on pets or parking, for example?

✔ *Environmental factors.* Do power plants, garbage incinerators, or airborne pesticides from farmland affect the area?

WHAT THE SELLER MUST TELL YOU

Although a prepurchase inspection can uncover essential information about a future home, no one knows the quirks and tics of a house better than the people who have been living in it. Until recently, home buyers almost always had to pay for major property defects discovered after purchase, based on the premise of *caveat emptor* ("let the buyer beware"). Today legal trends indicate greater recourse for buyers by placing the onus on the seller to disclose problems before selling a house. Although real estate disclosure laws differ from state to state and even city to city, they generally require sellers to reveal major defects that affect the property's value and habitability.

Depending on the locality, sellers may be required to disclose verbally what they know about a house's defects, to provide a written disclosure form, or merely to answer honestly any questions a would-be buyer asks. In some cases, a buyer can cancel the sale or sue for repair costs if a seller has knowingly concealed defects or purposely misrepresented the condition of a house. (See "Managing Your Home," page 30.)

Even if you do not live in an area with strict disclosure laws, you may be protected by implied warranties of habitability and fitness. State courts that recognize implied warranties acknowledge that home buyers have the right to expect their property to be free of material defect in the same way that a consumer buying a product expects it to be free of defect. (For more about implied warranties, see YOUR CONSUMER RIGHTS, page 404.) Ask a real estate attorney or the office of the state attorney general if your state recognizes implied warranties.

Avoiding New-House Woes

Just because a home is new does not mean it is perfect, as is evident from the high volume of litigation involving owners of newly built homes. The problems these homeowners encounter generally stem from the use of inferior materials, low-quality construction, or a combination of the two.

Inferior materials may be used because the high cost of raw materials and the pressures of competition prompt some builders to substitute cheaper products for high-quality items—as by using particleboard instead of plywood. Low-quality construction work may be the result of pressure to finish the home on deadline or on budget. Shoddy workmanship can result in all sorts of ills, such as malfunctioning of the electrical, plumbing, and heating systems; misalignment of doors and windows; lack of ventilation in bathrooms, kitchens, or laundry rooms; and dirt trapped under a polyurethane floor finish.

An awareness of these potential lapses should reinforce any buyer's determination to insist on a prepurchase inspection by a reputable home inspector and, if necessary, a structural engineer. If these professional prepurchase examinations reveal problems, insist on having them fixed immediately. If necessary, you may have to renegotiate the terms or timing of the sale or even cancel it.

Concerns With Older Homes

Older homes may well offer charm lacking in newly built houses. What's more, the fact that a house is older does not necessarily mean that it is not in good physical condition. The soundness of a building depends on its original quality and on the extent of maintenance done by previous owners. A 20-year-old house may be in better condition than a 10-year-old structure.

Nevertheless, an older house may host a roster of problems that could translate into major repair bills for a new owner. Whether a building is 20 or 200 years old, a buyer should learn as much as possible about its structural soundness through prepurchase inspections and information from the seller.

Be particularly aware of evidence of termites and wood rot, inadequate or antiquated electrical wiring, plumbing weakness because of old pipes and rusty fixtures, leaky roofs and useless gutters, and wet basements. While these problems usually can be identified in prepurchase inspections, the extent of the problems may not be clear until you take possession of the house. Wood rot, for example, may have been concealed with a couple of coats of paint; or an electrical system that adequately serviced the house's existing equipment may not be able to cope with the high-voltage demands of your appliances.

WARRANTY PROTECTION

Besides conducting a thorough prepurchase inspection, buyers of older homes may want to invest in a home warranty. Once restricted to new-home purchases, home warranties are now available for previously occupied houses. They can be paid for by the buyer or the seller as part of the purchase agreement. The warranty period is typically one year with an option to extend, and annual premium prices may run several hundred dollars plus deductibles. Older-home policies rarely cover structural defects like leaky roofs or cracked foundations, but they do protect against limited problems in the major systems of the home, such as plumbing, electrical, heating, and cooling.

Anyone buying an older house, especially one more than 30 years old, should expect to have to make repairs. Major prob-

---

Warranties: Legal Protection for Newly Built Homes

A variety of warranties are included with the purchase of a newly built home.

✔ *Express warranties.* These first-year guarantees of good workmanship from builders or developers come free with new homes and are spelled out in the sales contract. Some states require them, but few regulate their content; therefore the builder decides what is covered and for how long.

✔ *Implied warranties.* Almost every state guarantees implied warranties of habitability and workmanship, which legitimize the reasonable expectations of homeowners that a new home is safe, sound, and well constructed. For example, a sinking patio might breach the implied warranty of workmanship.

✔ *Extended warranties.* An extended warranty covers a home for 10 years against major design and structural defects. It may come free with a house when its builder belongs to a warranty company like Home Buyers Warranty, Home Owners Warranty, or American Home Shield.

✔ *Product warranties.* Products in a new home under written warranty from their makers are included in the first-year warranty of a builder or are covered by the implied warranties from the builder.

lems found before purchase often can be negotiated into the sale price. But buyers who agree to take a house "as is" must accept responsibility for all repairs and maintenance.

Do You Really Want to Build?

A custom-built home may be the answer to your dreams or it may be a financial and emotional debacle. Taking certain precautions can help protect you from disasters and arm you with legal recourse for worst-case scenarios. Before you start booking designers and builders for your custom home, take time to plan it out yourself. Decide what kind of house you want, how big a house you need, and how much you can spend on it.

If your design requirements are unique and your budget is ample, you may want to hire an architect. Interview several before choosing one, and consider their reputations and finished projects before making a decision.

Many custom-home builders can provide both design and construction services. Some builders keep files of house plans they have designed, and as long as the plans are not copyrighted, you can use them for your own home, modified to your needs. Full-service builders will not only design and construct the house but can advise you on interior design as well.

If you use builders to design your house, set the terms of the design in a contract. Make sure the contract clarifies who owns the design plans if you decide to use another builder for the construction; the breakdown of design and building costs; what kind of changes can be made to the design once construction begins, and at what cost.

To save money on the design side, you might buy one of thousands of house plans available in home and trade magazines. This approach is cheaper than hiring a builder/designer or architect, but the plan you choose may need tailoring (if your land is sloping rather than level, for example). Make sure all specifications, including electrical and plumbing, are included, or you will end up paying to have the plan redesigned for you.

YOU'RE THE BOSS

No matter whom you hire to design and build your home, you are at the helm of this mammoth undertaking. Before you begin, determine—and contractually clarify—the chain of command for the process. Does the builder defer to the architect? Who hires—and is liable for—subcontractors?

A builder must follow not only your design plan but also the building codes set by municipalities, counties, and states to protect occupants from hostile conditions, from fire to flood.

HOW TO CHOOSE AN ARCHITECT

These criteria can help you choose an architect to design a custom-built home:

1. Word of mouth. If a friend has a house you admire, find out who designed it. Ask the local chapter of the American Institute of Architects (AIA) about architects in your area.

2. Interview and compare. Meet with at least three architects to discuss your plans. (Ask first if they will charge for consulting time.)

3. Find out about fees. Some architects charge fixed fees plus expenses; others get a percentage of the cost of the house. Pin it down before going any further.

4. Explain your own ideas. Go to the interview with your own concept and priorities, including size and style of the house, budget, and special needs. Make sure the architect responds to your vision.

5. Ask how she works. What is her specialty? Would she execute the design of your project, or use assistants? What priority would your project take in her schedule?

6. Consider personality. You will be working with an architect for a long time. Is her company congenial?

7. Discuss the contract. Be clear about your payment terms and the architect's responsibilities. You might get a lawyer to look over the contract.

These codes vary regionally: Chicago prohibits wood-frame constructions, for example, while San Francisco requires seismic support. Since you are ultimately responsible for any building-code violations, be sure to review the requirements of these codes with your builder before construction begins.

Other Ways to Own a Home

Though the classic image of "home" may be a single-family residence on a private patch of land, there are other options available to potential homeowners. These include buying homes in a planned residential development, condominiums, cooperative housing units, co-owned properties, and rental properties that include an option to buy. Planned community developments, once the venue of retirees, have grown popular nationwide with those who want to eliminate some of the burdens and responsibilities of ownership.

PLANNED COMMUNITIES

A planned community of single-family residences often offers conveniences such as complete lawn service in summer and snow shoveling in winter; amenities such as common swimming pools and other recreational facilities; limited maintenance and repair service for the home; and on-site conveniences such as grocery stores or banks.

If you are considering buying a home in a planned but not yet completed development complex, be sure to investigate the reputation of the developers, the past projects they have completed, and their financial backers. Also, if you have seen only a model home, find out which features and fixtures will actually be included in your house. Ask specifically about such features as the dishwasher, carpeting, designer light fixtures, and bathroom fixtures. Take into account whether they are part of the overall price or whether you must pay extra for the ones you particularly want.

CONDOS AND CO-OPS

Along with homes in planned communities, condominiums and cooperative apartments are also gaining popularity. A condominium is a type of ownership, not a type of property. Whether a condo is an apartment or town house, you own the dwelling plus an interest in the common property. You contribute toward, and are jointly responsible for, building maintenance, lawn care, and shared amenities. A cooperative apartment, alternatively, is not owned individually: A person buys shares in a corporation that owns the real estate, and holds

Keeping It Cool With Co-owners

The details of co-ownership of property vary in complexity with the parties' relationships and their state laws. For unmarried co-owners a good way to avoid ambiguities and squabbles in the future is to sign a written agreement, separate from the deed or other ownership documents. Here are some points of potential trouble that it might nail down:

✔ *Mortgage.* How much of the monthly payments will each owner pay, and who will deal with the lender in business relating to the mortgage loan?

✔ *Maintenance.* Will the costs of keeping up the property be spread among the owners as they occur, or is there a joint repair and maintenance account? How will each owner's nonfinancial maintenance contributions be compensated?

✔ *Disputes.* How will arguments over dealing with the property be resolved? Mediation? Arbitration?

✔ *Incompatibility.* Who gets to stay in the house if two partners find they can no longer get along? How will that decision be made? And if one partner does leave, will the other have first option to buy his or her share?

✔ *Survivors.* What happens to the property if a co-owner dies? Will it pass to the other co-owner, or must it be transferred through a will?

a long-term lease on a particular unit.

Residents in planned subdivisions are automatically part of the homeowners associations that govern their common properties. These associations are legally entitled to enforce rules and regulations that residents must adhere to. Since these rules may both benefit and constrain a resident, you should consider them carefully before making a commitment to buy.

A final option for prospective home buyers is to share a property: parent and child, two sisters, an unmarried couple, or several friends might pool resources for a joint property. You should be careful to delineate in advance how ownership will be divided—who pays what proportion of which expenses, who will act as managing partner, and how the co-ownership arrangement can be dissolved. (See also "Keeping It Cool With Co-owners," page 17.)

With the high cost of real estate, some sort of joint ownership may be the only way new home buyers can hope to finance a home. It can be a legally intricate business, however, so hire a real estate lawyer to advise you.

Buying a Foreclosure? Beware!

Some home buyers look for value in properties whose mortgages have been foreclosed by lenders because of the owners' financial distress. You should know that houses in foreclosure may not be the bargains they seem. Watch out for these common difficulties:

• **You might not see what you get.** When homes with government-backed mortgage loans fall into foreclosure, they are boarded up and advertised for sale in local newspapers. The winning bidder buys the house sight unseen— and then may find it a shambles, thanks to former owners who have taken everything they could, including the kitchen sink. If the foreclosed property is offered by a private lender in public auction, however, you usually will be permitted to tour the property before bidding at auction—obviously a safer alternative.

• **A home may be riddled with financial woes.** Many foreclosures come with outstanding debt attached to the property. Mechanics' liens— claims against the home by unpaid former workers—can put in question the title of a home itself, not the credit of the previous owners. Mechanics' liens and any unpaid property taxes must be paid off before title to the house can be transferred. Both of these sorts of debts can be tracked down before purchase by a real estate lawyer.

• **Former owners may buy back the property.** Homeowners are sometimes able to buy back their homes even after a foreclosure sale, depending on the state's foreclosure laws. Half of the states permit homeowners to regain possession of their homes for anywhere from six months to several years after the foreclosure sale. If you are the new owner of a home purchased under these circumstances, you may not be able to take final possession of the home until this period expires.

• **The paperwork is highly complex.** Buying a house in foreclosure is a complicated legal procedure with rules that vary from state to state. In New Jersey, for example, it may take as long as two years to complete the process, while a foreclosure sale in Connecticut can be completed in less than six months. Wherever you live, you must have a real estate attorney to help you navigate through the muddle.

• **You may need cash on hand.** In some foreclosure sales, the full payment is required immediately, within a week or 10 days of sale. Most mortgage lenders will not finance foreclosure purchases. Therefore, you will need to make sure you have cash on hand when you are lining up the purchase of a foreclosure.

Negotiating and Settling

You finally found the right house, and now you have to come to terms with the seller. Know what your rights as a buyer are—and sharpen your bargaining skills.

Key Concerns in Negotiation

When your house hunting leads you to a home you want to buy, you can start negotiating the sale with the seller. This process typically entails three stages: the bids, the counterbids, and the agreed-upon price. The buyer then presents a final purchase offer accompanied by a deposit, called "earnest money." When this is accepted by the seller, it effectively becomes what is known as the binder, or deposit receipt. Often, the binder becomes the purchase contract. If changes are needed, the buyer and the seller set a date to create the final sales contract.

To prepare yourself for the negotiating process, you must define your priorities. First, know the top price you can afford to pay and the top price you will pay for the house under consideration. Second, determine which aspects of the house would be negotiable, such as trading off the inclusion of kitchen appliances for accepting that the house needs new carpeting. Finally, consider your requirements for particular features of the deal, such as a certain moving day.

HOW TO CALCULATE AN OFFERING PRICE

In order to calculate your initial bid, you must assess the fairness of a seller's asking price. You may well have looked at other properties in the area and thereby have firsthand knowledge of the asking prices for comparable homes. In addition, the real estate broker who showed you the house can prepare a list of homes similar in age, condition, size, and property called a "comparative mortgage analysis." The list should compare only similar homes in the same neighborhood sold within the last six months. (If you are not using a broker, you can look at deeds at the county clerk's office stating location and sale price of homes, then scout the area to find those of comparable size.) Be sure to factor in any value differences, such as the added worth of newly renovated bathrooms.

At this point you may have sufficient knowledge of comparable homes to make an appropriate offer. But if you are not confident of your own analysis, you may want to arrange for a professional appraisal. A state-licensed home appraiser assesses the current market value of your home. An appraisal service

Do You Need a Lawyer?

When it comes time to close on a house, many home buyers turn to a family attorney to handle essential documents. Other buyers feel they can manage by themselves, since it is not mandatory to have a lawyer represent you when buying a home.

But to ensure that your interests are promoted and legally protected, from purchase offer to title transfer, your best bet is to hire a real estate attorney.

Your lawyer can help draft a purchase offer that protects you with contingency clauses, unlike a standard purchase offer or one drawn up by the seller's broker or attorney.

A real estate lawyer can also conduct a title search on your prospective house; arrange an appraisal of the house; and review your mortgage lender's agreement. When you get to the final sales contract, the lawyer can add items that protect you, brief you on the complex procedure of closing on the home, and finally represent you at the closing itself.

Some real estate lawyers advertise a low flat rate for closing on a house but do not offer services over the course of the home-buying venture. Other lawyers charge an hourly rate, a flat fee, or a percentage based on the purchase price of a home.

can cost several hundred dollars but may save you thousands if it identifies an inflated asking price. Note, however, that mortgage lenders require home appraisals by appraisers of their choice, paid by the buyer, so you may prefer to wait until you apply for a loan to have an appraisal; otherwise, if your appraiser is not one of those normally used by the lender, you may pay twice for the service.

MAKING A PURCHASE OFFER

If you have been dealing with traditional real estate brokers, you are likely to be given their agency's standard purchase-offer form when you find a suitable house. While state laws mandate some provisions for the final purchase agreement that will be part of these standard forms, these provisions may not protect you enough. A buyer's best protection is to hire a real estate lawyer to write the contract. You can ask friends or the local bar association to recommend one. (See also "Do You Need a Lawyer?" page 19.)

Some basic points to include in a purchase offer, besides names, addresses, description of the property, and the offering price, are any other financial details, such as the amount of earnest money deposit and the down payment requested, and amount of mortgage loan to be sought. The offer should also describe any conditions, or contingencies, upon which the final sales agreement depends, such as home inspection, seller disclosure, loan approval, and so on.

THE IMPORTANCE OF EARNEST MONEY

The most effective purchase offers are accompanied by earnest money. You are not required by law to make a deposit, but sellers tend to judge the sincerity of buyers by the size of their deposits. In one way, less is best since you may lose your money if the deal falls through (this may depend on a contingency clause in your purchase offer about breaking the deal at the last minute.) Alternately, a big earnest money deposit might encourage the seller to agree to a lower purchase price.

Most real estate brokers expect to have a deposit check in hand when presenting your offer to the seller. The check should never be made out directly to the seller, however, but to the real estate brokerage as trustee or fiduciary agent—one of those terms should be part of the payee's name on the check—or to an escrow service that holds your money in trust. (Decide with your broker or attorney where your earnest money will go until the purchase is final.) If it is a big deposit, your purchase offer should stipulate that it be held in an interest-bearing account with interest credited to you. The offer should also set a date for refunding the money if the seller does not accept your offer or if you withdraw it before he accepts.

MAXIMIZING YOUR POWER TO NEGOTIATE

To clinch the best deal, you should arm yourself with firm facts about the local real estate market. You also must be careful not to reveal any clues that might give the seller leverage.

1. Before making an offer on a home, have a real estate broker (your buyer's broker or the listing agent) prepare a comparative market analysis. This will show you recent sales prices of similar homes in the area. When you then consider both the added features and notable problems of the house you are looking at, you can determine whether the asking price is fair.

2. Avoid talking to the seller about why you are buying a house. If a seller knows that you must buy quickly because you are relocating for a new job, he can use your urgency to his advantage.

3. Be sure the seller knows that you are considering other houses, even if his is the one you want most. The threat of competition for your interest will encourage him to keep his price and conditions within fair market value.

4. If you are home shopping with your spouse or a friend, save any show of enthusiasm for a particular house until you are in private. If the seller knows you really like the house, he will have an edge over you during negotiations.

Dealing With Final Details

After you complete your purchase agreement and before the closing, or settlement date, you need to make sure that the seller is the true owner of the home, that no claims exist against the property, and that the seller has the right to sell the property. If problems do arise, you might be able to renegotiate the terms or timing of your final contract and still complete the sale.

When someone owns real estate, he is said to hold "title" to the property. Bad or defective title to a property occurs for a variety of reasons: liens (financial claims) against the property; an unpaid second mortgage; an heir of the previous owner suddenly appearing to claim ownership; or a violation of community association standards.

To ensure that a house does not have a defective title, you need a "title search." This can be conducted by a title insurance company or a lawyer. The search traces the history of the

Put Legal Protections in Your Purchase Offer

Contingencies in your formal purchase offer are particular conditions that allow you to break or to renegotiate the purchase contract if certain aspects of the deal are not met to your satisfaction. (Remember, the purchase contract—or binder—can become the final contract.) Negotiate the following issues before you sign your purchase offer:

• Set a limit on the seller's response time to your offer. By giving him 48 hours, for example, you keep the seller from waiting for better bids from other buyers while keeping you in limbo.

• Make your purchase offer contingent on the results of a professional home inspection by an inspector of your choice. This may include a termite and environmental inspection.

• Insist that the seller provide you with a written disclosure of defects in the property before you agree on a final price.

• If you are applying for a mortgage, include an escape clause that lets you pull out of the deal if your loan is not approved within a designated time.

• If the purchase of your new home depends on selling your current residence, try to add a clause that frees you from the purchase contract if you cannot sell your home within a designated time.

• Establish the settlement (closing) date and date on which you will take possession of the house.

• Enumerate exactly which features and fixtures of the home will be included in the purchase, such as kitchen appliances, lighting fixtures, carpeting, bookcases, or a backyard swing set.

• Include a description of the condition you expect the house to be in at settlement time. Ideally, the house should be "broom clean," or swept of debris, and completely intact.

• Agree in advance to a specific amount of penalty if you need to back out of the deal or if you learn something about the property (other than a defect in the house, for instance) that makes the deal untenable for you. Known as a "liquidated damages clause," it is part of most purchase offers. State laws vary. If your state limits liquidated damages to the earnest money deposit, do not agree to a clause requiring more money.

• Watch out for arbitration clauses in purchase offers prepared by brokers. These clauses obligate the broker, buyer, and seller to arbitrate any dispute. If you agree to this and the offer becomes binding, you forfeit your legal right to sue.

Ways to Ward Off Defective Titles

If title to a home has liens against it from outstanding debts, you may have to postpone the settlement or even cancel your purchase offer. Protect yourself from defective general titles with these measures.

✔ *Assurance from the seller.* The seller has an obligation to deliver clear title by the settlement date, at which time she should sign a legally binding affidavit that the home's title is not claimed by anyone else and has no liens against it. Your purchase offer should spell out your legal recourse if that turns out not to be true.

✔ *Search of public records.* Your attorney or a title service can examine public records describing your prospective property and any title defects, liens, or encumbrances.

✔ *Owner's title insurance.* For a one-time fee, you can buy insurance from a title company that protects you against any title problems discovered after purchase. Title companies are regulated by state law but have various rates—usually two or three dollars per $1,000 of home value.

✔ *General warranty deed.* With this document the seller warrants that she legally owns the property in question, that there are no claims against the title, and that she has the right to sell the property. It offers stronger protection to the buyer than a simple affidavit.

property, determines whether there are any current claims or encumbrances against the property, and tells you what problems must be cleared up before you can have "clear title" to the property. You can then decide whether you want the seller to fix the problems (such as paying the property taxes due), or whether you should cancel the sale. Some title defects are simply due to recording errors (such as failure to show a paid-up second mortgage) and are easily fixed.

Even with a title search, most buyers opt for the protection of title insurance. There are two types: lender's and owner's. Lender's title insurance—required by lenders, paid by buyers—protects lenders from faulty title. Owner's title insurance protects the buyer from claims against the property that predate the buyer's ownership. Both policies carry a one-time fee, usually half a percentage point of the purchase price. The buyer might pay for both or negotiate to split costs with the seller.

GET THE VITAL DEED

Besides clear title to a home, a buyer needs a valid "deed." A deed is a written document signed by the seller that describes the property and confirms title or ownership. Deeds are held at the county recorder's office. If the signature on a deed has been forged or falsified, it could invalidate your right to ownership—even if you have already bought the home.

To protect against bad deeds, buyers usually require a general warranty deed (also called "full covenant and warranty"), in which the seller ensures legal soundness of the title of the home. While general warranty deeds allow the buyer to sue the seller if claims against the home are discovered, suing is a minor consolation to losing a home.

Other types of deeds offer less protection for the buyer. A "quitclaim deed," for example, merely transfers the seller's ownership to the buyer and does not guarantee clear title . A "grant deed" is more definitive, but does not include a promise by the seller to defend the buyer against future third-party claims. Be sure to clarify the type of deed you will receive from the seller before closing the purchase.

Strategies for Closing Day

When the purchase offer evolves into a final sales contract, the buyer gives the seller a down payment. Then the buyer works to secure a mortgage loan (see "Paying for Your Home," page 25), and the "closing," or settlement, date is set. This is also the time for a buyer to ensure the best deal possible with certain last-minute efforts. These include a final walk-through of the home, whether owner-occupied or newly built, which should occur a day or two before closing. You should look for glaring new problems (a floor badly damaged by the seller's moving service) or discrepancies with your purchase agreement (the seller removed a fixture that was part of the contract). Insist that problems be remedied, or prepare to negotiate a repair or replacement fee with the seller at closing.

A Bad Time to Change Plans

PROBLEM
Doug and Mary made a purchase offer on a newly built custom home, put down an earnest money deposit, and agreed to a final sale price with the builder. A week later, because of changes in their anticipated job transfers, they decided not to buy the house. Are they entitled to a refund of their earnest money?

ACTION
Because the builder was unusually generous, Doug and Mary got back their deposit though they could have ended up in court. While contingencies in purchase offers normally protect buyers from penalty if their mortgage falls through or other conditions aren't met, buyers who change their minds have to forfeit their earnest money deposit. If they hadn't been so lucky, Doug and Mary's builder could have sued them for damages arising from their breaking the contract. If he had, they could have tried to settle out of court by agreeing to pay the costs of the building plans and site work.

Before closing date, the buyer needs to buy a home insurance policy to protect the new investment in the event of damage or destruction. (See also "Managing Your Home," page 30.) This insurance also protects the mortgage lender's investment, and at closing the buyer must provide proof of purchase of the policy to the lender.

On closing day, the least anxious buyers are those who are well prepared. They have attended to all the prepurchase concerns discussed on the preceding pages and are fully informed about what will happen during the closing. According to federal law, a mortgage lender must provide the buyer with an itemized estimate of settlement costs and a detailed account of closing procedures and terminology. Brokers can also convey or supplement this information, but a buyer should rely primarily on the advice of an attorney.

The home buyer's closing costs typically include:

- Balance of the purchase price not covered in the deposit and in the mortgage amount being borrowed.
- Items payable in connection with the mortgage loan, which might include the lender's home appraisal fees and prepayment of insurance costs and property taxes for the year.

TEN CONTRACT ESSENTIALS

Be sure a contract includes:

1. A formal description of the property and its boundaries, including the physical terrain and the boundary markers.

2. Identification of features and fixtures that the seller is obliged to transfer to you as part of the property sale.

3. Total purchase price, including the amount of earnest money deposit, down payment, and the balance due in your mortgage loan.

4. The identity of the escrow agent who holds the earnest money deposit.

5. Agreement between you and the seller on who pays what costs, through what date, for municipal assessments such as property taxes.

6. For the purchase of newly built homes, the builder's guarantee of habitability and good workmanship.

7. Assurance of clear title to the home, unencumbered by claims against the property.

8. Promise of a valid deed that entitles the present owner to sell the home to you.

9. Firm date of occupancy. Without this you may have to leave your old home before the seller has left your new one.

10. A detailed written description of the house and contents upon occupancy.

- Title charges, for title search and both owner's and lender's title insurance.
- Government recording and transfer fees, for recording property documents at the county courthouse.
- Property and pest inspections (both buyer's and lender's).
- Bank attorney's fee, for presence at closing and preparation of documents.
- Buyer's broker commission, if applicable, and lawyer's fee.

Along with vigorous check writing to cover these costs, you also engage in final rites with the seller. These include: coordinating the payment of utilities; calculating property tax payments so that you pick up the tab where the seller leaves off; making adjustments for any missing fixtures. The seller should provide you with the "certificate of occupancy" for the home, a document confirming that the house meets building codes. The "C of O" is essential for refinancing, remodeling, and selling the home. If the seller does not bring it, the closing may be delayed. Last but not least, remember to get the keys!

Closing Costs You Can Negotiate

Closing ceremonies of a home sale consist mostly of the buyer writing cashier's checks to various parties. While local custom often dictates whether the seller or buyer pays certain one-time fees at closing, buyers should know that most of the following costs are negotiable:

• **Mortgage loan fee.** You can suggest that the seller pay your lender's fee for issuing a loan (usually one or two percent of the loan). After all, the seller gains if your loan is expedited. If you are buying a new house, try to get the builder to pay this fee to free your cash for the down payment.

• **Title insurance.** Lender's and owner's title insurance can both be paid by the buyer, or in some cases, shared by the buyer and seller. Your final contract should clarify who pays which costs.

• **Credit report.** Lenders charge a nominal fee to explore your credit history before issuing a loan. You can try to add this to other expenses charged by the lender and propose that the seller share the costs or pay for them outright.

• **Transfer fees.** If you are buying a home from a current occupant, the local municipality charges small fees to record the transfer of ownership into public records. Either buyer or seller can cover these costs.

• **Escrow fees.** When you make an earnest money deposit, you normally leave it in the hands of a neutral third party such as an escrow agent. Naturally, this person charges you for the safekeeping of your money. Since this money eventually goes to the seller as part of the sale price, you might want to ask the seller to pay for all or part of the escrow service.

• **Prorated monthly expenses.** If the closing date of your home purchase falls between billing cycles of property taxes and basic maintenance bills such as oil, water, gas, and electricity, you and the seller must negotiate the fair division of these costs. If you are signing toward the end of the month, you could bargain for the seller to pay the whole month's worth of property tax, for example.

• **One-year home warranty.** If you are asked to pay this warranty on your newly built home, ask the builder to include the warranty as part of your purchase price. In some areas, real estate brokers pay for the warranty.

• **Attorney fees.** Your mortgage lender runs up legal expenses in closing your loan. Although the buyer would normally pay this cost, there is no harm is asking the seller to split it with you.

PAYING FOR YOUR HOME

Most home buyers cannot afford to put down the total price of a house. Mortgage loans are the answer, but finding the best loan is no easy chore.

Prequalifying for a Mortgage

Most home buyers make a deposit on the home they want to buy and then apply for a mortgage loan to help finance the deal. If the buyer has trouble settling the loan, the closing date for the purchase may be postponed or the sale canceled. To avoid these problems, it is smart to "prequalify" before applying for a loan.

Prequalifying for a mortgage loan means finding out how much money a lender is likely to loan you, based on an analysis of your monthly income and outstanding debt. Lenders use two traditional ratios: they compare the anticipated monthly housing expense—mortgage payment plus property taxes and home insurance premiums—with the borrower's gross monthly income; and they compare the borrower's overall monthly debt (mortgage loan payments, credit card debt, car payments, and so on) with gross monthly income. Generally, lenders want monthly house payments to stay below 28 percent of gross monthly income and total monthly debt to stay below 36 percent of gross monthly income.

You can ask a mortgage lender to prequalify you at no cost. The lender states the amount it would be willing to put up, and you can search for a purchase that falls within the correct range. Prequalifying for a mortgage is not a promise that a loan will be made, but it does get the attention of real estate brokers, who can be more confident that a client is good for the money, and it also lures sellers, who want to deal with buyers financially qualified to purchase their homes.

Making the Most of a Mortgage

A mortgage is a legal agreement with a lender whereby you give a promissory note and receive a loan to buy a house, and the lender gets the right to own the house if you do not repay the loan as agreed. This arrangement between lender and homeowner is commonly referred to as a mortgage.

In a traditional 30-year mortgage, you pay fixed, monthly payments that in early years return mainly interest profits to

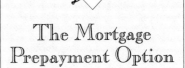

The Mortgage Prepayment Option

What if you have a sudden increase in cash flow and want to pay off your entire mortgage loan before it is due?

Although you might think lenders would be glad to get their money back as soon as possible, prepayment of mortgage loans actually deprives them of profit they expect to get from the interest you would otherwise be paying on the outstanding loan.

Some states prohibit prepayment penalties or limit the size of penalties, but in most states mortgage lenders can impose prepayment penalties that can be as much as three percent of the initial loan. A mortgage agreement can also provide for full or partial prepayment at specific intervals.

So it is important to inquire about prepayment provisions when applying for a loan. The financial flexibility of being able to pay the loan sooner can save you thousands of dollars in interest payments.

The prepayment option also becomes crucial when a homeowner wants to refinance the mortgage. A harsh prepayment penalty in the original loan could offset the significant benefits of refinancing in a period of low interest rates.

TYPES OF MORTGAGES/PROS & CONS

When you are considering the manner in which you are going to pay for your home, the primary financial concern is the type of mortgage loan you should assume. Mortgages come in myriad forms: fixed and adjustable, 10-year to 30-year, government-guaranteed or privately funded, all with varying interest rates,

Type	Definition
Fixed-Rate Mortgage (FRM)	Fixed-rate mortgages are available for anywhere from 10 to 30 years to maturity. The borrower makes a fixed monthly payment for the life of the loan, paying a much higher proportion of interest to principal in the early years.
Adjustable-Rate Mortgage (ARM)	Interest rates on ARMs are based on a financial index such as U.S. Treasury bills. Because these rates fluctuate over the life of the mortgage loan, a borrower's monthly mortgage payments may change frequently. Most lenders impose caps (limits) on these changes.
Stable Mortgage	This hybrid of fixed rate and adjustable mortgages comes in two varieties: one is 75 percent fixed and 25 percent adjustable, with a low down payment; the other is 50 percent fixed, 50 percent adjustable, with a higher down payment.
Balloon Mortgage	Balloon mortgages offer equal monthly payments based on a fixed interest rate, with one large final payment at the end of a relatively short term, usually 5 or 10 years. Monthly payments typically cover interest, while the last payment repays all the principal.
Government Loans	The Federal Housing Administration (FHA) and the Veterans Administration (VA) offer mortgage loan guarantee programs for war veterans and low-to-moderate-income families. Nearly a quarter of residential mortgages are backed by the government.
Jumbo Mortgage	A variation of traditional fixed-rate mortgages, a jumbo loan, which may be necessary to buy a very expensive house, involves larger amounts of money—generally $200,000 or more—than more common loans. Loan life usually varies from 15 to 30 years.
Graduated-Payment Mortgage (GPM)	This type of fixed rate loan is a crescendo of monthly payments that start small and rise steadily, until leveling off for the duration of the loan. Designed for younger home buyers with growing earning power who will not be able to afford higher payments for 5 or 10 years.
Shared-Equity Mortgage	Friends, relatives, or business partners buy property together and share down payments and /or monthly mortgage payments, but only one partner occupies the residence. Partners either share profits from the sale of the house, or one buys the other's share.
Assumable Mortgage	An assumable mortgage is passed on to the new homeowner at the former owner's interest rate. Generally, ARMs, FHA and VA mortgage loans are assumable, while fixed rate loans are not.
Seller Take-Back	In times of high interest rates the current owner may offer to finance the new owner's purchase, using the home as collateral. In effect, the seller takes a first or second mortgage on the property while transferring ownership to the buyer.

repayment requirements, and monetary boundaries. In addition, each one has advantages and disadvantages for you depending upon your financial situation, age, desires, and needs. If you are among the many borrowers who have trouble understanding their mortgage options, let alone figuring out which is best for them, this chart is designed to help. It describes the 10 most common types of mortgage loans and briefly discusses the most relevant pros and cons for each type of loan.

Pros	Cons
The borrower has the security of predictable monthly mortgage expenses and also benefits from long-term tax deductions on interest payments.	Lenders often charge a higher interest rate on FRMs than other types of mortgage loans to protect their interest income in periods of higher interest rates.
Initial interest rates of ARMs are two or three percent lower than fixed rate mortgages, and borrowers have lower monthly mortgage payments when interest rates go down.	When interest rates go up, so do mortgage payments. Even with caps on monthly increases, a steep rise in rates could cause mortgage payments to soar beyond what you can afford.
The low starting rate of a stable mortgage, compared with a fixed rate, affords borrowers a more expensive house. The partially fixed ratio provides stability against interest-rate fluctuations.	If you plan to be in your home less than five years and can afford a higher down payment, you may get an even lower starting rate from a balloon or other mortgage.
Starting costs and monthly payments are low, making this option especially attractive for first-time home buyers who have no profit from selling a former residence.	Monthly payments are mostly interest, so the borrower gets no equity in the home until the loan is paid. The final payment may be so big that it requires refinancing. A dangerous option.
Lower interest rates, easier qualifying requirements, and lower down-payment requirements make government loans attractive to many qualified borrowers.	Maximum loan amounts average less than non-government (conventional) loans. Depending on where you live, FHA loans may be limited to $125,000, VA loans to $184,000.
For home buyers who can afford a home priced $200,000 or more, jumbo mortgages provide necessary resources. Some jumbo loans offer both adjustable and fixed rates.	Interest rates are higher on jumbo loans than on conventional loans, by a half or one percent. Jumbo mortgages also require you to make larger down payments.
In the early years of the loan, when new homeowners can least afford monthly mortgage payments, rates are lower than average fixed-rate loans. Later, when you can better afford it, rates are higher.	If your income does not rise as anticipated by you and your lender, or you unexpectedly get laid off, you may have trouble keeping up with the escalating monthly payments.
One partner helps make the purchase possible and gets tax advantages and, hopefully, profit, while the other partner gets to live in the home and gets help with mortgage payments.	Resident partners give up equity in the home, while investor partners may lose anticipated profit if homes do not gain value. For both parties, equity sharing entails complex legal and tax issues.
In a period of high interest rates, a buyer who can assume the seller's lower-rate loan pays less total interest and smaller monthly payments. The seller enhances the value of her home.	Lenders may charge a fee for assuming a mortgage. Depending on the outstanding balance and the interest rate of the old loan, assuming the seller's loan can cost more than a new loan.
For the buyer, the interest rate of a take-back is usually lower than market rate, making this loan a no-lose prospect. Sellers can sell homes more quickly and still obtain their equity.	Take-backs usually require a final balloon payment, which the buyer may have to refinance. Sellers who do not arrange take-backs through traditional lenders assume financial risk.

What Makes Lenders Wary?

When you apply for a mortgage loan, the lender checks your financial history, and will note unfavorably any unusual cash flow within the previous six months. Lenders are looking for a steady income, not fluctuating highs and lows. As a result, home buyers who accept financial help from relatives or friends to make a down payment might be dismayed to find that gifts can hinder their eligibility for a mortgage loan.

If you get financial help from someone, ask her to write a "gift letter" to your lender confirming that the money is a gift and not a loan. This assures the lender that you are not going further into debt and jeopardizing your ability to repay the lender's loan.

Prospective borrowers who sell pricey personal assets, such as a boat or car, to fund the down payment may also be viewed unfavorably by lenders. Plan to sell personal assets more than six months before applying for the loan.

Lenders are also reluctant to lend money to people already in debt, so you should use any available cash to pay off your credit-card debt before applying for the loan.

If you are strapped for cash, consider trying to get a mortgage from the Federal Housing Administration or the Department of Veterans Affairs. They offer lower interest rates, and their mortgages are generally easier to qualify for than conventional mortgages.

the lender for your use of its money and in later years repay primarily the principal—the amount of money you actually borrowed. Through the process of "amortization," or paying off your debt, you increasingly gain equity (ownership) in the property. Variable or adjustable-rate mortgage loans offer different payment schedules and more flexible interest rates.

Mortgage loans are offered by a number of sources: (1) commercial banks; (2) savings and loan associations (S & L's); (3) mortgage bankers specializing in mortgage loans; (4) the government-run Federal Housing Administration (FHA) or Department of Veterans Affairs (VA); and (5) credit unions. Once you have decided which lender offers the best mortgage options and have made an application, the lender will find out if your income is sufficient to cover monthly mortgage payments and other debts, determine if you have enough assets to close the loan, investigate your credit history, and appraise the property value of your prospective home.

Meanwhile, you should try to get a loan commitment letter from your lender with a "lock-in agreement" that stipulates the exact interest rate of the loan that you are negotiating. This agreement protects you from rising interest rates during the application process. You may be charged a fee by your lender to lock in an interest rate. A few states forbid or limit this fee, but most allow it.

GETTING INFORMATION FROM A LENDER

Once you receive a commitment letter from the lender—formal receipt that your mortgage loan application is being processed—the federal Truth in Lending Act requires the lender to itemize all loan costs and provide you with a booklet entitled "Settlement Costs," which is published by the Department of Housing and Urban Development. (If you are not given this when you apply for the loan, the lender must send it to you within three business days.)

Loan costs include points (a one-time fee of several percentage points of the total loan); a loan application fee ; credit check fees; home appraisal, home inspection, and escrow fees; mortgage insurance; lender's title insurance; and title search fees. The lender must also tell you the finance charge (interest) on the loan and the annual percentage rate (APR) for the loan. Because lenders charge different points and interest rates, the APR is the closest thing consumers have to a standard measure of comparison (see also YOUR MONEY, page 297).

Many mortgage lenders sell mortgages to government-backed investors such as Fannie Mae (Federal National Mortgage Association) or to private firms. By selling the loans, lenders get cash back to reinvest, while those who buy the loans, referred to as the "secondary market," get the right to receive the principal and interest paid by borrowers. When you apply for a loan, lenders should tell you whether they intend to sell your mortgage. If so, be sure to ask what effect, if any, that would have on you.

WHAT IF YOUR BANK SAYS "NO"?

If you are rejected for a traditional mortgage, it may be that the size or steadiness of your income is insufficient, your overall debt is too high, or the cost of the home is more than the lender thinks you can afford. Or you may be the victim of discrimination. Federal fair housing laws dictate that if a lender rejects your loan application, he must tell you why within 30 days from the day you applied. The lender also must give you a free copy of the credit-bureau report that was used to gauge your qualifications. The credit report includes your history of on-time payments, the amount of credit available to you, and other pertinent information. Since credit bureaus make mistakes, borrowers should not hesitate to question their accuracy. (See also YOUR MONEY, page 316.)

If you cannot get anywhere with traditional mortgage lenders, you might consider government-sponsored or other lending sources. But be careful. Generally, the less proof of credit verification a lender requires, the higher the cost of the loan to the borrower—higher interest, extra fees, or larger down payments.

Who Needs Mortgage Insurance?

When you are accepted for a loan, you may be required to pay for mortgage default insurance. (This is different from "mortgage life insurance," an optional policy that pays off your debt if you die before the mortgage is paid off.) Mortgage default insurance protects the lender from borrowers who default on their loans by covering the lender's losses. The entire first-year premium on the insurance is often paid for by the buyer at settlement, with subsequent premium payments paid from the escrow account your lender sets up to cover this and other periodic costs.

Lenders normally require that mortgage default insurance on loans cover 80 percent or more of the cost of the property. In other words, the down payment is less than 20 percent of the appraised value of the house. Although the purpose of this insurance is to protect the lender, it can also help borrowers buy a home with less money down. Once you have acquired 20 percent equity in the home, your lender should no longer require you to maintain the default insurance.

Foreclosure: A Frightening Concept

A specter that haunts many homeowners with mortgage loans is the fear of default and foreclosure. The laws and rules governing procedures are dauntingly complex, but some salient features of the process are:

✔ *Default.* An owner can default on a mortgage loan by missing a payment or simply being late with one. Lenders generally overlook one or two late or missed payments, but do not have to.

✔ *Acceleration.* Once an owner is in default the lender has the right to demand the entire amount of the loan at once.

✔ *Workout.* The owner should contact the lender immediately to try to work out a solution; such as a new loan schedule. The lender, anxious to avoid the laborious foreclosure process, may be willing to negotiate.

✔ *Foreclosure.* If the owner cannot pay the debt or work out a solution, the lender usually must go to court to get a foreclosure judgment against the owner. The owner may be able to defend against it, but will need an attorney to do so.

✔ *Last resort.* Before the actual foreclosure sale, an owner has the right to get the home back by paying the mortgage debt and costs, or the "equity of redemption."

MANAGING YOUR HOME

Insurance, taxes, building flaws, mortgage lenders, utilities, and greedy governments may all have to be dealt with as you settle into your new house.

123...

FILING A PROPER CASUALTY CLAIM

In the wake of burglary, fire, or any other disaster, you can take these steps to file a complete casualty insurance claim:

1. Call your insurance agent or company immediately to report loss or damage. They will send you a claim form and arrange for an insurance adjuster to inspect the damage.

2. Insurance companies will ask you to supply reports of loss or damage as soon as possible. Be as accurate as you can—and if you later discover something additional that was stolen, for example, amend your list of losses.

3. Don't have permanent repairs made until the insurance claims adjuster has seen the damage. If you must have immediate work done, such as new locks or windows, keep receipts and take pictures of the damage.

4. Your claim form will ask you to itemize damaged or stolen possessions, including the original purchase price (or appraised value for an antique or high-value gift) and current replacement cost. Document your information with sales receipts and canceled checks, appraisals, pictures, and videotapes that identify the damaged or stolen belongings.

How Much Home Insurance?

As long as you owe money on a mortgage loan, your lender will require that you maintain a homeowners insurance policy. This insurance does more than just protect a lender's investment—your home—if it is damaged or destroyed. A homeowners policy also protects your stake in the property and your finances in case you are sued for accidents that occur on your premises.

A homeowners insurance policy should include two types of coverage: "casualty protection," which covers you in case of loss or damage to your home or personal property; and "liability protection," which guards you against lawsuits for injuries that occur to others on your property. You can buy one or several standard policies and supplement them with additional coverage, if needed. For homeowners insurance to be effective and worth the price you pay for it, you need to start with an appropriate amount of coverage and keep increasing it as your property increases in value.

CASUALTY INSURANCE

Three standard home casualty insurance policies, HO-1 (HO stands for homeowners), HO-2, and HO-3, protect you against a variety of perils that might damage your home and personal property. The HO-1 policy affords the barest protection of your property and possessions from 11 common perils including fire, windstorms, and theft. The more popular HO-2 offers protection from 18 perils, while the most common policy, HO-3, protects the dwelling but not its contents from all other perils except certain standard exclusions. Earthquake or flood damage, for example, is covered only by separate, more costly policies. HO-4 covers renters, while HO-5, like HO-3, protects a dwelling and it also covers its contents.

Homeowners must guard against being over-insured—paying too much money for excessive coverage—as well as under-insured—risking inadequate coverage during crisis situations. You can determine the right amount of casualty insurance you need by assessing how much it would cost to rebuild your house if it were completely destroyed. This "replacement cost" is different from the market value (likely sale price) of a home, because market value includes the value of the land and its location within the community. For example, if your ocean-view home that could sell for $300,000 is destroyed by fire, you may have to spend $180,000 to rebuild it. Because the fire has not diminished the value of your ocean-view lot, your casualty insurance need only cover the replacement value of the house and belongings. (It can work the other way, of course: An old house might well cost much more to replace than it could fetch on the current market.)

You need an appraiser to assess the value of your house, but you can calculate the value of your personal belongings by making a complete inventory of items, from furniture to clothing, including purchase date and price. Since standard policies limit reimbursement for damaged or destroyed personal property, you may need extra insurance, or "floaters," for valuable assets such as jewelry, art, or furs. A floater is either a separate policy (for an art collection, for instance) or an extension of a standard policy and may cost from several cents to several dollars per $100 of coverage.

Preventing Accidents on Your Property

According to personal injury law, you can be held responsible if someone is injured on your property. The degree of your fault depends on how serious the injury, how dangerous the conditions that caused it, and what you did to correct those conditions.

• Premises liability law requires homeowners to take reasonable care to prevent injuries to third parties on the property. Reasonable care, though not precisely defined by law, means using common sense to foresee and prevent problems whenever possible. This may include warning visitors about a temporarily exposed wire or a pet that may turn violent.

• The law in several states distinguishes between social guests and business visitors. Your responsibilities toward a social guest include a measure of reasonable care as generally defined above. A business visitor, such as a repair person or city worker, is owed a greater effort of care. If a roof shingle that the owner did not know was loose falls and injures a social guest, for instance, the owner is not liable; if it hits a business guest, the owner may be liable, since he owes such guests a duty to have discovered the loose shingle.

• A homeowner can be held responsible for intentionally causing harm to anyone entering the property, including trespassers. If a passerby is injured by touching an electrified fence that had no warnings, you may have to pay her medical damages.

• The courts are tougher on homeowners when children are injured, since children lack the judgment of adults and are therefore more vulnerable. You may be responsible if a child enters your property without permission—perhaps sneaking into your backyard, diving in the shallow end of the swimming pool, and cutting his head.

• You are personally responsible for on-the-job injuries of household employees, defined as anyone you pay to do part- or full-time work where you provide materials. A babysitter or secretary for a home business, for example, is a household employee. You should consider carrying workers' compensation insurance for these workers to protect yourself from lawsuits. The coverage is mandatory in several states. You may also need separate insurance for the home business.

• If you are sued for an accident and injury that occurred on your property, contact your lawyer and your insurance company immediately. Smaller claims are routinely settled outside of court, even if you are not legally at fault. Minor injury claims are paid by the medical-payments coverage part of a homeowners liability policy.

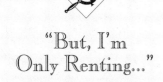

"But, I'm Only Renting…"

Many tenants believe that their personal belongings are insured under their landlord's insurance policy and that any injuries sustained in their rental unit will be the responsibility of the building's owner. But when they try to file a claim, they are surprised. Your landlord's insurance policy will not cover either of these things. It covers the actual building you live in and its common areas.

A special kind of homeowners insurance known as HO-4 is available to meet the insurance needs of tenants and it is worth your while to look into buying a policy.

A tenants policy will insure your belongings against the same perils regular homeowner's insurance covers, including: fire; riot; vandalism; theft; weight of ice, snow, and sleet; freezing of plumbing systems; certain leakage; and damage to some heating systems. This coverage also pays for living expenses you incur as a result of these perils. If your home is damaged by fire, for example, you may be covered for the cost of accommodation and living expenses while repairs are being made.

HO-4 liability coverage applies to injuries or damages caused by you, a family member, or even a pet in your home. For example, if a guest slips and falls in your home, your insurance will cover any medical expenses she incurs and your legal costs if you are sued.

Along with floaters, many standard policies offer complementary coverage for certain perils, including floods, earthquakes, hurricanes, and riots. The nationwide spate of these disasters in the early 1990's prompted insurers to lower their financial risk by increasing the cost of coverage. As a result, homeowners who want these high-risk policies may face higher premiums, higher deductibles (out-of-pocket expenses before the policy reimburses you), or outright denial of coverage. If you believe you have been unfairly denied coverage for insurance, you can contact your state insurance commissioner, whose office regulates the prices companies charge, the kinds of policies they offer, and whom they can refuse.

LIABILITY INSURANCE

As a homeowner, one of the risks you assume is that someone might be injured on your property and hold you financially responsible for damages. Liability insurance protects you from this risk. It pays the legal costs and actual damages of a claim against you (and your family) for bodily injury or property damage that you, or your pets, may cause to others on your property. Unlike casualty insurance, a liability policy does not require you to pay a deductible amount before the insurer covers your losses. However, your liability coverage is limited, typically to $100,000.

Premises liability law, as defined in nearly every state, requires homeowners to exercise reasonable care to prevent injuries to third parties on their property. If you are sued, and your liability insurer agrees that you have acted reasonably to prevent injury to others, your legal expenses and any damages should be covered by your insurer to the limits of your policy, after which you are responsible for costs incurred.

If you have a net worth greater than the limit of your liability insurance, you should consider extra, or "umbrella," coverage. This comes separately and pays for losses beyond the limits of a standard policy. You are covered, for instance, if a delivery person slips on your front steps, breaks an arm, and sues you for an exorbitant amount because he thinks you are wealthy. Umbrella coverage also protects against suits for libel, slander, or invasion of privacy.

VARIATIONS ON STANDARD POLICIES

Variations on standard liability and casualty insurance are also available for owners of condominiums, cooperatives, older homes, and vacation homes. As with traditional single-family dwellings, it is important for owners of other types of homes to buy the appropriate homeowners insurance policy in order to avoid being overcharged on premiums and underinsured in the event of damage or disaster. Homeowners 6 (HO-6) is the standard casualty policy for condo and co-op owners. It protects the personal possessions and interior space of the owner. It does not provide insurance coverage for the structure itself. That is usually covered by the condominium or co-op association. (See also "Condos, Co-ops, and Planned Communities," page 66.)

Property insurance companies offer different casualty policies for older homes, defined differently by each company, but usually 25 years and older. Because older homes are more likely to have outdated wiring or other systems and may not be modernized to meet new building codes, insurance companies often charge more for these policies. The standard older home casualty policy, HO-8, covers the basic perils of the HO-1 policy, such as fire and theft.

HO-8 does *not* cover a multitude of perils that are covered in newer homes: freezing or bursting pipes, electrical damages, collapse from weight of snow, and others. Historic homes—50 to 100 years and older—are the most difficult to insure, since architectural details may be irreplaceable or prohibitively expensive to replace. For insurers that specialize in historic homes, contact the National Trust for Historic Preservation.

Owners of vacation homes and second residences need to purchase liability and casualty coverage separate from their primary residence policies. Although casualty coverage generally protects your property against burglary and theft, for example, policy restrictions often apply to homes that are not occupied for 30 days or longer. (When you leave even your primary residence unoccupied for a month or two, your policy may require you to notify your insurance agency.) As with any type of coverage, you need to decide, with the help of an insurance agent or broker, which policy is most appropriate for you.

When to Challenge Property Taxes

Home ownership generally includes the obligation to pay property taxes. Collected by local governments (cities, towns, villages, counties), these taxes pay for such public services as sanitation, fire and police departments, streetlights, sidewalks, schools, parks, hospitals, and more. Property owners pay according to the value of their property, as determined by government assessment.

The assessed value of a citizen's property is multiplied by a tax rate usually set by the local government. This determines each property owner's tax burden. While states set a limit on taxation, local governments can adjust the tax rate periodically to fit their budgetary needs. They can also charge special assessments to fund one-time expenses, such as a new public library.

Refuting an Unfair Insurance Settlement

If you feel your insurance company shortchanged you in settlement of a claim, here are measures to take:

✔ *Reread your policy.* First you must know what situations your policy covers, as well as its financial limits. Only then can you decide if you are getting a proper response from the insurer.

✔ *Compare your estimate.* Add up your inventory of damages and losses and their approximate replacement value; compare your figures with the insurance adjuster's estimate. Then discuss the discrepancies with the adjuster.

✔ *Gather and offer evidence.* Before contesting your insurer's settlement, you must harness all evidence supporting your case. This includes written and pictorial evidence, such as the receipt for a stolen ring or a picture of an antique you inherited.

✔ *Talk to the boss.* If talking to the adjuster does not solve the problem, ask to speak with the claims department manager. Most companies will pay for an independent appraiser or arbitrator to help settle the disagreement.

✔ *Get government help.* If you are still unsatisfied, contact your state insurance department. This body regulates the industry and often provides free mediation services.

Making Sure Your Property Tax Assessment Is Fair

According to the standards of the law governing property tax assessments, homes of similar value must be similarly assessed, with adjustments made for individual variations in value—new roof, back deck, swimming pool, and so on.

Sometimes you can get your assessment reduced if you can show that you are the victim of one of the following unlawful judgments:

"Unequal assessment" occurs when your property has been assessed at a higher percent of value than other similar properties in the same assessment category.

"Excessive assessment" means that your property has been assessed at more than its true value.

"Unlawful assessment" occurs when a tax has been imposed on a property that should be exempt or partially exempt because you are a war veteran, for example, or because you are 65 years old and subject to a reduction for older homeowners.

If you think any of these situations apply to you, call your local tax assessment board or contact a real estate attorney.

Your local board of property tax assessors must notify you about the status of your property taxes and assessments for the upcoming fiscal year. (For fiscal years starting in July, tax-assessment notices are sent between November and January.) You have very little time—sometimes only 10 days—in which to challenge an unfair assessment.

According to legal standards, property tax assessments should be fair and just for all citizens, but the evaluations are often politically charged and economically complex. For example, a town losing money in commercial property taxes proposes major hikes in residential taxes, or a state finance board wants counties to raise the taxes of rural property owners.

MAKING SURE AN ASSESSMENT'S FAIR

Along with political and economic factors, it is common for assessors to make mistakes in calculating the value of your property. An assessor might inaccurately record the square footage of your home; mistake the size of your lot; see value-enhancing improvements where you made necessary repairs.

If you believe your property tax assessment is inaccurate or unfair, there are a number of steps you can take:

- Gather evidence to verify that your taxes are unfair. If the assessor's report incorrectly states that you have a two-car garage, take a picture of your garage to prove otherwise.
- Examine public records at the local assessor's office listing property values and taxes you and your neighbors pay.
- Join an organized community protest against tax increases or attend the next town meeting on rate hikes.
- File an appeal with your municipality, in writing, stating why the assessment is in error and include evidence; or meet with the local tax board and make an appeal.
- If necessary, appeal the decision of the tax board in court. A lawyer may take the case on contingency, collecting a fee only if you win.
- Hire an independent property-tax consultant (ask your accountant for a recommendation) instead of a lawyer to contest your assessment with the local tax board or in small claims tax court, if one exists in your state.

Your Escrow Money

A portion of a homeowner's monthly mortgage payment goes into a reserve fund, or escrow account, that holds sufficient sums to pay upcoming property taxes and homeowners insurance premiums. Your mortgage lender, who manages your escrow account, calculates your contribution based on anticipated yearly tax and insurance costs. The yearly cost is distributed evenly among your monthly mortgage loan payments.

Lenders generally review escrow accounts once a year to determine whether monthly payments need to be adjusted and then send you an annual notice. If you do not normally receive this notice from your lender, you can request one.

Homeowners should guard against two common problems with escrow accounts: inflated monthly payments and misappropriated interest earnings. Attorneys general in many states have successfully filed suit on behalf of homeowners against lenders guilty of cushioning escrow accounts. Some states insist that lenders should keep no more than a two-month cushion in an escrow account. Some mortgage agreements allow for only a one-month cushion or none at all. Thus if a homeowner's yearly tax and insurance costs are $1,200, monthly escrow charges should be $100 plus the stipulated one-month cushion. If the mortgagee is actually paying $250 a month for escrow, the lender is overcharging.

Mortgage lenders have also been found guilty of withholding interest profits from homeowners. Many states, however, do not require lenders to pay property owners the interest from their escrow accounts. In other words, lenders benefit from the extra cash pool of escrow accounts and also make a profit from the interest generated from them.

Undercharging on escrow accounts also can be a problem. A lender may collect too little every month, then hit the home-

Where large sums of money are concerned, it is advisable to trust nobody.

AGATHA CHRISTIE
Endless Night

Resolving Disputes With House Builders

If you discover structural problems in a house that is less than 10 years old, try to resolve the problems with the builder or developer. Even if you are not the first owner, you may still have recourse under state and federal laws. Here are some steps to take:

• Review your homeowner's warranties to determine whether your complaints are covered. Then talk to the builder and try to compromise on a fair solution for repair or replacement.

• If your builder is unresponsive, find out from your town or city planner's office whether it has a statement of intent and agreement from your builder. This statement cites the builder's responsibility for property repairs and improvements.

• Contact your local Better Business Bureau. Here you can get information on the builder's company and any complaints filed against it. The BBB in many areas offers mediation services that are free to homeowners. After a homeowner files a complaint, the bureau asks the builder for a written statement. The bureau mediator then tries to work out an agreement between the parties. It may take a month to reach a settlement. Sometimes no agreement is found, but it is worth trying.

• If mediation does not work, the Better Business Bureau may also offer binding arbitration, the results of which are enforceable by the courts. This process may last a couple of months. If settlement prospects look dim, talk to an attorney about suing the builder or developer.

• Some states have recovery funds to compensate owners for faults in new home construction. The state attorney general will help.

123…

IS YOUR ESCROW MONEY BEING MISMANAGED?

If a review of your escrow account makes you think you are being overcharged or denied interest due you, some of these steps should help:

1. Complain directly to your lender. Explain your position to the account manager and follow up your conversation with a letter that confirms your discussion.

2. Write to your state's banking regulation department to complain about your lender. You may be one of many complainants in an ongoing investigation of wrongdoing.

3. Call your state attorney general. Ask for the consumer frauds bureau and find out if your lender has been singled out for wrongdoing.

4. Contact the Federal Reserve Board, the Federal Deposit Insurance Corporation, or whichever federal regulatory body oversees your bank.

5. Call the U.S. Department of Housing and Urban Development (HUD) to register a complaint and find out the status of legislation on controversial escrow management practices.

6. Try to arrange an escrow release agreement from your lender, which would allow you to pay your tax and insurance costs directly. If the lender will not give it to you, consider refinancing your loan if interest rates are favorable.

owner for a large lump sum when taxes or insurance premiums are due. Or, if property taxes rise suddenly, lenders can impose an increase in escrow fees and require immediate cash payments. Homeowners unable to provide the lump sums in such situations risk defaulting on their mortgages.

You can analyze your own escrow account at any time by reviewing your original loan contract and then comparing it with the lender's annual statement of your escrow account. Also check your mortgage contract to determine whether it specifies a maximum amount of money the lender may maintain in your account. Or you can hire a private mortgage monitor who will analyze your escrow account and flag any irregularities.

Structural and Property Defects

When you buy a home, the law acknowledges your right to assume it will be decently constructed and safe to inhabit. As with any product you buy, your home should be free from major problems, defects, and dangers. Almost every state guarantees so-called implied warranties of habitability and workmanship with the purchase of a new home, and thousands of homeowners every year invoke legal protections in their claims against manufacturers, builders, and others responsible for a panoply of problems.

Owners of newly built homes have the most recourse under the law for complaints of major structural problems and property defects. But even if you bought a previously occupied, or older, home, you have a variety of options for recourse. Recourse can be based on two types of flaws: "material defect," which is a major physical problem that might prevent someone from buying the property or that significantly diminishes its value, such as seasonal flooding; or "product defect," such as a broken stove or bad house paint.

Seeking redress will be easier if you take measures immediately upon discovering a defect in the house or property. Contract laws in some states may allow you to sue for up to six years after contract agreement, but claims may need to be brought within one year of discovery. You may have a claim even 10 years after purchase if the problem is a "latent defect," which is a problem you could not have known about until it became obvious at a later date—such as discovering that the house was built on land that had been used as a toxic waste dump.

LEGAL PROTECTIONS
Depending on the age of your house, major structural problems may be repaired or replaced free of charge under the

terms of a written home warranty you received at settlement. If your home is newly built, you probably have a first year warranty from the builder or developer that guarantees good workmanship. An older house that is less than 10 years old may still be covered by builder's or seller's warranties.

You may also have bought an extended-term version of this warranty (typically 10 years, renewable annually) that continues to cover some major design and structural defects, but to a lesser extent than in the first year. For example, after the first year your warranty may require that you pay for repair service calls. For a plumbing problem too minor to be covered by your home warranty, you will pay for the service call on top of the cost of the warranty. But if your furnace fails, that major expense would probably be covered by the home warranty.

Dream House Turned Nightmare

PROBLEM
Nine months ago, Sara and Jon bought a one-family home on a new development site, part of a larger planned community. Other homes on the site were in various stages of completion. Except for Sara and Jon's landscaped yard (and one other), the grounds were still unsodded, without trees or vegetation. Heavy rains caused major drainage problems, ruining Sara and Jon's new sod and causing water damage in their basement. When they bought the home, the developer and real estate broker had assured them the site would be finished within three months of the settlement date. What recourse did they have?

ACTION
Early residents of unfinished developments with barren lots must often wait for completed landscaping until the developer sells or completes more homes. But Sara and Jon's problem was a property defect, and because they were the first owners of a newly built home, they had a good case for legal recourse. Upon the advice of a lawyer, they wrote a letter to the developer explaining the situation and requesting reimbursement for the damage. If the developer had not cleaned up the damage or made financial reparations, Sara and Jon could have sued him.

Even if you do not discover a problem until several years after your purchase, you may have a valid legal claim if you act immediately. (The time period in which a lawsuit must be initiated varies from state to state.) First gather whatever pertinent evidence you have, such as home and product warranties, purchase contracts, correspondence with the seller or builder, photos or videos that document physical damage, and records of any mediation efforts between you and the party you consider financially responsible. You might have notes on conversations with neighbors with similar problems whose houses were built by the same contractor. These records will give your attorney a more viable case.

What to Do About Defective Products

Every home is built and equipped with hundreds of manufactured products—doorknobs, dishwashers, ceiling fans, air ducts, plywood, plumbing, wiring, and so on.

If one of these products fails to function as it should, a homeowner may be legally protected by one of three warranties: (1) a written warranty from the manufacturer; (2) a homeowners warranty from the builder of the house, called an express warranty, which protects the first owner and sometimes subsequent owners of a newly built home; (3) an implied or express warranty from the builder or seller of the home. (See also :"Warranties: Legal Protections for Newly Built Homes," page 15.)

Product failure might be a breach of one of these warranties. If a problem occurs, contact the manufacturer to see if its warranty still applies.

If the company refuses to repair or replace an item, try the contractor, who may be even harder to pin down than the manufacturer. Next ask the office of the state attorney general if your state laws offer enough implied warranty protection to give you a case. Finally, consult a lawyer, who will consider your case under both federal and state commercial product warranty laws.

If a home product causes injury or illness to someone, the manufacturer could be responsible under a personal injury liability law. If such an injury occurs in your home, contact an attorney immediately.

Your Right to Challenge Utilities

Every homeowner relies on utility companies to provide basic services, including gas, electricity, oil, water, and local telephone service. Although utility providers are private companies, they hold local monopolies or near monopolies on these essential services. This means you can neither choose utility service providers from a competitive pool nor contest the rates they are allowed to charge for services.

To protect consumers from unfair pricing practices, states regulate utility companies. State public service commissions set rates, wrangle with utilities over the way costs and losses should be accounted for, and monitor billing procedures. Despite this watchdog surveillance, homeowners are still subject to a host of errors and unfair practices.

Utility problems experienced by homeowners may stem from technical or computer errors, inefficient or unethical business practices, lax laws, environmental factors. Some states, such as New York, require utility companies to provide more detailed utility bills than many other states, enabling customers to detect inaccurate billing more readily. But wherever you live, it is worth scrutinizing your bill periodically for irregularities that might tip you off to problems.

If you do question your bill and get into a dispute with a local utility, the utility company does not have the right to terminate your service without a fair hearing. Although unscrupulous utility companies have gone so far as to illegally enter residences to turn off service, a utility is supposed to use due process, and should terminate your service only after it has investigated your reason for not paying.

Most states require a hearing before service can be terminated. If your service is terminated without a fair hearing, first contact your state utility regulator. You service must be reinstated immediately, and remain "on" while the dispute is being investigated. If you experience problems, you may want to consult with an attorney about taking legal action.

Battling Condemnation

Federal, state, and local governments have the right to take your property for public use as long as they provide you with fair compensation. This governmental right to claim private property to serve the public good is called "eminent domain." It is severely restricted by law and often hotly contested in practice. The Fifth Amend-

---

1 2 3 . . .

TAKING ON YOUR UTILITY

If you think your utility bills are inordinately high or suspect that you are being charged for someone else's service, here is what you can do about it:

1. Before contacting anyone, make sure you have a viable complaint. If it is the electric bill that worries you, turn off all lights and electrical appliances (don't forget the refrigerator), take a flashlight, and look at the electric meter. If it is still running, you have fodder for a case that you are being wrongly charged.

2. Contact your utility company, explain your situation, and ask for a meter inspection. This is a more thorough examination than a meter reading.

3. If you plan to withhold payment of your bill while the utility responds to your complaint, put the complaint in writing and make sure that service will be continued in the interim.

4. If the utility company is unresponsive to your case, contact your state's public service commission, which regulates utility companies and investigates billing disputes. You can demand a formal hearing on your claim.

5. You can sue a utility company if the firm has denied you a fair hearing for your complaint. A letter from your attorney may be enough to get the attention of the boss so that you won't have to sue.

ment of the Constitution protects private property from being taken "for public use without just compensation."

Public use includes the building of railroads, highways, schools, hospitals, sewage systems, parks, and airports and may also include urban renewal housing, high-rise office towers, and shopping malls.

Homeowners, neighborhood associations, and environmentalists have increasingly challenged government development plans on the grounds that a project is taking more property than necessary, that the plans are not well enough formed to warrant condemnation, or that condemnation does not serve a legitimate public purpose. So far, however, the government has nearly always managed to persuade the courts that it is justified in taking private property for public use.

ON THE LOSING END

If the government decides to take your property, it will make an offer of compensation based on its appraisal of your property's value. The basis for determining compensation is the current fair market value, not the replacement value of a home. Nor are you compensated for the cost of moving, of financing a new mortgage on another home, or for emotional suffering you may experience when asked to leave your family domain.

You can contest the government's compensation offer in a condemnation hearing. Because condemnation proceedings vary by state and can be complex, consult a lawyer who specializes in this field.

I believe that every right implies a responsibility; every opportunity, an obligation; every possession, a duty.

JOHN D. ROCKEFELLER
American Oil Magnate
and Philanthropist
1839–1937

Your Right to Contest Compensation

Before the government can legally take your property for public purposes, it must negotiate with you a fair price of compensation. If you do not agree on a price, these are steps you can take to reach more acceptable terms:

• Arrange your own professional appraisal to determine the current fair market value of your property. The best approach is to measure your property against comparable homes in the neighborhood. If your appraiser's figure is higher than the government's, you can present this evidence in condemnation proceedings.

• Enlist your neighbors' support. If their properties are also targets of condemnation you believe is unjust, you might consider joining forces for a class action suit against the government.

• If only some of your property is to be taken, you are entitled to request severance damages in addition to compensation for property taken. This may take the form of monetary compensation or alternative benefits that you can suggest, such as new grass and hedges for the border of your property next to which a school will be built.

• Ask for a jury trial. As part of the condemnation proceedings articulated by law, homeowners are entitled to ask for a trial by jury. This can work to your favor, as juries are generally more sympathetic to property owners than to governments.

• Contact a lawyer who specializes in condemnation proceedings. You may not have to pay the lawyer unless you win your case. These specialists often work on a contingency basis: they take a percentage of the compensation fee.

REPAIRS AND IMPROVEMENTS

Whether you are fixing up your home or just coping with wear and tear, you need to know how to finance the work, get someone to do it, and stay within the rules.

Home Equity Loans: Your Best Bet For Improvements?

When you renovate your home, make essential repairs, or do some home maintenance, you have the option of financing these projects with several kinds of bank loans that use your house as collateral: a second mortgage, or home equity loan; a home equity line of credit; or a reverse mortgage. The amount of the loan is based on your "equity," or degree of ownership, in the home. One big advantage equity loans have over personal or credit-card loans is that the interest on home-secured loans is tax deductible (up to $100,000 borrowed).

To determine how much you can borrow, lenders generally calculate your equity as the appraised market value of your home minus the amount you still owe on your mortgage loan. Therefore, the more you have paid off on your first mortgage loan, the more money you can access. Lenders usually offer loans for nearly the full amount of your equity (75 or 80 percent). You can also qualify for these loans, of course, if you have no mortgage.

BORROWING FOR A NEW KITCHEN

A traditional second mortgage loan is a fixed-rate loan of a limited amount of money, repaid on a schedule of equal monthly payments for the life of the loan. Fixed-rate second mortgage loans often suit homeowners who need a lump sum for a set purpose, such as remodeling the kitchen for $10,000.

Although second mortgages are often referred to as home equity loans, home equity loans may be based on an adjustable interest rate rather than a fixed rate. This can give borrowers the advantage of lower interest rates in a favorable economic climate, but it leaves them vulnerable to unpredictable fluctuations and unfavorable rates.

Unlike a second mortgage or home equity loan, a home equity line of credit allows you to use the collateral of your home as a new source of cash up to the limit of your credit line. As with credit cards, you can borrow from and repay your credit line as often as you like. Typically, the lender gives you a checkbook, and you are free to write checks against your account (the loan) and make deposits (loan payments) to the account at any time. In some parts of the country, a credit card is used instead of checks.

Reverse mortgages are available usually to homeowners age 62 and over (in some areas, 60 or 65). In a reverse mortgage, your home is collateral for a loan that the lender advances to you in regular monthly installments—like your first mortgage loan in reverse. The debt is paid back when you sell your home, or, in the event of your death, is settled by your heirs. Reverse mortgages are more commonly used for supplementing pension or Social Security income, but may also be used to increase cash flow for home improvements and other expenses.

Whatever kind of home equity loan you choose, remember that your home is on the line. If you are careless about spending and repaying the loan, the convenience of a home equity loan can become squandered equity and, at worst, foreclosure. Borrow cautiously and compare lenders' terms as carefully as you did for your first mortgage loan.

Complying With Building Codes

When you reconstruct or add on to your property, whether building a shed or converting an attic into a home office, you have a legal obligation to comply with local codes. Building codes, written by the city or county in which property is located, set standards for construction materials, electrical, sanitation, and other systems of homes to protect the welfare and safety of residents. If your plans for home renovation or remodeling are going to alter the structure or systems of your home or even change the use of a room, you will be expected to comply with building codes.

Building permits are documents that indicate your compliance with city or county building codes. You probably would need a building permit or other type of professional permit for projects ranging from converting a porch into a bedroom to installing a new dishwasher to building a tool shed. You will have to comply with local electrical, plumbing, and fire-safety codes, as well as rules governing height, distance from property lines, and location of any structures you build.

THE DANGERS OF CHEATING

Homeowners sometimes ignore building codes under the false assumption that a little change in their own house is nobody else's business. If your house bristles with scaffolding, though, or is trafficked by contractors, an official may notice the activ-

How to Get a Building Permit

Before you start a major construction or renovation project, you will need a building permit from your municipality's buildings department. Permits are the way local governments enforce compliance with health and safety codes. Localities issue permits when they are assured that the construction will be done according to local standards.

To obtain a building permit, you must submit an application, along with a nominal fee, that describes the changes you are planning for your home. If possible, include architect's or builder's plans with detailed specifications. You will need to arrange with the city department for on-site garbage receptacles or another method of disposing of construction materials.

In some areas, obtaining a building permit is so complicated that architects, engineers, or contractors do it as part of their service to the homeowner—perhaps at a price. Once the permit is obtained and construction begins, you may receive visits from your town's building inspector, who ensures the project is in compliance.

If you proceed without a permit, your town can halt construction or fine you or both. If you finish the project without a permit, you may be denied an updated certificate of occupancy, a vital document certifying that the house meets local health and safety codes. Without a "C of O," you will have trouble selling your house.

ity and take steps to penalize you for noncompliance. Even if you do not get caught during the remodeling, you do yourself no favor. If you ever want to put your house on the market, it will have to be "brought up to code" before it can be sold.

INVESTIGATE ZONING CODES

Zoning codes divide municipalities into districts for specified use: commercial, industrial, residential, rural, and others. Zoning decisions are made locally by zoning boards composed of professional city planners and select local citizens. When you are planning a renovation or addition, for example, you will have to observe zoning laws as well as building codes.

For the most part, zoning codes are local and specific, and they change with time. So whether you live in a new neighborhood or inhabit a three-generation homestead, you should explore zoning codes before altering your home or how you use it. Your city or town hall houses the official zoning maps and regulations, which are available for public reading. The maps will indicate how zones are divided and subdivided.

Applying for an Exception to Zoning Rules

If you find that the reconstruction or addition you are planning for your home does not conform to local zoning regulations on size, location, or use, here are some steps you can take to request a variance—an exemption from the rules:

• **Acquaint yourself with the local zoning ordinances.** Three common categories of restriction are building height; distance that must be left between the new structure and your property lines, called setback standards; and the proportion of lot space taken up by the new structure.

• **Find out if your plans are subject to special exceptions.** Local zoning boards sometimes single out areas within a larger group of properties for potential adjustment to the zoning scheme based on individual circumstances.

• **Talk to a real estate attorney about your chances of winning a variance.** If she feels your case may meet resistance from a reluctant zoning board, she may advise you instead to consider modifying your construction plan.

• **Apply for a variance.** If you believe a zoning rule is unfair or should not apply to your property—a two-story height restriction for your low-sitting valley home, for example—you can apply for a variance. Your request for an exemption from zoning rules will be considered by the local zoning administrator.

• **Appeal a rejection of your variance request.** If the zoning administrator denies your application for an exemption from a zoning rule, you can appeal the decision to the local zoning board or in court. You should hire legal counsel to represent you. If your variance request concerns the size of a proposed structure, you (or your lawyer) will need to show that the exemption will not adversely affect the aesthetic character of the neighborhood, that you cannot achieve the benefits of the construction in any other way, and that a denial of the request causes economic hardship.

• **If you are applying for a variance for the use of property, prepare your case carefully.** Variances for changes in use (if you are planning, for instance, to use a new room as a beauty parlor) are more rarely granted than for physical alterations. You would need to show that the zoning rule makes it difficult or impossible for you to use the property to its full value, or that the property has a unique aspect that puts it at an unfair disadvantage under the rule. Finally, you would have to convince the board that the variance would not create noise, traffic, or other affronts to the residential integrity of the neighborhood.

Residential zones may distinguish among single-family home districts, condominium and apartment districts, historical home districts, and so on.

Zoning codes commonly regulate what you may build on your property, where you may build it, and how you may use a new or altered structure on your property. Planned communities, condominiums, and cooperatives usually add other rules (see also "Condos, Co-ops, and Planned Communities," page 66). If you ignore zoning regulations, you could be fined or, in a flagrant case, be forced to demolish offending structures. At the least you will have difficulty selling the property.

SETTING UP A HOME BUSINESS

Whatever kind of business you plan to set up in your home—day care, word processing, tax preparation, massage therapy, hair care—you should first investigate local zoning laws. Most problems occur when a home business attracts more visitors, makes the neighborhood noisier, increases commercial traffic to the home, or uses advertising on the property. As the number of Americans working from home increases, community regulations on home businesses are being reevaluated. You can help shape your local zoning rules by attending open community and city council meetings on the subject.

The Value of Keeping Records

Whenever you make a change to your house or property, you should always keep accurate records of your expenses, using two categories: repairs (necessary maintenance) and improvements. The distinction matters most in taxes: local property-tax appraisals and federal income-tax calculations after a sale of property take into account expenditures on repairs and improvements. Home repairs cannot be used in calculations to lower federal capital gains tax; improvements can, but they also increase your property value and therefore increase your property taxes.

By tax standards, a home improvement is work done to a home that fulfills at least one of three goals: (1) It increases the home's value (you convert a closet into a bathroom). (2) It extends its life (you modernize the entire electrical system of an older house). (3) It changes and enhances the use of the property (you convert a garage into a rental apartment).

In contrast, home repairs are changes that merely maintain the house's normal condition. Repairs include fixing a leaky faucet, patching a hole in the roof (but replacing the roof is an improvement), or repainting the chipped exterior of the home.

Important Records to Keep on File

Protect yourself against construction problems, tax challenges, and lawsuits. Keep records of home-construction projects until several years after selling your home.

✔ *Construction and design contracts.* Contracts with architects and contractors should indicate work and payment schedules and who takes responsibility for what.

✔ *Before-and-after photographs.* Pictures of the construction area can solve later problems with a contractor.

✔ *Names of suppliers, subcontractors, trade inspectors.* You should know who installed and inspected your electrical, plumbing, and heating systems.

✔ *Name of on-site city building inspector.* If you are found to have violated a building code, the city official who signed off on the project may be partially responsible.

✔ *Personal journal.* Keep records of conversations you have with contractors as evidence of oral agreements.

✔ *New product information.* From new wiring to new walls, make sure you keep all warranties and receipts.

✔ *Receipts of payments.* Keep canceled checks of payments to contractors. If you pay cash, keep a written receipt signed by both of you.

CHOOSING A CONTRACTOR

Many people think that the most important decision you will make when building or remodeling your home is picking the right contractor. Here are some suggestions as to how to go about it:

1. Check with local building agencies. Many cities offer a builders' exchange that matches licensed, reputable builders with clients.

2. Comparison shop. Let each prospective contractor know that you are obtaining several bids on your project.

3. Talk to former clients. Reputable contractors should willingly give the names of at least a dozen satisfied customers.

4. Make sure a contractor is state licensed, bonded, and carries both workers' compensation and liability insurance.

5. Ask for a bank reference to verify that the contractor is solvent and responsible.

6. Visit other jobs in progress that are similar to yours or ask for pictures of other projects.

7. Find out how many projects the contractor is currently handling, and whether he can keep to your schedule.

8. Ask how extra costs or charges for special services are calculated. A contractor may bid low for part of a job (plastering a wall), then offer to finish the job (painting it) and overcharge you badly.

Homeowners and the IRS or local property-tax assessors sometimes disagree on what constitutes an improvement or a repair—hence the importance of keeping accurate records of any construction or alterations. For example, the local property-tax assessor sees that you put new windows on one side of the house—a value-added improvement that raises your tax basis. You might argue and present evidence to the local tax board to prove that the windows were damaged during a recent storm and had to be replaced. Thus qualified as repairs, they should not result in higher property taxes.

Some home improvements qualify for special tax breaks, such as property-tax credits for improvements on older and historical homes. Or, if you add a work space to your house, you may qualify for federal tax deductions for home offices. A tax accountant can best advise you on these complicated matters—and he will want complete records of the project.

Hiring a Contractor

To take care of major home repairs and improvements, most homeowners hire building contractors. When working with a contractor, you should keep four standards in mind: (1) The contractor should complete work according to the terms of your contract. (2) He should be careful not to damage your property or cause personal injury. (3) His costs should be fair. (4) He should not be negligent or engage in unethical behavior.

Unfortunately, these standards are not always met. While licensed contractors are generally honest and capable, consumer-protection agencies can cite a huge number of homeowners' complaints against unscrupulous and unqualified contractors.

This is true partly because some states require no more than a registration fee for a contractor's license. The home builder is more protected in those states that have strict performance standards for contractors. Even better are the states and local municipalities that require contractors to be bonded and carry liability and workers' compensation insurance. A bond is a sum held by a third party (usually a bonding company) as a guarantee of good workmanship. There are several types of bond:

- **Contractor's license bond.** Required by most states as a qualification for licensing, these bonds can range from $2,000 to $20,000, depending on the type of contractor and the volume of work performed.
- **Performance bond.** This option guarantees that funds will be available if your contractor does not complete the job

stipulated in your contract. The fee that a contractor must pay for this bond is normally passed on to the homeowner.

- **Payment bond.** These bonds assure subcontractors that they will be paid by the general, or head, contractor. Payment bonds mean that no financial claims, or "liens," for labor or materials will be filed against your property. However, they are costly and often duplicate other protections.

Along with licensing and bonding, be sure that the contractor you are considering carries two types of insurance: liability and workers' compensation. The liability insurance will protect you if the contractor damages your property or causes injury to someone on your premises. Workers' compensation is required in some states for the contractor's employees and covers the treatment of injuries incurred on the job.

WHAT TYPE OF CONTRACTOR DO YOU NEED?

If you are planning a big repair or improvement project, you probably should consider hiring a "general contractor," the generic term for the person who maintains overall control of and responsibility for a project. The duties of a general contractor include meeting with you to discuss the plans and specifications for the project; preparing a bid, or estimate, for the project; and acting as liaison between you and an architect, interior designer, or subcontractors on the job.

A "specialty contractor," or subcontractor, works in one trade—as a carpenter, roofer, locksmith, or plumber. General contractors often have a roster of reliable subcontractors with whom they work. But when you take on small projects, such as replacing a heating system, you will probably hire the specialist directly. You should be sure to meet the specialty contractor, conduct a background check, and solicit bids just as you would when hiring a general contractor. When hiring any contractor, remember that the better you define your expectations, the more successful the project will be.

Dealing with Contractors

Just as knowing what you want in a project helps determine whom you hire for the job, knowing how much money you expect to spend protects you from committing to a financially draining affair. You can negotiate the costs and specifications of a project, such as the quality of materials to be used, when a contractor submits his bid to you for the job. Then compare that bid with those you get from other contractors. (If you do plan to compare the bids of several contractors, be sure you supply the same information to

The Protection of Cooling-Off Laws

Federal and state laws protect consumers from the pressures of aggressive sales techniques with so-called cooling-off laws. These laws state that you have the right to change your mind about certain purchases of goods over $25 within three business days if the contract was signed in your home.

The cooling-off laws are aimed primarily at protecting consumers from the importuning of door-to-door salesmen, but they also apply to services supplied by contractors.

Suppose that while a contractor is painting your living room he suggests installing a new molding. You like the idea and place the order. But if you change your mind, you have the right to cancel the order within three business days without penalty because you made the purchase away from the seller's place of business.

You must notify the contractor in writing: send the notice to an address that the contractor must provide and use certified mail with return receipt requested. The contractor must respond to your letter within 10 days of receiving it.

The cooling-off laws do not apply if you made a purchase or ordered a service over the telephone, by mail, or in the contractor's place of business; nor do they apply to contracts for emergency home repairs.

WORK ORDER

HOMEOWNER 1

Name _____

Street _____

City/State/Zip _____

CONTRACTOR

Name _____

Street _____

City/State/Zip _____

DESCRIPTION OF JOB 2

_____

_____

_____

_____

MATERIALS REQUIRED AND SUPPLIERS 3

_____

_____

_____

Total _____

COSTS

$ _____

$ _____

$ _____

$ _____

LABOR REQUIRED AND HOURS 4

_____

_____

_____

Total _____

$ _____

$ _____

$ _____

$ _____

TOTAL COST OF JOB 5 $ _____

WORK /PAYMENT SCHEDULE 6

Progress payments will be made in the following amount on the following schedule:
Work Stage and Date Completed:

1. _____

2. _____

3. _____

Amount to Be Paid:

$ _____

$ _____

$ _____

7 The homeowner hereby authorizes the contractor to furnish all materials and labor required to complete the job. 8 Any alteration or deviation from the above specifications involving extra cost of materials or labor will be executed only upon written orders for same, and will become an extra charge over the sum mentioned in this contract. 9 All work will be completed in a workmanlike manner according to standard practices, within the time period specified. 10 The homeowner agrees to pay the amount mentioned according to the terms thereof.

_____

Agreed: Homeowner

_____

11 Agreed: Contractor

_____

Date of Agreement

A Sample Work Order for a Small Project

This simple work order could be used for an inexpensive, straightforward project, such as painting a room or having minor electrical work done. It includes: **1.** Names and addresses of homeowner and contractor; **2.** A detailed description of the job; **3.** A list of materials, suppliers, and costs; **4.** The type of labor, hours required, and cost; **5.** The total cost; **6.** The payment schedule based on work completed. In addition, the contract should include clauses authorizing: **7.** The contractor to hire workers and buy supplies; **8.** Any changes in writing; **9.** That the work will meet standards of quality and time; **10.** That the homeowner will pay when work is complete and satisfactory; and **11.** Signatures proving that both parties agree. If you are planning extensive construction, you will need a stronger contract that includes more protections.

each.) You can compare contractors' bids on the basis of the following criteria:

- **Presentation.** Is the contractor's estimate scribbled on a piece of paper or neatly typed on letterhead? Is it supplemented by brochures or other materials pertinent to your job? A contractor who presents a well-organized presentation probably has a higher standard of professionalism on the job than someone who looks at your kitchen for five minutes and announces that the remodeling will cost $30,000.
- **Price estimates.** Bids will vary among different contractors, but should fall within about a 10-percent range of one another. If they deviate more than that, and you provided comparable information to each, it is possible that the low bidder forgot to include a certain element or is underhandedly trying to lure business with a low bid that will later rise.
- **Detailed measurements and materials.** Contractor bids should spell out, as much as possible, the specific sizes of rooms, windows, doors, and the like called for by the project, as well as the quantity and quality of the various materials that will be needed. If you specified a certain product brand, model, or quality level, make sure an inferior material has not been substituted to lower the bid price.
- **Installation.** If your bid includes the price of new carpeting, does that price include the usual fee to install it? Specify the same for dishwashers, cabinets, windows, and so on.
- **Payment structure.** To make sure that your job is completed on time and within the budget, structure your payments to tie completion of a specific task with periodic payments. You will have to pay a certain amount of money before the job begins and then make specified payments at specified times, as the work progresses. Be sure to withhold a percentage until the job is completed to your satisfaction.

Since this information will appear in your final contract, clarify as many details as possible in preliminary bid negotiations with prospective contractors. Otherwise you leave yourself vulnerable to bids that can be interpreted in the contractor's favor. Along with details on materials and costs, a homeowner should base the choice of contractors on personal appeal and responsiveness to your preliminary concerns. All else being equal, you want the contractor with whom you communicate best and whom you trust the most to work in your interest.

SIGNING THE CONTRACT

Once you have weeded out the competing bids for your job and checked licensing and references, you can select a contractor and sign a contract. Although it is always in a con-

---

HOW TO DEAL WITH POOR WORKMANSHIP

What if your contractor turns out shoddy work or fails to finish the job? Here are some ways to deal with him:

1. Talk to the contractor about the problems, then put your complaints in writing. You will soon discover whether or not he can rectify the problems.

2. Gather proof that the contractor did not live up to the terms of your contract. Include records of all written and verbal agreements and correspondence, and photographs of damage or poorly done work.

3. Call the local department of consumer affairs and the Better Business Bureau to file complaints. They can provide information on any other claims against the contractor.

4. Call the contractor's recovery fund if there is one in your state. This service is administered by the state contractor's license board, and provides protection to homeowners whose licensed contractor has not performed as promised or has defaulted on the contract.

5. Sue the contractor in small claims court. The court cannot make the contractor redo or finish the job properly, but it can order him to pay you damages if you win.

6. If the damages you claim are more than is allowed in small claims court, hire an attorney to sue the contractor in municipal court.

sumer's interest to have a qualified attorney review a written contract, you also can manage the agreement yourself, especially on smaller jobs. Be sure to spell out in the contract all basic information about the job, including timing; price; materials; responsibilities for insurance, permits, and cleanup; and a schedule for making payments.

Because few construction projects progress precisely as planned, your contract should stipulate how changes will be mutually agreed upon by you and the contractor. Changes from the original contract agreement should always be confirmed in writing so that you are protected in potential disputes. Most contractors use a "change order form" that refers to a specific alteration of an item listed in the contract—for example, "Substitute oak doors for pine doors in closets. Additional charge for materials, $600."

Homeowners should also include a contract clause on work stoppage. It ensures that if your contractor simply fails to show up for the job and stops answering your telephone calls for a certain period of time, you can send written notice to the contractor that you consider his actions a work stoppage and that you are implementing the part of the clause that permits you to hire another contractor and/or take legal action.

WHERE DOES YOUR MONEY GO?

Your new home improvement project begins, and after your second or third payment all you see is a pile of rubble and a gaggle of subcontractors yanking wires and pulling up floor-

Where we cannot invent, we may at least improve.

CHARLES CALEB COLTON

English clergyman and writer
1780–1832

Reducing the Risk of Mechanics' Liens

A contractor, subcontractor, or supplier has the right to put a lien, or financial claim, against a homeowner's property for unpaid bills. Even if you have paid the contractor in full, you are vulnerable to liens if he has not paid subcontractors. You can protect yourself with these measures:

• In most states, the right of a contractor to issue a lien can be waived upon request by the homeowner if the contractor agrees. Ask the contractor for a lien waiver or release before work begins. The waiver should state that the contractor forfeits any rights to file a claim under mechanics' lien laws.

• The contractor's lien waiver pertains only to his own work and not to that of subcontractors and suppliers. So you should insist that your contractor provide you with lien waivers from all such persons involved in the job. Withhold payments at each stage of the project until you have received notarized lien waivers from the subcontractors and suppliers involved in that stage attesting that they

have been paid in full and agreeing to release you from any obligations under state lien laws.

• Rather than make the contractor responsible for obtaining lien waivers from subcontractors and suppliers, you can arrange to pay these parties directly. This prevents the possibility of your paying a contractor for suppliers and his using the money for other purposes.

• Talk to subcontractors and suppliers throughout the course of the job to make sure they are getting paid by the contractor according to the terms of their agreement. Some courts actually put the onus on homeowners to ensure that the contractor is paying the bills.

boards. What exactly is happening, and where are your payments going?

The money you give contractors is funneled into four major categories: contractor's labor, cost of materials, cost of subcontractors, and profit percentage. Most contractors, when estimating the cost of a job, total the costs of material and labor, then add a percentage to cover their overhead costs (licensing, building permits, paperwork, taxes, and so on) and profit. The percent of profit contractors charge is typically around 10 percent, but may vary from 5 percent to 25 percent depending on the local marketplace, the contractor's popularity or specialty, and the region of the country.

THE PERILS OF A MECHANIC'S LIEN

Mechanics' lien laws are designed to protect workers and suppliers from contractors and homeowners who fail to pay for work done or supplies received. The laws put ultimate responsibility for these payments on the homeowner—even if he has already paid the contractor for work done by a subcontractor or for supplies delivered.

Warding Off a Lien

PROBLEM
Julian hired a contractor to put a new roof on his house and build a small deck. After the job was done, and Julian had paid the contractor in full, he decided to ask the bank for a home equity loan to build a swimming pool. But before he could do so, Julian received notice that a claim for $2,000 was being filed against his property by the carpenter who had built the deck as a subcontractor. The carpenter said he had not been paid and was basing his claim on the mechanics' lien law, which puts responsibility for paying the debt on the property owner. Julian, aware that if the lien was applied to the property he would have trouble getting a loan, had to make sure the lien was not approved.

ACTION
Julian went to the contractor, who admitted he had spent Julian's money to pay off debts and had nothing left to pay the carpenter. Acting on his lawyer's advice, Julian offered to settle with the carpenter for $1,500. Realizing it was probably the best he could do, the carpenter accepted the offer and signed a release of his mechanics' lien. Then Julian filed a suit in small-claims court against the contractor for $1,500. Persuaded by Julian's proof that he had paid the contractor and the carpenter's testimony that he had done the work but secured no money from the contractor, the judge ordered the contractor to pay Julian.

Lien laws exist in all states, although they vary widely in terms of the procedure a subcontractor or supplier must follow and in the degree of protection given to homeowners. Subcontractors generally have a certain amount of time after not

Beware of Improvement Rip-offs

State consumer-affairs departments are inundated with homeowners' stories, especially from senior citizens, of unscrupulous contractors.

Common tales of woe include gaping holes in walls, unfinished roof and siding work, disconnected gas lines, driveways blacktopped with oily gunk that washes away with the next rain.

Even more painful is the contractor who spends two months building an addition to your home, cashing your payment checks along the way, then skips town, and leaves you with an unfinished room.

Other typical scams involve your property's landscaping. A self-proclaimed contractor, seeing that your lawn is bare, claims he has topsoil left over from a previous job that he will offer you at a cut rate. What he really has is low-quality soil at an inflated price. Or you may encounter a tree "expert" who offers to trim your trees, then hacks away at your favorite maple before absconding with your deposit.

After a natural disaster, homeowners are particularly vulnerable to on-the-spot improvement offers. No matter how badly you want a job done, do your homework first: check references, licensing, and the Better Business Bureau for a record of complaints. Never pay cash in advance. Your home and finances are at stake.

1,2,3...

BUILDING
IT YOURSELF

Homeowners acting as their own contractors for home improvement jobs should understand these key issues before committing to a project:

1. Being your own general contractor makes you responsible for hiring subcontractors, such as electricians and plumbers. For each, you need to solicit bids, check credentials, draw up written contracts, confirm insurance coverage, and monitor work.

2. Construction jobs are extremely time-consuming. You may find yourself constantly juggling schedules, buying materials, conferring with workers to solve unexpected problems, and more.

3. When you are the boss, you assume all responsibility for unforeseen problems. If you order the wrong materials and thereby delay a subcontractor who charges you a penalty for wasting his time, you have no legal recourse.

4. If you apply for a loan to finance your home improvement project, you may find that lenders are reluctant to risk an unprofessional remodeling project that could actually lower the value of the home.

5. You must arrange for building and zoning permits and all other details, such as garbage disposal, that a contractor would normally organize. Be aware that owner-contractors are often more carefully scrutinized by city building officials.

being paid (two or three months) within which to file a lien claim. Although it seems unfair, a homeowner may well end up paying the subcontractor even if he has already paid the contractor for the work done. If a lien claim is found to be valid in court, the lien can become an encumbrance on the property, making it very hard to sell or borrow against.

To protect yourself from mechanics' liens, you may be able to have contractors and subcontractors sign a waiver of lien right (see "Reducing the Risk of Mechanics' Liens," page 48). If a mechanics' lien does get filed against your house, it will be recorded with the county clerk. When the claim has been settled, it is very important—and entirely up to you—to get the lien taken off the record.

Can You Do It Yourself?

The popularity of do-it-yourself home improvement manuals and television programs indicates the enthusiasm homeowners have for making their own repairs and renovations. For major construction projects, you can act as your own general contractor by registering for an owner/builder exemption at your building permit office. The exemption endorses your legal right to act as a contractor when building or improving structures on your own property for your own (and your family's) use. Without this permit, city officials could request that you cease construction or be fined.

Be realistic about the work you can, or should, handle. Before you try rewiring the electrical system in your attic, for example, call your local construction or buildings department for information on city codes. Systems that are subject to municipal health and safety standards generally require the work of qualified trade specialists.

PICK YOUR HELPERS CAREFULLY

If you choose to hire subcontractors to help you in your task as owner/builder, you are exempt from state licensing requirements that apply to general contractors, but you must still comply with state labor and other laws. You should avoid hiring subcontractors unless you have complied with state requirements on workers' compensation insurance, liability insurance, medical insurance, and employment taxes. You might also have to contend with legal minimum wage and overtime rates.

Avoid hiring unlicensed subcontractors, even if they seem competent and offer you a low rate. If anything goes wrong on the job—if they damage your property or cause negligent injury—you have little legal recourse, since these workers probably do not have enough assets to make a suit worthwhile.

NEIGHBOR PROBLEMS

Uncertain boundaries, delinquent dogs, late-night noises, trees, and trespassers all cause unneighborly friction. The law deals with most of these vexations.

Getting Your Boundaries Straight

Most homeowners have a basic idea of their property's limits, or boundary lines, and they generally respect their neighbors' boundaries. But the precise limits or boundary lines are often unclear and can become a source of conflict when someone believes his neighbor has transgressed his property line.

Property boundaries are detailed in the deed to your home, which you received at the time of your purchase. (Deeds are also available for review at the county recorder's office.) It is not uncommon for boundaries to be imprecisely recorded, since most boundaries are not simple, straight lines but irregular or undulating. Even boundaries marked by more permanent features, such as a stream or large rock, can change through time—as when a stream changes course or a rock is removed for construction.

Ownership boundaries apply also to the space above and below ground, with limits set by state and local laws. (Air rights, for example, vary by hundreds of feet in different areas.)

When boundaries are unclear or erroneously recorded in public records, homeowners have several options for clarifying their property lines without involving neighbors. These are:

- **Title insurance.** The title search conducted when you bought your home describes the boundaries of the property and is backed by the title insurance you bought. Title insurance guarantees that the purchaser has legitimate ownership of the property described in the deed. If this turns out not to be true, you can make a legal claim against the insurance company.
- **General warranty deed.** If you have this type of deed, the previous owner has assured you that the property description is true and accurate. If you discover that the property boundaries were misrepresented, you may be able to take legal action against the seller.
- **Quiet title.** If you discover an error in the recording of the boundaries of your property, you can take action to correct, or quiet, the title. The action to quiet title must be presented to a judge and is best managed by a lawyer.

123...

IF NEIGHBORS BLOCK A VIEW

If your neighbor builds or plants something in the middle of your favorite vista, consider these points before taking action:

1. The law allows your neighbor to block your view as long as the blocking item is useful to the property owner and not built specifically to annoy you. You have a valid case if you can prove malicious intent, as in the case of a so-called spite fence—an unnecessarily tall fence erected to irritate you.

2. City ordinances occasionally protect the view you had when you bought the property. You must have proof, such as photographs, that your original view has been blocked.

3. Municipal zoning laws usually include setbacks (distance between structures and property lines) and height restrictions—typically four feet for a front-yard fence, for instance, and six feet in back. See if the neighbor's addition that blocks your view is in violation.

4. An "easement" formally establishes a specific right-of-way between your and your neighbor's land. If you arrange a solar access easement, for example, your neighbor agrees not to block your sunlight.

- **Homeowners association.** Properties in planned developments and subdivisions are usually well defined, but if you find an error, contact the developer or association board.
- **Ordinances on water boundaries.** Property lines defined by streams, lakes, or oceans may change as the water's edge moves. Normally, a homeowner owns the land up to the water's edge, and in some cases to the center of a lake or stream. The federal government, however, owns navigable waters, and both federal and local governments may limit your right to build a dock or overhanging deck on the water.

BOUNDARIES MARKED BY FENCES

Whether white-picket or hand-hewn stone, fences are a clear way to mark territory. Because fences are at times the source of boundary conflicts between adjoining property owners, most states have fence statutes. These regulations apply to all types of boundary fences.

In rural areas, fence statutes usually impose either an open range or closed range policy. In open range areas, cattle, sheep, and other livestock wander freely, and neighbors may erect fences to protect their properties; in closed range areas, the livestock owner must fence in the herd.

Urban and suburban fence statutes usually regulate fence appearance, height, and location within the property. Planned communities often impose additional restrictions and specifications. In practice, few cities waste time enforcing fence violations. As long as no one complains, nonconforming fences may stay put for generations. In general, with the exception of subdivision rules, local laws allow you to determine how your fence looks, and as long as the materials used are not hazardous or dangerous to passersby, such as electric barbed wire, a fence can be made of whatever material you choose.

SHARING THE FENCE EXPENSE

When a boundary fence is shared by you and your neighbor, it is subject to additional state and local laws. Most states have statutes recognizing that a preexisting fence used by both of you belongs to both of you equally. You must share the cost of maintenance or replacement, and neither of you may remove it without the other's permission. If your neighbor refuses to contribute to necessary repairs after your verbal and written requests that he do so, you can sue him for half the costs in small claims court.

A more amicable solution if your neighbor does not want equal responsibility for maintaining the fence—perhaps because it is not visible from his house, but is quite close to yours—is to agree in writing that you will take primary or even full responsibility for it. If one neighbor moves out and a new homeowner moves in, however, the situation regarding the boundary fence reverts to local laws on mutual ownership.

If your neighbor erects a fence on the boundary line between your properties, that fence remains your neighbor's property. But if, once the fence is built, you use it to enclose your own property on one or more sides, many state fence laws provide that you pay your neighbor a portion of the value of the fence.

Occasionally, a homeowner will build a fence intended to put neighbors out of sight and mind—and out of sorts. Generally referred to as a "spite fence," it is likely to be a high, unsightly barrier constructed at the edge of his property, and under certain circumstances, it may be against the law. Several states have laws defining spite fences and give a neighbor the right to sue the builder of such a fence on the grounds that it is a nuisance with no reasonable use to the owner.

*Good fences
make good neighbors.*

ROBERT FROST
Mending Wall

Troubles With Trees

When trees grow on or near property boundaries, issues of who owns or cares for the trees often arise between neighbors. State laws on boundary trees, or "line" trees, are based on the premise that the location of the trunk determines ownership. If the trunk is on your side of the property line, even if roots or branches extend into your neighbor's yard, the tree is yours. If the trunk straddles the boundary, in most states you and your

---

Settling Boundary Disputes

If any boundary question arises with your neighbor that cannot be clarified in your property deed, take corrective action right away. Legally, anyone encroaching on your property without your objection has the right to continue such use after a certain number of years.

• **Make an agreement.** If you and your neighbor do not know your exact boundaries, and one of you wants to build on land that is in question, you can agree, in writing, to a new boundary.

• **Sign a quitclaim deed.** A more formal agreement is a quitclaim deed: Each neighbor waives any right to the disputed property on the other side of the boundary. (If it is recorded in public land records, the agreement is binding even on future owners.) Be aware, though, that some lenders demand full payment of a mortgage loan if the borrower transfers any interest in the property.

• **Hire a surveyor.** A licensed surveyor will determine the exact dimensions and location of your property boundaries. If the survey conflicts with earlier surveys and one neighbor is found to be on the other's property, consult a lawyer.

• **Try mediation.** Local government building departments or other municipal agencies may offer mediation for disputes between neighbors. Planned communities also may provide mediation services.

• **File a lawsuit.** To correct a disputed boundary line, you may have to file suit in district court. If your neighbor is building on ground that a recent survey shows is yours, and the neighbor does not respect the new boundary description, you may need to file a civil lawsuit.

If a Neighbor Hurts Your Trees

If your neighbor destroys or seriously damages a tree on your property, you need to know if the act was accidental or deliberate.

If the neighbor bulldozes your young maple tree while clearing space for a new deck, it is pretty clearly an accident, and he will likely offer to pay for damages.

But if he refuses to take responsibility, contact your homeowners insurance company. Many policies cover trees damaged unintentionally by others. Your neighbor's insurance may also cover the problem.

If insurance will not cover damages and your efforts to receive compensation from your neighbor fail, you can sue for the amount of actual replacement value. Some state courts additionally compensate tree owners for aesthetic loss and diminished property value.

If your neighbor deliberately injures or destroys your tree, civil penalties in many states provide punishment—in most states, double or triple the cost of replacing the tree. In other states, criminal penalties apply to the act of intentionally harming someone's trees, shrubs, or saplings.

Thus a spiteful neighbor, irritated by the blossoms falling in his yard, could be charged with a criminal violation for chopping down your cherry tree. To file a complaint, you might need a witness to the desecration or some other evidence.

neighbor are legal co-owners and should negotiate equal shares of maintenance and care.

When you and your neighbor co-own a tree, each of you has the right to cut limbs over your own property as long as no harm is done to the tree or the other person's property. At best, neighbors can agree that one person will arrange for the tree to be trimmed and send the bill to the other for sharing. But sometimes problems arise—for example, if you believe a costly procedure is necessary and your neighbor disagrees or refuses to share the expense.

As long as it has been established that the tree is a boundary tree, you can take action if the problem falls into one of these categories: legal necessity (conforming with a height ordinance), essential maintenance (protection against disease), or safety (attending to potentially hazardous falling branches).

Explain to your neighbor why the work should be done, if necessary with an expert opinion, such as from a tree service, to back you up. If he still refuses to share costs, make at least two written attempts at securing his cooperation. In your letter refer to your prior requests for his cooperation, provide an estimate of the work needed, and state your intention to have the work done and bill him for half the amount. If your neighbor still refuses cooperation, you might suggest mediation or file suit in small claims court to recover your expenses.

OVERHANGING BRANCHES

You may have the right to trim branches of your neighbor's trees that overhang your property. If your neighbor's trees interfere with your ability to use your property fully (if a newly planted tree throws deep shade on the garden from which you sell cut flowers, for example), some states recognize that you have a legal claim. Other states recognize a legal claim only when the trees cause serious harm to your property, as when its roots cause your driveway to crack.

If a neighbor's tree is diseased or hazardous, you should alert the tree's owner and can trim branches within your property boundary if the owner does not. Generally, however, you may not enter your neighbor's property to trim or destroy the tree except in an emergency situation (such as a violent storm or fire when a branch poses an immediate threat of danger). But courts increasingly are holding owners liable for damage caused by trees they know to be unsound or dangerous.

Therefore, if an obviously rotten limb of your neighbor's tree falls on your garage, you can sue for damages if you can prove the owner knew, or should have known, that the tree's condition made it hazardous. As in all relations with your neighbors, however, first try direct communication and then mediation before going to court.

Problems With Trespassing

Under the law, a trespasser is anyone who intrudes physically onto your property without permission or privilege, and you have the right to fend trespassers off the premises by putting up a sign or a fence or by telling them to leave. An unwanted door-to-door salesman who keeps ringing your bell is invading your property without permission. And if you find an unfamiliar neighbor lounging at your swimming pool, he too is invading your property without permission. All social guests and household workers, on the other hand, come onto your property by "permission," and firefighters who arrive to save your burning house have "privilege" to enter your property without permission.

But what if the trespasser is your pleasant neighbor Betsy who has extended her garden a few feet onto your property, or who regularly takes a shortcut to and from work through your yard? These are incidents of repeated trespass, or "encroachment," on your property to which you should respond, even if her encroachment does not bother you. Why? Because in almost every state, a trespasser can legally acquire ownership of your land by occupying it if you do not object.

Under this legal doctrine, called "adverse possession," the homeowner who allows someone to trespass for years (in most states, 10 or 20) without giving permission, complaining, or taking legal action loses rights to the land. In 15 years Betsy

Ultimately, property rights and personal rights are the same thing.

CALVIN COOLIDGE
President of the United States
1924–1928

Keeping Your Neighbors' Pets Out of Your Yard

What can you do if your neighbor's prized poodle has a penchant for eating your petunias? Pet owners are responsible for the behavior of their trespassing pets and in general must adhere to local ordinances. If you have a persistent problem, here is what to do about it:

• Dog and cat owners are not normally held responsible for their pets' occasional trespassing into your yard. But if a pet causes significant damage to your property—such as digging up new, expensive sod—you may be able to seek monetary compensation in small claims court under nuisance laws.

• Most towns have leash laws, or running-at-large laws, that require dogs to be restrained when they are not on their owners' property. If the owner of a dog that ranges around your neighborhood does not respond to your request to abide by leash laws, you have the right to report the dog to the police or animal warden, and the city might impound the pet.

• So-called pooper-scooper laws require pet owners to clean up immediately after an animal defecates on another person's property or on the street. If your town has no such ordinance, and if your neighbor's Great Dane seems to hang out in your rose garden, and if your neighbor is unresponsive to your pleas to keep his dog on his own property, your only recourse may be to sue him for nuisance or property damage.

• Local ordinances often restrict the number of animals allowed per household and usually restrict certain species as well, such as ducks, goats, reptiles, and other animals that might wander onto a neighbor's property. Check the laws in your locality, and don't hesitate to assert your rights.

may actually own the strip of land on the edge of your property where she planted that garden, simply because you never said anything.

AVERTING ADVERSE POSSESSION

As a homeowner, you have several options for preventing unwanted visitors, including neighbors, from gaining a legal claim to ownership of any part of your property. Fences, gates, and "No Trespassing" signs are basic measures. You may also need to "clarify," or claim, your property boundaries for the trespasser. For example, if your new neighbor, unsure of the boundary, innocently installs a swing set for his children in part of your backyard, you should quickly set him straight. You may let him leave the swing set, but you should ask him to sign an agreement that grants him and his family permission to use your property. The agreement should describe in detail the portion of land involved and state clearly that you have the right to revoke your offer at any time. If the bit of land in question is sizable—say he builds a playhouse next to the swing set and you have noticed that the kids are playing baseball every day in the area—you could suggest that he pay rent for it as well as signing the agreement.

EASEMENTS

Homeowners commonly grant, or sell, the right to use part of their land for a specified purpose, called an "easement." Unlike the agreement temporarily granting your neighbor permission to use a strip of your land for his child's swing set, an easement becomes part of the property and applies to the property no matter who owns it.

Easements are recorded in the title or deed to your property and are filed in the county records office. Cities and utility companies commonly hold easements allowing them to haul trash, install telephone poles, build sewer systems, and so on without constantly asking property owners for permission.

Homeowners can issue private easements to their neighbors, but problems often arise when a new owner is subject to an unexpired easement granted by a previous owner. (Easements can, but do not always, have a start and end date.) Thirty years ago the owner may have issued an easement for his neighbor to run a water pipe under part of his property. Now you own the home, and you start to build a driveway and run into the pipe. You must, by law, respect the right-of-way of the easement and work around the pipe. To eliminate the easement, you can seek a written release from the easement holder. You should first consult a real estate lawyer for advice.

An attorney can also help you grant an easement. (To be effective, the grant of an easement must be in writing.) You

---

What to Include in an Easement

If you decide to grant an easement, or legal right-of-way, on part of your property, you or your attorney need to prepare a written document that includes the following:

✔ *Names of both parties.* Identify yourself and the person to whom you are granting the easement, and make sure both of you sign the document.

✔ *Purpose.* You should describe the exact nature of the easement and the reason for it, such as providing a shortcut to the beach or using land for building a storage shed.

✔ *Property description.* Include the precise location of the area within your property affected by the easement and its exact dimensions.

✔ *Special use, duties, or conditions.* Clarify, for example, that the builder of the storage shed agrees to maintain the trees surrounding the shed as part of the easement agreement, or that your neighbor must pick up after her horse as a condition for granting an easement for a riding path.

✔ *The price paid to you.* The exchange of money legitimizes the easement as a legal contract. You and the easement holder can negotiate the amount.

✔ *Duration.* You can stipulate that the easement is effective from the date of signing until five, 15, or 25 years later.

have the right to sell a right-of-way or other use of your property. The amount may be a token to legitimize the easement, or it may be a significant sum if the easement diminishes your property's value.

Noisy Neighbors

In addition to trespassing, homeowners sometimes experience noise, odors, and other intrusions that are defined as "nuisances" under the law. Playing music loudly in your home at midnight, letting your dog howl at the moon, and revving up your lawn mower early on weekend mornings may appear to be privileges of ownership, but when your neighbor is trying to sleep, he may consider them nuisances.

Two types of nuisances are recognized by the law. A public nuisance is an offense against a whole neighborhood or community—such as excessive noise from a nearby airport—and legal action to correct it is usually taken by a public entity, such as the city or county government, against the offender. Private nuisances usually involve homeowners complaining about their neighbors, such as a barking dog or loud music, and complaints are filed by individuals in civil court.

Generally, a homeowner must show that the neighbor is responsible for an offending activity that interferes with the enjoyment or use of the homeowner's property. In addition, he must prove that the annoyance has caused harm, which may take the form of property damage, physical injury, or mental anguish. If his evidence is sound, the homeowner can seek redress for injuries inflicted by the neighbor's annoying activity and seek a court order to have it stopped.

FAMILIAR NUISANCES

Many of the annoyances that cause conflict among neighbors are common enough that laws are usually in place to forestall lawsuits. For example, almost every local community has ordinances prohibiting excessive, unnecessary, and unreasonable noise. (Homeowners associations may have noise prohibitions even more strict than municipal rules.)

Basically, the annoyance your noisy neighbor causes must be substantial enough and of a sufficient duration that any reasonable person would have the same angry response that you do. You would not have a valid complaint against a neighbor just because you are unusually sensitive to loud noise, for example, or because you cannot abide hard rock. Noise ordinances are enforced by the police, by special environmental noise-abatement organizations, and by the consumer-affairs office of local government.

123...

KEEPING THE NOISE DOWN

If your neighbor's noisiness interferes with your domestic peace, there are steps you can take before taking legal action:

1. Approach your neighbor amicably and discuss the problem. She may be unaware that her TV set, turned up so she can hear it over the vacuum cleaner, blasts directly into your office.

2. Visit city hall or the public library for a copy of the local noise ordinance. Then write a letter to your neighbor, citing the ordinance, pointing out that her noise violates it. Keep a copy of the letter.

3. Check with other neighbors to see if anyone else is having trouble You may want to join efforts.

4. Try mediation. Dispute-resolution services are free in many localities, especially in urban centers and in planned community associations.

5. If your neighbor still continues to agitate you, call the police or the department of environmental protection while the noisy activity is occurring.

6. Consider filing a nuisance claim in small claims court for monetary damages or in civil court if you have suffered major injury, such as loss of business. First, however, have your lawyer write a letter threatening legal action which may stop the noise before you have to go to court.

Before You File a Nuisance Claim

Can you prove that your neighbor has caused substantial interference with your use and enjoyment of your property? Have all your efforts to correct the matter failed?

If you answer "yes", then you may choose to file a nuisance claim. However, be prepared to face the common (and effective) defenses that (1) you must have known about the nuisance when you moved into the neighborhood (the "We were here first" logic), or (2) that the neighborhood has tolerated the nuisance for so long that it has, by inaction, endorsed it.

The party you accuse may say she is not responsible, or is only partially responsible, for the offense. For example, if her dog's howling occurs only when two certain neighborhood dogs get together, not when her dog is alone.

When you file a nuisance claim you must not only be prepared for effective defenses, but you must produce sufficient evidence that a nuisance definitely exists. Proof may take the form of testimony by neighborhood witnesses, expert or specialist witnesses, photographs, videotapes, or other factual evidence.

BLIGHTED PROPERTY

Among the list of woes that one neighbor can wreak upon another is poorly maintained, unsightly property. Most local ordinances regulate the appearance of property to some degree by prohibiting "blighted property," or property that has fallen into a state of disrepair. Ordinances typically forbid a homeowner from maintaining a property that creates a danger to others or is such an eyesore that it diminishes the value of neighboring homes. If your neighbors paint their house bright blue with yellow shutters, you may shudder at the sight but have no legal recourse unless you can prove that their color scheme actually reduces your property value, or unless neighborhood zoning laws prohibit the colors.

Quieting the Neighbors

PROBLEM

Jim and Linda had just retired and moved to a small house in a new neighborhood. They introduced themselves to their next-door neighbors, Bob and Katie, personable young newlyweds. Unfortunately, the newlyweds were also fans of popular music and played their high-tech CD system loud and long into the night. Jim and Linda liked to go to bed about eleven, but found that many nights they were kept awake by the music until two or three in the morning. Jim and Linda complained gently to Katie and Bob, and the music stopped for a few weeks. But when it started again, Jim and Linda found the situation untenable.

ACTION

First, Jim and Linda researched their local noise ordinance at the local library and the county clerk's office and decided the late-night noise was a violation of local law. They also kept careful notes on the times they were kept awake by the loud music and the ways in which they tried, vainly, to get Katie and Bob to do something about the problem. Then they took their problem to the local community dispute-resolution board, which formally mediates such cases. The board persuaded Bob and Katie to turn the music down six nights a week, and Jim and Linda agreed to put up with it until one a.m. on Saturday nights. Had no mediation group existed in their community, Jim and Linda could have reported the problem to a local government office or the police. As a last resort, they could have taken Bob and Katie to court.

Blighted property ordinances may also require that driveways and sidewalks be clear of debris and in good condition and not cracked, or that sidewalks and fences be free of graffiti—or even an innocuous hopscotch board. Communities usually regulate weeds and rubbish separately as health and safety hazards, although the trimming of high, unsightly weeds may be included in a blighted property ordinance. Planned communities often impose additional aesthetic restrictions on yard and home appearance and maintenance.(see also "Condos, Co-ops, and Planned Communities," page 66).

Environmental Concerns

As the hazardous side effects of modern technology grow more serious, homeowners have gained certain rights—but have just as many responsibilities.

Fighting Pollution on the Outside

Along with a house and the lot on which it stands, homeowners gain incidental rights to the use and enjoyment of the airspace above, the earth below, and the water that flows on or under their property. To protect these rights, federal legislation has set standards for air, water, ground, and noise pollution, such as the Clean Water Act and the Resource Conservation and Recovery Act. Many states have added their own environmental protection laws. Still, homeowners who want to sue for pollution damages under federal and state laws face a daunting legal battle, and may be better off joining local citizens' action groups to press for change or file a lawsuit.

NOISY NOISE AND DIRTY AIR

While homeowners own the airspace around their home, upper airspace is controlled and regulated by the federal government to facilitate airplane traffic. When residents live near local airports, the noise generated by airplane traffic may be aggravating enough to justify a claim against the government for the taking of property (see "Managing Your Home," page 30), or against a privately owned airport for nuisance. If you feel your right to use and enjoy your property is impinged on by airport noise, talk to your neighbors about a joint action or contact a lawyer.

Another common intrusion into homeowners' airspace is the harmful or noxious emissions from local industrial plants. Although federal government protections such as the Clean Air Act regulate air pollution, enforcement is difficult and often unsuccessful. The rules require precise and detailed proof that the accused company is emitting harmful substances that are causing, or will surely cause, damage to local residents or devaluation of their properties.

Since it is difficult to get action from the federal government, one way homeowners can seek recourse is to bring a private nuisance lawsuit against the offending property owner. For example, you could sue a nearby meat-packing plant creating noxious odors or a textile mill expelling excessive levels of dust. Other common pollutants that provoke property owners' com-

Are Electric Power Lines Dangerous?

In this electronic age, the health risks of electromagnetic fields produced by everything from toaster ovens to high-voltage power lines have become a subject of major controversy.

Several independent scientific studies have linked physical proximity to high-voltage power lines with unusually high rates of cancer in adults and children, including childhood leukemia. Other scientific opinions, however, say the evidence is inconclusive.

Because research is incomplete, the federal government is unable to define for homeowners what level of exposure may be dangerous. (Some utilities give homeowners meters to measure the electric fields around their houses, but the readings do not mean much without a definition of safe exposure levels.)

Meanwhile, parent and community groups have pushed local governments and utility companies to reduce the possible dangers of electric fields by keeping high-voltage power lines away from schools and densely populated areas.

For the latest information on this volatile subject, contact the environmental protection bureau of your state attorney general's office.

The nation that destroys its soil destroys itself.

FRANKLIN DELANO ROOSEVELT
President
of the United States
1932–1945

plaints are pesticides sprayed by crop-dusting planes, fumes and ash from garbage incinerators, and offensive smells from municipal landfills or composting facilities. In all such pollution-related nuisance claims, the court would have to weigh the benefit of the industrial activity for the public (such as local employment generated or state-mandated requirements for waste disposal) against the personal or property damage suffered by the individuals or groups of property owners who filed the complaint.

Watch out for common legal defenses of polluters: when the pollution has persisted over the course of many years, the polluter may claim that the statute of limitations, or time limit to file suit, has expired. The polluter may also argue that because he has been polluting for so many years without objection, he has gained an easement, or right, to pollute property, just as a trespasser might acquire an easement to a shortcut through your yard. It is therefore essential to take action right away if pollution is causing damage to you or your property.

DANGEROUS WATER

Your incidental rights as a homeowner extend to the water below your property, and being sure that water is clean is a critical matter if you pump your own drinking water. That vital source can become polluted by underground chemical and fuel storage tanks and by farm pesticides. Federal legislation has begun to address compensation to homeowners for damages caused by underground tanks, and many states impose rules

How to Fight for a Healthy Home Environment

From individual lawsuits to government intervention, there are numerous methods of recourse for homeowners who suffer personal or property damage as a result of pollution, both inside and outside the home:

• Local environmental and citizens' action groups can provide valuable information and assistance on local polluting culprits and pending cases. They can help connect you with others suffering similar damage from polluters.

• If you know and can prove who the polluter is in a local situation, you can file an individual lawsuit claim on grounds of trespass or nuisance. You need to show that you or your property has suffered actual harm or damage.

• The state attorney general's office will represent citizens in severe pollution cases, as when homeowners must leave their properties because of hazardous waste leakage.

• Under the Freedom of Information Act, homeowners can obtain information on government-monitored pollution. If, for example, you believe a local chemical company is dumping hazardous waste that is contaminating your well water, you can file a request for documents of state or federal agencies that regulate the company and that may confirm your suspicions.

• Many federal environmental laws, such as the Clean Water Act, allow individual homeowners to sue a polluting company for compensation for damages and decreased property value. But because these lawsuits must occur in federal court and are very complicated, they are prohibitively costly for most homeowners.

on underground tank disposal and placement, which may offer protection to property owners. Class action suits by private citizens against pesticide manufacturers have forced companies to install filters in affected homes. Homeowners may also have recourse under nuisance and trespass law.

Contaminants in the Home

Environmental problems just as likely lurk inside your walls as outside your home. The myriad products that go into the construction of a home are regulated to some degree by federal, state, and local laws that require testing and elimination or removal of dangerous products. Still, materials in your home may threaten your and your family's health and safety. The most common home contaminants are asbestos, formaldehyde, lead paint, and radon.

- **Asbestos.** A mineral fiber found in rock, asbestos was used in a variety of household and building materials—from appliances to floor tiles—to strengthen the product and provide insulation and fire protection. Asbestos can cause lung and stomach cancer if inhaled repeatedly over time. Banned in new products, asbestos is common in older homes. A homeowner can hire a qualified asbestos professional to survey her home and determine whether there are asbestos-containing materials that should be removed or encapsulated.
- **Formaldehyde.** A chemical used widely in building materials and household products such as pressed wood and carpeting, formaldehyde can cause burning sensations in the eyes and throat, breathing difficulties, headaches, depression, or exhaustion. Formaldehyde emissions are highest when products are new and when temperature or humidity in the home is high. Mobile homes tend to have higher than average, and often excessive, levels of formaldehyde. You can test for formaldehyde with a home test kit or through city or state health agencies. Excessive levels of the chemical can be controlled by removing the offending product and increasing ventilation.
- **Lead paint.** Most homes built before the mid-1970's were coated with lead-based paint. If sweet-tasting lead paint chips are ingested by children, or dust from the paint is inhaled, lead paint can cause brain damage. Victims of lead paint exposure can sue the paint manufacturers, but must determine which lead-paint company is responsible. While total removal of lead paint from a home is costly, special sealants may reduce the hazard. Call the your state office of the Environmental Protection Agency for information.

Watch Out for Radon Scams

By no means are all firms that test for and deal with radon contamination unscrupulous. But some are, and they take advantage of homeowners' concerns about the dangers of radon. Here are things to watch out for:

✔ *False fears.* Some dual-service companies, which offer both radon testing and radon reduction services, have been known to exaggerate the level of radon found during testing, then convince panicky homeowners to pay for costly radon reduction services.

✔ *Immediate cure.* Because radon levels fluctuate daily and seasonally, and in different areas within the home, even the quickest tests should take at least 48 hours. Long-term tests that provide the most accurate average radon levels take several months.

✔ *Scare tactics.* Beware the radon reduction contractor who insinuates that other homes in your neighborhood have tested high in radon. Certain communities do have higher than average radon levels, but neighboring homes often have greatly varying levels. Arrange an impartial professional radon test to be sure.

✔ *Do-it-yourself kits.* These are widely sold and are easy to use, but may be misleading. You can call the state office of the Environmental Protection Agency for recommendations of the most accurate kits.

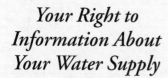

Your Right to Information About Your Water Supply

Under the mandate of the Safe Drinking Water Act, you have the right to know these facts about your drinking water:

✔ *The source.* Drinking water comes either from groundwater or from surface water such as ponds, lakes, and rivers. It is then treated by your community's water supplier. You have a right to be told by the supplier where the water comes from and how it is purified.

✔ *Contaminants.* You are entitled to know the precise contaminants for which your water has been tested, both at present and in the past.

✔ *Violation notices.* If maximum-level water contamination occurs (safety levels are defined by the EPA), the water supplier must give the public an explanation of the violation within 14 days of detection.

✔ *Potential health risks.* The notification of water contamination should include a clear description of the potential adverse health effects.

✔ *Corrective measures.* Your local water supplier must spell out for you what steps it is taking to correct a contamination problem.

✔ *Alternative sources.* The supplier must indicate whether alternative water sources, such as bottled water, are necessary, and if so, for how long.

■ **Radon.** A colorless, odorless radioactive gas that can cause lung cancer, radon occurs naturally. It is released from the breakdown of uranium in the soil and rock on which many homes are built and enters the home through cracks in floors and walls, openings around sumps (basement drains), and through water wells. Some states offer free radon testing; your state EPA office can provide more information. You can also buy a do-it-yourself radon test kit or hire a certified radon tester.

For more information about household hazards, contact the regional office of the Environmental Protection Agency, local and state government environmental offices, and local environmental groups.

Is Your Drinking Water Pure?

Most bacteria and parasites once present in drinking water have been eliminated through 20th-century technology. Nevertheless, American homeowners are still vulnerable to the contamination of their lakes, rivers, groundwater, and other essential water sources.

Modern-day toxic chemicals, from industrial, agricultural, and municipal sources, pollute water and can cause cancer and other serious health problems. In the 1970's, the federal government recognized the link between toxic chemicals consumed in drinking water and elevated cancer risks, and implemented new safety standards through the Safe Drinking Water Act and subsequent amendments. Some state laws offer further protections.

TRYING TO GET IT CLEAN

The standard purification method used in U.S. water treatment systems involves sand filtering the water and disinfecting it with chlorine. Yet this rigorous process is not foolproof, and the water that gets to your tap may not be as safe as you think. Some chemical by-products of chlorination have been shown to cause cancer. The Environmental Protection Agency sets limits on the amount of these chemicals allowed in drinking water.

Lead is another toxin that can contaminate water after it is treated. Lead leaches into water from the lead pipes and soldering of public water distribution systems and private household plumbing systems. Lead pipes and solder were banned in new construction in the late 1980's. The EPA now requires that large-scale water systems add lime or other chemicals to the

water to minimize the amount of lead, but homeowners with older houses should test their own plumbing systems for lead content in the water.

TESTING THE WATERS

Even when public drinking water meets national and state standards, it may still contain pollutants that you cannot see or taste, such as pesticides or herbicides, industrial solvents, bacteria, parasites, or radon that leaks into wells. If you have a private well, you are responsible for the quality of its water. Your local health department or water authority may provide free testing of your tap water, especially if you have specific cause for concern. Or you can pay a state-certified water testing lab for a thorough private test.

If you find that your water needs to be filtered or treated, there is a wide range of water treatment systems available. Be careful, however, not to buy the wrong product or become prey to deceptive sales practices by unscrupulous water treatment companies. Before investing in a water treatment system, you should consult a qualified water-quality contractor or plumbing inspector on the most appropriate treatment for your specific water problems.

Even if your water comes from a public utility, you may want to have it tested. If you discover that it contains contamination above the allowable federal standards or substances for which no standards are set, you should contact the utility company and your local health department. If your local water company or state or federal officials fail to comply with the Safe Drinking Water Act, you have the right to file a civil lawsuit. Talk to an attorney for advice.

The Hidden Dangers of Lawn Care

Pesticides, herbicides, and insecticides can help eliminate unwanted rodents, weeds, and bugs from agricultural crops and suburban lawns, and can greatly increase the productivity of farms and the beauty of private and public landscapes. But they can also damage human immune and nerve systems and cause cancer.

Although some pesticide toxins have been banned by the EPA, others are still legal and are commonly used in lawn pesticides at legally allowable levels. Toxins are present in some pesticides prepared for use by home gardeners as well as, more potently, in sprays used by lawn care and landscaping companies.

The cumulative effect of chemical lawn and farm sprays contributes to air pollution, and water runoff from treated lawns and fields is suspected of contributing heavily to the pollution

Pesticide Warnings

Landscaping companies that take care of people's lawns and gardens typically spray mixes of pesticide and fertilizer. When many lawns in a neighborhood are treated this way, the toxic chemical sprays remain, drifting about the neighborhood and permeating the air you and your family breathe.

In response to pressure from concerned citizens' groups, many communities now require lawn care companies to give local residents warning prior to, or while, pesticides are being sprayed. This right to fair warning about spraying allows residents—especially those with children, who are hypersensitive to pesticides—to vacate the area or stay indoors during spraying.

If you hire a lawn service, you have the legal right to know what your alternatives are when choosing a termiticide, pesticide, or herbicide, including nonchemical treatments. Insist on a thorough explanation of the health implications for the suggested chemical treatment.

You can check with the Environmental Protection Agency or a local environmental group. Then refuse to have any chemical you consider hazardous used in and around your home.

Homeowners can maintain a healthy lawn without pesticides by using a number of nonpolluting methods, including fertilizing with organic products. You can also check with your local environmental group for information on low-maintenance varieties of grass that grow in your climate.

of enclosed bodies of water. Because the toxic chemicals in pesticides are colorless and odorless, many people suffering symptoms of pesticide exposure may misinterpret the cause. Some learning disabilities and certain forms of depression, for example, have been linked to pesticide "poisoning." Clinical ecologists can often diagnose pesticide illnesses, and poison control specialists may be able to link physical symptoms to specific pesticide ingredients. The EPA, the Food and Drug Administration, and the Department of Agriculture are working together to reduce pesticide use in the United States.

Too Much Garbage

American homeowners produce millions of tons of garbage every year—garbage containing organic waste, plastics, paper, glass, metal, and all manner of toxic materials. Local sanitation departments and private haulers truck this garbage away, and for many homeowners that is the end of it.

Yet garbage continues to affect citizens as it is processed into the local environment and ecosystem. More than two-thirds of our garbage goes into landfills, whose effluents pollute local soil and trickle down into the groundwater supply. Some garbage is burned, polluting the air with toxic emissions and creating potentially toxic ash residue. Sometimes garbage is illegally dumped into local waters.

DEALING WITH TOXIC WASTE

Besides the environmental impact of the sheer tonnage of of garbage produced by Americans, there is also the problem of dealing with everyday products that are in themselves toxic. The Environmental Protection Agency sets safety standards for household products containing hazardous materials, and local pollution laws often require that certain hazardous fluids, such as oil and automotive antifreeze, be treated separately from other refuse.

In many communities, environmental groups have worked with cities or counties to institute hazardous waste collection programs such as paint-collection days for recycling unused, hazardous paints. Recycling of some materials is now mandatory in some localities but is often limited to certain types of papers, metals, and plastics.

Despite mandatory and optional means of disposing of or recycling hazardous wastes, many homeowners still pollute public waters and city dumps by casually dumping excess paint strippers, pesticides, and other hazardous wastes down drains and into trash cans. These homeowners, along with irrespon-

Taking Action Against Polluters

If a neighbor or local business is polluting your area, it may be up to you to take action. Every situation is different, and the law is complicated in this area, but here are some things you can do:

✔ *Try negotiating.* If your neighbor is dumping motor oil into the gutter, for instance, you may be able to deal with him directly. He may not realize that he is breaking the law.

✔ *Check local ordinances.* If your neighbor's yard is strewn with rubbish, or his front lawn is piled with leaves and trash, he may be violating local laws. Go to the library or check with a city hall clerk to find the appropriate agency to contact.

✔ *Report polluters.* Some areas have complaint lines that you can call and report activities such as illegal dumping. Check the blue pages in your telephone book or call the department of sanitation.

✔ *Form a coalition.* Taking action against a local business that is polluting the air or water supply may be difficult. Contact neighbors and others in your community to form a group to give your complaints more leverage.

✔ *Ask for help.* If your problem is important, but you don't know where to turn, contact local or national environmental groups or your state attorney general for advice.

sible industries, effectively pollute their own, and their neighbors', home environment—water, air, and earth.

TAKING ACTION AGAINST HAZARDOUS WASTE

Private citizens who want to reduce their contribution to toxic waste in the local environment can recycle hazardous products such as batteries and bug spray, and reduce the amount of hazardous products they purchase. They can also work to stem the tide of industrial hazardous waste by joining local governments, business leaders, and citizen groups that are committed to finding community solutions to waste management. Among the issues addressed are:

- Setting up community programs for recycling, composting, and collecting hazardous household waste.
- Community importation of garbage from other communities. Usually this is a revenue-raising program by the local government.
- Ensuring that landfills are lined to prevent leakage into surrounding soil and are monitored for leaking toxins.
- Initiating or supporting plans for source-separated waste facilities, such as separate programs for yard waste, food waste, and other materials that can be composted.
- Setting up a forum on solid-waste management that creates a dialogue between business and industry, government, environmentalists, and other concerned citizens.

Nobody can be in good health if he does not have, all the time, fresh air, sunshine, and good water.

FLYING HAWK
Oglala Sioux Chief

Homeowners' Pollution Primer

The crazy quilt of local rules governing waste disposal in the U.S. defies generalization. Homeowners can do their bit, nevertheless, not only by observing their local rules but by reducing their use of toxic materials. For the sake of your home and community, you can:

• **Recycle.** Some communities have passed laws requiring citizens to separate and recycle materials such as corrugated cardboard, colored paper, cans, glass bottles, plastics, and newspapers. Fines levied against violators can be high.To find out about recycling programs in your area, contact your local sanitation or health department.

• **Limit your use of hazardous materials.** Some drain cleaners, air fresheners, rug and upholstery cleaners, pesticides, and even certain laundry detergents contain chemicals that can cause ills ranging from dizziness or nausea to cancer. Local environmental groups or the Environmental Protection Agency can provide information on which products are unsafe and suggest alternatives.

• **Dispose of garbage properly.** Abandoning materials such as mattresses or appliances not only pollutes the environment, but may be illegal in your area. Many communities make periodic pickups of items too large to place in trash bins. Contact your local sanitation department or look in your local Yellow Pages under "Rubbish and Garbage Removal" to find out about such services.

• **Dispose of hazardous substances properly.** In most communities it is illegal to dump motor oil, certain paints, petroleum, and pesticides into the public sewer system via your drain, street gutters, or a local waterway. Call your department of sanitation or health to find out about proper disposal of hazardous waste in your area.

CONDOS, CO-OPS, AND PLANNED COMMUNITIES

These innovations in home owning offer many benefits—and a few pitfalls.

Key Concerns When Buying In

Condominiums, planned developments, and cooperative housing organizations are shared-interest communities that have gained great popularity among homeowners in the past 50 years. There are more than 150,000 such communities in the United States today, and by the year 2000 as many as one quarter of all homeowners may live in shared-interest communities instead of individual, independent homes.

Planned housing developments and condominiums are the most popular and widespread type of shared-interest community, while cooperatives are less common. The rules of ownership vary: Buy a condominium and you own a unit in a building or complex (of apartments or townhouses, for example), with full ownership of your unit. Buy a single-family home in a planned development and you get rights of ownership to your house and property. Buy a cooperative apartment and you own shares in a corporation that owns the property and you get a proprietary lease for your unit.

All three types of shared-interest communities are governed by homeowners associations consisting of members of the community, but usually run by an elected board of directors or board of managers. When you buy property in a shared-interest community, you are legally agreeing to abide by the governing rules and regulations set by the managing board. It is vital, therefore, that you understand the legal ramifications of those regulations—and the possible limitations of your rights—before you finally buy a house or an apartment in a shared-interest community.

WHAT HOMEOWNERS ASSOCIATIONS DO

The homeowners association of a planned community is like a government. It imposes laws you must abide by to remain a citizen, and it also offers protections and advantages to you, your family, and your property that you would not otherwise have. State courts of law generally accept the independent power of a homeowners association to rule its own territory, within the limits of certain federal and state laws. Some states have enacted legislation that specifically governs condominium and cooperative operations and management, and other states apply the same statutes and principles to co-ops and condos that apply to corporations in general.

Since a homeowners association is, like any corporation, essentially self-ruled, it is able to impose a wide degree of control over the daily lifestyle and environment of members of the community. It can place restrictions on what your house looks like; whether you may have pets, or how many; the hours during which you can perform noisy home repair work or play loud music; and so on. These rules are described in the covenants, conditions, and restrictions, better known as the CC&R's, of the property. You receive a copy of these rules when you purchase property in the association.

While the rules and regulations of homeowners associations constrain residents to some degree, owning a home in a planned, controlled environment offers a number of advantages over independent home owning. These benefits may include special facilities and services such as on-site security, swimming pools, playgrounds, parks, party rooms, social events, health care, tennis courts, golf courses, parking facilities, exercise rooms, and more.

WITH SO MANY OWNERS, WHO PAYS FOR WHAT?

To pay for the myriad services and facilities, homeowners associations charge each unit owner a monthly maintenance fee. In condominium developments, each unit—everything within and including the four walls, floor, and ceiling—is owned individually, while common areas and services are owned and paid for jointly by all unit owners.

Condominium owners pay a monthly fee based on the size and value of their individual units in relation to the whole development. Part of the condo owner's monthly maintenance payment is applied toward the building's mortgage and property tax costs.

For cooperative property owners, who do not own individual units but own a share in the property-holding cooperative, the co-op board pays all the building's mortgage, taxes, insurance, and maintenance and repair expenses. The co-op owner's monthly maintenance fee, proportional to shares of ownership, goes toward these expenses.

Property owners in planned developments pay their own taxes and other expenses for keeping up their units, and they also pay monthly maintenance to the homeowners association to cover the maintenance of common buildings and common grounds of the development.

Part of the monthly maintenance fees for all three types of common-interest ownership are kept in a reserve fund, or account, to cover emergencies such as a main water pipe rup-

---

123...

WHAT TO DO BEFORE BUYING

Looking at a home in a condominium, a cooperative, or a planned community? Take these steps before buying:

1. Get copies of the binding agreements, rules, and conditions to which you would be subject if you bought into the community.

2. Ask to see a copy of the most recent financial statement from the homeowners association or condo/co-op board. Look for unpaid assessments from shareholders defaulting on paying for common costs. If the homeowners association is cash poor, it may offer you a lower initial maintenance fee, then raise it steadily after you move in.

3. Find out the history or general pattern of maintenance fee increases.

4. How many units have already been sold? How many are occupied by renters? (Renters do not have the same stake in the association.)

5. How big is the operating budget for routine maintenance and repair, and how big is the reserve fund for unanticipated expenses?

6. You have the right to look at the minutes of a board meeting, which may tell you something about the association's directors. You may also glean valuable information, such as the details of a pending lawsuit against the association.

ture or broken elevator. Unit owners may be asked to pay occasional special assessments for unforeseen or new circumstances, such as lobby renovation or enhanced landscaping. These extra costs, and the necessity for incurring them, are often the source of conflict between individual unit owners and the homeowners association or condo or co-op boards.

Constraints of Community Rules

Homeowners association rules can affect many aspects of daily life. The color you paint your house, the trees you plant, the mailbox you put up, the lettering style of your house number, your kitchen remodeling, where your cat plays outdoors, which relatives can visit for extended stays, how loud you play music, the time of day you do home renovation—all are examples of the kinds of free choices you might have to forfeit when you become a member of a shared-interest property.

The Duties of Association Directors

Like any corporation's board of directors, the managing board of any homeowners association (which includes condo and co-op boards) has legal obligations to the shareholders of the corporation. Some states have specific statutes governing these associations, and some apply regular corporate laws, but all agree that an association board has several basic obligations:

• **Duty to adhere to the governing documents of the association.** These documents, including the declaration of incorporation and its bylaws, define the relationship between the unit owners and the association. A board may take action only within the authority allowed by these documents. If your condominium bylaws call for a two-thirds majority vote of shareholders to change or add a rule, the board may not make a rule in any other manner.

• **Duty to conduct activities responsibly.** The homeowners association must perform the activities it is chartered to do with diligence and due care. Without specifying what duties are owed, state courts generally describe an obligation to act prudently and avoid negligence in management activities. An association board would be exercising due diligence by keeping the reserve fund sufficiently financed to cover emergency and ongoing costs.

• **Duty to act in good faith.** The board is acting on behalf of the corporation and its shareholders. Management decisions must be made in the best interest of all unit owners and not based on personal gain or self-interest. Board members must be legally disinterested in the board's action, and there should be no self-dealing, as there was in the case of a cooperative board that approved of a board member's personal use of common space without adequate compensation. The court agreed with other non-board shareholders who filed suit that the act was an unfair appropriation of shared property, a breach of good faith.

• **Shareholders assume the same responsibilities.** Owners who are not on the board but who make occasional management decisions are subject to the same rules. In condominium and cooperative associations especially, shareholders are often given the power to approve actions that, in a typical business corporation, would be approved solely by the board. For example, owners may be asked to approve increased maintenance charges or to change the rules on swimming pool use. Thus, even unit owners who are not on the board have the power to make decisions on behalf of the association, and have the same obligation to exercise due care.

Community association rules, restrictions, and conditions are generally concerned with these basic issues: who occupies and uses your home, how you use it, how you alter its appearance, to whom you rent and sell it. Here are some specific areas in which an association's rules and restrictions might apply:

- **Members of the home.** Although in most cases the federal laws on fair housing prohibit discrimination in the sale of housing, homeowners associations have been permitted to prohibit roommates or unrelated adults to live in the same unit, limit the number of household members in a unit, and, in some cases, exclude children. For example, a condominium community might require that residents be at least 55 years old, and prohibit visitation children under the age of 16 to no more than 60 days per calendar year.

- **Pets.** Pets may not be welcome in many planned communities. Associations may impose an outright ban on pets or limit the number and kind of pets. They also may prohibit certain breeds of dogs, such as pit bulls, or nontraditional pets like geese or snakes. Associations that allow pets usually enforce restrictions such as leash laws, even for cats, and cleanup rules. Conflict may occur when pet rules change, as when a "No Pets" ruling is added to the association's declaration and bylaws after a resident has moved in. In this case, residents are usually allowed to keep their current pets but may not replace them when the pet dies.

- **Use of the home.** Associations often regulate zoning issues, such as whether home businesses are allowed. If your work is invisible to the community—you are a writer, for example—you will probably have no problem, but if your business requires visitors to and from your residence or bothers other shareholders in any other way, the association can require that you cease your home-based business.

- **Roommates.** Another home-use issue over which unit owners have clashed with their associations is the matter of roommates and unmarried partners. Generally, unrelated adults may stay for an unlimited period of time unless the bylaws of the association deem otherwise. However, the shareholder-tenant usually must use the apartment or house as a primary residence and in most cases cannot turn it into a commercial enterprise by inviting consecutive roommates to pay rent.

- **Home appearance and alterations.** Architectural restrictions may impinge on the freedom of maintaining your condo or co-op house and yard as you wish. Restrictions may include dictating the style of a home, the building materials (wood shingled roofs may be mandatory, while certain colors are forbidden), yard appearance and maintenance, the height

Your Rights When Rules Change

Condo, co-op, and subdivision unit owners have argued in lawsuits that it is unfair for the homeowners association to change rules governing their individual unit if the rules adversely affect the unit owner. But state courts have overwhelmingly rejected the argument that the individual owners should have been consulted about the rule change.

The disaffected owners have claimed that other shareholders should not be able to deprive them of rights that existed at the time of purchase, such as in a sudden decision to prohibit dogs in a condo building.

But whether the new or changed rule is significant or minor for the unit owner, the courts have held that owners are aware when they buy into the association that the board has the power to amend rules and regulations.

Furthermore, the courts have said, the deeds for condos and planned community homes state that the rules are subject to change, and state condominium laws generally permit changes of association bylaws without unanimous consent of unit owners.

Some states require unanimous consent for certain changes that affect the number of units, unit boundaries, common areas, or the voting power of each unit. Otherwise, if the board has acted legally and fairly, a unit owner will probably have to succumb to the majority or propose a viable alternative.

HOT SPOTS OF CONFLICT

Cooperative associations enforce and amend rules that sometimes conflict with the needs and desires of shareholders. Watch out for these common points of conflict:

1. Pets. Homeowners association rules on pets are usually more stringent than local municipal laws. Some associations restrict pets altogether; others tolerate only certain kinds of pets.

2. Architecture. Most associations have a committee that enforces the architectural restrictions of properties. You may not be able to add a porch to your subdivision home or plant a certain type of tree.

3. Parking. Associations often limit the number of parking places allotted each shareholder and may further regulate the type and weight of vehicle permitted.

4. Access to amenities. The use of common facilities is regulated by homeowners associations. In an attempt to limit its insurance liability, for example, a board may impose strict rules on the use of a common swimming pool.

5. Age. Condominium and subdivision associations can legally restrict the age of residents to serve the needs of a certain age group, such as 55 and older. Generally, there must be a legitimate reason for the age restriction—a no-children rule preserves the peaceful environment of a retiree community, for example.

and style of a fence, whether you can have a television satellite dish, or whether you may build a shed. Major structural changes such as an additional room as well as a minor alteration like adding a skylight may require approval by the association's architectural control committee.

- **Renting.** Condominium and cooperative developments often restrict the freedom of unit owners to rent or loan their residences to a third party. A board that permits renting or leasing typically sets parameters, such as a rental period not less than six months (to minimize traffic), only two rentals per year, no pets, board approval for the tenant, and so on. In addition, unit owners must sometimes pay a fee to the association for the right to sublet. Since these restrictions are spelled out in the association bylaws to which an owner has agreed, courts generally uphold them.

- **Resale.** Homeowners associations usually extend considerable control when a shareholder decides to sell a unit. They often have the first option to buy a unit, called "right to first offer," before it goes on the public market. They can charge a so-called flip tax, a one-time fee (often substantial) paid to the association when a shared-interest unit is sold. State statutes generally impose no restrictions on these practices and no limit on the amount of fee charged, as long as these rules are explicit in the bylaws and do not conflict with other state or federal laws (on discrimination, for example).

When shareholders have challenged resale or other restrictions, courts have usually held that property owners of shared-interest communities have reasonable grounds for wanting some control over who lives in their building or complex. As long as an association has acted reasonably and in good faith, homeowners have little or no recourse. The courts acknowledge that community members are financially interdependent, and must share facilities, preserve a certain desired character of community, and manage the community in an interdependent fashion. Most important, the courts recognize that homeowners consent to these rules when they agree to buy the property.

Handling Internal Conflict

While homeowners associations are granted much legal leeway in imposing and enforcing their governing rules and restrictions, sometimes they overstep their authority. Property owners may have valid legal cases against their association, not just differences of opinion.

In some cases, you may be able to negotiate exemptions from a rule or find creative ways to work around it. If advertising is prohibited, you may find a central but discrete place where all residents can post signs. One clever resident of a planned community that did not allow advertising signs to be posted in front yards put a sign in his car window saying, "For Sale, $120,000, house included."

Organizing your neighbors can be an extremely effective way to influence the association. As fellow shareholders, they may share your grievance and be eager and happy to help. Once you have joined forces, you can approach the board as a unified lobbying force against a new or unpopular ruling. (For more information about joint action, see YOUR RIGHTS IN ACTION, page 488.)

Instigating Change

PROBLEM
Michelle and John Hirsh had been living in their condominium for three years and had adhered to all homeowners association rules. As a gift, John received a basketball hoop and net and decided he wanted to hang it from the wall over his garage door. Michelle pointed out that installing recreation equipment outside of their unit was against the association rules.

ACTION
John and Michelle talked to a few of their neighbors and found that not only would they not mind a basketball hoop, they would welcome one. John and a group of residents drafted a proposal to put before the association board. They asked that the rule regarding hanging equipment outside each unit be repealed. After negotiating with the board, John and his group compromised, and part of the often-unused guest parking lot was converted into a basketball area for the use of all residents.

WHO IS LIABLE FOR INJURIES?

Courts have recognized homeowners associations as distinct legal entities with responsibilities to both unit owners and to outsiders. For example, if you are seriously injured on the common-interest property of your planned community, you may be able to take legal action against the association. A number of state laws assert that a unit owner may sue an association for any act of negligence on the part of the association for injuries suffered in a common area.

Complications may arise if a third party, such as a visiting friend, is injured on common-interest property. Courts have ruled that individual unit owners do not have control over the maintenance and management of common areas and are thus not considered liable when a third party is injured in a common area. The association, however, can be found liable

Making Changes From Within

A handful of municipalities now require condo and co-op homeowner associations to set up in-house mediation services. These services give disputing parties the chance to resolve differences outside of courtrooms. Where they exist, in-house mediation and arbitration services have significantly reduced the number of shared-interest property owners filing lawsuits.

If you have a conflict, find out if there is a mediation or arbitration clause in your association's rules. Settling your dispute may be much easier than you thought.

Make sure to be fully prepared to present your case at any mediation or arbitration hearing. Although the proceeding may be less formal than a court hearing, you still should have proof to back up your claims, including copies of contracts, agreements, photographs, and statements from witnesses. (See also YOUR RIGHTS IN ACTION, page 472.)

Another way for a shareholder to influence board decisions is to join the board. To prepare for this step, you may be able to enroll in one of the increasingly popular training courses for new board members. The Community Associations Institute is a national network of leaders in the common ownership field that offers such courses.

because, to the extent that it controls common areas, it acts like the owner of those areas.

WHO PAYS FOR REPAIRS?

The lines of responsibility for repairs in condominium and cooperative units are often blurred. Although condo and co-op associations are responsible for problems in the major structural systems of the complex, including main water pipes and electrical wiring, the unit owners must pay for problems inside the four walls of their units.

But what if the bathroom ceiling in your condo suddenly cracks open because of water damage? You have to determine the source of the problem to know who is responsible for repairs. If the main water pipes are faulty, the association is responsible. If your upstairs neighbor habitually lets water overflow his bathtub, then he may well be responsible.

To determine the source of a repair problem, you should hire a qualified contractor or other home professional, such as a plumber or electrician. Make sure you get a detailed written report to prove the cause of your problem. Damages caused by other unit owners may be covered by their homeowners insurance or yours. If the association is at fault and accepts responsibility, members will likely limit their payment to the actual costs of repair. If they refuse to pay for damages for which you are convinced they are responsible, you may need to call a lawyer specializing in shared-interest properties.

If a rule is reasonable the association can adopt it; if not, it cannot.

RULING OF A FLORIDA DISTRICT COURT

Do You Have a Case Against Your Association?

If negotiation and arbitration with your home association have failed, and if the board's actions have violated one of the following conditions in your case, you have a chance to succeed in challenging the association. Talk to a lawyer who specializes in community association law.

• **Unauthorized rule making.** If the board does not have authority either under state laws, such as a condominium statute, or under the governing documents of the association, the rule you dispute may have been made by the board without authority.

• **Arbitrary and capricious rule making.** If the board makes a rule that is not related to the health, happiness, or enjoyment of property of unit owners, courts may consider the rule invalid. For example, if for no apparent reason a board imposes a new rule that limits the size and weight of vehicles residents may keep in a spacious parking area, a unit owner who uses a minibus for business might have a legal case.

• **Discriminatory effect of rule making.** Boards may not make rules that isolate, discriminate against, or are unfair to the minority shareholders. A condominium board may not impose higher maintenance fees on the minority of condo owners who do not live in their units year-round unless it is specifically granted that power in its bylaws.

• **Unfair lien.** What if your association board fails to pay a landscaper who did major yard work, and he files a mechanics' lien or financial claim against the entire shared property? You may have a case against the board if you can prove it did not act in good faith—if, for instance, it had money in reserve that it used instead to refurbish a rooftop patio used mainly by several board members.

RENTING

Because the landlord-tenant relationship is often contentious, many laws and regulations exist to protect the rights of both sides.

Your Rights As a Tenant

If you rent rather than own a home, you are protected by state and local laws that govern landlord-tenant relations. Although these laws vary considerably depending on where you live, there are certain basic concepts with which you should be familiar in order to know when your rights are not being recognized.

First you want to formalize a rental agreement with the landlord. Your tenancy and many of its conditions can be established by either an oral agreement or a written lease. A verbal agreement is usually sufficient for short-term stays, such as week-to-week or month-to-month tenancy. In an oral understanding, the landlord agrees to rent the unit for a fixed term at a fixed price, and you agree to pay the rent. The agreement remains valid for as long as you keep paying rent.

Some states require landlords to give written notice of termination of such an agreement, while others allow for reasonable verbal notice of termination, such as one rental period.

LEASES LONG AND SHORT

Written lease agreements may bind you and a property owner for any length of time, from a month or less to one year or more. Because a written lease is always enforceable in a court of law, it is to your advantage to sign one in case your landlord transgresses your rights or reneges on his obligations. The landlord may not include in the lease any provisions that negate your rights granted by federal, state, or local law.

For example, a landlord might be permitted to limit the number of people living in your apartment. He cannot, however, add a clause to the lease to the effect that your rental agreement will be terminated if you, as a guardian or parent, have children under the age of 14 living in your apartment. Such a restriction contradicts your right to fair housing under the federal Fair Housing Act. (Certain senior-citizen complexes are exempted.)

Landlords do have the right to impose certain other restrictions on the use of their rental properties. A landlord can prohibit you from using a water bed, ban pets, forbid cooking with a barbecue, and even limit your use of air conditioners. If chal-

---

✦123✦ WHAT SHOULD BE IN A LEASE

A lease for more than a year must be written to be legally binding and should include:

1. The owner's name, or his agent's, his address, and his telephone number. You will need this information in emergency, or to file a complaint.

2. The date you take possession and the date you start paying rent. If your landlord enticed you with a free month's rent, make sure these two different dates are acknowledged in the lease.

3. Terms for refund of security deposit and interest generated from the deposit. Many states require landlords to pay tenants the interest from their security deposit accounts once or twice a year.

4. Permission to sublet. If the landlord allows subletting, you will have to agree to be responsible for the rent and that the sublessee will abide by the lease provisions.

5. Condition of the premises. If there are repairs to be made, include in a rider the landlord's duty to complete the work by an agreed date.

6. Pet rider. Some landlords dictate conditions of pet ownership. Make sure you agree to the terms before signing.

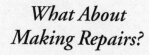

What About Making Repairs?

Your lease agreement, state statutes, and local health codes determine how landlords must handle repairs. The general guidelines are:

✔ *Emergency repairs.* If repairs are needed to correct a critical problem, such as a leaky pipe, the landlord may enter the unit immediately. (This is one reason a tenant may not change the locks of a unit without giving a key to the landlord or his agent.)

✔ *Repairs related to health and safety.* If the problem is not an emergency, the landlord must start repairs within a certain number of days, set by state law, after your notice. In some locales, you may be able to have the repairs done and deduct the cost from the next month's rent.

✔ *Miscellaneous repairs.* Landlords are bound by a good faith obligation to effect nonemergency repairs as soon as possible. Some states set a time limit during which a landlord must begin repairs after a tenant's notification.

✔ *General maintenance.* If the owner neglects standard maintenance chores, such as collecting garbage, you can report him to the county health or housing department.

✔ *Damages caused by tenant.* If you cause damage in your rental unit, you are responsible for arranging for the repair and paying the cost.

lenged, however, such rules and regulations usually are measured by these criteria:

- The regulations promote the convenience, safety, or welfare of all residents;
- The rules are reasonable in relation to their purpose;
- The rules apply equally to all residents;
- The regulations are clear and unambiguous;
- The rules have not been designed to evade the obligations of ownership.

You have the right to be notified of any regulations that will apply to you as tenant at the time you sign your rental agreement. If your landlord subsequently changes a rule or regulation, you should be given reasonable notice of the change.

Standard rental leases often include "riders," or additional provisions. If the rental property offers a parking space you want to use, a garage and vehicle rider to the lease will clarify the terms and conditions under which you rent the space; the additional rental amount, if any; whether you must pay a deposit; and allowable vehicle size.

You, as tenant, can propose adding a rider or extra clause to the lease. For example, if you prefer your own stove to the one in the rental unit, you can ask the landlord to add a clause stating that you will use your own stove and be responsible for moving and maintaining it. Otherwise, the landlord could later claim that it is part of the rental property, and you would have to leave it behind when you move.

WHAT TO EXPECT AFTER YOU MOVE IN

Once you move into your rental property, both you and the landlord must comply with local building and housing laws on health and safety. You cannot clutter common hallways with your bicycle and other personal objects, nor can your landlord allow garbage to pile up in the building lobby. If you believe your landlord is violating health or safety laws, complain to the local department of health or other government agency.

Although states offer different standards of the conditions a tenant may expect from a landlord, usually the landlord must:

- Have the unit ready for the tenant to move into at the time and in the condition agreed upon;
- Provide safe, healthy premises;
- Make necessary repairs to keep the premises in a livable condition;
- Maintain all electrical, plumbing, and other facilities in good working condition;
- Provide receptacles and arrange for frequent removal of

garbage (single-family residence renters usually must provide their own garbage bins) and be responsible for rodent and cockroach elimination;

- Provide hot and cold running water;
- Provide weatherproofing, such as unbroken windows.

If you are injured on the common property of the rental building or complex because the property has not been well maintained—say you trip on a loose stair and break your ankle—you may have a liability case against your landlord if he was aware of the problem and made no effort to warn residents or correct it. If, however, you live in a rental house and trip on a loose front step, your landlord probably cannot be held responsible—home renters are generally responsible for maintaining property in safe, working condition unless otherwise stipulated in the lease.

YOUR RIGHTS WHEN YOU MOVE OUT
You are obligated to leave the apartment in the same condition as you found it, except for ordinary wear and tear. If you have adhered to your legal obligations as a good tenant, you then have the right to reclaim your security deposit. However, the landlord has the right to apply part or all of your deposit to costs incurred for damages beyond ordinary wear and tear. For example, if you soiled the carpeting to the degree that it has to be replaced, your landlord can deduct the replacement cost from the security deposit. Any repair costs must be item-

For a man's house is his castle...

SIR EDWARD COKE
English Jurist
1552–1634

Renters' Basic Legal Rights

Generally, the law dictates that your rental property should be safe, healthy, and livable, in compliance with local health, housing, fire, and safety codes. In addition, renters are entitled to certain specific conditions guaranteed by local legislation on tenants' rights:

- Like a homeowner, you have the right of quiet enjoyment of your rental property. That means you should be able to live in your dwelling without unreasonable interference by your landlord.

- Your landlord must respect your right of privacy. If he needs to enter your apartment for non-emergency repairs or maintenance, he must give reasonable notice—at least 24 hours—and may do so only during normal business hours.

- You have the right to complain to your landlord if he neglects his legal duties, such as keeping common areas of the building safe and sanitary. The landlord may not retaliate against you for complaining by raising your rent or decreasing services.

- You have the right to join with other tenants to bargain the terms of the rental agreement. If your landlord has imposed an unreasonably stiff penalty for late rent payments, for example, you could form a coalition of neighbors to petition for a five-day grace period.

- Your landlord may not take your personal possessions for the purpose of recovering overdue rent. In some cases he may, however, withhold part of your security deposit when you leave.

- As long as you do what the rental agreement and the law require of you, you have the right of exclusive possession of the property until the lease expires.

ized for you, with copies of receipts included. After your lease expires, the landlord must give you notice of any repair costs within a period specified by state law, such as 14 days. If the landlord does not give you timely notice, you have the right to reclaim your entire security deposit, regardless of damages—but you must take action within one year of the end of your lease.

The Snoopy Landlord

PROBLEM
A few weeks after Betty moved to a new apartment, she realized that the landlord had come into her apartment when she was out during the day. One of her locks was left undone, and only the landlord had extra keys. When she confronted him, he said he was showing the place to a contractor making bids on renovating the building. Betty was furious, and when it happened again, she threatened to take action against the landlord.

ACTION
First, Betty called her local department of housing to complain about the landlord's behavior, and was told that a landlord must respect a tenant's right to privacy. In an emergency, or when the health and safety of residents is at stake, many states' rental laws tend to allow a landlord to enter a rental unit irrespective of the wishes of the occupants. But in nonemergency situations, a landlord must give a tenant reasonable notice—a day or two, often prescribed by state law—for limited purposes: to inspect the premises, make repairs, or show the unit to prospective tenants. Even then, a landlord is restricted to entering during reasonable hours. Armed with the housing department's recommendation, Betty confronted her landlord again and warned him that if he continued to invade her privacy, she would seek a court injunction against him on the basis of unreasonable entry. This was enough of a threat to convince the landlord to stay out of Betty's apartment.

Your Rights As a Landlord

Whether you lease a portion of your home, rent out your vacation property, or lease multiple-unit investment properties in exchange for money, you take on the legal obligations of a landlord. Local municipalities regulate the actions of anyone who rents out property. Landlords must also adhere to applicable federal and state laws, such as the federal Fair Housing Act. In many cities, certain legal exemptions are made for owner-occupied rental properties and other properties containing only two, three, or four units.

As a landlord, you are also entitled to certain rights. These rights begin when you first select tenants to occupy your premises. Although you must adhere to federal and state laws

---

THE DUTIES OF TENANTS

Besides paying the rent on time and meeting other specific conditions of the lease, tenants owe a landlord these considerations:

1. Tenants may not disturb other tenants with excessive noise or disturbances, such as nightly trumpet practice.

2. Tenants must use the apartment as it is meant to be used. They may not run a high-traffic business from the apartment when they have signed a residential lease. If there is no kitchen, they may not set up their own cooking facilities.

3. Tenants may not house an excessive number of relatives or friends. If a tenant says he will be living with his son, he cannot also put up the son's girlfriend and two children without written approval.

4. A tenant who damages the refrigerator, windows, carpet, or other items of the landlord's property in the apartment must repair or replace them.

5. A tenant can be expected not to carry out illegal activities, such as drug dealing, on the premises. In some cities, landlords have been held responsible for drug dealing under civil forfeiture laws.

6. When a tenant moves out, the property should be in the same condition as when he took possession except for ordinary wear and tear.

on housing discrimination against tenants based on race, religion, and the other fair housing criteria, you have the right to otherwise refuse rental to anyone you do not want as a tenant.

Unless your city has rent control laws, you have the right to set any amount of rent you choose. Additional rent charges, such as for a parking space, should be included in special clauses, or riders. You also have the right (but not the obligation) to charge a security deposit to cover various potential losses, such as damage caused by a tenant, the tenant's failure to return the keys at the end of tenancy, or a breach of the lease agreement. The security deposit is normally less than or equal to one or two months' rent, depending on state laws on security deposits. If, at the end of a tenant's lease, you have lawful grounds to retain all or any of the security deposit, you must notify the tenant in writing of the reasons for retention, with all costs itemized.

WHEN THE TENANT MOVES IN

Before a new tenant moves in, the property should be put in good condition—a broken air conditioner replaced, a fresh coat of paint applied, and so on. After you sign the lease and before the tenant moves in, you should inspect the rental property together and make note of slight damage, such as a dent in a wall, that does not warrant repair. Record these facts on an inspection form, and co-sign it with the tenant; this document protects both you and your tenant if you later argue over property damage.

Your tenant is legally obliged to maintain the premises in reasonable upkeep, which means operating electrical and plumbing fixtures properly and maintaining appliances in good working condition. The tenant may use or alter the space only within the limits and regulations set in your lease agreement, and must notify you promptly of problems with the property or its major systems, including electric, gas, water, or sewage.

In the normal course of maintaining your rental property, your tenant may notify you of broken or damaged items that need to be fixed. You must give the tenant reasonable notice that you, or a professional service such as an electrician, will enter the apartment at a certain time to remedy the problem. After fair notice, you can enter the dwelling to inspect, repair, make improvements, or supply necessary services.

DEALING WITH NON-PAYERS

Your rental agreement probably states what day of the month rent is due and details a grace period for payment, if any. If rent is late, send tenants a reminder letter. If your lease allows you to charge a late fee (usually a week or 10 days after rent is due), send a late-charge notice on the day the charge is effec-

Renting Out Your Home

If you are moving to a new home but having trouble selling your old one, or if you own a second home that you rarely use, you may want to convert your home into a rental property. Along with the financial benefits of rental income, you gain certain tax advantages, such as writing off all the business costs of renting the property.

Finding a good tenant is key to ensuring that you get a steady rental income and that your home is not damaged. You can advertise in your local paper or list your rental with a real estate agent. Ask applicants to fill out a form with their employment, credit, and rental histories.

Follow up by checking the references thoroughly. Although you must adhere to federal fair housing laws and antidiscrimination laws when choosing a tenant, you can be particular about your own rental criteria. For example, you may require that a tenant earn four times the monthly rent and have held the same job for at least eight months.

Once you have found a tenant you want, your obligations as landlord will include general repairs of the property, lawn upkeep, and responsibility during "emergencies" such as flooding. You may want to hire someone to handle these chores. You should also consult a lawyer and insurance agent about liability protection, and an accountant about how your rental income will affect your taxes.

tive. Eviction proceedings vary from state to state. Most states require a formal notice requesting rent due as the first step in a formal eviction procedure. There is also the "five-day form," which informs the tenant that she has five days to pay overdue rent, after which the landlord will start eviction action.

If the tenant does not comply, you can sue to evict. You must first notify the tenant in writing, by certified letter in some states. If the tenant still does not pay rent due, you will have to make a court appearance. In most states a landlord does not need a lawyer for eviction proceedings, although you may want to hire one to improve your chances—especially since the burden of proof that the the tenant should be evicted rests with the landlord, and since the law historically has favored tenants.

If the court determines that the tenant should indeed be evicted, she must leave voluntarily or she may be physically removed by local officials. Since winning an eviction case does not guarantee that you will receive the money owed you, even if that is ordered by the court, consider hiring a collection agency to track down the delinquent tenant.

How to Handle a Dispute with Your Tenant

Although local and state landlord-tenant laws and ordinances clarify most of the obligations of both parties, you and your tenant may disagree on issues that are not clearly defined. In many states the procedures for negotiating disagreements with tenants are clearly spelled out. You should consult with an attorney before taking any legal action.

• **Legal notice.** If your tenant is not complying with a provision of the lease or is the source of complaints by neighbors, ask your lawyer to draft a letter to the tenant. The letter should clarify the lease clause that you feel the tenant is violating and request a stop to the offending activity within a certain time.

• **Arbitration.** If you are in dispute over a matter concerning the physical condition of the property, you and your tenant can agree to have a neutral third party inspect the property to determine whether or not you are conforming to your obligations. You can agree that the findings of the arbitrator will be binding. Your local department of housing may be able to suggest arbitrators.

• **Termination of lease.** You can usually cancel your tenant's lease by giving notice within 30 days prior to the end of the lease agreement that the lease will be terminated. You can also cancel according to some other provision of the lease. Or your tenant might voluntarily offer to terminate the lease before the end of the rental period, in which case you can simply accept the termina-

tion. (In some states under certain circumstances, however, you cannot terminate a lease even at its end without legal cause.)

• **Termination notice.** If your tenant continues to violate your lease agreement for any reason other than nonpayment of rent, and you have carefully notified the tenant of the violation, you can issue a notice of termination of the lease. The notice must reiterate the reason for the termination, which must be based on substantial breach of the lease and not be simply a ruse to take back the premises. The termination notice document, which in some places has to be notarized, must also set a time frame for the tenant to quit the residence. A lawyer can advise you on your state's procedures for delivering a termination notice.

• **Eviction.** If your tenant disregards your legal notices, you may have to sue to evict. Eviction involves a court proceeding in which a judge determines whether the tenant has truly violated the lease and deserves eviction. You may never physically evict the tenant yourself—that is done, if necessary, by a sheriff under orders of the court.

OWNING A SECOND HOME

Whether your second home is for pleasure, business, or both, you should be aware of different options for dealing with renters, property managers, and the IRS.

Defining How You Use a Second Home

Homeowners buy a second residence for a variety of reasons. Urban dwellers may own a home in the country and a condo in the city. A young couple might buy a houseboat on the bay and use it as a vacation hideaway. Older homeowners may buy a home that will serve as their retirement retreat in a few years. And a few lucky people have the financial means to afford two or three residences in favorite areas of the country or the world.

Buying a second home is much like buying your primary residence. However, a unique set of concerns arises in terms of maintenance of the home and tax implications. If your home away from home qualifies as a second residence that you do not rent out when it is unoccupied, you can deduct the mortgage loan interest as you do on your primary residence (as long as you do not owe more than $1.1 million on either home or the two combined).

The Internal Revenue Service is not so generous on additional properties. For example, you cannot deduct the mortgage loan interest on a third home. Property taxes, however, are deductible on any number of homes you might own.

IS IT FOR WORK OR PLAY?

In addition to scrutinizing mortgage loan interest deductions, the IRS is interested in whether you use your second home as a personal residence or a business property. The distinction is this: If you rent your home for more than 14 days a year, you become a landlord and must report rental income. That in itself does not make the home a rental property if you can prove that you also use the place for your own enjoyment.

For the IRS to determine whether to tax you on the home as a personal residence or a rental property, you must report the amount of your personal use of the property as well as your rental income. If your personal use of the property totals more than 10 percent of the time that you rent the home, it is considered a personal residence. For example, if you rent the home out for 200 days a year and use it 21 days, you qualify for the

---

What Kind of Vacation Home

A vacation home can serve several purposes. There are various ownership options:

✔ *Personal use.* If you can afford it, a second home offers a cherished weekend or vacation getaway from the workaday life. If you live in it enough for it to qualify as a second residence, your mortgage loan interest may be tax deductible.

✔ *Investment.* Buyers often choose resort area condos and town houses for a mix of business entertaining, personal use, and selective rental periods. At best, the property earns money, is enjoyed, and is a tax shelter.

✔ *Fractional ownership.* This option allows the advantages of a vacation getaway without the full costs or responsibilities. A quarter share usually means you get the property every fourth week.

✔ *Time-shares.* Ownership in a time-share is usually divided in 52 parts. If you buy three parts, you get three weeks in the unit per year. Or the property developer remains the owner, and you buy a limited lease. Time-shares may be fun, but generally are not good financial investments.

What You Should Know About Time-Shares

Visitors often fall in love with a particular vacation spot and then are seduced by the notion of a "time-share" in a condominium, chalet, or beach cottage. A time-share is a fractional piece of ownership in a particular property.

You pay not only the purchase price of your share but also a proportional share of maintenance costs for the unit and its grounds. These fees are set by the developer of the time-share property, and he can raise them whenever and as much as he wants. He can even change the basic terms of your agreement.

Some time-shares entitle you to a prescheduled time slot each year in a specific place and may include a deed to that fraction of property that you own. Other arrangements offer a floating time slot or an alternative choice of units in which you can stay.

Some time-shares are part of a vacation club, where you buy access to different destination choices. Your choice may be reduced, however, by a developer who rents out time-share units to non-time-share owners in the most popular seasons.

If you try to sell your share of the unit, you probably will not succeed. You will be competing with the developer, who is probably using the same lures that brought you into the time-share. Most timeshare owners who try to sell cannot find a buyer and take a loss on their investment.

personal-use test. The IRS defines personal use of a second home when:

- The property is used by you or your family;
- You rent the property for a nominal, below-market fee, such as asking your son's friend to pitch in $100 a month to cover water, electricity, and telephone costs;
- The property is used by someone with whom you have arranged an exchange—such as trading your country home for a friend's mountain cabin;
- You temporarily donate the property to a charity organization, such as giving a coupon for a free weekend's stay to your church for a fund-raising auction.

Homeowners have two alternative strategies in using a second home for personal and rental use. If you claim the second home for personal use, you can take a tax deduction on your mortgage interest for the home. On the other hand, if you rent out the home enough to qualify it as a business property, you can often claim a significant tax loss on the property. Many second home owners use this business property to shelter other taxable income, such as a high salary. Because these tax issues are complex and subject to change, you should consult with your tax accountant or advisor before you buy a second home.

MAINTENANCE ON A SECOND HOME

If your home is for personal use only, very little maintenance may be required—locking up the home, turning off the water and draining pipes for winter, and other seasonal or occasional concerns may be the extent of your efforts. But if you rent or loan the home to others and constantly keep it in use, you are more likely to have additional maintenance and repair concerns, as well as landlord obligations.

You should clarify in a verbal or written agreement with a renter what her responsibilities are, such as calling the local plumber if a toilet clogs or a pipe bursts. If the situation is more complex or costly—if the plumber decides you need a whole new plumbing system, or a ceiling needs replastering—the renter should be obligated to contact you.

Because of the difficulty of managing a property far from home, many owners of second residences—particularly those that they rent to others—hire a local property manager. If your residence is part of a resort area, it should be easy to find a professional on-site property manager. If your home is tucked far away in the woods, you may need to find a trusted local person through the recommendation of neighbors or the real estate office through which you found your property. You can make a contractual arrangement with the property manager to check on your house regularly when you are away, to be on call in the case of emergency, and to personally handle or hire workers for routine maintenance chores such as lawn mowing.

To protect yourself from injuries to others on your property, you will need to carry homeowners insurance just as you do on your primary residence. The same principles of liability apply to your second residence as to your first. That is, you are responsible for maintaining the property in a safe and habitable condition and for correcting any potentially hazardous situations that may arise.

Resort Vacation Options

When you buy a vacation home in a resort area, the value of your property is dependent on the viability of the resort. So before buying a ski chalet or a condo on a golf course, you should determine the quality of the resort. If it is a publicly held development, you can ask for copies of quarterly statements and annual reports to get an indication of the resort's financial soundness. If it is a private resort, you can ask the opinions of local realtors, current residents, and employees of the resort. If the employees tell you they have not received paychecks in a month and management is in turmoil, you may want to reconsider investing there. Ask your banker or lawyer to research the financial stability of the resort and its owners.

If your vacation house is affiliated with a resort, you should also know exactly what rights of access you will have to the resort facilities. Do you have unlimited access to ski slopes, or do you have to pay extra usage fees? Are your privileges limited if you are not a year-round resident or if you do not use the property for a specified number of days each year? Put your agreements in writing.

A MOVABLE TREAT

Greater concerns arise when your vacation property is not a fixed location but is part of a time-share arrangement that offers a choice of locations. These vacation clubs are a popular choice for people who want to enjoy different properties and locations in different seasons. As a member of an international time-share network, you can trade your ownership interest with another time-share owner—your week in the tropics for a week in the Alps. Be sure to clarify your privileges and access to amenities. The last thing you want to hear upon arriving at an expensive beach resort is that you have to use the public beach a mile down the road because the time-share owner you traded with used up this year's private beach passes.

SHARING A SECOND HOME

If you decide to share the expense of a second home with a friend or relative, watch out for these potentially contentious issues:

1. How will ownership be divided? This should be specified on the deed. You will also have to calculate each partner's proportion of the down payment, monthly mortgage loan payments, maintenance, property taxes, and other operating expenses.

2. Who gets to use the property when? Rather than find yourselves arguing over desirable holiday time slots, arrange your schedules in advance.

3. How is voting power distributed? If it is not distributed equally among the partners, be very clear about which partners' opinions count the most.

4. Who will manage the property? Management includes not only physical upkeep but also the necessary bookkeeping. If you decide to hire a property manager, you must make it clear which owner the manager will report to.

5. What if one partner wants to sell her share? Decide ahead of time how much advance notice you must give each other and how you will determine the buy-out price.

HOME OPTIONS FOR SENIORS

More and more elderly Americans are taking advantage of imaginative housing schemes that pool their resources and help ward off the loneliness of old age.

Age-Exclusive Communities

Homeowners who are getting older and who perhaps have retired from full-time work often choose to trade in the responsibilities of owning an independent home for the benefits of common-interest properties. Many choose condominiums or homes in development communities that are age-exclusive. These communities of senior citizens offer the amenities and security of most planned communities as well as social activities and services geared specifically for older residents.

Federal laws generally forbid housing discrimination based on age, and the federal Fair Housing Act prohibits discrimination in the sale or rental of housing based on "familial status," which means a home inhabited by parents or guardians and their children under the age of 18. However, the Fair Housing Act makes an exception in the case of housing communities for older persons, which it defines in two ways: housing intended for and solely occupied by persons 62 years of age or older; and housing intended for and occupied by at least one person 55 years old or older per unit in at least 80 percent of all units.

Additionally, the housing complex for the elderly must feature significant facilities and services specifically designed to meet the physical and social needs of older persons. This means more than adding a wheelchair ramp or throwing a couch in a laundry room and calling it a recreation center. The Fair Housing Act does not define specifically what the physical features and services must be, but the federal Department of Housing and Urban Development (HUD) provides examples, such as recreational programs, continuing education, emergency and preventive health care, common dining facilities, counseling, and housecleaning services.

What does the law mean for seniors looking to move into an age-exclusive community? It means that if you are considering a complex that promotes itself as being for seniors only, make sure it is legally acknowledged as such. Otherwise you may move in only to discover that half your neighbors have children running around your hallways or that services you assumed to be available are not. Your local HUD office can tell

tell you if the housing complex you are considering qualifies, under their standards, as housing for older persons.

A One-Time Tax Break

O nce in a lifetime, all homeowners qualify for a generous tax break based on their capital gains when they sell a home. When you are over 55 years old, the Internal Revenue Service gives you a one-time $125,000 exclusion on profits from the sale of a home. (If you are married and filing separate tax returns, the limit is $62,500 each; if married and filing jointly or single, the full $125,000.) The savings from this one-time-only tax shelter can be substantial: if you are in the 31-percent tax bracket, you save nearly $40,000.

This exclusion is quite different from the opportunity offered by the IRS to avoid paying taxes on the profits from sale of a home by reinvesting them in another home. That option, popularly called a rollover, requires that the profits be reinvested within two years in a more expensive home, and imposes other limits as well, but it can be used as many times as you sell a home.

You can use the $125,000 tax exclusion only once; you cannot spread it among different home sales; and you must have owned and lived in your home for at least three of the five years prior to claiming the exclusion. It is not contingent, however,

I heard my father say that he never knew a piece of land to run away or break.

JOHN ADAMS
Autobiography

Sale and Leaseback

America's senior citizens own as much as $2 trillion in home equity, but many remain cash poor. If you are a home-owning parent, you might consider this popular strategy for staying in your home while cashing in on your equity:

• **The strategy.** Sale and leaseback is a method whereby owners over age 55 sell their home to their children, who in turn lease it back to the parents for life. The deal is often seller-financed, meaning parents receive a down payment and monthly mortgage payments from their children, then return some of it in rent payments.

• **Advantage for you as seller.** You stay in your own home, free of ownership responsibilities, with a steady income. You can treat up to $125,000 of profit from selling the home as tax-free income.

• **Advantage for your children.** They keep the family home in their possession without having to pay estate taxes on it when you die. They also earn

rental income, against which they can deduct, for tax purposes, the expenses of being a landlord.

• **Complications.** Sale-leasebacks are complicated arrangements involving a variety of contracts (sale, rental, mortgage, annuity) and tax considerations. The IRS requires the landlord (in this case, your children) to charge a market rate of rent, or it may suspect you of avoiding taxes and disallow some of the tax advantages.

• **For more information.** Consult your accountant and a real estate attorney. The American Association of Retired Persons (AARP) also provides information on this and other home equity conversion options.

123...

ASSISTED-LIVING OPTIONS

Older persons have an increasingly wide range of options for living in community residences offering varying levels of personal care and health services:

1. Independent apartments within a large complex may suit basically healthy individuals. A meal plan and housekeeping services as well as social activities may be included in the monthly fee.

2. For someone who needs the security of knowing that health care is available if needed, such as when recovering from a stroke, some assisted-living residences offer around-the-clock nursing care.

3. For seniors who are more acutely ill or need short-term care, daily nursing care can be included in the monthly rent at an assisted-living residence, along with the meal plan and other services.

4. Long-term health-care services in residential complexes can combine the level of care found in nursing homes with the continued comfort of private living quarters.

5. In facilities with several tiers of service, a person who needs full-time nursing care after a hospital visit and then becomes more self-sufficient can stay in the same apartment. Only the monthly fee changes. Seniors who need and can afford the extra health care often prefer this more congenial community atmosphere to traditional nursing homes.

on the subsequent purchase of another home. You can also take advantage of the exclusion if you already own a second home and elect to move into it after selling your more expensive primary residence.

You want to be sure, however, to make the best use of this one-time offer. You may have more than one opportunity to think about it if you move several times after reaching 55, so you should carefully calculate the advantages of each opportunity. Your best chance may come when you are about to move into what you think will be your final home and need the savings. Or it might come on an earlier sale, when you can realize the full $125,000 exclusion. In any case, many people whose home represents a large percentage of their personal equity use this ruling to great advantage in their later years.

Shared Housing

The steady increase in the numbers of Americans over the age of 65 has generated great interest in new housing options that offer alternatives to the often sad choice of living alone or, when necessary, in a nursing home. Federal and local government agencies, health policy experts, families and senior citizens are seeking and supporting housing innovations that are affordable, safe, and comfortable. Three increasingly popular options are group shared housing, matchup services, and adult foster care. (For more about these services, see YOUR MARRIAGE AND FAMILY, page 156.)

Group shared housing consists of apartments, condominiums, or houses in which several unrelated adults, including healthy, independent older people, live together and share expenses. Most shared-housing complexes are funded primarily by the residents' rent payments and private donors, but some are government funded, some are run by private nonprofit organizations, and others are profit-making real estate ventures.

VARIED ASPECTS OF SHARING

Shared-housing developments take different forms. They can be clusters of duplexes of two apartments each, for example, with each four-bedroom, two-bath apartment occupied by four residents. Or a large Victorian house with separate, private rooms and common living areas may serve as a group home. Residents pay rents, called "sharing fees," which may be quite low in homes where members make their own meals and are otherwise independent. In homes offering meal preparation, laundry service, or housecleaning, fees are much higher.

Like the homes they occupy, members of group shared housing are a diverse lot. Some still work full- or part-time outside

the home. Some are fully retired and living off their retirement income. Still others may need the help of a part-time nurse. All members share common facilities and spaces such as backyards and dining rooms. The agency with which they are affiliated may offer no social services except an occasional visit from the residence supervisor. For groups whose health or disability requires more help but not full-time care, a house manager can help shop, cook, and clean.

Group shared housing for the aging occasionally conflicts with zoning regulations and raises objections from local communities. Some zoning boards object to shared housing between unrelated adults on the grounds that group homes increase traffic flow. One group home planned for five residents, for instance, was not allowed to open until it assured the local zoning board that only one resident would have a car.

MATCHUP SERVICES

Matchup programs bring together individuals in need of housing with homeowners who are seeking a person to share their home and rent (or mortgage payments). The matchups are usually between an older and younger single person. The one seeking the home is most often an elderly person who wants added income, security, and companionship. The younger adult is often enticed by rent that is lower than market rate.

In some programs, the renter performs light household chores in exchange for free rent. Unlike group shared homes that can rely on higher rent income, matchup programs receive most of their funding from local and state governments or from private foundations and individuals.

ADULT FOSTER CARE

State-funded foster-care programs for the aging have placed tens of thousands of semi-independent older adults with families. Foster families are paid by the state to care for the adults, providing the amenities of home living and limited personal care. State laws vary, but foster families are usually allowed to care for up to three or more adults aged 65 or older. Besides welcoming the money, families with children welcome the presence of these foster "grandparents" in their homes.

The cost of adult foster care is about a third that of nursing-home expenses. Government or nonprofit agencies match families with foster adults and pay for care costs. In some programs, elderly people pay from their Social Security benefits or pensions. States are sometimes allowed by the federal Medicaid program to apply nursing-home funds to adult foster care.

All foster families are carefully screened by participating social service programs, and elderly participants can relocate if their match does not suit them. For more information, con-

The Benefits of Home-Care Social Services

Full-time private home care is of course the ideal way to look after the frail or elderly—but it is also extremely expensive. For those who cannot afford private care, health-care maintenance programs may be the best alternative.

These innovative programs merge medical care, home care, and social services into a comprehensive package for seniors who live at home but are not fully self-sufficient. Privately run, publicly funded, and affiliated with local hospitals, they require elderly participants to sign over their Medicaid and Medicare policies in exchange for unlimited use of program doctors and other health care professionals.

Comprehensive care services include helping relocate seniors to new apartments that are wheelchair accessible; sending an aide twice a week to clean the apartment, help bathe the resident, and pick up groceries; sending doctors on house calls; and transporting participants to a day center twice a week, where they join others in social activities.

Participants are guaranteed free health care for life, including hospital and nursing care. The support they receive through these programs far surpasses ordinary Medicaid care. And because their health is so closely monitored, participants are hospitalized only about half as frequently as other adults over 65 years of age. For more information, contact your Medicaid office.

MOBILE HOMES

Not-so-mobile "manufactured housing" is an inexpensive alternative to more conventional housing—but owners' rights are not well protected.

What to Look For in a Lease

If you rent a plot in a mobile-home park, try to get a long-term lease for a year or more. The lease should clarify the following:

✔ **Security deposit.** How big a deposit is charged, and under what conditions will it be returned to you?

✔ **Extra fees.** Are you charged an entrance fee when you move in? An exit fee on leaving? What if you sublet or re-sell your mobile home?

✔ **Utilities.** Are your expenses comparable with residential rates in the area? How does the park operator calculate each resident's share?

✔ **Basic services.** Are yard maintenance, septic systems, garbage collection, and other services included in your rent?

✔ **Extra amenities.** Does your rent include access to on-site swimming pools, tennis courts, clubhouse, and other facilities?

✔ **Children.** Are there any regulations on age or the number of children allowed?

✔ **Pets.** Are pets allowed, and if so, what kind and how many per homeowner?

Affordable but Vulnerable

Mobile homes, also known as manufactured housing, are factory-built residences made for year-round living. Unlike recreational vehicles or travel trailers that are towed along the highways, mobile homes travel only from factories to retailers to home sites chosen by consumers. Most of them never move again.

Because they are so much more affordable than conventional housing, mobile homes are the fastest-growing form of housing in the United States, especially in rural areas. Yet because they make up such a small part of the housing industry, and perhaps, because those living in mobile homes often have little economic clout, mobile-home owners in general have fewer rights than conventional homeowners.

A scarcity of federal laws and local regulations leaves mobile homeowners vulnerable to shoddy workmanship and unscrupulous salesmen and site operators. Industry activists are working with the federal government to improve regulation standards and establish fair practice rules, but in the meantime, mobile-home owners and renters must be on guard to avoid being exploited.

FINDING A PLACE TO SETTLE DOWN

Before you buy a mobile home, you need to find somewhere to put it. If you want to buy a plot of land in a residential area, check local zoning laws. Nearly half the states have passed laws preventing zoning discrimination against mobile homes, yet some regions still do so on the basis that they do not conform to local architectural standards and overburden municipal services such as garbage collection and water supply.

Most mobile-home owners settle down in mobile-home parks. There are thousands of these communities in the United States, some owned by mobile-home retailers or manufacturers and others independently operated. Even so, there is still a shortage of mobile-home sites, which gives park operators an advantage over their prospective tenants.

So watch out for unscrupulous mobile-home park operators who require that you buy a mobile home from them as a condition of renting a site on their property, or who charge more rent if you do not buy from them. Some states prohibit these unsavory practices, but they are still legal and all too common in many areas.

Negotiating a lease may also be a prickly matter. Only 13 states require that a lease of at least one year be offered to mobile-home tenants. Most tenants have to negotiate their leases month to month. This leaves them exposed to frequent rent increases without legal recourse.

If you are lucky, you will find a well-established, cooperative park community where residents, not a developer, are the rule-making owners.

GETTING THERE

Once you are ready to move your mobile home to the park site, your main concern is the safe transportation and installation of your home. To date, neither manufacturers nor dealers are fully responsible for damages to the mobile home incurred during transportation. For the mobile-home owner whose home arrives on-site damaged, the result may be additional expenses for repairs or a legal battle.

When it comes to installing the mobile home on-site, only half the states offer installation standards—there are no federal regulations to date—and many structural problems have been traced to improper installation of units. Lobby groups are working with government agencies to pass new legislation to mandate a five-year warranty on installation. In the meantime, be sure to use only professional, fully trained installers.

A house is a machine for living in.

LE CORBUSIER
Vers une Architecture

Things To Know About Mobile Homes

A single mobile home unit is usually 14 feet wide, may be anywhere from 32 to 80 feet long, and comes complete with carpeting, draperies, and appliances. Attractive as they may be, by the nature of their construction, mobile homes are not as safe as conventionally built homes.

• New mobile homes typically cost between $20,000 and $35,000, while used homes from the 1940s and 1950s often sell for a few hundred dollars. Mobile-home owners also must pay for the cost of renting or buying a site for the home and associated maintenance fees. Even so, mobile homes cost so much less than conventional homes that they are especially popular among young couples, retired persons, and other low- or moderate-income families and individuals.

• Manufactured homes that have been built since 1976 must comply with specifications established by the federal Department of Housing and Urban Development. (The law also requires that the homeowner be given adequate information about and effective warranties on the unit's equipment.) Even so, the existing regulatory system does not always ensure a quality product. Common problems in manufactured homes include weak caulking, disintegrating siding, improperly installed windows, inferior or nonexistent insulation, inadequate electrical systems, leaking roofs (especially in multisectional units), and improperly connected heating ducts.

• Most mobile homes are financed with personal loans, although you may be able to qualify for a traditional mortgage if you undertake to purchase the mobile home site as well. The Federal Housing Administration and the Department of Veterans Affairs also offer mobile-home loan programs.

SELLING YOUR HOME

Putting the house you live in on the market is a challenge, both financially and emotionally, and is best tackled with professional help.

YOUR CONTRACT WITH A BROKER

An employment contract with the real estate broker you hire to sell your home, called a "listing contract," should clarify these points:

1. Exclusivity arrangement. With an "exclusive right-to-sell" contract, you pay the broker's commission even if you find a buyer on your own. With an "exclusive agency" arrangement, you list your property with one broker but pay no commission if you find the buyer.

2. Length of contract. A relatively short listing period of 30 to 90 days is common, although it may take six months or longer for some homes to sell. Elect a shorter commitment with optional renewal.

3. Cancellation agreement. What if your broker does not perform a satisfactory job? Avoid contracts with penalty fees for sellers who cancel.

4. Commission agreement. Broker commissions are negotiable. You may be able to bargain below the typical six percent commission.

5. Showing the house. Will your broker bring interested buyers to your home individually? Do you need to be there? Will there be an open house?

Sell It Yourself or Get Help?

When it comes time to sell their homes, most homeowners choose to hire real estate brokers to handle the many details involved in taking a house sale to its closing rather than spend the time and effort themselves. Sellers find many advantages in using an experienced broker, who can:

- Advertise your home on the Realtors' computerized network—called the multiple listing service, or MLS—expanding sales potential to real estate offices nationwide;
- Offer advice on preparing your home for sale (from repainting and recaulking to repairing broken electrical switches and cleaning gutters);
- Write effective advertisements to sell the home, using tricks of the trade that maximize your home's fine points and mask deficiencies (by emphasizing, for instance, the historic authenticity of a house with small rooms and low ceilings);
- Use her experience, including knowledge of the neighborhood and local marketplace, to help you set the appropriate asking price;
- Screen buyers, weed out browsers who are not ready to buy, and assess their financial ability to make the purchase.
- Advise you on offering incentives in a slow economic market, such as paying for extra home improvements;
- Help review the buyer's offer and negotiate the best deal.

These pluses alone usually make a broker worth the typical commission of six percent of the final sale price of the home. If you are in a seller's market where there are more buyers than sellers, the broker may be able sell your home for at least six percent more than the original sale price, meaning that you essentially receive her services for free. (See also "Hunting for Your Home," page 10.)

If you have spoken to several brokers and found one you like, you should sign a contract that clarifies both of your rights and obligations. You can choose from a variety of arrangements. An exclusive right-to-sell agreement guarantees the broker a commission during the contractual time frame—even if you or someone else brings in the buyer—in exchange for the broker's dedicated effort to sell the home. This option is preferred by sellers who want the broker to do all the work involved in selling a home.

In contrast, an exclusive agency agreement exempts you from paying the commission if the broker does not find the buyer. This is often the best arrangement when the seller has a likely buyer or is willing to make the effort of finding a buyer by handling queries about the property and showing the home. Whatever your arrangement, a hardworking broker should stay in frequent contact with you. At all times, a broker hired by you has a duty to protect and promote your interests.

BROKER ALTERNATIVES

Discount real estate brokerages offer services midway between full-service, full-price brokers and selling a home by yourself. Discount services charge either a set fee or a reduced commission of two or three percent to list your home in the local marketplace and provide skeletal services. Discount brokers require you to do most of the marketing and all showings of your home. One national discounter, for example, charges $600 for a "For Sale" sign, a fixed number of print and television advertisements, a standard sales contract, and negotiating advice from staff members who are licensed real estate brokers. For an extra fee, sellers can also have their homes listed in the MLS electronic marketplace.

Another way of selling a home is to contact a local realtor and arrange an "open agency agreement." This is a nonbinding invitation for the broker to sell your home without listing it on the MLS and without performing even the minor services of a discount broker.

In an open agency arrangement, you do all the sale-end advertising and showing yourself, but agree to pay three percent of the sale price to any broker who brings in the buyer (that is, half the usual six percent a broker would receive for advertising the home and bringing in the buyer). This increases the flow of potential buyers to a seller's home. Sellers who choose this arrangement should advertise their homes as "for sale by owner with brokers welcome at three percent."

SELLING YOUR OWN HOME

Sellers sometimes choose to save the cost of a broker's commission by orchestrating the sale of their own homes with the aid of a few key professionals. If you are considering selling your home yourself, be prepared for a time-consuming task that will require much effort, patience, and flexibility. You will need to assess and set a fair sale price and calculate the value and condition of your home's main systems (electrical, plumb-

Tips for Selling Solo

In any economic climate, but particularly when sellers are competing for scarce buyers, homeowners who sell their own homes should keep these points in mind:

✔ *Set priorities.* Do you want a quick and easy sale at the risk of a lower price, or will you hold out for top price even if it means your house stays on the market longer?

✔ *Advertise wisely.* To create an effective newspaper ad, include a full description of the house that emphasizes its best features. Include the price, with your address (if you are having an open house) or telephone number. Put an eye-catching sign in your yard for passersby.

✔ *Remember fair housing.* Federal and state laws prohibit discriminating against potential buyers on the basis of race, gender, religion, and other criteria. Avoid judgmental statements that might be construed as discouraging buyers.

✔ *Get a home inspection.* Find out about problems that buyers might notice, before or after the sale, and either have them fixed or reconfigure your asking price.

✔ *Offer incentives.* Any inducement that adds value to a buyer's purchase works in your favor, from offering a home warranty to lending part of the down payment. Do not, however, represent the value of the house or the neighborhood falsely.

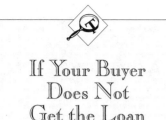

ing, and so on), appliances, and other features. Then you will have to advertise and market the home, respond to inquiries, screen potential buyers, and make appointments to show the home. Finally, you will negotiate financial agreements with the buyer and arrange for a sales contract.

To determine a reasonable sale price for your home, you will need to assess the current state of the housing market in your area. You should also be aware that while home improvements such as a new water heater or insulation add value to the sale price, home decorating, such as the new wallpaper in the master bedroom, does not. In the long run your best bet probably is to hire a professional home appraiser. For a few hundred dollars, using both objective calculations and personal opinion based on experience and familiarity with the area, he can assess the value of your home within a specific price range.

The Buyer and You

Before you open your home to prospective buyers, walk through each room with pen in hand and make a list of necessary improvements and minor repairs. Since you cannot anticipate the details buyers will notice—they may ignore the bathroom tiles you painstakingly regrouted while they peer at a tiny chip in the tub—focus on sharpening the overall condition and appearance of your home. Repainting, removing clutter from rooms, waxing floors, repairing dripping faucets, mowing the lawn, and other basic chores will make your home sale-ready.

Sellers should greet interested buyers with a fact sheet about the house. Include the dimensions of each room and the property; the average monthly costs of fuel, water and electricity; property taxes; and a brief history of recent value-enhancing repairs and improvements. Also have on hand all the relevant papers for appliances and other products, such as a water-sprinkling system that might still be under warranty.

SELLER TELLS ALL

Not only is it good business to be candid about the condition of your home; in many states, it is the law. Disclosure forms and disclaimers about the condition of the seller's home are becoming a requirement in many states and cities. You must tell the buyer the truth about all the physical defects of the house. Most states also require sellers to tell buyers about lead-based paint in and around the property, as well as the presence of radon and asbestos (see also "Environmental Concerns," page 59). Since more and more buyers are suing sellers for problems not disclosed before the sale (and since more courts

---

If Your Buyer Does Not Get the Loan

When you sign a purchase agreement, or binder, with a buyer, the final sale may be contingent upon certain conditions that must be met by a specified deadline. One of the most common contingencies involves the buyer's securing a mortgage loan. If your buyer has not done so by the deadline, you have several courses of action.

The option most preferred by buyers is to renegotiate a deadline for financing. Sellers should keep in mind that for buyers to secure a mortgage, they must not only be approved for the loan but also accept its terms, such as added points or fees. As the seller, you should know what constitutes an acceptable loan for the buyer. The terms should be spelled out in your purchase agreement.

If the market is slow for sellers, you will probably be anxious; so if your buyer has not secured a loan by the deadline, you might consider altering your arrangement. You could offer to pay for one of the loan points or other up-front fees, such as title insurance. This will make it easier and more appealing for a buyer to secure a satisfactory loan.

Finally, if you are wary of your buyer's sincerity or ability to secure a loan and one of the contingencies of your agreement has not been met, you have the right to terminate the purchase agreement and look for another buyer.

are favoring these buyers), you should protect yourself with a disclosure statement, even if it is not yet the law in your state. Many agents will not show a home without a disclosure form, as they, too, are being increasingly sued along with sellers.

One strategy is to hire professional home inspectors. You can attend to any problems they find in the structure or systems of your home, reduce the sale price, or make another financial deal, such as a buy down, to offset the probable cost to a buyer of repairing the defects.

By disclosing the problems, you lessen the chance of being sued for concealing a defect—potentially a much greater drain on your finances than a few repair jobs. To protect yourself against any inaccuracies in your disclosure form, you can get errors and omissions (E & O) insurance for sellers.

NEGOTIATING THE VARIABLES

Eager buyers will make bids to buy your home in response to both your asking price and their assessment of what your house is worth. While your asking price should be reasonable for the market, you can set it two or three percent above the current market value in order to leave room for bargaining. If you know that other sellers in your area with comparable homes are getting many offers, you might set your price at five or six percent over market range. In this way you can give in a little more on the price to make buyers think they are getting a deal, and still sell your home more quickly for an acceptable price.

While in the "offer" stage, you can accept offers from more

No man acquires property without a little arithmetic also.

RALPH WALDO EMERSON
American Author
1803–1886

Offering a Better Deal With a Buy Down

One incentive that can be offered by a seller who is having trouble finding a buyer is a buy down. In this arrangement, the seller agrees to reduce, or buy down, the interest rate on the buyer's mortgage loan for the full term of the mortgage. Here is how it works:

• A buy down is an extra incentive provided by the seller whereby he pays for, or buys, an agreed-upon percentage of the buyer's mortgage loan. For example, for a one percent buy down, you would pay the equivalent value of one percent of the interest on the mortgage, based on current interest rates. Thus if current interest rate on mortgage loans is 7.5 percent, your one percent buy down on a $100,000 house would be $7,500.

• At the closing of the sale, the seller writes a check for the buy-down payment to the buyer's mortgage lender. The lender puts the money in an escrow account and applies it evenly to the buyer's monthly mortgage interest payments over the period of the loan,

• Like an offer to pay points or some other part of the buyer's up-front mortgage loan fees, a buy-down offer reduces the buyer's cost in buying the home. Rather than paying the buyer a one-time fee, however, the seller's buy-down money is distributed over time into the buyer's mortgage payments, thereby lessening the buyer's monthly mortgage loan expense.

• The buy down also benefits the seller obliquely by making the property more attractive to a buyer who might otherwise not have taken it. Also, since a buy down is actually a reduction in the sale price, it reduces the taxable profits on the house. Finally, the seller pays less commission to the broker, whose fee is a percent of the final sale price.

Watching Improvements Pay Off

If you have kept careful records of improvements to your home over the years, you will reap rewards when you sell it. Remodeling projects add value that translates into quicker sales, greater leverage for pricing, and tax reductions. Remodeled kitchens, for example, typically return as much as 94 percent of their cost if the house is sold within a year of the job.

A major kitchen renovation might include new cabinets, flooring, laminate countertops, energy-efficient oven, ventilation system, custom lighting, and a central island of counter space. A minor kitchen job might entail refinished instead of new cabinets.

Along with updated kitchens, the highest-value remodeling projects are sun-space additions, which open up the house visually and can double as an office or family-room; family room renovations such as adding glass doors, a fireplace, or more floor space; and bathroom remodeling that might mean a new bathtub, a vanity counter with molded sinks, and new flooring.

Homeowners spend tens of billions of dollars a year on home repairs and improvements. To the extent you can afford them, you can enjoy these improvements and add value that pays off at sale time.

---

than one buyer at a time and make multiple counteroffers. You are free to take the best deal. All offers and counteroffers, whether negotiated through a real estate broker or directly between you and a prospective buyer, should be in writing.

Saved by an Escrow Account

PROBLEM

Marge, widowed for five years, decided to sell the old house she and her husband had lived in for many years, and move to an apartment she could afford. Through a broker she put the house on the market, and when a couple showed serious interest, she began negotiating for her new place. Then a house inspection commissioned by the buyers revealed that her home's electrical system might not be able to cope with their modern demands. Marge was devastated when they threatened to withdraw because of the potential expense the problem might lead to.

ACTION

On the advice of her broker, Marge got an estimate of the cost of replacing the electrical system and immediately offered to put that much, and a little more, into an escrow account out of which the buyers could draw to refurbish the electrical system should the old one fail within the first year of their ownership. Reassured, the buyers accepted her deal. Marge got less money than she had hoped for (since some of the sale money went back into the escrow account), but she still had enough to relocate and had rid herself of a property that could have turned into a serious financial burden.

When evaluating a purchase offer, be aware that the sale price alone does not convey the full value of an offer. For example, if a buyer offers less than your asking price but is willing to make a high down payment, or to accept the house without certain necessary repairs, it may be a worthwhile offer.

GETTING CLOSE TO MAKING A DEAL

If you have a buyer who is really interested, you should be amenable to allowing a home inspector of his choice to examine your home within a certain number of days. The report of a professional home inspector can actually help shift some liability for future problems from you to the professional. Show the buyer your disclosure statements as well as voluntary inspection reports, such as for termite inspection. Be careful not to guarantee too much—you can say the roof is five years old and under warranty, but do not promise it will not leak.

Negotiate a deadline, such as a day or two, by which you agree to make a counteroffer. You could use the time to weigh multiple offers, if you have them, and drive up the final sales price. Do not keep interested buyers waiting too long, or they may withdraw their offers. Also, buyers can take back any earnest money deposited in an escrow account if you do not make a counteroffer or accept their offer by the deadline. When you do accept a buyer's purchase offer, or the buyer accepts your counteroffer, you enter into a purchase, or binder, agreement, and you must stop accepting other offers.

Final Concerns of Selling

The purchase agreement is a legally binding contract that will become a sales contract (or the basis of a sales contract) when the conditions, or contingencies, of the agreement are met. Since it is a legally binding contract, you should have an attorney review the agreement and include certain legal protections.

If you and the buyer agreed that a certain known defect—say, loose floorboards in a bedroom—will remain unrepaired, you should state this specifically in the contract so the buyer cannot later blame you for concealing or neglecting the problem. Your purchase agreement should also clarify your agreement with the buyer as to which fixtures come with the home, such as laundry machine, dishwasher, and ceiling lights.

SMALL COSTS, BIG PROTECTION

There are a number of up-front costs to a home purchase that a buyer may have negotiated for you to pay, including title insurance and home warranties. You might offer to pay the title insurance costs not only as a sales incentive and goodwill gesture but because it protects you from being sued by the buyer in case of an error in the boundary records.

Similarly, home warranties protect the seller from unanticipated problems. Warranties guarantee the basically sound condition of a home's major systems, from heating to plumbing, for a limited number of years after the sale. Home warranties do not cover the structural elements of a home, such as the foundation, and are harder to obtain and less comprehensive for older homes.

Still, for a relatively low, one-time premium fee, home warranties can protect the seller from responsibility for undiscovered defects that might later prompt a buyer to file a lawsuit.

CLOSING IN ON THE CLOSING

Once a purchase agreement has been signed and a date of closing set—usually a month or two away to give the buyer time to secure a mortgage—there is not much left for you to do besides pack your belongings and make whatever repairs you have agreed to. You have the responsibility of leaving the house in a clean, habitable condition.

Closing, or settlement, day should bring few surprises to

The Facts About Sellers' Tax Breaks

When you profit from the sale of your home, you owe the Internal Revenue Service a capital gains tax. There are several ways of easing, delaying, or even avoiding, the payment:

✔ *Calculate adjusted basis.* You do not simply pay taxes on the sale price of your home. You pay taxes on the difference between the price you paid for it and the price you sell it for, plus the value of home improvements, minus losses from fire or other damage. This is called the "adjusted basis" of the home.

✔ *Two-year replacement.* You do not have to pay capital gains tax if, within two years, you reinvest the profit in a new principal residence that costs at least as much as your profit from the former house. (If you buy in a less expensive area, you can increase the house's value by making various qualifying improvements.)

✔ *Deducting sales costs.* Sellers can deduct many expenses incurred in preparing a home for sale, including repair costs during the 90 days before signing a sales contract, real estate broker's commissions, advertising, and legal fees.

✔ *The over-55 exclusion.* If you are at least 55 when you sell your home and have owned and lived in it for at least three of the five years prior to sale, you may qualify for a one-time tax exclusion for $125,000 of gain.

home sellers. To ensure this, have your attorney check with the settlement agent (usually chosen by the buyer) a day or two before settlement to make sure all the proper elements are in place, including the buyer's mortgage loan. If you hold joint title to your home, remember that your co-owner needs to have signed the deed to the property before settlement day.

You should gather all of the items you will need at settlement, including:

- Documentation that any contingencies you were responsible for have been fulfilled, such as repairs completed;
- Your homeowners insurance policy, if the buyer is taking over your policy for the home;
- The deed to the property to transfer the title from you to the buyer;
- Prorated expenses, such as property taxes and gas, water, or electric utility bills, with a copy of receipts indicating your most recent payments.

Do not expect to walk away from the settlement with a lot of cash or even freshly written checks. Settlement attorneys often hold on to buyers' checks until the necessary legal documents have been recorded, such as the deed in the county records office. Make sure your attorney has discussed with the settlement attorney or agent exactly when you will receive your checks. You can write these dates into the sales contract.

A friendship founded on business is better than a business founded on friendship.

JOHN D. ROCKEFELLER
American Oil Magnate
and Philanthropist
1839–1937

Selling a Property You Co-Own

Co-owners are two or more people who purchase and inhabit property together; they may be married with joint property, owners in a tenancy-in-common arrangement, or joint unmarried owners. When they sell the property, special concerns for each form of ownership must be addressed:

• Married couples usually own property in joint tenancy, each having an equal undivided interest. If they sell the property, any profits are shared equally. If married co-owners are divorcing, the sale of the house is part of the bigger issue of property acquired during marriage. State laws vary widely on community property and equitable distribution. Your divorce lawyer can advise you.

• If you own property with someone not related to you by marriage as "tenants-in-common," and if your co-owner wants to sell the property, you could be forced to sell against your wishes. A co-owner may sell his individual interest in the property, and in some instances, through a "partition lawsuit," force a sale of the property.

• Property law has not addressed many contemporary issues of joint ownership by unmarried persons. Such co-owners themselves need to address certain legal issues in a contract they write at the time of purchase. The contract between unmarried co-owners should clarify, for example, whether a joint owner has a first option to purchase the share of an owner who wants to sell. Another contractual consideration should be who will retain rights to live on the property if the joint owners can no longer live together.

• Any contract between tenants-in-common or joint unmarried owners should also specify how the fixtures, furnishings, and appliances in the house are to be distributed if the property is sold.

MOVING

A final step in the long process of finding a new home is getting your possessions from one house to another. Learn what you can do to minimize the cost and anxiety.

Avoiding Problems in the Move

As the sale of your home nears completion, and about six to eight weeks before you want to move out of your home, you should start planning the move. Unless you expect to do it all yourself, you will want to compare the services of several moving companies. Check the movers' qualifications with the Interstate Commerce Commission (ICC), or your local Better Business Bureau if the move is local. Ask for the mover's motor carrier (MC) number—without one, the mover is not authorized to carry goods.

To compare movers, ask for an estimate, either nonbinding or binding. A nonbinding estimate is the probable cost of your move, based on the company's on-site evaluation of what you are moving, and how far. The actual cost may differ, based on the total weight (or sometimes volume) of your goods, plus the amount of packing and other services provided. A binding estimate is a guaranteed final cost based on the company's inventory of your possessions. There may be a nominal extra charge for this guarantee. Binding estimates tend to be the best deal for consumers because they allow fewer variables in pricing.

MAKING A COMPLETE INVENTORY

Moving companies nationwide comply with a standard set of rate charges determined by a private agency, the Household Goods Carriers' Bureau, based on weight of goods and distance transported. The agency sets charges for packing, unpacking, and other services—all of which should be explicit in your job estimate. Walk through your house with the movers as they inventory your belongings to ensure an accurate assessment. Note any damaged items and insist on a statement in the estimate declaring that all other items are in good condition. Be thorough, for belongings the mover did not see, such as boxes in the attic or bicycles in the basement, will cost extra.

On moving day you will receive the actual contract for the job, called the "bill of lading." Read it carefully for any deviations from the estimate agreement. If the cost of your move is based on weight of goods (as it is in interstate travel), you have the right to watch the movers weigh the goods. Unscrupulous movers have been known to overload the scales.

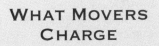

WHAT MOVERS CHARGE

1. Line-haul charge. This is the basic charge for a move, based on weight of goods and distance traveled.

2. Packing charge. Boxes, bubble wrap, packing tape, and the labor of packing and unpacking boxes are all extras.

3. Distance fees. If the movers must carry your goods more than 75 feet from truck to building, you may pay more.

4. Waiting time charges. If you are not ready when the movers come, you may be charged for delaying them.

5. Stair carry. You may not be charged for one flight of stairs, but any steps above the first flight usually carry a charge.

6. Charge per mover. Companies usually charge an hourly rate for each mover.

7. Additional charges for heavy furniture or appliances. Pianos, whirlpools, refrigerators, and other difficult or heavy items generally cost more. Get a price breakdown.

8. Special services. If you want your goods delivered quickly, you may decide to pay for exclusive use of a vehicle rather than wait for other customers' goods to be loaded with yours.

Regulating the Movers

Interstate movers that handle more than 100 shipments a year are regulated by the Interstate Commerce Commission, a federal agency.

The ICC sets rules regarding such issues as movers' rights to cross state lines, their basic liability for lost or damaged items, the certification of accuracy of scales used to weigh goods, and many other specific duties and responsibilities movers must fulfill.

The ICC also endorses moving rate charges set by the private agency, the Household Goods Carriers' Bureau. Companies offering highly discounted rates must apply to the ICC for a rate exemption. Check to see whether or not your discount movers have met ICC standards.

The ICC also handles complaints and claims that cannot be resolved between moving companies and customers—at an average rate of 4,000 complaints a year.

Local and intrastate moves (within the confines of a state) are not regulated by the ICC. Although moves may be regulated by state agencies, many states have no system for processing damage claims or investigating movers who overcharge and no enforcement system for levying fines.

If you hire local or in-state movers, take extra precautions to screen the companies. Check with the Better Business Bureau or the local consumer-affairs office for previous complaints.

Unless you have paid for private delivery, your belongings will probably be moved with other families' goods. In this case, delivery is made within a specified range of days. The mover must notify you of any delay. When the movers arrive at your new home, be there. Open any crushed boxes and make notes on the inventory forms about any damaged items inside.

MOVER'S LIABILITY

Your own homeowners insurance may be the best protection for your possessions, so check with your insurance agent before signing a contract with a mover. Movers offer valuation insurance, which is different from full insurance, in that you have to prove liability before the mover will pay. Valuation is the amount of value you place on your shipment; if something is damaged or lost, you can get reimbursement or replacement only if you can prove that the mover is at fault.

For items of extraordinary value, get a separate written appraisal. Movers offer different rates and deductibles for items of extra value. Your best bet is to move precious items yourself or hire a specialized service, such as art movers.

FILING DAMAGE AND LOSS CLAIMS

Because you have to prove the movers caused the damage to your belongings, your inventory list is the first piece of evidence you need. It cites the undamaged condition of goods before the move. You also need your notes from the delivery day, specifying any damages you and the mover noticed on-site. To file a claim on an interstate move, you have nine months from the date of delivery, but you should act as quickly as possible for best results. To prepare your claim, make sure you have your bill of lading (contract) number, a written assertion that the mover is responsible for damage incurred, and a dollar amount of replacement or repair value for items in question.

The mover must, by law, acknowledge receipt of your claim within 30 days and either deny or make an offer to settle within 120 days. If the company fails to respond in time or you are unable to resolve the claim with them, consider arbitration. The regional office of the ICC can suggest movers' dispute services in your area. Suing the movers would be your last resort.

TAX BREAKS FOR MOVING

Moving may not be quite so expensive as you think. Depending on your circumstances, in the eyes of the Internal Revenue Service you may be able to deduct some of the expenses of moving. If you are moving to a new job and qualify by IRS standards, you can deduct the cost of trips to the new area and other items. The regulations may change, however, so talk to your accountant about the latest IRS criteria.

YOUR MARRIAGE AND FAMILY

Nothing is more personal than your marriage, your children, and your family. But knotty legal questions can intrude on even the most private situations. Knowing your rights can help you find the best answers.

MARRIAGE ■ FAMILY PLANNING ■ ADOPTION ■ PARENTING ■ CHILD CARE ■ EDUCATION ■ DOMESTIC PARTNERSHIPS ■ DIVORCE ■ REMARRIAGE ■ ELDERCARE ■ FAMILY PETS ■ DEATH IN THE FAMILY ■ PROTECTING YOUR FAMILY

MARRIAGE

As well as being a sacred institution, marriage is also an important legal relationship. It brings great benefits and entails even greater responsibilities.

(See also "Domestic Partnerships," page 131.)

The Marriage Is Off: Who Gets the Ring?

The engagement is over and the groom-to-have-been wants his ring back. Can he sue his former fiancée? Maybe, but hiring a professional mediator might be a better solution. Such cases, called breach-of-promise lawsuits, are not popular with the courts and not even allowed in some states. So, before heading to court, consider the following:

✔ *Whose ring is it?* Traditionally, the ring is a gift from the prospective groom to his fiancée and is hers to keep. But if she breaks the engagement, or if the ring was an heirloom from his family, a judge might well force her to return it.

✔ *Who was at fault?* If you got cold feet, the court may rule against you. If your intended met someone else and backed out, the court may rule against him or her. If the breakup was mutual, you may both be required to return the gifts you gave each other.

✔ *Can fairness be decided?* If you go to court, the judge may have to weigh the relative value of the gift or gifts in question. While there certainly are exceptions, generally, a gift is considered a gift—including an engagement ring—with no obligation attached.

Can You Marry?

Marriage has been expected to last a lifetime. It may therefore seem surprising that this civil contract can be so easily entered into. The law, with some variations from state to state, requires very little from you or your prospective spouse before you take that first step down the aisle.

Perhaps the most basic of these requirements is age. Age regulations were originally based on the belief that the marriage candidates should have reached puberty. The bride was required to be at least 12, the groom 14. Today in most states the ages have been raised, with the intent of encouraging unions between people who are more socially and physically mature and more able to support themselves.

Generally, males and females can marry without parental consent at age 18, or with parental consent at age 16. There are exceptions in some states, particularly under special circumstances, such as pregnancy.

THOU SHALT NOT

Even if you are old enough to marry, you cannot necessarily marry anyone you want. Currently, marriage between members of the same sex is not legally valid in any state. (Some municipalities have legislated certain marital benefits to same-sex couples. See also "Domestic Partnerships," page 131.) You cannot marry someone who is already married. Nor can you marry certain close relatives. While marriage between first cousins is permitted in almost half the states, every state bans marriages between a parent and child, brother and sister, grandparent and grandchild, great-grandparent and great-grandchild, uncle and niece, and aunt and nephew. Some states also bar stepparent and stepchild marriages and those between in-laws.

State laws also restrict marriages when one or both parties lack mental competence, generally defined as the ability to understand one's legal responsibility and, therefore, to give consent. These laws are based on the perceived duty of the state to protect the incompetent person, but they are sometimes an area of dispute because incompetence is not always clear-cut or easy to define.

If a marriage takes place that is not legal, it can be voided or annulled. Reasons for such a measure include incompetence or failure to meet age requirements. Marriages can be voided because one or both parties withheld pertinent information from the other—such as being underage, the woman's pregnancy by another man, physical incapacity, impotence resulting from disease, malformation, or a defect that precludes the husband from consummating the relationship.

Forms and Formalities

You have never been more ready for marriage. You have applied for a marriage license at the county clerk's office or marriage license bureau, you have completed the application form, and paid the fee. Yet the chances are you will still have to cool your heels, for two-thirds of the states have "cooling off" periods ranging from one day to an entire week.

Sharing Your Life, Financially

Making the right financial decisions with your mate is important to your partnership's success. In money matters, it is never too soon to begin. The following tips will get you started financially and legally:

• **Joint bank account.** Once married, you are legally entitled to open a joint bank account, with shared responsibility for its activity. Each of you can make deposits and write checks. You and your spouse may also decide to maintain separate bank accounts. Many couples, particularly those with two incomes, choose this option to clarify where the money is coming from and where it is going.

• **Credit cards.** If you already have your own credit cards, you are not required to make them joint if you marry. When a husband and wife do open a joint credit card account, they both become responsible for it, no matter who actually incurs the charges. More and more, married couples consider it prudent to maintain at least one account in the name of just one of them to establish a separate credit identity and history.

• **Life insurance.** If you do not already have life insurance, marriage may provide the impetus to get it. If you are young, healthy, and have no children or large debts, you may not feel you need insurance just yet. But you should definitely start considering it. Many couples take out two policies, one for the wife, naming her husband as ben-

eficiary, the other for the husband, naming the wife as beneficiary. If you already have insurance, you should probably reconsider the amount of coverage you need and whom to name as the beneficiary. (See also YOUR MONEY, page 326.)

• **Health insurance.** Most company and private health insurance plans make provisions for family members. If you both already have coverage, you may want to maintain separate coverage, or it may be more cost-effective to switch to joint coverage under one policy. Check with your employer, and carefully read the provisions of your policies.

• **Income tax.** You can file joint federal income tax returns, but you are not legally required to do so. Speak to an accountant to assess how you can take best advantage of the changing tax laws and whether you should file separately or jointly.

• **Joint decisions.** You may want to share all financial responsibilities, or you may decide that one of you can handle them better. But it is important to make this decision and stick to it. Whatever you arrange, you should both know where all your legal and financial documents are located.

WEDDING INSURANCE: ARE YOU REALLY COVERED?

As wedding costs rise and couples realize that many expenses are nonrefundable if a wedding does not come off as planned, insurance to recover expenses gains popularity. Check your policy's fine print, paying special attention to the following:

1. Cancellation. Will you be covered if the event is canceled or postponed because one of you is transferred to a foreign job? What if the reason is that you or your intended has been injured? Policies generally do not cover costs if one of you is hurt while intoxicated or skydiving, and generally you will not be covered if one of you has a change of heart.

2. Wedding attire. Are you covered if someone steals the wedding party's dresses or suits? What if your dress is not ready on time, or you lose part of your tuxedo on your way to the wedding?

3. Bad weather. Usually you are covered if a tornado, blizzard, or other extreme weather forces you to cancel your plans, but not if you wanted sunshine and it rained instead. Are you covered if your tent does not function as expected?

4. Food. Will you be covered if the caterer cancels or if the restaurant closes before the reception takes place? In most cases you will not be covered if the food is unsatisfactory or not what you ordered.

Suppose you and your beloved decide to marry on the beach in Hawaii or perhaps in a foreign country. Will your marriage be valid? The answer is yes: every state will find the marriage legal as long as it was conducted with a license from and according to the laws in that locality. If, however, you specifically go to another state to marry your first cousin in order to evade your own state's restrictions, your marriage could be deemed invalid when you return.

MAKE IT OFFICIAL

You can marry practically anywhere—in a church, in a court office, on the beach; some couples have even tied the knot while skydiving. But wherever you choose to hold your wedding, you must find a person authorized by law to officiate at it, and by law the ceremony must be completed in the presence of one or two adult witnesses in addition to the conducting official. The license must be signed by you, your spouse, the witnesses, and the official, and finally recorded with the appropriate county office. Not every legal union requires such a civil contract, however. In states that recognize common-law marriage, couples do not need a license for a marriage to be legal, although other requirements pertain.

In recent years a new legal contract has sometimes been added. Before entering a marriage, some couples may decide to write a premarital (or prenuptial) agreement, setting forth certain agreed-upon conditions concerning property, support, children, or other important areas of their life together. While some premarital agreements may not be enforced by the courts, these agreements have become more common among couples marrying later in life and those who remarry with significant assets. (See also "Remarriage," page 146.)

Rights and Obligations

Historically, under common law, a wife was considered to be literally the property of her husband, totally dependent on him and subject to his will. Today's laws, increasingly gender-neutral, grant both spouses full civil rights to own property, get credit, negotiate and sign contracts, engage in business, and keep wages.

Moreover, while the law recognizes the right of a wife to be financially dependent on her husband, it also allows a husband to be the dependent spouse and rely on his wife's earnings. Both partners are legally responsible for supporting each other, the basic legal obligation of each partner being to provide necessities: food, clothing, medical care, and shelter. This assumes, of course, that he or she has the means to do so.

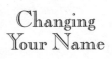

WHO OWNS WHAT

In all 50 states and the District of Columbia, you can keep individual control over any property you take into a marriage. However, most states are now "equitable distribution" states, which means that all property accumulated during a marriage is subject to division upon divorce, regardless of how it is titled, particularly if it has become commingled over the duration of the marriage. And if you live in Arizona, California, Idaho, Louisiana, Nevada, New Mexico, Texas, Washington, or Wisconsin, you are subject to community property laws, which say that all property acquired by the labor or skill of either spouse during the marriage is owned jointly and equally. In community property states, each spouse owns one-half of the property and if one spouse dies, the property does not pass onto the other automatically. It is distributed to heirs named in a will or according to intestate laws.

Issues relating to these laws usually do not come up unless the partners divorce and must divide their assets. Even so, when you and your spouse want to own property jointly—a house or stocks, perhaps—you may have to choose what kind of "tenancy" will be involved. ("Tenancy" here is used in a legal sense and does not refer to renting.) Married couples usually own property through "joint ownership," either through "joint tenancy with the right of survivorship," which guarantees a survivor the deceased partner's share, or "tenancy by the entirety," which forbids one spouse from selling the property unless the other gives permission.

In both of these cases, if one spouse dies, the other becomes the sole owner of the property. Joint owners cannot sell without permission from the other, although they each own equal, individual shares in the property. Some couples may be "tenants in common," each owning separate legal title to an undivided interest in a property. A tenant in common can sell off her part of the property. After death, it passes by will or intestate succession laws to the next of kin.

"Sole tenancy," or titling the property in one person's name, may also be an option. In many states, however, real estate purchased by one spouse will be considered to be owned by both spouses, even if there is only one name on the title.

THE SPECIAL NATURE OF MARRIAGE

Married couples are granted certain rights indicating the law's recognition of the "special nature" of the marital relationship. Married couples are entitled to the right of privileged communication: a spouse generally cannot be required to testify in court about confidential information exchanged with a partner, although if one spouse wants to testify against the other, he may do so.

Changing Your Name

Many people still assume that a married woman automatically takes her husband's name. That notion is derived from the long-past days when a married woman had no legal existence apart from her husband.

In fact, it is only when the wife uses her husband's name that it legally becomes hers. If that is your preference, you may want to change the name on your driver's license, Social Security card, credit cards, and other identification.

Then again, husbands sometimes want to take their wives' names or both husband and wife may decide to use both surnames hyphenated. Or a couple may decide to take an entirely new name together. In most states you do not need the approval of the court to take a new name; just begin to use it.

To avoid any confusion, however, or problems with government or other agencies that may insist that you use your "real" name, you may want to formalize the change. Every state has legal procedures for changing your name. In a divorce, women can minimize potential problems by including their name-change intentions in their final decree.

FAMILY PLANNING

Having a baby can be one of life's most satisfying experiences. But when to have a child is a matter to be thought about carefully. It carries legal consequences.

Birth Control by Sterilization

Perhaps surprisingly, sterilization is the second most common form of contraception in the United States, after birth control pills. More than 20 million women to date have chosen tubal ligations, and more than 10 million men have had vasectomies. In most states, candidates for the surgery are required to give written, informed consent 30 days before the operation. Depending on state laws, anyone under 21 years of age or mentally incompetent may be prohibited from giving consent.

If a woman becomes pregnant because the sterilization procedure failed, a wrongful pregnancy claim may arise; essentially, it is a a medical malpractice case.

Parents have recovered expenses for pregnancy and delivery care and collected damages for physical pain and mental suffering, but not for the costs of raising an unexpected child.

For women and many men, sterilization procedures cannot be reversed. Before consenting to sterilization, make sure you have thought the decision through carefully and have discussed the procedure extensively with your doctor.

Deciding About Pregnancy

The majority of American women between the ages of 15 and 44 use some form of contraception. Adults have had the right to buy and use contraceptives since 1965, when the U.S. Supreme Court ruling on the case of *Griswold* v. *Connecticut* asserted that such practice was protected by a constitutional right of privacy. This right, invoked against "unjustified governmental interference" in individual matters such as procreation, has also been part of the controversial legal debate over abortion.

The U.S. Food and Drug Administration is responsible for certifying the safety and effectiveness of birth control devices and drugs before they go on the market. Every form of contraception involves a combination of benefits, risks, and side effects that should be weighed with the help of your doctor.

If you are seriously injured because of the use of a contraceptive, you may in some circumstances have a claim against the manufacturer. In the case of an intrauterine device (IUD) known as the Dalkon Shield, thousands of injured women successfully sued the A. H. Robins Company when it was determined the company knew about, but did not communicate, the potentially harmful effects of its IUD.

ABORTION

In its 1973 landmark *Roe* v. *Wade* ruling concerning abortion, the Supreme Court judged that the constitutional right of privacy is "broad enough to encompass a woman's decision whether or not to terminate her pregnancy." Although it did not venture to resolve the difficult moral question of when life begins, *Roe* did establish relevant guidelines:

- During the first three months, or trimester, the government has no right to interfere in a woman's decision, made with the assistance of her physician, to terminate her pregnancy;
- During the second three months, the state can pass a law restricting where and how an abortion is carried out, if the purpose of the law is to protect the woman;
- During the final months, state law can prohibit abortion if a fetus is viable; that is, capable of living outside the womb.

Since that Supreme Court decision, many states have continued to impose restrictions. A handful of states—including Connecticut, Maryland, and Nevada—have expressly affirmed by law or referendum a woman's right to choose an abortion. But a 1992 Supreme Court decision, while ostensibly upholding *Roe,* upheld a Pennsylvania law requiring a 24-hour waiting period, counseling about abortion, and parental consent for minors.

NOTIFICATION AND CONSENT

The issue of notification and consent is one of the biggest areas of controversy regarding the state's right to place restrictions on abortion. The Supreme Court's stance is this: states may regulate abortion as long as regulations do not create an undue burden on a woman's decision to have one. According to the court, requiring a minor to notify her parents of her decision, or to get their consent before she can have an abortion, does not create such a burden. A number of states require either notification or consent of one or both parents before a minor can obtain an abortion.

Requiring the consent of a woman's husband (or the father of the unborn child) has been ruled "unduly burdensome" by the Supreme Court. In a 1976 decision, the Court ruled that states may not force a woman to obtain her husband's or partner's consent before having an abortion. It asserted a woman's primacy as the childbearer; therefore, she is the party "more directly and immediately affected by the pregnancy."

Although the Court has ruled on consent, it has never directly addressed the issue of requiring prior notification of husbands. However, a Pennsylvania provision requiring notification of the father by an attending physician before abortion was overturned on appeal.

Dealing With Infertility

Advances in reproductive technologies have changed the odds for couples who want children but have had trouble conceiving. In 1978, Louise Brown made international news as the world's first test-tube baby, conceived outside a woman's body. Today, several hundred clinics around the country offer in-vitro fertilization. This is the process by which a woman's eggs are fertilized with a man's sperm in a glass dish and then transferred to a woman's uterus. Some states have laws requiring insurance companies to include in-vitro fertilization in the policies they offer employers. The American Society for Reproductive Medicine can supply literature on the procedure and a list of clinics prac-

---

Rights for a Pregnant Teenager

What should you expect if your teenage daughter becomes pregnant and considers an abortion?

✔ *Must a parent be told?* Most states require that you as a parent must either consent or be notified before a physician can legally perform an abortion on your teenager. But currently, in 14 states your pregnant daughter is entitled to get an abortion without your involvement at all.

✔ *Giving your permission.* You may be required to accompany your child to a clinic, or you may be able to simply sign a notarized statement. In a few states, both parents need to give their consent.

✔ *A judge's decision.* States with consent and notification laws also provide what is called judicial bypass. This permits a young woman to seek approval for an abortion in a court hearing rather than from her parents. Judges are asked to assess her maturity and ability to understand her decision, but in some states this emotionally charged process may not be confidential. In most states that require consent, a teenager does not need to seek parental consent if she is a victim of rape or incest.

ticing in-vitro fertilization that meet the society's standards. (For the society's address, see RESOURCES, page 493.)

ARTIFICIAL INSEMINATION

Each year more than 170,000 women whose partner's sperm is not viable are artificially inseminated. In most cases, the couple relies on the sperm of an anonymous donor, but if they are married, the law presumes that the husband is the legal father of a child born during the marriage. Most states verify this legal status by requiring the physician who performs the insemination to obtain the husband's written consent.

The donor has no rights and no responsibility to the child unless he is known to the mother and acts as the father. Records related to anonymous donations are considered confidential, although some state laws enabling adopted children to learn about the health and genetic background of their biological parent may also cover children conceived from a donor.

One source of increasing concern is the risk of contracting a disease through donated sperm. Sperm banks usually screen donors for such diseases as HIV, gonorrhea, syphilis, herpes, and hepatitis B. To further decrease the chance of infection, the sperm is typically frozen for a period of time. Anyone dealing with a sperm bank should insist on these precautions.

The sperm bank should also perform a complete chromosomal analysis before accepting a donor. If the recipient gives birth to a child with a screenable genetic deformity, such as Tay-Sachs, for example, she may have a legal claim for dam-

The history of man for the nine months preceding his birth would, probably, be far more interesting and contain events of greater moment than all the three-score and ten years that follow it.

SAMUEL TAYLOR COLERIDGE

Miscellanies, Aesthetic and Literary

Fertility/Infertility: A Glossary of Terms

As more couples wait longer to have babies, infertility has become a growing problem. New technology has made childbearing possible when it had not been before, but the advances involved have caused a growing public debate on legal, medical, and ethical issues.

• **Artificial insemination.** Semen is deposited in the vagina by artificial means rather than intercourse. It is typically used in cases of infertility and for single mothers.

• **Sperm bank.** This is the depository that maintains sperm given by donors, who are usually paid a fee and promised confidentiality.

• **Frozen embryos.** These are fertilized ova, or eggs, that have been removed from a woman's ovary, fertilized with a man's sperm outside the human body, and then frozen, to be implanted later in the woman's uterus. If not all the embryos are used, the remaining ones have been the source of custody disputes.

• **In-vitro fertilization.** Also called IVF, this phrase literally means "in-glass fertilization." The woman's mature egg is removed from the uterus with a thin needle, fertilized with the man's sperm in a glass petri dish, and then reinserted into a woman's uterus.

• **GIFT.** A variation on in-vitro fertilization, GIFT, or *gamete intra-fallopian transfer*, involves combining the egg and sperm and immediately inserting them in the fallopian tubes (not the uterus) for natural fertilization rather than fertilizing them in a petri dish. ZIFT, or *zygote intra-fallopian transfer*, is a newer procedure in which the egg is first fertilized in a petri dish before being placed in the fallopian tubes.

ages against the sperm bank. She may also have a claim for damages if she is inseminated with the wrong sperm.

SURROGATE MOTHERS AND THE LAW

More than a dozen states have laws regarding the contractual arrangements between parents wanting a baby and a woman who agrees—usually for a fee—to be artificially inseminated with the husband's sperm or to have an embryo implanted and carry the baby. Surrogate motherhood, infrequently chosen yet widely reported on, remains an area of great dispute.

Michigan, for example, considers illegal any surrogacy contract that involves the exchange of money for the surrendering of a baby. In New Jersey a lower court ruled in the well-known "Baby M" case of 1984 that the surrogacy contract in question was valid. But Mary Beth Whitehead, the surrogate (and genetic) mother, who wanted to keep her baby, appealed, and the state's supreme court ruled the contract illegal and unenforceable. Then, based on its judgment of the child's best interests, the court granted custody to the genetic father and his wife, with visitation rights for Mary Beth Whitehead.

Whose Rights Come First?

As a woman's pregnancy progresses, questions of rights under the law can become distressingly complex. Sometimes the courts must evaluate the conflicting rights of the mother and the fetus she is carrying. Physicians are required, for example, to get the informed consent of patients before performing surgery or other medical interventions, and this right to choose or refuse medical treatment extends to pregnant women.

It is a woman's right, therefore, to decide to refuse medical treatment, such as having a cesarean section, even if her refusal could jeopardize her fetus. In order to protect the rights of the fetus, some courts have ordered doctors to perform cesarean sections despite a mother's objections. The resulting ambiguities create a legal confusion that is a long way from resolution.

IS IT CONFIDENTIAL OR NOT?

The same ambivalence applies to a patient's right to confidential medical records. That is what the law in many states promises, yet if a pregnant woman or a newborn baby is found to have traces of an illegal drug in the bloodstream, health-care workers in some states are mandated to report it on the grounds that the child has been abused. Although the law is still unsettled about the constitutionality of this practice, it has led to prison sentences and loss of custody for the mother.

Cesarean Sections

Nearly a quarter of all childbirths in the United States are performed by cesarean section, a surgical procedure for delivering a baby through the abdomen rather than vaginally. While most medical professionals would agree that this rate is higher than it should be, there is widespread disagreement regarding the reasons for this upward trend. Some believe that a physician's concern about a malpractice suit if a birth becomes unexpectedly complicated may be one factor driving this increase. Others blame it on the policy of performing repeat cesareans for all women who have once experienced a surgical birth (although this practice is diminishing).

Prior to labor, if your doctor advises a "C-section," you are entitled to seek a second opinion. Another doctor and another hospital may be less inclined to perform it. You can also ask your doctor early on when and why she performs cesareans. You may or may not agree with her reasons.

While most women prefer not to have a C-section, in rare cases, a woman may request one. She may fear the pain or stress of labor or may have had complications in an earlier delivery. A doctor generally will not perform a C-section for other than medical reasons, but if you have concerns, you should discuss them with your doctor. Severe stress or fear may indeed be a medical reason to perform one.

ADOPTION

Adoption has long been a means of creating or augmenting a family. But adoptive parents are required to prove their special fitness for parenting.

Entering the Adoption Maze

Perhaps you want to have your own child, but your partner is infertile. Perhaps you have two boys, feel too old physically to try again, but always dreamed of having a girl. Perhaps you are single, doubt that you will ever marry, but really want to be a parent. Adoption represents a viable way to form or extend a family and to provide a family for children whose relationship with their biological parents has been terminated.

Yet many legal, financial, and emotional hurdles stand between you and a successful adoption, and they dictate that you carefully research your state's adoption laws, whether you are working through an agency or on your own. And every adoption agency—public or private, for profit or nonprofit, religious or nondenominational, local or foreign—has its own requirements. Each of these agencies has developed criteria it hopes will ensure that adopting parents possess the personal qualities and financial resources to best serve the child's welfare. While natural parents can raise their children with the expectation of only minimal government intervention, adoptive parents are required to give clear evidence of their parenting potential.

AGENCIES, PUBLIC AND PRIVATE

To begin the process, you will want to find out what agencies are available in your area and what services they offer. The National Adoption Information Clearinghouse can give you referrals and advice. (For its address and telephone number, see RESOURCES, page 493.) Every state and some cities have agencies funded and run by the state. Private agencies may either be for-profit or nonprofit. At a public agency, you can expect to encounter extensive waiting periods and sometimes strict eligibility requirements. If you are seeking a healthy newborn, you may discover that there is a multiyear waiting list or perhaps even that no applications are being accepted at the present time.

Most public agencies almost exclusively place children who have already been given up for adoption and need parents. If you are prepared to adopt an older child or particularly a child with "special needs" (one with physical or mental disabilities, or possibly from an economically deprived or minority background), you can expect greater opportunities to adopt more quickly and with less stringent applicant requirements through a private agency.

Private agencies associated with a specific religious group may or may not consider applicants who fall outside that faith. They may, however, be more open than other private agencies to couples with limited incomes and may offer their services for a lower fee.

It is easier for a father to have children than for children to have a father.

POPE JOHN XXIII

Independent Placement

More than half of the infant adoptions today come about through placement outside of the private and public agency systems. Most states permit prospective adoptive parents to connect directly with a birth mother or her intermediary. Subject to court approval, you can expect to pay "reasonable fees" for adoption services, attorney expenses, and the birth mother's medical expenses.

In some states, you may pay for other pregnancy-related expenses, such as transportation, housing, maternity clothing, and counseling. If, however, you meet someone who offers to "find you a baby" or "place your child" for a fee, you have probably found a criminal.

Bringing a Foreign Baby Home

Thousands of Americans decide to look overseas to find a child to adopt. The process is not quick—it can take 18 to 36 months in all—and it may cost $10,000 or more. Each agency and country will add a layer of procedures, but here are the basic steps and documents involved:

• **Legal documents.** To obtain a foreign adoption, you or your attorney will need proof of the child's identity through a birth certificate, evidence that the birth parents have relinquished their parental rights, and receipt of an adoption decree.

• **Orphan petition.** You must file for the "Petition to Classify an Orphan as an Immediate Relative" with the U.S. Immigration and Naturalization Service (INS). This form will require the same documents as above. Once approved, you can get a visa for foreign travel.

• **Passports.** You may have to go to the foreign country for court proceedings or to pick up the adopted child, although perhaps an intermediary can act on your behalf. Be sure you have passports for the child as well as for yourselves. Contact your local passport office for information.

• **Adoption petition.** You will have to go through adoption proceedings in a U.S. court even if you have completed the adoption in the child's birth country. You will need the child's personal documents, proof of U.S. citizenship of at least one adoptive parent, evidence that the child was less than 16 when adopted, and an adoption petition.

• **Naturalization.** After the adoption, you should naturalize your child. In some cases, it can be done immediately; in others, it may take a year before the INS will grant a certificate of citizenship.

123...

BE PREPARED FOR THE HOME STUDY

Anyone who adopts must go through a home study. This is a series of detailed interviews conducted by a social worker to evaluate your "appropriateness" for adopting. Here is what to expect:

1. You may have to write an autobiographical statement and answer detailed questions about your life: education, family, work, religion, friends, and child-rearing ideas.

2. You will be asked for a report of a physical exam, including a tuberculosis test. You may need a doctor's statement that you are infertile.

3. To make sure you have no child abuse or criminal record, a form with basic personal data will be sent to your state's child welfare department and police agencies.

4. To verify your income and financial status, you will need copies of your tax returns and other financial records.

5. You will be asked to identify three or four people who know you well and who can provide references concerning your suitability for adoption.

6. Be prepared during the home visit for the interviewer to inspect the child's bedroom and make sure there are safety features such as smoke detectors and a plan for exiting in case of an emergency.

While six states—Colorado, Connecticut, Delaware, Massachusetts, Michigan, and North Dakota—prohibit independent adoption, adopting parents in these states may be able to file for adoption in the state where the birth mother lives and gives birth. But because fewer than half the states permit non-resident independent adoption, you will have to check whether this approach is an option for you.

For some people the expense of independent adoption may be prohibitive: It can run up to $15,000 or more. Although there are no set fees, some courts may evaluate fee reports in their approval decisions. If fees are too high, in some cases, an adoption may not be approved. Also, when you begin your search—personal contacts and newspaper advertising are the most common approaches—you can let it be known that you are looking for a birth mother who has her own health insurance. Another way to keep the costs down is to focus your search on those states that restrict a birth mother's fees to her legal and medical bills.

You may choose not to use an attorney as an intermediary to locate a baby. But, especially because you will not have the services of an agency, you will probably want the assistance of an attorney for other aspects of the process: doing a background and health check of the birth parent, providing counseling or doctor referrals, assessing the adoption for any potential legal difficulties, assisting the social worker who processes the case, preparing legal documents, and appearing in court when necessary.

Seeking a Special Child

Some adoptive parents wait years for a healthy infant. Meanwhile, tens of thousands of children are waiting for adoptive parents to choose them. Not everyone can or should adopt a "special needs" child, but you will want to consider whether you have the tolerance and the capacity to care for such a child.

No exact list of conditions defines special-needs children. They may have physical, mental, or emotional disabilities. They may have suffered physical or sexual abuse in their birth families. School-age white children may be "special needs" kids, as well as African-American children over four years old. Children who test positive for the HIV antibody, who were born to HIV-infected mothers or possessed traces of cocaine at birth, may all come into the category and so might those who are part of a sibling group that needs to be placed together.

Older children are another special group, because almost every state has laws requiring that older children consent to the adoption. The "age of consent" varies from 10 to 15 years old. Often these children are living within the state foster-care system, which provides a temporary home either in a state-run institution or with private, state-subsidized foster parents. Foster care is not intended to be a permanent parenting arrangement, and it sometimes becomes an intermediate step to adoption. (See also "Parenting," page 112.)

A NATIONAL NETWORK

Finding a special-needs child can be as simple as contacting a local adoption agency, either public or private. These agencies are usually linked to exchanges—state, regional, and national in reach—that match families and special-needs children. Many of these exchanges provide photos, biographies, and other relevant information.

You may be eligible for a financial subsidy if you adopt a special-needs child. This subsidy is available when reasonable efforts to place the child have been unsuccessful, the child cannot be returned to the parents, and a subsidy may make the placement attractive or will help pay for the child's particular special needs.

The Rights of Birth Parents

First and foremost, the birth parents have the right to give or withhold consent for a child to be adopted. This is the linchpin without which no adoption can be completed. A birth mother may decide before giving birth to have her baby adopted, but most states, recognizing the inherent emotional complexity of this decision, have laws that prohibit her from giving official consent until after the baby is born.

Many states also insist on a waiting period after the birth, typically four days, but it varies widely from state to state. (See "When a Birth Mother Can Change Her Mind," page 110.) In most states, a licensed social worker may witness the written consent; others request only that a notary public witness the consent. Some state laws are more stringent, requiring that the birth mother appear before a court.

THE BIRTH FATHER'S RIGHTS

Although the birth mother's consent is primary, the position of the birth father must be considered. If he is married to the birth mother who wants to give up her baby for adoption—a rare situation—his consent is also required.

In the majority of cases, however, the father is not married to the birth mother. Legally described as the "putative" or

---

Being There at the Beginning

If you have arranged an open, private adoption, you may be able to be present at the baby's birth if you want to be. Some adopting parents are reluctant to observe the delivery because the birth mother has not yet signed her consent. Otherwise, the decision rests entirely with the birth mother. Here are her rights:

✔ *Access.* Although she needs to get doctor and hospital approval, the birth mother may invite anyone she likes into the delivery room.

✔ *Consent.* It is the birth mother's baby until the consent form is signed, and it is up to her whether or not she decides to see the baby before giving consent.

✔ *Counseling.* A hospital social worker will check on the birth mother. The mother does not have to talk to her, but the worker will ask whether she has received or at least been offered adoption counseling.

✔ *Naming.* The birth mother is entitled to name her baby and receive a copy of the birth certificate. Later, when the adoption is complete, the certificate will be amended to show the child's adopted name and to identify the adoptive parents as the parents.

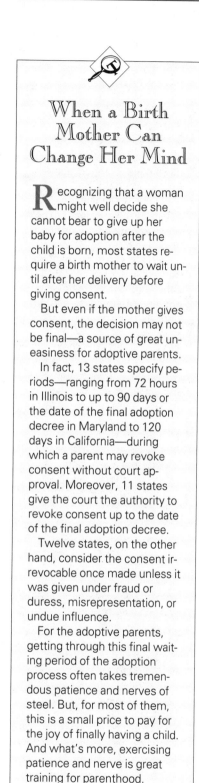

"alleged" father, he may not be required to give consent in most states; in many states, he must simply be given notice of the planned adoption. These laws are generally based on the notion that the unwed father may not wish to enter into the legal process or that he is not interested. After the notice is received, most states permit the father's rights to be terminated after a certain time period if he does not file an objection.

If he wishes, the unwed father can seek full rights to custody or to veto the adoption. Usually he has sought his parental rights prior to the adoption petition. To do this, he must prove he is the biological father; sign the birth certificate; support, communicate with, or try to act like a father to the child; and obtain a court order establishing his paternity.

Completing the Adoption

To complete the adoption process, you must prepare and file a petition. This document is usually filed in the state and county where the adoptive parents reside. Its exact contents vary from state to state, but generally the petition includes:

- The date and place of the child's birth;
- The person who placed the child with the adoptive parents and the date;
- The new adopted name of the child;
- The name, age, length of residence in the state, and marital status of the adopting parents;
- A statement attesting to the parents' desire and ability to care for the child and accept the rights and responsibilities of parenting;
- The name of anyone whose consent is required but has not yet been received.

If you adopted through an agency, the home study conducted by the agency when you applied for adoption may be a sufficient report. (See "Be Prepared for the Home Study," page 108.) In some instances, however, if you have made an independent adoption, you may have to let a social worker inspect and report on your home environment after the child's arrival.

At the court hearing that follows the petition, the judge usually grants an interlocutory decree, which is a document giving you temporary legal custody. After a certain waiting period, typically six months, the judge will grant a final decree. Finally, the adoption is complete: the child's name is changed, a new birth certificate is completed, and the confidential adoption records are sealed.

A Child's Right to Know

In recent years courts have increasingly recognized the desire of adopted children to know more about their biological parents and of biological parents to learn about their natural children. Every state now permits adoptive parents and adult adoptees to receive such general information (not including names and exact locations) as medical and genetic histories of the biological parents, and in some cases the general circumstances regarding the adoption.

Most states require that adoptees seeking access to confidential records provide sufficient reason for their release. A few states—including Alaska, Kansas, and Tennessee—allow adult adoptees to obtain their original birth certificates and adoption records upon request and without restriction.

A DELICATE BALANCE

Some states have "search and consent" guidelines that allow an agency or other intermediary to try to find the birth parent to obtain consent. If it is refused, the adoptee may still be able to have the adoption records opened by petitioning the court. Or adult adoptees and biological parents can voluntarily list their names in mutual-consent adoption registries. If one party makes a request for the release of records, the registry can verify if consent has been granted. Finally, some states will release information about deceased biological parents to an adoptee.

At every step the child should be allowed to meet the real experiences of life; the thorns should never be plucked from his roses.

ELLEN KEY
The Century of the Child

Tracking Down a Parent

Eventually, your adopted child will have questions about her roots. The knowledge may be important to psychological well-being, or she may need to know her medical or genetic history for health reasons. The following steps will help her track down her biological parents.

• The very best approach is to plan ahead. If you know from the beginning that you are going to want your child to meet her biological parents, you can probably make arrangements at the time of adoption for future information or contact.

• If you have to start from scratch later on, ask the agency or intermediary that handled the adoption to try to get in touch with the birth parent. If the state has "search and consent" rules, the agency may be able to contact the birth parents and get permission to reveal their identity.

• Write to your state's bureau of vital statistics, which can sometimes provide additional birth data, including the name of the birth parent.

• Register with your state's mutual-consent adoption registry or with a national registry service; the birth parents may have registered, too.(For registry addresses, see RESOURCES, page 493)

• Supply the Social Security Administration with a name and any other identifying data. If you have sufficient cause, they may be able to provide you with the address of one parent's last known place of employment.

• Besides "search and consent" guidelines and mutual-consent registries, some states keep identifying information about siblings of deceased adult adoptees or deceased biological parents who consented to a release of records.

PARENTING

The law recognizes the special, private nature of the parent-child relationship. But it will step in when parents fail to provide basic care.

When Discipline Becomes Abuse

It is a parent's prerogative to give a child a spanking once in a while. But the law considers excessive or "unreasonable" force abuse—and if parents are found guilty of it, the child can be taken from them. No two state laws defining abuse are identical, but most have elements in common and generally include:

✔ *Serious injury.* If a child suffers serious physical injury at the hands of a parent, especially if hospitalization or medical care is needed, nearly every state considers it abuse. Sexual molestation and intercourse are also abuse.

✔ *Potential threat.* Besides statutes against bodily harm itself, some states have laws that prohibit placing a child in a situation where he will be at risk of serious injury or psychological abuse.

✔ *Injury is injury.* Laws in some states consider any physical injury—not just "serious" injury—to be grounds for suspecting abuse.

Taking Care of Your Child

The role of the law in determining how you raise your children remains relatively slight. This is based on the belief that it is not the state's business to interfere in the private sphere of the family. It seeks only to ensure that every child's basic needs are met. Food, clothing, shelter, and usually medical care and education as well, are the minimum necessities parents are legally responsible for providing. Only if these basic parenting duties are not being met—through neglect or abuse—will the state become involved.

As the courts have been called on to determine child-custody arrangements, some states, such as West Virginia, have turned to the notion of a "primary caretaker." This is the parent—still typically but not necessarily the mother—who has taken the ongoing, day-to-day responsibility for the child's welfare. More and more, however, the courts are considering both parents to be responsible for meeting their child's basic needs. A Colorado court said it clearly: "No party shall be presumed to be able to serve the best interest of the child better than any other because of sex."

SUPPORT UNTIL EMANCIPATION

Both parents are responsible for support. Should one parent lose a job or leave town, for example, it is the responsibility of the other parent to ensure that the child's support and care are provided; this minimizes the risk that the child will become a public charge. This dual responsibility persists at least until the child has reached the age of majority or has been "emancipated," that is, gets married, joins the military, or is otherwise living independently. It applies even if the parents are not married or are minors themselves.

The laws that govern the tricky matter of determining whether parents have neglected to care properly for their children are narrowly defined. The court still has great discretion to evaluate each case individually. But child neglect—which, along with abuse, can lead to the termination of a parent's rights—is generally recognized to mean that a child's safety or health is put at risk.

Child neglect includes leaving a child without proper supervision for a certain period of time, letting a child's wound or illness go medically unattended, allowing a child to suffer malnutrition, and using drugs or excessive amounts of alcohol and thereby jeopardizing a child's emotional or physical safety. Some states consider a parent's conviction for a serious crime or failing to send a child to school to be neglect.

It is not only the parents' actions that dictate the appropriate care for the child. Parents may themselves request foster care because they cannot handle a child's difficult behavior, such as frequent acts of truancy or juvenile delinquency. But the court will not take action to begin outside supervision until a petition is filed and a court hearing has been held. The petition can be filed by a parent or a guardian, a police officer, a social worker, or even a citizen with a complaint.

Going Solo

The rise in the number of single parents in recent years has led to greater social acceptance of and respect for this often difficult and demanding parenting role. Whether they are alone because of divorce, death, or because they never married, single parents have the same responsibilities to provide basic care and support for their children as two-parent families, although they usually have to do it with more limited resources.

Following a divorce, the noncustodial parent will probably be entitled to visitation rights. This is not only the parent's right,

Second Thoughts About Single Parenting

PROBLEM
Before the birth of her son, Margo told his father, Rick, that he did not have to worry about taking care of the child. With or without Rick, she decided, she wanted to have the baby. But in the first months after the arrival of her son, Margo began to have second thoughts. Only then did she realize the full burden of single parenting and of the unfairness to her child—emotionally, financially, and in terms of time. She tried to talk to Rick about it, but he refused even to take her phone calls.

ACTION
Since Rick was the father, Margo had the right to make him provide support, whether he wanted to or not—but first Margo had to prove his paternity. She went to family court, and the court required Rick and Margo to take blood and other genetic tests. On the basis of the tests and Margo's testimony, the court decided that Rick was indeed the child's father and ordered him to accept his legal obligation of child support and related parental responsibilities. (If Rick fails to pay, Margo has the right to ask the court to garnishee Rick's wages.)

1 2 3

TIPS ON THE FAMILY LEAVE ACT

When your baby is born or when you adopt a child, you, as father or mother, may be entitled to 12 weeks of unpaid leave from your job. If you work for a firm with more than 50 employees, you are probably covered by the federal Family and Medical Leave Act, which took effect in August, 1993, and covers about half the nation's workers. But before you take advantage of the act, consider several points:

1. The leave is unpaid, which means that you may not be able to afford to take the it.

2. The act requires employers to guarantee their workers the same or an equivalent job when they return. But you may fear that you will be unhappy with the "equivalent" position you are placed in upon return.

3. Twelve weeks' leave can mean 12 weeks' total time off: The leave may include any paid vacation or sick time you have not yet taken.

4. If your salary is in your company's top 10 percent, you take the biggest risk if you take family or medical leave. The act does not guarantee you the same job (or its equivalent) upon your return. The firm can claim that doing so would cause it "substantial and grievous economic injury." (See also YOUR JOB, page 247.)

but also the child's. Visits can be frustrating and may cause confusion, but they should not undermine the primary parent's role. The custodial parent generally maintains sole responsibility for deciding on education, religion, medical care, place of residence, and other such basic parenting matters unless the courts have deemed otherwise. Nevertheless, one parent's primacy in decision-making does not absolve the noncustodial parent from financial obligations to provide child support. (See also "Divorce," page 135.)

If a single parent is a mother who gave birth out of wedlock, she can take steps to obtain the support of the natural father, whether he wants to acknowledge his paternity or not. Furthermore, if a single parent dies, the surviving parent automatically becomes responsible for a minor child's continuing care and support.

Your Children's Rights

Throughout this century, the Supreme Court has upheld parental authority. Usually these cases came up because of a conflict between the parent and the state. "The custody, care, and nurture of the child reside first in the parents," the court asserted in a 1944 decision. But in recent years the courts have been called on to consider the constitutional rights of the child when they may be at odds with parental authority.

The landmark 1992 case of Gregory K., in which an 11-year-old Florida boy in foster care filed a petition to terminate his relationship with his biological parents, may have been the first instance of a minor's being granted the right to act as an adult. Based on the 14th Amendment, the Florida court recognized the child's right to due process, equal protection, privacy, and access to the court. Child-initiated lawsuits are unlikely to become widespread, but the debate continues.

EMANCIPATION

The laws that establish the age of majority and the right to emancipation are the clearest indications of when children can assume most adult rights and responsibilities. At emancipation, a young person is no longer legally restricted by parental control or limited by the state in terms of age. He is also, under most circumstances, no longer legally entitled to support from his parents.

A child can be emancipated without a court decree by reaching the age of 18, getting married (with parental consent if necessary), or entering the military, all of which confer automatic emancipation in most states. If the parents and their child

---

Who Is Liable for Your Child's Behavior?

If your child damages property or causes injury, you may be held responsible for her actions, depending on the circumstances and your state's laws. Generally, parents can be held responsible for their child's behavior if it is willful or malicious, or if the parents' negligence contributed to the behavior.

If a parent allows his child to have a party where alcohol is being served to minors, he can be held responsible for any damages or injuries caused or suffered by intoxicated partygoers. By allowing underage children to drink, the parent is acting negligently, that is, failing to meet the standard of care that a reasonable person would have met under the same circumstances.

Suppose a parent allows his child to attend a party and reasonably believes there will be no alcohol served? In many states, he will not be held responsible for any damages his child then causes as a result of being at the party.

If your nine-year-old leaves his bicycle in a neighbor's driveway and someone accidentally trips over it, in most states you would not be liable for damages unless you acted irresponsibly regarding supervision, knew your son had a history of leaving his bike where he shouldn't, or otherwise acted negligently.

A Child's Life, Legally Speaking

Children reach adulthood, with most of its inherent rights and responsibilities, at the age of majority, which in most states is 18. Before that, unless children have been emancipated or have established independence from their parents, their rights are mostly contingent on their age. Here is how that affects them in various circumstances as they grow up:

• **Contraception.** Anyone can purchase over-the-counter contraceptives, whatever his age. About half the states require parental consent or notification for prescription birth control devices if the buyer is not of age or emancipated. States also vary on consent or notice requirements for abortion.

• **Criminal courts.** Persons under 18 who commit a criminal offense are usually charged in the juvenile court system. Some states set the age at 16, and in serious crimes such as murder or rape, a juvenile may be treated as an adult.

• **Curfews.** Local laws may restrict access to streets and public places after a certain time at night by people under a certain age. Although curfew laws vary widely, they usually allow young people to be out after hours in the company of an adult or to go to work. Some permit them to be out with a parent's permission. Many curfew laws are facing legal challenges in court.

• **Drinking.** Every state prohibits persons under age 21 from buying alcoholic beverages by making either the sale or the purchase of alcohol illegal, sometimes both. In some states it is illegal for a minor to drink or possess alcohol only outside the home or in a public place.

• **Driving.** Most states set 16 as the minimum age to get a driver's license and nearly all require parental consent before age 18. Several states—including Mississippi and Montana—allow licensing at 15. Several others set the age higher, at 17 or 18. Most states allow a young person to drive (with an adult driver in the vehicle) with a learner's permit in the months before that age.

• **Gambling.** In most states, a person must be at least 21 to gamble in a casino and at least 18 to bet in a lottery or at the racetrack.

• **Guns.** Many states prohibit the sale of handguns to minors and allow minors to own handguns only for hunting or target shooting. Federal law makes selling or giving a handgun to a minor an offense punishable by up to 10 years in prison.

• **Marriage.** In most states, marriage is legal without parental consent at 18 and with parental consent at 16. Some states have even lower age limits. A marriage that has taken place before the required age may not be valid. In most states it becomes valid if it remains unchallenged until the required age has been reached.

• **Medical treatment.** Most states require that a patient be 18 years old or the age of majority to give consent for medical treatment. Some states set the age as low as 14. Parental consent is not required for emancipated children and in cases of emergency.

• **Pornography.** In most states it is illegal for dealers to sell or distribute to minors any materials deemed obscene, indecent, or pornographic, including books, films, and magazines. But most state laws do not make it illegal for minors to purchase or possess such materials.

• **Schooling.** All states have laws regarding compulsory attendance for school-age children in either public, private, or home schools. All states allow children to be educated at home as long as certain provisions (which vary by state) are met.

• **Sex.** Every state defines how old a female must be before she may legally give her consent to having sexual intercourse. Prior to this age, which ranges from 12 to 18, a male can be found guilty of statutory rape by having intercourse with a woman below the legal age of consent. Some states will not find the male guilty unless he is above a certain age.

• **Smoking.** In many states, it is legal for children under 16 or 18 to possess and smoke cigarettes or other tobacco products. But it is illegal in every state to sell or give them such products.

• **Voting.** In 1971, the right to vote in federal elections was lowered from 21 to 18 with the enactment of the 26th Amendment.

• **Working.** Federal and state laws mandate work restrictions concerning age, type of work, and hours of employment. Minimum-age exceptions include such jobs as baby-sitting, yard work, farm work, golf caddying, and delivering newspapers. (For more information about child labor laws, see YOUR JOB, page 261.)

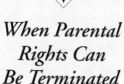

When Parental Rights Can Be Terminated

The law has great regard for the parent-child relationship. Courts are reluctant to intervene and terminate a parent's rights. Yet they will do so. When is such a move deemed necessary? The state needs solid evidence that the parent is not acting in the best interests of the child and is therefore unfit. Following are examples of parents whose parental rights could be terminated by the courts:

✔ *The abusive parent.* A parent who inflicts physical injury or commits a sex offense against a child will be deemed unfit, as will a parent who allows physical injury to be inflicted on a child or allows a sex offense to be committed.

✔ *The neglectful parent.* A parent who fails to provide a minimum level of care—proper food, shelter, clothing, and medical attention—is considered guilty of neglect and therefore unfit. So are parents convicted of a serious crime, parents who are incarcerated, and parents who use drugs or excessive amounts of alcohol.

✔ *The absent parent.* Typically, a parent who is away from the home or otherwise fails to provide normal supervision may be considered neglectful and deemed to have abandoned his or her child.

agree, emancipation can also be established if the child creates an independent household or otherwise establishes self-supporting independence.

In California a minor can petition the court to be emancipated. But the law requires that the child, if living apart, must be 16 or older, must derive his income from legal pursuits, and must have his parents' acquiescence to his living separately. Furthermore, the court must be convinced that granting emancipation will be in the minor's best interests. If emancipation is granted, he is free to establish residency, apply for a work permit, enroll in college, buy or sell real property, consent to medical care, enter into binding contracts, and sue or be sued in his own name.

Taking Over Custody

When parents cannot care for their children, the state or county will take over that responsibility. Any such action that exceeds 30 days, however, must be approved by a proceeding in family court. Courts transfer this responsibility reluctantly and only under compelling circumstances, such as when evidence of neglect, abuse, unfitness, or abandonment is strong.

No child can be removed from her home without a court hearing except in a life-threatening emergency. The parental role can usually be terminated only after the child has been removed from the parents' custody and the parents have failed to maintain contact or in other ways serve the best interests of their child. The criteria governing this legal action vary from state to state, but in every case, clear and convincing evidence that a parent is unfit must be demonstrated before a court will order final termination of parental rights.

GIVING PARENTS A CHANCE

In many states, the child must be removed from the parents' custody and be placed under state supervision for six months or more before termination proceedings may begin. Most states require that the conditions justifying termination remain unimproved for a certain period of time. The courts will also consider whether or not the parents have tried to maintain contact with or have attempted to rehabilitate their relationship with their child.

In some states, however, including California, no warning or waiting period is required if the conditions are considered particularly grave—when, for example, a parent is convicted of a felony, habitually abuses drugs or alcohol, or has a severe physical or mental disability that undermines fitness.

FOSTER CARE

If a child needs a custodian because injury, death, neglect, abuse, or another situation has rendered the child's parents unable to provide care, the child can be placed temporarily with another adult—a relative, a friend, or a stranger appointed by the court.

If the court decides to place the child with a stranger, the child will be placed either in an emergency home where he will stay for a few days while awaiting a court hearing or in a group home (with two to eight children) run by a public or private agency where he will live for a longer period.

Foster care is viewed as a temporary solution even if the child's stay in a foster home lasts for several years. A child may be placed in foster care with the consent of the natural parent. But in cases where abuse or neglect of a child is either suspected or proven, foster care is more likely to be involuntary and ordered by a court.

Typically, a local social services agency is legally charged with placing the child in foster care and is presumed to be acting in the child's best interests.

FOSTER PARENTS

Unlike adoptive parents, foster parents do not have legal custody of the children in their home. Some foster parents do begin proceedings to adopt their foster children, but the arrangement presumes that the natural parents will eventually obtain custody of their children, or that the foster children will be transferred elsewhere within the foster-care system, or that they will be adopted. The children remain in the custody of the state, and the foster parents usually have no special advantage over others if they want to adopt them. Some children remain in foster care for a number of years or until they reach emancipation.

Foster parents and foster homes must be licensed according to the standards of their state. This usually involves training the prospective foster parents to meet the special demands of foster children and a careful examination of the parents' physical health and personal characteristics, as well as checks that would reveal any criminal background. The licensing procedure also includes an inspection of the health and safety standards of the home itself.

AFTER TERMINATION

When a parent's rights have been terminated—whether they are curtailed voluntarily by the parent or involuntarily by public authority—the child legally has the same status as an orphan. In other words, a legal relationship no longer exists between the parent and child.

This means that the child cannot automatically inherit from

THREE WAYS THE GOVERNMENT CAN HELP

When parents cannot offer their children adequate support, the government will step in and provide assistance. Each state sets its own need standards for determining eligibility. The following may be available:

1. Money. Aid to Families With Dependent Children (AFDC) gives money to families with children who, because of death, absence, incapacity, or unemployment of one or both parents, are deprived of support. The children must live at home, be under age 18, or under 21 and attending school, and the family must qualify under stringent guidelines of impoverishment and other conditions.

2. Relative support. If a child has been placed in a relative's home, that family is also entitled to AFDC payments. It makes no difference that the care is provided by a relative.

3. Subsidies. Families that qualify for AFDC or welfare programs may be entitled to food stamps, a housing allowance, or medical care. Families or individuals who serve as foster parents are entitled to subsidies for the care and support that they provide.

the biological parent if there is no will. The parent is not required to provide child support, cannot gain custody or visitation rights, and has no right to participate in the child's adoption. The state as guardian has full power to approve the child's placement. The state also becomes fully responsible for the child's support, and some states will not terminate parental rights until they have determined that the child is adoptable.

WHO INHERITS WHAT?

State laws vary on the rights of a child to inherit from her biological grandparents after the termination of the parental rights of her natural parents if the grandparents have left no will. Some states expressly disallow any inheritance from anyone in the natural family after termination.

Other states allow the child to inherit if her natural parents die before her natural grandparents do. But an adopted child is usually entitled to inheritance without a will from his adoptive parents and grandparents. (For more information about inheritance see, YOUR MONEY, page 365.)

What Are the Rights of Parents?

Along with the duties of parenthood—to provide food, clothing, shelter, and medical care for their children—parents also have a basic right to their children's custody and many other rights as well, starting with the right to name them. Here are some of the other rights:

• **Consent.** Before medical treatment can be administered to a minor, the parents' consent is required. This is true for most types of medical care, with some exceptions such as abortion and birth control. Parental consent is usually required in various other areas of a minor's life, such as marrying and driving.

• **Religion.** It is left to the discretion of the parents to choose the religious training their children will get. If your child refuses to go to church, however, you have no legal means to make him do so. The state will step in if a parent's religious beliefs physically harm the child. If a parent refuses to consent to a medically necessary procedure on religious grounds, a court may determine that the parent is neglecting his child and intervene. This may be done when a judge believes that the parents' action (or lack of action) will be harmful to the child's health or welfare.

• **Education.** Parents are responsible for making every reasonable effort to see that their child attends school regularly, whether it be a public or private school. Parents have the option of educating their children at home if certain conditions are met. (See also "Educating Your Child at Home," page 126.)

• **Place of residence.** Parents can choose the place where they and their children will live, up to the age of the child's majority or emancipation. (Under a divorce order, however, a custodial parent may be prohibited from moving more than a certain number of miles away.)

• **Lifestyle.** It is the parents' prerogative to decide the standard of living of their children, assuming that basic needs are met. Should a marriage end, the courts will assess child support and will take a hard look at the financial capability of both parents to decide on an appropriate living standard and lifestyle.

• **Guardian choice.** If one parent dies, all rights of decision and control fall to the surviving parent. The surviving parent should name another guardian for the child immediately. This choice is subject to the court's confirmation in the event of the surviving parent's death. In some cases, the preference of the child will be considered if he has reached a certain age.

CHILD CARE

All parents worry about getting the best possible care for their children. States may set standards, but they cannot replace a parent's personal evaluation.

Choosing Home Day Care

Parents entrust their children to private-home day-care services more than any other kind of child care. Parents typically choose home day care over a day-care center because it offers flexible hours, a home setting, and relatively small numbers of children. And it usually costs less than having a baby-sitter come to their own home.

Nearly every state has established regulations for those providing care in their homes. While the regulations vary widely from state to state, they establish basic safety and health standards. They stipulate the number of children a provider can care for at one time, what kind of home inspections are necessary, what health and safety standards must be met, and what training or other qualifications are required. These regulations do not guarantee your child quality care, but they do provide some direction. Examples of such legislation follow:

- Most states set the maximum group size for day care in a home at no more than eight children including the provider's own children, although the number ranges up to 15 (Arizona) or 16 (Mississippi);
- Nearly all states require children in home day care to be vaccinated against illnesses such as polio, diphtheria, measles, and mumps;
- Most states require smoke detectors or fire drills or both in the home, and some also ban smoking;
- Several states, including Arizona, Kentucky, Montana, and Nevada, require the homeowner to carry liability insurance;
- About half the states require that the staff be trained in CPR or first aid or both;
- Some states require that providers have special training or professional experience in child care before they set themselves up as a day-care business;
- Some states require that a certain amount of space be available for facilities or recreational equipment.

At the very least, government standards offer parents the choice of providers who are licensed, certified, or registered. While no exact statistics exist, the majority of private-home

---

Checking for Safety

Although a day-care home may be regulated, that does not ensure its strict adherence to safety guidelines or cover all your concerns. It is important that you personally check the building where you will leave your child. Here are some things to look for:

✔ *In case of fire.* Are there fire extinguishers, smoke detectors, multiple exits, an emergency plan?

✔ *Risk of exposure.* Are radiators and electrical sockets covered? Are there exposed electrical appliances or sharp kitchen utensils? Are medicines kept locked up?

✔ *Home improvements.* Does the home need repairs? Is it well ventilated and well lit? Have window safety guards been installed on second and higher stories to prevent a child from falling out?

✔ *Domestic animals.* If the provider has pets, are they healthy and friendly?

✔ *Cleanliness.* Are the bathroom, the changing room, and the sleeping area clean? Does the provider wash her hands after diapering? Is there any evidence of mice or roaches?

day-care providers still operate outside the regulated system. When providers are regulated, the government may require the provider to make an application and pass an on-site safety inspection before obtaining a license.

For example, an inspector may go to the provider's home to check for fire extinguishers and smoke detectors. But some states permit providers to register by providing their own reports and conducting their own inspections. No regulations can determine for you whether the provider possesses the character or other personal qualities that you want for your child.

DAY-CARE CENTERS

Each state licenses day-care centers and sets minimum standards. These centers, either nonprofit or for-profit, may be connected to a church or synagogue, a school, or a corporation, or they may operate as independent commercial enterprises. As with family day care, government regulation is intended to guarantee parents a certain minimum level of care, but the standards vary widely from state to state. A crucial issue for parents to evaluate is the staff-to-child ratio, which affects the amount of attention you can expect your children to receive.

Every state sets guidelines that vary according to the age of the children. In Maryland and Massachusetts, for example, one staff member must be available to care for every three one-year-old children. By the time those children reach three, one staff member can care for a group of 10. In North Carolina and Delaware, however, the rules require only that there be one staff member for every seven one-year-olds. In Delaware one staffer can be in charge of 12 three-year-olds, and in North Carolina, one staffer can be in charge of 15.

A WELL-TRAINED STAFF

Nearly every state requires staff members to wash their hands and refrain from smoking, and most insist that staff members be trained in CPR and first aid. Most states also require personnel to complete some training in child care or possess professional experience before being employed and to continue training thereafter. Nearly every day-care center undergoes government inspections at least once a year.

Still, no regulations can substitute for a parent's own judgment about the quality of a center. Do the caregivers personally greet each child in the morning? How do they discipline bad behavior? Is staff turnover heavy? The answers to these questions will indicate much about the level of care. For example, low staff turnover indicates good management and also encourages stronger bonding with the children. One guideline, however, is always valid: never put your child anywhere you cannot drop in and visit any time you want.

Chicken Little Day-Care Center
632 Broadway • Montgomery, Alabama 32851
Susan Peters, Caregiver • 708-431-7870

AGREEMENT FOR DAY-CARE SERVICES

Child ❶

Name of child

Birth date

Child's allergies, medications, special conditions

Parents ❷

Home address

City/State/Telephone

Father (daytime telephone):

Mother (daytime telephone):

DAY-CARE SERVICES ❸

Days of care

Hours of care

Vacations/Holidays

Materials/Services provided:

FEES ❹

Payment dates

Hours of care

Overtime charge

If child is absent

EMERGENCY INFORMATION ❺

Name of close friend or relative: (Include address and phone number.)
❻
Name of pediatrician: (Include address and phone number.)

I grant consent for emergency medical treatment. (Parent's signature and date)
❼
Signature of caregiver

Date of agreement

Signature of parent

Date of agreement

Agreement for Day Care

To make sure that your child gets the best care, pin down the details of your arrangements with the center by executing a document like this one. The document can originate with the center or with you, but should include: **1.** Your child's vital statistics, including food or medicinal allergies; **2.** The numbers where both parents can be reached during the day; **3.** A detailed yearly schedule, including holidays. (Check for holidays that do not mesh with your work holidays, and make appropriate arrangements); **4.** A clear statement of fees, including charges if your child stays late or is absent; **5.** The telephone number of a friend who can be called if there is an emergency; **6.** Your pediatrician's name and telephone number and written permission for emergency medical care; **7.** Signatures that indicate that both parties understand and agree to the services provided.

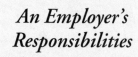

Some centers (particularly if they are nonprofit) offer rates based on what parents can afford to pay. Day-care-center fees generally range from about $50 up to $300 or $400 a week, with an average of about $150 for infants and $100 for older children. Often, the better the facility is, the higher the fee. Of course, high cost does not guarantee quality care.

Hiring a Baby-sitter or Nanny

In-home help offers parents the most control over their children's care. It is also usually the most expensive, averaging $200 to $400 a week in major cities. The in-home child-care provider could be anyone from a professionally trained nanny to a recent high-school graduate with limited experience.

She may live in your home full-time or work a regular daytime shift and leave. As the employer, you will have to determine what qualifications you need, what kind of care you can afford, and what your responsibilities are.

Finding the right person to provide your child daily, one-on-one care is not easy. You can try to do it on your own, by advertising or networking with your friends or business associates. Or you may use an employment or "nanny" agency that charges a fee to find and screen candidates, typically conducting a background check for any criminal or abuse-related record and to weed out aliens ineligible for the work.

THE "AU PAIR" SOLUTION

Some agencies specialize in placing so-called au pairs. Typically Western Europeans, these young women may be permitted one-year visas and receive about $100 for a 45-hour week. Only a few agencies are authorized by the U.S. Information Agency to match au pairs with American families. The agencies get a fee that includes the expense of transportation, health insurance, continuing support, and administration.

Issues to consider when hiring a babysitter or nanny include:

- Find out if state law requires you to buy workers' compensation insurance for in-home workers and whether your homeowners policy covers her in case of accident or illness.
- If you expect the worker to drive, make sure her license is valid, particularly if she is not a U.S. citizen. Find out if she is covered by your insurance policy.
- Clarify employment terms, including salary, overtime, raises, and benefits such as vacation and paid holidays, sick days, medical coverage, and Social Security deductions. You may also have other expenses, such as state disability insurance.

An Employer's Responsibilities

Once you start paying someone to take care of your child in your home, you have legal responsibilities as an employer. These include:

✔ *Taxing matters.* According to the so-called "nanny tax" act of 1994, if you pay a household employee more than $1,000 in a calendar year, you must make payment for Social Security, Medicare (FICA), and unemployment insurance (FUTA) taxes.

✔ *More taxing matters.* You must withhold Social Security and Medicare taxes from your employee's wages. If the employee asks you to, you can withhold federal income tax from his check as well, but you are not required to do so. You are required to provide your worker with a W-2 form by January 31, reporting the previous year's wages. To report the taxes and wages, you need to get an employer ID number, using form SS4.

✔ *Legal evidence.* The responsibility is on you to verify the legal working status of any employee. You are required to complete an I-9 form from the U.S. Immigration and Naturalization Service, and must actually see evidence of the individual's work eligibility: a U.S. passport, a Social Security card, an alien registration card, a green card, or a work permit. If you are caught hiring workers who do not have working status, you may face stiff fines.

EDUCATION

The right to free education is a cornerstone of American society, but it is often hard to sort out the duties and responsibilities that come with that right.

Who Gets a Free Education?

Every child living in the United States has the right to a free education. This historically has been true whether or not the child is a legal resident or English is her native language, although that has now been challenged in some states, notably California. In most states, the right to a free education continues through high school and until the student reaches the age of 21.

Perhaps surprisingly, the right to be educated is not established by the Constitution or the Bill of Rights. It has evolved over time as a matter of state law, supported by taxpayer dollars. In turn, all parents have a responsibility to make sure their children attend school, be it public or private, religious or nonsectarian. Attendance is compulsory until the age of 16, 17, or 18, depending on your state's law.

Parents may educate their children at home, but they must meet certain, sometimes stringent, requirements to do so. (See also "Educating Your Child at Home," page 126.) Parents who refuse to enroll their children in school or who do not ensure in some other way that their children are educated act in violation of state law and, in extreme cases, may face criminal prosecution.

ATTENDANCE

Although your child has a right to attend school, schools are not forced to accept students who have not been vaccinated against such illnesses as smallpox and diphtheria. Parents who refuse to have their children vaccinated are unlikely to find recourse through the courts, since most states maintain compulsory vaccination laws as a matter of public health policy.

Eligibility for attendance typically requires that the child and her parents or legal guardian reside within a district, which may be defined by the town, the neighborhood, or the community. Moreover, school officials are permitted to decide which schools local children will attend, based on such factors as school size and student population; the choice may not be the school closest to the child's home. Parents may make a request to transfer a child to another school within the local district, but school officials can reject it. Parents may also try to enroll their child in a school situated outside their commu-

Giving Your Child a Day Off

With the stroke of a pen, parents can excuse their children from school. Maybe Alice has a head cold and really should stay at home. Then again, maybe you decided to take her to your family reunion—and write a note saying she had a cold. A day's absence rarely leads to disputes with school authorities.

It grows more complicated, however, if you want to take your children on a two-week trip to Europe in the middle of the school year. State or local policies may set the ground rules for whether you can get such an excused absence.

If during informal discussions with teachers or administrators you can work out how the missed classwork or related exams can be made up, later or in advance, the school will often excuse the absence.

Should the school refuse your request and you take your children away anyway, they may face lowered grades or loss of course credits. Schools may turn to state laws or local school regulations concerning compulsory attendance to justify their action. (Some schools may also be motivated by the fact that they get federal grant monies based on attendance records.)

123

nity, but local officials can require the family to pay tuition if space is made available.

Absences from school are recognized as a reality of life. Children get sick, families sometimes get called away, and other special conditions occur whereby the parent and teacher must agree on the acceptability of the child's absence.

Students with unexcused absences, however, are considered truant. In such cases, particularly when unreasonable absences become habitual, court-appointed truant officers may require parents to explain the absences in court and even place them under bond to help ensure proper attendance. In extreme cases, habitual truants can be placed in juvenile reform schools.

Rights at School: A Primer

The right of free expression, established under the First Amendment, extends to students in school. The U.S. Supreme Court affirmed this in a 1969 decision, *Tinker* v. *Des Moines,* for Iowa students who wore black armbands to protest the Vietnam War. Free expression thus includes publishing newspapers and leaflets, distributing buttons, forming political clubs, and, of course, speech.

Free expression can be silenced, the Court ruled, only when it is "materially and substantially" disruptive to the work and discipline of the school. If you are uncertain about the legality of a school's action, particularly concerning censorship in school-financed newspapers, you or your child should seek a lawyer's advice.

SHORT HAIR AND UNIFORMS

Although hair and dress styles can be considered a form of expression, the courts have been split over the rights of students in public schools to dress as they please. Some states prohibit any regulation concerning hairstyles unless the school can demonstrate the rule's legitimate educational purpose or that the hairstyle results in a substantial disruption of the school's activities. In such instances, the school may contend that a hairstyle can distract other students or cause discipline problems. Other states permit hair regulations without requiring any specific educational purpose. Still others allow regulations based only on health and safety concerns.

In California, public schools can require students to wear uniforms as long as there is an opt-out clause and students will not be discriminated against for choosing to opt out. Uniforms must be provided for students who cannot afford them.

The equal protection clause established every student's right not to be discriminated against on the basis of race, religion,

---

YOUR RIGHT TO SEE SCHOOL RECORDS

In 1974, Congress passed the Family Educational Rights and Privacy Act that grants parents the right to see their children's school records if the school receives federal funding. The act, also known as the Buckley Amendment, requires the following:

1. Schools must give parents notice of their right to see records each year. School records include everything from grades and test scores to IQ test results, discipline records, and psychological evaluations.

2. Students who are over 18 have the right to examine their own records. Students under 18 can see their records if their parents request it in writing or if the school chooses to allow them to do so.

3. Records must be made available in a "reasonable period of time," and no more than 45 days after requested. Many states set shorter periods for releasing records.

4. If you find false or unfair information in a record, you can ask school authorities to change it. If they refuse, you are entitled to a formal hearing. Even if the hearing official rejects your request, you are entitled to include in the record a statement of your disagreement with the information.

or ethnic background. The Supreme Court's 1954 *Brown* v. *Board of Education* decision affirmed this when it ruled that racially segregated schools were by definition not equal. In recent years, the courts have frequently addressed discrimination on the basis of gender. Public schools cannot offer courses specifically for boys, for example. The courts have been divided about single-sex sports. Schools with only boys' teams in a particular sport may be required to allow both sexes to participate, although that right has often not been extended to include contact sports. Equal funding of girls' and boys' sports teams is not mandated either.

The First Amendment established the separation of church and state, and that is the basis for the Supreme Court's rulings that prayers and Bible reading should be prohibited in public schools. Instead of prayers, some states have legislated a moment of silence, but such laws have been judged unconstitutional if their intent is determined to be religious in nature rather than for some form of personal reflection.

When Your Child Is Disciplined

In 1975, the Supreme Court asserted students' right of due process—in layman's terms, the right to be treated fairly by government agencies—before any serious punishment can be carried out in a school. The court said that schools must follow "minimum procedures" before negative action can be taken against a student.

No national, uniform procedures exist with regard to discipline, but for the suspension or expulsion of a student, most schools provide oral or written notice of the charges to students or their parents, stating the evidence of the misdeed and noting the family's permission to respond to it. Many states have more-extensive formal procedures, particularly for expulsions and suspensions of more than 10 days. Some states match a specific range of disciplinary responses to specific misconduct. The more severe the punishment, the more likely the student is entitled to be represented by a lawyer at a hearing.

Suspension is typically considered a last resort, and schools are generally required to use alternative measures first. Suspensions that extend beyond what is deemed an emergency situation may be cause for review. Many states prohibit schools from expelling students on the principle that to bar them from school denies them the right to an education. Some states specifically limit the length of a suspension and specify the offenses for which it can be invoked. In Connecticut, for example, the limit is 180 days, and in Texas, the only ground for an expulsion is assault.

Injuries at School

Teachers and other school workers must act with reasonable care to protect students from injury. But injuries happen anyway, and some of them make schools, and perhaps their employees, liable for damages. Here are some legal issues that apply:

✔ *Reasonable care.* A teacher of a woodworking class using power tools can reasonably be expected to take extra precautions. Should he fail to give clear instructions and warnings and provide close supervision, he can be found negligent. If the school knew the teacher was unqualified to teach, it could be held liable as well.

✔ *Foreseeable danger.* Teachers are not presumed to be able to foresee extraordinary accidents. A math teacher in whose class a desk suddenly breaks and fractures a student's wrist is not likely to be held liable for injuries.

✔ *Student's contribution.* Even if a teacher or coach is found to be negligent, the school may argue that the student's deliberate and possibly careless action contributed to the injury—if the student, for example, was injured because he knowingly disobeyed a safety rule in shop.

✔ *Court awards.* If you prove negligence, a school or teacher may have to pay damages equal to the amount of loss the injury caused and additional money if malice, fraud, or reckless disregard for a student's safety is proved.

A whale ship was my Yale College and my Harvard.

HERMAN MELVILLE
Moby Dick

IS CORPORAL PUNISHMENT ALLOWED?

A few states bar corporal punishment in schools, but others allow it in their schools as an instrument of control, training, or education. In those states, the schools may be required to notify the parents, include an adult witness, or rely on the principal to carry out the punishment.

Should the corporal punishment seem excessive or unreasonable, however, it can justify criminal charges being brought against the teacher or educator who used it. Then various factors concerning the student and the offense would be evaluated to determine whether the punishment was reasonable.

When a Student Has Special Needs

Since 1975 the Education of the Handicapped Act (now renamed the Individuals With Disabilities Education Act) has required free and appropriate education to be provided for all children with a wide range of disabilities. These include hearing, speech, visual, and physical impairments, mental retardation, learning disabilities, emotional disturbances, and a number of other chronic or long-term health problems.

Besides education, the act also provides for related services to be made available. Speech therapy or physical therapy, medical diagnosis, vocational training, transportation, and parent counseling are among those mandated services.

Educating Your Child at Home

Every state has compulsory education laws to encourage able and productive citizens. Yet most states, with sometimes stringent restrictions, allow you to educate your children at home. If you want to pursue the idea of home schooling, here are some of the problems you may encounter:

• School officials may evaluate the teacher, the teaching methods, the curriculum, and the materials used in your home teaching program. This evaluation is designed to confirm that the home instruction is comparable, or substantially equivalent, to public schooling. It does not, however, have to be identical.

• School officials are permitted to assess the amount of time devoted to the home schooling and the tests and teaching materials used. The officials have an obligation to ensure that compulsory attendance laws are being fulfilled.

• School officials may request an occasional home visit to evaluate the "school setting." A New York State case affirmed the legitimacy of such visits, if infrequent and unobtrusive, to observe the nature and quality of the home education.

• Some states have laws restricting instruction of children to public or private schools, and although these laws have been challenged, courts are unlikely to find their restrictions unconstitutional. Courts in several states have insisted that such laws are valid because they are designed to ensure that children get an adequate education. To conform to such laws, parents in these states who want their children taught at home must establish their homes as private schools—which may in turn mean that the parents themselves have to become certified as teachers.

Under this law, schools must develop an "individualized educational plan" (IEP) for each child who is disabled or has other special needs. Reviewed annually by school officials and the child's teachers and parents, the plan should detail the child's educational performance level, services planned, and methods for measuring progress.

Getting Your Child in the Right Place

PROBLEM
Barbara thought that the best thing for her deaf son, Russ, was to attend regular public school. Aided by a sign-language interpreter, Russ could take any class, join clubs, and develop the skills he would need in a world that relies on speech and sound. But after a few months Barbara saw that Russ was having difficulty reading lips, did not speak clearly, and found the other children impatient with him. His self-esteem was low. Now Barbara wanted to switch him to a school for the hearing impaired, convinced that Russ needed a few years in classes with teachers and peers who consistently supported him. But because Barbara had consented to Russ's inclusion in a regular school and agreed to the school district's individualized educational plan (IEP) for him, school officials resisted her desire for change.

ACTION
First, school officials asked Barbara to consider letting Russ finish the school year where he was, at which time they would have to review his IEP anyway. But Barbara believed that was too long to wait and asked for a review right away. Again, the officials demurred, so Barbara exercised her right to demand an impartial hearing by the state department of education, which federal law says must take place within 45 days. The hearing official decided the boy's plight was serious enough to require quick action and ordered the school officials to transfer Russ immediately.

The law requires that parents receive written notice of the school's intentions and must give consent before the school can conduct any evaluation of the child's abilities or needs. In some cases, parents may also be able to have their child tested independently at the school's expense. Schools then must let the parents participate in the design of an IEP and, again, get their consent before placing the child in a special program. The law states that a child should be educated in the "least restrictive" environment. This practice, often called "mainstreaming," can lead to controversy if a mainstreamed child is disruptive in the classroom to the point that other students have trouble concentrating on their studies.

Special programs exist for gifted children as well as for those with handicaps. IQ and achievement tests are used to locate students for these programs. Since 1978, Congress has earmarked small amounts of money for gifted education after passing the Gifted and Talented Act. But most initiatives for gifted programs start with state and local efforts.

A Parent's Role in Designing an IEP

The "individualized education plan" (IEP) developed by your special-needs child's school will set the course for his education for the entire school year. Before signing off on a program, make sure to check the following:

✔ *The classroom.* Visit the classroom where your child will spend his days. Talk to teachers and faculty members to make sure the IEP will be properly implemented.

✔ *Goals.* The IEP should include clearly stated, measurable goals. For example, a goal could be for your child to learn her times tables by the end of the term.

✔ *Services.* Your child will receive only the services mentioned in the formal plan. Make sure it is specific, including for example, speech therapy twice a week and daily bus transportation to and from school.

✔ *Equipment.* Make sure the plan includes any equipment your child needs, such as braille textbooks for a blind student.

✔ *Your acceptance.* If you disagree with anything in the plan, ask the school to change it. If the school will not cooperate, you can ask for a hearing before an impartial hearing officer, and if that does not help, you can file a complaint with your state's department of education.

Parental Action

If your child is suspended and you feel the punishment is unwarranted, you can appeal the school's action. If your child is a slow learner and the school wants to place him in a special education class, you can reject its decision. In other matters, too, parents have recourse when they disagree with a school's action. But the law gives school officials substantial decision-making power, and a parent's ability to effect change is limited. It helps to know your legal rights.

On an individual level, you are entitled to examine your child's school records, something you may want to do at least once a year to determine whether the contents are fair and accurate. You also can take advantage of parent-teacher conferences to discuss your child's needs or your complaints. If dissatisfied with the teacher's response, you are entitled to take it up with the school's principal and, if the problem is serious enough, all the way up to the superintendent.

STRENGTH IN NUMBERS

On a broader level, you can join forces with other parents or groups like the Parent Teacher Association to pursue change affecting school policy. School board meetings must be open to the public, and parents have the right to be notified about them. At meetings, school boards can be petitioned, and question-and-answer sessions can provide a forum to raise issues.

Although parents have the right to take their grievances to court, the courts may be reluctant to circumvent a school district's authority over daily operations such as absenteeism, gross misconduct, or violation of laws or regulations. According to state and local law, state education officials and local school boards are responsible for choosing curriculum and texts, opening or closing schools, defining district boundaries, hiring and firing teachers and administrators, deciding on disciplinary codes, and settling disputes between parents and teachers.

Private Schools

Unlike public schools, private schools have the right to set standards specific to the kind of education and students they want. Unrestricted by the demands of public funding, they may, by and large, admit only females, males, or Roman Catholics, or require their students to wear uniforms and keep their hair short. They can set severe penalties for bad behavior and require high intellectual aptitude for admission. They can charge huge fees.

You may not want, or be able to afford, to send your child to private school. But if you are thinking of it, you should seriously consider your objectives and requirements. How intellectually demanding should the curriculum be? How open or traditional should the teaching methods be? Do you prefer a racially, economically, and ethnically diverse student body? Is it important that the school have a high percentage of students accepted into top universities?

ACCREDITATION

Find out if the school you are thinking about is accredited by a state or regional accreditation association. Accreditation requires higher standards than those set by state regulations; it is provided by periodic evaluations from a group of independent educators asked to judge the school's educational philosophy, methods, goals, and standards.

Of course, having found the right school, you will have to figure out whether you can afford it. While financial aid is widely available for colleges and universities, aid for private secondary education is more limited. Every school offers some scholarships, usually based on need and sometimes on merit. Most private schools do offer some financial aid, but you may have to calculate if you can afford one of the extended tuition-payment plans. Offered by the schools themselves or by banks or other lending institutions, these allow you to pay the tuition in monthly installments.

Paying for Higher Education

With annual bills that can run into tens of thousands of dollars, it is no wonder that many parents doubt they can afford to send their children to any college, public or private. Higher education has never cost more—but the competition among schools for good students as well as the opportunities for those students to land financial aid has never been greater.

Based on a formula set by Congress in 1986, the Congressional Methodology Need Analysis considers various factors in determining what portion of your resources can be contributed to your child's tuition: family income, family assets, living expenses, parents' age and marital status, number of children in the family and in college, and medical expenses. Most colleges require you to fill out the free application for federal student aid (FAFSA) or the family financial statement (FFS). Schools may ask you to fill out their own forms, also.

Your financial status is more complicated if you are divorced. Some schools consider only the income of the custodial par-

Reduce Your Worth to Get More Aid

Every family that applies for financial aid for college education is judged by the basic government formula for determining need. Parents are expected to make substantial contributions, as much as 47 percent of after-tax income. But there are legal ways to increase the amount of aid you can get.

✔ *Break the piggy bank.* Avoid putting large sums of money in savings for your children. The student has to pay a much higher percentage of her assets for college than the parent. She will be expected to spend part of her savings account on her education.

✔ *Put retirement funds into retirement accounts.* Put retirement savings in an IRA, a Keogh, or a 401(k) plan. The government aid formula does not consider them assets (although some colleges may call them assets in their analyses).

✔ *Don't wait too long.* Sell investments such as stocks or mutual funds the year before your child applies to college. Capital gains during the year she applies would be considered income, and you would be expected to pay a bigger chunk of the education cost.

✔ *Home sweet home.* Borrow money with a home equity loan rather than using credit cards. Mortgage debt reduces your net worth according to the aid formula; credit card debt does not.

ent. Others will consider the combined income of both parents. If you remarry, your new spouse's income may count when the school decides your child's need for financial aid.

WHERE THE MONEY COMES FROM

The aid system attempts to equalize families of widely disparate fortunes. It may be determined that you are capable of contributing $3,500 annually to your child's education or $10,000 a year. In either case, the aid package should make up the difference, whether the school costs $7,000 or $27,000 a year. A student aid package can be derived from a variety of sources:

- **Grants and scholarships.** This aid is essentially free money, with no responsibility to pay it back. Grants may come from federal or state sources or from the college's own funds. Scholarships usually come from the school itself and generally require excellence in academics, sports, or some other area that the school deems important.
- **Federal work-study.** This is a subsidy from the federal government providing funding for part-time work for students to offset the costs of tuition and/or living costs.
- **Student loans.** At most schools the largest source of support is student loans. These are generally subsidized by the state or federal government and carry much lower interest rates than regular unsecured loans. Moreover, students are not obligated to begin making payments or paying interest on these loans until they leave school or graduate.

Is This School on the Up-and-Up?

It could happen: You sign up for a course in a trade school and pay the fee, then discover that the school is not legitimate and cannot deliver what it promised; or, worse, that it has closed its doors altogether. Ask the right questions before you hand over your money:

• **Is the school certified?** This is good to know but be aware that while certification means the school has obtained a state license, in many states that may mean only that administrators filled out a few forms, paid a small fee, and, perhaps, bought a fire extinguisher and a smoke detector.

• **Is the school accredited?** Accreditation is the result of a more elaborate evaluation conducted by independent and respected educators who are trained to judge the educational quality of the school. Accreditation represents a meaningful stamp of approval.

• **What kind of background do the teachers have?** The school's instructors may have college degrees, but no practical experience in the trade you are studying. If so, you probably will not get the concrete, technical training you are looking for.

• **How long has the school been in business?** A school without a track record is a risk. You want to be sure that the school can deliver what it says it can, and you can determine that only if it has been operating for a number of years.

• **How have previous students fared in the job market?** If few of the school's students have actually found employment in their chosen field, that is a red flag. If the school is reluctant to give you such information or to put you in touch with previous students, think twice about attending.

DOMESTIC PARTNERSHIPS

Couples living together outside marriage have gained greater legal protection, but they still are denied the full benefits extended to married couples.

How Courts View Unmarried Couples

The U.S. Census Bureau estimates that 4.9 million adults live together in family-like arrangements outside of marriage. Unmarried couples were once stigmatized and existed in a kind of legal limbo, but in the last two decades their nontraditional arrangements have slowly gained support and protection from the courts. The 1976 *Marvin* v. *Marvin* case in California was a turning point.

When actor Lee Marvin and his live-in companion of some six years, Michelle Triola Marvin, broke up and he stopped supporting her, she sued him. She claimed that, in response to his oral promise for lifetime monetary support, she had given up her own career in order to become a full-time companion and homemaker.

The California Supreme Court's influential decision on the case asserted the right of unmarried couples to make contracts, written or oral. The court also stated that an "implied contract"—actions based on an unwritten agreement—can be applied to unmarried couples. As it turned out, the court decided that Michelle Triola Marvin had failed to prove her oral agreement with her partner and ultimately denied her "palimony," the term coined by her lawyer for support.

Nevertheless, the California court's decision opened the door to more liberal considerations toward unmarried couples in other states, most of which will enforce written contracts between unmarried partners. However, many states have passed anti-palimony statutes in response to the Marvin decision, requiring, for instance, that the agreement be in writing with certain formalities such as having witnesses present and the opportunity to consult an attorney (see also, "Put It in Writing," page 134).

SAME-SEX COUPLES

A growing number of municipalities and corporations have recognized the special nature and increasing societal acceptance of nontraditional domestic partnerships, particularly those of gay couples. They have allowed unmarried hetero-

---

Some Benefits of Tying the Knot

Unmarried couples have become more widely accepted, but the law still provides advantageous status to those who have made vows. The following are some of the benefits automatically extended to married couples:

✔ *Health benefits.* The right to get insurance coverage through your spouse's company policy, to authorize medical treatment, or to visit a spouse in the hospital (except where domestic partnerships are recognized).

✔ *Tax benefits.* The right to file joint tax returns and claim the spouse as a dependent or to qualify for rates allowed only to married couples.

✔ *Financial benefits.* The right to inherit from a spouse without a will, obtain an interest in pensions and retirement benefits, or take out an insurance policy on your partner.

✔ *Corporate benefits.* The right to take death or sick leave for a family member.

✔ *Leisure benefits.* The right to get discounts on family travel packages, share frequent-flier mileage and benefits, or get discount rates at health clubs or other private organizations.

COHABITATION OR COMMON-LAW MARRIAGE?

Many people assume that couples who live together for a long time inevitably become common-law husband and wife. However, only 13 states and the District of Columbia permit common-law marriages, although some states that do not permit common-law marriage will recognize those from states that do. While laws vary by state, to establish a common-law marriage, generally the following criteria must be met:

1. Both partners must meet the same basic legal requirements as for marriage: they must be single, in good health, and old enough to marry.

2. The couple must specifically present themselves in public as husband and wife by introducing each other as "my wife" and "my husband," for example, or by using the identifiers Mr. and Mrs., with the expressed intent to create a marriage.

3. The couple must live together for a specific period of time, which varies from state to state.

4. Some states recognize common-law marriage only if the couple began living together before a certain date.

sexual and gay couples some benefits previously available only to married couples. In New York City, Burlington, Vermont, and the District of Columbia, for example, unmarried domestic partners of city employees are eligible for health-care benefits. In Cambridge, Massachusetts, unmarried partners can get visiting rights at hospitals and jails, although to do so they must file a domestic-partnership declaration with the city.

Hawaii has been a leader in the move toward liberalizing the laws regarding same-sex marriages—a process that began in 1993 when the state's supreme court ruled that refusing to allow three gay couples to obtain a marriage license violated the state constitution's due-process clause. The decision is currently being challenged.

Eight states—California, Connecticut, Hawaii, Massachusetts, Minnesota, New Jersey, Vermont, and Wisconsin, as well as the District of Columbia—have all passed laws prohibiting discrimination on the basis of sexual orientation.

The Risks of Joint Assets

Many couples who live together outside of marriage may not adequately consider the financial ramifications of their arrangement. Perhaps they start out intending to keep their financial lives separate or think that having a small joint fund for household expenses will be enough to keep things running smoothly. But gradually they discover that living together can easily create more interdependence than they thought. Questions arise. Should we open a joint bank account? Co-sign a rental lease or a bank loan? Purchase an automobile?

While the law confers special rights and benefits concerning property and finances on married couples—particularly when a spouse dies or becomes incapacitated, or the marriage ends—unmarried partners lack the same protections. For example, if your partner's name is the only one on the title to your condo, even if you can prove that you contributed to the maintenance and mortgage costs for years, you might not be able to claim any ownership. Or if your partner suddenly dies without a will, his or her property will be distributed according to the laws of intestate succession. These generally specify that property is distributed to such blood or legal relations as spouses, children, parents, brothers, and sisters.

It is therefore important for unmarried couples to keep written records of all financial agreements. Without such written evidence of ownership or interest, there is very little chance that an unmarried partner will be able to assert her individual rights in court. If you open a joint bank account, for example,

keep a record of how much each of you puts into the account and how the money is spent to avoid disputes. Be aware that one person could empty the joint account at any time, and the other partner would have little or no recourse. A cohabitation agreement can help document who owns what and how assets are to be divided in the event that you break up. (See also "Put It in Writing," page 134.)

KEEP THINGS SEPARATE

Unmarried partners should also be aware of their liability for each other in joint agreements. Any jointly owned property, any jointly shared credit accounts, any co-signed lease makes both partners liable for payments. Let's say you both signed a lease or mortgage, pay 50-50 shares on it, and then your partner loses his job. You would become liable for the full amount of the money owed.

Unmarried partners should take special precautions when making purchases together. If you are buying a car, for example, will it be jointly titled? If so, both partners will be responsible for payments. If it is not jointly titled, an unmarried partner who owns the title could sell or take the car without the other partner's knowledge or agreement. Making a formal agreement from the outset can help avoid later problems.

If You Have a Child

Children born outside of marriage can be legally recognized as the offspring of both parents if the father asserts in writing that he is the father, the parents marry each other, the father openly acknowledges the child as his own and accepts him into his home, or the father is so-designated in a paternity action.

Once, children born out of wedlock were severely stigmatized and were cut off from benefits given children born during a marriage. They were limited in seeking financial support from their biological father, for example, or in sharing in his estate when he died. Today such a child is generally entitled to those rights as long as paternity can be proved. This is based on dozens of Supreme Court cases that invoked the equal-protection clause in the Constitution.

THE UNIFORM PARENTAGE ACT

More than a third of the states have attempted to move beyond the legitimacy issue by adopting the Uniform Parentage Act, which says that the parent-child relationship "extends equally to every child and to every parent, regardless of the marital status of the parents." Establishing paternity is a chief concern of

Who Gets Custody?

Unmarried parents who break up have an equal right to custody of their child if paternity has been acknowledged. The father does not have that right, however, unless he acknowledged paternity in writing or legitimized the child in some other way.

Unmarried parents can decide between themselves who gets custody of the child. Usually the courts will not question that decision unless the child's welfare is in doubt.

When parents cannot agree who will get custody of the child, courts recognize a concept in the case of children under five entitled "primary parent," which weighs in favor of the parent who has had primary responsibility for caring for the child's basic needs (food, clothing, hygiene, nursing, and so on).

In the United States these duties are still primarily assumed by mothers. Thus in the majority of cases, the mother becomes the custodial parent. But the final decision belongs to the judge who is responsible for determining the "best interests of the child."

the act, since paternity creates grounds for such rights as inheritance and child support and protects the father's rights in cases of custody and adoption. (See also "Adoption," page 106.) When a child's parents are not married to each other, paternity can be legally established if the father states in writing that he is the father. A father who denies his parenthood and the related financial responsibilities can, in the course of a paternity lawsuit, be made to take blood or genetic tests to evaluate his claim. (See also "Parenting," page 112.)

Like married parents, an unmarried mother and father have a legal duty to support, care for, and educate their children. So long as the partners can mutually determine how to handle these responsibilities, the courts generally will not become involved in their affairs. Exceptions can be made, however, in cases that involve rights of inheritance, or eligibility for social security, or welfare-benefits.

WHEN THE PARTNERSHIP FALTERS

When unmarried partners separate and cannot resolve the issues of child support, custody, and visitation rights between themselves, the courts will have to decide for them. For example, one parent, or a public agency such as the welfare department, can sue the other parent to obtain a court order establishing the level of child support to be paid. (See also "Divorce," page 135.) A noncomplying parent can be held in contempt of court and face stringent collection procedures.

Put It in Writing

Unmarried partners who live together without any written agreements risk getting saddled with debts and losing property. Since oral agreements are hard to prove in court, it is best to clarify the terms of the relationship in writing. Consider drafting the following types of agreements:

• **Written agreements.** An informal agreement can lay out the basic details of your arrangement, from who bought the stereo to who pays the rent. This document, while not enforceable in court, can clarify expectations. Written records of joint property, household finances, and debt become critical if you split up. A formal cohabitation agreement can pin down who pays what for the mortgage, taxes, and maintenance related to real estate. It can also define how property will be handled if the relationship ends. Consult a lawyer for advice.

• **Parenting agreement.** Not necessarily enforceable in court, a parenting agreement can detail support obligations and responsibilities for decision-making regarding the care of a child.

• **Medical proxy.** A medical proxy enables unmarried partners to take responsibility for medical decisions, consult with doctors, and visit in the hospital should the other partner become sick or injured.

• **Durable power of attorney.** This type of agreement allows a partner to take over financial decision-making should the other become mentally or physically incapable.

• **Will.** A will helps ensure that your partner receive your property when you die. Without a will, the courts automatically make your next of kin the recipient of your assets. Even if you have a will, it may be contested, so make sure the will is carefully written and properly executed.

DIVORCE

Even though no-fault divorce has helped reduce abusive, name-calling battles, divorce is almost always an emotionally trying experience.

Ending Your Marriage

The statistics speak for themselves: one out of every two marriages will end in divorce. To be sure, divorces are now easier to get, and the process poses far fewer legal hurdles, but rarely, if ever, is a divorce painless. By clearly understanding your options and obligations, you can reduce the difficulties of ending your marriage.

ANNULMENT

Not all failed marriages are dissolved by divorce. Annulment is a way of legally invalidating a marriage as if it had never existed. Annulments have become less common as divorce has lost its social stigma and no-fault divorce has simplified the process. In most states the courts will grant an annulment if you can prove that one of the following conditions existed at the time of the wedding: one partner was underage, incurably impotent, legally insane, or married to someone else; or one partner forced the other into the marriage under duress or misled the other by fraud.

Duress may involve the use of violence, blackmail, or intimidation. Fraud means that one partner concealed relevant information, such as drug addiction, criminal convictions, venereal disease, or homosexuality.

To get an annulment, you should seek the help of an attorney. Each state sets time requirements for filing an annulment, ranging from 90 days to four years, depending on the grounds. Usually only the parties to the marriage can file for annulment, but in some instances parents or guardians can do so.

SEPARATION

Some couples separate to test whether they really want to divorce. Some separate legally and never live together again, but for religious or economic reasons never divorce. Other couples—with children or debt or serious financial issues—use a separation to settle their affairs in writing, as soon as possible, to avoid having the divorce become a long and costly court battle. Whatever the reason, once you have completed a voluntary separation agreement, the divorce process is significantly simplified. For your document to be binding, a petition must be

---

1̣2̣3̣...
THE SEPARATION AGREEMENT

A separation agreement is the blueprint for a divorce. It resolves in writing your legal concerns, sets out a legal plan for living apart, and can be a framework for your divorce decree. You and your spouse can write a first draft, but you should also get a lawyer's help. Here are the general areas your agreement should address:

1. Distribution of assets. This aspect of the agreement concerns the way assets will be distributed. This may include furniture, photographs or wedding presents, as well as cars, money, investments, and real estate.

2. Children. This involves not only the question of custody, but also child support, visitation rights, medical costs, housing, and education plans.

3. Spousal support. The intimidating list of financial matters your agreement should deal with runs from insurance to income tax—and who pays for what. If alimony is to be paid, the terms should be decided. The agreement requires analysis and disclosure of both spouses' assets, including pension funds and financial investments and should also spell out details concerning inheritance rights.

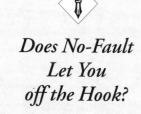

Does No-Fault Let You off the Hook?

You may file for no-fault divorce, but that does not mean judges will ignore questions of fault when determining property division, custody, and support payments. About half the states permit judges to consider the emotional pain or suffering, such as physical abuse or mental cruelty, one spouse inflicted on the other.

✔ *Adultery's price.* Courts in some states, including Georgia, Louisiana, North Carolina, and Virginia, will not award spousal support to anyone guilty of adultery.

✔ *Sex and custody.* During some custody battles, judges have been known to take a dim view of a parent, particularly the mother, if she is involved in sexual relations with another person. The relationship may cost her custody of her child or children.

✔ *Discreet conversation.* Some states require couples, particularly those with children, to speak with a marriage counselor, social worker, or other professional before they will grant a divorce. Other states require a separation or waiting period.

filed with the court, and a court order must be signed by a judge.

You may file for divorce without having legally separated in most states. But you will probably be required to live physically apart for a period of time, ranging from six months to three years, depending on the state in which you file.

GROUNDS FOR DIVORCE

Historically, a divorce was possible only if there was evidence that one partner had irreparably harmed the marriage through "fault." Today, every state has no-fault laws, although most states will grant fault divorces. The grounds vary, but in most states, "fault" includes adultery, criminal conviction, extreme cruelty, desertion, habitual drunkenness, or impotence.

Some states also consider the following as grounds: fraud, duress, insanity, nonsupport, pregnancy from a man other than the husband at the time of marriage, and disappearance. In some states, support from one spouse may be reduced or eliminated if the other spouse is found to be at fault.

The large majority of divorces these days are no-fault. They became widespread in the 1970's when changing state laws recognized that some couples were creating false evidence to get a fault divorce and individuals were being forced by the law to stay together when they could no longer get along. No-fault permits couples to do away with trumped-up fault charges and to simply state, as grounds, irreconcilable differences, mutual consent, or irretrievable breakdown of the marriage.

Most states require that you be a resident of the state for at least six months, and some, for up to a year, before you can file for divorce. Nevada permits divorces six weeks after residency is established. Some couples who are in a hurry may fly to the Dominican Republic or another foreign country with rapid divorce procedures. But don't expect the divorce to be legally valid if you get a foreign divorce on your own in an attempt to break away from a spouse who refuses consent.

CAN YOU DO IT YOURSELVES?

Some couples seek to simplify their divorce—and minimize the cost—by doing it themselves. Using a do-it-yourself kit, although certainly cheaper than hiring a lawyer, should be considered only by spouses who both consent to a no-fault divorce, have been married a short time, have little property to divide, are both working and in good health, and have no children.

In those cases, the process is relatively simple. One spouse initiates the divorce and sends a notice to the other through the court. The receiving spouse has 20 to 30 days to respond. Then the spouse who initiated the divorce will appear in court, state the circumstances of the case, file a petition for the dissolution of the marriage, and if there is property, file a property settlement. Both spouses must sign their property settlement before the court signs a decree of dissolution, which officially makes the divorce final.

One Lawyer or Two?

PROBLEM
Max and Dana Diamond, though divorcing, thought they could avoid conflict and settle their differences themselves. Yet after they began making outlines concerning their property, debts, spousal support, and visitation plans for their baby girl, Lillie, Max realized how complicated it all was and hired a lawyer. At first, Dana agreed to this, but she gradually began to feel that Max was trying to take advantage of her, and decided she should hire her own lawyer. But she had already verbally accepted, although reluctantly, most of the terms suggested by Max and his lawyer. She also knew how angry Max would be when she announced her intention. What should she do?

ACTION
Even non-adversarial couples frequently hire two lawyers to be sure that each understands his or her rights and that someone is advocating their individual interests. The moment Dana felt uncertain about whether her interests were being protected, she should have hired her own lawyer. As it was, since they had not actually signed anything, she still could renegotiate. Braving Max's displeasure, she hired an attorney recommended by a friend, and they began their negotiations all over again. In the end, the basic points of their settlement did not change much, but Dana went through the divorce proceeding confident that she was getting a fair agreement.

When looking for an attorney, it is best to choose someone experienced in matrimonial law. You are entitled to a written statement concerning fees, and you can also ask for a periodic report of expenses. Especially complicated and protracted divorces can generate huge legal fees. You should ask what will happen if you run out of money before your divorce is completed. (See also YOUR RIGHTS IN ACTION, page 479.)

Settling Finances and Property

Every state has its own guidelines to determine how a divorcing couple should equitably divide their property. These establish broad parameters, and judges will use them if you, your spouse, and attorneys cannot reach agreement outside of court. For couples without children, the hardest task will involve assessing their joint and separate holdings and deciding who gets what.

Nine states are community property states: Arizona, California, Idaho, Louisiana, Nevada, New Mexico, Texas, Washington, and Wisconsin. In these states, each spouse has the right

123

ORDERS THAT RESTRAIN AND PROTECT

Sometimes in the upheaval of divorce, assets disappear and tempers flair. You can seek a temporary restraining order to protect your assets until final division or an order of protection to safeguard yourself and your children.

1. If you suspect that your spouse might try to remove joint assets—money in a joint account or a safe-deposit box, for example—you can get a restraining order to prohibit the removal, sale, or transfer of that property.

2. If your spouse asks other parties—such as a financial manager, a broker, a banker, or anyone who has access to your assets—to help gain control of your assets, the restraining order can be served on them too.

3. If your relationship has been violent, or you feel you or your children might be threatened with physical harm during the period of divorce or separation, you should seek an order of protection. In most states, victims-advocacy groups or court personnel can help you file the papers to get protection. Your spouse can be restrained from coming near you, your house, place of work, school, or other defined location. You might also be awarded temporary exclusive occupancy of your shared home. If the order is violated, your spouse can be arrested and jailed.

to half of all property acquired during the marriage, without consideration as to whether each spouse equally shared in purchasing the assets. Both spouses are also equally liable for all debts. Property that is brought into the marriage, is obtained by one spouse through inheritance, or is received as a gift can remain separate.

The rest of the states are noncommunity, or so-called equitable-distribution, states. In these states, judges determine what is an equitable or fair distribution of the marital property, generally including everything except what was brought into the marriage, inherited, or received as a gift. To do this, judges generally employ certain guidelines:

- The length of the marriage;
- The age, health, and future earning potential of each spouse;
- The contribution that each spouse has made to the marital assets, including taking care of the home and children;
- The needs of the parent with custody of the children;
- Other financial prospects, including investments and savings.

Can Mediation Settle Your Differences?

Mediation can offer divorcing couples a less harrowing way to try to settle their differences than fighting it out in court. Mediation uses a neutral third party trained in conflict resolution to facilitate communication about and resolution of disputes over property, custody, or any other unresolved area. It is not the answer for everyone, however. Can mediation work for you?

• **An amicable parting.** Maybe you have already worked out child custody, most of the property issues, even who gets the beloved pet. But, because you are living 100 miles apart, you cannot agree on a visitation plan. Or, with little shared property, you have agreed on a basic separation arrangement but need help fine-tuning the details. The mediator can help clarify your options.

• **No substitute for lawyers.** Perhaps you want to keep down your costs, and see mediation as an alternative to a lawyer. But mediation is not a substitute for legal advice, even though with the court's final approval, it can become legally binding. The mediator will not represent your interests in particular (her job is to remain neutral), nor is she necessarily a legal expert. Furthermore, some states require each party in mediation to have a lawyer who works with the mediator to arrive at a mutually agreeable arrangement.

• **Future benefits.** Couples who use mediation are generally more satisfied than those who do not, and there are fewer post-decree problems with mediation settlements. In mediation, the parties "own" the agreement and have tailored it to fit their situation.

• **Not for the abused.** If you are a victim of domestic violence, some states prohibit mediation as the means to work out a divorce. Other states in which mediation is mandated may allow you to forgo this face-to-face encounter. Because it depends on conversation and negotiation, mediation can be a mistake if you are in a particularly aggressive or coercive relationship.

• **Not a substitute for therapy.** You should not look on the process of mediation as an opportunity to air grievances, to deal with lingering anger or bitterness against your soon-to-be ex-spouse. Mediation is no place for this kind of behavior, and the process will probably break down if you or your spouse enter into it in this spirit.

• **May be a money saver.** If a court has mandated mediation, the service may be free or nominal in cost. Even if it is not, you may spend fewer hours with your lawyers—and incur smaller bills—if you try mediation before going to court.

With the help of an attorney, you can assess your holdings and appraise their value. But you may want to complete as much of this time-consuming process as possible before you spend long, billable hours with a lawyer. You will need to gather together financial records, including bank statements, tax returns, insurance policies, and deeds, plus pension, retirement, and profit-sharing plans. You should also make an inventory of physical property, such as television sets and stereo systems, furniture and jewelry, kitchen appliances, cars, and, of course, your home itself.

KEEPING A HOUSE A HOME

The sticky issue of who gets the house gets more complicated when young children are involved. If one parent receives custody of them, the courts, to minimize disruption in their lives, may grant that parent possession of the house and mandate that it not be sold until the children reach a certain age. At that point the house may be sold and the funds divided, assuming the spouse with custody has not already bought out the other.

A divorcing couple without children or with older children might agree to hold on to their house until the real estate market improves. No matter who lives in the house, your court order or separation agreement should detail who is responsible for the monthly mortgage, maintenance costs, taxes and deductions, and repairs. And, even though you might expect a 50-50 split when the house is sold, a judge may decide in this case that "equitable" does not mean equal shares.

Your attorney can help clarify the tax consequences of your divorce on homes and other property matters. While you may or may not benefit from such changes, they should be incorporated into the final terms of your settlement.

Spousal Support

Into the 1970's, the awarding of alimony was a natural extension of the traditional marriage arrangement. The husband was the breadwinner and provider; the wife was the homemaker and caretaker of the children. If the marriage ended and alimony was awarded, it was the wife who got it—usually for as long as she or her former husband lived (or until she remarried). Today, the law aims to be gender-neutral, allowing either spouse to claim the need for alimony, depending on who has the greater income or wage-earning capacity. Statistics demonstrate clearly that the living standard of the spouse with custody of the children will drop precipitously.

Alimony, also known as "spousal support" or "rehabilitative maintenance," is rarely awarded for a lifetime anymore,

Joint Credit Card Debt: Who Pays?

Like many couples, you and your spouse may have tangled over the credit card bills every month. Now that you have decided to call it quits, be sure you do not simply put that memory out of your mind. Old debts, like new ones, can be a continuing financial burden.

If you are worried that your spouse may run up new bills with unused credit, contact the credit card company immediately and ask it to close the account. Generally the creditor will demand that you pay off the balance first, but you can ask that the card be made inactive in the meantime.

Credit card debt, like other joint marital property, is a shared responsibility. So you and your spouse must work out how it will be paid. You can sell off joint property and apply the proceeds, or one of you can pay the debt in exchange for a greater share of the property. You may decide to split it all down the middle, but be aware that if your partner declares bankruptcy later, you will be left holding the bill.

Furthermore, a divorce decree will not protect you from debt collection if credit was granted to you jointly, even if the court has assigned your spouse sole responsibility for a particular debt; the creditor can still collect from either one of you. If you end up paying a bill assigned to your ex-spouse, you may have to go back to court to force your ex-spouse to reimburse you.

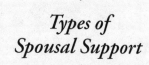

Types of Spousal Support

Alimony often comes in the form of a weekly or monthly check, but there are several other ways of arranging spousal support.

✔ *Lump-sum payment.* Some couples agree to a single lump-sum payment based on a set number of inflation-adjusted years. Once paid, both sides can call it quits if no children are involved. It is a gamble for both sides, however—the recipient cannot go back for more money, while the payer might see the former spouse remarry a year later.

✔ *Property settlement.* Not everyone can afford a large lump-sum payment. You can agree instead to exchange property such as the house, stocks, or the new car.

✔ *Anticipate the IRS.* Spousal maintenance is deductible for the payer, but is taxable income to the recipient. Your monthly support check may be enough, but calculate how much the IRS will take.

✔ *Pension benefits.* Depending on the length of your marriage and your age, you may be entitled to pension and Social Security benefits under your former spouse's accounts.

✔ *Life insurance.* Usually your right to receive spousal support dies with your ex-spouse—although your need for it may not. Consider negotiating for an insurance policy on your ex-spouse's life.

except where there has been a marriage in excess of 20 years with a traditional division of labor—one partner is a wage earner and the other a homemaker. Several states—including Delaware, Indiana, and Kansas—have mandatory time restrictions for alimony. Usually it will not extend beyond a period comparable to the length of the marriage. In general, judicial decisions reflect the assumption that a spouse needs support only for a specific period of time while getting back on his or her feet. Whether or not this assumption is valid, the courts generally consider the following in determining alimony:

- The length of the marriage;
- The earning capacity of both spouses and their ability to pay;
- The age and health of each spouse;
- The work experience, skills, and education of each;
- The couple's standard of living during the marriage.

If you are awarded spousal support, you may be offered a choice between one lump-sum payment or periodic payments. Each option has its risks. Should you find at a later time that the lump sum is inadequate to cover your needs, the courts are highly unlikely to add to the earlier agreement. Spouses paid periodically, on the other hand, often receive late checks or no checks at all. If you are the one making payments, you might try tying the amount of the payments to your own fluctuating financial status or that of your spouse. The payments would rise when you earn significantly more, for example, or go down should you lose your job.

There may be a late-payment penalty built into your support agreement, but you still might have a tough time collecting your payments. This is a common problem, along with unpaid child-support payments. Some spouses incorporate clauses to help secure payment. These might include a provision permitting the posting of a bond or garnishment of wages.

Child Support

Parents are responsible for supporting their minor children, and divorce does not end that responsibility—although, unfortunately, the noncustodial parent, usually the father, frequently acts as though it does. Unpaid child support represents billions of dollars annually, a fact that has enormous social consequences.

In 1984, the Uniform Marriage and Divorce Act expressly mandated that every state establish basic levels of child support—that is, the cost of food, clothing, and shelter. But those minimum standards vary, and the courts may set a significantly higher level of support in individual cases, depending primarily on the ability of the parent to pay and the perceived needs of the child. Parents negotiating support agreements should consider additional expenses such as health insurance for medical and dental costs, child care for a working custodial parent, schooling, and even camp or other hobby-related activities.

A FOCUS ON ENFORCEMENT

A court will intervene in a divorce settlement if it feels the child-support arrangement does not meet certain standards. State formulas for support payments generally fall into three categories: amounts based solely on the noncustodial parent's income; amounts based on the income of both parents, either their gross or net income; and amounts that establish a basic subsistence for each parent before allocating the remaining resources. Check with an attorney or the local office of child support for the guidelines in your state.

Federal and state laws are focusing more and more on increasing compliance with child-support orders. The Family Support Act of 1988 requires employers to withhold wages of delinquent noncustodial parents. Under this act, a local child-support-enforcement agency can help a mother locate a non-paying missing father, establish paternity, and get and enforce support orders. Punishments for nonsupport will likely continue to get stiffer.

If the noncustodial parent of a child is in arrears, the custodial parent is entitled to a court hearing to request back payments or authorize the seizure of assets to pay off the support owed. If the delinquent parent cannot be located or has no income or assets, there is not much to be done about getting back payments.

If the delinquent parent has a steady income or sufficient funds, however, the court can issue an order to his employer to withhold money from his wages, or a judge may attach funds the delinquent parent may have in savings accounts, stocks, or other assets. A delinquent parent whose reasons for nonpayment are not valid can be held in contempt of court and even be jailed in very aggravated cases until payment is made.

MODIFYING THE SUPPORT ORDER

In some cases, a judge may alter a child-support order if there is a significant change of circumstances in the status of either parent. Such changes might include a significant increase or decrease in one parent's income; increased expenses, such as for a new child in the household; a change in the child's needs; or the loss of a job. To have the original order modified, the need for change as well as supporting evidence must be presented at a court hearing.

Finding a Deadbeat Parent

The United States is a big country, and finding a father who has skipped out without making his child-support payments can be a daunting task. Still, there are ways to track him down. (More and more women now pay child support, it is true, but the vast majority of delinquent parents are fathers.)

Armed with the name, Social Security number, and an existing support order, your state child-support-enforcement agency can contact the federal Parent Locator Service. The service can consult records in the Department of Defense, National Personnel Records Center, the Social Security Administration, and the Veterans Administration.

Locally, your state child-support-enforcement department can search records of motor vehicle registration, unemployment insurance, state income tax, and correctional facilities for information.

You can also hire an investigator—but it's best to do so only after other options are exhausted. Try to arrange to pay the investigator on a contingency basis to provide incentive and to protect yourself from paying more than you collect.

If you find the deadbeat, consult a lawyer or your local welfare or child-support-enforcement unit. They may be able to help you get a court order to force the delinquent parent to pay what he owes or have his wages garnisheed.

Rebecca Shipley
1665 Coolidge Street
Phoenix, Arizona 52210

June 29, 1995

Mr. Martin Shipley
555 Mesa Avenue
Phoenix, Arizona 52210

Dear Martin:

This letter is a reminder that you are behind in your support payments for our child.

As stipulated in our final decree dated April 10, 1994, ❶ you are required to pay $350 by the 7th day of each month. ❷ As of today, you are 22 days late. ❸ You also know that the decree stipulates a late penalty of $50 for each month you are behind. In total, then, you are now $400 in arrears. ❹

According to the terms of the court's child-support order, your wages may be withheld if payments fall 30 days into arrears. I want to avoid involving the court again to resolve this. But you know that I very much need this money to provide the proper care for our child, Molly. Please take care of this as soon as possible before the problem becomes larger and other enforcement efforts become necessary. ❺

Sincerely,

Rebecca

Putting Pressure on Your Ex

If your ex-spouse has gotten behind in his child-support payments, act swiftly to avoid bigger problems later on. Start with a letter like this one. Specifically: **1.** Make note of the date of the final divorce decree, which is useful information should this letter be handed over to a judge as evidence later on; **2.** Include details of the decree to preclude any misunderstanding with your ex-spouse (and to jog the judge); **3.** State the exact amount your ex-spouse is behind, including any penalty; **4.** Carefully calculate the total; **5.** Make it clear that you are acting in good faith, that you prefer to handle the problem amicably. You do not want an angry letter to turn a temporary situation into a permanent problem. You might give your ex-spouse a chance to explain why he is behind, but don't let him forget that he has an enforceable, commitment to you and his child.

Child Custody and Visitation

The courts are charged with the responsibility for establishing child custody according to the "best interests of the child." But too often custody disputes between acrimonious parents become emotionally exhausting tugs of war. In the best circumstances, divorcing parents decide between themselves on a reasonable plan for custody and visitation.

This agreement is then put in writing—with schedules, financial obligations, and so forth—for the court's approval. Couples may want to try, or may be required to use, mediation, arbitration, or other resources to help resolve impasses before the plan is presented to a judge for final approval.

SOLE OR JOINT CUSTODY?

When the court is called upon to weigh the best interests of the child, sole custody is most likely to be awarded to one parent. Some states rely heavily on information about which parent has been the "primary caretaker," that is, who has provided the day-to-day child-rearing. In today's society, this most often has been the mother. Most states have the right to appoint a social worker, investigator, or even an independent attorney to provide the court with a report on the family. Some states require parents to meet with a court-monitored counselor, who then prepares a custody evaluation to aid the judge in making a decision.

Although there is conflicting evidence concerning what custody arrangement is really best for the development of the child, several states now affirmatively support joint custody. Courts distinguish joint legal custody from joint physical custody. In joint legal arrangements, both parents must jointly make major decisions about the child's health, education, and religion. Where parents share joint physical custody, the child may spend significant time living in each parent's home, or in rare cases, the parents will take turns living in the home where the child resides permanently.

A BALANCING ACT

Most states require that the parents spell out exactly how they will implement such a joint arrangement, which requires constant communication and interaction between them. Other states will not finalize the joint custody until the parents have shown it can work. In a growing number of states (such as California), a court order may prohibit a custodial spouse from moving more than 100 miles away from the noncustodial parent unless she has a compelling reason to do so.

ASSESSING THE CHILD'S BEST INTERESTS

If parents cannot decide on child-custody and visitation arrangements, the courts must determine the "best interests of the child." It is a difficult job with wide room for interpretation. Here are six factors judges may consider:

1. Who is providing primary care? The courts will consider which parent can best provide day-to-day care.

2. What does the child really need? Maybe the child is emotionally troubled and needs a lot of attention. Dad often travels for work. Mom freelances at home—and gets custody because of that.

3. Are Mom and Dad healthy? The courts are unlikely to grant custody to a parent who is physically ill or mentally unstable.

4. What about siblings? Judges resist splitting up brothers and sisters, especially when they are close.

5. Should the child leave home? Divorce is hard enough on children, and the courts hesitate to make them adjust to a new home, school, and neighborhood as well. If Mom plans to move away, a court might decide that Dad can offer more stability.

6. What does the child say? A child under 10 is unlikely to be asked his or her preference. But in many states a teenager's opinion (given privately) may be considered.

What Are the Rights of Grandparents?

Grandparents are sometimes recognized by the courts as being legally entitled to visit their grandchildren. In states that grant these rights, the inherent value of children maintaining contact with their grandparents is recognized.

These rights apply whether they are parents of the custodial parent or the noncustodial parent. Usually, however, the grandparents spend time with their grandchildren if they are the parents of the custodial parent (that is, maternal grandparents spend time with their grandchildren when the kids are with their mother).

Situations may arise in which the custodial parent does not want grandparents to visit. Grandparents are not legally entitled to visit if a parent objects unless a court awards visitation (or a state law provides otherwise).

A court may deny grandparents visitation rights if it decides that visitation would not be in the best interests of the child—if, for example, the request is an attempt to harass an ex-daughter- or son-in-law, or if the grandparent has a drug or alcohol problem.

Until recently, some state courts allowed dissatisfied parents to reopen custody cases decided in another state. This had the effect of encouraging kidnapping by frustrated parents who hoped that another jurisdiction might return custody to them. The Parental Kidnapping Act of 1980 requires state courts to abide by child-custody decrees issued in other states. Sneaking your child across state lines is now a criminal violation. Should you fear or face this, contact a lawyer immediately.

VISITATION

In the best circumstances, divorcing parents include their agreed-upon plan for visitation in the divorce settlement or decree. They can detail the length and the frequency of visits—for instance, every other weekend plus certain holidays. Such an agreement is preferable to leaving the decision up to a judge.

When the parents cannot agree, the courts will decide visitation rights for the noncustodial parent and include the plan in a visitation order. The court may be asked to intervene, particularly after a bitter divorce or custody battle, if the custodial parent continues to refuse to abide by the order. If visitation becomes a problem, these are things you can do:

- Document refused or missed visits and their circumstances;
- Write a letter to the custodial parent, stating your concerns;
- Contact a mediator, social service worker, or lawyer to act as an intermediary;
- Make sure to continue paying any support payments, even if visitation is denied;
- Request that a counselor talk to your child if she refuses to see you;
- Ask the court to reconsider the custody and visitation arrangement if the refusal continues;
- Obtain a court order enforcing your visitation rights, but only as a last resort.

If you are the custodial parent and your ex-spouse is abusive or there is another good reason to refuse visitation, you can ask the court to terminate visitation rights or provide for visits to be supervised. If your former spouse refuses to visit, the courts cannot force the issue. You might, however, be able to get the court to order an increase in your child-support payments to offset the loss of the noncustodial parent's caretaking services during regular visitations.

REPORTING CHILD ABUSE

If you suspect physical or sexual abuse of your child by her parent, you can deny visitation while you talk to a lawyer, clergy person, or mental health professional. Lawyers and the clergy are not legally obliged to contact investigating authorities. Most states have mandatory reporting laws that require certain professionals (such as police officers, mental health professionals, and teachers) to report suspected abuse.

A report of child abuse can lead to criminal charges being filed and even imprisonment. Reporting mere suspicions of abuse is a dramatic measure, however, and you may want to have a confidential conversation with your attorney.

After the Divorce Is Final

In most states, unless fraud was involved, there is no right to modify your property-settlement agreement, although if your ex-spouse agrees in writing to changes, the court will in most cases approve them. A judge might consider extending spousal support beyond the agreed-upon termination date, but judges generally are unwilling to grant spousal support if you did not originally ask for it.

Child-support and custody and visitation issues are modifiable under certain circumstances until your child reaches the age of majority. Both a custodial parent seeking an increase in support payments and a noncustodial parent unable to pay can file a petition for a hearing to show why a change is needed. Changing a custody ruling is much harder. You must show a significant change of circumstances and rebut a presumption that favors the custodial parent's retention of custody.

Happiness in marriage is entirely a matter of chance.

JANE AUSTEN
Pride and Prejudice

Starting Over: Changing Your Personal Records

With a certified copy of your divorce decree in hand, you are ready to begin a new life. And since you are in effect establishing a new identity as well, you want to be sure to make the necessary changes on various personal and legal documents to avoid any troubles later.

• **Property records.** Record documents for transfer of ownership or interest in real property with the county recorder's office. This may include the deed to your home if it was jointly owned during your marriage. You may also have to change the title to your car with the state Department of Motor Vehicles.

• **Name change.** If you decide to take back your maiden name or otherwise change your name, notify all the institutions and firms that have your old name on file, such as the Social Security Administration; the Department of Motor Vehicles if you hold a driver's license; all banks where you have accounts; credit card companies; and stores whose charge cards you hold.

• **Joint bank accounts.** Close and divide joint bank and investment accounts as agreed in your property settlement.

• **Creditors.** Inform your creditors—banks, credit card companies, and so on—as to who is responsible for any debts that are outstanding from your married days. If you are not responsible for the debts, ask the creditors to remove your name from the account.

• **Beneficiaries.** Check the beneficiaries of pension plans and insurance policies and make necessary changes. If you want to alter the way your estate is to be settled, don't forget to have a new will drawn up and executed.

REMARRIAGE

The second time around you know more. But to make it work, additional obligations demand that you understand your options and responsibilities.

Should You Combine Assets?

Being careful about finances is important in every marriage, but particularly in a remarriage when your former spouse and children from a previous marriage require continuing support. One important decision will be whether to combine all resources and file joint income tax returns with your new partner. Consider the following:

✔ *Spousal support.* Your former spouse is entitled to sue for increased spousal support. Your and your new spouse's combined incomes and expenses will be evaluated.

✔ *Child support.* A stepparent's income, even when jointly held, is rarely considered in resetting child support.

✔ *Debts.* Money you put into a joint account could be at risk if your new spouse has lingering debts.

✔ *Inheritance.* Your new spouse is entitled to a share of your combined assets, as are dependent children from this and any previous marriages. To maintain control over how your estate is to be divided, you need to rewrite your will.

How Remarrying Can Affect Your Finances

More than a million marriages a year are remarriages, an encouraging statistic for many who are divorced and widowed. But it is a sobering reality that remarriages, often weighed down by complicated responsibilities to both a new family and a previous one, are even more likely to end in divorce than first marriages. Even if you are entering into a second marriage without children or financial obligations to your previous spouse, you will be faced with the challenge of coordinating complex new domestic arrangements.

If you currently depend on spousal support, be prepared to forgo that support if you have not negotiated an exclusion in your original divorce decree. Typically, such payments cease when you remarry. If you currently pay spousal support, it is highly unlikely that it will be reduced, even if you can provide evidence that your new marriage cuts into your ability to pay. Also, in many states the courts will consider your new spouse's income in assessing your responsibility.

INSURING BOTH BROODS

With the additional responsibilities of a new family, you will need to reevaluate your life insurance coverage. Perhaps you can be carried on your new spouse's health insurance plan—or vice versa. You can change the primary beneficiary of a life insurance policy to your new spouse, but a stepparent is usually under no legal obligation to provide for your children in the event of your death or otherwise.

To ensure that both your new spouse and your children from a previous marriage will be provided for, you may have to take out a second policy—one that will benefit your new family—and keep the existing policy that protects your children from a previous marriage and perhaps your obligations to your former spouse according to your divorce settlement. Also, with two families depending on you, you may need to increase your disability insurance.

Older people who want to remarry are especially sensitive

to the prospect of losing assets that they—and perhaps a deceased spouse—spent years accumulating. Or, their children may resent a new spouse's arrival. Legally, they have a reason to be concerned: if there is no premarital agreement a spouse cannot be disinherited and can make a claim of one-third to one-half of an estate.

Can You Protect Your Inheritance?

PROBLEM
Betty Oliver, a widow, named her only daughter, Jackie, as the sole heir in her will. But after she decided to accept Joe Anders' proposal and marry again, she worried that once she was married to Joe, her daughter Jackie's inheritance might be jeopardized.

ACTION
Although she trusted Joe completely, Betty asked a lawyer how she could make sure Jackie was her sole heir. The solution was a contract or premarital agreement between Betty and Joe in which he waived his statutory inheritance rights as a widower to Betty's assets if she died before he did. Joe also consulted his own lawyer. Betty had to list her assets, giving a full and fair accounting of her financial condition. She and Joe signed the contract drafted and reviewed by their lawyers before they married. Betty also made a new will which clarified her intentions to leave her estate to Jackie—referring to the premarital agreement and her intention not to leave her assets to Joe.

One way to balance the rights of your new spouse and the expectations of your children is to (with the help of an attorney) write a premarital contract spelling out the disposition of the assets you take into the marriage. Another is to leave property in a will by "life estate." This arrangement enables you to leave the long-held family home to your children but ensures that your spouse can go on living there after your death. The children cannot force a sale and claim their share before your surviving spouse dies.

If you and your new spouse buy property together, you may want to establish the title as tenants in common. This allows you to leave your share of the property to anyone you want.

What About the Children?

As a reflection of the nationwide scale of divorce and remarriage, more than 20 million Americans are stepparents. An estimated one out of of every three Americans is currently part of a stepfamily, and one out of every two will, at some point, be part of a stepfamily. Yet despite these growing numbers, stepparents do not have the same legal rights and responsibilities as biological parents. Even

REMARRIAGE AND SOCIAL SECURITY

Any Social Security benefits you earn in your own right are yours whatever your marital status. But what happens to your spousal or survivor's benefits if you remarry?

1. If you are divorced from your former spouse, or if you were widowed but are not yet 60, you lose your right to collect spousal benefits on your former spouse's benefits when you remarry.

2. If you were married for 10 years or more and then widowed, and if you are now age 60 or older, you may collect survivor's benefits from your late spouse after you remarry.

3. If you are 62 or over, or if you are taking care of your new spouse's child—who is under 16—you may collect spousal benefits after you have been remarried at least a year. If you have been collecting your late spouse's benefits, however, you will not be able to collect both benefits.

4. If your new spouse dies after you have been married at least nine months, you may collect survivor's benefits. But you cannot collect from both spouses' benefits.

5. If you divorce your new spouse after being qualified to collect on his spousal benefits, you remain qualified. To get survivor's benefits after divorce, however, you must have been married 10 years.

if the stepparent chooses to provide financial support or education, for example, the courts in the large majority of cases consider the position of the natural parent to be primary.

If you pay child support, your payments continue until your children reach the age of majority, unaffected by remarriage of either parent. You can seek a modification of the court order if a change of circumstance affects your ability to pay. But most courts will not allow a modification just because a noncustodial parent remarries. If you stop the child support without permission from the court, collection efforts can be taken against you. (See also "Divorce," page 135.)

STEPPARENTS AS CARETAKERS

Under most circumstances, a stepparent is not financially responsible for supporting stepchildren—the biological parents are. But the courts may require a new spouse to provide support under certain conditions: if the biological noncustodial parent refuses or is unable to pay it, or if the child is at risk of becoming a public charge, for example.

Child support may be your main concern if you want to begin a new family. But there are other matters you should consider. If you have minor children, you may want to rewrite your will after remarrying. If you were to die, it is unlikely that the courts would give a stepparent custody of your children. The biological parent is entitled to custody unless he is deemed unfit. If you designate your new spouse to have custody in your will, your preference is not controlling, but it could be taken into account if custody must be determined by a court. You can also name a stepparent as guardian of your child's financial affairs if you wish.

ADOPTING STEPCHILDREN

To strengthen the family bond and provide continuity should your spouse die, you might consider adopting your stepchildren if their other biological parent is no longer living. Adoption overcomes the legally weak position of stepparents: even if they choose to give financial support or in other ways participate in the raising of stepchildren, stepparents legally remain unable to assume a full parental role. Adoption gives the stepparent the same legal rights and financial responsibilities as a natural parent, whether or not the marriage lasts.

Because the courts are very reluctant to deprive a natural parent of his legal parenting rights, stepparent adoption is generally possible only if the noncustodial parent has died. However, if you decide to undertake the often difficult process of separating a child legally from his biological parent, you should by all means speak to an attorney. Then you can begin the process by serving the parent with a formal adoption request.

123..

STEPPARENTS, STEPCHILDREN, AND THE LAW

The legal relationship between stepparent and stepchild is a tricky one. Legislation varies widely from state to state, but the law's basic position is that a child's biological parent takes precedence in legal matters over a stepparent, even if the latter is, in fact, much closer to—and more important to—the child. Here are some examples of how the law can further muddy the complexities of stepparenting:

1. A stepparent cannot authorize basic medical treatment for a stepchild unless a biological parent gives specific permission. Experts recommend having on hand a notarized document in which the biological parent authorizes the stepparent to order medical treatment of the stepchild.

2. Generally, the law does not recognize the right of a stepparent to visitation rights with a stepchild if the remarriage ends in divorce. A few states, however, now recognize that a relationship may be close, and grant visitation rights to a stepparent if it is in the best interests of the child.

3. As a rule, stepchildren cannot inherit from a stepparent who dies without a will. In a few states a stepchild can inherit if the deceased stepparent leaves no other heirs. Otherwise, if you want a stepchild to have some of your estate, it is vital that you make a will specifying that wish.

If the natural parent refuses to give consent to the request, you then must be able to give reasons why his parental rights should be terminated, such as that he abandoned the child or is otherwise unfit. (See also "Parenting," page 112.) If you succeed in adopting a stepchild, you may suggest that the child maintain his birth-family name as a middle name, to minimize the inevitable feelings of divided loyalty.

If your marriage breaks up, you are highly unlikely to obtain custody of your stepchild unless you can give evidence that both natural parents are unfit. While visitation rights may be granted in a some cases, they are generally not given to stepparents either. (See also "Stepparents, Stepchildren, and the Law," page 148.)

Premarital Agreements

No one enjoys preparing a premarital agreement. But it can be an important way to clarify ownership and define financial expectations for the future, especially for remarriages, when both partners are more likely to enter the union with assets and children. Nearly every state now enforces premarital or prenuptial agreements under certain conditions.

This increased enforcement of premarital agreements reflects the growing belief that couples who think about financial matters early on can minimize or avoid courtroom property disputes later. You may be among the many couples who reject the expense or the pragmatism of a written agreement that addresses the prospect of divorce. Yet a frank discussion about your finances can help build the foundation of a healthy relationship. It can also be important and useful if one partner should die unexpectedly.

MAKING IT STICK

If you do want such an agreement and want it enforceable, the key requirement is full disclosure of financial information by both partners. What property, stocks, cash, or other assets do you own? What debts do you have from credit cards or other loan accounts, child support, or alimony? How much is your income? By listing all assets and liabilities, you can clarify what ownership and interest existed before the marriage took place and avoid any suggestion that the agreement is based on false or misleading information.

You also should be aware of other reasons an agreement may be questioned. If, for example, the court determines that you gave up your right to alimony in the agreement without understanding the state law, the agreement can be deemed invalid.

Who Pays for College?

Generally speaking, a stepparent has no legal financial responsibility for a stepchild, but the picture changes slightly if you are remarried and trying to get financial aid to help pay for your child's college education.

College financial-aid forms often ask for financial information about the parent whom a child seeking financial aid has been living with for the last 12 months, usually the custodial parent. That information will include the stepparent's income and assets as well as the custodial parent's, and the decisions made by colleges about whether to give aid, and how much, are influenced by the combined incomes of the parent and the stepparent.

In effect, then, your child's stepparent becomes directly involved in whatever financial arrangements are made for the stepchild's higher education.

If you are the custodial parent and if your ex-spouse was ordered, at the time of your divorce, to pay college expenses, do not expect the college to collect the contribution. That responsibility is the custodial parent's. Thus you—with, possibly, the help of the child's stepparent—may have to pay what is owed the college and then file suit to make your ex-spouse fulfill his or her financial responsibility. (See also "Education," page 123.)

Some states may reject outright any agreement that waives all rights to alimony; such action is considered against public policy because it risks making the spouse a public charge.

The premarital agreement also can be denied if you agreed to receive one-tenth of your partner's property after his death without knowing that state inheritance laws generally provide a surviving spouse with one-third or one-half.

BUT IS IT FAIR?

Lastly, courts may evaluate the agreement on the grounds of fairness and reasonableness. Both parties need to have legal representation. Was the agreement entered into voluntarily and with full disclosure? Does it undermine the living standard of either party at the time they entered into the marriage? Does the agreement create an incentive for divorce or separation? Does it strongly favor the spouse who has the most assets? The answers to questions like these will weigh heavily in the court's evaluation of your prenuptial agreement.

What Goes Into a Prenuptial Agreement?

Some prenuptial agreements simply list the assets that each partner owns and will keep if the marriage ends and state that everything acquired during the marriage is shared equally. If your holdings and responsibilities are complex, you may need a more complicated agreement. Here are some questions you should be prepared to ask, or answer, when you meet with your lawyers:

• **Premarital assets.** What assets does each partner own before the wedding? What property do you want to maintain separately? What do you want to include as shared family assets?

• **House and car.** If you live as a couple in the house you now live in alone, will it become jointly owned? How about the car you now drive? How will you distribute any increased value of property you owned separately before your marriage? Will you split that 50-50 or keep it separate?

• **Life insurance and pension.** Who are the beneficiaries of your life insurance, pension, or other retirement benefits? Will they change, or do the current arrangements meet the terms of a settlement from a previous marriage that requires certain insurance be maintained for an ex-spouse or children? Should you consider buying another life insurance policy?

• **Joint accounts.** Will you have joint checking and savings accounts? Do you want to have joint credit card accounts? Who will ultimately be responsible for the bills?

• **Debt.** Are you coming into the new marriage with old debt or other liabilities? Will your spouse be compensated if joint marital assets are used to pay off your preexisting debts?

• **Children.** Do you and your new spouse plan to have children? If so—and even if you do not plan it—how will that affect the terms of this agreement? Will you participate in the support of your new spouse's children from a previous marriage?

• **Divorce.** How will you divide jointly owned property or property acquired during the marriage if there is a divorce? If there is a divorce, will one partner pay spousal support to the other?

• **Death.** What percentage of your premarital assets will your spouse be entitled to if you die first? Will the percentage change with the length of the marriage? (For example, the percentage might rise with each additional year of the marriage, up to a certain ceiling.) How do you plan to change your will to reflect the changes your new marriage may bring to existing family relationships, particularly children?

ELDERCARE

Whether or not you are the primary caregiver of your aging parent or relative, you need to know your rights and their rights—to ensure protection.

Planning for Eldercare

Illness, physical disability, and the other inevitable changes brought on by aging can make life for the elderly—and their adult children—both difficult and confusing. While your aging parents may be perfectly capable of taking care of themselves and making decisions at the moment, you as their child can raise issues and express concerns in order to help them make their later years more comfortable.

Begin by asking your parents if they have begun to make plans in case of incapacity or death. Find out the names of their lawyer, insurance agent, and banker and the location of any important documents such as title deeds, stock certificates, insurance policies, their checkbook, and other financial information. Encourage them to make a list or write a letter detailing all of their assets and monthly income. Ask if they have a will, who the executor is, where it is kept, and find out if they have already made arrangements regarding funerals. Although you may be reluctant to bring up such issues, remember that having this information will only make things easier for both you and your parents.

Protecting Assets

Whether your parents are rich or poor, you should encourage them to make a properly executed will. If they die without a will, their assets will go to probate and will be distributed according to the laws of the state they live in. These decisions may or may not be consistent with their wishes.

If their estate is relatively small, they may be able to write a will on their own, using a do-it-yourself kit available at local bookstores. Make sure all laws for your state are followed. If a question arises, or if large sums of money and property are involved, contact a lawyer.

THE ADVANTAGES OF A LIVING TRUST
Another way for your parents to maintain control over their financial affairs while still keeping the future in mind is to estab-

---

Easing Stress With a Letter of Instruction

If a parent dies or gets seriously ill, loose ends may have to be taken care of quickly. A letter of instruction from the parent will make those chores easier. Here is what such a letter might include:

✔ *People.* A list of the names, addresses, and telephone numbers of doctors, family members, neighbors, lawyers, financial advisors, insurance agents, stockbrokers, and bankers.

✔ *Documents.* The location of birth, marriage, and divorce certificates; a will; powers of attorney; military discharge papers; a deceased spouse's death certificate—and, if there is one, the safe-deposit box.

✔ *Financial data.* Records of stocks, bonds, funds, IRA's, and checking, savings, and other bank accounts.

✔ *Health information.* The location of insurance policies, Social Security card, and any Medicare information.

✔ *Household documents.* Mortgage information, the title deed, and the homeowners insurance policy. The location of car registration and insurance information, as well as the keys to the car.

THREE TYPES OF POWER OF ATTORNEY

If you are going to need to handle real estate, banking, insurance, health care, or transactions on behalf of your parent, you need to acquire a power of attorney. Consider these three types.

1. Power of attorney. This is a written document stating that one person (the principal) delegates another person (the attorney-in-fact) the authority to act on his behalf. An attorney-in-fact can be given authority to make almost any type of decision or decisions and can sign legal documents for the principal.

2. Durable power of attorney. Generally, a power of attorney expires automatically if the principal becomes mentally or otherwise incompetent. A durable power of attorney remains in effect if the principal becomes incapacitated. It then ends only when the principal dies or becomes legally competent again and revokes it.

3. Springing power of attorney. If a principal wants to retain control until he becomes incompetent or otherwise unable to make decisions, he may create a springing power of attorney, which takes affect only when a specified event—such as his becoming mentally incompetent—occurs. A springing power of attorney can be general or for something specific, such as health care, so that the attorney-in-fact can make health-care decisions if the principal cannot.

lish a "living trust." A living trust allows them to transfer the legal title of their property to a trustee, who manages the property on their behalf. When they die, their assets belong to the trust and are not subject to probate. If your parents wish, they can name themselves as trustees and name you as a cotrustee. If the trust is revocable, your parents may be able to cancel or amend it at any time.

Living trusts are complicated and should not be created without serious consideration and the advice of a lawyer and financial advisor. Such trusts mainly benefit people who have large estates and wish to minimize probate costs and delays. Also, a living trust does not eliminate the need for a will.

PREPARING FOR POSSIBLE INCOMPETENCE

Protecting the distribution of assets is essential but may not be enough. If your parent becomes incompetent and neither you nor he has made advance preparation for such a situation, you may have to go to court to get conservatorship or guardianship to take control of his affairs. (See also "Declaring a Parent Incompetent," page 153.)

To avoid such problems, many people establish some form of power of attorney to maintain control over the way their affairs are handled—and by whom—should they become physically or mentally incapacitated. (See "Three Types of Power of Attorney," at left.)

To establish a power of attorney or health-care proxy, your parent must be legally capable of understanding the power that he or she is turning over. The law varies in each state as to whether witnesses or a notary are required to make a power of attorney or health-care proxy legal. The participation of witnesses, as well as a lawyer's counsel, can help ensure the validity of the document.

Your parents may also want to inform banks, insurance companies, investment firms, doctors, and other institutions that a designated attorney-in-fact will be dealing with their affairs. Some institutions, such as the bank, may ask your parents to sign a form, including a clause holding the bank blameless for any act performed at the request of the attorney-in-fact if the power of attorney is later revoked. Your parents can revoke or change the power of attorney or health-care proxy at any time.

LIVING WILLS

Even if your parents are reluctant to give up control of their assets or decision-making power, they may be open to creating a living will. A living will is a document that informs family, friends, and doctors of a person's wishes concerning health care in the event that they are incapacitated by serious illness. For example, a living will might state that a person does not want to be kept alive by artificial means if she is suffering from a terminal condition and death is imminent. Unlike a health-care proxy or power of attorney for health care, a living will specifically states a person's wishes instead of naming a person to carry them out.

Although statutes vary from state to state, most explicitly provide civil and criminal immunity for physicians who follow a valid living will's directions. Moreover, these laws establish that a decision not to prolong life does not constitute suicide and, therefore, insurance is not affected. To be valid, the document must be signed and witnessed. All states allow a person who has made a living will to revoke it. (See also YOUR HEALTH CARE, page 232.)

Financing Eldercare

Since its passage back in 1935, the Social Security Act has served as the backbone of financial support to retired workers, their spouses, and children. Relying primarily on contributions made from workers and their employers, the Social Security Administration provides monthly benefits for retired and disabled workers and their dependents.

Applying for benefits is not difficult, but some older people—a widowed housewife, for example—may need help. Contact your local Social Security office for advice and assistance. (See also YOUR MONEY, page 353.)

If your parent does not qualify for Social Security or if Social Security does not cover his financial needs, other income is available. Since 1974, the federal government has provided for Supplemental Security Income, or SSI, to low-income and aged or disabled individuals. This program is administered by the Social Security Administration and may be available to your parent. To qualify for low income and aged benefits, he must be at least 65; have limited assets totaling no more than $2,000 (individually) or $3,000 (as a couple) except for a house and household goods, a car valued at no more than $4,500, and burial plots. In addition, the recipients cannot earn more than $953 a month (individually) or $1,389 (as a couple), including Social Security benefits. The average monthly federal payment is not large and may be supplemented by state contributions.

To apply for SSI, your parent will need a Social Security card or other proof of his number, his birth certificate, and records concerning his income and assets, such as bank statements, title deeds, car registration, and tax returns. After he has been approved, he is eligible for these benefits until his financial circumstances substantially improve.

Declaring a Parent Incompetent

One of the hardest things an adult child may have to do is to declare her parent incompetent. It may happen that you have no choice, however, and you should know the proper steps to take.

State courts have the power to appoint one or several persons to take over responsibility for your parent's care. This power, known as "parens patriae," or parentage of the state, allows the government to protect people who cannot take care of themselves by appointing a guardian or conservator, even against the allegedly incompetent person's wishes.

Before the state can appoint a guardian or a conservator, however, a probate court hearing must be held to prove that the person has a specific disabling condition and that as a result he cannot take care of his personal or financial affairs.

An allegedly incompetent person has the right to challenge allegations against him. Doctors, friends, business associates, relatives, and others may testify at the hearing.

By and large, any concerned person can petition the court to hold a hearing. In fact, the allegedly incompetent person can file a petition to have himself declared incompetent.

If you decide to take such measures on behalf of an older relative, hire a lawyer to guide you through the legal labyrinth.

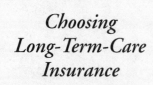

Choosing Long-Term-Care Insurance

Medicare and Medicare supplement policies provide benefits to help pay for hospital care, but they provide little for nursing home care. Long-term-care insurance is purchased to prevent the cost of nursing home care from eating up substantial assets, Such policies, however, can be very expensive. If you or your parents are thinking about buying one, be sure to review the terms of the policy. Ask the following questions:

✔ *Is the policy renewable for life?* Some policies expire at a certain age, possibly before the policyholder can even benefit from them.

✔ *What kinds of care does the policy cover?* It may cover only skilled care and not intermediate, or custodial care, such as rehabilitation centers and some nursing homes.

✔ *What conditions are covered?* Some policies will not cover Alzheimer's disease, senility, and similar conditions.

✔ *Where will I be covered?* Some coverage is limited to care in Medicare-certified nursing homes.

✔ *What is the daily benefit rate?* Find out if it compares to the actual charges where you live to determine if coverage is cost-effective. Find out if there is a clause that increases benefits with inflation.

GOVERNMENT MEDICAL INSURANCE

Most older people, even if they are healthy and well-off, at some point fear catastrophic illness and the financial ruin that could easily result. The federal government funds two programs to provide health-care security, one for the elderly, one for low-income people of any age: Medicare and Medicaid.

Medicare, administered by the Social Security Administration, helps those over 65 to pay for health care, no matter what their income level. The program has two parts: hospitalization and outpatient services. Hospitalization covers services for patients who are hospitalized or who require post-hospital inpatient care in a nursing home, at home, or in a hospice. Those covered are not required to pay premiums.

Outpatient services include ambulance transportation, oral surgery, artificial limbs, radiation treatment, and psychiatric services. Participants pay monthly premiums. Both parts of the program carry yearly deductibles and require coinsurance payments. For example, your parent will have to pay a deductible for each 60-day period she is hospitalized. If she stays longer than 60 days, she will have to start paying part of the daily cost for each day. After 90 days, her part of the cost goes up.

Anyone over 65 who is eligible for Social Security benefits qualifies for hospitalization benefits and has the option of enrolling for other services. Anyone not eligible for Social Security may obtain coverage by paying monthly premiums, as long as he is 65 or over and has been a legal U.S. resident for at least five years. (See also YOUR HEALTH CARE, page 208.)

MEDIGAP AND MEDICAID

Although Medicare is helpful, it may not be enough to pay for all expenses. It does not cover regular checkups, dental care, hearing aids, eyeglasses, or cosmetic surgery, and for some, the required coinsurance and deductibles can be quite costly. Therefore private health insurance, known as "Medigap," is available to supplement Medicare. Federal law regulates Medigap insurance, and you should check with your state's department of aging for more information on Medigap policies in your state. (See also YOUR HEALTH CARE, page 213.)

Medicaid is a government program to help those with limited incomes pay for medical care, whatever their age. Funded jointly by the federal government and each state, Medicaid is usually administered by a local social service or health department. State requirements vary on the maximum monthly income one can receive and still be eligible (usually around $400) and what assets will count toward eligibility. In some circumstances Medicaid can supplement Medicare, paying costs that might be out-of-pocket for the patient. Medicaid pays for physician's care, ambulance service, home health care, outpatient hospital care, and inpatient nursing-home or hospital care. In some states other services are covered as well.

Paying for Nursing-Home Care

Nursing homes are not cheap. In 1994 the national average cost for a year of nursing-home care was about $37,000. So if you and your elderly father see the nursing-home option as the best solution for him when he gets too old to take care of himself, you are going to have to figure out how to manage it financially.

Your parent's private health insurance or Medicare plus Medigap policy may cover all or part of his nursing home expenses. If not, he may be eligible for Medicaid. Medicare will pay for care in an approved skilled nursing facility, but only if your parent is admitted within 30 days of a hospital stay of three days or more, and it will pay for the full cost of care only during the first 20 days of your parent's stay.

A Senior's Guide to Planning Ahead

Although you trust your children to carry out your wishes after you die or if you become incompetent, it is up to you to make sure they handle your affairs the way you want them to. Here is a brief review of the elements you need to keep track of to make your survivors' job easier:

• **Will.** The need for a will may seem obvious, but many people neglect to write one. Speak to a lawyer and decide how you want your assets divided after you are gone. It is far better to have a will that you may change later than not to have one at all. Don't keep a will in a safe-deposit box that will be hard to open after your death.

• **Power of attorney.** You need not give up immediate power over your assets in order to create a power of attorney. A "springing" power of attorney allows you to name someone at will to act on your behalf after you become incapable of making your own decisions. You can appoint a springing power of attorney for a specific function, such as health-care decisions. A durable power of attorney allows you to choose someone to act on your behalf even after you become unable to do so on your own. You can change the attorney or the terms of a power of attorney at any time.

• **Living trust.** If you have a large estate, you may want to set up a trust while you are still alive. This way you can determine how your property and money will be managed after your death, giving written instructions. You can name yourself the trustee, naming a successor who will take over only after your death or disability.

• **Health-care proxy.** This document, now recognized everywhere in the United States and available in do-it-yourself kits sold in bookstores, allows you to designate someone to have the legal authority to make decisions regarding health-care treatment. It can be specific, detailing exact treatments, or it can give broad decision-making power and can be revoked or changed at any time.

• **Living will.** This document outlines your wishes regarding your health and medical care. Primarily, it is a statement describing your preferences about medical care in the event of a terminal illness. You can specify exactly how far you want physicians to go in providing care when death is imminent.

• **Funeral arrangements.** You can buy a plot, pay for funeral arrangements, and even set up a trust payable to a specific funeral home after your death. (See also "Death in the Family," page 163.) If you have special desires—about your funeral arrangements, for example—write a letter of instruction to make them clear.

For longer stays, Medicare will pay only a percentage of the cost up to 100 days. After that, you and your parent will be on your own. Medicaid, on the other hand, will pay for long-term nursing care for those who are eligible as long as the care is medically necessary. Some seniors deplete their resources until they become eligible for long-term-care assistance through Medicaid. This is known as "spending down," and it must be done carefully so as to comply with state and federal laws. For example, most asset transfers must be made 30-36 months in advance of application for Medicaid. Also, certain assets or resources are exempt when Medicaid eligibility is determined.

By inventorying assets and resources in advance of application and making decisions about them, seniors may protect some personal resources and also meet eligibility guidelines. Spending down is an extremely complex process. Be sure to contact a lawyer or eldercare specialist before your parent signs assets over to you or someone else.

LONG-TERM NURSING-HOME INSURANCE

Many people buy private long-term nursing-home insurance. These policies are designed to provide funds for costs that exceed coverage through private health insurance, Medicare, or Medigap insurance. Long-term-care insurance usually pays a certain amount of money per day for each day your parent spends in a nursing home. Long-term-care insurance is expensive and is usually only worth buying if your parents have substantial assets they want to protect. If assets or funds are limited and your parent is spending what he has on health care already, he will most likely be eligible for Medicaid soon.

If your father decides, or is forced, to pay his nursing-home bills himself, the only financial relief he can expect is that medical expenses exceeding 7.5 percent of his adjusted gross income are tax-deductible.

Home Care for the Elderly

Whether your parents live in their own home or in yours, they may at some point require full-time care. While nursing homes can provide a viable option, recently a network of home health-care providers for the elderly—volunteer, nonprofit, and for-profit—has appeared to provide in-home alternatives. The result: greater independence for the elderly, less guilt for family members, and less expense for all.

People are living longer, and more medical attention has become focused on the elderly. One relatively recent development is the emergence of eldercare specialists, also called "geriatric care managers." Usually nurses or social workers by training, they act as consultants and can help develop a comprehensive plan for care, based on an elderly person's needs, finances, and insurance coverage. They are knowledgeable about the in-home and community services that are available and can help organize care, evaluate the quality and costs, and then monitor the services. These managers can help ease the emotional strain, particularly if the older person lives at a distance from her family, but they can be expensive, up to $150 an hour. Contact your state's Department on Aging or local senior citizen center for information on finding an eldercare specialist in your area.

MAKING YOUR OWN PLAN

You and your elderly parent can organize a plan for services on your own, using the guidance of local or national referral agencies and researching health-care providers in your area. Your local Department on Aging is a good starting point for finding out what is available. You may be able to hire individuals to assist you and your parent, or you can seek out a home-care agency. (See also "Services for the Elderly," page 158.)

A home-care agency is either a for-profit or nonprofit entity that specializes in providing services for the sick or elderly. These services include nursing care; physical, speech, or occupational therapy; personal assistance; meal preparation; and even companionship. Home-care agencies are listed in the Yellow Pages, and your local Department on Aging may be able to refer you to an agency in your area that will meet your particular needs.

Although you may prefer to hire an individual to take care of your parent on your own, your parent's source of financing (such as insurance) may require you to use a particular kind of agency. Some nonprofit agencies will waive their fees if you cannot afford to pay for their services, whereas most for-profit private agencies ask for payment, which is often covered by private insurance policies. Other nonprofit, for-profit, and hospital-based agencies accept Medicare and Medicaid.

FINDING A LICENSED AGENCY

To choose an agency that provides home-care services, you should determine its legal status. Is it licensed, certified, accredited, bonded? Contact the state or city department of health or office of consumer affairs to find out. You can also call your local Better Business Bureau to find out if there have been any complaints logged against the agency.

Nearly every state requires licensing for agencies that provide more than minimal personal-care services (such as bathing and grooming). Exceptions include some agencies that provide only single services or highly specialized ones. You will

Helping From a Distance

Your mother may no longer be able to live on her own, but she refuses to leave her familiar home. If you live far away, how can you help her from where you are?

✔ **Get information.** Various referral agencies, both local and national, provide advice by telephone, and often for no charge. They can tell you what in-home and community services are available for your parent. A starting point is the national Eldercare Locator Service, (800) 677-1116.

✔ **Recruit helpers.** With your mother's help, make a list of people who are important to her and their phone numbers—friends, neighbors, doctors, lawyer, banker, and insurance agent. They can advise you, help you make decisions, or make a home visit in an emergency.

✔ **Arrange finances.** Have all Social Security or benefit checks deposited directly into your mother's checking account. If possible, have companies deduct their monthly charges from her account, so her service will never be interrupted due to unpaid bills.

✔ **Take leave from your job.** If your company employs 50 people or more, you are entitled under the Family Leave Act to take up to three months of unpaid leave to care for your elderly mother if she is ill.

receive payments from Medicare or Medicaid only if a given home-care agency is accredited by them. To be accredited, an agency has to be evaluated and approved by professional organizations in its field. Accreditation is sometimes required for reimbursement by insurance companies.

Bonded agencies, which must put aside money in case of lawsuits, provide a further level of security should your parent be mistreated or should another problem arise. But remember: determining an agency's legal status is no substitute for a personal check of its references, range of services, and personnel.

One more option to consider for an elderly parent or relative who can no longer live alone is foster-home care. Some states have developed foster-care programs for the elderly in which families or individuals are paid to take in elderly adults, provide them a safe and comfortable home, meals, a bed, and companionship. Since costs average about $1,000 a month, well below the cost of nursing-home care, such an arrangement may turn out to be just the solution you have been looking for.

Services for the Elderly

Many programs are available to provide support for elderly adults and to connect them to their local communities, whether they are housebound or out and about. Call your local Department on Aging and ask about the following:

• **Senior centers.** At one time senior centers primarily provided recreational and social activities, but many now offer a wide range of information and referral services to help older people manage their affairs. Centers may offer meals, educational programs, health services, tax-return advice, as well as social or recreational activities. Most are free or charge only nominal fees

• **Adult day care.** For the elderly who need more care and supervision than those who usually attend senior centers, adult day-care centers often provide physical therapy, nursing care, meals, counseling, and many other services also found at senior centers. Services and quality and fees vary widely. The senior person may be eligible for financial help from Medicaid or from a long-term-care insurance policy, depending on the individual state's guidelines.

• **Local agencies for the aging.** This national system of agencies is funded by federal, state, and local governments as well as private contributions. Agencies provide services to those over 60, including adult day care, legal advice, tax advice, job training, meal delivery, referrals, health-insurance information and counseling, protection services, and much more. Contact your state Department on Aging to find out what is available in your area. Many services are free or offered at low cost.

• **Companionship and reassurance.** Local religious and social service groups provide volunteers to make regular visits to the homes of older adults, to help with chores or just to sit and talk. Many organizations also provide daily checkup telephone calls to make sure the person is safe.

• **Meals on wheels.** This delivery service provides hot meals to housebound people either free or for a small fee. Originally a volunteer program, the service is now supported by a combination of private, community, and federal funding.

• **Transportation services.** Many communities have some kind of transportation available for the elderly, often sponsored by churches or other social service groups, using volunteers' private cars, vans, or small buses. The services also may have special buses or vans with ramps for wheelchairs and walkers. Many communities provide discounts on public transportation.

FAMILY PETS

Animals are often beloved members of a family, but they may not be so beloved by everyone else. Knowing the law will help keep you and your pets out of trouble.

Taking Legal Care of Your Pet

As every parent tells his child, owning a pet means taking responsibility for its care. It also means recognizing your legal obligations. These may include getting licenses and vaccinations, abiding by local ordinances, and making sure that your pet does not cause trouble in the neighborhood.

Almost every municipality requires dog (and sometimes cat) owners to obtain a license for their pet and make sure that the animal wears it at all times. Without a license it is often difficult to locate the owner of a lost animal, so your straying pet could be adopted by someone else or, worse, be put to sleep at the local animal pound.

Licenses also serve the public health because it is a way that owners must show proof they have had their pets vaccinated for rabies. Check your telephone directory for the city or county licensing office, or call your city hall to find out the regulations in your area. Usually you must reregister your pet annually and when you move to a different locale.

You may be subject to a number of other pet laws in addition to licenses and vaccinations, depending on where you live. Some jurisdictions set restrictions on the number of dogs or cats you can keep in your house or apartment, and in an effort to minimize pet problems outdoors, many cities have leash laws and "pooper-scooper" statutes. In addition to municipal laws, many apartment buildings and homeowners associations have their own strict rules about pets.

When the Vet Treats Your Pet

Like the family doctor, your pet's veterinarian should be a trusted health adviser, and you are entitled to expect quality care from her. Veterinarians must have received a doctor of veterinary medicine (DVM) degree, passed the state's written test for veterinary medicine, and secured a proper state license to treat animals.

Under guidelines adopted in 1960 by the American Veterinary Medical Association (the vets' equivalent of the AMA),

---

Puppy Lemon Laws

Pet sellers are bound by the same warranty laws that apply to products. (See also YOUR CONSUMER RIGHTS, page 404.) Here is how you are protected:

✔ *Reasonable expectations.* It is reasonable to assume that a pet for sale should be healthy. This is an implied warranty, and if your new puppy is sick, you may be able to get your money back. Some states have pet laws comparable to "lemon laws" for car buyers, which require a seller to pay for veterinary expenses if he sells you an unhealthy pet. You will probably need certification from a veterinarian.

✔ *Promises made.* You buy a dog on the strength of a seller's statement that it is a pure-bred—an express warranty; later you find out it is not. Under warranty law, you can sue for your purchase price. You are more likely to win if you have the seller's promises in writing.

✔ *Fit recommendations.* You are looking for a dog to breed, and a seller recommends a German shepherd. But the dog turns out to have been neutered and is clearly not fit for your stated purpose. The seller failed to fulfill the warranty of fitness for a particular purpose, and you may have a claim against him.

WHEN A PET IS BEING MISTREATED

Every state has anticruelty statutes that make it illegal to mistreat animals. Some laws are vague, restricting "needlessly cruel" or "inhumane" treatment, while others are more specific—for example, making it illegal to use any animal as a lure on a dog racetrack Contact your local animal-control office to find out what the exact laws are in your state. In general, you can expect the following:

1. You are responsible for taking care of your pet. You must make sure your animal receives adequate food, water, exercise, and shelter and does not suffer from abandonment or unnecessarily cruel confinement. Cruelty to animals can be reported to the local police.

2. If an animal is tortured or used to provoke a fight with other animals, criminal charges, fines, and imprisonment may result. Pets that are mistreated can be taken from their owners.

3. To determine negligence, evidence that actions were intentionally cruel is not required. Usually it is sufficient to prove that a person knowingly neglected an animal.

4. Acts of malicious cruelty, which are presumed to be intentional, are treated the most severely.

vets are required to prevent or relieve the suffering of animals, to offer proper medical attention to all animals, and to treat animal medical emergencies as well as they are able.

PROBLEMS WITH THE VET

If you have a dispute with a vet over a bill, your best option is to pay it first and file a suit in small claims court later, since in many states a veterinarian is entitled to keep your pet as collateral until outstanding bills have been paid.

If you have a serious complaint about a vet, you can notify the veterinarian licensing board in your area. Whether or not your claim is investigated, your complaint will be recorded and may end up helping others avoid problems. If your pet was injured or died while under veterinary care, and you believe your vet acted incompetently, you may have a legal claim.

The Negligent Veterinarian

PROBLEM
Tina and Russ Bloom's dog, Scout, was hit by a slow-moving car. Although Scout did not seem to have any injuries, he was yelping continuously and so Russ and Tina rushed him to the nearest veterinarian. After examining the dog, the vet told Russ and Tina that Scout had suffered no more than a few bruises. The Blooms paid $50 and went home. Later that night when Scout still had not stopped whining, Russ and Tina took him to another vet, who found that the dog was bleeding internally and required surgery. Sadly, Scout died before the operation began.

ACTION
Russ and Tina were crushed by their dog's death, and upset that a timely diagnosis might have saved him. They talked to a third veterinarian, who agreed to testify in court that he believed that a veterinarian of ordinary competence should have recognized that Scout was bleeding internally and that the first vet made a negligent diagnosis. The veterinarian also said that had surgery been performed in a timely manner, Scout probably would have lived. Russ and Tina wrote a letter to the first veterinarian, explaining the malpractice case they were building and asked for a settlement for the cost of their dog as well as for both veterinarians' bills. The vet agreed and paid them $350. Tina then called the veterinarian licensing board in her state to report the malpractice.

You can try to settle your differences directly with the vet, or you may have to turn to a mediator or file suit for reimbursement of costs incurred, for negligence, or for malpractice. Usually, however, the legal costs of such a case will exceed what you can reasonably expect to recover.

Veterinarians are not liable for keeping animals indefinitely if their owners fail to pick them up and pay for them. Many states have guidelines as to how many days vets must keep a pet before seeking a new owner or putting the pet to sleep.

Keeping Wild or Exotic Pets

You might not consider your pet ferret or your baby boa constrictor a threat to anyone, but most municipalities prohibit what they call "dangerous animals," such as wolves, alligators, and poisonous snakes. Some cities allow only dogs, cats, certain birds, rabbits, hamsters, gerbils, and mice to be kept as pets and may even prohibit owning certain breeds of dog, such as rottweilers, pit bulls, or wolf hybrids, without a permit.

Generally, the law recognizes two categories of animals: wild animals that cannot be tamed, such as lions, tigers, bears, wolves, snakes, and alligators; and domestic animals that may be tamed by humans or are naturally docile, such as dogs and cats but also including horses, chickens, goats, and rabbits.

Under the law, wild and domestic animals are subject to different regulations. Owners of wild or exotic animals are subject to a higher duty of care to protect others from harm from their animals. In most areas, particularly nonrural ones, you need a special permit to keep a wild animal and are responsible for any injuries or damage it causes, whether or not the animal is provoked.

If your domestic-animal pet bites someone, you may or may not be responsible, depending upon the animal's history and your knowledge of its behavior. If your golden retriever, for example, has been a kind, placid dog but suddenly nips a child who pulled its tail, you may not be liable for its actions. On the other hand, if your pit bull jumps the back fence and attacks a toddler, chances are you will be held accountable.

Although farm animals such as horses, cows, sheep, and goats are considered domestic, local zoning laws often prohibit keeping them in residential neighborhoods or, if they are allowed, limit their numbers.

Pet Misdeeds and the Law

It is up to you to see that your pet does not cause injury or damage property. If your rabbit escapes from its hutch and ruins your neighbor's rosebushes, or if your dachshund strays next door and bites your neighbor's ankle, you will be responsible for paying for the damages. Most states have "dog bite" statutes, which make an owner financially responsible for any injury or damage caused by his pet.

However, if your pet was provoked, your pet had no history of biting or attacking, or if someone came onto your property despite signs warning to "beware of dog," you would proba-

Your Dog and Your Neighbor's Rights

Your dog Wellington wanders off your property and down the street, attracted by a little boy playing in his front yard. The child's father gets nervous when he sees your big dog approaching his child. If Wellington stops across the street and merely watches the boy, your neighbor has no right to harm the dog. If your dog barks and growls, but in no way threatens attack, your neighbor has no right to harm the dog either.

However, if Wellington growls at the child, lunges, and bares his teeth in attack, your neighbor can take appropriate action to stop the animal (such as causing it physical harm) in order to protect the child. In extreme circumstances, a person may be justified in killing a known vicious or dangerous animal that is on the attack. In such cases, you would be unlikely to win a suit for injury to your pet.

On the other hand, your neighbor cannot harm your pet for digging in his yard or destroying his property. You may be financially responsible for your pet's actions, but if your neighbor harms your pet when the animal presents no danger of injuring a person, you may be able to recover the costs of veterinary bills or compensation for damages.

*The greatness of a nation and
its moral progress
can be judged by the way its
animals are treated.*

MAHATMA GANDHI

bly not be at fault, but state laws vary. When someone is injured by another person's pet, the dispute is often settled out of court by the victim and the pet owner. Still, if you are the injured party, you should immediately obtain the name and telephone number of the owner of the pet and find out if the animal has had its rabies shots. You should also find out if there were any witnesses. If you get medical attention, be sure to save copies bills and records related to treatment.

Some homeowners insurance policies cover owners whose pets bite or cause injury. If you cannot agree to a settlement with the owner, or if he is not covered by insurance, you may seek resolution through mediation, arbitration, or small claims court. Find out what the dog-bite laws are in your state. If the damages you are seeking exceed the small claims limit because your injury is severe, contact a lawyer for advice. You should also report the incident to the local animal control board. If there have been any previously reported cases involving the same animal, or if it has already been determined to be "vicious," the owner may face fines or have to put it to sleep.

A Roundup of Dog Laws

Every state and municipality, large and small, has laws or ordinances dealing with dogs as pets. These rules set limits on owners and protect the public's health, safety, and property—in other words, they define the dog's place in human society. Here is a distillation of the laws:

• **Dog-bite statutes.** Laws in half the states hold owners liable for any injury caused by their dogs. They are called dog-bite statutes but usually cover any injuries caused by canine misbehavior.

• **Pooper-scooper statutes.** In some large, crowded cities such as New York, these laws require that the owner immediately remove and properly discard of any excrement his dog deposits in any public or private place other than his own property.

• **Leash laws.** These regulations require owners to keep their dogs on leashes or face a fine. Dogs need not be leashed on their owner's property, and some cities have set aside certain parks or fields on which dogs can be unleashed.

• **Guide dogs.** Guide dogs for the blind or other specially trained dogs that provide assistance to the disabled are typically exempted from the restrictions placed on other dogs. Such animals have access to public places and private workplaces, the right to travel on public transportation, are exempt from pooper-scooper statutes, and may live in rental housing that forbids pets. Most

municipalities will provide an identification tag and license for these dogs without charge.

• **Dog fighting.** Provoking a dog to fight is prohibited by anticruelty statutes. Using an animal for organized dog fighting, or even training it to fight, is a felony in most states, punishable by large fines and imprisonment.

• **Vicious dogs.** Many communities have laws restricting dogs that are deemed dangerous or potentially so. In recent years, for instance, many communities have singled out pit bulls for their viciousness and banned them outright. Laws regarding dangerous dogs usually require someone who has been injured or threatened to file a formal complaint. A judge can then decide whether the dog is vicious and needs to be constrained. In an extreme case the judge can rule that the dog be removed or put to sleep.

• **Barking dogs.** A dog does not have to be dangerous to be a nuisance. If a neighbor complains about your pet's barking, you can be forced by law to pay a fine, or be subjected to a civil claim by a neighbor, or you may have to get rid of the dog.

DEATH IN THE FAMILY

No family is ever fully prepared emotionally for death, but you can lessen the stress by knowing what tasks have to be done and how to do them.

When a Family Member Dies

At a time of great emotional and psychological stress, family members are called upon to make a number of difficult decisions and arrangements. The most immediate decisions concern the funeral and disposition of the body of the loved one; later, survivors may have to take steps to claim benefits to which they are entitled.

In every state, surviving spouses are granted the authority to make these decisions unless they are incompetent or refuse to accept the legal and financial responsibility. If that happens or if there is no living spouse, states typically rely on kinship or bloodlines to determine the right of control. This begins with children, then parents, siblings, and other relatives. When the next in line is a minor, the authority will be passed on to the next relationship.

DECISIONS ABOUT THE REMAINS

The deceased may already have established an executor for his estate with instructions about how to handle the costs of his funeral and burial. Even in such instances, the spouse generally retains control over the disposition of the body—that is, she can decide where the burial should be, whether to have a funeral, and where. (If the dead person was indigent, and if no one takes responsibility for the burial or cremation, city or county governments must deal with the remains.)

When a person dies, his spouse or other close family member in effect inherits and is responsible for the body. The survivor then has the right to consent to an autopsy, which involves an examination of the body to help learn the cause and time of death, or to withhold consent for religious or other reasons. Even if the survivor refuses consent, the coroner or medical examiner may order an autopsy in certain circumstances, including cases of suspected wrongful death.

AUTHORIZING ORGAN DONATIONS

An individual can agree that when he dies his tissue or organs will be donated to be used for transplants, or he can give his body for medical research. Under the Uniform Anatomical Gift Act, such a donation is legally binding on the survivors if the

---

1̲2̲3̲..

WHAT TO DO RIGHT AWAY

When someone dies, members of the family need to take certain actions right away:

1. Find, and sign, any documents relating to the wishes of the deceased regarding the disposal of his body, including the donation of his organs or tissue or the body itself.

2. Get the death certificate from the doctor or medical facility where he died.

3. If the deceased belonged to a burial or memorial society, notify the society.

4. Pick a funeral home and make arrangements to transfer the body.

5. Buy a burial plot if the deceased had not already made arrangements for one.

6. Contact a clergy member who can provide spiritual support and assist in decisions about a funeral.

7. Make final arrangements for the funeral and burial or for cremation.

8. Place an obituary notice in the local newspapers.

10. Notify relatives and friends of the place, date, and time of the funeral.

Why Death Certificates Are Necessary

When somebody dies, every state requires that a death certificate be issued, stating the time, place, and cause of death. This is filled out by the attending physician, a medical examiner, or a coroner, and provides legal proof of the death.

If the death was from natural causes, as most deaths are, a certificate should be filed within a few days. If the cause of death is unknown or suspicious, an autopsy may be performed before the death certificate is issued.

If you are the surviving relative taking care of such matters you should obtain several certified copies of the document. If you need additional copies later, they will be available at your state or local health department or vital statistics registry.

With the certificate, you can file for probate of the deceased person's will and seek any Social Security, life insurance, and pension benefits to which you are entitled. You also will need a certified copy of the death certificate to gain access to a safe-deposit box.

You should also make sure that the death certificate states the exact cause of death, because that may affect decisions concerning survivors' benefits.

individual signed a Uniform Donor Card. However, such donations are unlikely to be accepted by medical professionals if the surviving kin does not approve of the deceased person's wishes. (See also YOUR HEALTH CARE, page 232.)

APPROVAL FOR ORGAN TRANSPLANTS

If, on the other hand, the surviving kin wants to donate the organs for transplants or research, she can authorize removal. Assuming that the organs are medically acceptable and there is appropriate personnel to perform the operation, they will be removed and then the body will be returned to the place indicated for final disposition. This can be done without delaying the funeral or disfiguring the body.

The deceased person may have specified a final resting place before her death. The legally responsible kin must then decide whether or not to carry out the expressed desires of the deceased. Some states have laws recognizing the right of each person to decide on the disposal of her body. In these states, if you ask to be buried, your family cannot cremate your body. In some cases, the deceased family member may have already arranged and paid for her funeral, but the decision of how and when to bury, cremate, or entomb rests with the surviving kin as long as they comply with state law.

Arranging the Funeral

Disposition of the body is only one of the many decisions grieving survivors will be called upon to make. Among the others are: Where will the funeral be held? Who will conduct the service? Will there be an open casket? What clothes should the deceased wear? Will he be embalmed? Who will carry the casket? Will transportation have to be provided? Who will arrange for the obituary notice? Who will pay for all of this?

You may decide to purchase a complete funeral package from a funeral home. This typically includes transfer of the body to the home; embalming, restoration, and dressing of the body; the cost of a coffin; the use of a hearse and limousine; staff services; and the use of funeral-home facilities. Other services include providing pallbearers, ordering flowers, and providing a guest register.

A funeral home may also organize the service, take care of the burial permit, obtain copies of the death certificate, and place the obituary in the newspaper. Music, flowers, a clergyman's honorarium, and additional limousines are extra. So are burial costs, including the opening and closing of the grave and, in some cases, the purchase of a cemetery plot. All told, the costs of a a funeral can add up to a major expense. The national average is over $3,500, but even an unelaborate funeral can cost many thousands more. The price of the coffin alone can range from $1,200 to more than $4,000.

Although funeral homes are granted authority by the state to embalm bodies and conduct funerals, as well as to perform burials, cremations, and entombments, no one is required to use their services. Some states have mortuary companies that perform only burials and cremations at minimum cost, but all states or localities, of course, have laws to ensure that all burials or cremations, whoever performs them, will be carried out in a way that is consistent with local health and safety standards. Call the Department of Health for more information.

PROTECTING THE VULNERABLE

Occasionally, unscrupulous funeral operators will take advantage of the vulnerability of the survivors when someone in a family dies. By pressuring them into using unwanted or unnecessary services, raising prices, or billing for goods not provided, these crooks add to the survivors' distress, inflate the costs—and reflect badly on all funeral homes.

In an attempt to control such practices in the multibillion-dollar funeral industry, Congress in 1984 passed a law generally known as the FTC (Federal Trade Commission) Funeral Rule. It requires funeral providers to tell clients in advance which of their services are not required by state or local law, and how much the goods and services under consideration will cost. (See "Regulating the Funeral Parlors," page 166.)

Planning Your Own Funeral

You may decide to ease the financial and emotional pressures on your family by planning and paying for your funeral in advance. One way to do this is join a memorial or burial society. Such societies do not sell goods or services themselves, but for a small, one-time fee they will organize agreements based on your wishes with low-cost funeral providers who will take care of things at the time of your death. Most memorial societies are members of the Continental Association of Funeral and Memorial Societies.

Pre-need funeral plans are another method for protecting your survivors from hard-sell tactics at the time of death. Generally they have two components: an agreement for specific funeral goods and services you want, and a method for prepaying the costs. Remember, the FTC Funeral Rule requires funeral-home operators to give you over-the-phone and in-person price information. You can confidently sign the agree-

Finding the Right Cemetery Plot

Although cemeteries vary widely as to quality, price, and care, all are regulated and supervised by an agency of the local, state, or federal government. Before buying a cemetery plot, consider these points:

✔ *Who owns the cemetery?* Cemeteries can be owned by religious groups, fraternal or charitable organizations, profit-making companies, or public agencies that get tax money. The choice is yours, provided that you qualify. A Catholic wife might not be allowed to bury her Jewish husband in a Catholic cemetery.

✔ *Second thoughts.* You may change your mind later. Be sure that you can resell the plot. Find out whether the cemetery will buy it back and for what price.

✔ *Size.* You may buy a plot for yourself, for you and your spouse, or for your whole family. Some cemeteries permit one casket to be buried above another, which uses less space and costs less.

✔ *Maintenance.* Visit the cemetery before you buy to see whether the grounds are well maintained. The cemetery may require you to pay a one-time fee for perpetual care. Or you may have to pay an annual upkeep fee. If so, make sure that your survivors can afford the fee, or make arrangements for the annual payments.

ment for the specific goods and services you want, because it is not legally binding without a prepayment arrangement.

There are various ways to arrange prepayment of your funeral. Make your arrangements carefully to avoid the risks of fraud or other problems. For example, if you pay in advance, there is a chance that the funeral home might close before you die, an operator will misuse prepayments invested with him, or a home will refuse to give you or your survivors a refund if you move to another city.

One way to avoid such problems is to open a regular interest-earning savings account at your local bank with money to cover the costs of the funeral, earmarked as payable to the funeral home upon your death. Or you might open a joint savings account with a family member and grant that relative the right of survivorship to pay for the funeral. This joint tenant will not be obligated to use the funds for the funeral, so make sure he knows what the funds are for and can be trusted.

A TRUST FUND FOR YOUR FUNERAL

Another prepayment possibility is to arrange with a funeral director for a state-regulated trust, available in every state except Vermont, Alabama, and the District of Columbia. You and the director both sign an arrangement agreement; then you give the director a sum equal to the funeral's cost. He must place all or a portion of that money into a trust account to become available upon your death. More than half the states require funeral operators to keep all the money in a trust

There is no cure for birth and death save to enjoy the interval.

GEORGE SANTAYANA

Soliloquies in England

Regulating the Funeral Parlors

To protect consumers who may be emotionally vulnerable after a death in the family, the Federal Trade Commission's Funeral Rule sets strict standards for what undertakers and others in the funeral industry can and cannot do when dealing with the public.

• Funeral homes must allow customers to buy the products the homes sell and the services they offer individually rather than only through a package. Packages, however, can be offered.

• Funeral homes must reveal the prices of their goods and services over the telephone. When inquiries are made in person, they must detail the prices in writing.

• Embalming, which is very expensive, cannot be done without authorization unless state law requires it. Customers must be informed in writing if embalming is not required by law. (If the casket is to be open, embalming is usually a practical necessity.)

• Funeral homes must provide itemized statements for all goods and services ordered by the customer. The statement must include the individual costs and total cost as well as a listing of the laws or provisions that require customers to buy certain goods and services. Customers are not obligated, for instance, to pay for a casket for use in cremation, even if a funeral director tries to convince them otherwise.

• Funeral homes must detail in writing any fees being added to the price of an item purchased or service hired on the consumer's behalf. If the customer asks for a simple funeral service, he must be informed if the costs of flowers, an organist, burial clothes, or limousines are going to be extra.

account. The rest allow them to retain some percentage of what you prepay, but require that they provide the funeral selected.

A popular alternative uses life insurance policies. You sign the agreement, buy life insurance that covers the cost of the funeral, and designate the funeral home as the beneficiary. In some cases, you may designate the money to an independent agency or a special trust that is responsible for paying the funeral home.

ANTICIPATE FUTURE PROBLEMS

You should be careful that any prepay mechanism is inflation-adjusted or otherwise rises in value so that it will cover the costs of the funeral, particularly if you organize your pre-need plan while you are relatively young and in good health. The dollar amount you settle on now may not be enough to cover expenses in a decade or so.

You also should find out what happens to any money in excess of the funds needed to cover the inflation-adjusted cost of the funeral. Does the funeral home keep such interest, or does your estate get a share of those excess earnings?

Make sure to ask whether the pre-need plan can be canceled or transferred should you later change your mind or move. Individual plans can be maintained from out of state, but state laws vary regarding cancellations.

Finally, before choosing a pre-need plan, make sure to do your homework on the agency or funeral home that will be managing your funds. If the firm goes bankrupt, you may be left with nothing.

Survivor Benefits

After the funeral, the survivor may have a number of other responsibilities, such as contacting the deceased's lawyer, arranging for a tombstone or marker, notifying insurance companies with which the deceased had policies, and claiming a number of survivor benefits for which she may be entitled. (See also "Eight Tax-free Death Benefits," at right.)

The most significant sources of help for survivors in paying for funeral and burial costs are Social Security and Veterans Administration benefits. Social Security provides a one-time, lump-sum death benefit of up to $255. This amount is paid to the surviving spouse or to the surviving child or children of the deceased if there is no surviving spouse. A child, to be eligible for any Social Security benefits, must have been entitled to them on the deceased worker's record as of the month the worker died.

---

1 2 3...

EIGHT TAX-FREE DEATH BENEFITS

After a family member dies, it is easy for survivors to overlook possible sources of income. Here is a list of death-related benefits. Some are obvious, some are not, but none counts as income for federal income-tax purposes.

1. Social Security. Social Security pays survivors a lump-sum death benefit.

2. Veterans' benefits. The Department of Veterans Affairs pays various funeral-related benefits to veterans' survivors.

3. Life insurance. For many survivors, the deceased's life insurance becomes a major source of support.

4. Workers' compensation. Almost all employers are required to carry workers' comp insurance that pays off for work-related deaths.

5. Health insurance. Health and hospital insurance policies help pay medical expenses.

6. Personal injury awards. Court settlements awarded as compensation in death-related legal actions are not taxable.

7. Employer's death gratuity. Some companies offer payments to their employees' survivors. Up to $5,000 is tax-free.

8. Gifts in memorium. Money given as a gift to survivors in memory of the deceased is tax-free for the recipients.

Tracking Down a Missing Policy

Your widowed mother has recently died, and you are sure she had a life insurance policy. But a search of her papers has not turned up the policy. How can you track it down?

✔ *Look in her check registry.* There may be a reference to an insurance company. Or, better still, try to find a canceled check or a premium notice.

✔ *Call her insurance agent.* If you do not know who that was, try a local agent whom she or other family members might have used.

✔ *Contact her employer.* Or, if your mother was in a union or a professional association, contact them. She might have been insured under one of their group policies.

✔ *Contact her banker, mortgage broker, or automobile club.* She may have been insured under a policy related to their services.

✔ *Call the American Council of Life Insurance (ACLI).* The council may be able to conduct a policy search among most of the major insurance companies. The address of the ACLI is: 1001 Pennsylvania Ave. N.W., Washington D.C. 20004-2599, (202) 624-2000.

CLAIMING SURVIVORS' BENEFITS

Survivors have two years from the date of death to submit an application for this death benefit. Social Security also provides monthly benefits to survivors after the death of a spouse, parent, or child. A spouse at least 60 years old, a disabled spouse at least 50 years old, a spouse of any age rearing an eligible child, dependent parents at least 62 years old, dependent and unmarried children under 18 (or 22 if disabled), and in certain situations, a divorced spouse may be eligible.

You will have to contact your local Social Security office to apply, either by phone or in person. To verify your claim for benefits, you will need documentation such as your birth and marriage certificates, the death certificate, the Social Security number, and the most recent federal tax form or W-2 form of the deceased. If you are applying for benefits as the dependent parent of a deceased child, you will need evidence verifying that your child provided at least half of your support.

Any Social Security benefit checks sent to the deceased during the month of the death must be returned. Whether the person died at the beginning of the month or on the last day, the money is not payable.

VETERANS' BENEFITS

Military veterans or service personnel may also be eligible for funeral and burial benefits. Most military veterans are entitled to burial without cost in a national or public cemetery with a grave marker, transportation of their body to that site, and a United States flag to drape the casket. In addition, the Department of Veterans Affairs (VA) will pay a funeral benefit if the veteran dies from a service-connected cause. The VA will also provide an allowance for burial in a private cemetery and an additional benefit if the death was not service-connected and if the deceased was receiving a veteran's pension or compensation or died in a VA facility.

The following are entitled to have their bodies or remains, if cremated, placed in a national cemetery:

- Any honorably discharged veteran;
- Any member of the armed services who died while serving in active duty;
- Any reserve member or member of the National Guard or Air National Guard whose death took place under honorable circumstances during active duty, during inactive duty for training, or because of an injury related to that duty;
- Any U.S. citizen who served honorably in the military during wartime for a government allied with the United States;
- The spouse of an eligible military member regardless of where the military member is buried or intends to be buried.

PROTECTING YOUR FAMILY

No one can say when trouble will strike, but you must be aware that it might, and be prepared if it does. Different modes of defense are available.

Financial Considerations

One way to help insulate yourself from some of life's grievous surprises is through insurance. The law does not require you to be insured—except for a certain minimum amount of automobile insurance in some states—but you can protect yourself, your home, your car, and your health from disaster by making sure you are properly insured. These safeguards can make the difference between coping and devastation if a tragedy occurs.

In addition, life insurance can be both a protection and an investment tool. Indeed, life insurance accounts for much of the estate many middle-class Americans leave their families when they die, particularly if they die prematurely. By underestimating your life insurance needs, you could leave your survivors without the necessary income to live. (For more information about life insurance, see YOUR MONEY, page 326.)

HOW THE GOVERNMENT HELPS

Insurance, however, is expensive, and many families cannot afford enough of it to protect themselves from disaster. Government support programs have come under serious scrutiny in recent years and undoubtedly will change through the years ahead, but if you are unemployed, disabled, or otherwise unable to provide for your family's daily expenses, many federal and state assistance programs provide a safety net.

Social Security is one of the oldest of these programs. In addition to retirement income, Social Security provides insurance for widows, insurance for children of workers who have died, and disability benefits for disabled workers who are injured and unable to work. Medicare, which provides health insurance for the aged, and Supplemental Security Income (SSI), which supplies extra income for the aged, disabled, or blind people with limited assets, are also administered by the Social Security Administration.

Among other state and federal programs are Medicaid, which pays for medical care to the poor; Aid to Families With Dependent Children (AFDC), which gives cash payments to a parent or other relative who is caring for a child and whose income places them in a poverty category, depending on state

IF YOUR APPLICATION IS DENIED

What happens if you apply for public assistance, such as Aid to Families with Dependent Children (AFDC), and are found ineligible or awarded smaller benefits than you feel you are entitled to? Federal law allows you to appeal such decisions. Here's how:

1. You should have received notice of an agency decision, describing its reasons and explaining your appeal rights.

2. From the date of notice, you have a "reasonable" time, usually a maximum of 90 days, to appeal the decision and seek a hearing, which may be at a local or a higher, state level. Benefits already being received should not be stopped or changed during this period.

3. Before the hearing, you are entitled to examine the case record and all documents the agency may have used to make its decisions.

4. At the hearing, you have the right to be legally represented, to provide evidence, and to question and cross-examine witnesses.

5. The agency must comply with the hearing decision within 90 days of the date the hearing was requested.

standards; food stamps, which are intended to ensure that every American receive proper nutrition; and state unemployment insurance, which provides temporary assistance to those who become unemployed through no fault of their own.

Consult the government listings section of your local telephone directory for the state or local welfare or human resources agency that can assist you, or call the Federal Information Center at (800) 347-1997 for the name and number of the federal agency to contact for your needs.

THE WILL AS FINANCIAL PROTECTION

Regardless of your age and financial circumstances, the importance of executing a will cannot be stressed enough. If you were to die "intestate," or without a will, your assets might be distributed according to state law rather than your personal wishes. Do-it-yourself kits are available at stationers, but if you have significant income, it is wise to consult a lawyer.

You should consider carefully who should be the beneficiaries of your will, your life insurance, and any other investment vehicles you own, such as a 401(k) plan. If you do not designate a beneficiary, the money may be subject to probate taxes, whereas if you have designated beneficiaries, the money will not be included in the estate and will not be subject to such costs. (See also, YOUR MONEY, page 365.)

Owning a Weapon

The Unreasonable Use of Deadly Force in Self-Defense

Using a gun or other deadly weapon to defend yourself or your home from a burglar may seem like an effective way of protecting your family. But be careful: emotionally, you may be right; legally, you are probably wrong.

It is not legal to use a deadly weapon solely for the purpose of protecting your property. To do so would be considered excessive or unreasonable use of force. Unless the intruder clearly threatens your life, attacks you, or otherwise places you or a family member in grave bodily danger, you will have a hard time proving in a court of law that you acted in self-defense.

In fact, if you fire your weapon and kill an unarmed burglar, or if you jump on and kill the burglar with a knife, you could be charged with the homicide. Even if you were subsequently found innocent, the slain intruder's family might sue you in civil court for damages.

The prohibition against using unreasonable force applies even more strongly outside of the home. You are permitted to use whatever force is necessary to defend yourself, but it must not be deadly force—a gun, for instance—unless you can prove that you yourself were in mortal danger.

Many people believe that owning and carrying a weapon, be it a gun, knife, or protective equipment such as Mace, is a good way to ensure the safety of their person, their family, and their home. The Second Amendment to the U.S. Constitution guarantees that "the right of the people to keep and bear arms, shall not be infringed," but a national debate simmers over the thorny question of whether some weapons are more dangerous than protective.

Federal and state legislation has long prohibited convicted felons, drugs users, and others from owning firearms. It has also placed some limitations on citizens' rights to buy and carry weapons—such as handguns, assault weapons, and switchblades—likely to produce death or bodily harm or be used to commit a crime. The so-called Brady Bill, enacted in 1994, imposed new restrictions including a waiting period for buyers of certain weapons.

As long as you obtain the permit required by state or local law, you can keep a weapon in your home, but make sure it is stored in a place that is completely inaccessible to children.

YOUR
HEALTH CARE

The problems of health care—who receives it, how much it costs, and who pays—are complicated. Knowing your rights can keep you healthy—both physically and financially.

THE HEART OF HEALTH CARE ■ YOU AND YOUR DOCTOR ■ YOUR RIGHTS AS A PATIENT ■ DEALING WITH A HOSPITAL ■ ALTERNATIVE HEALTH CARE ■ DECODING HEALTH INSURANCE ■ GOVERNMENT INSURANCE ■ LONG-TERM CARE ■ NURSING HOMES ■ DYING WITH DIGNITY

THE HEART OF HEALTH CARE

As health-care practices are transformed, it is imperative that you understand the meaning of the changes in order to make sure your rights are protected.

The Right to Quality Care

I t has long been the policy of the United States government that all its citizens should have the right to health care. Inherent in this philosophy is the belief that such health care should be "quality care," which includes the right to choose one's own physician, the right of access to state-of-the-art medical technology, and the right to patient satisfaction. Quality care, however, is often available only to the patient's who can pay, and increasingly in recent times, many patients cannot.

THE COST CONUNDRUM

In 1969, approximately seven percent of the national income went to health care. Today, expenditures have doubled, comprising almost 14 percent of the national income and exceeding $800 billion per year. Americans spend more per capita on health and medical services than any other country in the world.

The reasons health-care costs continue to rise so dramatically are numerous, complex, and interrelated. Americans are living longer, and, as a result, greater numbers of people are seeking treatment, especially the elderly. In past generations, acute, short-term illnesses like the flu, smallpox, and typhoid often killed men and women in their prime. Today, chronic, long-term illnesses like heart disease, cancer, and AIDS are the villains, but because of scientific breakthroughs, doctors are able to extend the lives of many patients with these conditions. However, many of medicine's new treatments involve specialized procedures that can be administered only by highly trained physicians and technicians.

The cost of treating more patients for a longer period of time using more specialized procedures and experts has inflated the cost of health exponentially. Furthermore, to pay for their own escalating costs, doctors and clinics are also charging more for basic services like checkups and immunizations. In order to cover all this, the price of insurance premiums has spiraled.

THE INSURANCE DEBATE

In the face of these rising health-care costs, when medical and hospital care insurance becomes an increasingly urgent need

The health of the people is really the foundation upon which all their happiness and all their powers as a state depend.

BENJAMIN DISRAELI
From a speech
1877

for most people, more than 35 million Americans are not protected by health insurance. Nevertheless, when the unprotected become injured or ill, they are entitled to receive treatment in a hospital or clinic. What is more, whether through increased taxes, or increased prices, someone pays the bill.

For decades, private groups and public officials, including the president of the United States, have tried to come up with a solution to the knotty problem of ever-escalating health-care costs. Among the various suggested plans are managed care, managed competition, national health insurance, mandatory employer-provided health insurance, and scores of variations on these themes.

While the debate continues, managed care seems to be emerging as the most practical alternative. More than 30 percent of Americans already belong to a health maintenance organization (HMO) or some other managed-care plan, and the numbers are rising rapidly. But whatever type of health insurance proves to be the best answer, you should know what the various options mean, as defined in the box below.

New Health-Care Terms

The debate over health care continues. Many plans have been suggested, by many influential people, but none have been universally adopted. The debate has spawned terms you should know in order to understand the developments in the way health care is delivered and paid for:

• **Managed care.** A general term for many types of health insurance plans, such as HMO's, that attempt to provide quality health care at reasonable costs. A network of providers (doctors, dentists, hospitals, etc.) is paid a fixed rate per patient by an employer or a consortium of groups or individuals to provide a spectrum of health services. With some managed-care plans, you have the right to retain a traditional fee-for-service arrangement if you are willing to pay the higher cost. (For a description of various plans, see "Comparing Health Insurance Options," page 203.)

• **Health Maintenance Organization (HMO)** This is the prototype of managed-care plans whereby members pay a fixed monthly premium for access to a range of medical services provided by the organization.

• **Managed competition.** A controversial form of cost control whereby the federal government would define a standard minimum benefit package. Large employers would contract directly with insurance companies for this coverage for their employees, and large health cooperatives would contract with private insurers on behalf of small employers, the self-employed, and the unemployed. Tax deductions for employer-provided health insurance would be capped at the cost of the cheapest plan, and a steep tax penalty would be placed on those choosing costlier alternatives. Thus "competition" would keep costs down.

• **National health insurance.** Also called a "single-payer" plan. Under this system, the government would act as health insurer for all citizens, paying for it with taxes. In some plans, the option for private care would be included.

• **Mandatory employer-provided insurance.** Here employers would provide health insurance to employees directly or by paying a percentage of payroll into a public pool through which employees would be covered. Some plans include government subsidies with which low-income, unemployed people can purchase insurance.

• **Individual mandate.** Under this plan, each person would be required to buy her own health insurance, shifting responsibility from employers to individuals. Some plans include restructuring the tax system to subsidize premiums.

YOU AND YOUR DOCTOR

Since the relationship with your doctor is one of the most important professional associations you will ever have, be sure that it works for you.

How to Choose a Doctor

Remember Marcus Welby, M.D., the smiling, affable doctor on television who always had time to chat and listen sympathetically? Whatever your idea of the perfect doctor, the best way to find what you are looking for is to shop around.

Once you have the name a of prospective doctor, schedule a consultation. Prepare a list of questions about any symptoms you have been experiencing, medications you are taking, or treatments you are receiving. Try describing any pain on a scale of one to ten, one being comfort and ten being unbearable. How long does pain last? What triggers it?

Let your doctor know your expectations and the kind of treatment you want. Make sure she has copies of your past medical records before your visit. Do not be shy about telling your doctor about events in your life that could be affecting your physical or emotional health. The smallest aches and pains could be clues to a larger medical problem. And be honest—if you are a smoker, for instance, don't try to hide it.

YOUR RIGHT TO ASK QUESTIONS

It is a good idea to ask your doctor about her medical education and training. Find out if she is on the faculty of a major medical school or on the staff of a teaching hospital. Ask if you will always be seen by her, or if she will use her colleagues, nurses, or assistants for some procedures.

You also have the right to ask about fees. If you are covered by traditional insurance, find out if she will accept insurance as payment in full. Is there a copayment? Will she let you pay in installments if necessary? If you receive Medicare or Medicaid, are her fees commensurate with government programs?

Feel free to write down anything your doctor says. You might even ask her to put your treatment plan in writing, including any medications she prescribes and their risks. Or take along a family member or friend who can remind you to ask certain questions or can ask questions on your behalf. Remember: You are paying your doctor to work for you. If you don't like the way she treats you, you have the right to complain or to take your business elsewhere.

Types of Health Providers

Doctors pursue dozens of specialties within the medical profession, and having a general idea of who does what will help you find the best care. Unless you have an acute problem, you should probably start with someone who will coordinate your medical care, from monitoring a chronic disease to referring you to the appropriate specialist. In other words, you need a general practitioner, now known as a primary-care physician, or PCP.

Think of a primary-care physician as an orchestra conductor. He does not play each instrument, but he knows how each should be played to create a symphony. Your primary-care doctor conducts your health care. He considers all aspects of your personal and medical history when making a diagnosis. Ideally, he should be able to teach you about diet, exercise, and other illness-preventing habits. If you are chronically ill, your primary-care doctor will monitor your condition. If you need a specialist, he will make the referral and save you the trouble and expense of running from doctor to doctor.

SPECIALISTS WHO PRACTICE GENERAL MEDICINE

Although primary-care doctors practice general medicine, most are board-certified to specialize in a particular area as well. Internists, for example, specialize in internal medicine; they do not perform surgery. An internist might be a cardiologist, treating diseases of the cardiovascular system, or an endocrinologist, treating disorders of the hormone system. Internists also diagnose and treat diseases of the digestive system (gastroenterology); the joints, muscles, and tendons (rheumatology); the kidneys and urinary problems (nephrology); and blood disorders (hematology). Despite all these specialties, internists usually see patients as general practitioners as well.

A primary-care doctor may be in "family practice," a branch of medicine that includes the treatment of children as well as adults. Family practitioners are trained in pediatrics, surgery, internal medicine, obstetrics and gynecology, and orthopedics. Unlike internists, they are trained to perform general surgery, such as tonsillectomies and appendectomies.

Pediatricians specialize in child development and diseases. You may choose to use your child's primary-care doctor from birth through adolescence. Like internists, pediatricians may subspecialize in particular areas, such as the care of newborn and premature babies and their mothers (neonatal-perinatal medicine), or the treatment of children with cardiovascular problems (pediatric cardiology).

Obstetrician-gynecologists treat the female reproductive sys-

---

QUESTIONS TO ASK YOUR DOCTOR

Don't hesitate to interview your doctor thoroughly and directly; it is the best way to find out if you will have a good relationship. You have the right to ask these questions:

1. Education. Where did you attend medical school and serve your residency?

2. Specialization. Are you board-certified in your area of specialty?

3. Medical philosophy. What is your medical or treatment philosophy? Do you tend to spend much time with patients? Will you discuss test results and other issues?

4. Hospital affiliation. At what hospital do you have admitting privileges?

5. Availability. Are you available 24 hours a day for emergencies? If not, who covers for you? How long does it take to get an appointment? What is your policy regarding telephone consultations?

6. Fees. What are your fees? Will you accept Medicare or Medicaid? Are you associated with any managed-care plans?

7. Malpractice. Have you ever been sued for malpractice or disciplined by a federal or state agency?

tem. Their care includes regular examinations; preventive tests like Pap smears for cancer detection; the surgical removal of cysts or tumors; and the prescription of medications, such as hormones or birth control devices; the treatment of infertility; and the management of menopause. Obstetricians care for women during pregnancy and delivery and immediately after. Many women use their gynecologist as their general practitioner, and many managed care organizations recognize gynecologists as primary-care physicians or "gatekeepers."

Doctors of osteopathy (D.O.'s), are fully trained physicians who have graduated from a four-year college of osteopathic medicine rather than a medical college. They focus on the musculoskeletal system (muscles, bones, and joints). Osteopaths approach illness as a possible disruption in one or more of the body's systems and may use hands-on manipulative therapy.

Nurse practitioners are registered nurses with advanced training in specific areas of medicine. You will find them in doctors' offices or hospitals. They can conduct physical examinations; order laboratory and other diagnostic tests; assess,

What to Expect From Your Dentist

A dentist, like a doctor, should be licensed and board-certified, and qualified to treat your particular needs. While it is important to have a good rapport with your dentist, every detail of his practice counts. Here are some things to look for when you are choosing a dentist:

• You should be able to talk comfortably and candidly with your dentist, and he should be willing to explain what your dental problems are and how he will go about fixing them.

• The dentist's office should be scrupulously clean. All of the dentist's equipment should be completely heat-sterilized. To reduce the possibility of transmitting germs, the dentist should use disposable items, such as the needles to administer anesthetics. Disinfecting all the switches, buttons, and drill handles that he or his assistants touch should be routine. Similarly, rubber gloves and protective face masks should be worn during every procedure.

• It is your right to ask your dentist if he and his assistants have been vaccinated against hepatitis B, measles, rubella, and influenza. You also have the right to know that your dentist's assistants are specially trained and licensed to take X-rays and final impressions, and clean and polish teeth.

• Ask your dentist how often he recommends X-rays. If your dentist is cautious, he will take the minimum amount of X-rays necessary. Because

of the possible danger of radiation, some experts suggest that full-mouth X-rays should not be taken more often than every five years and that children under 16 should not have them at all unless problems are suspected.

• When your dentist or his assistants do take X-rays, they should take every safety precaution. For example,they should cover your chest and lap with a lead apron. They should always check with you that it is safe to take an X-ray; do not allow X-rays to be taken if you are pregnant.

• A good dentist is prevention-oriented. The dentist should carefully explain during each visit the best home-care techniques and put you on a regular schedule of office visits.

• If your dentist treats your children, make sure he instructs them how to take care of their teeth, teaches them about cavity-causing foods and eating habits, and sees that they are sent home with a new toothbrush. It is also a good sign if the dentist has other children as patients or even specializes in treating children or, at least, is thoughtful about family health care.

diagnose, and monitor medical conditions; and prescribe medications. They cannot perform surgery.

Physician's assistants work under a doctor's supervision and can diagnose and treat common medical problems. They can provide preventive services and are trained to deal with routine emergency situations. Some physician's assistants can help surgeons in the performance of routine procedures, but they cannot perform surgery themselves.

When You Need a Specialist

Your primary-care doctor is concerned with your overall health, but if she thinks you need a test or procedure, she cannot provide, or if she wants a second opinion on a diagnosis she has made, she will probably refer you to a specialist. You have the right to search out a specialist on your own, but your best bet is first to follow the recommendation of your primary-care doctor.

Specialists deal with specific body systems, diseases, or age groups. They focus on the part of the body that is presenting problems, rather than concerning themselves with the complete medical condition and history of the patient. A good primary-care doctor will not forget about you after he sends you to a specialist. He will confer with that specialist and monitor your progress.

BE YOUR OWN JUDGE

While it makes sense to take your doctor's advice in the matter of a specialist, you are nevertheless entitled to question a recommendation. Specialists are far more expensive than primary-care doctors. They also tend to perform more tests and procedures.

Before acting on your doctor's referral, insist that she explain what she thinks is wrong with you. If she does not feel you need a referral, find out what treatment she feels is best for you. If she does recommend a specialist, find out why she has chosen that physician—and what that specialist's reputation and credentials are.

A specialist should be board certified in the treatment area you need. Board certification represents a minimum standard of excellence. It means that in addition to graduating from medical school, a specialist has completed at least two years of supervised specialty training or residency and has passed a written and oral exam given by a national board of professionals in that field. Each specialty has its own board, but not all boards have high standards. Specialists with the most complete training and testing generally are certified by the American

Mental-Health Experts

Before looking for a mental-health professional, you should understand the different disciplines that treat mental or emotional disorders.

Psychiatrists are physicians licensed to practice medicine and prescribe medications as well as provide psychotherapeutic help. After medical school, they complete a year internship and three years of psychiatric training.

If board-certified, they have practiced for at least two years and have passed the written and oral examinations of the American Board of Psychiatry and Neurology.

Psychiatrists can determine when emotional disorders are medically-related and require drug intervention. They can also provide psychotherapy. They are the only mental-health professionals who can write prescriptions.

Psychologists are not physicians, but can provide psychotherapy. They usually hold a master's or Ph.D. degree from a university program and have passed a licensing examination. They can counsel individuals, groups, or families.

Psychiatric nurses are registered professional nurses with advanced degrees in the prevention and treatment of mental health-related problems.

Psychiatric or clinical social workers usually have a master's or Ph.D. degree in social work. They are licensed in social work and some form of psychotherapeutic counseling.

The following warning signs could be evidence that the person you are consulting is practicing quackery, not medicine:

✔ *Dodging questions.* He will not tell you where he attended medical school, where he trained, or how much experience he has had with specific procedures and treatments.

✔ *Making serious errors.* He prescribes antibiotics when you have a cold, for instance, even though antibiotics do not work on colds. Or, for a young child with flu he prescribes aspirin instead of acetaminophen.

✔ *Cutting corners.* He writes a new prescription without examining you first.

✔ *Refusing to translate.* He uses pseudo-medical phrases, such as "strengthen your system," "detoxify," or "rejuvenate your body" and will not explain them.

✔ *Shunning second opinions.* He will not refer you to other doctors to confirm his findings and will discourage you from seeking second opinions.

✔ *Blaming your diet.* No matter what ails you, he links most diseases with poor nutrition and relies on vitamin supplements as remedies.

✔ *Offering vague diagnoses.* Be cautious of catchall, indefinite diagnostic terms given without a comprehensive diagnosis, such as "environmental illness."

Board of Medical Specialties. (The ABMS recognizes only 23 of the 150 existing medical boards.) To find out about your doctor and his specialty, call the ABMS at (800) 776-2378. They will also provide a list of board-certified doctors in your area.

Don't be satisfied with the term "board-qualified" as opposed to "board-certified." All doctors are board-qualified if they have graduated from medical school and completed residency in their specialty. Doctors who are board-qualified must still pass the certification exam in their specialty in order to be board-certified.

Two important directories, both of which should be in your local public library, list virtually all the doctors in the United States who have been board-certified together with their complete credentials. These directories are: *The Directory of Medical Specialists,* and *The American Medical Directory: Physicians in the United States.* Doctors who are recent medical school graduates may not be listed.

A doctor who passes a specialty board examination is awarded the status of Diplomate. Most board-certified doctors also become members, or fellows, of their medical-specialty societies. Doctors who earn the title "Fellow" have met the full requirements for membership in their specialty society. They are considered qualified to practice a specialty due to their education, training, and experience.

Even though board-certification is the best indication of specialty training, it does not guarantee excellence. Older, general practice doctors who have been specializing for years may lack board-certification but still be excellent doctors.

Any doctor can call herself an expert or specialist. For instance, a doctor who is a sports enthusiast may advertise himself as a "sports medicine specialist." A state license does not instantly qualify your doctor as a specialist. A license indicates only that a doctor has completed medical school and one year of internship or residency.

Working With Your Surgeon

Surgery, among the most expensive and high-risk specialties, is one of the most important areas for you to be informed about. When surgery is done on an emergency basis, making choices about doctors, hospitals, and procedures is out of your hands. Most surgery, however, is elective, which gives you time to arrange it according to your best interest.

Before you agree to surgery, make sure you understand exactly why it is recommended. Your doctor has the duty to explain the benefits and the risks to you and whether you can avoid surgery altogether by undergoing alternative treatment.

You have the right to get a second opinion on any medical issue, but it is especially relevant when surgery is the issue. Some insurance companies actually require second opinions before agreeing to pay for an operation.

When looking for a surgeon to give you a second opinion, choose one who is not affiliated with the surgeon who wants to operate: co-workers may tend to agree with each other. Make sure the second-opinion surgeon has seen all of your medical records and test results. If you remain unsure, get a third or even a fourth opinion. (Be aware, though, that insurance may not pay for the extra opinions.)

SELECTING YOUR SURGICAL TEAM

One way to control your fate in the matter of surgery is to stipulate that specific doctors perform the procedure. Choosing a surgeon, like any specialist, calls for research. Get one or more referrals from your primary-care doctor. Then visit each surgeon under consideration. Investigate their credentials. Make sure they are board-certified in the area you require. Find out if they are fellows of the American College of Surgeons or other appropriate board. Find out with which hospitals the surgeon is affiliated, and to which one he plans to send you.

Besides choosing your surgeon, you also have the right to request that specific doctors, including the assistant surgeon and anesthesiologist, be part of the surgical team. Since the assistant surgeon typically gets paid a fixed 20 to 25 percent of the surgeon's fee, he should have equal qualifications.

Selecting your anesthesiologist may be tougher, since most anesthesiologists contract with hospitals, which make the surgical assignments. Still, you may ask your surgeon to request the anesthesiologists most appropriate for your operation. Then, discuss with the anesthesiologist the type of anesthetic to be used and the associated risks and side effects.

Once you have selected your surgical team, meet with each member and find out exactly what will happen during surgery. You are entitled to know what to expect, from the time you get to the hospital to the time you leave. You also should be informed about how you may feel afterward, how long your recuperation is expected to take, and how you can make yourself more comfortable.

SET YOUR OWN SCHEDULE

Deciding where to have surgery will depend on your surgeon's hospital affiliation, the type of procedure you are undergoing, and your overall health. Some simple procedures that require only local anesthetics may be done right in the doctor's office or on an outpatient basis in the hospital.

BEFORE YOU SAY YES TO SURGERY

Surgery is risky and expensive. If your doctor recommends it, make sure you understand what is at stake—and do not feel obliged to consent until you get every question answered. For example:

1. Your illness or injury. Has your doctor explained to you precisely what is wrong and how surgery will help?

2. The operation. What is the nature of the operation and how will it be performed, step by step? How long will the operation take?

3. Risks. What are the risks and how serious are they? Will there be side effects, residual or permanent damage, or extreme pain? If you will experience pain, how long will it last?

4. Your doctor's experience. How many times has your surgeon performed this procedure? What is his success rate? Has he ever failed?

5. Costs. How much will the operation cost? Will your insurance cover all surgical and hospital costs adequately?

6. Recurrence. Might the condition recur after you have had surgery? What are your options if the condition recurs?

7. Alternatives. What will happen if you choose not to have surgery? Are there alternative ways to treat your condition that you could try first?

Know Your Surgery Coverage

O nce you have decided to have an operation, be sure to find out how much of its costs will be covered by your insurance. The language of insurance policies is notoriously hard to decipher. Don't hesitate to question your insurance agent until you are sure you understand your coverage.

Hospital insurance covers both the cost of inpatient and outpatient services. It usually specifies the number of days of hospitalization the policy covers, as well as the maximum cost the policy will pay. Find out if your hospital insurance policy pays the daily room-and-board rate of the hospital you have chosen, and make sure you know whether there is a waiting period before benefits go into effect.

Medical-surgical insurance is divided into two parts. The medical part covers your doctor's visits while you are in the hospital, and may pay for office visits. Find out how much your policy pays for the doctor's hospital visits and how many visits it covers. The policy should also pay for prescription drugs, medications, X-rays, anesthesia, and tests performed outside the hospital. Find out if it includes special treatments such as intensive and coronary care, and physical therapy.

Your policy should cover the surgeon's fee, but ask if it covers fees for an assistant and an anesthesiologist. Don't rely on what your doctor tells you about your policy; check with the insurance company.

If your operation requires general anesthesia, you will need close, constant monitoring, or complications may develop. As a result, you will probably be safest in a hospital. Find out why your surgeon has recommended a particular hospital before agreeing to have surgery. Generally, doctors actively utilize one or two hospitals. Using a hospital where your doctor is recognized and perhaps teaches or supervises residents may assure you of better health care and attention.

When You Are Dissatisfied

I f you are lucky, the treatment you receive from your doctor or other health-care professional will always be satisfactory. Unfortunately, many people become unhappy or dissatisfied with their doctor for any number of reasons. Your problem with your doctor may be personal; you may feel she is treating you in a less than professional manner, perhaps by keeping you waiting too long before appointments. Your complaint could be more serious: you may suspect your doctor is under the influence of alcohol while she is treating you, or that she is overcharging you. The agencies that regulate a doctor's license to practice are individual state agencies. There is no federal legislation that protects you from unethical or unsatisfactory medical conduct. If you are not actually harmed by your doctor's behavior and do not have grounds for a malpractice case, your recourse lies within your state.

NONMEDICAL COMPLAINTS

Problems between doctors and patients that are not directly related to improper medical conduct but to personality or other conflict may best be dealt with directly. If you find yourself in a situation where you are unhappy about your treatment, it is your responsibility to speak up and make your concerns known. Tell your doctor exactly why you are dissatisfied. For example, she never fully explains why she is prescribing a particular medication. If you do not speak up, she has no reason for her to change her customary procedure and she is not likely to do so. However, if your doctor does not change her practices after you have talked to her, you may want to look for a new physician. If the problems are serious, you may also want to complain to local medical associations and hospitals where your doctor is on staff, or to your insurance company.

WHAT ARE UNETHICAL PRACTICES?

The following are practices your state medical examiner's offices may consider unethical. In fact, in some cases, certain of these practices may be illegal:

- Incompetence;
- Gross negligence or repeated negligent acts;
- Falsifying medical records or patients' bills;
- Evidence of mental or physical illness that impairs the doctor's ability to practice medicine;
- Prescribing drugs without giving a proper examination;
- Abuse of drugs or alcohol or being under the influence of either while attending a patient;
- Sexual harassment—unwelcome sexual advances toward a client or patient.

Suppose you suspect your doctor is not billing you correctly. First, study your bill carefully. Check to see if your doctor is charging you for services that were not rendered, charging you twice for the same procedure, or billing you for his time when a nurse actually treated you.

If you suspect your doctor is guilty of unethical or illegal practices such as falsifying records or negligent behavior, inform your insurance company and your state's medical examiner's office. Every state has boards and agencies that investigate and sanction medical personnel and facilities, and you may want to make a report to a such an agency or board. Call your local health department to find out which state agency to contact.

If you are still not satisfied with the response you get from your state medical agency, you may consider contacting your state attorney general's office, your senator, or your congressman to lodge a complaint.

When a doctor does go wrong, he is the first of criminals. He has nerve and he has knowledge.

ARTHUR CONAN DOYLE
The Adventures of Sherlock Holmes

Filing a Complaint Against a Doctor

Whether you feel that your doctor is not giving you the attention and time you deserve or that your doctor is acting unethically, you have a right to speak out and let your concerns be known. If you have a complaint against a doctor, keep the following in mind:

• If you suspect your doctor of unethical conduct, merely speaking to him may not be enough. If you suffer physically, mentally, or financially because of your doctor's incompetence, you may have a malpractice case against him. Contact a lawyer immediately if you think you do.

• If you have not suffered any real harm, but still suspect your doctor is incompetent, is too mentally or physically impaired to practice medicine safely, or is committing fraud, take your complaint to a state regulatory agency.

• Making a formal complaint can be time-consuming and complicated. Call your local department of health to find out where to register your complaint. You can also file a written complaint with the state licensing board that pertains to your physician.

• When you file your complaint, make sure you include the name of the doctor or other health provider; a complete description of the incident or incidents on which you are basing your complaint, including dates and locations; and any witnesses who can support your position.

• Make sure you have all the documents that relate to your complaint: medical or hospital records, lab reports, and bills. Always keep the originals, making copies if necessary. If you do not have these, indicate where they can be found.

Understanding Malpractice

If you suffer injury and disability because a doctor, nurse, or other health provider was negligent in treating you, you have the right to sue for malpractice. Failing to cure you is not necessarily grounds for malpractice. But you may have a claim if your condition worsens because your doctor has been negligent; that is, if he has failed to treat you according to the minimum standards of skill and care that have been established by his specialty and would be observed by other practitioners under the same circumstances.

If your doctor prescribes medication to which you have a known allergy and you suffer harm as a result, he may be liable due to his negligence. Similarly, if you are hurt because he injects a drug in the wrong area of your body, improperly sets a broken bone, or misdiagnoses a fracture as a sprain, he may be liable for damage caused by his negligence.

A doctor is not being negligent if he abides by standard medical practice, even if his treatment fails to help you. For instance, you do not have grounds for suing your doctor if he refuses to make a house call, prescribes an expensive but unsuccessful treatment for an incurable disease, or if he orders expensive, exploratory tests that come out negative. Not making house calls is considered standard medical practice, as is ordering expensive exploratory treatments.

Doctors and all health providers are required to inform patients about their illness, the proposed treatments, the chances of success, and any risks involved. They are then required to obtain a patient's consent to begin treatment. If a health provider begins a treatment without consent, he may be liable for his negligence.

HOW TO GUARD AGAINST MALPRACTICE

Being your own advocate is the best way to protect yourself against malpractice. Before committing yourself to a doctor's care, be sure to exercise your right to research his credentials and record. If he has been sued before, you might think about choosing a different doctor or finding out why.

If you already have a doctor, but have doubts about his competence, you can protect yourself against possible malpractice by looking for certain clues. For example, a misdiagnosis or an improperly prescribed medication is a sign of incompetence. Your doubts would be strengthened if your doctor shrugged off your complaints or avoided your repeated phone calls.

Be alert for signs of physical decline—if the doctor appears ill, unkempt, or intoxicated. Look for the qualities you once admired about him. Have they changed? If so, his professional

---

I will follow that method of treatment which, according to my ability and judgment, I consider for the benefit of my patients, and abstain from whatever is deleterious and mischievous.

I will give no deadly medicine to anyone if asked, nor suggest any such counsel.

Into whatever houses I enter, I will go into them for the benefit of the sick, and will abstain from every voluntary act of mischief and corruption.

While I continue to keep this Oath unviolated, may it be granted to me to enjoy life and the practice of the Art, respected by all men, in all times, but should I trespass and violate this Oath, may the reverse be my lot.

HIPPOCRATES
From the
Hippocratic Oath

skills and standards could be slipping. Obviously, such a scenario is not common, but being mindful of such subtleties might help keep you out of trouble if it turns out your doctor has indeed lost his grip.

SEEKING REDRESS

If you believe you have suffered significant damage to your health or well-being due to a negligent doctor, you may have grounds for a malpractice claim. Your first step should be to get your medical records from the doctor. A lawyer or another doctor will need these records in order to evaluate the treatment you received and determine if you have a claim. Next, ask another doctor for a second opinion. Keep careful records of any incidence of pain, conversations you have with any doctor, dates of appointments, diagnosis, treatment plans, or anything relevant to your condition.

A Doctor's Carelessness

PROBLEM
Ed was new in town and did not have a primary-care doctor. After pulling a muscle in his back, he called a doctor whose name he found in the Yellow Pages under "Back Specialists." The doctor prescribed extra-strength aspirin, since Ed did not want anything that would make him drowsy. The physician did not tell Ed to come in for an examination; nor did he ask Ed if he was taking any other medications. Ed took notes as the doctor spoke and followed his advice. As it happens, Ed was taking a drug called Coumadin, which prevents blood clots from forming. After a few days of taking both drugs, Ed began experiencing severe stomach pain. He noticed blood in his urine and stool. Alarmed and unable to reach the doctor, he went to the emergency room.

ACTION
The emergency-room doctors explained to Ed that his stomach lining had become irritated and had started bleeding due to the combination of aspirin, which is known to cause stomach bleeding, and Coumadin, which prevents blood from clotting. According to standard medical practice, the doctor should have insisted on examining Ed before prescribing anything over the phone. Then he should have asked Ed if he was taking any other medications. Ed sued the doctor for malpractice and was able to prove that he suffered harm due to the doctor's negligence. He collected damages for pain and suffering and was reimbursed for the emergency-room and hospital expenses that his insurance did not cover.

If you still feel you have been mistreated and want to file a claim, consult an experienced malpractice lawyer to make sure you have a case. If your lawyer thinks you have a strong case, then bring a malpractice claim. (For more information about bringing suit, see YOUR RIGHTS IN ACTION, page 476.)

Do You Have a Malpractice Claim?

To win a malpractice suit, you must prove the following:

✔ *The doctor owed you a duty.* The doctor's duty is to fulfill the doctor-patient relationship, providing medical treatment that meets an acceptable standard of care. When your doctor agrees to treat you, he makes a professional commitment to provide appropriate care.

✔ *You were given substandard care.* When a doctor provides care that does not meet the standards upheld by the medical community, he commits a breach of duty. If he does not use the degree of knowledge and skill that a "reasonable physician" in the same specialty would have used under the same circumstances, he is similarly at fault. You must prove this point to win a malpractice claim.

✔ *You suffered harm.* You must prove that you suffered an injury or damage to your health, your financial well-being, or both.

✔ *The doctor's negligence was the cause of harm.* This is perhaps the most difficult point to prove. You must show that your injury or harm was a direct result of having received substandard care from your doctor. Unless you or your attorney can establish a link between your injury and your doctor's failure to provide proper care, you will have a difficult time winning a malpractice claim.

YOUR RIGHTS AS A PATIENT

When you are ill or injured, you feel especially vulnerable. But as a patient, you have many rights available to you, and you should not hesitate to use them.

Know What What Your Are Signing

To make the best decisions about your health care, you need to be fully informed about your condition and understand how any medical or surgical treatments will affect you. You have the right to this information. Without it, you cannot give your informed consent, which health care professionals are obligated by law to obtain from you before giving you treatment.

Specifically, your doctor must get your consent before treating you. The only exceptions to this occur if you need life-saving medical treatment and cannot give your consent, and there is no time to find someone to consent for you. Also, if your doctor has evidence that informing you about your condition or a treatment might harm you or prevent you from making a rational decision, he may withhold the information or give it to someone designated by you.

The concept of informed consent means that you agree to treatment based on your understanding of its benefits and risks. If you consent to a treatment when your doctor did not fully inform you of its risks and you are harmed as a result, then your doctor may be liable for a claim of negligence.

HOW BINDING IS A CONSENT FORM?

Printed consent forms usually are not legally required. State statutes vary. Your verbal consent is legally valid, but should you and your doctor disagree about whether your consent was obtained for a specific procedure, a written form is most likely to hold up in court.

A consent form must contain all the elements required for informed consent, plus any other relevant information you have discussed with your doctor. If you disagree with something on the form, it is your right to delete or change it. Even so, not all consent forms are legally binding. Blanket consent forms, which seek to authorize a physician to perform any procedure he deems advisable, are the least binding. You probably will be asked to sign one when you check into a hospital so that medical personnel can perform routine procedures on you.

Detailed consent forms are more binding. They specify your medical condition; the proposed treatment or procedure; and

Patient's Bill of Rights

The Patient's Bill of Rights is a set of guidelines describing the level of care you are entitled to in various medical settings. These guidelines are not federally mandated and have not been adopted by all states, providers, or facilities. According to most versions, you have a right to:

• Receive proper medical care regardless of your race, color, religion, national origin, or source of payment for your care.

• Receive prompt emergency services without being questioned in advance about your ability to pay for them.

• Receive considerate and respectful care in a clean and safe environment, including reasonable responses to reasonable requests for service.

• Receive complete, relevant, and understandable information about your medical condition, the course of your treatment, and the prospects for your recovery.

• Know the name and position of the doctor who is in charge of your care in a hospital and be able to talk with that physician.

• Know the names, positions, and functions of any members of a hospital staff involved in your care, including students, residents, or other trainees.

• Have an interpreter if you do not speak English or if you are hearing impaired.

• Receive as much information as you need about a proposed treatment—including risks, benefits, alternatives, and the name of the person administering the treatment—in order to be able to give informed consent or refuse the treatment.

• Make decisions about the course of your care, including the right to seek additional consultations, before and during treatment, and make decisions about your discharge from the hospital. You are entitled to a written discharge plan, as well as a written description of how you can appeal your discharge.

• Be notified of your impending discharge at least one day in advance, as well as have a consultation with an expert on the reason or reasons for the discharge. You are also entitled to have a person of your choice notified in advance regarding your discharge.

• Refuse treatment and be told how your refusal may affect your health. (If you are not conscious or competent and there is no evidence of your treatment wishes, a court may order treatment to save your life.)

• Refuse transfer to another facility unless you have received a complete explanation of the need and benefits of the transfer, the other facility has accepted your transfer, and you have agreed to it.

• Be given every consideration of privacy and confidentiality regarding all information, discussions, and records pertaining to your care. You have the right to know why anyone not directly involved with your care is present.

• Have an advance directive, such as a living will, health care proxy, or durable power of attorney for health care that clearly states your treatment wishes or designates a surrogate to make decisions for you. You also have the right to know a hospital's policy on advance directives.

• Review all records of your care and have them explained, as necessary, except when restricted by law. You also have the right—which cannot be denied due to inability to pay—to a copy of your medical record for a reasonable charge.

• Ask or be informed if a hospital or physicians have a financial interest in a health-care facility, educational institution, or insurance plan that may influence your treatment and care.

• Agree or refuse to participate in research studies or human experimentation that might affect your treatment and care and to have those studies fully explained before consenting.

• Be informed of hospital policies and practices that relate to patient care, treatment, and responsibilities. You have the right to be informed of available resources, such as ethics committees or patient advocates, and be informed of any charges for such services.

• Leave the hospital, even against the advice of doctors. You will be asked to sign a "Discharge Against Medical Advice" form, relieving the hospital of any responsibility for harm you suffer by leaving.

• Receive an itemized bill and explanation of all charges.

its risks, benefits, and alternatives. You might be asked to sign a surgery consent form, an anesthesia consent form, and so on.

Remember, you do not sign away your rights with a consent form. Your doctor or hospital still may be held accountable for malpractice; and even after you have signed a form you may withdraw your consent.

Medications and Devices

You have the right to refuse any medication, and the right to question your doctor about medication he prescribes. Your doctor is legally obliged to tell you the name of the drug and what it is supposed to do, when it should be taken, and in what dosage. He also should explain what to do if you forget to take the medication or if you want to stop taking it altogether.

If you have ever experienced an allergic reaction to any medications, inform your doctor immediately. Also, tell him if you smoke or drink caffeinated or alcoholic beverages. Any of these substances may mix badly with certain medicines. Should you get a serious or unexpected reaction from a drug, you should immediately report it to your doctor. If the drug proves particularly toxic, you also may want to report it to the Food and Drug Administration (FDA), the federal agency responsible for monitoring drug safety.

KNOW THE RISKS OF MEDICAL DEVICES

Federal law requires every medical device to be classified as relatively harmless such as slings and bandages; potentially harmful; such as wheelchairs or home pregnancy tests; or one that can be implanted in the body or pose a serious risk to health. Devices in the third category include breast implants, pacemakers, and intrauterine devices (IUD's).

A different law requires hospitals, nursing homes, and manufacturers to report deaths and serious injuries caused by medical devices. The law also authorizes the FDA to order a manufacturer to stop distributing harmful devices and recall them if necessary.

In 1993 the FDA issued new rules requiring manufacturers of potentially life-threatening devices to provide the current names and addresses of all customers within 10 days of an FDA request, in the event of a recall. Such devices include implants, pacemakers, heart valves, and breathing monitors.

You have the right to be informed by the manufacturer if a permanently implanted device is defective, but the manufacturer must be able to locate you. This involves filling out a warranty card and leaving a forwarding address if you move.

Your Rights in Medical Research

If you participate in any special medical research project, you have a right to:

✔ *Understand the research.* Obtain an explanation of its purpose, procedures, and experimental components.

✔ *A time frame.* Know how long your participation is expected to last.

✔ *Understand the risks.* Ask for an explanation of possible consequences, including risks, discomforts, and benefits.

✔ *Privacy.* Find out how confidential your identity and your records will be.

✔ *Potential compensation.* If you are taking a risk, you should be told whether you will receive payment and what compensation you will receive should you suffer injury.

✔ *IRB approval.* Most hospitals have an Institutional Review Board (IRB) that reviews proposed research projects and makes sure they meet federal guidelines. Make sure the project is IRB-approved.

✔ *Meet the director.* Insist on knowing who is in charge of the research project and whom you can call for answers to your questions.

✔ *Withdraw.* Your participation is voluntary, and it is your right to refuse to continue at any time without being subject to a penalty.

CAN YOU SUE FOR DAMAGES?

If a medical device makes you ill or causes injury, you should first inform your doctor, who should respond to the problem in some way. You may also file a product-liability lawsuit against the manufacturer of the device and anyone involved in its sale. To win, however, you must prove that the product's defective manufacture or design led to danger, that you were not informed of the product's risks, or that the instructions were inadequate or unsafe.

Getting Your Records

The information contained in your medical records can be characterized as your property, but the records themselves generally belong to the doctor or medical facility that holds them. Depending on the facility and the state in which you live, your ease of access to your medical records will vary.

Regulations differ among states. The majority grant individuals a legal right to see and copy their medical records, either through state statute, regulation, or judicial decision. Your access probably will be easiest and most direct if your records are held by a federal facility, such as a Veterans Administration hospital. According to the federal Privacy Act of 1974, records in federal facilities generally must be made available to patients.

If your records are not in a federal facility, you may have some negotiating to do. Sometimes your doctor or the medical records department of your hospital will honor your request by phone. More likely, however, you will be asked to provide a written request, possibly in person. You also may be charged for the cost of retrieving and copying records.

In states that do not require availability, some doctors and hospitals may be unwilling to give you your records. They may argue that you would not understand them or would misinterpret them. Insist on seeing them anyway and on having copies made. (You may even base your relationship with your doctor on the provision that you have access to your medical records.) The chances are that your request will not be denied. In some cases, however, like those involving substance abuse or some psychiatric services, doctors may withhold your records if they feel that seeing them could harm you.

IF YOUR REQUEST IS DENIED

If your doctor or hospital denies your request to obtain your records, you are entitled to get in writing the reasons for the denial. If time permits, you may stop seeing the doctor who

---

123

YOUR MEDICAL RECORDS

If you request and receive a copy of your medical records from your doctor, here is what you should find:

1. Information that identifies you, including your name, address, height, weight, and other physical descriptions.

2. An account of your medical history, including family illnesses, surgeries, hospitalizations, and medications that have been prescribed.

3. Results from your most recent physical examination, including laboratory reports and X-ray results.

4. A copy of your written informed consent for any recommended medical or surgical procedures, or a written note explaining why you have withheld informed consent.

5. A description of your medical condition and its progress, as well as recommendations for treatment made by your doctor and the results of your treatment.

6. Reports of all tests or procedures that have been performed and their results.

7. Your doctor's findings and suggestions at the end of treatment or hospitalization.

8. Findings and correspondence from other doctors regarding your medical condition and treatment.

refuses to show you your records and find one who will. Then have the file transferred to the new doctor. Doctors and hospitals generally honor requests for patient records if they come from other providers. If polite verbal or written requests fail, you can try filing a complaint with the hospital administrator, the hospital's patient representative, or the ethics committee.

The patient must combat the disease along with the physician.

HIPPOCRATES
Aphorisms

Your Right to Privacy

You are guaranteed a right to privacy in most health-care settings. Doctors, nurses, hospital personnel, and other health-care providers involved with your care are legally and ethically bound to protect any information about your medical condition. However, there are a few exceptions.

If you are hospitalized, dozens of staff members are likely to be involved with your care in addition to your primary-care doctor. Each will stake a legitimate claim to your records, which is why you should know what they contain.

Another exception involves public health. When the health of others is involved, a doctor may be legally required to disclose medical information. For example, doctors must report births; deaths; infectious, contagious, or communicable diseases; child abuse; and violent injuries such as gunshot wounds.

Sexually transmitted diseases are considered threatening to public health; therefore if you have one, your privacy may be

---

Keeping Your Own Medical Records

An up-to-date medical file is an excellent way to keep track of your health care, and to help your doctors plan necessary treatment. A medical record is especially important if you move, change doctors, travel frequently, or become incapacitated. Your records should include:

• **Overall medical history.** Write down your name, date, and place of birth, your insurance-company name and identification number, and your Medicare and Social Security numbers. List any medical conditions, acute or chronic, that you have suffered. If certain conditions run in your family, like diabetes or cancer, record them.

• **Office Visits to Physicians.** List each visit to a doctor, with the date, the reason for the visit, the condition that was diagnosed, and the treatment prescribed.

• **Medications.** List every medication you take or have taken, including prescription drugs, vitamins, and over-the-counter drugs; the name of the doc-

tor who prescribed them; the pharmacy where you bought them; and any side effects you may have experienced.

• **Major hospitalizations.** List the date, the hospital name, the doctor overseeing your care, and the reason for your hospitalization. Record laboratory tests, dates, and results.

• **Eye examinations.** Record the results of each examination, and include a copy of your prescription for eyeglasses.

• **Dental examinations.** List the name of your dentist, the dates of visits, any unusual problems you have suffered, and all treatments.

infringed upon. Laws in 33 states authorize health authorities to notify sexual partners of HIV-positive people that they are at risk of contacting the disease. These laws, however, depend on the willingness of infected patients to reveal their partners, and cannot force you to identify partners.

PRIVACY AND INSURANCE COMPANIES

Protecting your privacy from insurance companies may be tricky. Technically, insurance companies are permitted only limited access to your medical records and may see only the parts that pertain to a particular condition or treatment. If an insurance company learns of a preexisting medical or psychiatric condition, it could deny you coverage. You may want to ask your doctor or hospital to give an insurance company only those records that pertain to the coverage you are seeking.

When you authorize the release of your records to an insurance company, you may also unwittingly be releasing them to the Medical Information Bureau (MIB), a Boston-based nonprofit organization of 750 insurance companies that gathers medical information on more than 15 million customers. Although MIB members cannot deny insurance applications based on information they get solely from the MIB clearinghouse, negative information in your MIB file may affect you adversely. If your application for insurance is rejected, you are entitled to know why. You have the right to obtain your MIB file and correct any errors it contains. For the address and telephone number of MIB, see RESOURCES, page 493.

Children's Medical Rights

Usually parents have the right and responsibility to make all health decisions on behalf of their minor children. Doctors cannot treat a child without parents' informed consent except in an emergency. Barring certain emergencies, parents have the right to stay with their child, whether in the doctor's office or in the hospital.

Unfortunately, there is no standard protocol for doctors or parents to follow when a child and parents disagree over the child's medical treatment. Policies regarding children's medical rights vary among states.

In general, doctors prefer to act according to children's best interests, but children by no means have the final word. A doctor who believes that a teenager's health would be threatened by parental involvement may treat her without notifying her parents. In the case of an older child, a doctor is not likely to give tests or treatment without obtaining that child's explicit permission, regardless of parents' requests. Courts also recog-

Hospital Privacy

Privacy is one of your most important rights as a hospital patient. Be aware that you have the right to:

✔ *Refuse visits.* You may turn away family, friends, or anyone not officially connected with the hospital. You also may refuse to see anyone from the hospital not involved with your care, including interns.

✔ *Safeguard your records.* You may forbid anyone not directly involved with your care to look at your records, including hospital personnel.

✔ *Wear your own clothes.* You can wear your own pajamas, slippers, and robes, if they do not interfere with your treatment.

✔ *Have an attendant of the same sex.* You have the right to have a person of your own gender present during examinations by a medical professional of the opposite sex.

✔ *Remain robed.* After an examination is completed, you have the right to put your clothes back on immediately.

✔ *Expect confidentiality.* Medical personnel are bound to treat information about your condition as confidential and are not permitted to discuss it openly in the hospital.

✔ *Change rooms.* If you are disturbed by someone sharing your room, you have the right to insist on being transferred to another room.

Must Children Be Immunized?

All children have the right to immunization. But state requirements vary widely as to when they should or must be immunized and when parents are allowed to prevent immunization.

In general, your child must be immunized against certain diseases before entering school without exception. The diseases for which there are vaccines include diphtheria, pertussis (whooping cough), tetanus, measles, mumps, rubella, poliomyelitis, and hemophilus influenza type B.

Most doctors recommend that immunizations begin as early as age six to eight weeks and continue, with boosters, until age 14 to 16. But because children have been known to suffer complications from vaccines, some parents oppose immunizations. Parents also may oppose immunizations for religious reasons.

Only a few states allow exemptions from immunizations if parents obtain a doctor's signed explanation or if the child's religion specifically prohibits immunization.

In states that allow exemptions, public schools cannot refuse entry to a child who is legally exempt from immunization, but private schools and day care facilities may.

If you have questions about immunization laws, contact your state's health department to clarify your rights.

nize that children have the same rights as adults to refuse medical treatment, as long as they are considered to be competent and mature enough to understand the consequences of their decisions. However, there is no legal consensus about what age or what mental state signifies maturity.

WHEN CHILDREN'S RIGHTS PREVAIL

As a child approaches adolescence, she may be able to seek or refuse certain types of medical care without parental consent, acting as an "emancipated minor." Depending on state law, the child must show that she is self-supporting, manages her own financial affairs, and does not live with her parents.

In other states, some children over 14 may be considered "mature minors" and be permitted to give informed consent to medical care. The care must be considered medically necessary but not high risk.

A Question of Confidentiality

PROBLEM
Sara, a 16-year-old, went to a gynecologist for testing and treatment of a sexually transmitted disease. She asked her doctor to keep her visit confidential, but when a laboratory report arrived in the mail, her parents discovered that she had sought treatment. They called the doctor and demanded to know what was wrong with Sara, claiming that because she was underage, they had a right to know the details of her condition.

ACTION
The gynecologist refused Sara's parents' request. He had a legal obligation to keep Sara's diagnosis confidential despite her age, because she was seeking treatment for a situation related to her sexuality, and his obligation was based on the theory of privacy regarding sexual activity. Almost all states have laws specifically permitting a doctor to treat a minor for a sexually transmitted disease without parental notification. (If her condition had been unrelated to sexual activity—for instance if she had broken her hand, or had leukemia—her parents might have been entitled to information.) The doctor decided to ask Sara if he could tell her parents that she had no threatening condition. When she agreed in writing he informed her parents that she was all right.

In some situations, a child will seek treatment for a sexually transmitted disease or some other sensitive condition only if she is guaranteed confidentiality. In such instances, which also include seeking substance-abuse treatment or pregnancy-related services, the doctor is free to oblige the child's wish except in some states which require either parental notification or judicial permission when a minor seeks an abortion or if the child's life is in danger.

DEALING WITH A HOSPITAL

Checking out hospitals when you are healthy will give you a head start on knowing what to expect if you have to check into one.

Choosing a Hospital

Ideally, a patient should be able to choose the hospital where he would like to be treated. Unfortunately, in a number of situations, such as is an emergency, or when your doctor or health practitioner is only associated with one facility, you are not in the position to do so. If you are lucky enough to be choosing—if your doctor has privileges at a number of facilities for example—you will want to consider a hospital's quality of care, the credentials of its staff, its location, and cost. Also, check your insurance policy and make sure it will cover the hospital you are considering. Then call the hospital administrator and arrange to take a tour.

A hospital's services and technical capabilities should also factor into your decision. If you need specific services, such as facilities for magnetic resonance imaging (MRI), or organ transplants, make sure they are available. Ask what the hospital charges for the procedures you need, and compare costs with other hospitals.

Based on the Hill-Burton Hospital Construction and Survey Act of 1946, hospitals that receive federal funds to build or expand their facilities must provide certain services including aid to those who cannot afford to pay and must participate in Medicare and Medicaid. In addition, all hospitals must be licensed and/or accredited by the Joint Commission on Accreditation of Health Care Organizations (JCAHO), especially if they want to qualify for Medicare or Medicaid funding. JCAHO accreditation shows that a hospital maintains relatively high standards in such matters as patients' rights, food, medical records, and the quality of care. To find out a hospital's accreditation rating and receive a performance report, contact the JCAHO at (708) 916-5800.

DISTINGUISHING TYPES OF HOSPITALS

Different kinds of hospitals have different strengths. General hospitals, as the term implies, handle all types of medical and surgical treatment, while specialized hospitals focus on specific illnesses and procedures. Community hospitals, which may have anywhere from 50 to 300 beds, are private, nonprofit, and owned and operated by community groups, religious institu-

---

123...

SIZING UP A HOSPITAL

Before checking into a hospital you may want to find out how well trained the doctors and nurses are and what percentage of doctors are board-certified. You may also want to:

1. Ask for a nurse count. Since nurses are the major caregivers in hospitals, find out how many patients each nurse sees, and how much attention you can expect.

2. Get a mortality rate. If you are about to undergo a risky procedure find out how many people with the same illness have been through the same procedure and have died as a result. If you can't get information from the hospital, check with your city or state health department to compare information from area hospitals.

3. Ask about infections. It is common for hospitalized patients to pick up infections when their resistance is low. Check with the health department and find out how many patients got infections after being admitted to the hospital and compare the numbers with other hospitals.

4. Check accreditation. Check to see if the hospital's radiology department, for example, is accredited by the American College of Radiology.

tions, a consortium of doctors, or other volunteers. These hospitals concentrate on providing health care for the local community and provide a full range of services, still managing to give personal attention in most cases.

Teaching hospitals may be public or private. These are generally affiliated with medical schools, providing a training site for students and recent graduates. Patient care is usually handled by resident physicians, with an attending physician supervising. A patient in a teaching hospital can refuse to be examined by medical students and has the right to know exactly the qualifications of those who are proposing treatment. If you do not want to participate in the education of medical professionals, a teaching hospital is not your best option.

For-profit hospitals are usually owned by corporations and are likely to put a premium on cost efficiency. Public hospitals, are owned by federal, state, or city governments and their corresponding health departments. They provide care for all citizens, and especially the poor.

It may seem a strange principle to enunciate as the very first requirement in a hospital that it should do the sick no harm.

FLORENCE NIGHTINGALE
British nurse
1820–1910

Admission and Discharge

If you know you are going to be hospitalized, plan ahead. Call the admitting office to arrange a time when you can stop by and do all the preliminary paperwork. Be sure to take your driver's license, Medicare or insurance identification card, checkbook, and any other documents the office

---

Advance Directives: Giving the Doctors Orders

An "advance directive" is a document such as a living will, health care proxy, or power of attorney that stipulates your medical-treatment desires before you become seriously ill. Here are some things you should know before creating an advance directive:

• The Patient Self-Determination Act (PSDA), passed in 1991, protects patients' rights to control the care received in facilities or hospitals that receive funding from Medicare or Medicaid. It requires institutions to inform patients, on or before admission, of the institution's policies regarding patients' rights, particularly the right to request or refuse life-sustaining treatment.

• According to the act, federally funded hospitals must give patients a written description of both state law and their own institutional policies regarding living wills and patients' rights in making end-of-life treatment decisions.The act also requires facilities to indicate in a patient's medical records if the patient has an advance directive and

to provide education about decision-making in the matter of life-sustaining treatment.

• Being fully informed about the Patient Self-Determination Act should be part of the hospital admission procedure, but you should understand it before checking in. The act does not guarantee that a hospital will respect your treatment wishes; it requires only that the hospital tell you how it handles patients' requests to direct their own care.

• To ensure that your directive will be carried out, check with your doctor and with any hospitals where you are likely to be treated before creating the document. For more about advance directives, see "Dying With Dignity," page 232.

requests. You will also be asked for your Social Security number and, in some cases, your mother's maiden name.

You probably will be asked to sign a form indicating how you plan to pay your bill and a form declaring whether you have insurance. When you actually check in, you may also be asked to sign a form listing the personal possessions you have with you.

Once you have completed the paperwork, find out exactly when the hospital begins billing you for your stay. You will save money by checking in the day of your procedure rather than the night before—ask your doctor if a same-day check-in is permitted or perhaps even required in your case.

CAN YOU BE REFUSED ADMISSION?

If you are not an emergency patient, a hospital can turn you away if it has no free beds or if it cannot deal with your condition. But no hospital may refuse to admit you because of your race, religion, or national origin. Nor may it demand a deposit if you receive Medicare or Medicaid.

Some states have laws forbidding hospitals to reject non-emergency patients who cannot pay. Whether your ability to pay affects your admission depends on the hospital. Hospitals that received federal assistance for construction are required by the Hill-Burton Act, for 20 years after construction is completed, to provide care to a reasonable volume of patients who cannot afford to pay for it. Such hospitals must publish notice of the availability of such funds and must alert those seeking care that funds are available. There may be eligibility requirements, and the hospital's funds for such care are not unlimited.

Once you have been admitted to a hospital, you cannot be prevented from leaving, even if you are unable to pay your bill. As long as you are mentally competent, you may leave at any time. If the hospital staff thinks you are too ill or physically incapacitated to leave, you may be asked to sign a "discharge against medical advice" form, but you have the right to refuse to sign it.

Emergency-Room Rights

You have a legal right to emergency-room care as long as you truly have a medical emergency. If a hospital cannot treat you in an emergency, it must refer you to one that can—after the staff has determined that you do indeed require immediate care. Some examples of true emergency conditions are heavy bleeding from major blood vessels, heart attack, stopped breathing, deep shock, ingestion or exposure to fast-acting poison, a penetrating wound to the

---

Patients' Representatives

If you have questions, problems, or needs concerning your hospital care, a useful person to talk to is the patients' representative, or ombudsman. Her job is to act as a mediator between you and the hospital organization to ensure that your needs are met. The patients' representative's primary duties are to:

✔ *Tell you what your rights are.* If you are unsure of exactly what you are entitled to, a patients' representative should be able to clarify things for you.

✔ *Voice your complaints.* She should be able to take your problems to appropriate department heads and get a quick response.

✔ *Steer you in the right direction.* If she cannot help you directly, a patients' representative should be able to refer you to someone who can. For example, she can tell you where to get a second opinion or hire a private nurse.

✔ *Work with the hospital staff.* A good patients' representative will keep increasingly harried and impersonal hospital staff aware that a patient's comfort is vital.

123...

DON'T PAY FOR THINGS YOU DON'T WANT OR NEED

You will be billed for almost every item you receive in the hospital, whether you asked for it or not. You have the right to refuse these items:

1. A private room. If you need a private room for medical reasons, you should have one. But realize that private rooms cost more than semiprivate rooms and often are not reimbursable by insurance companies unless they are medically necessary.

2. A telephone. Your room will probably have a telephone. Even if you do not use it, the hospital may charge you for calls others make to you. If you do not want a telephone, say so; or bring your own cellular telephone.

3. A television set. A TV can keep you company during sleepless nights, but the charge is often steep. If you do not think you will use the TV, ask that it not be connected. If you want one, ask if you can bring your own.

4. Personal items. Bring personal items such as a comb, toothbrush, sanitary napkins, even aspirin and vitamins, from home. Hospitals will provide these for you, but may charge you more than you would pay in the store.

5. Simple requests. Be careful about asking for simple amenities like a second pillow. You will probably be charged.

heart or lungs, severe head injury, or an acute psychotic state.

If possible, have a friend or relative accompany you to the emergency room to help you make decisions if you are in too much pain or too upset to understand the nature of your condition or the treatment that is proposed. Make sure you understand and approve all tests and treatments that are ordered. Remember, you have the right to refuse proposed emergency care, as long as you are mentally competent to make that decision. These precautions are not always possible in an emergency situation, but it is important to know you have rights.

Try to get your primary-care doctor involved immediately, either by calling him before you leave for the hospital or by asking emergency-room staff to call him once you get there. You have every right to expect your primary doctor to oversee your care, even on an emergency basis.

How to Control Your Care

Knowing your health care rights and how to protect them is of paramount importance when you are hospitalized. Unless you enter the hospital on an emergency basis, you have the right to ask that specific doctors care for you. You also have the right to refuse care or treatment from any medical personnel. Don't hesitate to ask about the experience of a medical student or resident who is assigned to administer treatment or perform medical procedures, or to request a more experienced practitioner.

GETTING HELP TO GET YOUR RIGHTS

It is all very well to know your rights in a hospital, but sometimes you need help to assert them. Several sources of help may be available:

- **Patients' rights advocates.** The job of a patients' rights advocate is to communicate your complaints to the hospital administration and bring the responses back to you while you are in the hospital. A patients' rights advocate might work for the hospital, an insurance company, a consumer group, or directly for you. His role is to help you understand, exercise, and protect the rights described in the Patient's Bill of Rights. If the hospital staff notifies you of your discharge when you do not feel well enough to go home, you can call on a patients' rights advocate to help you delay discharge.

- **Patients' representatives**. Unlike patients' rights advocates, most patients' representatives work for the hospital. Rather than championing your cause, a patients' representative will

work to ease trouble between you and the hospital. He may be able to settle billing disputes or help you work out a payment schedule.

- **Ombudsmen.** An ombudsman does not help with direct problem resolution. He instead identifies broad problem areas in the hospital, researches them, and offers solutions to the hospital administration. If you were unhappy with a hospital policy, whether you had a problem with treatment, admission procedures, or visiting hours, you could complain to the hospital's ombudsman.

- **Ethics Committees.** An ethics committee is a hospital group that helps develop hospital policy and deals with issues regarding difficult ethical dilemmas, such as right-to-die cases. The committee usually includes doctors, a lawyer, a nurse, a social worker, and a member of the clergy. If a relative was being kept alive by life support systems, and you and the doctor disagreed over whether or not to discontinue their use, the ethics committee could be asked to review the case and make a recommendation.

OTHER WAYS TO COMPLAIN

All hospitals must be licensed by the state, so any complaints about their facilities should be made to a state department of licensing for hospitals. Complaints about the professional conduct of medical personnel should be directed to the board that oversees each profession. You would contact the Board of Medical Examiners for doctors, the Board of Nurse Examiners for nurses, and so on. Billing complaints should be directed to your insurance company. If you have any indication that you are the victim of hospital billing fraud, contact your state attorney general's office.

Understanding Your Bill

According to a recent national audit, approximately 97 percent of hospital bills contain some kind of overcharge. The best way to avoid being overbilled is to keep an eye on charges, recognize common errors, and know your rights when it comes to disputing charges you never incurred.

Make note of tests and procedures you receive. Also, record all services and seemingly small items (like toothbrushes), as well as all visits from all doctors. Have someone note how much time you spent in the operating and recovery rooms, since you will be charged by the hour for their use.

Having your own written record of hospital charges will make your bill more understandable. Insist that the bill be item-

Patient Dumping: Cruel and Illegal

Your rights—and your health—are in jeopardy if you need emergency care, cannot pay for it, and as a result are possibly shunted from one hospital to another.

The most dangerous aspect of this deplorable practice, graphically dubbed "patient dumping," is that patients who cannot pay are sometimes shifted from the emergency room of one hospital to another before they have even been treated or stabilized.

Hospitals have been known to avoid giving the best care to patients who lack medical insurance or to be stingy about giving time to patients who belong to HMO's. Some hospitals have even been known to avoid treating high-risk patients that pose a threat of developing medical complications that could lead to malpractice suits against the hospital.

In 1986 Congress adopted legislation that places severe limitations on the practice of patient dumping. If you are moved to another hospital, you have the right to find out why, and a doctor must certify in writing that the benefit of the transfer outweighs the risk.

If you bring a friend to the hospital with you, ask the friend to get the names of anyone who treats you and to take notes about what is said to you about your condition.

Finally, be aware that your emergency treatment cannot be delayed while hospital staff confirms your insurance status.

ized rather than presented as a lump sum. Make sure you are being charged for the correct number of days you stayed in the hospital, for only the medications and procedures you received, for the right kind of room, and for only the doctors you saw.

If you do not understand the description for each treatment, insist on an explanation from your doctor or a hospital administrator. If you do not get an itemized bill from the hospital at the time of your discharge, request it by mail and do not pay it until you have had a chance to study it carefully.

WATCH FOR COMMON BILLING ERRORS

Typical billing mistakes involve confused numerical codes that indicate specific procedures. A single-digit error could cost you hundreds of dollars. Another expensive mistake could result if a hospital charges you for all the tests and services normally associated with a procedure, even if you had only the procedure itself. For example, hospitals often routinely charge for birthing-room services, but sometimes a mother delivers her baby without using one.

"Unbundling" is another common cause for overcharges. When a hospital unbundles, it splits the price of a single medical procedure into several costs, then bills you for each one. Instead of charging you $2,500 for an emergency hysterectomy, for instance, it would charge you $2,000 each for removal of your fallopian tubes, ovaries, and uterus, at a total cost of $6,000. While unbundling is not technically illegal, it is considered unethical by AMA standards. Confront the hospital's billing department and withhold payment until the charges are properly explained if you suspect such practices.

Being charged more than once for the same procedure is another source of billing errors. Sometimes this is due to an administrative mistake. At other times it results from a technician's insistence on repeating a test. Refuse repeated tests unless they are medically necessary, then study your bill for duplicate charges; if a test is repeated because of a technician's error, you should not have to pay for it.

Your bill will also be fatter than it should be if it contains "exploding tests," a process by which separate tests from several samples are conducted, when a combined test from a single sample could produce the same results. If you are charged for a number of tests and only recall having one or two, you may be a victim of "exploding tests."

If you are suspicious or do not understand any part of your bill, make sure a hospital representative explains it to you. If your insurance company refuses to pay a part of your bill that you thought you were covered for, check for inappropriate or unethical billing practices on your bill before you question your insurance company.

Contesting Your Bill

If you don't think you owe what your hospital bill says you owe, here are some steps to follow:

✔ *Don't pay the whole bill.* Pay only for charges you accept, and mark any you do not think are justified.

✔ *Approach the hospital.* Ask the billing office to explain your bill. If you still are not satisfied, request a formal audit by the hospital and withhold payment until it is complete.

✔ *Inform your insurance company.* Ask for a "utilization review;" an in-depth examination of your hospital stay and the charges incurred. Provide the insurance company with any records you kept, and ask it not to pay your bill when the hospital submits it.

✔ *Write a letter.* Whether you deal with the hospital billing office or your insurance company, put it all in writing.

✔ *Check codings.* If your insurance company claims that charges are inappropriate or excessive, make sure the codes for your procedures were correctly recorded. Call the hospital billing department to check the coding.

✔ *Call the local medical board.* If you suspect a hospital billing department has purposely recorded the wrong codes, you may consider fraud charges. Your local medical board or society or an attorney can tell you what action to take next.

PATIENT ACCOUNT STATEMENT

GENERAL INFORMATION

Patient's Name	Account No.	Birth Date	Admission Date	Discharge Date	Statement Date
James N. Smith	123456	12-15-55	12-15-95	12-18-95	1-6-96

Primary Insurance Co.	Group No.	Policy Number
Health America/Maxicare ❶	584003	185329253

BILL TO   MAKE CHECK PAYABLE TO   AMOUNT OF YOUR PAYMENT

BILL TO	MAKE CHECK PAYABLE TO	AMOUNT OF YOUR PAYMENT
Rebecca R. Smith 14 Hermitage Nashville, TN 08526	Parthenon Central 18 Westlake Road Nashville, TN 08526	$2,881.20

Important: To ensure proper credit, please detach and return the top portion of this statement with your payment.

GENERAL INFORMATION

Patient's Name	Account No.	Statement Date	Admission Date	Discharge Date	Page No.
James N. Smith	123456	1-6-96	12-15-95	12-18-95	1

If you have any question about this statement call:

❷ Frances Jones 546-2791   Monday through Friday 8:30-4:30

SERVICE DATE ❸	❹	DESCRIPTION ❺	TOTAL AMOUNT ❻	INSURANCE PORTION ❼	PATIENT PORTION ❽
		SUMMARY OF CHARGES			
12-15-95	120	Room & Daily Care 9 Days @ $582/day (12/15/95 to 1/3/96)	5,238.00		
12-15-95	115	Patient Tray-Towels, Pillow, Slippers	380.00		
12-15-95	250	Pharmacy	1,275.00		
12-15-95	258	IV Solutions	2,872.00		
12-16-95	260	IV Therapy	1,850.00		
12-16-95	270	Medical-Surgical Supplies	28.00		
12-16-95	300	Laboratory Tests	612.00		
12-16-95	301	Laboratory Tests	612.00		
12-17-95	392	Diagnostic X-ray	827.00		
		Total Charges	$13,694.00		
		Amount Billed to Insurance		$10,812.80	
		Pay This Amount			$2,881.20

Thank you for choosing Parthenon Health Services for your medical care.

Final Diagnosis	Please read reverse side of this statement.
Acute Exhaustion	

Your Hospital Bill Defined

Ask your doctor or your hospital's billing office for the name, fee, and billing codes of the procedures you will undergo during your hospital stay. When you receive your bill: **1.** Check that your insurance company's name and your group number is correct. **2.** Look for the name of a hospital contact in case you have questions. **3.** Make sure the "Service Date" column lists the correct dates you received each procedure. **4.** Check that the billing codes refer to specific procedures you received. **5.** Check that the "Summary of Charges" itemizes each of the procedures you received. (It may be broken down in greater detail in an actual bill). **6.** Scrutinize each corresponding charge. **7.** Make sure the amount that your insurance company will pay reflects a reasonable and accurate percentage. **8.** Check that the amount you must pay is correct.

ALTERNATIVE HEALTH CARE

Certain remedies practiced outside of the medical mainstream may be helpful to you, but don't jeopardize your safety or your rights when you use them.

Recognizing Fraudulent Cures

While many alternative remedies are effective and many practitioners are on the up and up, fraudulent cures and dishonest practitioners are numerous too. Here are some "red flags" to look out for:

✔ *Not enough information.* Find out if an alternative remedy is harmful and what the potential side effects are. If a product does not list its ingredients on its label, it may be because they are harmful.

✔ *Exclusive therapies.* Think twice if a practitioner recommends that you stop using therapy or medication that your doctor prescribed. An alternative remedy sanctioned by the medical community is one that can be used in conjunction with traditional medicine.

✔ *Miracle cures.* Beware of a seller who claims that a product or therapy works for all kinds of conditions, including yours. There are no cure-alls.

✔ *No proof.* Previous testimonials that the cure is a success are not enough. For all you know, the number of dissatisfied customers may far outweigh the number of happy ones. Call the FDA and find out if the product has been tested.

Types of Alternative Care

Mainstream medicine is not your only health-care option. Nontraditional treatments for ills ranging from aching joints to cancer are gaining increasing numbers of disciples among those dissatisfied with established procedures.

Some of the more popular alternative practices and procedures are described below, with guidelines as to what kinds of procedures caregivers are allowed to perform.

CHIROPRACTORS

According to chiropractors, the key to good health is a balanced spine and nervous system. They believe that without that balance, the spine and its related nerve roots become irritated and make the body vulnerable to disease. People use chiropractors for relief from backaches, spastic colon, and headaches.

Chiropractors are licensed in all 50 states. They earn a Doctor of Chiropractic degree after at least two years of college and four years of chiropractic college, followed by a clinical internship. Their training includes course work in anatomy, physiology, neurophysiology, and kinesiology. They cannot prescribe drugs or perform invasive procedures. In addition, they may not hospitalize patients and must refer them to a physician for a condition that they cannot treat. Currently, 41 states require private health insurers to cover chiropractic care.

ACUPUNCTURE

The ancient Chinese practice of acupuncture involves the use of very fine needles inserted at various points on the body to treat numerous symptoms and illnesses. Stimulating these points by inserting and twirling needles is believed to send impulses throughout the nervous system that, in turn, sends healing signals to the organs and restores the body's balance.

Acupuncture has been promoted as a cure for obesity, hypertension, ulcers, headaches, back pain, drug addiction, and numerous other ailments. In some states acupuncturists must be licensed physicians, but not all physicians who practice acupuncture are specially trained. Some states do not require that acupuncturists be physicians but require instead that they work under a physician's direct supervision. In other states, acupuncturists need no medical supervision. Six states now require private insurers to cover acupuncture treatment.

MIDWIFERY

Midwifery is enjoying renewed popularity. Most midwives are registered nurses who have taken additional training in obstetrics, gynecology, and newborn care; have passed an extensive examination; and have been certified by the American College of Nurse-Midwives. Midwives also are usually licensed by the states in which they practice. Lay midwives are not registered nurses, but they have been trained in midwifery. Some states license lay midwives and require a rigorous examination; some allow nonlicensed lay midwives to practice.

Midwives may employ massage or relaxation techniques during delivery; they monitor the progress of labor including the presence or absence of fetal distress; and they determine if a doctor is needed. They also assist in the delivery and examination of the newborn. Midwives are restricted to caring for women with normal, uncomplicated pregnancies. They must work in association with a physician, and usually a hospital, in order to obtain assistance if complications develop. Check with your state medical licensing board to find out what accreditation is required for midwives in your region.

ALTERNATIVE THERAPIES

The fear and desperation that the diagnosis of a potentially terminal disease arouses sometimes compel patients to seek treatment outside of regular medical practice. Such treatments include special diets, experimental drugs, vaccines, salves, even psychological approaches.

While proponents of alternative treatments claim that they can provide cures, some medical professionals claim that some may do more harm than good. For example, some salves are said to burn away certain surface skin cancers. Yet they may contain corrosive agents that do damage to the skin and are useless against the cancer. Many physicians believe that the danger in using alternative therapies is in lost time. By the time a treatment is found to be ineffective, the disease may have progressed too far for traditional medical treatments to do any good. However, many organizations and professionals, including the American Cancer Society, do not discourage patients from using alternative therapies, as long as they are used in conjunction with traditional medicine.

The types of therapies available and the opinions regarding them seem endless. It is difficult to know whom or what to believe. One measure of reliability may be the U.S. Food and Drug Administration. The FDA does not test remedies itself

---

WATCH OUT FOR FAD DIET PLANS

Dieting is never easy. Warning bells should ring if any plan or weight loss center tells you it is. Here are some basic truths about dieting to keep in mind:

1. Weight loss should be slow. Avoid any diet or clinic that promises fast weight loss. Shedding weight too fast can be dangerous, and the weight usually returns anyway.

2. A good diet includes variety. Diet plans that restrict you to a few foods will bore you and put you at risk for nutritional deficiency. The healthiest way to lose weight is to change your eating habits so that you eat nutritionally balanced, low-fat meals that allow for your individual tastes.

3. Diets should be proven. No plan should be based on a secret formula. The credibility of a regimen is based on the number of people it has helped—the more the better. You are safest choosing a plan that has been shown in controlled studies to be effective and that has been published in a respected scientific or medical journal.

4. A diet should make sense. You should be able to adapt it to your family situation and to restaurants. If you cannot live with it, you are not likely to stick with it and probably will regain any weight you lose.

5. No diet can change your life. Any diet or food plan that promises life-changing miracles is misleading and bogus.

but permits others to test new products. In order to begin testing, the product's sponsor must show scientific evidence that a product might work and that precautions will be taken to protect those it will be tested on. After testing, the product's sponsors show the results to the FDA, which then decides if the product's benefits outweigh its risks.

A miracle drug is any drug that will do what the label says it will do.

ERIC HODGINS
Episode

Promoters of alternative treatments do not always submit information to the FDA about their products, but if the FDA knows about a product or device and believes it is unsafe, it can ask the manufacturer to issue a recall. The FDA may also ask the U.S. Attorney General to have an unsafe product seized, file a criminal complaint against the violator, or seek an injunction to prevent distribution of a product.

Because the FDA regulates products—foods and drugs—not all alternative therapies fall under its jurisdiction. Generally, experimental therapies sanctioned by mainstream medicine are reviewed within the medical community and are held up to high standards and evaluation. Studies are outlined in detailed reports so that others can verify findings. Ask if a remedy you are interested in has been approved by the FDA, and if not, ask to see the research on it.

If an alternative treatment proves harmful, or if you are misled, you may be a victim of fraud. Report suspected health fraud to the Food and Drug Administration (FDA), and false or misleading advertising to the Federal Trade Commission (FTC). Also contact the FDA to find out if a particular drug or device has been approved for a specific use.

Your Rights Outside the Mainstream

Trying alternative methods of health care does not mean you lose your right to protection. Here are some organizations you can contact if you want to research an alternative practitioner, if you think you have been misled, or if you believe your rights have been violated:

• **American Cancer Society** publishes reports and maintains a clearinghouse on questionable cancer treatments. Write or call: 1599 Clifton Road, N.E., Atlanta, Ga. 30329, (800) ACS-2345.

• **Consumer Health Information Research Institute (CHIRI)** publishes and distributes studies of misinformation, fraud, and quackery. Write or call: 3521 Broadway, Kansas City, Mo. 64111, (816) 228-4595

• **Food and Drug Administration (FDA)** answers questions about foods and drugs, and is empowered to take regulatory action against manufacturers of foods, drugs, and devices that are unsafe, not clearly or completely described, or illegally mar-

keted. Write or call: 5600 Fishers Lane, Rockville, Md. 20857, (301) 443-1240.

• **Federal Trade Commission (FTC)** investigates false advertising claims and has the authority to file civil lawsuits on behalf of consumers who have been harmed by unfair or deceptive trade practices. Write or call: Public References Branch, Room 130, Pennsylvania Avenue at 6th Street, NW, Washington, D.C. 20580, (202) 326-2222.

• **National Council Against Health Fraud** has a Task Force on Victim Redress to advise and assist people who think they have been harmed by an unscientific practitioner. Write or call: P.O. Box 1276, Loma Linda, Calif. 92340, (909) 824-4690.

DECODING HEALTH INSURANCE

Insurance safeguards your health only if you know how to use its benefits.

Understanding Health Plans

Wending your way successfully through the world of health insurance depends on knowing how different plans are organized, figuring out which one will best suit your needs, or making the best use of the plan most readily available to you.

First, you must decide between individual and group coverage. If you (or your spouse) are employed full-time and the employer offers a health insurance plan, you are probably eligible for it. If so, your employer will pay all or part of the required premium. Employer-sponsored health insurance is a substantial benefit. Most people elect to participate in their employer's plan. To get maximum use out of yours, you should understand the terms of the plan offered.

For decades, employer-provided health insurance was commonplace, and many corporations provided top-of-the-line, expensive insurance. However, since insurance costs have skyrocketed, many businesses have turned to some form of managed care, such as that provided by health maintenance organizations (HMO's), or in the case of small companies, to not offering health insurance benefits at all. If you belong to a professional, fraternal, or some other organization, you may be eligible for group coverage under its auspices. Large groups are charged a fixed premium which is generally less costly than the premium an individual would be charged

If your employer does not offer health insurance, and you are not affiliated with an organization that offers a health plan, you will have to secure individual coverage. Unfortunately, individual coverage is usually expensive and sometimes difficult to get. Generally, you have two choices: a traditional fee-for-service plan or some form of managed care.

Traditional Health Insurance

The traditional type of medical insurance most Americans relied upon until recently is known as "fee-for-service" health insurance. Generally, such plans are divided into three parts: 1) medical and surgical expenses in or out of the hospital, 2) hospitalization, and 3)

Health-Plan Lingo

Here are some basic insurance terms you should know:

✔ *Deductible.* The amount of money you must pay—usually within a calendar year—before your insurance company begins to reimburse you. If your deductible is $200, you must pay the first $200 for covered services before your insurance company pays anything.

✔ *Copayment.* Also known as "coinsurance," this is a fixed percentage of covered charges that you must pay after you have paid your deductible. Both managed-care plans and traditional plans may require co-payments.

✔ *Usual, customary, and reasonable charges.* The amount that the insurer will reimburse the provider, based on the most commonly charged fees for the particular procedure in that provider's region. You may be responsible for any amount above these charges.

✔ *Stop-loss provision.* This component of a policy limits the total amount that you must pay during a given period. After you have paid the stated deductible and coinsurance, the insurance company pays 100 percent of the remaining covered expenses for that particular period.

Besides asking about cost, location, and what services are covered, you should ask the agent or representative of an HMO the following:

1. Is there a wide selection of primary-care doctors as well as specialists from which to choose? Are all of the doctors board-certified?

2. How many doctors affiliated with the HMO a year ago are no longer there? Is the turn-over rate high?

3. Is the doctor of your choice accepting any new patients at this time?

4. Do doctors, nurses, or physician's assistants handle routine visits?

5. Can you see the same doctor every time? If not, can you specify other doctors you would like to see?

6. Are doctors paid on a salary basis or according to the number of patients they see? Are they financially penalized for ordering too many tests, procedures, or hospitalizations?

7. What provisions are made for emergency care? Will you be charged for seeking care outside the network?

8. What are the most common complaints that the HMO receives, and what is the grievance procedure?

9. What is a doctor's obligation if he leaves the plan while his patient is in the hospital?

major medical or catastrophic care, which pays for the costs of treatment for major illnesses and injuries.

Medical and surgical coverage usually includes doctors' and surgeons' fees, as well as surgery-related costs and laboratory and diagnostic tests. Usually you pay the fee directly (thus the term "fee for service") and then submit a claim to the insurance company, which reimburses you in whole or part.

A Freelancer's Insurance Dilemma

PROBLEM
Kate worked for a restaurant that paid her health insurance. When she decided to open her own catering business, she failed to realize how much she would have to pay for her own insurance. Kate found that the average monthly premium for either a traditional fee-for-service plan or an HMO seemed too expensive, so she decided to forgo insurance. When a few months later Kate was in a bicycle accident and banged up her knee and severely injured her ankle, she faced the prospect of losing all her savings in a series of costly medical procedures.

ACTION
Fortunately, Kate's injuries were not as bad as she had feared, and her doctor's bills were not overwhelming. However, she was scared by her close call and realized that she could no longer take the risk of having no insurance at all. By making some sacrifices, she found room in her budget for the monthly premiums of a "bare bones" insurance policy with a substantial deductible. Although she had to pay for routine doctor visits out of her own pocket, she was at least protected against the catastrophic costs of a major illness or injury.

Hospitalization coverage is for in-hospital expenses such as room, board, and regular nursing, as well as X-rays, laboratory tests, and medications. Often the insurance company pays the hospital directly. The fee is usually a fixed, maximum amount for each day you are hospitalized. Limits are set on the length of your stay, and you are responsible for any difference between the amount paid to the hospital and the total cost of your stay.

If you have major medical (or catastrophic) insurance, however, which covers major expenses associated with serious illness or injury, it will fill in any gaps left by your hospital or medical/surgical coverage. After you have paid an initial deductible, the major medical portion of your insurance will usually pay most of the remaining charges for physicians' and surgeons' fees, hospital room and board, general nursing services, and ancillary hospital services like anesthesiologist services, X-rays, blood and transfusion costs, and medical appliances, such as crutches. You may also be reimbursed for prescribed out-of-hospital treatments and medicines, rental of equipment, such as a wheelchair, and, in some situations, medically-necessary transportation.

Comparing Health Insurance Options

Distinguishing among types of insurance plans may seem daunting. Health insurance falls into two basic categories: traditional fee-for-service plans and managed care. This list will help you to understand how to choose the plan that is best for you and your family:

TRADITIONAL PLANS

• **Fee-for-service plans.** With this classic plan, patients choose their own doctors, specialists, and hospitals, and pay them directly on a fee-for-service basis. Then, the plans reimburse patients for out-of-pocket costs after the patient has paid an annual deductible and any copayment requirements. On average, traditional plans cover 80 percent of all medical costs above the deductible amount, and patients pay the remaining 20 percent. With some plans, a "stop-loss provision" kicks in if charges run very high, after which the plan covers all costs. Fee-for-service plans usually cover all care involving hospitals, including doctors and tests. Traditional plans rarely cover preventive care, such as routine physicals, well-baby care, vaccinations, birth control, and dental care.

MANAGED-CARE PLANS

• **The common denominator.** In these plans, health care is "managed" through a primary-care physician, known as a "gatekeeper" who is usually required to provide health-care services, recommend and authorize specialists and laboratory tests, and review all treatments, either short-or long-term. Financial incentives are used to keep costs down.

• **Managed indemnity.** This type of plan combines traditional fee-for-service compensation with such managed-care techniques as the use of a gatekeeper to review and authorize treatment.

• **HMO's (Health Management Organizations).** HMO's require patients (or their employers) to pay a monthly premium to the organization to cover all medical and hospital costs. No fee for service or deductible is required, although some plans require a small copayment for service (usually five to ten dollars. An HMO plan often focuses on preventative medicine and is less expensive than traditional health insurance plans

• There are three basic types of HMO's: In a "staff model," practitioners are employed directly by the HMO; in a "group model," a group of doctors, including primary-care physicians and specialists, is paid a given amount for each patient they agree to treat; and in a "network model," independent doctors or group practices contract with a plan to provide patient care, but often retain private, non-HMO patients as well.

• The HMO pays the doctor or group a monthly fee based on the number of patients enrolled in the plan. Groups then decide how the fees will be distributed among individual doctors or their own HMO-approved doctors. The gatekeeper approves all referrals to specialists which are usually part of the HMO. Therefore, choices may be limited. HMO's also tend to discourage extensive testing, the use of specialists, and extended stays in the hospital.

• **IPA's (Individual Practice Associations).** With this type of plan, an association, the IPA contracts with individual doctors who remain in private practice but provide care on a discounted fee-for-service basis. The scope of services covered depends on the particular plan. Because doctors stay in private practice, they see both private patients on a traditional fee-for-service as well as those covered by the IPA.

• **PPO's (Preferred Provider Organizations).** Doctors and other health-care providers contract with the PPO to provide care to patients at a discounted rate. Patients receive the discount as long as they see doctors associated with the PPO. They may still receive care from providers outside the plan but will receive less reimbursement from the insurance company. PPO's are offered primarily through traditional insurance companies.

• **EPO's (Exclusive Provider Organizations).** An EPO operates similarly to a PPO. The difference is that patients must receive *all* their care from the plan-affiliated doctors and specialists in order to benefit from the discounted fees. If they seek care outside the plan, they must absorb the entire cost of the treatment.

• **POS's (Point-of-Service Plans).** These plans permit patients to choose between insurance plans when they go for care; that is, at the point of service. As with an HMO, patients choose a primary-care doctor, or gatekeeper, from a panel of plan-affiliated doctors—the network. The gatekeeper provides direct clinical care and approves referrals to specialists. As long as patients choose providers from within the plan they pay only a token co-payment or nothing. In some circumstances, if the patient goes outside the network, he will be reimbursed on a fee-for-service basis, but only in part.

Managed-Care Plans

More businesses, families, and individuals are enrolling in managed-care plans. Central to the philosophy of managed care is cost containment. This is achieved because the employer or the individual pays a monthly fee to a managed care organization for a comprehensive package of health services including hospital care. Plans charge minimal deductibles or copayments, and often cover prescription drugs and preventive health care, but discourage excess testing and the use of specialists.

An integral aspect of managed care is the assignment of each member of a plan to a primary-care physician (PCP), also known as a "gatekeeper." The gatekeeper, who is usually a general practitioner, provides direct clinical care and also refers, approves, and coordinates care with specialists. Without the gatekeeper's approval, a plan member may not be reimbursed for the cost of seeing a specialist. If you do not like your assigned gatekeeper, you generally can choose a different one, which may be easy or difficult, depending various aspects of the plan's policies.

The HMO (Health Management Organization) is the most common type of managed-care plan. Members are covered only for services received from HMO providers or with HMO authorization, except in emergencies. There are a number of types of HMO's, differentiated by the way they contract with doctors and offer services to plan members. (For details, see "Comparing Health Insurance Options," page 203).

CRITICISMS OF MANAGED CARE

One strong criticism of managed-care plans is that patients usually must choose only among the doctors and the services that a plan provides. Some plans allow you to select unaffiliated doctors, but in that case may offer only partial reimbursement.

Another criticism is that, in order to control costs, some managed-care plans weigh the cost of treatment against its long-term effectiveness for the patient. For example, many HMO's do not regularly perform mammograms on women under 50 because doing so has not proven conclusively to have long-term benefits. In other words, treatments are approved if they make both medical and financial sense.

One of the ways managed-care plans cut costs is by restricting patient's access to specialists. If you feel you should see a specialist and your gatekeeper refuses authorization, you may still have some rights. First, appeal in writing to the plan's medical director. If the matter is urgent or life-threatening, you might simply see a specialist and try to get reimbursed for it later, especially if a private doctor indeed finds a problem.

Insurance You May Not Need

Soaring health-care costs might scare you into thinking you need every kind of health insurance policy you can find. Evaluate the cost of coverage versus your risks, and how full the coverage actually is, and look out for the following:

✔ *Hospital indemnity.* There is a danger of getting little payoff with this kind of policy. In exchange for your premium you are reimbursed a set fee for each day you spend in the hospital. The fee may represent only a tiny fraction of your actual daily bill.

✔ *"Dread disease."* These are policies designed to cover specific diseases, like cancer. Their benefits are limited, however, and rarely come close to compensating you for what you pay in treatment costs. Also, many of the services covered are already included in more comprehensive plans.

✔ *Accident insurance.* The components in an accident insurance policy are generally offered in a traditional, comprehensive health insurance package. Most specialty accident insurance does not come close to covering the cost of serious injuries.

✔ *Student accident.* These policies often reduce your reimbursement when your family's plan has paid for a claim, so that your combined benefits probably would still not fully cover the expenses after an accident.

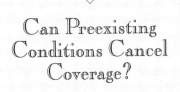

If a managed-care plan refuses to pay for treatment you believe you need, you can initiate a formal grievance. Some states allow plan members to appeal to the state health or insurance department. Some states require members to go through binding arbitration to settle disputes, or you can also consider contacting a lawyer and taking formal legal action. In the past, customers have brought suits claiming their HMO was guilty of breach of contract, bad faith, and reckless infliction of emotional distress. Of course, lawsuits are a very expensive option.

Other Insurance Sources

The U.S. government also provides a number of other types of health insurance programs, including Medicare and Medicaid. (For more about government health benefits, see "Government Insurance," page 208.) Much controversy surrounds the extent to which voters feel that federal or state governments should assume health-care costs, and apparently the debate will not be resolved in the near future.

The federal government may also provide assistance for disabled individuals through the Social Security program. Disability insurance provides income when illness or injury prevents you from working. It ranges from payments during short-term sick leave to long-term coverage and is provided through private plans, as well as Social Security, workers' compensation, or civil service. (See also YOUR JOB, page 247.) If you buy private disability insurance, be sure it covers both accidents and illness.

Veterans of the armed forces are entitled to a wide range of medical services, including comprehensive care, hospitalization, nursing home care, medication, and treatment for alcohol or drug dependence. Some benefits require a veteran's condition to be service-related, while others are in effect only if the veteran served on active duty during particular periods. To determine your eligibility, call your regional office of The Department of Veterans Affairs. (For the address and telephone number, see RESOURCES, page 493.)

Eligibility for Coverage

One of the central issues in health-care debates is the individual's right to be insured. Even if you can afford insurance, your eligibility is not guaranteed. In most states, insurance companies (including HMO's) are permitted to deny or limit coverage and charge a

Can Preexisting Conditions Cancel Coverage?

One of the loopholes that most insurance companies put into individual (and sometimes group) policies is a clause dealing with preexisting conditions. A preexisting condition is any health problem, such as chronic back pain or a heart condition, that existed before the policy was bought.

Some policies exclude coverage not only for the preexisting conditions but for any illness or injury related in any way to a preexisting condition—even if that specific illness or injury occurred after the policy was bought. For example, if you have suffered from high blood pressure, you may not be covered for any future related illness, such as heart attack.

Group and other policies often stipulate a period, say six months after a policy goes into effect, during which no costs pertaining to a preexisting condition will be covered. After the waiting period, the policy will begin covering costs.

Even though a "preexisting" clause may seem unfair, be honest when giving information on an insurance application about any preexisting condition you have. The chances are that if you make a claim related to that condition and you have lied, the company's investigators will find out, and then your policy will most likely be canceled and the coverage you sought denied.

higher premium to anyone who is already ill or considered to be a poor health risk because of a history of disease or a job that poses major health risks.

If you become seriously ill after buying insurance through your employer, your insurer may be able to reduce your benefits, whether it is you or your employer who is paying the premiums. To do that, however, your employer must also reduce the benefits of everyone else in your company, an action he may well be reluctant to make.

An individual policy with a noncancellation clause will cover you through the end of your contract at an agreed rate. An insurance company may cancel your policy, however, if you do not pay your premiums on time or fail to report a changed medical condition—but only after it has given you written warning. A "guaranteed renewable" policy, while difficult to get, offers the best protection from losing coverage.

IF YOU LEAVE YOUR JOB

If you are a member of an employer-sponsored plan, you do not immediately lose your right to health insurance if you leave or lose your job, unless you are fired for gross misconduct. If your company has 20 or more employees, the federal Consolidated Omnibus Budget Reconciliation Act (COBRA) requires your group health plan to continue your coverage for up to 18 months. Although you must pay the premium, it allows for continuing coverage regardless of previous conditions. (For more about COBRA, see YOUR JOB, page 251).

The Act of God designation on all insurance policies means, roughly, that you cannot be insured for the accidents that are most likely to happen to you.

ALAN COREN
British humorist
1993

Keeping a Lid on Insurance Costs

Securing the right health insurance plan means finding the most comprehensive package you can afford. If you are shopping for complete protection, here are several tips that will help you save money:

• **Avoid duplication.** Do not duplicate your coverage. Buying more than one policy may make you feel more secure, but it will probably not bring you any more cash or savings. Most policies do not allow you to collect from two companies for the same claim. Also, try to find a policy that covers your spouse and children without increasing your premium too drastically.

• **Consider managed care.** Think about an HMO or other managed-care policy that pays the hospital or doctor directly, leaving you with little or no out-of-pocket expenses

• **Take the highest deductible.** Elect the highest deductible you think you could afford if you were to get seriously ill. You will have to pay for most or all treatment for minor health problems and may face a hefty initial payment if you face more serious illness or injury, but you will pay substantially lower premiums while you are healthy.

• **Pay annually.** If you can afford it, arrange to pay your premium annually rather than monthly. Many companies offer a discount for lump-sum payments of annual premiums.

• **Invest in a major medical plan.** If you cannot buy a comprehensive insurance package, choose a basic major medical policy that will pay for most doctors' and hospital bills to avoid serious financial loss from catastrophic illness or injury.

Pressing Your Claim

Chances are, if you are insured, eventually you will need to file a claim for medical care. To ensure proper payment, keep copies of all your medical bills; do not simply send the originals to your insurer. If your insurance company should refuse to pay your claim, you will need your bills to protest properly. If a claim is denied, tell the company in writing why you believe you are entitled to reimbursement and ask for a written explanation of why your claim was denied.

If the company denies your claim because of excessive charges, it will usually do so right away. If this happens, ask your doctor to send the company a letter explaining the charges in detail. If the insurer cites lack of "medical necessity" for denying a claim, ask your doctor to assure your carrier that your treatment was essential.

An insurer may also refuse to cover your treatment if it was related to a preexisting condition. If you can show that the condition developed after you bought the policy, you may be able convince the company to cover you. Again, have your doctor write a letter, this time explaining your condition and what caused it. Have your doctor explain in writing how this new condition is unrelated to the previous one.

If the insurance company still refuses to pay, find out whether your plan provides for compulsory arbitration to settle claim disputes. You may then be permitted to present your case in front of a neutral arbitrator. (To learn about arbitration, see YOUR RIGHTS IN ACTION, page 474.)

If none of these measures works, write to your state insurance department and include copies of all correspondence between you and your insurance company. They may be willing to investigate. You may also find it necessary to contact the National Insurance Consumers Organization (NICO), which can find a lawyer to help you. (For the address of NICO, see RESOURCES, page 493)

CHOOSING PRIVATE INSURANCE

Most states require insurance companies to be licensed. If your insurance company is licensed and goes bankrupt, your state's guaranty fund will help cover your claims. The guaranty fund is funded by other licensed insurance companies operating in the state. Choose an insurer that has an "A" rating from independent financial rating agencies, such as Standard & Poor's. Also, check with your state insurance department to make sure your insurance company is licensed and financially solvent. (For more about insurance, see YOUR MONEY, page 326.)

What the "Blues" Have to Offer

Blue Cross and Blue Shield is a nationwide network of community health service corporations. Known as the "Blues," the plans are part of the Chicago-based Blue Cross and Blue Shield Association, although each operates independently, sets its own rates, offers its own package of benefits, and is regulated by laws in each state.

Sometimes Blue Cross and Blue Shield work together in a region; sometimes they work separately. Traditionally, Blue Cross has covered hospital costs, although some plans now cover outpatient care, home care, and other institutional services. In the past, Blue Shield plans covered only doctors' services, but some now cover dental, vision, and outpatient services.

Blue Cross and Blue Shield are nonprofit organizations and operate differently from commercial insurance plans. The Blues operate in communities where they contract directly with doctors and hospitals, paying them for the full cost of service, unlike commercial insurance companies that often only pay for a portion of services and do not work directly with providers.

Many of the blues offer open enrollment periods, when they accept anyone who needs insurance, regardless of preexisting conditions. And some Blue Cross and Blue Shield plans are now offering reduced-rate "core" plans that provide limited, basic coverage and lower premiums.

GOVERNMENT INSURANCE

Uncle Sam offers several bargains in health insurance that you pay for with your taxes. Here's how to make them work for you when you need them.

Medicare

Medicare is the federal government's health insurance program for individuals who are 65 or older. It also covers people of any age with certain disabilities or with permanent kidney failure. Medicare is run by the federal Health Care Financing Administration (HCFA), of the U.S. Department of Health and Human Services, which contracts with regional insurance companies to process claims. HCFA also issues regulations that govern the organizations that administer Medicare.

You can qualify for Medicare if:

- You are 65 and are a U.S. citizen and resident, or are a permanent resident with at least five years of continuous residency in the United States;
- You are 65 and married to a Medicare beneficiary;
- You are younger than 65 but you are receiving Social Security disability payments and will be receiving them for at least 24 months;
- You are under 65 and have "end-stage renal disease" and you or your spouse qualify for Social Security or Railroad Retirement Benefits.

Medicare insurance is divided into two parts, known simply as "Part A" and "Part B." In general, Part A covers hospital costs, and Part B deals with medical expenses. After you pay a deductible, Part A will pay for part of your inpatient care in a hospital. It will also pay for a portion of nursing-home care, home health care, hospice care, and inpatient psychiatric services. If you or your spouse qualify for Social Security or Railroad Retirement Benefits, you do not have to pay a monthly premium for Medicare Part A.

In 1995, the Part A deductible requires you to pay approximately the first $700 of your hospital expenses. Deductible requirements change annually, so check with your local Medicare or Social Security office to learn the amount currently applicable. Furthermore, with Medicare funds in danger of running out, changes in the system have been proposed in Congress and may take effect in the near future. After you have paid the deductible, Medicare picks up almost all hospital expenses for the first 60 days, including costs of a semiprivate room, regular nursing services, operating-room and recovery-room costs, intensive care, drugs, laboratory tests, X-rays, and all other services or supplies considered medically necessary.

Medicare Part A pays in full only for the first 60 days of hospitalization (after you pay the deductible). From the 61st to the 90th day of hospitalization, you must pay a coinsurance fee. From day 91 to day 150, Medicare will pay some portion of hospitalization costs, but those days are considered "lifetime reserve days," and you must pay an even higher coinsurance. You have only 60 lifetime reserve days.

Another complication involves the deductible payment. Suppose you go into the hospital in January. You must pay your Part A deductible of about $700. If you are readmitted to the hospital the following month, you do not have to pay the hospital deductible again because that is within the 60-day benefit period. But if you enter the hospital again in May, you will have to pay the hospital deductible again.

What Medicare Pays, What You Pay

Here is an approximate breakdown of who pays for what when it comes to Medicare. Some services are covered by both parts A and B. "The Medicare Handbook," available at your local Social Security Administration office, has a complete, up-to-date list of Medicare benefits:

MEDICARE PART A

• **Hospitalization.** For the first 60 days, Medicare pays for everything except your Part A deductible. For days 61 to 90, you pay a daily copayment. For "reserve days," 91 to 150, you pay a higher daily copayment. After 150 days you pay all costs.

• **Skilled-nursing facility care.** If you were in a hospital for at least three days and enter a nursing home within 30 days of discharge, Medicare pays all approved costs for the first 20 days. For days 21 to 100 you pay a co-payment. After 100 days you cover all costs.

• **Home health care.** For those without Part B coverage, Part A pays the full cost of medically necessary services and 80 percent of the approved amount for durable medical equipment.

• **Hospice care.** Medicare pays for core costs of all pain-relief and support services but only partially covers outpatient drugs and "respite care."

• **Blood service.** Medicare pays for all procedures and supplies involved in transfusions, but you must pay for the first three pints of blood per year.

MEDICARE PART B

• **Medical expenses.** For doctors' fees, physical and speech therapy, tests, and other expenses, Medicare pays 80 percent of an approved amount. You must pay a deductible and the remaining 20 percent.

• **Home health care.** Medicare covers all approved costs of medically necessary skilled care, medical supplies, and home-health aide services, and 80 percent of approved costs for durable medical equipment such as wheelchairs or crutches.

• **Clinical laboratory services.** Medicare pays 100 percent of approved costs of blood tests, urinalyses, and biopsies.

Outpatient hospital treatment. Medicare pays 80 percent of approved services to diagnose or treat illness or injury. You pay a deductible and the remaining 20 percent.

• **Blood service.** Medicare pays 80 percent of approved costs of procedures and supplies; you pay a deductible, the remaining 20 percent, and the cost of the first three pints of blood.

Medicare Terms

Understanding these basic terms will help you claim your rights as a Medicare patient:

✔ *Actual charge.* The amount a doctor or other medical supplier bills for a particular medical service or supply.

✔ *Approved amount.* The amount Medicare sets as the maximum fee to be charged for a service it covers.

✔ *Assignment.* The agreement by a participating doctor or medical supplier to accept the Medicare-approved amount as total payment for services.

✔ *Customary charge.* The amount a doctor or supplier usually charges for a service.

✔ *Excess charge.* The difference between the actual charge for a procedure and the payment on that charge allowed by Medicare.

✔ *Limiting charge.* The most a doctor is permitted to charge a patient for a Medicare-covered service if he has not taken assignment.

✔ *Prevailing charge.* The maximum charge Medicare can approve for any item or service. This is based on customary charges.

✔ *Reasonable charges.* The lowest of customary, prevailing, or actual charges approved by any private insurer that handles Medicare claims.

If you are eligible for Medicare Part A, you will automatically be offered the option of enrolling in Part B. You might not want to enroll if you are employed and want to take advantage of an employer benefit plan. When you retire, you can enroll in part B without the late-enrollment penalty.

Medicare's Part B is less bountiful than Part A. You must pay not only a deductible and some coinsurance but also a monthly premium. Your coverage will then pay for most of your doctor bills, outpatient hospital care, clinical laboratory tests, flu shots, and medical equipment.

DRG's: "Sicker and Quicker"

Since 1982, Medicare has used a system to estimate how much a hospital should be paid for a particular patient with a particular ailment. This system is called "diagnostic-related groups," or "DRG's." With DRG's, a hospital is paid according to a patient's diagnosed illness or injury, which is assigned when the patient is admitted. Each DRG is assigned a specific number of days an average patient should be expected to stay in the hospital with a given illness or injury, and the hospital is paid that amount, no more, no less.

The DRG system recognizes more than 500 categories of illness and injury. The assignment is not supposed to limit the patient's care in any way, although it does indicate to the hospital staff how long the patient is expected to receive hospital care. For example, the DRG category for pneumonia allows for eight days of hospital care. If you are admitted with pneumonia, but leave before your eight days are up, the hospital keeps the money it saves; if you stay longer than your DRG-allotted time, the hospital absorbs the cost and, as a result, loses money.

Some hospitals have been known to be rigorous about discharging patients according to DRG limits, even if it means sending them home "quicker and sicker." In fact, federal law prohibits hospitals from discharging patients on the basis of DRG's or Medicare payments. A discharge date must be based solely on a patient's medical needs.

If you believe a hospital is trying to send you home too soon, you have the right to protest. Complain to your own doctor, and to the doctor who approved your discharge date. If necessary, mention the federal law that forbids premature discharge. Also, remind him that the hospital can apply for extra funds for patients like you who need longer hospital stays than the DRG suggests.

Ask the hospital's patient's representative to help you deal with the problem. Finally, put your complaint before the hospital's Peer-Review Organization, or PRO. To do this, ask the hospital representative for a written "notice of noncoverage," which explains the process of appealing before the PRO. Even if you fail your appeal, you will have secured at least two additional hospital days.

When and How to Enroll

If you do not want to miss a day of Medicare coverage, enroll for the plan three months before you turn 65; your insurance will begin the first day of the month of your 65th birthday. You also may enroll up to three months after you turn 65, with no penalty. After this, you may sign up only during the open enrollment period between January 1 and March 31 of each calendar year, and your benefits will not begin until the following July 1.

You will be charged a 10 percent penalty on your premium for each year after retiring that you postpone enrolling in Medicare. You do not have to pay that penalty, however, if you are still working and are covered by an employer's health insurance plan. If that is your situation, you should apply for Medicare Part A, since it is free; and then apply for Part B when you retire or when you are no longer covered under your employer's group plan.

If you already receive Social Security or Railroad Retirement Benefits when you turn 65, you will automatically get a Medicare card in the mail. The card will show whether you are covered by Medicare Part A or Part B or both. It also will show the date your coverage began.

Even if you qualify for Medicare, you will not automatically receive a Medicare card in the mail if any of the following apply to you or your situation:

- You have not yet applied for Social Security or Railroad Retirement Benefits;
- You are a government employee;
- You suffer from kidney disease.

In these cases, you must file a Medicare application. To avoid a delay in receiving benefits or incurring late enrollment penalties, apply as early as you can at the nearest Social Security Administration office. To enroll, you will need proof of your age, your earnings records for the past two years, such as W-2 forms (or tax returns for the self-employed), and your Social Security number.

Before You Join a Medicare HMO

If you join a Medicare HMO, Medicare makes monthly payments, but you still pay your Part B premium. You may also have to pay a premium to the HMO for services not covered by Medicare. Here are some other conditions:

✔ *You must have Parts A and B.* You must be enrolled in both parts of Medicare.

✔ *Not just any HMO will do.* You can join only an HMO that has a contract with Medicare.

✔ *You must live in the area.* You must live where the HMO is licensed to enroll members.

✔ *You must join during open enrollment.* You must enroll during the HMO's open enrollment period, which may last all year or only for a few months.

✔ *If you quit, put it in writing.* Although you can leave the plan at any time, you must submit your request in writing.

✔ *Preexisting conditions are no bar.* Your enrollment cannot be denied because of the state of your health, and once you are a member, the HMO cannot cancel your membership due to poor health or the cost of your treatment.

✔ *Services must be available.* All services covered by Medicare must be available within a reasonable amount of time, and emergency facilities must be available 24 hours a day.

How Medicare Billing Works

Usually, the hassle of submitting Medicare claims falls to your doctor or other health-care provider. Part A claims are filed by hospitals or skilled nursing facilities. Part B claims are usually filed by doctors or medical suppliers. Neither the hospital nor the doctor has the right to charge you extra for preparing and submitting your claim.

If your doctor or medical supply company does not accept the amount that Medicare pays as payment in full, it must submit a Part B claim within one year of providing service or they may be subject to certain penalties. If your doctor or medical supplier refuses to submit a Part B claim, you have the right to, and should, complain to the insurance company that carries your Medicare policy.

In submitting a Part B claim, your doctor or supplier completes what is known as an HCFA-1500 form and shows it to you. You must sign the form before it can be sent to your Medicare carrier. If the claim includes rented or purchased durable medical equipment, it must be submitted with a doctor's prescription with a written note demonstrating medical necessity. The prescription must indicate the kind of equipment you need, why you need it, and for how long.

After your doctor or supplier submits the Part B claim, you will receive an "Explanation of Medicare Part B Benefits"

A man ought to handle his body like the sail of a ship, and neither lower or reduce it much when no cloud is in sight, nor be slack and careless in managing it when he comes to suspect something is wrong.

PLUTARCH
Moralia

Managing Your Medicare Claims

As a Medicare recipient, you do not have to submit your own insurance claims to Medicare; however, you can be caught in a jumble of rules that are confusing—sometimes even to your doctors. Here are some tips for keeping your Medicare bills as straightforward as possible:

• **Use participating physicians.** Over 60 percent of practitioners are Medicare participants. Participants agree to accept what Medicare pays less deductibles and copayments on all services rendered. By law, nonparticipating doctors can charge no more than 115 percent of the Medicare-approved charge for any procedure.

• **Review your Medicare bill carefully**. Check your Explanation of Medicare Part B Benefits (EOMB). If you find a discrepancy between the approved amount for the procedure and your doctor's charge to you, call your Medicare intermediary (the insurance company that processes Part A claims) or your Medicare carrier (for Part B claims) at the number listed on your EOMB.

• **Watch out for waivers.** Some doctors try to skirt Medicare limits on fees by asking Medicare patients to sign a waiver stating that the patient agrees to pay privately for services rendered and that no claim will be sent to Medicare. For a waiver to be binding, Medicare must not cover the service being provided and the doctor must so inform the patient. Alert Medicare if a doctor presents you with a waiver for covered services.

• **Report overcharges to Medicare.** If a participating doctor overcharges you, report him to Medicare by calling the number on your EOMB, as well as Medicare's fraud and abuse hotline at (800) 628-6833. Medicare will notify the doctor to refund the overcharge and may impose a fine.

(EOMB) form from Medicare. The form is not a bill. It tells you whether and how much of the claim Medicare will pay.

The amount Medicare agrees to pay a doctor for a particular procedure is called an assignment. If your doctor does not accept the Medicare assignment as payment in full, then Medicare will reimburse you, and you must pay the doctor directly. If your doctor or supplier accepts the assignment, the company in your area that has a contract with the HCFA to process Medicare claims pays the doctor directly.

In certain cases, such as when you consult with a doctor who does not accept the Medicare assignment, you will have to file your own claim for Medicare Part B with your insurance carrier. As with any insurance carrier, you usually have 15 months to submit your claim, but it is best to file a claim as soon as possible after treatment.

WHAT IF A CLAIM IS DENIED?

You generally have six months to appeal a claim that has been denied or has not reimbursed you for as much as you believe you are owed. You will find the reason for the denial printed on the EOMB. If your reimbursement is smaller than you believe it should be, write the carrier to request a review of your claim. (Be sure to include a copy of your EOMB.) If your claim was denied for a specific reason, such as lack of medical necessity, ask your doctor to respond, in writing, explaining why the procedure was medically necessary. Then write the insurance carrier and state why your claim should be covered, along with your doctor's supporting evidence.

If you still are not satisfied, and more than $100 is in dispute, you are entitled to request a formal hearing with the insurance carrier. If the amount in dispute is at least $500, you may appeal to an administrative-law judge; if the amount in dispute is more than $1,000, you can take your case to a federal district court.

Medigap

Although Medicare pays for basic medical and hospital-related needs, some expenses are not covered, such as deductibles, co-payments, and the bulk of long-term care. To fill some of those gaps, Medicare clients often get Medicare supplement insurance, or Medigap.

You can buy a Medigap policy through a private insurance company. There are 10 standard Medigap policies, labeled Plan A through Plan J, and most states have adopted regulations stipulating that no plans other than those 10 policies be sold. All policies must start with a basic core of Medicare coverage,

MEDIGAP PLANS

Following are the 10 standard Medigap benefit plans:

1. Plan A. Covers basic benefits, including the daily co-payment for hospital days 61–90 per benefit period, the higher daily co-payment for hospital days 91–150, and the full cost of 365 additional hospital days per lifetime.

2. Plan B. Pays basic benefits plus the Part A deductible.

3. Plan C. Like Plan B, but includes the Part B deductible. It includes a daily co-payment for days 21–100 in a skilled nursing home and covers foreign emergency care.

4. Plan D. Like Plan C, but excludes the Part B deductible and includes short-term home health care.

5. Plan E. Like Plan D, but excludes home care and includes preventive health screening.

6. Plan F. Like Plan C, and pays for all doctor fees not covered by Medicare.

7. Plan G. Like Plan D, and pays for 80 percent of doctor fees not covered.

8. Plan H. Like Plan D, but excludes home care and includes limited coverage for prescription drugs.

9. Plan I. Like plan G, but includes 100 percent of doctor fees not covered by Medicare and limited coverage for prescription drugs.

10. Plan J. Covers everything above, plus prescription drugs.

"Spending Down"

If you must enter a nursing home and cannot afford to pay for it, or run out of funds while there, you may be eligible for financial help from Medicaid. However, you must carefully plan in advance to ensure that your assets do not disqualify you from Medicaid, or you could end up spending your entire life savings on long-term care. To avoid this, some people deliberately deplete their resources in a process known as "spending down."

For those who already receive benefits, Medicaid will foot the nursing home bills. However, if you have not received Medicaid in the past, you must prove your eligibility. Requirements for Medicaid vary by state, but often a house, a car, and a small savings such as $2,000 are considered exempt assets. All other money and property must be transferred to others or placed in a special trust.

Spending down is a complicated process. If it is done incorrectly, a patient may give away assets and still not be eligible for Medicaid. For example, you must spend down at least 30 months before applying for Medicaid.

Some people feel uneasy about moving assets to increase the Medicaid eligibility. While this strategy is perfectly legal, it is complicated. To best protect yourself, contact a lawyer or an accountant—ideally one familiar with both Medicaid regulations and finance—for advice before transferring your assets.(See also YOUR MARRIAGE AND FAMILY, page 156.)

specified by law. Some policies are more extensive than others, covering a range of services that Medicare does not cover, but except for the basic policy, Plan A, not all policies are available in every state. The policy you choose should be tailored to your medical needs.

You can buy any of the 10 Medigap policies without worrying about preexisting conditions, as long as you do so within six months after enrolling in Medicare Part B. After that six-month open-enrollment period, an insurance company may deny you coverage because of your health status.

Since all new Medigap policies are guaranteed to be renewable, they cannot be canceled unless you fail to pay your premium. If you are dissatisfied with a policy, you may return it within 30 days of receiving it and get a full refund or select another, more appropriate, policy.

WHAT THE BASIC PLAN MUST COVER

Of the 10 Medigap policies, Plan A is the core plan that covers basic services and must be available to all Medicare recipients. The other nine policies must include the Plan A core package, which pays the patient's share of basic hospital and doctor cost covered by Medicare, including daily charges for long hospital stays, and 20 percent of doctor bills. All the plans must also pay for the first three pints of blood per year and for the cost of 365 days of hospitalization over a policyholder's lifetime. Medigap policies are not required to pay for either the Part A or Part B deductible, although most do.

EXTRA COVERAGE YOU MAY NOT NEED

The cost of a Medigap policy depends on how much extra coverage you buy. In addition to basic benefits, the 10 policies include a range of extra benefits, from emergency health care during foreign travel, to basic drugs, to preventive care. (See also "Medigap Plans," page 213.)

Before choosing a policy, make sure to carefully evaluate your needs. If you do not travel internationally, for example, you will not need foreign travel coverage. Similarly, if your doctor accepts Medicare-set fees, you will not need a plan that covers excess charges. Remember, you will pay more in premiums for every extra benefit you buy.

Federal law protects you against Medigap fraud. An insurer may not sell you a policy that duplicates your Medicare, Medicaid, or any private coverage you may have. An insurer also may not sell you a Medigap policy that is not one of the 10 state-approved standard policies. If you suspect an insurer of fraud or illegal sales practices, report it to your state insurance department. You may also complain to federal officials on the Medicare Hotline at (800) 638-6833

Medicaid

I f you cannot pay for the services that Medicare does not cover, or if you don't qualify for Medicare and cannot afford any health care, you may be eligible for Medicaid. Medicaid is the government program that pays for health care for the poor, including the elderly, the chronically ill, and the disabled.

Federal and state funds pay for Medicaid; it operates within federal guidelines, but each state runs its own program and sets its own eligibility standards. In general, you qualify for Medicaid if you receive Aid to Families with Dependent Children (AFDC) or if you receive Supplemental Security Income (SSI) because you are 65 or older, or blind or disabled.

If you earn too much to qualify for AFDC but have lost most of your income and assets by paying for large medical expenses such as long-term nursing home care, you may be considered medically needy and eligible for Medicaid. Also, if you qualify for Medicare but your income is not more than 100 percent above the federal poverty line and your financial resources are not more than twice the SSI resource-eligibility level, you may also be eligible to have Medicaid pay for your Medicare Part A and Part B premiums, deductibles, and coinsurance.

You can apply for Medicaid at your local welfare office. In some states the elderly can also apply at senior citizen centers or agencies on aging. You probably will need to show proof of your age, income, and any disability you have, as well as your Social Security number and the amount of your Social Security check if you receive one. It is advisable to bring copies of your medical bills for the previous year.

Pregnant women and women with infants under one year who are not eligible for AFDC but whose income is no more than one third higher than the state poverty level may qualify for Medicaid as well.

DO ALL DOCTORS ACCEPT MEDICAID?

Federal law requires Medicaid to pay for basic health services, but it does not require doctors or clinics to accept Medicaid patients. Those that do are prohibited from charging more for any service than Medicaid will pay. While Medicaid pays the providers directly, some states charge patients a minimal co-payment. Find out whether a doctor accepts Medicaid before you schedule an appointment. As for hospitals, the law requires those that take federal funds to accept Medicaid patients; since most hospitals need federal funds, there are very few that do not take Medicaid patients.

Services Medicaid Must Cover

Although coverage varies among states, there is a generous list of core services that Medicaid must cover. It includes:

✔ *Hospital care.* Medicaid pays for physician-ordered inpatient and outpatient hospital care in hospitals that are licensed and approved for participation in Medicaid.

✔ *Practitioners' services.* Medicaid will pay for services of doctors, nurse-midwives, pediatric nurse practitioners, and family nurse practitioners.

✔ *Tests.* Medicaid pays for laboratory tests and X-rays ordered by a physician in a hospital, doctor's office, or other facility.

✔ *Home care.* Medicaid will pay for health services provided in your home, if they are ordered by a physician.

✔ *Nursing-home care.* Medicaid will pay for services in a skilled nursing facility licensed and approved for participation in the program, if care is ordered by a doctor.

✔ *Transportation.* Medicaid will pay transportation costs for recipients to travel to and from health care providers.

✔ *Optional services.* In some states, Medicaid also covers chiropractic care, podiatry, dental care, occupational therapy, prescription drugs, and other medical supplies.

Long-term Care

With chronic or terminal illness, you need the strongest, most reliable health care safety net your money can buy.

Help for the Helpers

You may provide only minimal assistance to a disabled or homebound person, or be completely responsible for a terminally ill patient. Regardless of the amount of care you give, you can do number of things to make your job easier:

✔ *Find information.* Having a solid resource to call on can be instrumental in getting needed referrals and advice. Ask your local hospital or the patient's doctor for advice on finding an appropriate resource.(See also "Resources for Caregivers," page 224.)

✔ *Join a caregiver support group.* Often sponsored by social service agencies and hospitals, support groups can be a way to help you cope with the pressures you are facing. They may also be good resources for caregiving advice and information.

✔ *Use respite care.* Volunteers or paid workers, known as respite caregivers, may be able to come to the home to provide short-term relief.

✔ *Seek out employer assistance.* Some companies offer support groups and counseling or allow "flex time" schedules to make caregiving more convenient.

What Is Long-Term Care and Who Needs It?

Long-term care has many meanings. In general, it includes a broad spectrum of medical, personal, and social support services ranging from home meal delivery to skilled nursing care. Such assistance is provided over an extended period for people who are severely disabled, terminally ill, or have a chronic mental illness.

Long-term care is usually associated with old age. But the elderly represent only part of the long-term care population. People with cancer or AIDS, as well as people suffering from chronic, debilitating diseases associated with age such as multiple sclerosis, constitute a substantial portion of those who receive long-term care.

Long-term care is not limited to the sick. Someone who is physically disabled, such as someone with a spinal cord injury or born with a condition like muscular dystrophy or spina bifida, may require long-term care. The mentally retarded and the mentally ill—individuals suffering from schizophrenia or severe manic-depressive (bipolar) disorder—also may need long-term care. Blind or deaf people may also need long-term assistance, whether they are able to receive it at home or at a specially-designed facility.

Caring for the Chronically Ill

There are essentially three types of long-term care: in-home services, community-based services, and institutional care. In-home services assist people who live at home with a certain degree of independence but who need regular assistance with the activities of daily living. Community programs are geared toward people who need constant care and observation, especially during the day when those who normally take care of them are at work or simply need a rest from caregiving. People who require extended around-the-clock care but not hospitalization may need institutional care. Varying levels of institutional care are provided in nursing homes, convalescent homes, and rehabilitation hospitals. The scope and nature of the services depend on the condition and needs of the individual. In some instances, services in different categories may overlap.

IN-HOME SERVICES

Persons who are recovering from surgery or a heart attack commonly need home care, as do people who are in the early stages of a terminal illness or progressive neurological disease. Home care might also benefit someone who is suffering from a chronic illness or condition or who is physically disabled.

In-home services for the terminally ill may include medical care provided by a nurse or therapist, as well as personal support services, such as help with grooming, dressing, and daily household chores. Social support services, such as home-delivered meals, friendly visitor services, and telephone reassurance to the elderly who live alone, are also in-home services.

COMMUNITY-BASED SERVICES

Senior centers and adult day-care centers that provide social and recreational programs for older individuals are examples of community-based services. These centers commonly offer meals, counseling, legal, financial, and (sometimes) health care.

Nutrition sites are community-based programs that provide seniors with inexpensive meals along with opportunities to socialize. They are often located in senior citizen centers, housing projects, churches or synagogues, or schools.

Exercise and temperance can preserve something of our early strength even in old age.

CICERO
On Old Age

Continuing-Care Retirement Communities

A continuing-care retirement community (CCRC) integrates housing, social activities, and health-care services for older adults. If you or someone you care about is considering moving to a retirement community, keep the following in mind:

• **Know what you want.** Some communities allow residents to live independently; some offer assisted living, providing help with bathing, dressing, or other daily activities; others provide full-time nursing care; some provide all these services. Decide which type you are looking for before considering actual communities.

• **Check finances.** Before making a commitment, be sure that the community you are considering is financially sound. Find out if your monthly fee includes the cost of nursing or hospital care. And see if the community will guarantee you a nursing home or hospital bed when you need one.

• **Changing your mind.** Make sure you know the community's refund policy. You also should know if the facility can cancel your contract or if it will require you to purchase Medicare, Medigap, or long-term-care insurance.

• **Accreditation.** More than half the states have passed laws regulating continuing-care retirement communities, but no uniform level of protection exists. Accreditation by the Continuing Care Accreditation Commission indicates that a community meets certain standards for financial stability, management, and resident care. To find out if the CCRC you are considering is accredited, contact the commission at: Continuing Care Accreditation Commission, 901 E Street, NW, Washington, D.C. 20004; (202) 783-2242.

A Plan for Post-Hospital Supervision

In most states, hospitals are required to develop a discharge plan for patients. A discharge plan maps out the steps a patient needs to take in order to arrange for housing, income, medical care, and other support services after leaving the hospital.

A good discharge plan should consider where a patient will live; how a patient will meet her basic need for clothing, food, and shelter; what kind of medical care she may require; and what kind of financial assistance she may need.

A good plan will also help the patient or family members find agencies to locate housing, employment, medical services, or disability income.

Besides developing discharge plans, most hospitals are also required to work with a patient's family in developing the plan. This can be especially helpful when a family realizes that it cannot care for a loved one after discharge but wants to be closely involved and informed about ongoing care.

If your hospital does not follow through on a discharge plan, you have the right to insist that a social worker, therapist, or other hospital staff member complete one.

Some communities offer alternative living arrangements for individuals—the elderly or the mentally or physically disabled—who can no longer live at home. For instance, board-and-care-homes, sometimes referred to as congregate housing, provide people with a room; three meals a day; help with bathing, dressing, and other daily activities; and transportation. These homes may house anywhere from 30 to 100 residents and generally are privately owned and managed. Not all board and care homes are licensed, however, and quality standards vary from region to region.

House sharing is another type of community-based program where two or more people live together. Each person has a private bedroom but shares all common living areas. Household chores and expenses are also shared. Similarly, some communities have adult-foster-care programs, placing elderly and disabled adults in private homes.

Respite care is a type of community-based service that offers several hours or days of relief to family members who are caring for frail, ill, or disabled loved ones. This care is generally provided by volunteers who work with churches, synagogues, nursing homes, home health agencies, or volunteer agencies and who visit a person at home, in an institution, or an adult day-care center. To find respite care, use resources such as your local hospital, department on aging, a social worker, or any religious organizations you belong to or know of.

Hospice care provides care and counseling for the terminally ill and their families. Hospice workers help patients and families cope with the dying process and provide physical, psychological, social, and emotional support. The care may be provided in a designated hospice facility or in the patient's home.

INSTITUTIONAL CARE

There are three basic types of skilled institutional care:

- **Skilled nursing care** is designed for people who need intensive, 24-hour-a-day medical care. The patient might be recovering from a serious accident or illness, such as a heart attack, stroke, or spinal cord injury. Skilled nursing facilities are staffed by registered nurses who work under the supervision of a doctor.
- **Intermediate nursing care** is designed for patients recovering from less-serious medical problems. They may be somewhat independent but still need some nursing assistance and supervision that is neither intensive nor full-time.
- **Custodial care** is the least intensive level of institutional care. It is geared toward people who need room and board and some help with personal services but do not require health care services.

Financing Long-Term Care

Not all long-term care poses a financial dilemma. Cost depends on many factors, including the level, location, and duration of care. Some social services are free or provided at a low fee by nonprofit organizations. On the other hand, nursing-home costs can be so high, many wonder if they can even afford it.

Medicare, Medicaid, and private insurance policies all offer some assistance, but in most cases they are not enough. Many people decide to buy long-term care insurance, which offers the most extensive coverage for long-term care, although it can be expensive. For example, if you are 50 years old, a policy could cost you anywhere from $400 to $1,100 a year. If you are 65, you could spend from $980 to $2,200 annually on a long-term care policy. By the time you reach age 79, a policy could cost you $3,900 to $7,000 a year.

PURCHASING LONG-TERM-CARE INSURANCE

People usually buy long-term-care insurance when they anticipate going into a nursing home and want to avoid spending their assets on nursing home care when Medicare runs out. Medicare pays for only a small percent of short-term, skilled nursing home care after hospitalization. It also pays for only a very small portion of short-term, skilled at-home care.

But anticipating nursing home care may not be a financially sound reason for buying long-term-care insurance. For instance, if you have slender savings and have to use it all to pay for a long-term-care policy premium, you should not buy it. If your annual income is under $15,000 and you have less than $50,000 in savings, you do not need it. With such relatively-limited income and assets, you would quickly spend most of your resources on nursing-home costs—at which point you will be eligible for Medicaid.

Long-term-care insurance probably is not a wise buy unless your assets are between $30,000 and $50,000 or more and you have the income to afford the annual premiums. Even then, you should know exactly what benefits you are entitled to under Medicare and your Medigap policy if you have one, before investing in a long-term care policy.

If you decide on long-term care insurance, make sure your policy comes with inflation protection. Nursing-home costs climb every year, but the protection offered by long-term-care policies may not. If, for example, you buy a policy but do not claim benefits for five or ten years, by the time you are ready to enter a nursing home, costs may have soared.

Of course, such protection does not come cheap. The bet-

Getting Help to Make Your Home Accessible

Physically disabled people often need to modify their homes to accommodate wheelchairs. Government funds to pay for alterations for the disabled are scarce, but here are some alternative source ideas, depending on the state and status of the disabled individual:

✔ *Disabled vets.* If you are a veteran who was disabled on duty, you may qualify for a Home Improvement and Structural Alteration Grant or for a Housing Grant for Catastrophically Disabled Veterans. Both grants are administered by the Department of Veterans Affairs.

✔ *Vocational rehabilitation.* Often, state departments of vocational rehabilitation will provide financial or other assistance if you can prove that modifying your home will help allow you to return to work and prevent you from needing hospitalization.

✔ *Insurance.* If you need specific items, like a chair lift or an air conditioner, and if you can get your doctor to write an explanation of your need for it, your private health insurance might cover the costs.

✔ *State loans.* Some states have loan programs that allow the physically disabled to borrow money at low interest rates to buy medical equipment or to modify their homes.

ter your protection, in most cases, the more expensive the policy, and inflation protection will add from 25 percent to 40 percent to a long-term-care insurance-policy premium.

POOR HEALTH MAY EXCLUDE COVERAGE

Before you even consider the costs of long-term care insurance, check with your doctor and the insurance company to make sure you qualify for coverage. Insurance companies are in business to make money, and they do not like to sell policies to people with preexisting illnesses such as diabetes, multiple sclerosis, asthma, macular degeneration (an eye disease), or severe high blood pressure.

You are a bad risk as well if you are recovering from a stroke, recent cancer surgery, or even if you have undergone a hip-replacement operation within the last 18 months. If you already have a physical disability that keeps you from doing basic activities such as dressing, bathing, and eating, acquiring long-term insurance is probably impossible. One of your few legal protections in this area concerns Alzheimer's disease: the law in many states requires all insurance policies to cover this disease, as long as it develops after you buy the policy.

Insurance policies that cover people with preexisting health problems often cost much more than standard policies and offer fewer benefits. Even so, it is probably worth finding a policy that does not exclude preexisting Alzheimer's or Parkinson's diseases or stroke-induced dementia, since these are major causes of nursing-home stays.

All human beings
are born free and equal in
dignity and rights.

STEVEN MITCHELL SACK

Attorney at law
New York City

Guardianship of a Mentally Disabled Child

If your child is mentally retarded, mentally ill, or in some other way developmentally disabled and cannot make decisions for himself, you may want to apply for plenary legal guardianship once he becomes an adult. If you are considering this, here are some things you should know:

• You do not have to be a parent to become a legal guardian; you can be a relative or a close friend.

• Guardianship is not a lifelong commitment. You can terminate your legal guardianship at any time after following appropriate legal procedures.

• As a parent applying for guardianship, you must show a court that your child cannot manage his affairs due to mental incompetence. But it is not easy to declare someone—even your own child— incompetent, because the law vigorously protects the civil liberties of the mentally disabled. Courts generally require certification from two doctors, one of whom must be a psychologist or some other mental-health specialist.

• Legally, a guardian is responsible for such duties as paying the debts of her ward, entering into contracts for him, and managing his financial affairs.

• Attaining legal guardianship can be an especially important form of protection for a child who is mentally ill. Mental illness can be erratic and may be controlled with medication, enabling a person to function independently at least some of the time. Becoming his guardian assures you of having the legal authority to make decisions on his behalf when he is incapacitated.

• If a guardian fails to put her ward's best interest first when conducting the ward's business, the courts can take the responsibility away.

EVALUATING DIFFERENT POLICIES

When you read a policy for long-term insurance, you generally will see that it pays benefits when care is considered "medically necessary." That means care must have been prescribed by a doctor or is needed because a person can no longer take care of herself. Most policies cover skilled, intermediate, and custodial nursing care in state-licensed nursing homes. Policies may also cover home-care services, including physical therapists, homemakers, and home health aides that are provided by state-licensed or Medicare-certified home health agencies.

Long-term care policies are either "disability based" or "service based." Disability-based policies cover any type of long-term care, so long as the insured has become disabled. Service-based policies, which are more common—and less advantageous for the consumer—pay only for services that meet insurance-company standards. A service-based policy may pay only for custodial care in a skilled or intermediate nursing facility or in a facility that has at least 25 residents. A disability-based policy does not place such restrictions. (See also, "Limits on Long-Term Care," at left.)

Most policies pay for a least one year of nursing-home care. There are also policies that cover costs for from two years of care to care for the rest of a person's life. Find out if your policy requires a hospital stay before it will cover nursing-home benefits—this can end up being quite expensive.

LONG-TERM-POLICY WRINKLES

Some policies come with a "waiver of premiums," which means that you do not have to pay your premiums during nursing home stays. Most insurance companies do not, however, waive premiums when nursing care is given at home. Some policies also provide "nonforfeiture benefits," which means that the insurance company will return some of the money you have paid if you forfeit, or discontinue, your policy.

An insurer may cancel your long-term-care policy and return your premiums if the company learns that you have not honestly disclosed information about your health. (On the other hand, it may give you a price break for being in good health.) In most states, insurers offer a 30-day "free look" period, during which time you can closely examine a policy while being covered by it. If you do not like the policy, you are entitled to return it for a full refund.

Be wary of insurance companies that promise you long-term care coverage that goes into effect within a day or two of purchase. Such companies often attempt to determine your eligibility only after you have filed a claim. As a result, you might be in for a disastrous surprise after it is too late to do anything about it.

Rights and Responsibilities of Long-Term Caregivers

Suppose your elderly mother, who lives with you, suffers from Alzheimer's disease. She often forgets to take her medicine and sometimes gets disoriented; you are afraid that she might wander off and come to harm. You worry about her, but you also worry about whether you would be to blame if she caused injury or damage. So you think about putting her in a nursing home. Now your concern is whether you would be forsaking your responsibility. These dilemmas are facing more and more Americans as the elderly live longer and taking care of them gets more complicated.

Caregivers often do not realize how great a burden it can be to provide constant, long-term care. Then, when they learn firsthand that the load may be more than they can carry, they may not know if they have the right to stop providing care or, if they do, who will take their place.

The rights and responsibilities of long-term caregivers vary according to state laws and, of course, the condition of the person receiving care. A patient's rights do not change, however, insofar as they are intended to protect the privacy, dignity, and autonomy of every patient. All patients everywhere have the right to be fully informed about the nature of their illness, proposed treatments, and any possible risks or benefits.

When patients lack the mental capacity to defend their rights or make competent decisions about treatment, they are entitled to the protection of a caregiver who can and will. That protector could be a relative, a loving friend, or a court-appointed guardian, and it is the caretaker's duty to make treatment decisions that uphold a patient's rights and best interests.

LIABILITY FOR THE MENTALLY ILL

Most people with mental illness are not violent. Nevertheless, some mentally ill individuals, when not treated, may pose a threat to themselves or others. Under such a circumstance, can a caregiver be held responsible?

There is no easy or single answer to that question. Each circumstance depends on a patient's condition and on state law. If a person suffering from some form of mental illness causes property damage, for example, the caregiver may or may not be held financially responsible.

If a guardian of a minor or an adult had some way of predicting that he was going to harm a person and negligently failed to supervise or otherwise prevent the harm, then the guardian might be held liable for his actions. But foreseeing

potential injury by the actions of another individual is difficult to prove; therefore, a guardian is rarely held responsible.

Some states, like New York, have laws that tailor and limit a caregiver's responsibility to a patient's specific needs. For instance, a caregiver might be assigned to help a patient do his laundry. If he allows the patient to go to the laundromat alone, the caregiver has breached his duty of care in a negligent way and might be responsible if the patient intentionally damages a washing machine.

CAN YOU COMMIT SOMEONE?

It is difficult to commit someone against his will to a long-term care facility, be it a nursing home, a drug treatment center, or a psychiatric hospital. A person who refuses commitment is entitled to a court hearing. In most cases, caregivers, doctors, and anyone else involved with the person's care must prove to a judge that an individual poses a substantial physical danger to others or that he requires some form of institutionalized long-term care for his own well-being.

Battling a Loved One's Addiction

PROBLEM
George became aware that Rita had a problem with drugs when he discovered that she was sipping brandy and taking sleeping pills during the day. When he suggested she go into treatment, she refused. Feeling frustrated and frightened, he told her that if she did not sign herself into a substance-abuse treatment center, he would do it for her.

ACTION
George made an empty threat. The only way he could force Rita into a treatment center would be to prove to the court that she is incompetent or a danger to herself and others. He could, however, ask family members and friends to join him in directly confronting Rita—when she is sober—about her growing, excessive dependence on sleeping pills and alcohol, a process known as an "intervention." George opted for such a "tough love" confrontation. Shaken by the concern her family and friends showed, Rita acknowledged her problem, and agreed to try treatment.

If the problem is acute, and you think someone is in immediate danger of harming himself or others, you should dial 911 and request emergency assistance from the police or a mobile-crisis unit. A mobile-crisis team will send a psychiatrist or a social worker to evaluate the individual's state of mind and determine whether the person poses a risk.

Usually, though, the caregiver's dilemma about whether to commit someone, and how to go about it, develops slowly and does not involve mental illness or violent behavior. After years of caring for a relative with Alzheimer's disease, for example,

Substance-Abuse and Alcohol Treatment

Federal regulations state that people in rehabilitation programs for alcoholism and substance abuse have a right to confidentiality. But there are certain exceptions:

✔ *Elder and child abuse.* Programs and their staff are required to report suspected child or elder abuse.

✔ *Criminal threat.* A court order may require a treatment center to confirm or deny that they are treating a particular client who is suspected of being a criminal and a threat to the public. A person enrolled in a substance-abuse program who commits a crime is not protected by confidentiality.

✔ *Acute medical hospitalization.* Regulations that protect confidentiality also may not apply if, during the course of regular hospitalization, a patient is found to be chemically dependent. That information becomes part of the patient's general medical record, which may then be shared with hospital staff or anyone else involved with his care, as well as with insurance companies.

✔ *Employment applications.* Individuals applying for employment with the armed forces and federal or state agencies may be asked if they have ever participated in a treatment program and may be requested to release their treatment records.

a caregiver simply may be too exhausted or financially drained to continue providing care. Moreover, if the patient becomes incompetent, the supervision and care that can be provided at home may no longer be adequate.

In such a case, a long-term care facility will have to affirm that the patient indeed has Alzheimer's and is incompetent. After accepting a patient, the facility will design a treatment plan. It must also inform both the patient and the caregiver of its policies regarding discharge and transfer to another facility.

Just as you cannot commit someone against his will, you also cannot force him to take medication. Even hospitals and medical staff cannot do so. To make a patient take medication, you or the hospital staff have to prove that the patient is in medical danger by not taking it. Or a judge has to determine that a patient is incompetent and does not understand the need for medication. In that case, the judge could appoint a legal guardian to make sure a patient takes the medication.

HOW LONG IS LONG-TERM CARE?

The duration of long-term care depends on where the care is given, the severity of a patient's condition, and the financial resources and emotional stamina of the caregiver. For a patient with Alzheimer's, care can last until the patient dies. For a person who is addicted to drugs or alcohol, the length of care may last only as long as the rehabilitation process.

In some circumstances, a caregiver's role depends on legal guardianship. Depending on the state, most legal guardianships have time limits and are subject to regular court reviews to determine if they should be continued.

WHEN CAREGIVERS STOP GIVING CARE

Sometimes families can no longer care for their loved ones and must find alternative settings. If a caregiver dies without making provisions for care and support, and a patient has no other family, the state may declare the patient a ward of the state and find an alternative care setting. It will use any money the patient has to pay for care. If the patient has no financial resources, then Medicaid will finance care. If you are a caregiver, make sure you investigate alternative arrangements to provide for those under your care in case of your death.

A caregiver who feels unable to continue providing care can always ask the court for help in finding either an alternative caregiver or a new care setting, such as a group home, adult foster care, or a hospital.

Nursing Homes

At least one-third of Americans who reach age 65 will spend time in a nursing home before they die. Be sure you know what you or a loved one can expect.

Three Levels of Care

Approximately 25,000 nursing homes operate in the United States, and the service they provide has become an essential part of the social fabric. As more Americans survive into old age and fewer families are able to take care of their elderly relatives at home, the prevalence of nursing-home care will continue to grow. So it is important to learn what to expect if the time comes when you or a loved one needs to take this difficult step.

Nursing homes are classified according to the level of care they provide:

- **Skilled-care facilities** provide intensive care—such as intravenous and respiratory therapy and tube feedings—to patients who are bedridden and unable to help themselves.
- **Intermediate-care nursing homes** are for patients who need help with bathing, meals, and other daily functions and with health-related activities, such as taking medications and managing their diets.
- **Custodial-care facilities** serve those who can function independently but need some assistance getting out of bed, walking, and bathing.

Of these three, only skilled nursing facilities are reimbursed by Medicare; intermediate and custodial-care facilities are not. Intermediate care facilities may be certified to participate in the Medicaid program. Custodial care facilities generally are ineligible for Medicaid and Medicare certification. All facilities must be licensed by the state in which they operate. Facilities that receive Medicare and Medicaid funding must also comply with federal regulations regarding physical construction, fire safety, medical services, sanitation, nutrition, recreation, and record-keeping.

Rules vary by state, but in general, both skilled and intermediate nursing homes must have a registered nurse on duty eight hours a day, seven days a week, and a licensed nurse on duty at all times. Annual inspections are required for recertification, and a nursing home's inspection report must be made available. If it is not posted, ask for it.

123…

IS IT TIME FOR A NURSING HOME?

If you are unsure when it is time for you or a family member to enter a nursing home, you may want to consider the following questions:

1. Can the prospective nursing home resident cook for herself and manage her household? If not, it may be time for residential care.

2. Is there another family member who can help with caregiving? If there is not, you may be able to hire a home health aide to assist with meals and daily living.

3. Is there another family member who depends on this person for care? Although assistance in the home may be helpful, there may come a time when married couples can no longer look after each other.

4. Is the prospective patient planning to undergo surgery that will disable her for a period of time? If so, a temporary arrangement will have to be made, either in a residential facility or in the patient's home.

5. Does the patient need a new living arrangement, or does she merely need a place to stay during convalescence? There are facilities that specialize in convalescence.

Choosing a Nursing Home

To get a true picture of a nursing home you or a family member are interested in, plan to make both announced and unannounced visits. First, make an appointment with the nursing home-administrator or admissions director. Ask for a guided tour and arrange to speak with staff and residents.

Make your second visit unannounced. Stop by during evening or weekend hours, when administrative heads are least likely to be around. Or visit during the late morning or mid-day, to see if residents are out of bed, groomed, and dressed. A visit during and after mealtimes will give you a sense of the quality of the food and how well the dining area is cleaned.

If after careful consideration, you like what you see, it is time to discuss costs and availability of space. A patient or resident in a nursing home will be asked to sign a contract before being admitted. If someone is not mentally competent, then a guardian or other legal representative must sign.

Carefully review the contract before signing it and make sure it states the rights and responsibilities of a nursing-home resident. It should indicate how much you are obliged to pay each month, including prices for items not included in the basic charge. The contract should also explain the home's grievance procedures and its policy on holding a bed, should a patient leave temporarily.

Nursing Home or Home Care?

Nursing-home residents are often people who need 24-hour nursing care and supervision. Nursing homes are expensive and only partly covered by Medicare. You may want to look at home care services instead. Consider the following:

• If 24-hour medical care and supervision is not necessary, you might consider home care. Services, provided by a variety of professionals such as nurses, nurse's aides, physical therapists, and volunteers, are available in most communities.

• Home care is significantly less expensive than nursing-home care and in many cases provides similar services. For a reasonable fee, a nurse may come to the home, for instance, to administer intravenous medication, change a dressing on a wound, or take blood for testing.

• Home care can be highly specialized and tailored to a patient's needs. For instance, someone who has suffered a stroke may be visited regularly by a speech therapist. She may also benefit from the assistance of a nurse's aide who can help her bathe, dress, and prepare meals.

• For those who need minimal assistance, your state's department on aging may be able to put you in contact with organizations that send volunteers to help with chores such as housekeeping and shopping.

• For a senior who needs companionship more than medical care, an adult day-care center or an assisted-living arrangement might suit her better and cost less than a nursing home. Some of these programs offer recreational and health services as well as community living.

Before signing a contract, ask about the home's policy on advance directives. Any nursing home that receives Medicare or Medicaid funds is required by law to record end-of-life treatment wishes in each patient's medical record and to tell you if it will honor those wishes. If not, the nursing home is obliged to transfer the patient, upon your request, to a facility that will.

Monitoring Care

Federal law requires nursing homes to develop individual care plans for all residents. A care plan specifies how the staff will deal with a resident's medical and nonmedical needs. You, as the resident or as a friend or relative of a resident, have the right to be involved in the process.

The nursing-home staff must first complete an evaluation of a resident's functional abilities, including how well he can walk, talk, eat, dress, bathe, see, hear, understand, and remember. An assessment must be completed within 14 days of admission and at least once a year after that. It must be reviewed every three months and also when a resident's condition changes.

SAFEGUARDING A RELATIVE'S CARE

You are entitled to ask the staff to schedule a care-planning conference when you, the patient in your family, and other interested family members can attend. It is helpful to involve the nursing-home resident in developing the care plan.

After the care-plan meeting, follow up on what was discussed. Make sure the plan is being followed. If it is not, take your concerns or complaints to nurses, the doctor, or the nursing-home administrator. Some nursing-home personnel may resent your involvement, but remember that you have the right to protect your relative's welfare.

Financial Considerations

Nursing-home residents may start paying for nursing-home care out of their own pockets, but at a cost of $25,000 to $30,000 a year, or more, the bills will quickly deplete personal finances. Unless your income is well above average, you probably will need some type of financial assistance.

Private long-term-care insurance policies are one way of paying for nursing-home care. Such policies vary in their coverage. Those that pay for unlimited days of nursing-home care have the steepest premiums. Yet, the fixed daily rate of most

---

Creating a Nursing-Home Care Plan

Care plans for nursing-home residents ensure that they get the treatment they need. As a friend or relative of a nursing-home patient or as a resident, you should take an active role in drawing up these blueprints for care. The information in the assessment should include:

✔ *Medical information.* The plan should include a record of the patient's medical history, current conditions and medical status, dental condition, any drugs currently being taken, and any sensory or physical impairments.

✔ *Mental status.* The plan should include comments about the patient's current cognitive abilities and an analysis of his general psychological and emotional state.

✔ *Nutritional status.* The plan should detail the patient's diet, eating habits, and any special requirements, deficiencies, or requests.

✔ *A strategy.* The plan should take into account the patients needs and requests regarding food, activities, personal care, and mobility. It should also outline longer-term strategies.

✔ *Potential.* The plan should outline the doctors' opinions regarding the potential for both rehabilitation and discharge. This analysis should be updated whenever the patient's condition changes.

long-term-care policies does not cover all nursing-home costs. Also, many policies have waiting periods, plus stringent requirements and exclusions, such as requiring hospitalization immediately prior to entering a nursing home, or requiring skilled care before paying for custodial care. You cannot rely on Medicare either. It pays for only part of the cost of 100 days of skilled nursing care following related hospitalization.

If you cannot pay for nursing home care, or if you exhaust all your personal resources, you may be eligible for Medicaid. Medicaid will pay the balance of your nursing-home bill after your contributions from Social Security or other income have been included. You will be allowed to keep only a small amount of income each month for personal spending.

BEWARE MEDICAID DISCRIMINATION

Because Medicaid generally pays nursing homes at a lower daily rate than private-pay patients, some unscrupulous nursing homes have been known to discriminate against Medicaid patients. They may engage in the illegal activity of trying to convince families to pay privately for a period of time before applying for Medicaid. And although it is illegal, some nursing homes try not to keep residents once they have spent all their own resources and become eligible for Medicaid. If you suspect any kind of Medicaid discrimination or fraud, report it to your state or local Medicaid fraud and abuse unit. Call your local Medicaid office for the number.

On the other hand, nursing homes are not required to accept

No costs have increased more rapidly in the last decade than the cost of medical care. And no group of Americans has felt the impact of these skyrocketing costs more than our older citizens.

JOHN F. KENNEDY
Campaign speech
1960

Beware of Nursing Homes' Hidden Costs

The monthly or daily costs of nursing care may not include everything you think it does. Nursing homes may add on a number of extra charges. Some of these charges are legal, and some are not. Most, however, are regulated by state laws. Look out for the following:

• **Illegal admission fees.** This is one of the ways that unscrupulous nursing homes cover the difference between private and Medicaid or Medicare patient charges. If you are a Medicaid beneficiary, do not pay an admission fee. Contact your Medicaid fraud control unit or your state department of health to find out your state's requirements.

• **Inflated rates.** Some homes charge private-pay residents higher rates than Medicaid residents, giving them private or newer rooms in exchange. If permitted by state law, they may also require private-pay patients to pay their room and board bills 30 or 60 days in advance, and require them to put down a large sum of money to receive care.

• **Personal expenses.** Depending on state law, nursing homes may be able to bill patients for personal-care expenses. They are permitted to charge Medicaid patients extra for a television, telephone service, and visits to the beauty parlor or barbershop for more than a periodic hair trim, shave, or shampoo.

• **Supply charges.** Nursing homes can charge for supplies and specially ordered items, like a favorite soap or brand of shampoo, if it is an item that a nursing home does not regularly use. Medicare beneficiaries, especially, may be charged for items they assume are covered, such as facial tissues and wheelchair cushions, enema bags, and laundry and dry cleaning.

Medicaid patients, and not all do. Those that do, however, are legally prohibited from charging Medicaid residents or their families for items and services covered by Medicaid. They also are prohibited from charging Medicaid beneficiaries admission deposits or fees to supplement the Medicaid rate.

Nursing-home admission deposits are also illegal when patients are covered by Medicaid. By law, nursing homes that accept Medicaid patients must provide a list of the items and services that are included in the basic Medicaid or private rate as well as any extra charges that may be incurred. If you are asked to pay a deposit, contact your local or state Medicaid agency or department of health.

Patients' Rights

You are guaranteed certain rights in most nursing homes, no matter how you pay for care. Those rights will vary, depending on whether they are ordained by the federal Nursing Home Reform Act or individual state statutes. In many cases, you must be informed of your rights both orally and in writing.

Those rights include accepting or refusing medical treatment and being told how your decision may affect your health, being fully informed about the status of your health, having complete access to your medical records, and being guaranteed that your records will be kept confidential.

Nursing home patients also have the right to choose their own doctor, to be seen by a doctor whenever they need one, and to participate in planning their care. They should be protected from unnecessary physical restraints, tranquilizers or other drugs not medically prescribed, forced seclusion, or physical or verbal abuse.

A nursing-home patient is entitled to use certain personal possessions, such as clothing and furnishings, and to manage his own finances. If you and your spouse are residents in the same facility, you have the right to visit privately and share the same room, barring any medical risks.

THE RIGHT NOT TO BE TRANSFERRED

Some nursing homes may attempt, illegally, to discharge or transfer patients once they stop paying privately for services and begin collecting Medicare or Medicaid benefits. It is also illegal for a nursing home to transfer or discharge a patient who is unable to pay a Medicare deductible or coinsurance.

A nursing home is permitted to transfer or discharge a resident only if it cannot provide proper care, if a resident no longer needs nursing-home care, or if the resident poses a dan-

---

123

ALTERNATIVES TO NURSING HOMES

For patients who need extra care, but cannot afford or do not want to move into a nursing home, one or more of these alternative therapies may help:

1. Consider adult day care. An alternative to nursing home care, adult day care often offers the best of both worlds. It provides daytime supervision, meals, and recreational activities, while allowing an infirm person to live at home.

2. Hire a visiting-nurse service. This form of skilled home care is significantly cheaper than a nursing home and may be appropriate for people who do not need constant monitoring. Check your Yellow Pages for a visiting-nurse association in your area.

3. Call meals-on-wheels If the person cannot cook nutritious meals for herself, consider this service, which delivers balanced meals to the home. Check the Yellow Pages for an organization near you.

4. Use hospice care. Hospice care, for the terminally ill, is available in homelike hospice facilities or in the family home. It does not provide life-prolonging medical treatment but does offer basic medical care, counseling, and pain management. Most hospices require a doctor's prognosis stating that a patient probably has less than six months to live. Ask your doctor for guidance.

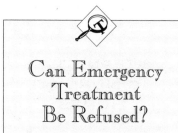

Can Emergency Treatment Be Refused?

Nursing-home residents have the same right to self-determination as any patient, as long as they are judged to be competent.

This includes the right to refuse emergency medical treatment, whether it is given in the nursing home or requires transfer to a hospital. The only stipulation is that the patient understands the consequences of his decision.

You do not need to have an advance directive defining your end-of-life treatment to refuse emergency medical treatment. Nor, although it might help, do you need to have signed a "Do Not Resuscitate" order, also known as a DNR.

A DNR is a statement a patient can make if he does not want his life needlessly prolonged, directing that all forms of resuscitation, such as cardiopulmonary resuscitation (CPR), be withheld in the event of a medical emergency. A patient can execute a DNR at any time during a nursing home stay. To make it effective, however, it must be signed by the patient's doctor and posted on his chart, where nurses and nurses' aides can see it easily.

A DNR can be revoked at any time. Even in the middle of a medical crisis, if a patient suddenly decides to change his mind and accept lifesaving medical treatment, he may verbally request it and overrule the DNR he wrote.

ger to others. It can also discharge a patient who has refused notices to pay a bill. Before transferring or discharging a patient, however, a nursing home must provide written notice explaining the reason for the move at least 30 days in advance, along with information on how to appeal the decision.

A patient has a right to protest at a hearing if he is being moved. He may request that his bed be held while he protests the action. He can expect to be told how many days Medicaid will pay to hold his bed.

If you or your family member is being illegally discharged, you can contact your state or local department on aging for advice. You may also be able to seek help from your local Medicaid fraud and abuse unit. As a last resort, lawsuits can also be filed against nursing homes who fail to provide adequate care, whose services do not meet state or federal standards, or whose charges exceed those permitted by law. Contact a lawyer for advice.

IF YOU BECOME INCOMPETENT

According to the Federal Patient Self-Determination Act, nursing homes that participate in the Medicare or Medicaid programs are required to inform residents of their rights to have advance directives and to note their end-of-life treatment decisions on their medical records. In an advance directive, a patient commonly names a relative or friend to make medical decisions for him should he become incompetent.

If a nursing-home resident who has no advance directive becomes incompetent, the facility must contact the next of kin for guidance on medical decision-making. If the patient has no family or relatives, the facility or its doctor will make medical decisions on a person's behalf until the courts can appoint a legal guardian to assume decision-making responsibility.

Dealing With Problems

If you have a complaint about a nursing home, and the staff does not respond according to your wishes, you may need outside help. All states are required to have "long-term care ombudsmen" who, as part of their job, serve as advocates for nursing-home residents. An ombudsman will investigate your complaints and convey them to the home without revealing your identity. To locate the ombudsman in your area, contact your state's department on aging; check the Blue Pages of your telephone directory for the number.

Another good source of help is the National Citizens Coalition for Nursing Home Reform, an advocacy group that represents the rights of nursing-home residents and their families.

The national telephone number for the Coalition, which is located in Washington, D.C., is (202) 332-2275. Call for additional information.

Your state's department of health is another resource you can tap to help you deal with problems. In addition to licensing nursing homes and conducting annual inspections to evaluate their quality of care, health departments also handle consumer complaints. Try to call the situation to the attention of the health department inspectors who periodically survey nursing homes. They regularly set aside time to speak with residents and sometimes with residents' families to discuss their perceptions and problems. Find out when your facility is being inspected and be prepared to talk with inspectors while they are there. Again, check the Blue Pages of your telephone book for the telephone number.

What If You Suspect Abuse?

Abuse can take many forms: physical, emotional, or even financial. The nursing-home patients' bill of rights specifically prohibits all kinds of abuse, and most states have laws forbidding patient or elder abuse. Under the federal Nursing Home Reform Act, state licensing inspectors are supposed to monitor facilities for a number of criteria, including all forms of abuse, every 9 to 15 months.

If you suspect that someone you know in a nursing home is suffering some type of abuse, broach the subject with him to confirm your hunch. Ask him to tell you specifically if he is being mistreated, how this has been perpetrated, and which staff member is responsible. After you have compiled detailed information, take your concerns and the supporting facts to the nursing-home administrator and ask for an investigation.

If voicing your complaints to the nursing-home staff does not help, contact the long-term-care ombudsman for your area through your local department on aging. In addition, contact the department of health, and your state attorney general. You might also report the nursing home to the local Medicaid fraud control unit, which is responsible for prosecuting people who allegedly have physically or financially mistreated nursing-home residents. Finally, again, get in touch with the National Citizens Coalition for Nursing Home Reform.

For extreme cases of abuse that present an immediate threat to the patient's safety or well-being, call your local police department. If abuse or battery has taken place, criminal charges may be brought against the nursing home.

Nursing-Home Warning Signs

As a friend or relative of a nursing home patient, you will want to be assured that she is getting good care. Here are some indicators of neglect:

✔ *Unanswered call bells.* A call bell may be a patient's only link to the nursing staff, so observe for yourself and ask the patient whether her call bell is answered promptly.

✔ *Overuse of restraints.* Physical or chemical restraints may be used to keep patients from harming themselves. Bed rails and wrist restraints may be legitimate preventive measures for some patients, and sedatives may help patients sleep. But drugs and wheelchair harnesses have sometimes been used only to make life easier for the nursing-home staff. Be sure the patient is not needlessly tied into a chair or unduly lethargic as a result of too much medication.

✔ *Bedsores.* Bedsores are a clear sign that a person is not being moved often enough and also may be suffering from malnutrition, dehydration, or lack of bathing.

✔ *Toilet distress.* The elderly often need help going to the bathroom and may have to be taken as often as every two hours. Neglect can lead to incontinence, urinary-tract infections, or other problems.

DYING WITH DIGNITY

Ultimately, we cannot overrule death, but by making informed decisions about how we want to die, we can assert our right to a dignified end.

Life-Prolonging Treatments

Before exercising your right to accept or refuse certain life-sustaining medical measures, make sure you understand your condition and the risks associated with the following:

✔ *CPR.* Cardiopulmonary resuscitation involves restarting the heart manually, mechanically, or with injectable drugs. If begun too late, CPR may restart the heart after the brain and other vital organs have been permanently damaged.

✔ *Respirator.* Mechanical respirators help people who cannot breathe on their own by providing oxygen through a tube that is inserted into the windpipe. If breathing cannot be restored, a person might become dependent on the respirator.

✔ *Feeding tube.* This is given to people who cannot swallow food or fluids. A tube, placed through the nose or the wall of the abdomen, delivers liquids and nutrients. It can permanently sustain unconscious or severely brain-damaged people for many years.

Final Treatment Decisions

In this age of life-sustaining medical technology, it is vital to decide—while you can—how much treatment you want at the end of life. Making such predictions with finality is almost impossible. Today you may feel certain that you want no heroic measures to prolong your life. Tomorrow you may want every effort made to keep you alive.

As long as you are mentally sound, you will be able to make your own treatment decisions—and to reverse them. If you become incompetent, the people closest to you will probably face the task of making those decisions for you. Therefore you should inform family, friends, and your doctor of your end-of-life treatment wishes, especially as those wishes change. It is the medical community's standard to sustain life any time there is no clear and convincing evidence that a patient would have wished otherwise.

You can express your wishes verbally. Some states recognize verbal statements as evidence of a person's wishes. In fact, many states have laws authorizing families to make medical decisions for loved ones who cannot decide for themselves and have not made advanced directives. Of course it is best (and may be required in some states) to put your wishes in writing and to give copies to family, friends, and your doctor.

Try to choose more than one person to make treatment decisions for you, in the event that someone will not be available when needed. Also, specify under what circumstances you do or do not want life-sustaining treatment, how long you want to be treated, and the kinds of treatment you will not accept.

DECIDING FOR SOMEONE ELSE

Being appointed as a "surrogate," or substitute decision-maker, gives you the authority to make treatment decisions on someone's behalf. You are entitled to know everything about a person's medical condition in order to make well-informed decisions. If that person never wrote down her wishes, you will have to recall the most recent conversations in which she discussed the kinds of treatment she would have wanted. Your request to stop a loved one's medical treatment is appropriate, as long as it is what she requested of a medical practitioner, friend, or family member. If she never expressed her desires not to be kept alive on life support, a doctor cannot legally terminate such treatment.

PREGNANCY AND RIGHT-TO-DIE LAWS

While all Americans in general have the right to refuse medical treatment, some states have "pregnancy-exclusion" laws that may prohibit pregnant women from exercising those rights. For instance, some states forbid the withdrawal or withholding of life support from a woman who is pregnant, even if she has expressly requested it in a living will. A few states allow a woman to appoint a surrogate decision-maker who can decide to withhold or withdraw life support if she is pregnant, while others explicitly forbid surrogates from making end-of-life treatment decisions on behalf of pregnant women.

Such diversity from state to state makes an already thorny decision even tougher. Your state attorney general's office will be able to tell you if you or someone you know is subject to pregnancy-exclusion laws.

EUTHANASIA AND ASSISTED SUICIDE

There is a difference between ending medical treatment that is prolonging life and ending life itself. Disconnecting a respirator that is breathing for an individual who otherwise would not survive is a form of passive euthanasia. Giving someone a lethal injection to hasten their inevitable death is active euthanasia, also known as mercy killing. Active euthanasia is illegal in

Between the idea
And the reality
Between the motion
And the act
Falls the shadow

T. S. ELIOT
The Hollow Men

The Definition of Death

In earlier times, people were declared dead when their hearts stopped beating. But since the 1960's, medicine has been able to restart the heart with CPR and sustain life with artificial respirator. As a result, death is currently defined by number of other criteria, including:

• **Medical criteria.** The medical community has not formulated a precise definition of death. Most doctors and scientists agree that definition is important both because medical science has created so many life-support vehicles to sustain life, while the success of organ transplants depends upon the organs being taken from the donor as soon as possible after death.

• **Legal criteria.** The Uniform Determination of Death Act, which was adopted by 26 states in 1992, defines death as the cessation of all brain activity resulting in the the cessation of respiratory and circulatory functions. In other words, the patient's brain has stopped giving orders to the autonomic nervous system and therefore the

patient stops breathing and his heart stops beating, thus stopping blood circulation.

• **Other criteria.** Some doctors determine death by a complete state of permanent unconsciousness. Doctors also consider the patient's total unreceptivity to external stimuli and complete absence of movement of the body's muscle system to be additional signs. Particularly, doctors look for absence of reflex in the eyes, including lack of dilation of the pupils and blinking.

• **Elapsed time.** The protocol of declaring death varies from state to state, and even from hospital to hospital, but must include a combination of the above criteria.

The Legacy of Nancy Cruzan

In 1983, an automobile crash left 25-year-old Nancy Cruzan permanently comatose. She had not made an advance directive stating how she would want to be cared for should she be incapacitated. But she had told family and friends that she would never want to live as a "vegetable."

Nancy's verbal wishes were not enough for the Missouri rehabilitation hospital that had connected her to a feeding tube. When it became apparent that her coma was permanent, Nancy's parents asked the hospital to disconnect the tube. The hospital refused, claiming there was no "clear and convincing evidence" that Nancy would not have wanted to be kept alive.

Nancy's parents went to court, and the U.S. Supreme Court upheld the rehabilitation center's right not to remove the feeding tube in a ruling that gave the states the authority to decide "right-to-die" cases. At the same time, however, the court recognized all Americans' constitutional right to refuse unwanted medical treatment, as long as their wishes are clearly known.

In 1990 friends of Nancy's testified at a new trial that Nancy had indeed expressed her wishes never to be kept alive artificially. Accepting their testimony as "clear and convincing evidence," a Missouri court allowed the feeding tube to be disconnected.

Nancy Cruzan died on December 26, 1990, but an individual's "right to die" lives on as her legacy.

the United States. A controversial variant of active euthanasia known as doctor-assisted suicide is also, in most states, a criminal act, although a handful of states do not have specific statutes against assisted suicide.

Passive euthanasia—allowing a terminally ill person to die by withholding or withdrawing medical treatment—is a legal right of the patient. So, while a doctor may not give a patient a lethal dose of drugs with the specific intent of causing death, she may legally turn off a respirator in honor of a patient's request not to be kept alive artificially.

Formalizing Your Wishes

Protecting your right to die with dignity may involve a number of actions on your part, such as verbally expressing your end-of-life treatment wishes, informally writing them down, or creating a formal advance directive. You can even do all three.

An advance directive is a legal document in which you explain what kind of medical care you want at the end of your life. You may not need a lawyer to prepare an advance directive, although you should consult one for advice. You may need witnesses to sign the document, depending on the state you live in. Most states honor advance directives, but each one regulates them differently. Every state has its own peculiar requirements for such a document, so much so that if you move to a new state, you should draft a new document to ensure that your wishes are honored.

Two kinds of advance directives are most commonly recognized by states: living wills and durable powers of attorney for health care. Each takes effect as soon as you sign them in front of witnesses, although they will not be used as long as you can make decisions about your own medical care. (See also, YOUR FAMILY, page 151.)

WILL YOUR WISHES BE HONORED?

Most states and the District of Columbia recognize living wills and durable powers of attorney for health care. If your state has a living-will law and you complete its state-recognized form correctly, then your wishes should be honored.

In addition, the Patient Self-Determination Act requires every federally funded health-care facility that does not honor advance directives to agree to transfer patients to one that does. In some states, doctors who refuse to honor living wills may be subject to malpractice suits.

Be aware that in an emergency situation your advance directive may not be honored, because emergency medical technicians are charged with stabilizing you and getting you to a hospital where your condition can be evaluated. Indeed, the first obligation of all medical practitioners is to keep the patient alive. That is why it is so important to make your end-of-life wishes known while you are still able to do so.

Dying at Home

Every person has the right to die at home. There, patients may be more likely to receive the close, supportive quality of care that only family can provide. They also are likely to save significantly in medical costs, most of which are spent in the last 10 days of life.

Yet dying at home is an emotional strain for patients and caregivers, especially when it comes to pain management. Although patients have the right to as much pain medication as they need to stay comfortable, getting enough medication for a patient at home can be difficult. Doctors and nurses are not always present to monitor a person's pain level and authorize the administration of medication. Doctors may also underprescribe pain medications for fear of hastening death.

Therefore it is important to develop a cooperative relationship with a doctor or other health-care provider who can prescribe pain medication for the person dying at home. Specify in your living will that you want enough pain medication to keep you as comfortable as possible. Make sure your doctor is willing to provide the amount of medication necessary to keep you pain-free.

WHEN TO CHOOSE HOSPICE CARE

Hospice care provides comprehensive palliative or comfort care, aimed at easing pain but not curing disease. It also provides supportive social, emotional, and spiritual services to both the terminally ill and their families.

Hospice care can be given in a patient's home, in a hospital, or in an in-patient facility. It may include nursing care from registered nurses, social services, physician services, spiritual support and counseling, homemaker health-aide services as well as respite care and bereavement support for caregivers. Some hospices provide 24-hour care. Others require family members to be with a patient full-time and to work with hospice workers.

To qualify for hospice care, patients generally must be considered to have no more than six months to live. They must not be on curative radiation or chemotherapy, since hospice focuses on peaceful, natural dying. Drugs are usually given only to ease pain. To find an accredited hospice in your community

Living Will Terms

If you are writing an advance directive or have a parent or someone else whose life may be in your hands, you should understand these terms:

✔ **Extraordinary measures.** Also called "heroic measures," these are life-sustaining treatments considered "above and beyond" ordinary care.

✔ **Guardian.** A person authorized by the court to make decisions for another person who cannot make decisions.

✔ **Surrogate decision-maker.** A person authorized to make decisions for an incompetent patient who has no advance directive.

✔ **Incompetent.** Lacking the mental capacity to make decisions or to understand the implications of them.

✔ **Life support.** The use of machines to take over bodily functions and keep a patient alive, usually while attempts are made at cure.

✔ **Natural death.** Death that occurs when the body's basic functions are permitted to stop on their own.

✔ **Terminal illness.** A hopeless condition that shows no promise of recovery. The exact definition varies among states.

✔ **Immunity clause.** A provision in a living will that relieves health-care providers and others of any liability for honoring a patient's end-of-life wishes.

Living Will

① To my family, doctors, and all those concerned with my care:

I,_____, being of sound mind, willfully and voluntarily make known my desire that my dying shall not be artificially prolonged under the circumstances set forth below:

② If at any time I should have an incurable injury, disease or illness, or be in a continual profound comatose state with no reasonable chance of recovery, where the application of life-sustaining procedures would serve only to prolong artificially the dying process, I direct that such procedures be withheld or withdrawn.

To arrive at this conclusion, I direct that my condition be certified to be terminal and irreversible by two physicians who have personally examined me, and have determined that my death will occur whether or not life-sustaining procedures are utilized. Specifically, I do not want **③** cardiac pulmonary resuscitation (CPR), mechanical respiration, or artificial nutrition or fluids administered by tube. **④** I wish to be permitted to die naturally with only the administration of medication or the performance of any medical procedure deemed necessary to provide me with comfort and relieve pain. If time and opportunity permits, I would prefer to die at home.

⑤ In the absence of my ability to give directions regarding the use of such life-sustaining procedures, it is my intention that this declaration shall be honored by my family, my physicians, and anyone else concerned with my care. This is my final expression of my legal right to refuse medical or surgical treatment, and I accept the consequences from such refusal. In so doing, I free anyone who carries out these directives of any legal liability.

I understand the full import of this declaration, and I am emotionally and mentally competent to make this declaration.

⑥

Declaration made this day of 1996.

_____
Signed

_____
City, County, and State of Residence

The declarant has been personally known to me and I believe him or her to be of sound mind.

_____
Witness name

_____
Address

⑦

_____
Witness name

_____
Address

Preparing a Living Will

To ensure that your end-of-life wishes are followed, it is wise to prepare a living will. Since statutes vary by state, write down your wishes using these general guidelines, then ask a lawyer to check that it abides by your state's laws. **1.** Address those who will most likely be making decisions regarding your care should you become incompetent; **2.** Make a simple directive that medical treatment be withheld at a particular time (or, you can express your wish to have every effort made to prolong your life); **3.** List specific treatments you do not want; **4.** Add instructions about the care you desire; **5.** Indicate whom you wish to carry out these wishes if you are unable, and, if necessary, relieve them of liability; **6.** Sign and date your living will; **7.** Make sure the will is witnessed according to the laws of your state; usually two adults are required.

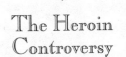

or to find out if the hospice you are considering is licensed and Medicare-certified, call the National Hospice Organization. (For the address and telephone number of the organization, see RESOURCES, page 493).

Are Autopsies Mandatory?

Autopsy is the dissection of a body to determine cause or circumstances of death. Every state has its own laws stipulating when autopsies must or may be ordered. Generally, autopsies are ordered when someone who appeared to be in good health dies suddenly. For example, in some states, a coroner may be required by law to

What Would Roger Have Wanted?

PROBLEM
Roger was a lifeguard, too young and healthy, he thought, to worry about illness, death, or anything like an advance directive. One day Roger suffered a heart attack while swimming underwater. Emergency medical personnel who pulled him from the pool gave him cardiopulmonary resuscitation to restart his heart. In the hospital, doctors put him on a ventilator so that they could evaluate his chances of fully recovering. When it became apparent that Roger was permanently comatose, his doctors refused to turn off the respirator, having no idea of what he would have wanted.

ACTION
Fortunately for Roger's family, they lived in state that allowed family members to make "substituted judgment" end-of-life decisions for a relative when he is unable to do so. Although Roger left no living will, he had repeatedly told his parents and fellow lifeguards that he would never want his life to be artificially prolonged. He took great pride in his physique and athletic prowess, and could not bear the thought of being "totally out of it," as he had put it. His family told the doctors what they knew, and persuaded the doctors to talk to Roger's fellow lifeguards as well. The doctors then asked Roger's family to go to the hospital ethics committee and explain the situation. After a hearing, the committee decided that there was "clear and convincing evidence" of Roger's final treatment wishes. The doctors agreed to disconnect Roger's life-support equipment.

perform an autopsy for all infant deaths or for those involving people under the age of 40 where no obvious cause of death is present. In some cases a medical examiner or coroner may perform a "death investigation," a process to determine whether or not a full-scale autopsy will be necessary.

If an autopsy is not required by state law, a hospital must obtain permission from the next of kin of the deceased to perform one. If a hospital asks permission to perform an autopsy

The Heroin Controversy

It is generally established that the terminally ill are entitled to receive as much pain medication as they need to be comfortable. It is also recognized that doctors may underprescribe medication for fear of causing drug addiction or hastening death.

To encourage doctors to give patients sufficient amounts of pain medication, some states have enacted "intractable pain measures." These laws codify the well-established medical practice of giving terminally ill patients pain medication in doses needed to relieve pain, even if the doses might themselves hasten death.

A more ambitious piece of legislation, the Compassionate Pain Relief Act, has been proposed as a federal law to allow doctors to prescribe heroin for terminal cancer patients who are in intractable pain and receive no relief from conventional painkillers.

The bill has been introduced in Congress every year since 1984 but has repeatedly "died in committee." Although the measure has had some support in the Senate and the House, it has met strong opposition from the medical establishment, which fears that legally prescribing heroin would foster an increase of inappropriate drug use.

For more information on the Compassionate Pain Relief Act, write to the National Committee on the Treatment of Intractable Pain, P.O. Box 9553, Friendship Station, Washington D.C., 20016-1553.

not required by state law, you do not need to consent. You may be able to sue a hospital for mental anguish for performing an unauthorized or unordered autopsy.

Organ Donation

123..
FACTS ABOUT ORGAN DONATION

Here are some things you should know about the donation of organs for transplantation or research:

1. To qualify as an organ donor, you must die in a hospital, usually after undergoing surgery or following intensive-care treatment. You must be declared brain dead, while circulation to other organs is sustained to keep them viable for transplantation.

2. The kidneys, heart, liver, lungs, intestinal organs, and pancreas are the solid organs generally considered for donation. Certain are called "solid" because they have a major blood flow through them.

3. Tissues, which include heart valves, corneas, skin and bone, are not considered solid organs, but still can be transplanted successfully.

4. You are ineligible to donate organs if you have some types of systemic or malignant cancer, if you are positive for the HIV virus, or if you have leukemia or hepatitis B. Your organs may be useful to researchers; however, you can sign a donor card if you wish.

5. If you donate only part of your body, the rest of it will be returned to your surviving relatives for burial.

6. For more information on organ donation, contact the United Network for Organ Sharing at (800) 24-DONOR.

As medical technology gets ever more sophisticated, organ transplants are being performed in hospitals all over the world. The concept of donating organs for transplant into someone else's body has changed from bizarre to routine. In fact, every state in the union has a version of the Uniform Anatomical Gift Act, which allows you to donate your organs or your entire body for transplantation or research. The medical need for organs is so great that all 50 states even encourage donation by including organ-donation request provisions on driver's licenses.

You have the right to donate any part or all of your body to science as long as you are 18 years old or older and understand the consequences of your actions. To become an organ donor, you may make a specific provision in your will, or you may sign an organ-donor card in the presence of two witnesses. You may name an individual or an institution to whom you want your donation to be made, and you also may specify which organs you want to be donated. Even if you have not filled out a donor card, your relatives or next of kin may consent to have your organs donated after your death.

Most states recognize the legal authority of a donor card. But most also rule that your decision to donate your organs can be revoked. The revocation does not have to be in writing—you may simply destroy your card or verbally withdraw your wishes in front of two witnesses. In addition, when families oppose the wishes of a person who has died, states tend to honor the family's wishes.

ORGAN DONATION IS VOLUNTARY

Organ donation is a completely voluntary, altruistic act. You cannot be forced or coerced into it. Nor can you be offered monetary payment or gifts in exchange for donating your organs or those of a loved one. Moreover, a hospital cannot refuse to release your body to your relatives if they refuse to consent to organ donation.

Yet most states have "required request" legislation, which requires that someone on the hospital staff ask the next of kin of every potential organ donor if he or she wants to donate. If they refuse at that time, doctors must discontinue mechanical ventilation (which maintains organ function in preparation for donation) and release the body for burial.

YOUR JOB

From your first job search to retirement, a complex legal network protects you from discrimination, dangerous conditions, and unscrupulous practices in the workplace.

THE CHANGING WORKPLACE ■ FINDING A JOB
■ EMPLOYEE BENEFITS ■ DISCRIMINATION ■ BASIC
RIGHTS ON THE JOB ■ TERMINATION ■ LABOR
UNIONS ■ WORKING FOR GOVERNMENT ■ SMALL
BUSINESSES ■ STARTING A BUSINESS
■ WORKING AT HOME

THE CHANGING WORKPLACE

New laws as well as new economic and social realities make the place where you work far different from what it used to be.

New Terms for the New Workplace

Today's increasingly complex job market is developing a new vocabulary. Here is a glossary of some new words:

✔ *Downsizing.* A company downsizes when it makes staff reductions (often on a large scale) to cut costs and remain competitive. A refinement of the term is "rightsizing," which describes the more precise policy of consolidating jobs and responsibilities.

✔ *Restructuring.* Changing the corporate organization. The chain of command shortens, with fewer managers and more low-level employees.

✔ *Lean and mean.* A description of the new corporation that has to produce more with fewer assets and that may care less about its employees.

✔ *Global economy.* The meshing of economies around the world that has led to dislocations of traditional jobs and market alignments.

✔ *Telecommuting.* This is when an employee works primarily at home and communicates with the office by way of computer, electronic mail, modem, and fax.

A Harsher Job Market

For a number of years after World War II, many Americans became accustomed to a high degree of job security as a healthy, growing economy promised plenty of steady work and a solid future for anyone who buckled down and stuck it out. But such job security is no longer guaranteed.

Foreign competition, a larger work force, and a fluctuating economy have forced U.S. companies to change, and the impacts of these changes have been felt from the assembly line to the executive suite. The old social contract that swapped corporate loyalty for job security has been broken. Today, workers are in charge of their own careers and often cannot look to a large corporation to provide a career path. Instead of working for one or two companies in your lifetime, you will probably work for seven or eight. You may even end up switching careers two or three times, even after you have turned 50.

New Ways of Working

Technology has also contributed to the changing face of the American workplace. Whole job categories are being wiped out, and if you are not computer literate, you may have a harder time getting and holding a job. On the other hand, if your computer skills are top-notch, you may find yourself to be quite marketable.

Computers and other modern technologies are reshaping the workday. Many more employees work at home, communicating with the office or with clients via phone, electronic mail ("E-mail"), computers, and facsimile, or "fax," machines.

Legislation, too, has affected the modern workplace. Although government once took a hands-off approach to employer-employee relations and you were offered relatively few legal protections, today's laws, as well as court decisions, specifically define what your employer can and cannot do, and what your recourse is should laws be broken. (See also "Glossary of Federal Job Laws," opposite.) Knowing your workplace rights is your best defense against having them violated.

Glossary of Federal Job Laws

Over the years the federal government has created many acts to protect the rights of citizens in the workplace. (Individual states have also passed laws affecting employment that are sometimes stricter than the federal ones.) Here is a glossary of the most important federal laws:

• **Age Discrimination in Employment Act of 1967 (ADEA).** Prohibits employers from discriminating against workers who are between the ages of 40 and 70 on the basis of age. Does not apply where age is an actual occupational qualification. Enforced by the Equal Employment Opportunity Commission (EEOC).

• **Americans With Disabilities Act of 1990 (ADA).** Prohibits employers from discriminating against qualified disabled workers and requires employers to make reasonable efforts to accommodate the disability of an otherwise-qualified individual if the accommodation does not place undue hardship on the employer.

• **Civil Rights Acts of 1964 (Title VII) and 1991.** The 1964 Act prohibits employers, unions, and employment agencies from discriminating against job applicants and employees on the basis of race, sex, age, handicap, religion, or national origin. The law prohibits discrimination in hiring, firing, discipline, compensation, and other conditions of employment. Exceptions are made for bona fide occupational qualifications (BFOQ). The 1991 act amends the earlier one and makes discrimination laws applicable to all facets of the employer-employee relationship, and it specifically allows women, disabled individuals, and members of religious minorities to sue for damages for intentional discrimination.

• **Consolidated Omnibus Budget Reconciliation Act of 1986 (COBRA).** Requires employers to offer to continue coverage for employees (and their covered dependents) in the company's group health insurance plan for 18 months after termination of employment except in cases of gross misconduct. The former employee must pay the entire premium and loses coverage if she fails to pay the premiums or when she becomes eligible for another group health plan.

• **Employee Retirement Income Security Act of 1974 (ERISA).** Applies to all employers who sponsor pension or retirement plans for their employees. Outlines specific requirements regarding plan participation, vesting of employer contributions, funding, reporting, and disclosure. Administered by the U.S. Department of Labor, the U.S. Treasury Department, the IRS, and the Pension Benefit Guaranty Corporations.

• **Equal Pay Act of 1940.** Applies to all employers with two or more employees. Requires equal pay for equal work, regardless of sex. Does not apply where different wages are paid according to bona fide merit, seniority, or any merit system not related to gender.

• **Family Medical Leave Act of 1993. (FMLA).** Requires employers to allow employees to take a 12-week-per-year leave of absence without pay to care for a sick spouse, child, or parent; a newborn, adopted, or foster child within a year of the child's arrival; or because of an employee's medical condition, such as pregnancy. The employer must continue health-care benefits during the leave, and when the employee returns, is guaranteed either the same job or a comparable one.

• **Immigration Reform and Control Act of 1986 (IRCA).** Prohibits employers from employing illegal aliens and requires employers to verify that job applicants are eligible to work in the United States and to supply appropriate documentation to the Immigration and Naturalization Service (INS).

• **Labor-Management Relations Act of 1947 (LMRA).** (The Taft-Hartley Act) Gives employees the right to organize and bargain collectively, and prohibits employers from using unfair labor practices, such as coercing employees to join or refrain from joining a union, refusing to bargain in good faith, or retaliating against employees for union activity. Doesn't apply to agricultural workers, housekeepers, independent contractors, managers, or employees of railroads or airlines. Enforced by the National Labor Relations Board.

• **Occupational Safety and Health Act of 1970 (OSHA).** Requires employers to comply with a broad range of safety and health standards. Administered and enforced by the Occupational Safety and Health Administration.

• **Worker Adjustment and Retraining Notification Act of 1988 (WARN).** Applies to employers of 100 or more full-time workers, or 100 or more full- and part-time workers whose weekly work time totals more than 4,000 hours. Requires employers to give workers, union representatives, and local government officials at least 60 days' notice of a plant closing or mass layoff. Does not apply to temporary seasonal workers.

FINDING A JOB

Being out of work is tough; the frustrations of the job hunt can be tougher. But you have rights from the moment you start looking. Make them work for you.

Choosing an Employment Agency

Finding an employment agency you are comfortable with is worth the effort it takes. Here are some tips to help you:

✔ *Experience.* Find out how long the agency has been in business and whether or not it has a good track record. In many states, agencies must be licensed, and you can contact the local licensing bureau.

✔ *Specialties.* Agencies often specialize in certain types of employment. Ask people in the field you are interested in whether they know of any specialty agencies.

✔ *Assistance.* Look for an agency that offers facilities for improving your on-the-job skills. This amenity can be critical for learning modern office skills such as word processing and desktop publishing.

✔ *Fees.* Beware of agencies that ask you to pay before you accept a job. You may not get any more for your money than a list of names and addresses or "job-hunting tips."

✔ *Contract.* Find out early on about the agency's terms. Ask to see a copy of the contract. If there is anything in it you do not like, keep looking for an agency that is right for you.

Putting Agencies to Work

Sooner or later you will be looking for a job—either your first one or a new one—and one of your options will be to get in touch with an employment agency to help you find the right spot. An employment agency, for a fee, matches job openings with appropriate personnel. Many agencies place workers in jobs and charge the employer for the placement. Some get the fee from the employee. This fee can be a percentage of the annual salary of the job, a month's pay, or a predetermined lump sum.

PAYING OFF THE AGENCY

If you have to pay an agency fee, you will most likely be asked to sign a contract. Usually, such a contract will require you to pay up after you have accepted a position and rules out a refund if you change your mind, quit, or are fired. You may also owe the agency if you land a job within a designated time (often 12 months) of signing the contract. An agency may send you out on an interview, for instance, but you are not offered a job at that time. A few months later, the employer calls to tell you the position is open again. You will most likely still be obliged to pay the agency's fee if you accept the position.

Since an agency profits only when a position is filled, it will be eager to get you working in a position it represents. No one can force you to take a job you do not want. Trust your instincts. Do not accept a job that you do not think is right for your skills or disposition just because an agency tries to pressure you. If you are not satisfied, go to other agencies. (See also "Choosing an Employment Agency," at left.)

Working as a Temp

If you are not looking for a permanent job, but need work for only a set length of time, you should consider employment agencies that specialize in short-term assignments. The most common jobs handled by temporary agencies fall under the category of general office work, such as word processing, data entry, typing, filing, and reception.

A temporary worker, or "temp," is paid by the temporary agency. Although the worker may report to several different job sites, the agency is the employer and has the same responsibilities under the law as any other employer. The agency must pay you for the work you do, pay you when it is supposed to, and supply you with equipment and a safe place to work.

The agency must also obey all federal employment mandates, such as wage and hour laws, income tax withholding, and Social Security contributions. Most states also require that temporary agencies carry workers' compensation insurance. (See also "Employee Benefits," page 247, and "Basic Rights on the Job," page 261.)

If you work as a temp for an extended period of time, your agency may offer you employee benefits. After logging a set number of hours, some agencies may allow you to buy health coverage at a group rate or may provide sick, holiday, and vacation pay. Be sure to ask your agency which benefits they offer and what you can to do to qualify.

The Interview and the Law

Stringent restrictions limit the kinds of questions an employer may ask when interviewing, either in conversation or by written application. The Title VII amendment to the Civil Rights Act, enforced by the Equal Employment Opportunity Commission (EEOC), prohibits discriminating against job applicants (and employees) on the basis of sex, race, age, religion, disability, or national origin. Anyone who employs 15 or more employees must comply with this federal legislation. Most states have similar laws that extend the same rights to employees in smaller companies.

Acceptable questions include your name and address, previous work experience, education (but only if it is relevant to the job), and citizenship (not national origin). Asking questions that have nothing to do with job performance can lead to charges of discrimination, unfair hiring practices, or invasion of privacy.

An interviewer should not ask your age (unless you are required by law to be a certain age to perform the job—for instance, to serve alcohol), your maiden name or your spouse's, your sexual orientation, whether you own or rent your home, whether you are pregnant or plan to be, or with whom you live. Questions about your nationality, ancestry, religion, and race are forbidden; even questions about your height and weight are off-limits in most cases. You can, however, be asked such questions after you land a job if the information is necessary for insurance or other legal purposes.

Laws vary from state to state regarding questions about past criminal activity. Most states let employers ask about convictions if they are relevant to the job, but you do not have to disclose information about arrests that did not lead to convictions.

If you are asked a question you believe is discriminatory, try to document it. If it is part of a written application, ask for a copy. If it is asked during an interview, ask your interviewer to repeat it or to elaborate so that you are absolutely certain of what you are being asked. Take detailed notes after the interview.

If you believe you did not get a job because of your answer to (or refusal to answer) a discriminatory question, you may have a legal claim for damages or compensation. Contact your local EEOC office to file a complaint, or consult a lawyer.

PREEMPLOYMENT TESTING

A prospective employer may ask you to take a preemployment test to help determine whether you are qualified for a particular job. In certain cases, employers can use tests to measure your intelligence, determine your physical strength and agility, or evaluate your personality. Under Title VII, however, employ-

Employment Tests and Your Rights

If your present or future employer asks you to take any kind of test, make sure it is a legal request and that the test is given under the proper conditions. You may be reluctant to challenge an employer in this way, but it is important because skewed test results can hurt your job prospects. Here are some common tests and your rights regarding them:

• **Lie detector.** The Employee Polygraph Protection Act of 1988 forbids private employers from requiring lie detector tests as a condition for hiring, except for certain security jobs, persons in sensitive-information occupations (such as defense workers) and people who work with controlled substances (such as prescription drugs). The law does not cover state and federal government employees, although some states have separate legislation regarding polygraph testing. The law permits employers to conduct tests under certain conditions: If a theft has cost the company money, your employer may ask you to take a polygraph test, but strict guidelines must be followed.

• **AIDS.** The Americans with Disabilities Act (ADA) says employers cannot make you take a test for HIV unless your employer can show that if you carried the virus, you would be an "immediate danger" to others.

• **Medical.** The ADA makes it illegal for employers to require medical tests as a requirement of hire. You may be asked to take a medical exam, but only if you have already been offered a job and all newly hired employees are required to as well. Results of such tests must be kept confidential, and exams must be geared to job performance.

• **Drug.** Employers may give applicants drug tests, provided a job offer has already been made, and all applicants are tested. Many states have legislation that restricts drug testing in private workplaces and forbids selective or random drug testing of job applicants. Government employees may be tested for drugs if the job is "safety sensitive"; that is, it involves carrying weapons or having access to classified information, although state laws may restrict tests in this area.

• **IQ, personality, and physical ability.** An employer can ask you to take a written, verbal, or physical exam to measure skills and knowledge required to perform a job. Such tests must be given to all applicants under the same conditions and cannot discriminate against a "protected group," such as women, minorities, or older applicants. The test must measure a bona fide occupational qualification and may not adversely affect the hiring of women or minorities.

ers can require these tests only if the test measures some asset needed for a job—such as a physical exam based on actual job-related tasks to evaluate a firefighter, or a typing test to rate a word processor.

Moreover, the law specifies that tests may not be discriminatory in terms of race, gender, age, or disability, unless there is a bona fide occupational qualification (BFOQ) that can be considered. If you believe a test you were given was biased and you were denied employment because of it, you can file a complaint with the EEOC. (See also "Employment Tests and Your Rights," page 244.)

Problems With References

Another aspect of the hiring process to worry about is providing references. Before an employer makes you an offer, she will probably want to talk to your former employer or colleagues. It is helpful to know that various federal and state laws limit what references can contain. (See "Keeping References Fair," at right.)

Civil rights laws prohibit employers from giving out information regarding your age, sex, race, color, national origin, or disabilities. The Americans with Disabilities Act (ADA) prohibits employers from revealing information regarding your medical condition or any medical examinations. Most states have laws that protect your right to privacy and your right to take action against someone who gives false information about you (known legally as "defamation").

You may have a legal claim against a reference giver if a reference contains particularly defamatory information about you. For example, if a former employer tells your prospective boss that you were let go for insubordination when in fact you were laid off for economic reasons, you may be able to sue for defamation. You will have to prove, however, that the statement was false and that your reputation or credibility suffered—for example, that you were denied a job—because of the statement.

Contract or No Contract

Most employees today are working "at will." This means in most states that a worker can be fired without cause, at the will of the employer. It also means the worker can leave the job at any time without giving notice or being penalized. Employers, however, do have to obey federal and state laws that prevent them from

Keeping References Fair

A good reference can give a job searcher a boost, while a bad one can be devastating. Therefore, if you are the one giving a reference, you need to be cautious. Here are some general guidelines regarding references:

✔ *Authority.* No one who does not have explicit authority to do so, should ever give a job reference.

✔ *Honesty.* Comments in a reference should be fair, objective, and true. In most states, a reference giver is protected by a concept called "qualified privilege" when discussing a former employee, and can make a subjective, negative statement as long as she believes it to be true and relevant to job performance.

✔ *Relevance.* Information should be limited to the purpose of the inquiry and appropriate to job-skills evaluation. If the reference giver is asked whether someone can operate a cash register, she should not answer the question and then volunteer, "...but he has an unprofessional phone manner."

✔ *Neutrality.* Opinions and personal feelings should be kept to a minimum or avoided whenever possible, especially if they are not directly related to job performance. A reference should give only the information requested.

firing workers because of their gender, race, religion, or national origin. (See also "Glossary of Federal Job Laws," page 241.)

Some states restrict an employer from firing employees without cause, but for the most part, as long as your employer does not violate any laws, he can fire you whenever he feels like it—unless you have a contract. An employment contract is a written, legally binding agreement between an employer and an employee. Contracts usually deal with matters such as compensation, fringe benefits, vacation, arbitration, termination, and any special provisions appropriate to the business.

Patching Up a Breach of Contract

PROBLEM
Monica Smith was hired by Susan and Todd Lawson to run their small knitwear company. The Lawsons offered Monica a fair salary and an employment contract. The contract, which was to be in effect for two years, stipulated that Monica could not be fired without cause. In exchange, Monica would run all day-to-day operations of their company. But at the end of the first year, the Lawsons told Monica that although she was doing a great job, they would no longer be needing her services. When she asked why she was being fired, she was told that the Lawson's niece was moving to town, and they wanted her to run the company.

ACTION
Monica showed a copy of her contract to a lawyer, who immediately sent a letter to the Lawsons pointing out that they had fired Monica without cause during the term of her contract. He asked the Lawsons for a settlement to compensate Monica for the broken contract, and provide her with money to live on while she looked for another job. The Lawsons, now aware of their legal obligation, and convinced that Monica would probably win a case against them, agreed to her terms.

An employee contract does not protect you against dismissal for cause, although just what comprises cause may be hard to determine, beyond the obvious—incompetence, insubordination, theft, criminal activity on the job. If you are in a position to do so, urge your employer to define "just cause for dismissal" in your contract.

IMPLIED CONTRACTS
Employment contracts can be "implied" even if you do not sign a formal document. An implied contract is one that is not in writing, but which, because of an agreement or other acceptance of employment condition, can often be recognized in court as binding. Any workplace rule, personnel policy, or employee handbook can have the effect of an implied contract. If you believe that your written or implied contract has been violated, or if you have been unjustly terminated, contact a lawyer to find out exactly what your rights are.

123...

CONTRACT CLAUSES TO WATCH OUT FOR

Employment contracts often include stipulations meant to protect the company from certain activities by employees. Here are three provisions to be aware of before you sign:

1. Work for hire. As a regular employee, most of what you produce for the company is "work for hire," meaning that the product, formula, computer program, or whatever you produce is created or prepared as part of your job. Unless a contract says otherwise, that work is owned by the employer, who is entitled to all benefits received from it.

2. Noncompetition agreement. This clause specifies that you may not work for a competing company within a specified geographic radius of your previous job for a specified length of time. Such a clause may not be binding, however. Courts have determined that the time period and geographical area must be "reasonable."

3. Nondisclosure clause. This prohibits an employee from sharing trade secrets, information, formulas, or inventions with competitors. You may be bound to this type of agreement even without signing anything. Many states have laws stating that the disclosure of confidential information, such as private client lists, marketing plans, even ideas, can be punishable as a crime.

EMPLOYEE BENEFITS

Some employee benefits are federally mandated rights; others are privileges your employer may—or may not—offer. Be sure you know the difference.

Government-Mandated Benefits

As an American worker, you are entitled to a number of government benefits, the most universal of which are Social Security and Medicare. Taken together, these programs provide retirement insurance, survivor benefits, and federal health insurance—benefits that you have paid for through taxes or through other deductions from your paycheck.

Starting at age 62, you can elect to receive Social Security retirement benefits. Your benefits will be higher if you wait until you are 65 to start receiving them. The amount you receive depends upon how long you were employed and paid into the Social Security fund, and the amount of money you earned. Spouses are eligible for benefits as well.

To receive Social Security benefits, you must apply for them at one of the 1,300 Social Security Administration offices throughout the United States. Check your local telephone directory for the office nearest you. (For more information about Social Security, see YOUR MONEY, page 353.)

GOVERNMENT DISABILITY

The Social Security Act also provides for disability coverage for persons under 65 who become physically unable to work. In order to be eligible for government disability, you must have an impairment that prevents you from being employed, and you must have worked long enough to qualify. (See also YOUR MONEY, page 353.) These disability benefits are different from workers' compensation benefits for job-related injuries and from private disability insurance. (See also "Different Types of Disability Payments," page 250.)

MEDICARE

As an employee, 1.45 percent of your income is withheld from your paycheck as a Medicare tax, and you become eligible to cash in on Medicare's federally funded health insurance at age 65. Medicare covers some, but far from all, of your medical bills. In addition, after becoming eligible, you must pay for part of the insurance on a quarterly basis. (For more about Medicare benefits, see YOUR HEALTH CARE, page 208.)

Government Benefits For Workers

The government offers employees a number of benefits. Here is a checklist of government benefits and when you are eligible for them:

✔ **Social Security**. A monthly benefit for retired workers (or their survivors) who have earned enough Social Security credits while working. You can apply any time after age 62.

✔ **Medicare.** A health insurance program, administered by the Social Security Administration, for persons 65 or over. Enroll for Medicare at your local Social Security office.

✔ **Social Security disability.** Monthly payments for those suffering long-term or terminal illness or disability, who have earned enough Social Security credits.

✔ **Unemployment insurance.** Monetary compensation for workers who are fired, laid off, or forced to quit a job.

✔ **Family and Medical Leave.** Federal legislation ensures employees of companies with 50 or more workers up to 12 weeks of unpaid leave to care for a newborn, a newly adopted child, or an injured or ill family member.

UNEMPLOYMENT INSURANCE

Unemployment insurance provides benefits if you lose your job. These benefits are administered jointly by the federal government and your state, but your employer pays for them and is, in fact, required to do so. You qualify if you have been fired or permanently dismissed because of business or economic conditions (known as being "laid off"). In some cases, you may be eligible even if you left your job voluntarily, for "good cause." Each state has its own definition of good cause. If you quit to care for a sick family member, or because you have been sexually harassed, or even because transferring to a new location would be a hardship, you may still be entitled to unemployment benefits depending upon the state in which you live.

Most states exclude temporary laborers from eligibility, as well as minors working for their parents, student interns, and the self-employed. State law also determines how long prior to filing for benefits you must have been working in order to qualify. In some states you must have been on the job for at least 12 months before you become eligible for benefits.

Family and Medical Leave

The Family and Medical Leave Act (FMLA) of 1993 entitles you to take up to 12 weeks of leave during a year to attend to a family or medical emergency. The leave is unpaid, but your employer must reinstate you in your job when you return. Here are some of the act's provisions:

• You are covered by the act if you work for a company with 50 or more employees deployed within a 75-mile radius of your work site. You must have worked for the same employer for a 12-month period, logging 1,250 hours of service.

• You can ask to take FMLA leave for the birth or adoption of a child, to provide foster child care, if you have a "serious health condition," or if you need to provide care for a sick child, spouse, or parent. Siblings, aunts, uncles, cousins, grandparents, in-laws, or unmarried domestic partners are not covered.

• You must give 30 days' advance notice of the need to take FMLA leave whenever possible, and you may have to show proof that you qualify, such as by medical certification of a serious health condition affecting you or a family member.

• Your employer can require a second or third medical opinion and can ask for reports of your or your family member's condition during the leave.

• Your employer has the right to include your regular vacation time as part of your FMLA leave. For instance, your employer is not required to give you 12 weeks' unpaid leave in addition to 4 weeks' paid vacation time.

• Many individual states have similar laws, and the FMLA does not supersede any state or local laws that provide more generous family or medical leave protection.

• If your employer already provides health benefits, he must continue to do so while you are on FMLA leave. This continued coverage is not free, however, so if you paid part of your health insurance costs while working, you must continue to do so on leave.

• The law allows for a category of "key" employees—those whose salaries put them in the top 10 percent pay level of the employer's work force—to whom the law's protection does not apply. These employees can be refused reinstatement or given different jobs upon return, but only if the company can prove it would suffer "substantial and grievous economic injury" by reinstating the employee and if it has given notice of its intention not to reinstate the employee.

The unemployment office does not simply mail compensation checks to you. In order to receive unemployment benefits you must be available to work and be actively seeking employment. Generally, you are required to report in person each week at your local unemployment office and sign a statement saying that you sought work during the week. In some states you can report over the telephone. The amount of compensation you receive varies by state and is determined by your salary during the previous year and the average weekly wage earned by all workers in your state. In most cases, you can receive benefits for 26 weeks after losing your job, but the federal government may extend this period during hard times.

If you are laid off or fired, call your local unemployment office immediately to find out when and where to apply for benefits. When you appear in person, take any documentation you have regarding your termination, including your paycheck stubs and your Social Security card. Your application must be reviewed and processed before you start receiving benefits.

How "Workers' Comp" Works

Workers' compensation is a system set up to provide employees the right to monetary compensation for job-related injury and disease. If you are a construction worker and suffer a severe back injury or a maintenance worker who slips and falls on the job, workers' compensation insurance, purchased by your employer, will probably pay your medical bills and a portion of your salary for any work missed because of the injury.

Although the system is not governed by federal law, all 50 states have workers' compensation laws, most of which require employers to purchase insurance for their employees. Before these laws were enacted, the only recourse for a worker injured on the job would have been to sue the employer to get compensation. Workers' compensation was set up to avoid court battles. The intent was to make employers pay for occupational accidents or illnesses, regardless of fault. One trade-off is that employers with workers' compensation cannot be sued by their employees for work-related injuries.

WHO IS COVERED?

Almost 90 percent of the work force is covered under government-mandated workers' compensation. Workers' comp is compulsory in 47 states, the exceptions being New Jersey, South Carolina, and Texas, where it is elective. (Employers in these states who do not carry the insurance face heavy legal penalties if an employee is injured on the job.)

---

1 2 3...

PURSUING UNEMPLOYMENT INSURANCE

Although most unemployment claims are approved, some may be denied. Your former employer may insist, for example, that you were dismissed for a reason other than the one you claimed. Each state system is different, but here are the steps commonly taken after a claim is denied:

1. Either the employee or the employer can file an appeal to an unemployment decision. Both are entitled to a hearing before an officer from the state department of labor.

2. At a hearing, both you and your former employer can testify regarding the circumstances of your dismissal. Have all available documentation and witnesses to support your case.

3. A referee may confirm, modify, or reverse the initial decision. If he rules in your favor, you will be entitled to benefits from the time of your original application. If the ruling goes against you, you have the right to another appeal.

4. In a second appeal, the review panel looks at the record of the original hearing and decides whether or not they agree with the decision.

5. If you are still unhappy with the decision, you may be able to take your employer to court. Consult a lawyer for advice.

DIFFERENT TYPES OF DISABILITY PAYMENTS

Suppose you slip and fall and are temporarily or permanently unable to work. Three types of disability benefits exist that may help support you and your family.

1. Government disability. If you were seriously injured and are eligible for Social Security benefits, you might be entitled to government disability insurance. To be eligible, you must have a severe impairment that leaves you unable to work for a year or more or is expected to result in death. These benefits are relatively small—probably much less than your salary.

2. Private disability insurance. If you break your hip and are unable to work for a few months, you may qualify for the type of private disability many employers carry. Such benefits are usually for short-term disabilities and pay you a portion of your wages while you are out of work. If you have purchased disability insurance on your own, your policy may pay you up to 70 percent of your gross income while you are out of work.

3. Workers' compensation. Almost all employers must carry this insurance, which covers work-related injuries. Benefits differ widely in the various states and fall into three basic categories: cash to make up for lost salary, payment of medical bills, and the cost of rehabilitation.

While almost all industrial employment is covered in most states, some states exempt firms with fewer than a stipulated number of employees. Most states also exclude certain job categories. New Jersey, for example, excludes maritime and railroad workers engaged in interstate commerce. North Carolina exempts volunteer ski patrollers, among others.

Farm labor, domestic help, and casual workers may be exempt, although private employers can choose to cover workers. Volunteers and employees of nonprofit organizations may also not be covered in many states. But by and large, most employees who work for a company at the time of an on-the-job accident are eligible for workers' compensation benefits.

WHAT IS COVERED?

Workers' compensation covers injuries suffered that are directly related to a job. If you are injured or become ill while performing the normal duties of your job, you will be covered. Most states will cover you even if you are in the employee lunchroom. Travel to work is not considered on the job, although a salesperson injured while traveling on the job probably would be covered.

If you hurt yourself deliberately or knowingly violate a safety rule, you probably will not be eligible for coverage. A welder who knows that safety goggles are required while on the job but who removes his anyway probably will not be covered for injuries sustained as a result. If, however, he is injured because of mere carelessness—for instance, if he wears his goggles but unknowingly fastens them incorrectly—he will probably be eligible for workers' compensation for injuries suffered, even if they are due to his mistake.

Laws offer coverage for only some of the health problems workers face. What are known as "ordinary diseases of life," or illnesses that are not "peculiar to or characteristic of" an occupation, are usually not covered. Each state has its own regulations regarding how much is paid for what kind of injury.

HOW TO FILE A CLAIM

Any time you are injured at work, even slightly, you should notify your employer or supervisor immediately. If necessary, ask for a claim form, which will probably ask you to give the basic information—the where, when, and how of the accident or the illness. In some states, your employer will require you to be examined by a doctor. Make sure to save any receipts for care that you prepay. You should start receiving benefits as soon as your claim is accepted.

Should your claim be denied, either in part or totally, you can call the workers' compensation board in your state to find out the procedures for initiating an appeal or review. You will probably want to contact an attorney who specializes in workers' compensation claims.

Voluntary Corporate Benefits

Although in today's "lean and mean" workplace more and more firms are forgoing added benefits in order to cut costs, you still may be offered a variety of additional benefits by your employer. These might include life and health insurance, a prepaid legal plan, a pension or retirement plan, sabbatical leave, payment during jury duty, profit sharing, bonuses, moving expenses, and such services as parking, recreation programs, and day-care centers.

All of these benefits are completely voluntary and your employer is under no obligation to offer them. If, however, your employer does offer benefits such as medical coverage, life insurance, or a pension, they become rights protected by the Employee Retirement Income Security Act. (See also YOUR MONEY, page 357.)

ERISA sets minimum standards that "sponsors" (employers) must meet. For example, ERISA requires employers to make sure a plan is not discriminatory, to provide an abbreviated summary plan description to all employees, and to manage funds prudently. Pension plans are subject to even stricter guidelines and must meet requirements for funding, participation, and vesting that do not apply to other plans. (See also "ERISA and Your Pension," at right.)

Plans not covered by ERISA include government plans, church plans, and plans maintained solely to comply with workers' compensation, unemployment insurance, or disability insurance laws. If you think you are not getting all benefits due you, check with your attorney or the EEOC to find out if you are protected under ERISA.

COBRA

If your employer offers group health insurance, you will most likely be entitled to continued coverage upon termination. The 1986 Consolidated Omnibus Budget Reconciliation Act (COBRA) requires companies with 20 or more workers to offer employees the opportunity to continue health insurance when their jobs end, whether they quit or were let go. Only employees who are fired for gross misconduct are ineligible.

You can get coverage for 18 months after you leave the job, but you must pay the full group rate, which will probably be higher than your current premium. You will probably save money if you look for affordable insurance on your own, using COBRA as an alternative.

ERISA and Your Pension

The Employee Retirement Income Security Act (ERISA) sets forth the minimum requirements that private pension plans must meet. These provisions concern:

✔ *Vesting.* This refers to how long an employee must have worked for the company to be entitled to employer pension contributions. By law, an employee may be 100 percent vested after five years or be gradually vested by increasing percentages over three to seven years. These are the employer's only options.

✔ *Fiduciaries.* Companies must appoint fiduciaries, or trusted administrators of funds, who are responsible for investing funds according to rules endorsed by the U.S. Treasury Department.

✔ *Information.* In addition to the summary plan, pension plan participants are entitled to a statement of total benefits accrued each year, as well as one financial update per year.

✔ *Survivor benefits.* ERISA requires that most retirement benefits in the form of a life annuity (a sum paid out each month to the retiree) must also provide for an annuity for a surviving spouse, unless the widowed wife or husband waives the right to receive it.

PREGNANCY BENEFITS

The Pregnancy Discrimination Act of 1987 regulates employers with 15 or more workers who provide medical coverage or short-term, private disability benefits. If your employer provides paid leave for employees who suffer debilitating diseases or injuries, she must provide the same benefit to employees (or their covered wives) who are pregnant and unable to work or have just given birth. If she pays 100 percent of the hospital bill for an employee with an injury or disease, she cannot then pay only 80 percent of the cost of a stay in the maternity ward.

BENEFITS THAT INVOLVE THE IRS

Some benefits may be subject to various tax laws, which may or may not work in your favor. According to the IRS, some employee benefits, such as parking spaces, car allowances, and tuition reimbursement are equivalent to additional income. If you have any questions regarding employee benefits and taxes, check with your employee-benefits department, your accountant, or the IRS.

EAP's: Help for Personal Problems on the Job

Employee assistance programs (EAP's) are becoming popular in both large and small companies. An EAP can assist employees with personal, medical, legal, and other problems. Here are some things you should know about EAP's:

• An employer or corporation funds an employee assistance program as a service to workers. The service works both ways, of course: well-adjusted employees with good morale contribute strongly to company productivity.

• EAP counselors are usually social workers who refer employees seeking help to the appropriate resources. If you have a problem and are not sure where to turn, an EAP may be able to help.

• Some of the issues EAP counselors deal with include marital problems, relationships in the workplace, family difficulties, stress and tension, alcohol and drug abuse, grief over the loss of a loved one, domestic violence, depression, financial and legal concerns, single-parent issues, and career development.

• EAP counselors generally meet with employees from one to six times to determine their needs. If further counseling or help is necessary, the counselor will give a referral.

• Many EAP counselors work with employees who need drug and alcohol rehabilitation, finding them an appropriate facility that their insurance policy will cover. An EAP counselor may also be able to grant an employee unpaid leave for treatment without revealing the nature of the problem to his supervisor or other employees.

• EAP administrators scrupulously safeguard the identity of their clients. Confidentiality is guaranteed in most programs. If your EAP wants to release any information about you, you must sign a release first.

• Some employers use EAP's as a screening process for their health insurance coverage. For example, you may have to go to an EAP counselor for a referral before your firm's health insurance plan will cover a visit to a psychiatrist or before you can be admitted to a rehabilitation center.

• A supervisor can suggest that an employee get in touch with the EAP counselor if the supervisor believes there is a problem that affects the worker's job performance. If the problem is serious enough, the supervisor can require the employee to check in with the EAP. This may or may not be the first step in a progressive discipline system.

DISCRIMINATION

Discrimination in the workplace can take many ugly forms. A comprehensive package of laws aims specifically at protecting you from the worst of them.

Legislation to Protect Your Rights

A protective network of federal legislation guards against discrimination in the workplace. The Americans With Disabilities Act prohibits discrimination on the basis of disability; the Age Discrimination in Employment Act prohibits it based on age; a series of civil rights acts forbid discrimination due to race, religion, national origin, or sex; and the Equal Pay Act requires equal pay for equal work, making it illegal to discriminate against women when it comes to salary or wages.

Perhaps the most far-reaching and significant federal legislation regarding discrimination is Title VII of the 1964 Civil Rights Act, which applies to all private employers with more than 15 employees. The Civil Rights Act of 1991 refined the 1964 act, giving all workers who have been discriminated against the right to seek monetary compensation and to request a trial by jury.

If you are ever refused a job because of your race, are denied a promotion due to gender, or subjected to harassment on the job because of your membership in a so-called "protected group," you will probably be able to seek redress under the provisions of the civil rights acts.

Most states have similar laws protecting employees of smaller companies and may even be more strict or inclusive, forbidding discrimination on the basis of sexual orientation or marital status, for example. As a general rule, when an issue falls under both federal and state law, the stricter law prevails.

DISPARATE TREATMENT

If you are treated differently from other employees primarily because of your race, religion, sex, or national origin, you may be a victim of discrimination and protected by the civil rights acts. Such behavior is called "disparate treatment," and it is prohibited in hiring, firing, promotions, discipline, compensation, and any other employment decisions. For example, you are Hispanic, and because you took four sick days in one month, your employer reprimanded you and placed you on probation. However, a non-Hispanic co-worker in the same situation was not disciplined at all. If your employer's only reason for treating you

It shall be an unlawful employment practice for an employer: (1) to fail or to refuse to hire or to discharge any individual, or otherwise to discriminate against any individual with respect to his compensation, terms, conditions, or privileges of employment, because of such individual's race, religion, sex, or national origin, or (2) to limit, segregate, or classify his employees or applicants for employment in any way which would deprive any individual of employment opportunities or otherwise adversely affect his status as an employee because of such individual's race, color, religion, sex, or national origin.

CIVIL RIGHTS ACT
TITLE VII
1964

The BFOQ Exception

Not all discrimination is illegal. A legal exception known as a "bona fide occupational qualification" (BFOQ) gives employers the right to specify a job in a way that might be considered discriminatory in other circumstances.

A moviemaker could presumably require that a young girl play the role of Heidi. Municipal governments have argued successfully that people over a certain age can no longer be firefighters. A hotel could reasonably advertise for a male men's-room attendant. A theater company might—or might not—get away with insisting on an African American actor to play a role stipulating someone of that race.

Such legal exceptions are rare. The Equal Employment Opportunity Commission (EEOC) lays down strict guidelines as to what is indeed an allowable bona fide exception. Determining what is acceptable can be tricky.

An employer has to prove that the limiting requirement is necessary to business operations, and that the requirement, say as to age or height, applies equally to all those in the excepted category.

Thus, an airline might impose an age limit on its pilots, the BFOQ being that their vision would be impaired by age; yet if some of those pilots over the limiting age still have perfect vision, they could plead discrimination without reasonable cause.

as he did was your ethnicity, you are the victim of disparate treatment—but you must show that your employer purposely discriminated against you. If your employer has another legitimate reason for punishing you, such as your history of calling in sick, he is probably not in violation of the law.

ADVERSE IMPACT

"Adverse impact" takes place when the effect of a company policy or rule has a disproportionally negative effect on a protected group. Whereas disparate treatment refers to deliberate discrimination because of your membership in a protected group, adverse impact can be more subtle and is often unintentional. For instance, requiring that police officers meet certain height and weight requirements when job duties do not necessitate it may be discriminatory. Such requirements may have an adverse impact on women, who are generally shorter and weigh less than men.

It is legal for an employer to be discriminatory in hiring in some instances. If the employer can show that a certain criterion is a "bona fide occupational qualification" (BFOQ) for a job, he can refuse to hire those who do not meet that criteria. An example of a BFOQ would be requiring a woman for a specific acting role or hiring someone over a certain legal age to serve alcohol.

Building an adverse-impact case is not easy. If an employer places male workers in certain jobs and females in other, lower-paying jobs, claiming that the men's jobs require heavy lifting, you will have to show that the requirement is actually a pretext for discrimination, that some women are capable of doing the men's jobs, and that your employer is placing females at a disadvantage by not giving them the same opportunities.

OTHER KINDS OF DISCRIMINATION

An employer may be perpetuating past discrimination if a seemingly neutral policy continues to reinforce workplace bias. For example, if an employer generally asks employees to recommend friends for open positions and the workplace is predominantly made up of white males, he may be guilty of discrimination if white males continue to be hired, and minorities and women do not have an opportunity to be employed.

Laws also offer recourse if you are subject to a hostile environment because of your membership in a protected group. Ethnic slurs or racially based jokes that continue even after you have voiced an objection can be judged discriminatory, whether or not your employer is actually participating in the behavior himself. If an employer is aware of discrimination, or even if it is judged that an employer should be aware of it, and does nothing to stop it, he can be held accountable for it.

Anytime you feel you are being discriminated against, try to document the behavior. If it occurs during a job interview, take notes if you can. If possible, keep a copy of an application or an employment test that asks discriminatory questions. If the suspected discrimination is happening while you are on the job, save memos, written reprimands, performance reviews, forms, or any policy statements that you think are discriminatory. If you are the victim of a verbal attack, find out if anyone else heard it.

Keep detailed notes and records of anything you were told that may be grounds for a discrimination suit. Include names, dates, and any other pertinent information, even your feelings at the time. If you file a complaint with the Equal Employment Opportunity Commission or a state agency, you will need to prove you are being or have been discriminated against; documentation may be essential in proving your claim.

MAKING A COMPLAINT

If your supervisor is not directly involved in the discrimination, you may want to put a complaint in writing and send it to the supervisor (certified mail, return receipt requested). Briefly describe the discriminatory behavior you are complaining about and state what you think ought to be done about it. If you cannot get results on your own, or if you feel that there is no one in the company you can complain to, you may want to seek outside help.

First see if a state or local agency will hear your claim. If not, you can file a complaint with the EEOC. Depending on the particular law that has been violated, you may have to file with the EEOC before you can file your own lawsuit. Whatever you choose to do, it is a good idea to contact a lawyer for advice.

Age Discrimination

The Age Discrimination in Employment Act (ADEA) protects workers over age 40 from being dismissed or refused a job because of age. It also applies to discrimination regarding pay, promotions, benefits, and other employment issues. Employees of all private businesses of 15 or more workers are covered, as are all federal, state, and local government employees. State laws may be more inclusive, setting lower age limits and covering smaller companies.

If you are over 40 and your employer fires you and then turns around and hires someone younger than you for your position, he may be acting in violation of the ADEA. There are exceptions, but in general, the ADEA says you cannot lose your job because of your age, because your salary has become too

FORCED RETIREMENT: DISCRIMINATION?

The Age Discrimination in Employment Act (ADEA) makes it illegal, in general, to fire someone or force someone's retirement because of age. Yet there are exceptions. You may be fired or forced to retire if:

1. You are 65 or older, have been in an executive position for the past two years, and are entitled to a pension of at least $44,000.

2. A BFOQ exists that makes your age a relevant factor in your job performance. In the past, positions that affect public safety, such as police officers and firefighters, have been subject to mandatory retirement under this exception.

3. An EEOC-approved, bona fide (nondiscriminatory) seniority system, retirement plan, or apprentice program exists in your workplace.

4. You work for a company with fewer than 15 employees and your state does not have an age-discrimination law that protects you.

5. Your salary is too high for current market conditions and your employer can prove true economic hardship, such as an impending bankruptcy. This decision must be purely financial and cannot have a discriminatory impact on all older workers.

high, or because you are about to become vested in a pension plan. Overall, the law does not allow forced retirement, but it does not forbid employers from instituting layoffs based on a seniority system reflecting on length of service. (See "Forced Retirement: Discrimination?" on page 255.)

SAME TREATMENT, OLD OR YOUNG

The ADEA requires an employer who offers employee group health insurance coverage to offer it under the same conditions to all employees in the same job classification, regardless of age. If you are over 40, your premiums and benefits must be the same as those of younger workers.

Age-discrimination complaint guidelines are similar to those for civil-rights-act violations. If you are being discriminated against, find out if a state or local agency handles such claims. If no such agency is available to you, you can file a complaint with the EEOC. In order to file a lawsuit for ADEA violation, you must first file a complaint with the EEOC or an equivalent state agency.

How to Deal With the EEOC

The Civil Rights Act of 1964 mandated the Equal Employment Opportunity Commission (EEOC) to enforce antidiscrimination laws. The EEOC investigates allegations of bias, negotiates agreements after charges are filed, and occasionally goes to court as a plaintiff to fight discrimination. Here are some things you should know if you are considering filing an EEOC claim:

• First find out about your state's equal-opportunity procedures and antidiscrimination laws. Many states and even some cities have their own agencies to deal with such claims.

• You must file a claim with the EEOC within 180 days of the incident you are citing. If there is a state or local agency that can handle your complaint, the EEOC will defer action for 60 days to give the other agency time to act. Your time limit for filing can then be extended up to 300 days.

• Once the EEOC receives your complaint, it will contact your employer and investigate your case. If your claim is proved, the EEOC may order your employer to do one or more of the following: cease the discrimination; hire, rehire, or promote you; award back pay; or establish an affirmative action program.

• Only in very few instances does the EEOC go to court on behalf of a complainant. If the commission is unable to resolve your problem within 180 days, it will give you a "right-to-sue notice" and you will then have 90 days to file a lawsuit if

you so choose. You will need to get your own lawyer, but if your case is strong, a lawyer may represent you without charging in advance.

• You can file a claim by mail (return receipt requested) or in person. Your complaint must be in writing and be notarized, including enough information for the EEOC to understand the nature of your complaint. Include copies of any documentation you have, names of witnesses, and the specific dates the discrimination took place.

• You do not need to include your name when filing a complaint with the EEOC, which will honor your request for confidentiality. In some cases, however, it may be impossible to take your case very far without revealing your name.

• Your employer cannot take any action against you for filing a complaint or cooperating in an EEOC investigation. If you are fired or disciplined because of your involvement with an EEOC claim, contact a lawyer. You may be able to bring a lawsuit against your employer based on wrongful treatment.

Gender Discrimination

Job discrimination on the basis of sex is legislated by Title VII of the Civil Rights Act of 1964. This includes pregnancy discrimination. If an employer refuses to hire you because you are pregnant or fires or demotes because you would like to have a baby, he may be violating the law. Gender discrimination in general can take on many forms and is prohibited by a number of laws.

EQUAL PAY FOR EQUAL WORK

The Equal Pay Act of 1963 requires employers to pay equally for equal work. Jobs that require the same level of skill, effort, and responsibility under similar conditions should pay the same. If you are a woman and work as a bank teller, your pay should be the same as that of male tellers, as long as your qualifications, experience, seniority, and training are similar.

To prove unequal pay, you will have to prove that the skills, effort, responsibility, and working conditions of your job and that of the person in question are all substantially equal.

If you are the victim of unequal pay, you do not need to file a complaint with the EEOC. You can file your own lawsuit against your former or present employer and may be able to recover the difference between what you were paid and what you should have been paid for the previous two years, plus attorney fees, and in some cases additional damages for distress and mental anguish. Many states have their own equal pay acts. If yours does, you may be able to sue under state statute. If you have any doubts about the equality of your pay, or if you think you have a case, contact a lawyer.

SEXUAL HARASSMENT

Sexual harassment can be defined as unwanted sexual advances or visual, verbal, or physical conduct of a sexual nature. It is illegal under Title VII of the 1964 Civil Rights Act, and virtually every state has its own laws as well.

The definition of sexual harassment is broad, and includes graphic or negative comments about an employee's appearance or anatomy, unwelcome sexual advances or propositions, unwelcome descriptions of personal sexual experiences, questions about an employee's sex life, the display of pornographic materials in the workplace, and threatening to fire or demote an employee for rejecting sexual advances.

Sexual harassment can be committed by anyone. The harasser may be the victim's co-worker, supervisor, or associate and can be of either gender. The courts recognize two general types of sexual harassment: "quid pro quo" and "hostile

A MODEL POLICY AGAINST SEXUAL HARASSMENT

In today's workplace, it is essential for every company to make it clear that sexual harassment will not be tolerated, letting employees know how it will be dealt with. An effective sexual harassment policy should do the following:

1. Be published. The policy should be in writing, be posted, and given to all employees when they are hired.

2. Educate. All employees should know how to recognize sexual harassment. Seminars or workshops may work better than a written statement.

3. Encourage participation. Employees should be encouraged to report any and all behavior they feel uncomfortable with or offended by.

4. Promise results. Victims should be assured that a speedy investigation will take place after charges are made.

5. Discipline violators. Quick action against violators sends a clear message. Punishments must be carried out.

6. Assure job security. Victims need to know that their job security and prospects for advancement will not be jeopardized if they participate in an investigation.

7. Designate policy administrators. Employees should know exactly whom to report abuse to. It is best to have more than one administrator.

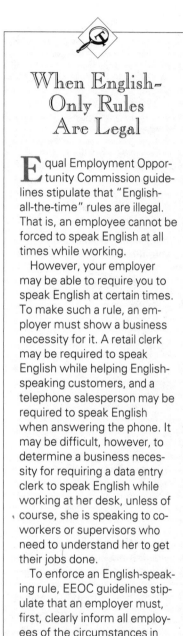

Equal Employment Opportunity Commission guidelines stipulate that "English-all-the-time" rules are illegal. That is, an employee cannot be forced to speak English at all times while working.

However, your employer may be able to require you to speak English at certain times. To make such a rule, an employer must show a business necessity for it. A retail clerk may be required to speak English while helping English-speaking customers, and a telephone salesperson may be required to speak English when answering the phone. It may be difficult, however, to determine a business necessity for requiring a data entry clerk to speak English while working at her desk, unless of course, she is speaking to co-workers or supervisors who need to understand her to get their jobs done.

To enforce an English-speaking rule, EEOC guidelines stipulate that an employer must, first, clearly inform all employees of the circumstances in which they will be required to speak English, and second, must notify them of the consequences of breaking the rule.

If an employer takes disciplinary action against an employee for not speaking English without having fulfilled those two rules, he may be being discriminatory.

environment." The Latin phrase *quid pro quo* means something received in exchange for something given. A classic example of this situation is when a supervisor informs a female subordinate that if she does not cooperate with his sexual advances, she will be fired. This type of sexual harassment is usually clear-cut. If the victim has any proof of the harassment, she will most likely win a lawsuit.

However, some forms of quid pro quo are more subtle, such as promises of advancement, better working conditions, higher compensation, or some other workplace issue. This type of harassment also includes threats of retaliation against an employee who does not submit to a harasser's demands, or who complains to a co-worker, a supervisor, or the EEOC.

HOSTILE ENVIRONMENT

Conduct that interferes with a person's work performance or creates an "intimidating, hostile, or offensive working environment" is also considered sexual harassment.

An individual may be a victim of sexual harassment even when she does not lose her job or get passed up for a promotion. In the courts, conduct is considered sexual harassment if it is conduct that a "reasonable person" would find hostile, abusive, or disruptive to working conditions.

No two cases of sexual harassment are exactly alike. In some cases, such as a quid pro quo situation, you may want to take immediate legal action at even a hint of harassment. If you are being subjected to conduct you are not comfortable with and do not know what to do, do not hesitate to file a complaint, call the EEOC, or consult a lawyer.

Race and Affirmative Action

The year after signing the Civil Rights Act of 1964, President Lyndon B. Johnson issued an executive order requiring all contractors working for the federal government to take "affirmative action," to make sure minorities were hired. Affirmative action is an effort to improve job opportunities for members of minority groups and women. Affirmative action laws are administered by the EEOC's Office of Federal Contract Compliance Programs (OFCCP); state laws are usually administered by the state's human rights commission or an equivalent agency.

Private employers are generally not required by law to have affirmative action plans, unless a pattern of discrimination has been noted by the courts. However, some employers may voluntarily or because of a union contract choose to implement one themselves.

Affirmative action plans can involve recruitment, hiring, promotions, transfers, and other conditions of employment. For instance, a state, local, or federal government employer may be required to publicize job openings where women and minorities are likely to see them so as to encourage these underrepresented groups to apply for positions and help balance the work force. The OFCCP sets affirmative action plan guidelines, such as requiring employers to encourage applicants and employees to identify themselves as members of protected groups in order to receive preference under the law.

An affirmative action plan cannot, however, automatically exclude nonminorities, or it may be considered "reverse discrimination." The courts would not approve of a minority employee being favored by an affirmative action plan if he was not qualified for his position. The courts also do not look favorably on strict quotas that ignore the number of qualified minorities in the community's work force. However, if two candidates for the same position are equally qualified for a position, the plan may call upon the employer to give the job to a minority or female candidate if they are underrepresented in that position in the workplace.

Religion in the Workplace

The law protects your religious beliefs as an employee just as it does your other rights. It is illegal to discriminate because of religion, but there are legal limits. Religious practices are not allowed to interfere with "neutral" laws regulating employment such as child labor laws and Social Security tax payments. No matter what your religious beliefs, you must observe both.

In most cases the law says employers should make "reasonable accommodation" to their employees' religious beliefs and practices. If work interferes with an employee's Saturday Sabbath for example, an employer should, if possible, find somebody else to work a Saturday shift, reschedule work, or make other changes. Not every religious accommodation is reasonable, however. A large company can juggle schedules more easily than a small company. When the economic toll becomes too high, employers are justified in refusing to make special accommodations or give time off for religious reasons.

To establish a charge of religious discrimination you will need to show that employment requirements conflict with your religion or a specific religious practice, that you notified your employer of the conflict, and that you were punished or negatively affected in the workplace due to your inability to comply with your employer's requests because of your religion.

What If Religion Interferes With Work?

Employers are entitled to ban certain religious activities from their premises. Here are some practices that can be legally forbidden:

✔ *Proselytizing.* You cannot proselytize for your religion at work without your employer's consent. However, the company may not bar one religion from seeking converts and give free reign to another.

✔ *Daily prayers.* You cannot organize prayers, meditation, a religious sing-along, or a Bible reading without employer consent. Some employers will allow such activity it if it does not interfere with the orderly flow of work.

✔ *Wearing religious costumes.* Your employer may prohibit religious dress such as turbans, yarmulkes, long hair, or beards in the workplace if it interferes with job performance. But beyond that restriction, the employer cannot prohibit some workers from wearing religious garb while permitting others to dress however they want.

The Disabled

Work keeps at bay three great evils: Boredom, Vice, and Need.

VOLTAIRE

Candide

The Americans with Disabilities Act (ADA) of 1991 bars employment discrimination against "qualified individuals with disabilities." It defines the disabled as those suffering from "a physical or mental impairment that substantially limits one or more major life activity." On the list of impairments are problems with seeing, hearing, speaking, walking, breathing, performing manual tasks, learning, and caring for oneself. It also includes alcoholism, epilepsy, mental retardation, paralysis, contagious and noncontagious illness—and specifically includes AIDS.

Companies with 15 or more employees must comply with the ADA. The law covers more than five million employers that must make it easier for the qualified disabled to be hired and to perform their jobs. "Qualified" means being able to do a job well, even if employer-financed assistance, such as wheelchair ramps or computer equipment, is necessary.

On the other hand, an employer can refuse to hire a disabled worker who poses a threat to the health and safety of others in the workplace. (Professional advice and documentation are necessary to prove that such a threat exists, however.) Furthermore, the ADA does not protect illegal drug users and alcohol abusers. If an alcoholic's disease interferes with his work, he can face termination. However, employees who are participating in or have completed rehabilitation are protected.

"Reasonable Accommodation" for the Disabled

One aim of the Americans with Disabilities Act is to make the workplace more accessible for the disabled by requiring employers to make "reasonable accommodations" to help the disabled perform the duties demanded of a specific job. It is the employer's responsibility to:

• Modify the application procedure so that a disabled person can be considered for the position. This would include reading a written application to a blind person, or altering a preemployment test as necessary.

• Adjust the work environment or job duties so that a disabled person can perform the essential function of the position. For example, if a clerk-typist spends 20 percent of her time filing, it is not an essential function of the job and can be performed by someone else.

• Meet the job-related needs of the disabled individual. The employer does not need to come up with the ideal accommodation, just a reasonable one. If raising the height of a workstation to meet the needs of an employee in a wheelchair is sufficient to make it possible for the employee to do the job, the employer does not need to buy other specialized equipment at the employee's request.

• In general, make all accommodations that are reasonably affordable to facilitate a disabled person's job performance. The employer may not need to make an accommodation, however, if it would be too expensive, difficult, or disruptive to the point of creating an "undue burden" on the business. Such undue hardship must be specifically proven by the employer, and cannot be a result of fear or prejudice. (The ADA requirements apply specifically to people with AIDS.)

BASIC RIGHTS ON THE JOB

Every employee enjoys fundamental rights at work. You must know what they are and how to make sure you get them.

Wages and Hours

The Fair Labor Standards Act (FLSA) was created in 1938 to ease the burden of underpaid workers during the Depression. Today the FLSA is the basic document that governs minimum wage and overtime pay, and protects workers from being taken advantage of by their employers. The act also sets child labor standards.

The Wage and Hour Division of the Department of Labor administers and enforces the law, which covers more than 80 million full-time and part-time workers in the private and public sectors. Exceptions include some federal employees, retail or service employees whose firms conduct business within one state, and workers in companies with fewer than 15 workers.

The FLSA divides workers into two basic categories: exempt and nonexempt. Most salaried employees at the executive and professional levels are exempt from FLSA rules, as are almost all office workers who earn more than $250 per week, as well as outside salespeople. These exempt employees are not subject to minimum wage or overtime laws.

The exemption, however, may be revoked if an employer treats such employees as if they are nonexempt. For example, if an employer docks an executive for missing part of a day's work, the employee may be entitled to overtime pay as defined by the FLSA.

A host of other exceptions covers smaller groups of employees, those in the fishing industry, cab drivers, amusement park workers, switchboard operators of small telephone companies, baby-sitters, and employees of small farms.

PROTECTION FOR THE NONEXEMPT

Nonexempt workers must be paid at least the current minimum wage (which has been $4.25 an hour since 1991) for the first 40 hours worked in any seven-day period. An employer who pays a receptionist less than $170 a week for a regular 40-hour workweek is violating federal minimum wage laws. If you are a typist and are paid by the page and are covered by the FLSA, you must earn at least $4.25 an hour regardless of the amount of work you complete. Employees who receive tips as part of their job, such as waiters, waitresses, and bartenders

CHILD LABOR LAWS

The Federal Fair Labor Standards Act has specific child labor provisions. Here are some things you should know if your child is working or if you hire young people (many states have additional restrictions):

1. No one under age 18 may be employed in hazardous occupations such as coal mining, meat packing, and roofing, or in jobs involving radiation exposure or handling explosives.

2. Minors of any age can work in "casual employment" such as delivering newspapers or baby-sitting, and on a family farm. They may also be employed as actors or performers or by their parents in nonhazardous situations.

3. A 17- or 18-year-old may hold almost any job not classified as dangerous, without any restrictions on hours.

4. Children under 16 may not work during school hours but may work up to three hours a day on school days and eight hours a day on nonschool days between 7:00 A.M. and 7:00 P.M. They cannot work more than 18 hours a week when school is in session. In summer, 14- to 16-year-olds can work until 9:00 P.M., up to 40 hours a week.

WHAT THE FLSA DOESN'T COVER

The job-related issues discussed below may be covered by a verbal or written contract between you and your employer, but they are not guaranteed by the Federal Labor Standards Act (FLSA):

1. Vacation and paid holidays. These are not legal requirements, but privileges your employer may offer.

2. Sick and severance pay. Your employer is not legally required to pay you for days missed due to illness or injury, and does not have to offer you any monetary or other compensation if you are let go, unless such an arrangement is part of a benefits package.

3. Holiday pay. Your employer is not required to pay you overtime for working on Christmas or any other holiday if it is part of your normal 40-hour workweek, unless a union agreement or other contract stipulates overtime.

4. Meals or rest periods. These are a matter of union or private negotiation, or state law. Most states have laws regarding lunch breaks; you are usually given a meal period of 30 or 45 minutes, depending on how many hours a day you work, such as six or eight.

5. Pay raises. You are not legally entitled to cost-of-living or merit raises unless they are part of an established employer policy or a written, implied, or union agreement.

may be paid 50 percent of the minimum wage, as long as they are permitted to keep all of their tips. If, however, an employee's hourly tip earnings and the cash wage the employer pays do not equal the minimum wage, the employer must pay the employee the difference so that he earns at least $4.25 an hour.

Most states have minimum wage laws that extend to employers not covered by the federal law, and they may be higher or lower than the federal minimum. Employers subject to wage and hour laws must pay the higher of the state or federal minimum wages. Employers who are not subject to those laws—a mom-and-pop business with a couple of employees, for example—may pay less than the federal minimum wage if their state's minimum is lower.

OVERTIME PAY

In some circumstances, your employer may be required to pay you more than the minimum wage. If you are a nonexempt employee, any hours you work in excess of 40 a week must be compensated at the rate of one-and-a-half times the regular hourly rate. In some states you are also entitled to overtime for hours worked over eight in a day. Under federal law, however, your employer may have you work four days a week, 10 hours a day, without paying you overtime.

Overtime Must Be Compensated

PROBLEM
Adam Parker worked in a retail electronics store. His regular schedule was from 9:00 A.M. to 6:00 P.M. every day with an hour for lunch: a 40-hour week. The week before a big sale, his employer, Mark Tanner, told him to go home an hour early each day that week. When Adam asked if he would be docked pay, his employer replied, "No, I need you to stay late every day next week. It will even out."

ACTION
It would not even out. Adam called his state department of labor and learned that under the Federal Labor Standards Act, Adam's employer must pay him overtime if he works more than 40 hours in a week. It was legal for Mark to pay Adam for only 35 hours the first week, but he had to pay the time-and-a-half overtime rate for the extra five hours in the second week. For those two weeks, Adam earned an extra two-and-a-half-hours pay.

Some public-sector employees, such as firefighters and police officers, are often offered the option of receiving compensatory, or "comp," time instead of getting overtime pay. Comp time is paid leave, usually taken during the same period the overtime was worked. If your employer gives you the option of taking compensatory time and you are nonexempt, you are entitled to get an hour-and-a-half of leave for every hour of overtime

worked. So, if you work three hours of overtime, you are eligible for four-and-a-half hours of paid leave.

Safety and Health at Work

The Occupational Safety and Health Agency (OSHA) aims to keep you safe and healthy at work. Part of the Department of Labor, OSHA has jurisdiction over virtually every private employer in the country and is responsible for implementing the Occupational Safety and Health Act of 1970.

In addition to OSHA, most states have their own laws regarding safety in the workplace. OSHA encourages states to implement such laws, as long as they are at least as strict as OSHA standards. Companies with fewer than 10 employees may be exempt from some of OSHA's standards, as are family-owned and -operated farms and self-employed individuals.

Under the Occupational Safety and Health Act, your employer has "a general duty to provide a workplace that is free from hazards that are likely to cause death or severe physical harm." In addition, OSHA has established numerous specific standards covering every aspect of the workplace. Some of the basic standards require that:

- Workplaces be kept clean and orderly;
- Medical and first aid treatment are readily available;
- Emergency exits and fire protection plans are implemented;
- Temperatures are maintained at a comfortable level;
- Workers receive proper training on machinery and equipment;
- Suitable drinking water is available;
- Adequate lighting is available;
- Noise levels do not exceed a certain level (unless protective gear is provided);
- Smoking is not permitted in elevators.

OSHA keeps track of how well employers meet these specific standards and the "general duty clause" standards though random inspections and through alerts from employees and other observers who notice conditions that might endanger the health and safety of workers.

INSPECTIONS

OSHA can inspect any premise at any time without prior notice as long as a warrant is issued. A representative of the employer and an employee are permitted to accompany the OSHA inspector during an inspection. Employees may be questioned, records inspected, and photographs of the workplace taken.

Smoking in the Workplace

Whether you have a right to smoke or a right to be smoke-free is a subject of national debate. Increasingly, city ordinances, state laws, and federal court decisions restrict or forbid smoking in the workplace, restaurants, and public buildings.

If your goal is a smoke-free environment, you can probably find support from a majority of your fellow workers as well as from the new laws. Present a united front to the management, citing the numbers of smokers and nonsmokers in the workplace, and pointing out where smoke is a particular problem or where ventilation is inadequate.

If you suffer from allergies or an illness that is aggravated by secondhand smoke, get documentation from a doctor to bolster your argument.

If you cannot get smoking banned altogether, ask for a designated smoking area far away from your work space.

If you are a smoker, you probably will have a harder time getting satisfaction, given the stringent restrictions being imposed, such as requirements for solid walls around smoking areas and ventilation equipment.

If you can rally enough fellow smokers to your cause, however, you may be able to convince your employer to create smoking areas that meet the restrictions.

Protective gear may be evaluated and emergency procedures and fire protection measures inspected. If the employer is violating an OSHA standard, a citation will be issued and a penalty proposed. The Department of Labor will then review the case and decide whether or not to impose the penalty.

The agency can also issue temporary emergency standards to deal with imminent health or safety hazards. If, for example, it were to be discovered that exposure to a toxic chemical commonly used in a particular industry is health threatening, OSHA could issue a temporary safety standard for employers. Such standards remain in force for six months and are then either revoked or replaced by permanent standards.

OSHA also requires employers to post OSHA notices, which include a "Job Safety and Health" poster, copies of any OSHA violations issued to the employer, and the annual summary of occupational illness and injuries that OSHA requires employers to complete each year.

HOW TO COMPLAIN

When you suspect a health or safety problem at work, it is best to go to a union or management representative first. Management is often aware of safety and health issues, and in many cases will respond to your complaint.

If you get no response, you may be able to file a complaint with your state department of labor. If this recourse is not available, you can file a complaint with OSHA. Include the company's name and address, the nature of the problem, how long

In order that people may be happy in their work, these three things are needed: They must be fit for it; they must not do too much of it; and they must have a sense of success in it.

JOHN RUSKIN

Pre-Raphaelitism

1851

Safeguards for Whistle-Blowers

An employee who reports a crime his employer has committed or who notifies authorities of safety violations in the workplace is known as a "whistle-blower." Federal and state laws may protect employees from retaliation by their employers under such circumstances.

• The Occupational Safety and Health Act (OSHA) stipulates that employees may not be discharged or discriminated against in any way for exercising their rights under OSHA.

• To be protected, employees must make their complaints in good faith and not merely to "punish" an employer. If you report false information not knowing it is false, you are still protected. But if you knowingly make false statements about your employer you will not be protected from retaliatory action, such as being fired.

• Currently, more than half the states have whistle-blower statutes that offer protection for workers who report job-related crimes. Some of these laws cover only public or government employees; others cover only workers in the private sector.

• If you feel you are being retaliated against for reporting a crime your employer committed—by being fired or in more subtle ways—find out what your state's laws are regarding whistle-blowers. You will most likely have to go through all of the appropriate channels, such as filing a complaint with OSHA or some other federal or local agency, before you have the right to pursue legal action against your employer under state law. You can usually file another complaint with OSHA within 30 days of the retaliatory action. In any case it is a good idea to consult a lawyer as soon as possible, especially if your job is at stake.

it has been going on, and what if anything has been done about it. You can request anonymity, but you must give OSHA your name when you file the complaint.

Usually the agency will follow up by sending an inspector to the work site. But that may take time, as much as a year or more, because OSHA investigates complaints by category, moving first on life-threatening dangers. As the complainant you are entitled to participate in OSHA inspections and prehearing conferences. You also have the right to talk privately to the inspector.

You have the right to refuse to work under conditions that are unsafe, but be aware that you may face disciplinary action if you do. If you walk off a job, OSHA legislation offers some protection, provided there is a risk of serious harm, the employer has done nothing to remedy the situation, and the situation is so urgently dangerous that there is not enough time to call OSHA and follow the customary complaint procedures. Expect to wait up to two years for such a case to be settled, however. Unless you feel your life or safety is in immediate danger and your employer will not remedy the situation, it is best to contact OSHA before refusing to work.

Working Part-Time

When you work part-time or in a temporary position, you may not have much job security. Part-time and temporary workers are often hired for specific assignments and let go when the assignments are done. But when it comes to health and safety at work and freedom from discrimination and sexual harassment, part-time employees have the same rights as full-time employees.

Coverage under the Family and Medical Leave Act depends on the hours you work per week. The law says you must have worked for an employer for a period of 12 months and have logged 1,250 hours, slightly more than 24 hours a week. If you qualify you can take the 12 weeks of unpaid leave and still have your job when you return. Employers must also withhold and deposit income tax and Social Security payments for part-timers and must carry workers' compensation insurance. (See also "Employee Benefits," page 247.)

UNEMPLOYMENT INSURANCE

Part-time and temporary employees may or may not be eligible for unemployment compensation when they leave their jobs. In some states, compensation is calculated according to your base pay. If your salary or wage is less than the minimum amount, you may not qualify. You may be eligible for benefits as a full-time temporary employee after you have worked a cer-

Part-Time Employee Protection

If you are considering part-time work, you should know that in some areas your rights are the same as those of full-time employees; in other areas, you are not so well protected.

✔ *Wages.* The Federal Labor Standards Act (FLSA) applies the same standards to part-time employees as to full-timers. But state minimum wage laws (which often apply to small companies not engaged in interstate commerce) may exclude part-timers.

✔ *Health insurance.* Part-time workers are rarely covered by employee health plans. Some employers allow part-timers to pay the premium themselves and be covered under the company's group policy.

✔ *Unemployment.* If you do not work the minimum number of hours set by your state, you will not qualify for unemployment benefits.

✔ *Workers' compensation.* Most part-time employees are covered by workers' compensation insurance. How much money you get if you are injured, however, will probably depend on how many hours a week you work.

✔ *Discrimination.* Your protection against discrimination does not depend on how much you work. If your company is covered by Title VII of the Civil Rights Act or state legislation, you will be covered as well.

tain number of hours. The length of time required varies from state to state, but temporary agencies generally pay unemployment taxes for the "temps" they place. Contact your local unemployment office to find out if you qualify.

Privacy on the Job

Your right to privacy in the workplace can be a very tricky issue. Although there are a number of federal laws that protect individual privacy, federal legislation that specifically applies to privacy in the workplace is scarce. For example, the Federal Privacy Act deals mainly with access to employee records, but it applies only to government agencies. The Omnibus Crime Control and Safe Streets Act of 1968 includes provisions that may be interpreted to restrict employer eavesdropping on private conversations, but the restrictions are limited.

Many states have laws that give employees the right to view their personnel files; others limit the release of records to third parties. Some states also have laws regarding workplace communications such as telephone calls, correspondence, and electronic mail.

Still, your private life may not be immune to employer scrutiny. Companies can sometimes insist on moral codes whose violation, on or off the job, can lead to discipline or dismissal. Employers have been allowed to fire people involved in illicit activities or who were moonlighting at another job.

Your employer may also be entitled to know if you abuse alcohol or use illegal drugs, although drug testing crosses a fine legal line. Federal testing guidelines exist for the transportation industry, people who carry weapons, and people with classified information. Truckers, pilots, and train engineers are subject to random testing. Few others are. However, state laws on drug testing differ greatly. Find out what the laws are in your state before submitting to a drug test. (See also "Finding a Job," page 242.)

PERFORMANCE REVIEWS

No law requires an employer to evaluate your performance on a regular basis, but many companies have made performance reviews an integral part of their employee relations. What was once an employer privilege has now come under court scrutiny, and the courts have held that reviews must be fair, unbiased, objective, and professional. If they are not, employees may be entitled to sue for reinstatement or back pay should they be fired, and they may be able to protest reviews that smack of personal bias or do not live up to the company's own policies.

Thus, the courts have heard cases of "negligent job evalua-

---

1 2 3...

PERFORMANCE REVIEWS

If you are asked to review an employee, you owe it to the employee to conduct a fair and constructive interview by following the suggestions below. If you are on the receiving end of a review, be aware of these guidelines as indicators of how an interview should go. Make sure to let your reviewer know if you feel you were not treated fairly.

1. Be candid. Identify weaknesses and strengths, and give clear, specific suggestions as to how the employee can improve on-the-job performance.

2. Document it. Put the review in writing and sign it. In most states the employee is entitled to see the review and write a rebuttal to it.

3. Be prepared. Keep written notes of the employee's performance throughout the review period.

4. Listen. Make a special effort to hear what the employee has to say, and take it seriously. If you disagree with anything, offer your own opinion, backing it up with examples from your notes.

5. Note disparities. If the review contains information that the employee feels is false, briefly note the objection on the document before having the employee sign it. This can be a peaceful way for the employee to voice disagreement without causing a scene or an argument.

tion," charging that reviews were unfair or were not performed on the basis described in the employee handbook. If your employer fires you after one bad review, you may have a negligent-job-evaluation suit. You will need to prove that you were fired for a reason other than the negative review, and that the review was only a last-minute cover-up.

In many cases, your review may be the only documentation of your job performance your employer has. Make sure you take it seriously. Save all copies of reviews you receive as well as your notes. They can offer protection further down the line. If you feel you have been reviewed unfairly or, more important, your job is at stake, you may want to consult a lawyer.

MANAGEMENT AUTHORITY

In today's workplace, employee discipline has become a major issue—specifically, how much of it management may impose on employees without crossing legal limits. Employers have a right to discipline you for cause. Use of abusive language, shoddy work performance, habitual tardiness, refusal to obey lawful instructions, use of drugs or alcohol, dishonesty, and breach of trust all qualify as legitimate reasons for discipline.

What your employer may not do is impose what the courts have called "outrageous" discipline. Making an example of you in front of other employees, forcing you to stay on the premises against your will, docking your pay for time you have worked, and any physical abuse or harassment inflicted on you are all examples of what might be deemed "outrageous" discipline, and give you a legal claim against the employer.

COMPLAINING

Grievance procedures, known as "corporate due process," can take many different forms. Some firms use panels, boards, or committees to consider both sides of a dispute and then hand down a decision. At other companies the task is assigned to an objective investigator who checks out the facts and then resolves the complaint.

If you work under a union contract, filing a grievance with management is a strictly defined procedure that your shop steward or other union official will explain. Otherwise, you should find out all you can about your company's grievance procedure before taking action. Prepare all documentation detailing dates, circumstances, and any witnesses or other parties involved with your complaint. Research appropriate laws and state agencies to determine if you have recourse outside the workplace. Write down everything you are told regarding your complaint. If you suspect your employer is breaking the law or that your job is in jeopardy, consult a lawyer and find out exactly what your rights are.

When the Boss Can Invade Your Privacy

However much you treasure your privacy, you may not be able to protect it fully from your employer.

✔ *Searches.* A private sector employer may search your desk, locker, workstation, or computer as long as you have no legitimate expectation of privacy and he has a reasonable suspicion of illegal behavior and has notified you in advance that a search is likely.

✔ *Telephone calls.* Private sector employers may monitor telephone calls if you consent to being monitored, or if listening to your phone conversations is considered part of the "ordinary course of business." If it is clear that a call is personal, however, the listener is supposed to hang up.

✔ *Surveillance.* Employers can observe employees in the workplace with video cameras, but cannot create an unnecessary invasion of privacy by installing cameras in areas such as employee rest rooms.

✔ *Electronic mail.* The courts are still setting precedents in this relatively new area, but in general, if your employer tells you that all communications or computer data are subject to monitoring, he can read your electronic mail, since he has removed your expectation of privacy in this area. If he owns the computer, he may be able to monitor your data even if he has not notified you.

TERMINATION

Whether you resign from your job, are laid off, or get fired, you have certain rights, and your employer has certain responsibilities to you. Insist on them.

Termination Rights and Benefits

When you leave a job, your employer is supposed to tell you what benefits are due you. Here is what you are entitled to and should insist on:

✔ *Pay.* By law in every state, when an employee leaves a job, she must be paid on her last day of work or on the next regular payday.

✔ *Health insurance.* You are entitled to continue on a company health plan for 18 months, although you must pay the premiums yourself.

✔ *401 (k) proceeds.* If you have contributed to a 401 (k) retirement plan, you are entitled to all money you invested. Find out how much time you have to transfer your funds if you are required to do so. You have various options regarding the account, such as transferring it to a qualified plan at your new job, or opening your own Individual Retirement Account (IRA). (See also YOUR MONEY, page 357.)

✔ *Pension.* The share of your pension fund that you are entitled to get depends on the policy of your pension fund and the length of time you have been employed by the company. Find out the pension policy and insist upon any benefits you are owed.

Resigning Gracefully

An employee's resignation is not normally governed by any federal or state laws, although business courtesy suggests that an employee give an employer at least two weeks' notice before leaving a job. Nor is your employer under any legal obligation to allow you to remain at your job for an unlimited amount of time after you submit your resignation. You must work out a mutually advantageous schedule.

Your employer, however, does have certain legal obligations to you when you resign. First, your employer must clarify when and how all sums of money owed to you will be paid. She must arrange for you to receive your final paycheck, and if you have participated in a 401 (k) plan, she must turn your savings over to you directly or roll the funds over into an appropriate account. (See also YOUR MONEY, page 357.) By law, she must inform you of your right to continued group health coverage under the Consolidated Omnibus Budget Reconciliation Act (COBRA). (See also "Employee Benefits," page 247.)

It is both courteous and practical to write a formal letter of resignation, stating why you are leaving, and confirming the verbal agreements you have made concerning your departure date and the financial details that remain outstanding. (See "A Termination Letter That Does the Job," page 271.)

Termination and the Law

If you are an "at-will" employee (that is, you are not protected by an employee contract or other agreement), your employer has the legal right to fire you at any time and for any reason, as long as the firing is not discriminatory or is not considered "wrongful discharge." If you are protected by a union agreement, employee contract, state law, or if illegal discrimination is suspected, your employer may need "just cause" to fire you. Many reasons can be considered "just cause" for dismissal: lying on your job application; excessive absences or latenesses; sleeping, drinking, fighting, gambling, or taking drugs on the job; stealing from your employer; harassing co-workers; or being physically, mentally, or emotionally incapable of doing your job.

Just cause does not simply refer to unacceptable behavior, insubordination, or poor job performance. Just cause also can involve legitimate business issues: bad economic conditions can force a business to trim its staff; or reorganization or technological changes may render some jobs obsolete. Still, it is important to find out exactly why you are being let go. Despite the broad parameters defining just cause, several strong laws protect employees from being fired unfairly or "discharged wrongfully." You are protected by law if your employer:

■ **Violates state or federal laws.** This would be the case if you have been discriminated against because of your gender, age, religion, disability, or national origin; if constitutional rights such as freedom of speech, press, or religion have been breached; or if you have been let go because you participated in union activities.

■ **Violates "public policy."** Public policy is what a court would

When You Have to Do the Firing

If you are an owner, manager, or supervisor, you will probably at some time have to fire an employee. The process can be painful for both parties—and it can also lead to legal hot water. To protect yourself and your employer against possible claims, follow these guidelines:

• **Be aware of protected groups.** Many groups are protected by law: racial and ethnic minorities; females; workers over age 40; the handicapped. Members of these groups can be fired for just cause, but you must do it with extra awareness of the employer's responsibility, the possible impact of the firing on that particular worker, and your company's past history of hiring and firing. (See "Discrimination," page 253.)

• **Use progressive discipline.** If you have an employee who needs discipline, plan a system of steps that has the primary goal of improving his performance, and not getting him fired. (See also "Progressive Discipline," page 270.)

• **Document performance.** Keep a written record of the employee's wrongdoings. For example, if chronic lateness is the problem, keep a file of attendance records, warnings, and any written policy regarding excessive tardiness.

• **Know the regulations.** Read your company's rules regarding discipline and termination policy. If you work in a union shop, stay informed about grievance procedures and union regulations. Know and understand the current laws in your state regarding discharge.

• **Use the chain of command.** If you think you will have to fire an employee, be sure to get the approval of your own supervisor. Never discuss the matter with any other employees.

• **Consult a lawyer.** Seek the advice of legal counsel, particularly if you are experiencing problems with a member of a protected group. Be aware that if a member of a nonprotected group is fired to retain a protected-group member you may be in legal trouble.

• **Prepare for the termination.** If you must fire the employee, clearly and calmly communicate the reasons for the dismissal. Inform him of when he will receive his outstanding pay, his rights with regard to his health benefits, the rules regarding unemployment compensation, and the company's proposed severance pay, if any. Prepare a dismissal letter, and have it reviewed in advance by your superiors, the personnel director, and legal counsel. Be aware that the terminated employee has the right to refuse to cosign the letter.

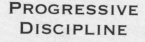
deem activities for the public good. You may be protected from discharge if you are summoned to serve on a jury, if you report your employer for breaking a law or violating safety standards, or if you engage in other other activities that a court would deem to be in the public interest.

- **Violates a written employment contract.** Specifically, your employer cannot fail to honor any facet of a legal employment agreement he has with you.
- **Violates implied agreements with you.** "Implied agreement" may apply to rules in an employee handbook; verbal promises made when you were hired; written or verbal reviews or other acknowledgments of good work; or, in some cases, simply having given long, "good faith" service.

CONSTRUCTIVE DISCHARGE

Under certain conditions, you may have a wrongful termination claim, known as "constructive discharge," even if you have quit your job. If you are forced to leave because of intolerable working conditions or harassment, you may be the victim of constructive discharge. In order to win a constructive discharge case, the intolerable conditions must have been extreme, and you must have had no other recourse but to resign.

Your Rights If You Are Fired

Even employees who are fired for misconduct have rights—some legal, others customary. First, you are entitled to receive prompt payment of any wages owed you. Some states require that you receive your last paycheck the day after you are dismissed; others require that you be paid by the next pay period. Depending upon the law in your state and your company's policy, you may also be entitled to payment for unused vacation days, holidays, sick days, or other accrued benefits.

Many, but not all, companies provide severance pay, depending upon how long you have been employed and the reasons for your dismissal. Severance pay is not a legal right, but it is a custom in many corporations. If your employer does not offer you severance pay, you should ask for it, especially if you are being fired without notice. If you are promised severance pay but are offered payment over a period of several weeks or months, request a lump-sum settlement, so that you can collect unemployment compensation immediately.

GETTING WHAT OTHERS HAVE GOTTEN

Your employer may agree to pay you other benefits, such as anticipated bonuses, pension and profit-sharing, career coun-

418 Longbeach Parkway • Sparta, New Jersey 08560

August 3, 1995

Mr. John Jones
Vice President, Human Resources
The Ajax Tool Company
25 West Ames Highway
Sparta, N.J. 08560

Dear Mr. Jones,

I am writing this letter to confirm the points we agreed on with regard to my termination from Ajax Tools. At our meeting on August 1, 1995, we settled the following:

1 Ajax will keep me on the payroll through August 31, 1995, and my last paycheck, due on that date, will reflect my regular salary through that date, as well as five unused vacation days and my annual bonus of $3,000.

2 Ajax will also pay me a severance check on August 31 reflecting eight weeks' pay or one week for every six months I have been employed at Ajax.

3 Ajax will pay the premiums on my health and dental insurance through September 30, 1995, and will arrange to convert my health policies to me under COBRA at the Ajax group rate.

4 Ajax will not oppose my claim for unemployment insurance and will provide me with any help required in completing all the necessary documentation.

5 Ajax will give me positive references, explaining to anyone calling for a reference that I was laid off as a result of economic cutbacks, not because of misconduct or inadequacy with regard to my work.

Thank you for your help in this matter.

Very truly yours,

Sylvia Scott

A Termination Letter That Does the Job

When you leave a company, for whatever reason, you should clarify your termination agreement in writing. If your employer does not write a letter to this end, write one of your own. **1.** Clarify when you will receive your final paycheck, how much it will cover, and if it will include any addi-tional payments such as bonuses or unused vacation or sick days. **2.** Discuss any severance pay that may have been offered to you, as well as when and how it will be paid. **3.** Put in writing your company's obligation by law to transfer your health insurance to you, including when and how it will go into effect. **4.** Remind the employer that you will be applying for unemployment compensation, and that you expect the company to support the claim. **5.** Explain why you are leaving, and what you expect the employer to say when asked for a reference.

BEFORE YOU BLOW THE WHISTLE

If you are thinking of blowing the whistle on criminal behavior by your employer or other employees, or reporting to the media or a law-enforcement agency a hazard in the workplace, you should take the following steps first:

1. Research. Find out if your employer has a previous record of violations of the law and, if possible, what has happened to prior whistle-blowers. Find out how state laws, union agreements, or OSHA will protect you.

2. Find proof. Be absolutely sure your accusations are well founded. Take detailed notes of illegal behavior and anything said regarding it. Having solid proof of your employer's illegal activity is essential to making a case, and protecting yourself and your job. (It is also vital, after you blow the whistle, to be able to prove any steps taken against you for doing so.)

3. Weigh the consequences. Decide if blowing the whistle is worth the risk. You could lose your job or be blackballed in your field. Although you may have legal recourse, lawsuits take time and money. Make sure you can afford both.

4. Talk to a lawyer. Discuss your accusations and intentions with a lawyer. Your employer may accuse you of defamation or libel if he refutes your charges, so you need to be on firm legal ground.

seling services, or the use of company offices. If your employer has offered any of these to other terminated employees, you may or may not have a right to them, depending on your status and your states laws, but it is worth asking for them.

Unless you were fired for misconduct, you may be eligible for unemployment insurance when let go from a job. Discuss the procedure for receiving unemployment compensation with your employer before you depart so that you do not run into problems when you apply for the benefits. Even though the benefits are paid by the state, the cost is recouped from employers, who sometimes try to avoid payments. If you are denied benefits, you have the right to appeal. Procedures vary by state. (See also, "Pursuing Unemployment Insurance," page 249.)

WRITTEN CONFIRMATIONS

Confirm your separation agreement by writing a letter to your employer that details your termination terms. Better yet, ask that your employer write the letter to you, and request that it be signed by both you and your former boss. (For a sample of such a letter, see page 271.)

Be wary if your employer asks you to sign a release or any other documents, particularly in the immediate aftermath of being fired. Your employer may be taking advantage of your distress by offering you a severance package in exchange for your relinquishing your right to sue. Carefully read exit agreements, releases, and any other forms that your employer wishes you to sign. If you are in doubt about their meaning, discuss the documents with your lawyer.

Bringing Suit

If you believe you have been discriminated against or your civil rights have been breached, think carefully before taking action against your employer. Do not ask yourself if you "deserved" to be fired; ask yourself if your employer had a "legal right" to fire you. If you think that your discharge was discriminatory or in violation of a written or implied contract, you may have a claim.

If you believe your employer has discriminated against you on the basis of race, gender, religion, or national origin—in other words, if you believe your employer to be in violation of Title VII—you must first file a claim with the Equal Employment Opportunity Commission (EEOC) within 180 days of your firing. If the EEOC agrees with your charges, it can reach a settlement with your employer, it can take the employer to court, or it can give you a right-to-sue letter that empowers you to sue the employer, which you must do within 60 days.

Most states and many cities have local EEOC offices; check your telephone directory for the number. (See also "How to Deal With the EEOC," page 256.) You may also want to check with your state's labor board to find out if your termination violates any state laws.

Before going to court, decide if it is worth the expense, the energy, and the emotional stress. Also, clarify your objectives: Do you want your job reinstated? Monetary compensation? Rectification of a serious problem in your former workplace? If you still want to take your case to court, hire a lawyer immediately. (See also YOUR RIGHTS IN ACTION, page 479.)

If the Firm Fails

Sometimes firing is the result of economic problems beyond the worker's and the employer's control. Often, large companies find that they must make large temporary or permanent layoffs. However, if you work for a company with more than 100 employees, the Worker Adjustment and Retraining Notification Act of 1988 (WARN) entitles you to 60 days' warning before mass layoffs or a plant closing. Employers can be exempt if news of possible plant closure would make it impossible to secure necessary financing, or if the closing is due to a natural disaster or other circumstance beyond the firm's control.

WARN defines mass layoffs as termination in any 30-day period of 50 or more workers, amounting to a third of the company's work force; if 500 or more employees are involved in the layoff, the one-third rule does not apply. Once the law is triggered, the employer must issue a notice written in understandable language that states the name and location of the plant to be closed, the date of the closing, and whether the closure is temporary (and for how long) or permanent.

MAKING THE BEST OF IT

If you are laid off, you are entitled to continue with your health benefits under COBRA for at least 18 months, and will most likely be eligible for unemployment insurance. Depending upon your company, you may also be entitled to severance pay, retraining programs, job-search assistance, and a number of other optional benefits.

A number of states and some municipalities may have closing and layoff laws that supersede the federal WARN law, including mandatory compensatory benefits such as health coverage during the layoff, rehabilitation and retraining, or severance pay. Check with your state's department of labor for further information.

Taking Some of the Pain Out of a Layoff

It may not seem to make much difference whether you are laid off or fired—either way you are out of a job. But it does make a difference. Being laid off may not be as bad as you think. Here are some things to keep in mind:

✔ *It's not your fault.* Unlike firings, layoffs are not the result of bad on-the-job performance on your part; they are a function of economic conditions.

✔ *You may get your job back.* You cannot count on it, but sometimes laid-off workers are rehired. Workers may be laid off when sales or profits are down, and if business improves, may be reinstated. Union members who are laid off usually have a contractual right to be called back to work first when a company resumes full production.

✔ *You can collect unemployment.* Laid-off workers are entitled to unemployment benefits if they otherwise qualify—for example, if they have been working long enough. As a general rule, employers do not contest the right of laid-off workers to collect unemployment insurance.

✔ *Your reputation does not have to suffer.* Telling a prospective employer that you were laid off is not a shameful admission. Employers know that being laid off is not the fault of the worker and generally do not hold it against job applicants.

LABOR UNIONS

*Although labor unions do not have the power they once had
they can still benefit workers in a number of ways.*

What Employers May Not Do

The NLRA prohibits employers from interfering with an employee's right to organize. An employer specifically cannot:

✔ *Strong-arm.* An employer cannot retaliate against or threaten an employee for participating in union activities or for trying to form a union. Nor can an employer "blacklist" an employee in order to prevent him from finding work somewhere else.

✔ *Censor.* An employer cannot prevent employees from distributing union material during nonworking hours away from the workplace.

✔ *Unfairly question.* An employer cannot ask new hirees or employees about past union membership, or about their views on unions.

✔ *Spy on employees.* An employer cannot use surveillance or any other means to monitor union activities, meetings, or conversations.

✔ *Unfairly bargain.* An employee cannot be coerced into joining or not joining a union by an employer's promises regarding pay or benefits.

Union Laws

The dominance of labor unions in the American workplace has declined since their peak of power during the years after World War II, but unions are still a force to be respected. Roughly 16 percent of the workers in the United States belong to unions and are therefore protected by various federal and state laws that govern union activity.

The National Labor Relations Act of 1947 (also known as the Taft-Hartley Act) is the basic law that covers union activities in the United States. The law bars firing or refusing to hire workers because they are union members and it guarantees employees the right to join a union, and the union the right to bargain collectively on behalf of workers. (See also "Must You Join a Union?," page 275.)

The NLRA law prohibits "unfair labor practices" which it defines as activity by an employer that: interferes with an employee's right to join a union; seeks to promote an employer-sponsored "company union"; backs one union over another; or refuses to bargain with labor organizers. The National Labor Relations Board was formed to interpret and enforce the act. The NLRB supervises union elections, punishes employers who interfere with union members' rights, and can make rulings in labor disputes.

KEEPING LABOR FAIR

Another piece of union legislation, the Landrum-Griffith Act, was enacted in 1959 to protect workers from their own unions—which may also be accused of unfair labor practices. This act set up a Bill of Rights for union members known as the Labor-Management Reporting and Disclosure Act. The LMRDA guarantees a union member's right to equal treatment, free speech, and assembly.

Union members are entitled to meet in groups to discuss union policies without fear of retaliation from union leaders. Members are entitled to speak at union meetings and cannot be forbidden to criticize labor leaders and their policies. Overall, the act requires unions to "make an honest effort to serve the interests of all its, members without hostility to any."

Collective Strength

You do not have to be a union member in order to be covered by a collective bargaining agreement. If you are a fork-lift operator, for instance, and the union was formed to bargain on behalf of fork-lift operators, you are part of the bargaining agreement, whether you are in the union or not. If your job is not covered by a collective bargaining agreement, however, you do not have union rights, although federal, state, and local laws still apply.

STRIKERS' RIGHTS

Unions have a right to organize a strike; that is, encourage employees to refuse to work in order to increase wages, benefits, or working conditions, or to refuse work as a protest if the employer is engaged in an unfair labor practice. You have a right to go on strike as long as the strike is legal. Illegal strikes are either those not authorized by your union or those that violate a no-strike clause in the union contract.

Workers who are out on strike do not get paid. If a worker is permanently replaced during a strike, he may become eligible for unemployment benefits. In some states striking workers are denied benefits for a specified period of time. These states then provide unemployment benefits if the striker is available for work.

The union will usually pay nominal strike benefits comparable to unemployment benefits. Workers can picket—hold signs and stage organized protests—as long as it is done peacefully and for no longer than 30 days. (You may be held personally responsible for any property you destroy while striking.) As a union member you agree not to cross a lawful picket line; and if you do, you can be fined by your union.

BACK TO WORK

Under the Taft-Hartley Act you are entitled to get your job back after a strike called to protest unfair labor practices, and your employer must dismiss any replacements he hired. But if the strike was for a wage increase, you are not automatically entitled to your job when the strike is over, although you are entitled to be placed on a preferential hiring list. Despite this law, many union contracts have a clause requiring employers to dismiss replacements after a strike, no matter what its cause.

If you are a member of a union, it is up to you to find out what your benefits are and how to obtain them. Ask your union representative or shop steward to answer your questions. You can also get a copy of your collective bargaining agreement to see exactly what benefits you deserve.

MUST YOU JOIN A UNION?

The union's relationship to workers varies from place to place, the main differences being whether or not an employee must join a union or pay dues. Nearly half the states have right-to-work laws making it illegal to require an employee to join a union. Your state's department of labor will know which of these four types of shops are legal in your state:

1. Open shop. This type of union shop is legal in every state. It makes union membership completely voluntary. The employee is not required to pay dues, and the union must represent all workers, members or not, who are part of the collective agreement.

2. Agency shop. In an agency shop, workers can choose whether or not to join a union, but they must pay union dues either way. Employees who decline membership do not have to follow the union's orders. In some states, agency shops are illegal.

3. Union shop. In a union shop, all workers must pay dues and join a union within a specified period, usually 30 days after being hired. Union shops are illegal in almost half the states, but where they are legal, they are quite common.

4. Closed shop. Like an agency shop, a closed shop requires an employee to join the union, in this case before being hired. Closed shops are against federal law, prohibited by the Landrum-Griffith Act.

WORKING FOR GOVERNMENT

If you work for government—federal, state, or local—you should know how the laws relating to public employers differ from those that apply to private industry.

What You need for a Civil Service Job

Not everyone is eligible for most civil service jobs. Requirements usually include:

1. You must owe your allegiance to the United States. When you apply for an exam you have to fill out a detailed questionnaire that tries to determine, among other things, your loyalty to the government. Evidence of disloyalty to the American form of government, such as your belonging to certain organizations, could disqualify you from jobs that involve national security.

2. Your private life and history must be satisfactory. Grounds for disqualification include making false statements in your application, excessive use of alcohol, and various kinds of "immoral conduct."

3. You must meet mental or physical fitness requirements for certain jobs.

4. If two members of your family living in your household work for the federal service, you are ineligible. (This stricture is waived for veterans.)

5. With few exceptions, you cannot be an employee of any state, municipality, or territory and also serve in the federal employ at the same time.

Who Is a Civil Servant?

Nonmilitary employees of national, state, and local governments who are responsible for day-to-day operations are called "civil servants." Police officers, firefighters, public-school teachers, administrative assistants to elected officials, and state hospital employees are all part of the civil service. The civil service system refers to the manner in which these government employees are hired, fired, paid, and promoted.

The Office of Personnel Management (OPM) is responsible for recruiting and managing federal employees, and requires all applicants for government jobs to take an exam to prove their qualifications. The Merit Systems Protection Board is responsible for safeguarding the rights of federal workers. Most states have civil service systems modeled after the federal one. In general, people who work for government—local, state, or federal—have better job protection than those in private industry because of the legislation designed to protect their rights. Once hired, civil servants can be fired only if they do not adequately perform their work.

The U.S. Supreme Court has held that only policymakers, managers, and those who give advice to elected officials can be dismissed when one party replaces another. For example, workers who are in support positions or whose day-to-day activities are unaffected by their political affiliation cannot be fired simply because another party gains political power.

GOVERNMENT HIRING AND FIRING PRACTICES

A number of laws require government contractors and subcontractors to take affirmative action in hiring, to assure veterans, the disabled, women, and minorities equal employment opportunities with the government. (See also "Discrimination," page 253.) Strict guidelines, regulated by the Office of Federal Contract Compliance Programs (OFCCP) have been laid out regarding these affirmative action policies, which specify how employers must advertise job openings and the type of notice they must give unions and employment services. These government employers also have written policies detailing the plan and must follow them to the letter.

Your Rights in the Military

The Uniform Code of Military Justice of 1950 (UCMJ) sets forth procedures that must be followed by all branches of the armed services and sets penalties for violations. The military therefore has its own customs, behavior codes, and even its own laws and courts.

Minor charges brought against a member of the military are usually dealt with by the unit's commanding officer, who hears evidence and then determines guilt and imposes punishment. For more serious offenses, a military member may face a trial conducted by a court-martial—a military court used to try military offenses.

Defendants in a court-martial do not have the right to a jury trial; cases are generally decided by one to five military officers. Otherwise, defendants are entitled to the same basic rights as civilian defendants in trials: the right to legal counsel, to call witnesses, and to cross-examine accusers. There is also a U.S.

Your Rights as a Government Employee

Rules covering federal employment are relatively uniform, but the rules vary widely among state and local jurisdictions, reflecting regional, cultural, and economic variations. Nevertheless, it is possible to give some general guidelines regarding the rights of government employees:

• **No strikes.** Government employees may join a union but may not participate in labor strikes (unless a collective bargaining or other agreement specifically gives them that right) because their work involves public welfare and safety.

• **Access to personnel files.** Federal government employees and government employees in states that have record-access laws have the right to see their personnel files, make copies of documents in them, and dispute any information.

• **No polygraph protection.** Employees of federal, state, and local governments are not covered by the Polygraph Protection Act. They can be required to take a lie detector test and are not protected from being disciplined because of the results.

• **Pension fund participation.** Federal government employees can participate in the Thrift Savings Fund, which is similar to the 401 (k) plan available to private-industry employees.

• **No Social Security tax.** Federal workers hired before 1984 are covered by the Civil Service Retirement System and do not have to pay Social Security taxes.

• **No political campaigning.** The Hatch Act of 1939 prohibits almost all employees in the federal executive service and state and local employees who work for agencies that receive federal funds from "taking an active part in political management or in political campaigns." Specifically such employees cannot participate directly in any partisan campaigning or fund-raising. For example, a federal employee cannot take part in a campaign to elect a Democratic mayor, but can campaign for a non-partisan issue, such as the Clean Water Act. Federal employees cannot, however, be prevented from political expression in the form of free speech or association.

• **Notification of dismissal.** A government employee must be notified of any charges against him at least 30 days before a proposed dismissal, allowing the employee a chance to demonstrate acceptable performance before being removed from his position. The employee may also appeal his dismissal afterward to the Merit Systems Protection Board.

Court of Military Appeals, the decisions of which are final.

Freedom of expression is limited in the military. Members may vote, attend political rallies, and even join a political club, but may not wear their uniforms to any such event. They cannot seek election, campaign for a candidate, or speak at political rallies. The matter of the rights of homosexuals in the military is a controversial one and is in flux; in general, however, the rights of homosexuals are less protected by military regulations than by civilian law.

Veterans' Benefits

Today, more than 27 million former servicemen and women and more than 46 million of their dependents are eligible for some kind of veteran's benefits. (Almost every veteran with an honorable or general discharge is eligible for veteran's benefits.) The Department of Veterans Affairs is in business to administer a wide variety of programs created and funded by the federal government. The Veterans Administration, the operating arm of the department, runs the various federal programs that help veterans with everything from health care to education to burial benefits.

The VA's major focus, however, is the delivery of quality medical care for all eligible veterans. It does so through a nationwide system of hospitals geared to veterans' needs—from traditional hospital and surgical procedures to outpatient services, mental health, and dentistry. While services are offered to all veterans, priority is given to those whose illnesses or disabilities are service-related. The VA also gives priority to low-income veterans. If a veteran's income is not considered low, he may have to pay an amount for hospital care that is equal to co-payment under Medicare.

LEGISLATION TO AID VETERANS

The Vietnam Veterans Readjustment Assistance Act of 1974 and the Veterans Reemployment Act protect men and women who serve in the armed forces from losing their jobs upon returning from duty. This includes members of the National Guard and reservists.

A returning military member must be reinstated within 90 days, as long as the job he worked in prior to serving was not a temporary position, he was away for less than four years, and discharge was honorable. Leave to serve in the military is without pay, and an employer is not required to pay health benefits to military members on leave. An employer cannot require an employee to use vacation time to serve military time and cannot penalize the employee in pension-vesting or seniority.

VA Benefits

The Department of Veterans Affairs offers a cornucopia of veteran's benefits. Here is a selection of them:

✔ *Insurance.* Military personnel on active duty are automatically enrolled in a group life insurance program. They may buy low-cost group insurance from the VA after discharge.

✔ *Medical care.* Institutional long-term and short-term care programs, including home and nursing-home care, are available in veteran's hospitals, especially for disabled and low-income veterans.

✔ *Mental health care.* Hospital inpatient programs and extensive outpatient programs offer help ranging from counseling to treatment for post-traumatic stress disorder to programs for mentally ill veterans who are homeless.

✔ *State programs.* These often duplicate federal services. Some states employ special counselors who help veterans cut through red tape to receive the maximum benefits they are entitled to under the law.

✔ *Burial.* Any veteran is entitled to burial in a U.S. military cemetery, with benefits including an American flag and a headstone.

✔ *Loans.* Veterans and certain surviving spouses may be eligible for special VA-guaranteed housing loans, to buy or build a home, or to repair, improve, or alter existing property.

SMALL BUSINESSES

Big corporations dominate the economic skyline, but millions of Americans work in small businesses, and the law protects their rights in many ways.

What Is a "Small Business"?

The Small Business Administration defines a small business as a company with 500 employees or less; yet the National Federation of Independent Businesses, which boasts a membership of 600,000 companies, says that among its membership the average independently owned business has only seven employees. Thus, by definition, a small business can run the gamut from a flourishing computer software manufacturer with large offices in five countries to a jewelry design firm that has only one employee—the jewelry designer.

Another way of thinking of a small business is as an independently owned and operated firm that is not considered a dominant force in its particular area of commerce. The reason small businesses have been singled out for consideration by the government is that the policy of the United States historically has been to encourage, assist, and protect such independent entrepreneurial enterprises. To that end, Congress established the Small Business Administration in 1953, its purpose being to aid small businesses in a number of ways. (See also "How the SBA Does Its Job," at right.)

Employee Rights and Benefits

Because several federal laws apply only to companies with a certain minimum number of employees, some workers fear that small businesses offer less legal protection for employees than large corporations. It is true that many federal laws come into effect only if a company employs a minimum number of people, including the Age Discrimination in Employment Act (at least 15 employees), the Americans with Disabilities Act (at least 25 employees), the Civil Rights Act of 1964 (at least 15 employees), the Family Medical Leave Act (at least 50 employees), and COBRA (at least 20 employees). However, many individual state laws that address the same issues demand that all companies, regardless of size, comply with the tenets of these laws.

In addition, many of the most compelling federal employ-

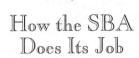

How the SBA Does Its Job

The Small Business Administration was created by the Small Business Act of 1953 with the goal of protecting, counseling, and promoting the interests of small businesses. Specifically, it ensures that small companies receive a fair portion of government contracts, subcontracts, and property. It make loans to small companies, or offers incentives to banks or other investment firms that back small business.

The SBA also provides extra assistance to businesses in areas that have been hit by economic disasters such as floods, hurricanes, and earthquakes. It also encourages businesses owned by or concerned with minorities, women, or handicapped persons; and helps small-business owners cope with new or complex laws concerning the environment, energy, health and safety, and employee benefits.

To find the number of the SBA regional office nearest you, call toll-free: (800) U-ASK-SBA, or write to the Small Business Administration, Washington Office Center, 409 Third Street, SW, Washington, D.C. 20024.

The Worthy 401 (k) : An Easy Step Toward Retirement

If you own a small business that is currently unable to provide a pension plan for your employees, consider establishing a 401 (k) plan. It may not be as difficult as you think, and can be advantageous to both you and your employees. Keep the following in mind:

✔ *Inexpensive.* These plans are inexpensive to originate, costing only about $2,500.

✔ *Uncomplicated.* Funding for the plan can come entirely from deductions from employee salaries and therefore cost the business nothing.

✔ *Growth potential.* As your business grows, you can elect to match a percentage of employee contributions, providing an attractive benefit to your employees and a tax deduction for the firm.

✔ *Personal benefit.* If you contribute to the plan yourself, you will give yourself a personal tax deduction and an added retirement investment.

ment laws apply to all companies, no matter how large or how small. These include the Fair Labor Standards Act, the Equal Pay Act, the Immigration Reform and Control Act, the Occupational Safety and Health Act (OSHA), and the Labor Management Relations Act.

Even if your company employs only two people—you and your boss—the boss is required by law to pay you the minimum wage plus overtime if you work more than 40 hours in a given week; to provide a safe working environment; to refrain from discriminating against you in equality of pay because of your gender, to make certain that you are eligible for work by immigration standards, and to permit you to join a union.

By law, certain benefits are mandated and assured by federal or state government, including Social Security, workers' compensation, and unemployment insurance. These benefits, too, must be provided to all employees, however small the company. (See also "Employee Benefits," page 247.)

WHEN BENEFITS ARE LIMITED

It is undoubtedly true that many fringe benefits are provided only at the discretion of the company, including life insurance, pension plans, profit-sharing, paid vacation and sick days, and, of course, health insurance. As much as they might wish, many small-business owners simply cannot afford to foot the bill for these extra benefits.

So it is true that employees in small businesses may get fewer perks and less luxurious fringe benefits than their counterparts in Fortune 500 companies. Yet other considerations, such as the higher odds for promotion, greater flexibility, more relaxed atmosphere, and congenial working conditions offered by a small company may more than make up for the fewer monetary benefits available.

As an employee, you certainly have the right to suggest to your employer that it could be beneficial to look into group health insurance plans that may be offered by professional societies with which your business is affiliated. Or, you can point out to your employer that a 401 (k) plan costs very little to start, and can provide benefits both for employer and employees. (See "The Worthy 401 (k): An Easy Step Toward Retirement," at left; see also YOUR MONEY, page 357.)

As an employer, you do not have to provide employee benefits that are not mandated by law, but you should look into the options carefully. You may discover that providing "fringe benefits" produces rewards that justify the cost. Starting a 401 (k) is an easy first step. Setting up a pension plan that meets certain ERISA requirements, for example, will entitle you to a number of specific tax benefits and will make your enterprise more appealing to employees.

STARTING A BUSINESS

If the entrepreneurial spirit spurs you to set up your own business, you will need to know how the law affects you, and when to seek professional help.

Becoming an Entrepreneur

Becoming your own boss may be part of the American dream, but running a business can also keep you awake nights. Your efforts as a small-business owner may be highly rewarded, but along the way, major decisions, petty details, money worries, and, all too often, legal problems may well plunge you in over your head.

Even before you devise your creative and marketing plans for a new business, you need to consider some personal issues. For example, are you a risk-taker or a conservative? Do you have personal funds to support you while your business grows or to lose if your business fails? Are you a workaholic, prepared to spend most of your days and nights working? Do you have a family that takes your attention away from your business? And, finally, how much experience do you have, particularly in this business?

The answers to these questions should clarify your goals, and give you an idea of how much money you will need to borrow, for instance, and, indeed, how much you may be able to borrow, given your experience and credit. Your responses will also tell you how fast and how far you can expect to take your fledgling venture.

FORMING A PROFESSIONAL TEAM

Every business presents a different set of considerations for legal interpretation. What's more, laws vary from state to state and from locality to locality. Despite some initial expense, it will save you time, stress, and probably money if you form a "professional team" to provide advice: a banker, an insurance broker, an accountant, and a lawyer. (See also "Help for Small Businesses," at right.) In fact, some experts believe that if you cannot afford such professional help, you cannot afford to go into business at all!

You can finance your business in many ways—from getting a simple personal loan from a bank or other financial institution, a family member, or a friend; to selling ownership in your business (equity financing), or securing a business loan (debt financing). However you get the necessary start-up funds, all methods have legal ramifications, particularly equity financing

The Legal Entity of Your Business

When you are considering creating your own business, you must carefully consider the sort of entity you wish to establish to ensure the greatest success. For a business, three types of organizations are legally viable: the sole proprietorship, the partnership, and the corporation.

SOLE PROPRIETORSHIP

• **Description.** This is a business with one owner who makes all business decisions. Few legal formalities are required. Some localities require a license for certain businesses (such as a liquor license) or registration if you are doing business in a name other than your own. Some localities also charge an unincorporated business tax. You must pay your own Social Security tax (which is paid through a self-employment tax), and make periodic estimated tax payments on income from your business. All income or loss, which includes deductions for business expenses, belongs to you.

• **Employees.** If you employ full-time workers, you must supply them with W-2 forms, and you must withhold federal and state income tax, Social Security tax (FICA), and Medicare tax from their wages, and deposit it with the government. You must also pay unemployment insurance as well as a Social Security tax on behalf of your employees. Your state may have requirements as well.

• **Liability.** The sole proprietor is personally liable for all the debts of the business, including loans, defective products, and employee accidents.

PARTNERSHIP

• **Description.** A general partnership is an association of two or more persons as co-owners who contribute money or property to form a business for profit. No legal contractual agreement is required by law, but certain state laws establish rules for partnerships when its members do not have a written agreement. Each partner has an equal say in managing the business unless authority is given, in writing, to a particular partner. The partnership must apply for a federal employer identification number through the IRS. The partnership must file an annual federal income tax return (Form 1065), but the business itself is not taxed. Instead its net income (or loss) is attributed (although not necessarily distributed) directly among the partners in proportion to their investment; they report the profit or loss on their own tax returns (Schedule E, Form 1040.)

• **Employees.** If the partnership employs full-time workers, it must withhold income taxes and FICA from wages and pay unemployment insurance and matching Social Security taxes, Medicare deductions, and any state taxes.

• **Liability.** Whatever property each partner contributes to the partnership becomes the property of the partnership as a whole, and is used to pay the costs of the business. If the partnership assets are exhausted, each partner is liable for the debts incurred by the business. In a "limited partnership," a limited partner's liability is limited to the amount of money or property he contributed to the partnership, but he has no rights regarding corporate management.

CORPORATION

• **Description.** A corporation, the most complex business organization, is formed by a group of investors and has rights and liabilities separate from the individuals involved. A corporation is created legally through a charter granted by the state, and those who hold shares are stockholders. The investment in shares is used to buy property and equipment to conduct business. If the corporation makes money, the profits are paid to the stockholders either in dividends or in reinvestment in the company, making the stockholders' original stock more valuable. If the company loses money, the stock of the owners becomes less valuable, but the personal assets of the owners/investors are protected from failure of the venture. A corporation must pay taxes on its income and must file its own tax returns. Stockholders are individually taxed on their corporate dividends or profits. (See also "Is an "S" Corporation Right for You?," page 284.)

• **Employees.** The corporation must withhold federal and state income tax and FICA from its employees' wages, take Medicare deductions, and pay unemployment insurance and matching FICA. States may have other requirements.

• **Liability.** A chief characteristic of the corporation is that the stockholders (owners) are liable only for the amount they have invested in the corporation. Corporation stockholders are not personally liable for the corporation's debt; creditors cannot go after stockholders in ordinary circumstances. If a corporation has trouble securing a loan, however, stockholders may be asked by a lender to guarantee the corporation's loans and accounts payable, and in some states, stockholders may be personally liable for unpaid wages of employees, other failures to follow the law, or gross misconduct.

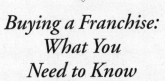

and debt financing, which are subject to complex laws and regulations. Work closely with a lawyer who understands financial and corporate law.

Depending on the kind of business you wish to start, you may want to buy an existing business or a franchise. An existing business or franchise can be less risky because it has a track record and, especially with regard to a strong franchise, can reduce the impact of sole financial responsibility.

Finally, how you decide to fund your business will have a direct impact on the sort of entity you wish to create: a sole proprietorship, a partnership, or a corporation. (See also "The Legal Entity of Your Business," page 282.)

STARTING UP

In the early days of getting your business going, you will be concerned with a host of matters, including setting up bank accounts, getting insurance, hiring employees, and planning how to market your product or service. You must check federal, state, and local requirements for all licenses, permits, and tax issues. You must pay close attention to insurance to protect yourself and your business. You will probably need to establish company policy with regard to personnel, including salaries and benefits.

The list of your company's needs depends upon the kind of business you are starting, where you are setting it up, and how large it is. Depending upon the nature of your business, you will be concerned with labor law, tax law, environmental concerns, consumer protection, credit law, commercial practices (such as distribution of goods under the Uniform Commercial Code and international trade laws), antitrust laws, credit laws, and the intricacies of finance.

Buying a Franchise

A franchise is a license or permit that allows you to operate a business that sells a particular product or service, such as a retail clothing outlet, a fast-food restaurant, a gas station, or a temporary employment agency. The basic franchise business is created and developed by the franchiser, and you, the franchisee, are permitted to sell the product or service for a fee or royalties, and sometimes additional costs such as rent and equipment leasing fees.

A franchise allows you to start and run your business with less risk than if you started from scratch, but it also reduces your potential profit, since you will have to share it with the franchiser. It also reduces your autonomy and therefore your ability to develop the business in ways you might like.

Buying a Franchise: What You Need to Know

If you are thinking seriously about buying a franchise, the first thing to do is see a lawyer. Here are some other useful steps to take:

✔ *Study the disclosure document.* Under FTC rules, a franchise seller must give you a full-disclosure document showing all pertinent details of the franchise operation. Analyze it very carefully.

✔ *Shop around.* If there are several different franchises in your area that deal in the kind of product or service you are interested in, ask for disclosure documents from them and compare offerings.

✔ *Talk to current owners.* The disclosure document must list others who currently operate the franchise. Interview them and try to verify the franchiser's earnings claims.

✔ *Check on inheritance rights.* Some franchisers refuse to pass the franchise on to the spouse even if he or she has been working at the place and is well qualified to run it.

✔ *Get professional advice.* Write to the International Franchise Association (for their address and phone number, see RESOURCES, page 493.) For general information, write the Federal Trade Commission, Sixth & Pennsylvania Avenue NW, Washington, D.C. 20580.

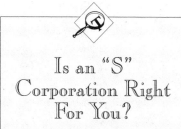

Is an "S" Corporation Right For You?

If you and several others are thinking of starting a small business in partnership, you might consider setting it up as a Chapter S Corporation. This is a hybrid business entity that combines some of the advantages of a corporation with those of a partnership.

As in a true corporation, the shareholders in an S Corporation are not personally liable or responsible for corporate losses beyond their original contribution. Yet the business is taxed like a partnership because the profits (and losses) from an S Corporation are not distributed as dividends, but are passed directly to the owners, or shareholders, who have to pay personal income taxes on them.

This arrangement can be very beneficial to a small business. Its profits are taxed only once, since corporate dividends are not issued and therefore are not taxed. Also, corporate profits accrue directly to owners and can be offset by other losses.

To form an S Corporation, you must file Form 2553 with the Internal Revenue Service. The corporation must be based in the United States and may issue only one class of stock. It may have no more than 35 shareholders, which can include individuals, married couples, estates, and certain types of trusts, but may not include partnerships, other corporations, or investors who do not reside in the United States.

WHAT KIND OF FRANCHISE?

There are three basic types of franchises, which vary according to the amount of control exerted by the franchiser:

- **A turnkey operation.** The franchiser exerts full control over the business. In other words, all you do is "turn the key and open the door" of your new business. With a turnkey operation, the franchiser builds the outlet, furnishes it, hires the employees, and dictates all sales and marketing decisions.
- **Trade-name franchise.** The franchiser permits the franchisee the exclusive right to sell a product manufactured by the franchiser in a particular area. The franchisee operates according to specified guidelines.
- **Business-format franchise.** The franchiser dictates quality and sometimes marketing techniques, but the franchisee produces an outlet and manufactures (or cooks, as with a fast-food chain) and sells the goods.

Franchises are not risk-free business. Just because a business works well in one location under certain conditions does not guarantee it will be successful everywhere. Even well-known fast-food and retail franchises go under. Also, buying a franchise can be costly and complicated. Despite stringent laws, fast-buck artists can con the unwary.

The 1979 Franchise Disclosure Law requires a franchiser to make available certain information about the franchise, including costs, expenses, contractual obligations if any, the owner's name, and data on the history of the franchise. This information is due 10 days before you sign a contract with a franchiser. Go over the information carefully with your lawyer. Understand the restrictions the franchiser imposes, and make sure any promises are in writing.

KEEP CLEAR OF "SHIPS"

Odds for success with a franchise are better than average for a new business owner because you are dealing with a known quantity. Franchises offer a good way for inexperienced entrepreneurs to start out on their own. But if the franchiser fails to keep its end of the bargain, you may have to go to court to sue for breach of contract. If the franchiser is bankrupt, you may not get all your money back. As with any business, there are always risks. Do your homework and know what they are before you begin.

Another word of advice: Be wary of business opportunities that sound like franchises but are called "distributorships" or "dealerships." Unscrupulous entrepreneurs may use these terms to avoid the strict disclosure requirements imposed by the Franchise Disclosure Rule.

Working at Home

Corporate downsizing and technological developments have combined to place many working Americans in a new venue: their homes.

On Someone Else's Payroll

More and more employers are discovering that having some employees work at home is good business. Eliminating a worker's daily commute not only saves time, but it can also increase productivity and improve morale (to say nothing of reducing pollution and traffic congestion).

"Telecommuting," a term recently introduced into the workplace vocabulary, refers to employees who work somewhere other than the workplace and communicate via cellular telephones, computers and modems, pagers, and fax machines. These devices can move information virtually instantaneously, thereby cutting office expenses and in many cases helping meet the changing needs of an employee's lifestyle.

If your employer gives you the option of working at home, ask whether it is really the best option for you. If you have children at home, you may want to be near them. On the other hand, you may be subject to a number of distractions at home that you would not be at the office. You may be the kind of person who works best with direct supervision or who needs constant contact with co-workers or customers on a daily basis. Although working at home may give you a great deal of flexibility, it can be isolating as well.

Be aware of the fact that if you are an employee (rather than an independent contractor), you are permitted to deduct the cost of a home office only if the office itself is created or used for your employer's benefit. If you are working at home solely for your own convenience, your home-office costs are not deductible.

Independent Contractors

Independent contractors, or freelance workers, constitute one of the fastest-growing segments of the economy. They are people who own their own businesses and who contract to do specific jobs for other individuals or companies. This kind of arrangement, while freeing you from the constraints of the 9-to-5 routine, also brings responsibilities.

123...

EMPLOYEE OR INDEPENDENT CONTRACTOR?

The difference between an employee and an independent contractor can be a fine line. If you work odd hours or not full time, your employer might try to classify you as a freelancer rather than as an employee in order to avoid paying for your benefits, such as Social Security taxes and workers' compensation insurance. But if you answer yes to more than one or two of the following questions, chances are you are an employee, not a freelancer.

1. Are you trained or instructed how to do your job by the employer?

2. Do you have to perform the job in person, on the company premises, at certain hours?

3. Do you have an ongoing work relationship, rather than being hired on a job-by-job basis, as needed?

4. Do you work for one company only?

5. Are you paid hourly or weekly instead of by the job?

6. Are you reimbursed for business expenses instead of paying for them yourself?

7. Does the company provide the tools necessary to complete the job?

As an independent contractor you must set your own work hours and arrange for a place to work that is properly insured, licensed, and zoned for the work you are doing. You will have to keep careful records, bill your clients, file taxes for your business, and be very careful about paying Social Security taxes on the money you earn.

Other distinguishing marks identify you as an independent contractor as opposed to a full employee. (See "Employee or Independent Contractor?" at left.) These distinctions are important, because it is not uncommon for an employer to try to hire independent contractors to do work that a regular employee used to do. Firms do not have to pay freelancers such benefits as Social Security, unemployment insurance, workers' compensation, or health and life insurance. Nor are they bound by long-term agreements. Therefore the temptation to call an employee an independent contractor is great, but the IRS takes a dim view of this practice. An employer who falsely characterizes employees as independent contractors can be subject to heavy fines.

ARE YOU DEDUCTIBLE?

The most important distinction, however, is that you, as an independent contractor, are in charge of the work you do and are responsible for its content. That can have legal ramifications. When an employee makes a mistake, the company is responsible and pays the penalty or the compensation. The employee may get fired for the mistake, but he is rarely held legally responsible for it. Independent contractors, however, can be named as codefendants in a damage suit if they are responsible for a shoddy product. This is why a carefully drawn contract can be so important in safeguarding your work.

Independent contractors usually work at home or at a location away from the employer's workplace. In recent years the IRS has become stricter in what it allows independent contractors to deduct for home offices on their tax returns. Today a home office must be a legitimate place of business where you earn more than fifty percent of your income. Your home "office" must be a separate room that is your principal place of business, and it must be used only for that purpose.

RETIREMENT PLANS

Regardless of where you work, if you are self-employed you must remember that you are responsible for putting aside money for your retirement. Several kinds of Keogh plans are available into which you can put tax-deferred savings, and a SEP/IRA (Simplified Employee Pension/Individual Retirement Account) also offers an easy way to put your self-employed earnings aside for the future. (See YOUR MONEY, page 357.)

YOUR MONEY

Handling your income, credit, investments, and estate affects every aspect of your life—so it pays to know your rights

BANKING ■ BORROWING MONEY ■ CREDIT CARDS ■ CREDIT BUREAUS ■ DEALING WITH DEBT ■ LIFE INSURANCE ■ INVESTING YOUR MONEY ■ INCOME TAXES ■ SOCIAL SECURITY ISSUES ■ SAVING FOR RETIREMENT ■ ■ WILLS AND ESTATES

BANKING

The basics of banking are changing daily—and you need to know how to use these services to your best advantage.

Choosing the Best Bank Account

What services do you need from a bank? For most people, the answer is simple. You need a checking account to pay bills and a savings account where your money can grow, even if only very slowly, or be kept safe for a rainy day. But finding the best deal in a bank account is no longer a simple process. The deregulation of banks in the 1980's has led to a bewildering variety of banking services. Some types of checking accounts, called NOW accounts, pay interest. Some types of savings accounts, such as money market deposit accounts, offer check-writing privileges. Today both checking and savings accounts come laden with an array of fees, maintenance charges, and minimum-balance requirements. In this confusing environment, be prepared to shop around for the best arrangement for your day-to-day money transactions.

When you shop for a bank, first of all make sure that it offers insurance from the Federal Deposit Insurance Corporation (FDIC) for your deposits. Among FDIC-insured banks, you can choose from the following:

- Commercial banks, which are chartered by either a state government or the federal government, and which have long offered a wide range of services, including savings and checking accounts.
- Savings and loan (S&L) institutions, which before deregulation provided mainly savings plans and mortgage loans and now also offer savings and checking accounts.
- Credit unions, which are nonprofit financial cooperatives that offer many of the services of a commercial bank. (See "Credit Unions: A Good Banking Alternative," page 294.)

THE RIGHT CHECKING ACCOUNT

Though the checking accounts that banks offer go by many different names, they can be divided into two main types: those that pay interest and those that do not. The best type for you will probably depend on your answer to this question: What is the lowest average balance you are going to be able to leave on deposit every month?

To earn interest, banks usually require a minimum balance of at least $1,000, and if your balance falls below that amount, you must pay a fee. Thus, if your balance is usually below $1,000, you should choose a checking account that pays no interest. However, even if you are able to keep a balance that meets the minimum for an interest-bearing checking account, find out from the bank's customer-service representative precisely how that minimum balance is figured.

The more favorable way for consumers is the "average-daily-balance" method, by which the bank takes the amount you have in your account each day and averages it across the entire month. Less favorable to you is the "low-balance" method, by which a bank considers only the lowest balance in your account for the month. For example, if you kept $2,500 on deposit for 30 days, but you withdrew all of it on the 31st, the bank would figure your interest based on a zero balance for the month. Not only would you earn no interest, you would pay a fee for falling below the minimum balance.

Bankers are just like anybody else, except richer.

OGDEN NASH
I Have It on
Good Authority

SMART BANKING STRATEGIES

Banking experts predict that bank fees will only continue to escalate. To hold down the costs of maintaining your checking account, try these "defensive-banking" strategies.

If you currently have a low-interest savings account with a stable balance, and a non-interest-paying checking account, consider asking your bank to link your savings and checking accounts into a single account. You may then have enough

---

How Fast Should Your Checks Clear?

By federal law, banks cannot place excessive holds on your deposited checks. The 1987 Expedited Funds Availability Act requires banks to clear your checks according to deadlines based on the type of check and its place of origin. Here is a guide to the maximum time limits allowed:

• **After one business day.** Federal, state, and local government checks; checks drawn on the same bank; cashier's checks; certified checks; postal money orders; electronic payments (direct deposit of a regular paycheck); the first $100 of any check.

• **After two business days.** All local checks, generally meaning those drawn on banks in the same city and often the same state, deposited with a teller in the bank. All cash, cashier's checks, and state and local government checks deposited into a bank's own ATM before noon.

• **After three business days.** Local checks fed into the bank's ATM machines before noon.

• **After five business days.** All nonlocal checks in the continental United States. (Banks in Hawaii, Alaska, the U.S. Virgin Islands, and Puerto Rico can take an extra business day to credit checks that do not originate inside their borders.)

• **After seven business days.** All deposits made before noon into ATM's not owned by your bank.

• **After 30 business days.** Funds from checks deposited into new accounts may not be available to you for the first 30 days after the account is opened. The same applies to checks for amounts greater than $5,000. If you are redepositing a check that has previously been returned, you may also encounter longer delays.

Beware of Checking-Account Scams

Crooks are using new ploys to gain access to your checking account. A typical scam involves a fraudulent telemarketer calling to say you have won a free prize. He asks you for the number of your checking account, claiming that the account information will help ensure that you "qualify" for the prize. Your answer to this request—or to any attempt to get such numbers as your credit card number or PIN code—should be a firm "no."

A crook armed with your name, address, and checking-account number can use the information fraudulently in a number of ways. He could initiate a "demand draft," which is processed like a check—but does not require your signature. Your bank would then debit your account, and you might not discover the loss until your next statement.

He could also change your home address on your line of credit and direct funds to his own address, cleaning you out without a trace. Or, again by changing your address, he could apply for a bank credit card in your name and go on a shopping spree.

To protect yourself, never give out checking-account information over the telephone unless you initiate the call or know the person who is calling. Report any unauthorized drafts on your account to your bank immediately.

money to qualify for an interest-paying checking account as well as assurance that your average daily balance will be stable.

Beware of "overdraft protection" programs that, though convenient, often prove to be very expensive. Overdraft protection is actually a line of credit that lets you write checks for more than you have in your account. If you exceed your balance, that amount is treated as a loan and you will be charged interest. In addition, some banks calculate overdrafts only in $100 increments, and if you are $150 short, the bank will charge you interest based on a $200 overdraft, even though you did not need that extra $50 that was deposited into your account.

If you do not routinely need your canceled checks, you may want to ask your bank to "truncate" your account. With a truncated account, you will receive only a monthly statement listing the checks you wrote, not the actual canceled checks. Because truncated accounts are cheaper to administer, banks will sometimes waive the monthly fee and minimum-balance requirements on them.

The High Cost of Saving

A bank savings account may seem like a good place to keep your money, but it may not be the most profitable. Although you have ready access to your cash, you will earn a low rate of interest on these accounts. When you earn so little on your money, inflation combined with an array of fees and penalties can eat into any money you accumulate. It can be a good idea, however, to keep some money in conventional savings accounts, so that you have some cash readily available in case of emergency. Also, if you link your savings account to your checking account, you may be able to avoid many expensive bank fees.

Depending on when and how you need to use your money, you should consider the following savings vehicles:

- **Savings accounts.** Old-fashioned passbook as well as newer "statement" savings accounts keep your money accessible , but they pay low interest rates. With passbook accounts, you take your passbook to the bank whenever you make a deposit or withdrawal, and the bank enters the transactions into your passbook. With the now more common statement accounts, the bank periodically (usually once a month) sends you a statement of your account's activity, and you pay a fee for the statement and your account activity. If you use the account regularly, your fee may be high, possibly exceeding the amount of interest you earn. Thus your savings could actually diminish.

■ **Money market accounts.** Although they're primarily savings accounts, these accounts allow limited check writing, usually three checks a month. If you write more, you usually pay a penalty. Banks require a minimum balance for these accounts and will apply a sizable fee if the balance falls below the minimum. Banks often claim they are paying "market rate" interest (usually higher than the rate of interest for regular savings accounts) on these accounts, but then apply that rate only to accounts with larger balances. Be sure to ask whether the interest applies to the entire balance.

■ **Certificates of deposit (CD's).** CD's require you to commit your money for a period of time ranging from six months to 10 years. CD's yield higher interest than savings accounts or money market accounts, but banks are allowed by law to exact a penalty (usually 180 days' interest) if you withdraw your money before the certificates have matured. Because banks are under no obligation to notify customers that their CD's are maturing, pay attention to the renewal policy in your CD contract. Some banks automatically "roll over" the money at the end of the term, locking you into a renewal rate you may not want, while others give you a grace period during which you can withdraw your funds without penalty.

It is important to remember that savings accounts, money market accounts, and certificates of deposit are not the best investment vehicles for long-term goals such as retirement income. However, bank savings accounts are probably the safest way to save money for a relatively short-term goal, such as a new car or the down payment on a house. Moreover, these savings vehicles are protected by federal law, and, as a result, although you may not earn as much, your investment is safe.

TRUTH IN SAVINGS

Banks used to advertise a complicated variety of interest-calculation methods. Most consumers who tried to compare one savings account with another found that they were comparing apples and oranges. Who could tell the difference between a "daily rate," an "average daily rate," or a "current rate"? Now, the Truth in Savings Act (TISA), enacted in 1993, obligates all banks, S&L's, and credit unions to state the interest rates they pay in the same way—as the "annual percentage yield," or APY. The annual percentage yield represents the amount of interest your principal would earn if you left it on deposit for one year, taking into account such variables as the interest rate and the bank's frequency of compounding it.

In addition, TISA requires that interest be paid for all the days you maintained the required balance. In the past, some banks would cancel an entire month's interest if your balance

Savers Beware: TISA Won't Always Protect You

The federal Truth in Savings Act (TISA) of 1993 eliminated many of the most confusing bank practices but still left room for banks to take advantage of unwary customers. Protect yourself by asking your bank's customer service representative the details about:

✔ *Interest crediting.* Banks still have the right to delay paying interest on your savings-account deposit until a deposited check clears. Bank only where you are paid interest from the day of your deposit.

✔ *Fees.* Some fees—such as the cost of certain transfers—are excluded from the list banks are required to give new customers. Make sure you know about all bank fees before opening an account.

✔ *"Free" checking accounts.* Banks have the right to sell "free checking" in ads even when the account may remain free for only a limited time, after which you must maintain a minimum balance to avoid future fees. Always confirm the terms and conditions of any account.

slipped below the minimum even once. Finally, TISA obligates banks to disclose in their promotional handouts the minimum balances, fees, and other conditions imposed on any savings vehicle. As a result, customers can now "comparison shop" for the safest and most productive accounts.

If a bank or savings and loan association fails to provide the information, it can be penalized. If a consumer suffers financial loss because of lack of disclosure, the financial institution is subject to being sued for damages and a fine.

Electronic Banking

By now most consumers take for granted the computer technology that enables banks to offer a variety of automated services, known as the electronic funds transfer (EFT) system. Whenever you use an automated teller machine (ATM) or arrange for a paycheck to be directly deposited into your account, you are tapping into

---

If Your Bank Makes a Mistake

It will probably happen to you someday: Your bank will make an error. Most errors are detected when you reconcile your monthly bank statement (the bank's version of your monthly transactions) with your checkbook (your own version of events). If you discover an error, double-check to make sure the error is not your own, then be prepared to take action:

• It is the policy at most banks to allow 30 to 60 days for customers to correct errors in their accounts. However, even if it has taken you longer than 60 days to discover and report your problem, you still maintain the right to insist that your bank resolve the error. In general, banks will respond positively to your demand.

• Call or visit the bank, find out the name of the bank's branch manager or customer service representative, and register your complaint with that person. Make a dated notation of your call or visit; record the branch manager's name and telephone number together with comments about the content of the conversation.

• Follow up in writing, addressing the letter to the branch manager or service representative with whom you dealt. In the letter, describe in detail what the problem is, and how and when you expect it to be resolved. For example, if the bank issued you an overdraft notice when you in fact had plenty of funds in your checking account, make it clear you want the overdraft penalties revoked and letters of apology sent immediately to the people to whom you wrote the checks that were returned because of the bank's mistake. (Don't forget to include names, addresses, and telephone numbers, if possible, of all the people involved.)

• Make a copy of the letter to keep in your own file, then send the letter to the bank by certified mail, return receipt requested.

• If the mistake involves any of the bank's automated services, such as a malfunctioning ATM, call the customer service representative of your bank immediately, or use a local ATM courtesy phone, then follow up in writing. Errors involving ATM machines are subject to rules of the Electronic Funds Transfer Act (EFTA). (See Electronic Banking, page 293.)

• If you are not satisfied by the bank's response to your problem, write to the Federal Reserve Board's Division of Consumer and Community Affairs, 20th and C Street NW, Washington, D.C. 20551. If the problem lies outside its jurisdiction, the office will refer you to the appropriate agency.

the EFT system. The EFT system offers consumers convenience and quick access to their money. But when errors occur in this system, they can wreak instant havoc—as more than 100,000 customers learned in 1994 when a bank mistakenly deducted a total of $15 million from their accounts in a single night.

When you bank electronically, be especially careful about monitoring your accounts. Errors may be hard to prove and may have serious consequences. For example, if you expect a loan payment to be automatically deducted from your account but the EFT system fails to transfer it, you could be charged a late fee; worse, your credit rating could be damaged. Your best

---

A Bank's Liability

PROBLEM
When Sheila tried to pay for a store purchase, she discovered her wallet was missing. She immediately called the police and also informed her bank that her ATM card had been stolen. In the meantime, the thief had withdrawn $500 from her account using the ATM card. The bank insisted that Sheila was liable for the $500 because, as it turned out, Sheila had written her personal identification number (PIN) on her ATM card.

ACTION
Sheila wrote to her bank's branch manager immediately, citing her rights under the Electronic Funds Transfer Act (EFTA). The regulation limits a consumer's liability to $50 if she reports a stolen card within two business days after discovering the error on a bank statement. This liability limit is based solely on the amount of time that has elapsed between discovery of the loss or theft and the reporting of it. No matter how an unauthorized user obtains the PIN, the liability limit still applies. So by law Sheila was covered, even if it was not smart of her to write her PIN on the card. When she got her new card, she memorized her PIN for her own protection.

---

defense is to keep accurate records of all electronic transactions and to reconcile your account statement with your own figures within a week after you receive it. If you find an error, quick action improves your chances of correcting it. Delay will make it harder to reclaim any lost interest, avoid bad-check charges, or rectify other mistakes resulting from the initial error.

Fortunately, the Electronic Funds Transfer Act (EFTA) of 1978 set up procedures for resolving errors that afford consumers a lot of protection. Specifically, the law provides that:

- If you report a lost or stolen ATM card within two business days after discovering the loss (even if it is on a bank statement), your liability for unauthorized transfers is limited to $50. If you report it between two and 60 days, and the bank can prove it could have stopped the unauthorized transfers

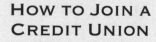

HOW TO JOIN A CREDIT UNION

Although most people join credit unions through their employers, you may be eligible to join on the basis of other criteria. These include:

1. Family ties. You may be able to join a credit union if your spouse, parent, child, or someone else in your immediate family belongs to one.

2. Common-interest groups. Groups with common religious, ethnic, or other unifying interests or ties have formed credit unions.

3. Neighborhood groups. Many communities have created credit unions based on local interests or even on zip codes.

4. Armed services. Most branches of the armed services, including the U.S. Army, U.S. Navy, and U.S. Marine Corps, have their own credit unions.

5. Academia. Students, alumni, professors, and other employees of some colleges and universities may join their school's credit union.

For the names of credit unions you may be eligible to join, write or call the Credit Union National Association, P.O. Box 431, Madison, Wis. 53701, (800) 356-9655, Ext. 4045.

had you informed it earlier, your liability increases to $500.

- If you notice an error on your bank statement or on an ATM receipt, you are required to notify the bank orally or in writing within 60 days.
- If you do not report an unauthorized transfer on your account within 60 days after the statement was mailed to you, you are completely liable for the amount withdrawn.
- If the bank asks you to put your complaint in writing and you do not, it does not have to re-credit your account.
- If unauthorized transfers are made with an ATM card that you never received, you are not liable and the bank must cover the loss.
- If the bank fails to complete its investigation of an error within 10 business days, it must provisionally re-credit your account for the disputed amount.
- When the bank completes its investigation, it must notify you in writing of the results.

Take advantage of these procedures whenever you think an error has been made. If you disagree with the decision, you can appeal to higher authorities within the bank or to state or federal bank regulators.

Credit Unions: A Good Banking Alternative

In annual surveys of consumer satisfaction with banking institutions, credit unions rank consistently at the top. A credit union is a not-for-profit financial cooperative that is both owned and operated by its members. Most people join through their place of employment, but you may also be eligible through some other affiliation.

Most credit unions offer both checking accounts (called "share draft" accounts) and savings accounts, and many of the larger ones also handle credit cards, payroll deductions, and loans. Because credit unions have lower operating costs, they are able to offer lower-cost loans and pay slightly higher rates for savings. Credit unions return part of their profits to members at the end of the fiscal year, usually in the form of a small dividend or as a rebate of loan interest.

Since the 1991 closing of 10 non-federally insured credit unions in Rhode Island, some consumers have questioned the safety of credit unions. Since then, however, many states have enacted laws requiring credit unions to be federally insured. Now more than 95 percent of credit unions are insured by the Share Insurance Fund of the National Credit Union Administration, which insures credit-union deposits just as the FDIC insures bank deposits.

If you are considering joining a credit union, make sure it carries federal deposit insurance. You will also want to make sure it is conveniently located, especially if you prefer to do your banking in person. Most credit unions have only one office. Furthermore, some credit unions offer only limited banking services, so be sure the one you are considering will be able to handle all your needs. For example, smaller credit unions may not be equipped to handle electronic fund transfers or may send out statements quarterly instead of monthly.

As with any banking institution, determine in advance all the rates, fees, and penalties that would apply to you. Since January 1995, credit unions have been held to the same disclosure laws as banks and savings and loan institutions under the federal Truth in Savings Act (TISA).

Is Your Money Safe?

As safe as money in the bank" may have been a popular phrase in the past, but as recent bank failures have shown, consumers need to know precisely how their deposits can be affected by bank failure and what they can do to protect their assets.

Most people—those with less than $100,000 in a federally insured institution—are fully covered if their bank fails. (See "Federal Protection for Your Money," page 296.) But some unpleasant surprises can await even customers of federally insured institutions. If a bank fails and then is taken over by another banking institution, customers could encounter any of these situations:

- **A credit dry-up.** The new bank has the right to cancel unused lines of credit, such as those that are backed by home equity loans.
- **Certificate-of-deposit rate changes.** The new bank has the right to lower interest rates on CD's to prevailing market rates. However, the new owner must notify you of any rate change within two weeks, and you have the right to withdraw your funds penalty-free if the rate has been changed.
- **Mortgages sold.** Like any bank, the acquiring bank has the right to sell your mortgage loan to another financial institution or mortgage-servicing company. Follow up with the new owner's customer service representative to ensure that your payments are being properly credited.

If your bank fails and is not taken over by another buyer, the FDIC steps in. Typically, the FDIC will pay off all deposits in full, with interest, to the day of closing. Usually this process

Reclaiming Lost Accounts

You can lose a bank account by doing nothing at all. For example, if your failed bank is acquired by another and you do not contact the acquiring institution within 18 months to perform some kind of transaction (such as a deposit or withdrawal), your funds will be considered dormant and, depending on local law, can revert to the state.

You can also lose an account to the state, even without a change of bank ownership, if your account has been dormant (no activity other than interest posting) for a certain period—in some states, as little as five years. Yet, no matter how much time has passed, you still own any unclaimed funds that are due you.

To collect the funds from a long-dormant or "lost" account, write to the state agency that took the funds. (Your bank will tell you which one to contact.) Include the name of the bank, the year the account was opened, your Social Security number, and your current and previous addresses. Once you prove ownership, the state will refund the money. Depending on your state's law, you may be entitled to interest as well.

takes less than three days after the bank's official closing.

If you have an outstanding loan, the FDIC will inform you where to send your future payments. If you have a loan that is delinquent and a checking or savings account at the same failed institution, the FDIC has the right to deduct the overdue amount from your accounts before returning your deposit.

Be aware that although the federal insurance programs guarantee the safety of your deposits, they do not necessarily guarantee that you will be able to withdraw your money on demand. Sometimes, if a bank has kept incomplete or inaccurate records, you will be required to provide proof of your own deposits. As a precaution, keep all recent bank statements and savings books in an accessible file.

OTHER SECURITY PRECAUTIONS

It is very difficult for the average consumer to tell if a bank is in trouble. Although some states issue ratings of banks' solvencies, researching the government and public sources can be costly and time-consuming for an individual customer. The simplest solution for most people is to bank with a federally insured institution.

If you still feel insecure, and if the possibility of being denied access to your cash for two or three days concerns you, consider one of these options: place an emergency cash fund at a second bank; take out a credit card that allows cash advances from another institution; or buy a savings bond that can be cashed at any savings institution.

Put not your trust in money, but put your money in trust.

OLIVER WENDELL HOLMES
The Autocrat of the Breakfast Table

Federal Protection for Your Money

Federal deposit insurance is the consumer's main defense against bank failure. The FDIC offers information about federal banking insurance on a toll-free telephone service. (See "Resources," page 493.) The following guidelines will help keep your money as safe as possible:

• Be sure that your banking institution is a member of either the Bank Insurance Fund of the Federal Deposit Insurance Corporation (FDIC), which protects commercial banks, or the Savings Association Insurance Fund (SAIF), which is administered by the FDIC and covers savings and loan associations and federal savings banks.

• If you bank with a credit union, make sure it is covered by the Share Insurance Fund (SIF) of the National Credit Union Administration (NCUA), which covers federal and state credit unions.

• Avoid putting your money in institutions covered only by a state-regulated insurance fund, which in some states have defaulted on their obligations.

• To find out whether an institution is protected by the FDIC or NCUA, look for prominently displayed advertising in the bank's lobby or ask the bank's customer service representative.

• Bear in mind that your accounts in a federally insured institution are covered up to a maximum of $100,000 per person, per bank. If your balance exceeds $100,000, the best protection is to open accounts in several banks insured by the FDIC, or to place funds in increments of less than $100,000 in the name of a different family member.

• Remember that mutual funds and various other investment products sold by banks are not covered by the FDIC.

BORROWING MONEY

Most of us need a loan occasionally—but since it costs money to borrow money, be sure you know how to get the best loan for the lowest price.

Choosing the Right Kind of Loan

Borrowing money can be a sensible way to achieve important life goals. Yet it is important to borrow for the right reasons, to make sure that the cost of a loan does not bog you down with a debt you cannot afford. The best reasons for taking out a loan are to buy something you truly need right away and could not otherwise afford, such as a house or car, or to buy something that profits you in the future, like a college education. If you consistently borrow money to pay for nonessentials like vacation trips or holiday gifts, you may put yourself in constant financial jeopardy without getting any lasting benefits.

When you take out a loan, you are, in effect, buying money from the lender. So you need to shop around for one as carefully as you would for any other major consumer item. Federal law does not set interest rates or other credit charges, but it does establish clear consumer rights to protect the borrower. The 1968 Truth in Lending Act (TILA) requires all creditors —banks, stores, car dealers, credit card companies, and finance companies—to state the cost of borrowing in clear, understandable language so that you can more easily compare costs. Most states have also enacted consumer credit-disclosure laws.

The two terms that TILA requires lenders to disclose to borrowers are the finance charge and the annual percentage rate (APR). The finance charge is the total dollar amount you pay to borrow money from a lender. It includes interest charges, compounding, and costs you pay up front, such as transaction fees. The APR is the interest rate you pay on a loan, expressed as an annual percentage. Many of the up-front fees you pay when you take out a loan are factored into the APR. Creditors who violate the Truth in Lending Act are subject to both civil and criminal penalties. A consumer may file suit against creditors who have misled them.

FINDING THE RIGHT LENDER

Many different kinds of establishments are in the business of lending money. Banks probably come first to mind. If you have dealt with a particular bank for at least five years, you probably should start your loan search there. Banks are more

---

Hidden Costs and Sneaky Add-ons

Lending institutions have many ways of charging for their services. Study the loan forms for the loan you are considering, and watch out for terms that are not advantageous to you:

✔ *Front-end load.* With this kind of installment loan— usually from a bank—you pay more of the interest cost in the early months than you do later. Should you decide to pay off your principal early, such a plan penalizes you because you will lose the extra interest you have paid. Look instead for loans that spread the interest evenly over every payment.

✔ *Prepayment penalty.* This clause means you must pay an extra fee if you repay your mortgage or other loan ahead of its due date. Since prepaying is often to your advantage financially, avoid a loan that comes with this restriction.

✔ *"Teaser" rate.* These are usually low rates—often highlighted in ads—that ratchet up after a certain period, such as three months. In a contract, this kind of lure is called the "initial loan rate." Be sure to ask when—and how much— the rate will go up.

willing to offer preferred rates on loans to long-standing customers.

Do you belong to a credit union? These not-for-profit financial cooperatives consistently offer their members loans that are two to three percentage points cheaper than the average rates of national banks and savings and loan institutions. Furthermore, while banks typically want to loan a minimum of at least several thousand dollars, credit unions will allow you to borrow a much smaller amount—sometimes as little as $100. (For more information, see also "Credit Unions: A Good Banking Alternative," page 294.)

Consumers with credit-rating problems often turn to finance companies, which are solely in the business of lending money to individuals or institutions. Finance companies usually charge higher interest rates than other lenders, and often penalize you if you pay off the loan early. Also, because finance companies do business with higher-risk borrowers, credit bureaus may look askance at anyone who has ever dealt with one.

A Glossary for Borrowers

Loans come in many different forms with a wide variety of terms and conditions that are described in a specific language full of unfamiliar words and phrases. Here are some common terms you are likely to encounter when negotiating a loan.

• **Adjustable rate.** The interest rate, also called a variable rate, that is raised or lowered periodically on the basis of a specified index (see below).

• **Annual percentage rate (APR).** The actual rate you pay on a loan over the course of a year. The APR is higher than the actual interest charged because it also factors in service fees as well as mortgage points.

• **Collateral.** Assets or property, such as a car, home, or certificate of deposit (CD), that you offer as security to back up a loan.

• **Finance charge.** The total cost of your borrowing, including interest and service fees. Finance-charge disclosures are required by the Truth in Lending Act.

• **Index.** A set standard, such as the prime rate given to banks, or the rate on one-year Treasury bills, against which interest rates for variable-rate loans are adjusted.

• **Points.** An up-front fee charged by a lender, separate from interest. A point equals one percent of the principal borrowed. For example, on a $100,000 mortgage loan, a charge of three points would equal $3,000.

• **Prime rate.** The interest rate banks charge their most creditworthy, income-producing customers, such as other banks and blue-chip corporations.

• **Principal.** This is the amount of money you have actually borrowed. What you owe the lender will be considerably more, depending on the interest charged, service fees, and other expenses.

• **Secured loan.** A loan guaranteed by collateral such as property or other assets. Mortgage loans and automobile loans are two common types. The lender can take back the collateral—that is, the house or the car—if the borrower does not make payments on time.

• **Unsecured loan.** Instead of collateral, the borrower pledges "full faith and credit" to repay the loan. If payments are not made, the lender can take legal action against the borrower. Credit card purchases and cash advances are common types of unsecured loans.

BORROWING FROM YOURSELF

Borrowing against your own resources can be a quick and convenient loan source. Often the cheapest loans are of the home-equity variety, when you borrow against the equity built up in your house.

Your own retirement plan can be a good loan source, so check to see if your plan permits loans. Most of the defined-contribution plans, including 401 (k), 403 (b), and company profit-sharing plans, allow participants to borrow from them. But the loans usually must be repaid within a designated period of time, or immediately if you leave your job.

You can use an independent retirement account (IRA) as a no-interest loan for short periods. If you replace the money within 60 days after the date of withdrawal, you do not have to pay the usual 10 percent penalty for early withdrawal, nor do you pay income tax on the amount withdrawn. You have this option only once a year per each IRA account. It is not a good idea if your IRA is in long-term certificates of deposit: You will be subject to a substantial early-withdrawal penalty for cashing in CD's before they mature.

Your savings account offers still another loan option. You pledge your savings account or CD as collateral, and the bank lends you money at a rate pegged to what your savings are earning. But be forewarned: The rate banks charge for loans secured by savings is often two to four percentage points higher than the rate they pay on your savings.

Most people do not think of the overdraft privileges on their checking account as a loan source, but in fact every time you overdraw your account and trigger the credit option, you are taking out a loan. Since banks often charge more than 16 percent on these overdrafts, this kind of loan is very expensive for you. Avoid the temptation to overdraw your account for routine bill paying; overdraft credit is best used for emergencies and protection against the occasional bounced check.

INSURANCE AS COLLATERAL

Most cash-value life insurance provides a savings and investment feature (the cash value) as well as a death benefit. (See also "Safety Net or Savings Plan?," page 326.) Your policy will have a loan provision. Usually you can borrow up to 95 percent of the policy's cash value, which, in effect, is used as collateral. All your cash goes on earning interest, but at a lower rate. Ask your insurance agent how your policy works.

Typically, you are not required to pay back a life insurance loan. The main drawback of borrowing against a life insurance policy and failing to repay is that if you die with the loan outstanding, the policy's death benefit will be reduced by what you owe. If you do repay it, you set the terms.

Consumer Rip-off: Credit Insurance

Would you willingly overpay for a product you do not need? Consumers spend more than $6 billion a year on credit life and disability insurance policies, but few people actually need them.

The policies cover loan payments to the lender should you die or become totally disabled. Lenders often try to bully borrowers who are getting substantial loans—such as a car or mortgage loan—into buying credit insurance from them instead of from an insurance company. (They are often motivated by the hefty commissions they get for selling it.) But their credit insurance is almost always overpriced. And if you are already adequately insured with life insurance and disability policies, credit insurance is unnecessary.

Except in a very few states lenders cannot require this insurance as a condition of the loan. If you must buy it, go through a legitimate insurance agent; it will cost much less. After you have paid off about half the loan and have demonstrated reliability, ask the lender to allow you to drop it.

Be sure to ask potential lenders in advance whether they require credit insurance. If an institution really wants your business, it may well drop the requirement for you.

LOAN OPTIONS CHART

If you want to buy a house, you go looking for a mortgage loan. For other borrowing needs, however, you can easily become confused by the number of possible options. This chart describes eight common varieties of loans, where you can get them, what to use them for, and their relative merits. It will help you decide what kind is best for your financial situation.

Type of Loan	Source	Best Used For	Advantages	Disadvantages
Checking-account overdraft privileges	Banks, S&L's, credit unions	Emergencies	Easily accessible	Expensive; easy to over-access
Home equity line of credit	Banks, S&L's, credit unions, mortgage brokers	When you need to make large payments over an extended period	Good rates, usually variable; tax-deductible interest	Variable-rate risk; requires discipline to repay promptly; home is collateral
Home equity loan	Banks, S&L's, credit unions, mortgage brokers	When you have a large, onetime expense	Good fixed rates; also tax-deductible	No flexibility in repayment schedule; home is collateral
Individual retirement account (IRA)	Banks, mortgage brokers	Short-term needs	Offers use of an interest-free sum for 60 days; good rates, flexible terms	Harsh penalties and immediate income-tax consequences if borrower does not repay
Life insurance	Life insurance policy	Most borrowing needs	Good rates; interest payments go into your own account	Potentially diminished death benefit
Retirement plans	Employer	Housing, tuition, emergencies	Can allow your savings to remain intact	Usually must be repaid within five years; job changers must repay immediately
Secured loan (by stocks, savings account, etc.)	Banks, S&L's, credit unions	Short-term needs; improving your credit rating; emergencies	Can be a better alternative than credit cards and other high-interest sources	Assets used as security may be tied up until loan is repaid
Unsecured personal loan	Banks, S&L's, credit unions, friends, family	Short-term needs; emergencies	When from family or friends may not require credit check; interest rates are usually good	When from banks, usually have very high interest rates; much higher than your savings earn

Negotiating Mortgage Loans

Choosing a mortgage loan requires special care. Mortgage loans are the biggest loans most consumers will ever assume, so even a small difference in interest rates and other costs will add up to a large amount of money. Many consumers believe they have to accept the first terms, rates, and closing costs that a lender stipulates. This is not true. Especially if you have a good credit history, lenders may be willing to bargain with you to get your business.

To negotiate convincingly, you need to do your homework first. Start by making calls to several lenders to get an idea of what mortgage-loan deals are available in your community. Mortgage banks usually offer lower-cost mortgage loans than commercial banks, for instance. Once you know the cost range of a mortgage loan in your community, you are in a better position to ask for changes in rates or fees that a lender would find reasonable. When you talk to a loan officer, be firm and specific about what terms you expect. Make it clear that you know what the competition is offering and that you are resolute about shopping around until you find the best deal.

A bank that will not consider reducing the interest rate on a mortgage loan, for example, may be willing to haggle over the up-front points instead. And some other bank probably will, in fact, negotiate its interest rate. (Two costs that lenders are not likely to reconsider are the up-front fee for simply applying for a loan and the cost of checking your credit with a credit bureau, but these are comparatively minor costs.)

Above all, read the small print of the mortgage agreement, and don't hesitate to ask someone you trust to explain anything that is not clear to you. A mortgage is likely to be a 15- or 30-year business commitment. Know what you are getting into before signing anything. For a full discussion on mortgage loans, see also YOUR HOME AND COMMUNITY, page 25.

Home Equity Borrowing

A loan against your home equity is among the best—and potentially the most dangerous—loans you can get. These loans come in two forms. With the home equity loan, also called a *second mortgage*, you borrow a fixed amount in one lump and repay it in monthly installments over a set period, such as 10 years. With a home equity line of credit, you arrange for a fixed amount of money to be available to you; then you are able to give yourself a loan when-

123...

MORTGAGE BARGAINING HINTS

Mortgage loan contracts can be intimidating documents, but they are not set in stone. You can bargain with lenders over many of the contract's terms. Here are some likely areas for negotiation:

1. Automatic payments. Many lenders will lower the interest rate at least a point (one percent) if you agree to have monthly payments automatically debited from your savings or checking account.

2. Points. Try asking for at least a quarter-point break on percentage points. On a $100,000 mortgage, a quarter of a point reduction will save you $250.

3. Preparation fees. Creditworthy customers should ask that the document-preparation fees be reduced, or waived.

4. Attorneys' fees. Many competitive banks have eliminated their attorneys' fees as part of the mortgage closing costs. You may find your lender willing to do so, too.

5. Prepayment penalties. These penalties are becoming much less common and are even forbidden on mortgages in some states. Don't accept a loan that includes them.

6. Refinancing. When refinancing, in many states you can save money on taxes by having the second lender assume the mortgage loan of the first lender.

ever you choose by drawing against that amount. You pay interest on the balance due, just as you would with a credit card.

But unlike the interest on credit cards, the interest rate on home equity loans is usually lower and the interest on up to $100,000 of the loan is tax-deductible. These benefits, coupled with easy availability, make home equity loans very appealing to consumers. Most lenders limit borrowing to 75 percent of a home's current value, minus any existing mortgage debt.

So what is it that makes this good deal dangerous? If you cannot make the payments, the lender can foreclose on your home, just as the primary lender could if you defaulted on the mortgage loan. So be certain you can carry this extra debt before you succumb to the tempting notion of having another source of cash available.

WHAT DO YOU NEED THE MONEY FOR?

Before deciding between an outright loan and a line of credit, be very clear how you plan to use the money. Will you be using it for expenses that are due periodically, such as tuition or a home-improvement project that will be done in several phases? That is when the flexibility of a line of credit works best. Or do you have a major onetime expense that you must pay in a lump sum, such as a surgical operation? In such situations, you may prefer the home equity loan with fixed rates. Be certain, however, that you borrow an adequate amount in the first place —if you go back to borrow more, you will have to pay a new set of fees.

Banks and savings institutions dominate home equity lending, but some credit unions, finance companies, and mortgage brokerage houses offer them as well. Whatever lender you settle on, use these guidelines when negotiating the loan:

- Base the size of your loan on your ability to repay.
- Understand the repayment terms of your loan or line of credit.
- Confirm how your interest rate is set.
- Don't be fooled by "teaser" rates that start you off with a low interest rate and then jump up later.
- If you are getting a credit line, ask about the interest rate "cap," or limit.
- Find out what costs and fees you will have to pay in the process of getting your loan.

Just because the lender allows you to borrow a certain percentage of your equity does not mean you should take the full amount. Begin at the other side of the question—instead of asking "How big of a loan can I get?" ask "How much can I afford to pay for it?" Financial experts believe your mortgage

---

The Home Equity Loan Consumer Protection Act

Since home equity lines of credit are generally cheaper than other loans and are also easier to get, you may be tempted to overlook the potential pitfalls of using one. In 1988, Congress passed the Home Equity Loan Consumer Protection Act to stipulate consumers' rights and to help borrowers assess the pros and cons of various lenders' credit-line offerings. The law provides for:

✔ *Complete disclosure.* You must be informed of all rates and fees connected with the credit line, as well as the index used and the index's 15-year history of rate fluctuations.

✔ *Unchanging terms.* The lender cannot add on new fees or increase the original ones during the term of the credit line. (On loans taken out before the act was passed, lenders can change terms at will.) And unless you fail to make timely payments, the lender cannot "call," or terminate, the loan and demand a complete repayment.

✔ *A cooling-off period.* You can cancel the credit line for any reason if you act within three days after opening it. The lender must then return all fees to you.

loan and home equity loan payments together should not exceed 35 percent of your gross monthly income.

Different lenders have different rules for repayment of a loan or line of credit. Many lenders, for instance, require you to pay only the monthly interest each month. Although that makes the loan seem more affordable, you could be unpleasantly surprised by the whopping balance—called a "balloon payment"—that you will be required to pay when the loan finally comes due.

Most credit lines have variable rates tied to an "index," the base for rate changes that the lender uses to decide whether and how much the annual percentage rate will change. Some variable-rate loans are tied to the prime rate plus three or more percentage points. Other indexes that lenders use include the 90-day Treasury bill rate and the average 30-day "jumbo" ($300,000) certificate of deposit (CD) rate.

Home equity lines of credit are among those often advertised with "teaser rates." Don't be fooled by very low interest rates offered in the first six months or year on a line of credit. These rates could jump substantially later on and surprise you with substantially increased payments, even on funds you have already borrowed.

Federal law requires all home equity line-of-credit agreements signed after December 8, 1987, to set a cap on how high your interest rate can rise over the lifetime of the variable loan. A common cap is five to six points over your initial rate. If you opened your home equity line of credit before interest caps were legally mandated, request that a cap be added to your loan agreement.

Closing a home equity loan, or second mortgage, can involve a host of incidental expenses. Various up-front charges such as the property appraisal and credit investigation can cost hundreds of dollars. If you live in a state with a mortgage-recording tax, you could pay several hundred dollars more. Home equity lines of credit have annual fees, which can range from $25 to more than $100.

THINKING OF RENTING OR SELLING?

If your short-term plans include either renting or selling your house, think twice about taking out a home equity loan. Some home equity agreements prohibit leasing your home, either full or part-time. This is within the lender's rights, so make a point of asking about it before getting involved in negotiations.

Finally, if you decided to sell your house, you probably would be required to pay off your home equity line or a second mortgage in full. Ask yourself whether it really makes sense to take on the trouble and the substantial costs of acquiring such loans for a short-term benefit.

Don't Gamble Your Home to Consolidate Debt

It sounds like a good idea: You are swamped with high-interest credit card or overdraft checking account debt. Home equity loans are cheaper, relatively easy to get, and the interest is often tax-deductible. Why not take out a home equity loan to pay off all of those other debts hanging over you? What could possibly go wrong?

Plenty, if you do not change the spending pattern that got you into heavy debt in the first place. Remember that you are not getting that loan for nothing—your house is at stake.

The Consumer Bankers Association notes that most of the home equity credit lines and loans that lead to foreclosures were used for debt consolidation. So before deciding that a home equity loan is the cure-all for your debt problems, make a resolve to curb your appetite for credit. It would be foolish to create new debt while you are still paying off the loan you took out to clear up your old debt.

If you think you need help disciplining your spending habits, consider seeking credit counseling before taking out that loan. For additional ways to help consolidate your debt, see "Dealing With Debt," page 319.

Guarantees from the ECOA

The law cannot guarantee that you will get a loan anytime you apply for one. But in 1974, Congress passed legislation that helps ensure that you will be judged fairly when you do apply: the Equal Credit Opportunity Act (ECOA). The act was aimed particularly at protecting women and minority groups, who in former times often found themselves being given the cold shoulder by lenders. ECOA requires a lender to apply the same criteria for judging loan applications from women and minorities that it applies to requests from white males or any other applicants.

You must supply your Social Security number on a loan application. You must also give your gender, race, and country of national origin on mortgage applications, because the government uses that information to monitor banks for patterns of discrimination. Before the ECOA was passed, however, lenders had the right to ask women for details about their marital status, childbearing plans, and even the kind of birth control they used. Creditors frequently canceled a woman's individual credit once she was married. The result was that many women could not establish credit in their own names. Today, creditors risk severe fines if they are found to discriminate on the basis of sex or marital status. (In 1976, the ECOA was expanded so that the prohibition extended to religion, national origin, and age as well.)

EXTRA PROTECTION FOR WOMEN

Special protections apply to women applicants for unsecured loans such as credit cards, overdraft lines of credit, and personal loans. For such credit, under the law, lenders cannot ask about gender or marital status. Indeed, a woman does not even have to indicate whether she prefers to be called Ms., Mrs., or Miss. The only situations in which a lender can ask a woman questions about marital status and her spouse are when she indicates: (1) that her husband will use the account; (2) she is opening a joint account he will share with her; (3) she is using her husband's income to qualify for a loan; (4) she is listing alimony and/or child support as income; or (5) she lives in a community-property state.

If the loan is "secured" (backed by collateral), as are mortgage and car loans, other rules apply. Then the lender may ask if an applicant is married, unmarried, or separated, because the property could be owned jointly. However, the law prohibits the lender from using that information to discriminate against an applicant. If you feel that you have been discriminated against, contact your state attorney general's office or your local consumer affairs office for advice on how to file a discrimination complaint.

Lending Money to Others

Not all loans have to involve institutional lenders. Suppose you have a friend who needs money to buy a car, and you have some money in a savings account that you do not think you will need to use for a while. You can offer your friend a loan on terms that will benefit both of you. You might suggest an interest rate of, say, seven percent, which is probably more interest than your money is earning in your savings account, but still cheaper than the 15 percent your friend might have to pay to get an unsecured loan at a bank. This stratagem is perfectly legal and is a good arrangement all around: it makes you some extra money and saves her some.

Be aware, however, that loans between friends or family members can go sour if you are not careful about the details. For one thing, even friends and family need to spell out the specific terms of their agreement, write them down, and sign the document to guard against problems later on. If the loan is not properly handled, the lender may suffer significant tax consequences. (See also "A Gift of a Loan," page 306.) To ensure financial peace of mind—and to avoid losing a friend or the goodwill of a family member—consider the following guidelines when making private loans:

- **Draw up the right papers.** A simple "promissory note" will specify the full amount as well as the interest terms. In addition, it will spell out the repayment schedule, and identify any collateral offered. You may want to consult a lawyer about the proper wording. (See also "An Installment Promissory Note," page 307.)
- **Choose a reasonable rate of interest.** The IRS sets minimum rates you must charge or risk owing a gift tax, as well as regular income tax, on the money loaned. Those minimum percentages, called the "applicable federal rates" (AFR's), are adjusted monthly, based on market rates. You can find out current AFR's by calling your local IRS office. (Check your phone directory for the number of the office in your locality.)
- **Structure your loan as either a demand loan or a term loan.** A "demand loan" provides leeway to the borrower because it sets no timetable for repayment, but its AFR can change monthly, and the loan can be recalled at any time. A "term loan," alternately, is one that has a set repayment schedule, and the AFR stays fixed.

🖼️

Debt is a kind of household tool. It's like a rope. You can use it for lifting or many other tasks. Or you can use it to hang yourself.

JAMES GRANT
Grant's Interest Rate Observer

🖼️

WHEN SOMEONE OWES YOU MONEY

If a person to whom you have loaned money has not repaid it, you have three legitimate options to pursue to get it back:

1. Start by contacting the borrower directly—by letter, telephone, or personal visit—and trying to work out a repayment arrangement. Consumer law advocates advise that to avoid charges of harassment you should *not* make such contact in an abusive way or at annoying times or unusual places.

2. If you get no satisfaction with a personal approach, and if the loan is relatively small, you can go to small claims court. Each state has its own definition of a "small claim," and procedures vary.(See also YOUR RIGHTS IN ACTION, page 476.)

3. If a large sum is involved, you may want to consult a lawyer about filing a complaint in a state, municipal, or district court. You could request a judgment authorizing a garnishment, which in some circumstances may permit you to collect the debt from an outside source, such as the borrower's bank account or paycheck. Your chance of success is best if you have a written document, such as a promissory note, to prove you did indeed lend the money. But even oral promises can stand up if the loan and its terms can be proved with clear evidence and credible witnesses.

■ **Observe the necessary formalities.** If you are making a mortgage loan, for instance, you must include in the promissory note the information that the debt is secured by your borrower's residence. If the borrower intends to deduct the interest on your loan from his income tax, the mortgage must be filed with county authorities.

A Mother's Dilemma

PROBLEM
Marian's son Jeff did not make enough money at his part-time job to qualify for a car loan, so he asked his mother to co-sign a loan at a local bank. By co-signing, she would become responsible for Jeff's debt if he did not meet his payments. Marian was happy to help Jeff but wanted to limit her liability as much as possible. At the same time, she also wanted Jeff to learn how to handle his debts maturely.

ACTION
Marian consulted with the loan officer at the bank. From him, she learned that the law in her state permitted her to be responsible for paying only the principal balance on Jeff's loan if he defaulted—but not any late charges, court expenses, attorney's fees, or other costs that could be generated. The lender included a statement in the contract: "This cosigner will be responsible only for the principal balance on this loan at the time of default." Marian also asked the lender to notify her if Jeff missed a payment, so that she could address the problem with Jeff before he actually defaulted. As a final step, Marian called her state attorney general's office to see if any other laws applied to her rights as a cosigner.

A GIFT OF A LOAN
Sometimes people want to extend a large loan to a family member or close friend but wish to charge only minimal interest. For example, a parent may want to loan a child a down payment on a house or part of his or her college tuition with little or no interest.

Beware, however. Your generosity could put you in hot water with the Internal Revenue Service, because the IRS could tax you for "imputed interest," or the interest the IRS believes you should have collected based on current market rates. Thus, if you give your child a mortgage loan at three percent, and the IRS says you should have charged six percent, you could be taxed on the six percent imputed interest instead of the actual three percent.

This IRS rule does not apply on loans up to $10,000 that are used to buy non-income-producing property, or on loans up to $100,000 if the recipient's net income from other investments is under $1,000. As a result, you could lend a friend $9,000 for a house or a child $25,000 for college at a very low interest rate, or interest free.

Gail L. Mathews • 201 Main Street • Tulsa, Oklahoma 43820

Promissory Note

For value received, I, Gail L. Mathews, of Tulsa, Oklahoma, ❶ promise to pay to Robert H. Mathews, of 277 Cheyenne Road, Norman, Oklahoma, or any subsequent holder of this Note, ❷ the sum of six thousand dollars ($6,000), with annual interest at 10 percent on the unpaid balance.

Payments shall be made in 24 installments of $278 each, with a first payment due on October 1, 1995, and the same amount due on the first day of each month thereafter until the entire principal amount of this note and earned interest is ❸ fully paid. All payments shall be applied first to earned interest, and the balance to principal. I may prepay this note in whole or in part without penalty.

The full unpaid principal and any earned interest shall be fully due and immediately payable upon demand of the holder of this note in the event that the borrower shall default in making any payments due under this note within 60 days of the payment due date, or upon the death, bankruptcy, or insolvency of the borrower. ❹

I waive presentment, demand, protest, and all notices thereto, and agree to remain fully bound to this note notwithstanding any extension, indulgence, or modification under this note, unless personally released, discharged or having fulfilled its terms.

❺

Signed this 25 day of September, 1995.

_____   _____
Borrower: Gail L. Mathews   Witness: Karin Martin ❻
Payment schedule attached

An Installment Promissory Note

An installment promissory note expresses the terms of a loan to be repaid in equal payments of principal and interest, in this case by a daughter to her father. **1.** The name of the state whose laws the note is in accordance with must be included; **2.** If the lender dies before the loan is repaid, the borrower is obligated to his heirs and estate; **3.** The sum of the loan, the interest rate, the number of installments, the amount of each payment including interest, and the payment due dates are clearly specified; **4.** If the borrower defaults, the lender can demand immediate payment; this note works in the lender's favor because he is not required to follow certain procedures for repayment; **5.** Indulgences (like chronic late payment) may be condoned but will not negate the agreement; **6.** Witnesses are not required but can be present for protection.

CREDIT CARDS

Credit cards affect the way Americans spend their money—and the way people go into debt. The right knowledge will help keep your debt under control.

Can You Qualify for a Low-Rate Credit Card?

Among the glut of credit cards on the market, a few offer especially low interest rates. Almost 80 percent of applicants for such cards are turned down, but you may qualify if your credit profile looks something like this:

✔ *Income.* You have a minimum income of $12,000 to $20,000.

✔ *Debt-to-income ratio.* Your monthly credit card and mortgage or rent payments total less than 35 to 45 percent of your income.

✔ *Residency.* You have lived at your current address for at least two years.

✔ *Employment.* You have worked for one employer or within the same field for at least two years.

✔ *Credit references.* You have other credit sources, such as a car loan or major credit card account at least one year old.

✔ *Delinquencies.* Over the past four years you have not been more than 60 days late with debt payments on mortgage or car loans, credit cards, or store charge cards.

Finding the Best Deal in a Credit Card

Millions of offers for easy-to-get credit cards flood Americans' mailboxes every year. Banks, non-profit organizations, department stores, travel-and-entertainment companies, oil corporations, and a host of other enterprises dazzle us with their versions of buy-now-and-pay-later convenience. How can you make your way through the maze of offers?

BANK CARDS

The most common type of credit card, issued by banks, offers you access to small personal loans, which the bank gives you each time you buy something with the card, and which you repay with interest over time. The card may be called Master-Card or Visa, for example, but it is issued by a particular bank that sets its own terms for the use of the card. Policies about interest rates, annual fees, billing practices, and other costs vary widely from issuer to issuer—which makes it essential to shop around and compare terms.

Small differences can add up to real savings; therefore, the lower the interest rate and the less onerous the fees, the more desirable the card. So while there is a plethora of cards available, getting one of the low-interest cards is not so easy, because the issuers of such cards, not surprisingly, are the most finicky about whom they offer cards to.

The general terms that banks typically offer cardholders are a credit limit of at least $500 and the option of making small monthly payments in lieu of paying the entire amount charged. Interest is charged on what is left over. Most bank cards also offer loans in the form of cash advances, almost always at very high interest rates. (See also "Choosing the Right Kind of Loan," page 297.)

"T & E" AND DEBIT CARDS

The term "credit card" is applied somewhat casually to all the pieces of plastic that allow you to buy without using cash or a check. But two kinds of cards differ from most of the others.

CREDIT CARD TYPES

Credit is issued by thousands of different financial entities: banks, oil companies, retail establishments, as well as travel-and-entertainment enterprises (like American Express), whose cards are not really credit cards, but a form of charge card. Debit cards, such as automated teller machine cards, are another type. Even among the true credit cards, there are many important differences. This chart summarizes the differences and relative merits of each type.

Type	Terms	Advantages	Disadvantages
Affinity cards	Like bank credit cards, but sponsored by professional associations and charities that promise to donate part of the annual fee (often more than $20) or part of each purchase to the sponsoring organization	Convenient way to donate money	Usually high costs
Bank credit cards	Can include annual fees, credit limits, interest rates ranging from 9 percent to 22 percent, depending on the state in which the card is issued; minimum monthly payments	Convenience and wide acceptance	Often high interest rates, and high fees for cash advances
Debit cards	Do not offer credit; a charge is electronically deducted from a bank account linked to the card	Easier than writing checks; you can't spend more money than you have in your account	May be harder to keep track of account activity without a check register or passbook on hand when using
Gasoline cards	Balance must be paid in full every month	Easy to obtain; may offer such benefits as travel clubs and credit card registration	Can cost more to use than paying cash; use limited to car- and travel-related expenditures
Retail cards	Issued for use in specific retail establishments; interest rates from 18 to 26 percent are charged on unpaid balances	Easy to obtain; no annual fees; often provide access to special sales and discounts	Extremely high interest rates make carrying a balance very expensive
Secured credit cards	You deposit money in a savings account as collateral to ensure you will meet your monthly payments; interest rates on your balance can range from 8 to 24 percent	A way to establish a credit rating or repair a bad one	Application, processing, and annual fees can be very high
Travel-and-entertainment cards	Do not offer month-to-month credit; bill must be paid in full every month; no preset charge limit	Convenient for travelers who might quickly reach their limit on a bank card; offer financial services geared toward travelers and executives	Accepted at fewer locations than bank cards; high annual fees

Getting Students Started on Credit

More than half the nation's 2.5 million college students carry some kind of credit card. According to financial experts, a student needs only one card, both for the student's convenience and to help her build a good credit history. Because a student's income is likely to be too low to qualify normally, various options are offered for obtaining a card:

✔ *Co-signed card.* A parent or other adult co-signs, and the payment history is reported in both names. If neither co-signer pays the bills, that negative information will likely be reported to a credit bureau under both names.

✔ *Secured credit card.* The student makes a deposit in a bank and obtains a bank credit card with a credit line based on that deposit. Usually, however, she must have at least part-time employment to qualify.

✔ *Special programs.* Many large credit card issuers have special application procedures for college students. Usually the cards have a smaller credit line than conventional cards, and the applicant must have proof of college acceptance. Most major banks and college admissions offices have information on these programs.

The so-called T&E card (issued by travel-and-entertainment companies like American Express) is more accurately defined as a "charge card," since it does not offer credit on a month-to-month basis. In other words, you cannot carry an ongoing balance but must pay in full each month whatever you charged to the card that month.

The other kind of "plastic" that is not a true credit card is the debit card, which is basically an electronic check: whatever sum you charge on your debit card is taken directly out of your bank account. An ATM card is a kind of debit card—the machine gives you some cash, and that amount is instantly deducted from your bank account. Since T&E and debit cards do not offer you ongoing credit, interest rates are not a factor. Annual fees, late-payment charges, and many other kinds of fees add up, however, as they do with any other type of card.

LEARN THE LANGUAGE

Before applying for a bank credit card, you should be familiar with the following terms: "interest rates," "grace periods," and "balance calculation methods."

Federal law requires that banks state their "annual percentage rate" (APR) in credit card offerings. The banks state that rate as simple interest charged on purchases not paid in full each month. But the cost to you may be more than you realize, because most card issuers in fact compound the interest you pay on new purchases *and* interest charges carried forward each month. The law lets card issuers change the interest rate at will if they give consumers 15 days' written notice.

Some cards allow a 25- or 30-day grace period during which you do not pay interest on expenses charged to your card. Usually, however, you are guaranteed a grace period *only* when you do not carry a balance forward from the previous month. The small print explains that if you carry any balance forward, your grace period is forfeited on all new purchases, which means that interest will accrue not only on the carry-over balance but also on new charges from the date of purchase. In other words, you get a grace period on your credit card only if you do not use it to get credit and pay it off in full at month's end.

The balance calculation method most favorable to consumers is the "adjusted balance method." With this method, the interest is applied to the amount you owe after your monthly payments are made. The most widely used method, however, is the "average daily balance method," which averages the amount of debt you had in your account each day during the month and charges interest on that amount.

The least advantageous method for consumers is the "previous balance method"; you are charged interest on the balance you owe on your account at the end of the previous month, with no credit at all for payments made since then.

A general guideline for choosing a credit card is that if you are in the habit of paying your whole bill every month, you need a card with no annual fee and with a grace period; since you do not carry a balance from month to month, the interest rate is less important to you. If most months you do carry a balance, however, you should look for a card with the lowest interest rate and the most favorable billing method.

HIDDEN CREDIT CARD COSTS

By law, credit card costs—interest (and how it is calculated) plus all fees—must be displayed in an easy-to-read box format on most applications and solicitations. But some credit card costs are harder to find out about. For example, card issuers usually charge interest on purchases from the date the charge slip reaches the issuer and is placed on your account. But many issuers have begun "backdating" interest to the date of purchase, which adds anything from one day's interest to as much as several weeks' worth of interest to your bill on each purchase. You should also be aware that when you charge a cash advance against your card, interest is always charged from the first day.

Dealing With Credit Rejection

PROBLEM
Although Barry had been steadily employed for a number of years, his application for a credit card was rejected. As reasons for its action the bank noted that Barry had been at his present job for less than a year and that he already held six other credit card accounts.

ACTION
Barry called the bank's credit manager. He pointed out that although his present job was new, he had been in the same field for several years and his present employer had hired him away from his former job. He offered to close some of his existing credit card accounts, but the credit manager refused to reconsider. Barry took action by canceling a few of his other cards, and then applying to another card company, which accepted his application. (Barry could also have waited until he had been at his current job for a year and reapplied to the original bank.)

Many cardholders mistakenly believe a credit card repayment schedule that requires the lowest minimum monthly payments is the best deal. True, the payments may seem easier when you sit down to pay the bills, but low monthly payments can mean shockingly high costs in the long run. Most card issuers require payment of three to five percent on the outstanding balance each month, but some offer minimums as low as two percent a month. A $1,100 balance at a 12.9 percent

Credit Card Travel Troubles

Hotels, motels, and car-rental companies sometimes use an irksome but legal tactic that can put a big dent in your travel or vacation plans, and may even severely inhibit your travel enjoyment.

When you check in to a motel room or rent a car that you have reserved with a credit card, the clerk may put a hold on your card account for the estimated amount of the rental or the hotel bill. This ploy ensures the merchant's payment, but it can create serious problems for you.

For example, if you book a hotel for eight days and the room costs $150 per day, the hotelier can put a hold of $1,200 on your card. If the cost of the auto rental is $400 for the same period of time, plus insurance of, say, $100, you may have used up $1,700 in credit before your vacation even begins. This may put you close to the credit limit on your card, and the hold can remain on your card for as long as two weeks, even if you pay your hotel or auto-rental bill in cash or by check before you leave on your trip.

Perhaps the best way you can handle this irritating situation—except for finding a hotel or car rental agency that will help you out—is to use two cards. Put lodgings and car rentals on one card, and use the other for restaurants, shopping, and other incidentals.

123...

HOLDING CARDS CLOSE TO YOUR CHEST

Credit card fraud is a billion-dollar problem in the United States. To avoid being a victim, always keep track of your cards and use them carefully, as follows:

1. Make a list of your credit card numbers, expiration dates, and the phone number of each card issuer—and remember where you put it. If a card is lost or stolen, the quicker you report it, the less hassle you will experience.

2. Keep an eye on your card whenever you give it to a clerk. Take it back promptly after he is finished with it and make sure it is yours.

3. Take possession of all carbons used in credit card transactions.

4. Never sign a blank credit card receipt. When you sign a receipt for a purchase, draw a line through any blank spaces above the total.

5. Don't give out your credit card number for mail-order purchases to strangers who solicit you over the phone.

6. Sign new cards as soon as they arrive. Cut up expired cards and throw them away. If you cancel a card, cut it up and return it to the issuer.

annual percentage rate would take 13 years to pay off at a minimum payment of only two percent (not counting any new charges). At the end of that time, you would have paid $919 in interest alone.

Using Your Card Wisely

The convenience of credit cards makes it tempting to use them indiscriminately. Indeed, studies show that people who shop with credit cards spend more than those who pay by cash or check—which is one reason retailers such as department stores urge their customers to sign up for the stores' credit cards. Common sense and a little discipline are the best remedies for overspending, of course, but there are also some strategies in both using the card and paying your bills that will help keep a rein on expenses.

Some merchants prompt consumers to spend more by requiring a minimum dollar-amount purchase for the use of the card. Minimum-purchase requirements are legal under federal law, but the major credit card companies do not allow them. Other card issuers may have their own policies; so call your card issuer's customer service department to find out. If a merchant insists on a minimum-purchase in violation of the credit card company's policy, inform the company as well as the local Better Business Bureau.

Usually, it is best to own no more than two credit cards. Keep one card that has a low (or no) annual fee and a grace period, and use it when you expect to pay off your balance on time. Keep another that has a low interest rate for occasions when you won't be able to pay the entire amount when due. Canceling all your other cards will save money and simplify your record keeping.

Whatever cards you have, you can save money when it is time to pay your bills by observing these tips:

- Try to pay off your entire credit card bill every month. You will spare yourself the finance charges, which are no longer tax-deductible.
- If you cannot manage to pay in full, pay what you can the moment you get your bill. The sooner the bank gets your payment, the less interest you will usually pay that month, and in the long run.
- Never accept a card issuer's enticing offer to skip a payment for a month. Although you would not be paying, interest charges would be accruing. That means you would just be adding to the amount you owe.

- Pay as much as you can on the highest-rate cards first. Then make minimum payments on your other ones. This reduces your debt more quickly than if you spread partial payments evenly among all your cards.
- If you are a good, longtime customer, try asking your card issuer to waive your annual fee. Many will do so, but you must initiate the request.

Keeping Private Information Out of the Wrong Hands

Often when you pay for a retail purchase with a personal check, the store clerk asks to see your driver's license and a major credit card to validate your payment. He then writes those numbers on your check and may even ask for your telephone number, too. But this form of "validation" exposes you to fraud, invades your privacy, does nothing to protect the merchant from bad checks—and may be illegal besides.

How does it put you at risk of being defrauded? Many eyes see your check between the time it is written and when the bank returns it to you. If the check has your name, address, telephone number, and credit card number on it, anyone can use that information to buy merchandise by telephone or from mail-order catalogs. One New York crime ring specialized in mail-order fraud by paying dishonest store clerks for credit card information.

You have the right to refuse to allow a merchant to write your credit card number on your check—15 states actually prohibit this practice. If you do not live in one of those states, however, the merchant in turn has the right to refuse you the purchase if you won't put your credit card number on your check. Mostly, merchants who want your credit card number do so because they think they can charge your credit card if your check bounces. In most cases they are wrong. The major card companies all forbid merchants from charging a customer's credit card account to cover a bounced check.

In credit card transactions, too, some merchants ask customers to write their telephone numbers on the credit card sales slips. Most people comply, not realizing that, again, the major card issuers prohibit this practice. Remember that the more information you divulge about yourself, the easier it is for someone to defraud you. Recognizing this problem, some states, including California, Delaware, Georgia, Maryland, Minnesota, Nevada, New Jersey, and New York, have enacted laws prohibiting the recording of *any* personal information in connection with credit card transactions.

Tactics for Protecting Your Privacy

To limit the chance of being victimized by credit card fraud, do not allow a salesclerk to write your credit card number on your personal check or your phone number on a credit card sales slip. If the clerk insists even after you have explained your position, take these steps:

✔ *Speak to the manager.* Ask to speak to the store owner, or manager, or someone who has the authority to alter store policy if necessary.

✔ *Clarify your position.* Inform the merchant that Visa, MasterCard, and American Express prohibit stores from refusing sales to customers who decline to provide personal information such as telephone numbers.

✔ *Verify with a credit card.* If you are trying to pay by check, offer to allow the merchant to verify that you hold a major credit card, but do not let him write the account number on your check.

✔ *Refuse the purchase.* If the merchant insists on recording personal information on your check or on the bank card sales slip, take your business somewhere else.

✔ *Complain to the credit card company.* Be sure to inform your card issuer of the name and address of the intractable merchant.

Coping with Billing Errors and Disputes

Skirmishes with credit card companies over billing errors have become almost as inevitable as death and taxes: a bank incorrectly totals your charges; you get charged for something you did not buy; or a mail-order merchant delivers items different from those you ordered. Fortunately, the Fair Credit Billing Act (FCBA) of 1974 provides legal ammunition for you in such exasperating situations. To take full advantage of FCBA's protection, however, you must understand its provisions, because customer service representatives often do not understand the procedures. Even more complex are the Truth in Lending Act rules for dealing with disputes over defective goods or unsatisfactory services that you have charged to a card.

The law allows you to withhold payment on a disputed charge and to ask your card issuer to investigate and resolve the matter for you. Card companies cannot try to collect while the dispute is being looked into, but they *can* treat the disputed amount as an outstanding charge when determining how close you are to your credit limit.

Here is a guide to steps that will improve your chances of getting a billing error satisfactorily resolved:

- Respond in writing within 60 days of the date the credit card bill was sent to you. Telephoning will not preserve your rights under FCBA. The address for billing problems should be printed on your monthly statement. (Usually it is different from the address to which you mail your monthly payments.) Note in your letter that you are asserting your rights under FCBA. The card issuer must respond within 30 days.
- Give clear details of the disputed transaction. Your letter to the creditor must contain your name, address, account number, the dollar amount of the erroneous billing, and a description of what you believe the error to be. Send photocopies of the relevant receipts or other documents, and keep the originals as well as a copy of your letter.
- Send your complaint by certified mail, return receipt requested, so that you can prove the card issuer received it.
- Pay any charges you do not dispute. Although interest on the disputed amount will continue to accrue until the matter is settled, the issuer cannot report your account as delinquent to a credit bureau if you pay all undisputed charges.

Within 90 days, the creditor must make a "reasonable investigation" of the error, which involves sending documentation

---

YOUR RIGHTS IF YOUR CARD IS STOLEN

Credit card crooks and con artists cause card companies massive losses every year. If your cards are used illegally, the immediate loss to you, however, is usually the time you spend clearing up the fraudulent charges rather than any money for purchases charged against your card illegally. Your liability for unauthorized charges is strictly limited by law. Specifically, these are your rights if you:

1. Report the loss quickly. If you report the loss or theft of a credit card before it is used fraudulently, you have no liability for any charges.

2. Report the loss after illegal use. If you report the loss of cards that have already been used, you must pay the first $50 charged on each card.

3. Are the victim of a mail order scam. If a lost or stolen card is used for a mail-order purchase and has not been presented directly to the merchant, you are not liable for any amount, whether or not you have reported the loss of the card.

4. Are offered insurance. If your credit card company offers you "credit card protection" insurance, think twice before signing up. After a few years, the fees you pay would probably exceed the $50 a loss or theft can cost.

on the disputed charge back to the merchant. If the investigation shows you are correct, you will not have to pay either the charge or interest accrued on it. If the card issuer decides against you, it must give you a written explanation and a statement of the amount you owe.

At that point, the creditor has met all its legal obligations under the FCBA and can treat the charge as correct. You are legally obligated to pay the disputed amount and any associated finance charges.

If you still think the charge was in error, you can seek legal advice or contact your local consumer protection agency. If you decide to continue withholding payment, you must immediately inform the issuer in writing. Be aware that this option could damage your credit history. The card issuer can report you to a credit bureau for not paying the disputed charge, but the issuer must also report that the matter is being challenged. Should you finally win the dispute, the credit card issuer must promptly clear your record with anyone who received that version of your credit report.

Protection Against Faulty Merchandise

The Fair Credit Billing Act protects you against billing errors made by a card issuer or the merchant. But if you used a credit card to buy merchandise that turned out to be defective, the Special Credit Card Provisions section of the Truth in Lending Act (TILA) outlines your rights when disputing charges on a credit card bill. The TILA legislation allows you to:

• **Withhold payment.** You have the right to refuse payment for the amount of the disputed charge still outstanding on your account at the time you contact the card issuer or merchant about the problem.

• **Dispute only legitimate complaints.** You must have a legal complaint in order to withhold payment. An appliance that malfunctioned would be a justifiable complaint. You cannot withhold payment merely because you "just don't like it."

• **Dispute only sizable charges.** The charge under dispute must be for a purchase or service of $50 or more. You are not protected for incidental items.

• **Dispute only in your own state.** The charge must have been made in the same state as your card-billing address; or, if you shopped in another state, the charge must have been made within 100 miles of your billing address.

• **Attempt a resolution.** You must have made a good-faith effort to resolve the problem on your own with the merchant or supplier involved.

• **"Asserting claims and defenses."** If the former qualifications apply, you can begin disputing the charge by notifying your card issuer—by telephone, in writing, or in person—that you are "asserting claims and defenses." After you inform the card holder, you are under no time restriction or limit to resolve your problem. The disputed charge becomes put on hold, and you can try to resolve the problem with the merchant without risking a blemish on your credit record.

• **Avoid delinquency.** The card issuer is not legally obliged to follow any particular procedures but usually will place the account under dispute and report it as such to a credit bureau. It cannot, however, report that the account is delinquent.

• **Secure a refund.** If you win the dispute, you do not get back your money from the card issuer. You must deal directly with the merchant.

• **Ask for more information.** Call your state attorney general's office or the Federal Reserve Board, the government agency that interprets this law. For the address of the Federal Reserve Board, see RESOURCES, page 493.

CREDIT BUREAUS

These electronic warehouses bulge with details of your credit history—and some of them are wrong. It is up to you to make sure your credit record tells the truth.

Your Rights to Accuracy and Confidentiality

To many, credit bureaus are mysterious, faintly sinister agencies that no one knows much about but that seem to exert enormous power over their lives. Whether you are looking for a loan, an insurance policy, an apartment, or a job, the chances are that your interviewer will ask a credit bureau to run a check on you. The resulting report will reveal such details as who has extended credit to you, whether you pay your bills on time, whether you have ever defaulted on a loan, even how much you owe each of your creditors at the moment.

Credit bureaus compile this data from many sources—financial institutions where you have car loans or charge cards, department stores, municipal tax lists, court records—and boil it down into a credit report. The three largest national credit bureaus alone—Equifax, Transunion, and TRW—collect more than 2 billion pieces of credit-related information each month and generate more than 400 million consumer credit reports on 160 million people each year. (There are roughly 800 more credit bureaus at the local level.) If your report contains an error—and studies show that nearly half of all reports do—you could be denied a loan or credit card you are applying for, the apartment you want to rent, or even a job.

FEDERAL LEGISLATION TO THE RESCUE

The 1971 Fair Credit Reporting Act (FCRA) was designed to protect you in this type of situation. The act spells out important rights that go into effect if you are denied credit, a loan, a job, or an apartment rental because of erroneous information in a credit report. You have the right to know the name and address of the credit bureau that supplied the information to the inquirer; you are also entitled to a free copy of the report if you request it within 30 days of being notified of your application's rejection. Furthermore, if the rejection of your application for credit was based on an erroneous report, you can force the bureau to correct it.

When you dispute an error, credit bureaus are not required to explain your rights to you, so you should know them and insist on exercising them. Here is a summary of the rights that the FCRA guarantees you:

- The right to review your credit report. You may do this in person, by phone, or by mail.
- The right to have investigated within a reasonable period (not defined by law, but generally within 30 days) any information in your credit report that you dispute.
- The right to have the erroneous information deleted from your record if the investigation finds that the information was, in fact, wrong.
- The right to have negative credit-related entries such as late payments deleted from your record after seven years and a bankruptcy report deleted after ten years.
- The right to have the credit bureau notify—at no expense to you—those creditors you name who previously reviewed the incorrect information.
- The right to know who has received a copy of your report over the last two years for employment purposes, and over the past six months for credit-granting purposes.
- The right, if a credit bureau investigates and insists its information is correct, to include a 100-word statement telling your version of the dispute.

GETTING YOUR REPORT

Your best protection against having errors creep into your credit reports is to check them periodically, whether you have had any trouble with creditors or not. Some credit bureaus will send one free report annually, while others charge up to $15 a copy, although some states have imposed ceilings as low as $3 on such charges.

Each of the three major credit reporting agencies has regional offices around the country. To find the major credit bureau in your area, ask someone in the consumer-loan department of your local bank. Then call that bureau's regional customer service office and ask how to order your report. For the addresses of several of the best-known credit bureaus, see RESOURCES, page 493.

Understanding Your Report

After you have taken the prudent step of ordering a credit report, you will see that although different bureaus use different formats, the type of information on all of them is basically the same. Most often, the printed reports use a series of codes and abbreviations that are designed to be read by computers, not humans. These nota-

---

HOW TO CORRECT A BLEMISHED CREDIT REPORT

A credit bureau is legally required to investigate and correct wrong information on a credit report. But it is usually up to you to discover the error and see that it is corrected. Here is how to go about it:

1. In a letter describe the error and request a prompt investigation, citing your rights under the Fair Credit Reporting Act. Include your full name, address, Social Security number, and phone number.

2. Send the letter by certified mail, return receipt requested, so you will have proof that the credit bureau got your letter.

3. If the investigation shows that one of your creditors incorrectly reported the information that you dispute, contact the creditor directly and explain the error. Ask the creditor to send a written correction of the error to all its credit bureaus.

4. If you disagree with the results of the credit bureau's investigation, you can insist that a 100-word statement telling your version of the dispute is included with the report.

5. After you have set the bureau straight, always request a copy of the revised report to ensure that it is now correct.

tions can be difficult—if not impossible—to read and comprehend; however, the bureau is required to give a clear explanation of its terminology.

Often, the only intelligible entries will be your name, birth date, address, Social Security number, and employer, as well as your spouse's name and employer. (Interestingly, sometimes even this information can be wrong if your credit history has somehow been crossed with another's, which has happened on many occasions.) Because the purpose of the information is to help a lender decide whether you are a good credit risk, your report will usually include the payment history for your bank loans, any major retailer accounts, and your bank or credit card accounts. For each account, you will see listed the creditor, type of account, terms, amount of the original debt or credit limit, and the balance outstanding on the most recent report or bill.

Your credit report will also include a list of "inquiries" made by any credit grantors who have accessed your file in the last six months. Any credit-related information that is a matter of public record—bankruptcies, foreclosures, judgments, or tax liens, for instance—will also appear. In addition, more and more frequently, the state agencies in charge of enforcing child-support agreements are reporting delinquencies in child-support payments.

WHAT IS NOT ON THE REPORT

You may be surprised that your credit report does not describe your bank accounts, including either your checking or savings accounts, your mortgage loans, or any other major assets. Furthermore, unless a debt collection has been launched against you, you probably will not be cited for owing money on oil and gas credit cards, utility bills, medical bills, or attorney's fees. A credit bureau's report is not, strictly speaking, a financial rating. Basically, your potential creditors usually evaluate the report and decide for themselves how much of a potential risk you may be.

However, some credit bureaus now use scoring systems to help creditors evaluate your creditworthiness. They instruct lenders to identify credit-related factors, such as income, length of employment, and payment history, and assign various "point values" to each characteristic, resulting in a score that either meets or does not meet the lender's requirements.

At the same time, the Federal Trade Commission has ruled that if a credit bureau uses such a system, it must provide you with your score, together with an explanation of how the score was determined, when you ask to see your credit report.

DEALING WITH DEBT

Millions of Americans live permanently in debt. For most it is a manageable problem, but when it gets out of control, it could cause serious trouble.

Practical Steps to Take
When You Are in Trouble

Mortgage payments, car loans, credit card charges —these are debts that most of us manage to cope with. Being in a serious financial crisis, however, can be a frightening and crippling experience. Some fiscal emergencies, such as getting laid off or becoming seriously sick, are beyond our control. Other acute debt problems are caused by poor financial management. Whatever the cause, it is important to face up to such a problem, then take steps to resolve it, and so avoid the serious legal problems caused by unpaid debts.

Most financial experts believe that consumers who spend more than 20 percent of their after-tax income on non-mortgage debt are dangerously overburdened. Non-mortgage debt includes all your other borrowed money, such as car loans and credit card debt. For example, John and Jane together earn $60,000 a year, with a net income after taxes of $3,500 per

A fool and his money are soon parted.

ANONYMOUS
English Proverb

Debt Danger Signals

You can often detect the warning signs of overindebtedness long before the collection notices from creditors arrive. If more than two or three of these danger signs apply to you, you need to get help developing a budget and debt repayment plan.

• You have begun charging to a credit card such essentials as food or daily expenses that you used to pay cash for.

• You make only the minimum payments on your charge accounts each month and perhaps do not pay one or two at all, even though it will mean additional finance charges on your next bills.

• You take a cash advance from a credit card to make the minimum payment on another or to use for incidental expenses.

• You no longer contribute to a savings or retirement account or, worse, have closed your savings account altogether.

• You put off all maintenance activities—from visiting your dentist to painting your house—because you cannot afford them "right now."

• You consistently have to work overtime, or are holding down a second job, just to make enough money to pay your creditors.

•You are at or near the limit on the line of credit on all of your credit cards. In fact, you have too many credit cards.

• You are unsure of how much you owe creditors, are unwilling to admit to yourself or anyone else just how big your debt might be, and avoid actually adding up the total debt.

A Respected Source of Help

Each year, over one million debt-burdened Americans turn for low-cost help to the Consumer Credit Counseling Services. CCCS is a nationwide network of nonprofit counseling agencies that give advice on money management techniques and can also negotiate with creditors on a consumer's behalf.

Depending on your needs, a counselor will work out a budget for you and may advise you to enroll in a debt-management program. If you choose the debt-management program, the counselor intercedes with your creditors and works out a repayment schedule with them. From then on, your creditors are asked to contact your counselor, relieving you of collection calls.

If you go into the debt-management program, any of your creditors may report that fact to a credit bureau, and a future creditor could hold it against you. But credit experts point out that a mark indicating you have been through debt counseling is far preferable to one indicating that you have not paid your bills or that you declared bankruptcy.

For help in finding the nearest CCCS office in your area, check the Yellow Pages of your telephone directory, or see RESOURCES, page 493.

month. They have a car loan of $250 a month, and they owe $5,000 to credit card companies on which they must pay a minimum of $800 per month. The result is that they are paying 30 percent of their income to cover non-mortgage debts—a very dangerous position indeed.

To find your ratio, add all your monthly non-mortgage loans or credit card payments and then divide the total by your monthly net income. If your debt-to-income ratio, like Jane's and John's, is above 20 percent, you should take immediate action to get your debt under control.

First, find out where you stand. Summarize all your debts, including the total amount due, the amount overdue, and the minimum monthly payment requirements. Figure out what you can afford to pay each creditor; it is best to pay some amount on all your bills. If you ignore a creditor, the account may be sent to a collection agency.

If you cannot keep up to date with your payments, contact your creditors. Your position will be stronger if you are the one to initiate contact and you have a clear idea of what you can afford to offer. Speak to the credit manager or whoever can approve a repayment plan. Most creditors prefer negotiating a new repayment schedule to taking costly and time-consuming legal measures. (This renegotiation will appear on your credit record, however.)

Explain your situation and offer a modified payment plan, such as paying 75 percent of the normal amount for four months, then resuming the normal payments. Even small, consistent payments prove to your creditor that you are a responsible customer experiencing temporary difficulties, not a deadbeat. Be sure to follow up with a letter that restates your agreement, and send it certified mail, return receipt requested, so that you have proof it was received.

AVOID BACKSLIDING

Now resolve to stick with your revised payment plan. This is especially important if your debt is secured by collateral that a creditor can seize if you fail to pay your bill. The bills that should have priority include: your rent, utility bills (if your service is disconnected, you will probably have to pay larger security deposits for future services), and credit cards (late payments are reported to credit bureaus, which will make it difficult for you to get credit in the future). Some creditors write off accounts to "profit and loss" if they are 90 days or more delinquent. If you put off paying any bill for more than 90 days, the possible profit-and-loss mark on your credit file is an extremely negative entry.

You will have somewhat more leeway in delaying payments to doctors and dentists, who generally do not report to credit bureaus and rarely charge interest or late fees, although they may send your bills to a collection agency. Recently, hospitals have begun reporting some delinquent accounts to credit bureaus, but they are usually receptive to patients who offer a revised payment plan when they cannot pay in full. The local business people you deal with regularly, such as appliance repairmen and dry cleaners, do not generally report late bill paying to credit bureaus. Rather than taking advantage of them, however, you should overcome your embarrassment and tell them you are in temporary financial trouble; if you have been a good customer, they may agree to take reduced payments until you are back on your feet.

If you feel unable to resolve matters on your own, credit counseling is available. Many banks and credit unions offer formal or informal debt counseling for their customers or members, and valuable advice is available nationwide at nonprofit credit-counseling services. (See also "A Respected Source of Help," page 320.)

Coping With the Bill Collector

Creditors are quick to act when payments are late. If you miss more than a few payments, often creditors will ask for the full balance of the loan or debt to be paid immediately. The creditor has the right to do this if your loan agreement contains an "acceleration clause." If you immediately bring the payments up to date, the creditor may then decide not to insist that you pay the rest at once.

But when you do not respond with a payment, the creditor may threaten to turn the matter over to a collection agency, a business that collects debts for others. Often collection agencies work on commission, collecting between one-third and two-thirds of the amount they bring in. You can expect debt collectors to use high-pressure tactics to collect a debt, although the 1978 federal Fair Debt Collection Practices Act (FDCPA) protects consumers from unnecessary harassment and offensive strong-arm tactics. The act—which applies only to debt collectors, not creditors—makes very clear what a collection agency may not do in its efforts to get you to pay.

A bill collector may not contact any third parties about your debt except your lawyer, credit bureaus, and those who might help the agency locate you. If a collector does contact someone else to help locate you, he or she cannot indicate that debt collection, or your debt, is the reason for the call.

Contact can be made only during normal hours. You cannot be called before 8:00 A.M. and after 9:00 P.M. Nor can a collector call you repeatedly simply to annoy or intimidate you.

How to Stop Bothersome Bill Collectors

The federal Fair Debt Collection Practices Act protects consumers against the bullying tactics that were once stock-in-trade practices of collection agencies. If you feel you are being unduly pressured, or are actually being harassed by a bill collector, the FDCPA offers a simple way to put a stop to it.

All you have to do is send the bill collection agency a letter saying that you will not or cannot pay the debt and that you want the agency to leave you alone. Send the letter by certified mail, return receipt requested, so you can be sure the agency receives it.

Once you have done this, by law the collection agency may not contact you again, except to say that collection efforts have ended or that some legal action is being taken against you. (Your letter has not absolved you of your debt; you may still be taken to court for it.) If a collection agency continues to badger you after you have sent the letter, be sure to keep notes about the offending contacts. Then you should notify your state attorney general's office—you may well have a legal case against the collection agency.

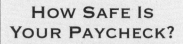

HOW SAFE IS YOUR PAYCHECK?

If a creditor takes you to court and wins, he may be granted the right to garnishee your wages. This means that unless and until you satisfy the debt, your employer may be required to withhold part of each paycheck and send it to the creditor. Garnishment can bring harsh consequences but also has its limitations.

1. Besides straight wages, your commissions, bonuses, retirement-program payments, and vacation pay can be garnisheed.

2. By federal law, you must be able to keep 75 percent of your weekly *net* wages (or 30 times the federal minimum hourly wage, whichever is greater). These items are deductible from your gross wages: federal, state, and city income taxes; Social Security contributions; Medicare payments; state unemployment taxes; and state employee retirement deductions.

3. Restrictions on garnishments do not apply if the debt is for federal or state taxes, delinquent child support payments, or bankruptcy.

4. If your wages are garnisheed for one debt, you cannot be fired; but if the garnishment is for more than one debt, you can be fired.

5. If you receive notice of wage garnishment, you may want to seek legal advice.

You have the right to demand that the debt collector stop calling you at work. If you have indicated that you are represented by an attorney, a bill collector may not call you in person at all.

No one can use false or deceptive collection methods, such as threatening you with arrest if you do not pay the debt, using a false name, or pretending to be a law enforcement officer or government official when calling to collect the debt.

Within five days of initially contacting you, a debt collector must send you written notification of the debt, giving the name of the creditor and the amount owed. You must also be advised of what to do if you disagree about the debt.

If you believe a collection agency has been acting illegally, you can take any of the following steps: notify the collection agency in writing that you do not wish to be harassed; write to the Federal Trade Commission, the Bureau of Consumer Protection, or the nearest regional office of the FTC and file a complaint. Or call the consumer protection division of the state attorney general's office.

COMING TO TERMS

The protection that the FDCPA offers you does not prevent debt collectors from exercising *their* rights. These will vary from state to state but may include the right to sue you in court. To keep matters from going that far, consider some tips for dealing with bill collectors:

- As you would with the actual creditor, be honest about your financial problems. If you are being pressured to pay more than you can afford, you may want to draw up a statement of your income and expenses to show what you can afford to pay.
- Resist pressure to agree to a repayment schedule you cannot afford or to pay with a postdated check. Ask for more time, and call back with a reasonable counteroffer. Often debt collectors have a great deal of flexibility both in terms of time and in negotiating the amount of the payments. However, if the collector's agreement with the creditor specifies a minimum acceptable amount, you will be unable to negotiate an alternative.
- Get the name of the person you spoke to. Record when and where you were contacted and any agreements you made with the bill collector. Keep copies of all correspondence pertaining to the debt. If you agree on payment terms, spell them out in a letter to the collector.
- If you agree to settle a debt for less than the total amount, take two precautions. First, write a disclaimer on the check that states "cashing this check constitutes payment in full." In some states, this will prevent the collector or creditor

from suing you for the difference between the check and the total amount of the debt. Then send a certified letter that spells out your agreement and asserts that if the debt collector cashes the check you have enclosed, it will satisfy the debt in full. Check with an attorney to make sure that this practice is legal in your state.

Is Bankruptcy the Answer?

At first glance, bankruptcy may seem like an easy way to get rid of debts and make a fresh start. Indeed, this country's bankruptcy law is designed not as punishment but as a stepping-stone to rehabilitation. Still, declaring bankruptcy can have a devastating effect on your life, and it should be pursued only as a last resort.

A bankruptcy filing generally stays on your credit report for 10 years, but the impact can last much longer. With a bankruptcy on your record, you could have trouble getting a job or renting an apartment, because of the black mark on your credit reports. You will also find it almost impossible to take out a loan, obtain a credit card, or be granted a mortgage. Most mortgage applications ask if you have ever declared bankruptcy—your "yes" will count strongly against you.

Why then did more than 800,000 Americans choose to file for bankruptcy in 1993? Because despite its ruinous effect on a credit record, bankruptcy can be a flexible and humane alternative for

Annual income twenty pounds, annual expenditure nineteen nineteen and six, result happiness. Annual income twenty pounds, annual expenditure twenty pounds ought and six, result misery.

CHARLES DICKENS
David Copperfield

Two Ways to Go Bankrupt

Two sections, or "chapters," of the federal bankruptcy code apply to individual bankruptcy: Chapter 7 and Chapter 13. (Chapter 11 usually applies to businesses.) Here are the basic differences between them. Before filing, consult a lawyer about which type best serves your situation.

• **Chapter 7.** Chapter 7 (or S) is designed for people who want to make a new start but cannot pay their debts from their current income. It requires immediate liquidation of whatever assets you may own except for certain exempt property such as a particular amount of equity in a home. Your remaining property is sold by a court-appointed trustee, and the money is then distributed to your creditors.

Once your bankruptcy is discharged—in the final court act that clears you of your debts—creditors can no longer try to obtain payment from you, even if all your debts were not paid off. However, you are still responsible for certain taxes as well as alimony, child support, and various other payments. Chapter 7 can be filed every six years.

• **Chapter 13.** Chapter 13, which involves a reorganization of your debts, is designed for people who want to pay off their debts but need more time to do so. You must be employed or have a regular income to be eligible to file for it. After a court approves your repayment plan, it appoints a trustee to make the payments (usually less than what you owe) to your creditors. These payments may be spread over three years. During this time, creditors cannot start or continue collection efforts.

After you have met the requirements of your plan, your bankruptcy will be discharged and your case closed. Certain debts, such as taxes and child support, must be paid in full, while others can be adjusted. Chapter 13 can be filed as often as necessary.

people who are so far into debt that there is no other hope of recovering. This is why federal law protects your right to file for bankruptcy—you cannot be fired from your job, for example. The law offers two types of personal bankruptcy: Chapter 7, called straight bankruptcy, and Chapter 13, known as the wage-earner's plan. (See also "Two Ways to Go Bankrupt," page 323.)

WHEN NOT TO CHOOSE BANKRUPTCY

Before seriously considering bankruptcy, ask yourself the following questions, which will help reveal whether your situation really requires that you take the fateful step.

- **Do I have much property to protect?** For consumers who have little money or property and no joint debts, a creditor who chooses to sue would have little chance of ever collecting the debt. In that case, filing for bankruptcy would mean unnecessary time and expense.
- **Will I lose property I need to keep?** Laws vary from state to state on what property is exempt in a Chapter 7 filing. If you are concerned you may lose essential property, avoid filing Chapter 7 and clarify any questions with your lawyer.
- **Could someone else get saddled with my debt?** If you had a cosigner on a loan, or if you have joint accounts, the lender can require the cosigner to make the payments once your liability has been discharged under Chapter 7.
- **Will I need to borrow again soon?** Getting credit after declaring bankruptcy is a difficult undertaking. Though most people considering bankruptcy have already severely compromised their credit reports, actually filing for bankruptcy is the worst mark you can put on your credit file.

If the answers to these questions are no and you still favor bankruptcy, most experts agree that because of the complexity of bankruptcy laws, you should have professional advice. Legal fees range from around $500 to more than $800 for a Chapter 7 filing and can be double that for a Chapter 13 filing.

Refurbishing Your Credit Image

Often people who have been through a major economic setback such as bankruptcy fear they will never get credit again. Because federal law allows negative information to remain on your credit report for seven or even ten years (for some levels of bankruptcy), it may seem as though only time will take care of a bad credit report. No doubt about it: cleaning up a blemished credit history will take time, but with persistence and a focused strat-

---

Credit for Delinquent Debtors

If you have a history of not paying your bills on time or of bankruptcy, you may be forced to apply for a "secured" credit card from a bank, savings and loan association, or credit union. As a security against default, you are required to deposit money with the bank or institution issuing the card. If you use this recourse, be sure to ask about the following:

✔ *Fees.* Often application and processing fees are levied as well as annual fees.

✔ *The deposit.* The amount required to secure the card ranges from a few hundred to a few thousand dollars. You will not be allowed to withdraw your money for as long as you have the card, so be sure you can afford to have the deposit unavailable to you.

✔ *Deposit interest.* Some card issuers pay you interest on only part of your deposit, or pay below-market rates.

✔ *Line of credit.* The amount you will be able to charge may not equal the amount you deposit. Some issuers give a credit line of only 50 percent of your deposit; others let you use all of it. Shop around for the best terms.

egy, within a few years you can reestablish your credit to the point where lenders will start talking to you again.

Your first step should be to review your credit report for any outdated or inaccurate information. (See also "Understanding Your Report," page 317.) If accounts you have paid in full are still listed as unpaid on the report, immediately notify the credit bureau. Try to pay off any accounts that are in arrears. Before you send a check, ask the creditor to remove all negative information from your credit file in exchange for your taking care of the outstanding balance. Although under no obligation to agree, the creditor may be willing to remove at least some of the negative information. For example, if you overextended yourself to a department store, it may be eager to keep your business and may remove a problematic notation.

ACCENTUATING THE POSITIVE

You will also need to get positive information in your credit file as soon as possible. This is where strategy counts. A good first step is to take out a savings passbook loan at a bank that will report this loan to a credit bureau. For passbook loans, you deposit a certain sum and ask the bank to give you a loan against the money in your account. In exchange, you turn your passbook over to the bank. Banks are willing to do this because they incur no risk: If you do not pay back the loan, the bank simply takes the money out of your account. As you repay the loan, month by month, you rebuild your credit standing.

Holding a major bank credit card is usually considered a stronger reference than any other type of account, even a mortgage. If you had a credit card that was canceled, try to reopen the account. Often, paying what you owe will enable you to get your card back. If you cannot get your account reopened, consider a secured credit card, which is backed by a deposit in the bank that issues the card. (See "Credit for Delinquent Debtors," page 324.) For a list of secured credit card issuers, call a nearby Consumer Credit Counseling Services office.

KEEP YOUR EYE ON THE GOAL

Not all credit accounts will enhance your creditworthiness. Some creditors, such as furniture stores and most gasoline card issuers, do not report accounts unless they become delinquent, so that kind of credit activity will not bolster your credit standing. Until your credit standing is restored, avoid opening any accounts that will not help you achieve that goal, so that you do not further overextend your ability to pay.

Finally, don't think you can get away from your bad credit record by moving. The major credit bureaus operate nationwide, and they will find you. Only by rebuilding good credit can you set the record straight.

BEWARE CREDIT-REPAIR SCAMS

Credit-repair companies that promise to "clean up credit reports" prey on debtors looking for a quick fix for their credit problems. Most of these companies charge hefty fees for advice but do nothing to improve credit ratings that the average consumer could not do alone.

If, nevertheless, you decide to pay a credit-repair company to deal with your creditors and credit bureaus, protect yourself by following these guidelines:

1. Contact your state attorney general or local Better Business Bureau to see if any complaints have been lodged against the company.

2. Make sure that the company is licensed or bonded in your state.

3. Avoid firms claiming that accurate negative data can be changed or erased. Such claims are false.

4. Be wary if you are asked for a large fee up front. Choose a company that charges only if it succeeds in getting information removed or corrected.

5. Ask whether you will receive a refund if the negative or incorrect information reappears on your file. Use only credit companies that offer this guarantee.

LIFE INSURANCE

Two out of three Americans buy life insurance, but almost everyone is confused by it. To protect your money, get all the information you can.

How Much Life Insurance Do You Need?

If anyone besides yourself is dependent on your income, you should have life insurance. But how much should you buy? Enough to fill the gap between the amount of income your dependents would have at your death, and the amount they would need to live on.

Before consulting an insurance agent or broker, make your own estimate based on an honest assessment of your present financial situation. Here is one useful rule of thumb: Buy life insurance worth five to seven times your gross annual salary. That figure is your starting point. From it, subtract the resources that will be available at your death, such as income from investments and savings, your spouse's earnings, death benefits from your company insurance policy, and Social Security and pension benefits.

Armed with this estimate of how much extra your family will need, you can better judge the figure that an insurance agent will suggest. The money your family will need changes with time, so every year or two, review your financial picture and compare it with the coverage you have.

Safety Net or Savings Plan?

When you buy life insurance, you are buying protection for your dependents from a loss of income if you die prematurely. But life insurance can also be a savings program, an investment opportunity, a source of collateral—or perhaps a waste of money. One thing life insurance is not, is simple. Buying it presents one of the most perplexing financial decisions consumers face: whether to buy, how much to buy, what type to buy, and from whom?

Although Americans spend around $65 billion annually on various forms of life insurance, few people really understand it. Consumer experts report that buyers of life insurance are less knowledgeable about the product than are the consumers of almost any other product in the country. One reason is that life insurance comes in a baffling array of forms. To find one that matches your needs and your ability to pay, you should begin by learning the vocabulary of life insurance. (See "Basic Life Insurance Language," on the next page.) Then start asking questions about how life insurance can work best for you.

The first consideration is whether you need it at all. Does anyone besides you depend on your income? If not, life insurance is probably the wrong way for you to spend your money. If you have dependents who would not otherwise have enough money to live on should you die, then you undoubtedly do need some kind of coverage.

TERM LIFE INSURANCE

Life insurance goes by many names, but comes in two basic varieties: "term insurance" and "cash-value insurance." Term insurance provides protection in much the same way that auto or homeowners insurance policies do: you pay premiums, and in exchange the policy pays a sum of money to your beneficiaries if you die. As the name implies, a term policy is for a set period of time, usually one or five years. When the term ends, so does your coverage unless you renew. You get back nothing—neither your money nor any interest—from the policy. However, for people with average incomes and family responsibilities, term insurance is appropriate.

BASIC LIFE INSURANCE LANGUAGE

Almost as many different life insurance policies are available to confused consumers as different kinds of loans. Because life insurance is a major financial commitment for most families, before you start shopping for a policy, you should familiarize yourself with the basic types, their advantages, and their drawbacks.

Policy type	Features	Advantages	Disadvantages
Term	Offers protection for a specified period of time. A physical exam is usually required. The insurance premium buys you simple risk coverage. Some policies are renewable, covering you for a fixed period of years or until a specified age. Many offer a "level term": the annual premium stays the same for a designated period, such as five or ten years	Most affordable and simplest form of insurance protection when you are young; easiest to comparison shop	Premiums increase periodically as you become older; after age 55, term becomes very expensive
Whole life	A cash-value policy that covers you for your entire life and offers a guaranteed sum payable to your beneficiaries when you die. Part of your premium pays the actual cost of the insurance risk, part pays the insurer's expenses, and part goes into the reserve fund known as the cash value. The cash value builds up annually on a tax-deferred basis	You can borrow against the cash value at favorable rates; you pay the same premium into old age; simplest type of cash-value insurance	Premiums start and remain high because some of the money goes toward cash value; not all policies offer dividends; even if they do, the amount of the dividend is not guaranteed
Universal life	A variation of whole life insurance that allows flexible premium payments. The premium is first used to pay for insurance protection and expenses. Any excess (the cash-value portion) is put into an interest-bearing account. When money has accumulated, you can increase or decrease the premium—or even skip a year or two—without affecting your coverage	Flexibility in amount of coverage and the amount of premium; you can see how your premium is divided	The return on your cash value is tied to an interest-rate index, and your return will vary; flexibility feature means you may have to put extra money aside each year in premium payments to make sure the death benefit remains at the desired amount
Variable life	Also a variation of whole life, with the cash value invested in one or more stocks, bonds, or money market funds that the insurer offers. You choose among fixed annual premiums	Fixed premium payments mean a guaranteed death benefit; investment options are the opportunity to participate in the stock market	You assume the risk for your cash-value investments; if you choose to buy stocks, for example, and the market declines, you could end up with little or no cash value to your policy

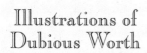

Illustrations of Dubious Worth

A convincing sales tool for insurance agents pitching cash-value life insurance is the so-called policy illustration. This is a computer printout with impressive columns of figures that are supposed to show how much you can expect to pay for a particular policy and what any investment account that comes with it might earn in interest. Can you trust these figures?

Unfortunately, no. In drawing up the illustration, an insurance company can make whatever assumptions it wants to about such variables as the interest rates it will be paying 20 years from now. Often such projections are not realistic. The illustration may also be embellished with intimations of premium bonuses that in fact are not guaranteed.

Furthermore, the illustration may fail to show the true costs of your policy—the amount the insurance company takes from your earnings to cover the cost of administering the policy and its investments. And, should you borrow against your cash-value policy in the future, that, too, might darken the rosy picture painted by the illustration.

How can you protect yourself? Be skeptical of optimistic speculation and ask your agent to point out and confirm those factors that are guaranteed in your contract: the premium, the actual cash value, and the death benefit.

CASH-VALUE INSURANCE

"Cash-value insurance" (also known, in various forms, as whole life, universal, or variable insurance) is more complicated because it is essentially a combination of a life insurance coverage and a savings plan. You pay periodic premiums, and the insurer pays a specified death benefit when you die. But the policy, in addition to covering your life, also builds a savings account or a "cash value" that is worth something even before you die. You can borrow against it, cash it in, or, with some policies, invest it. This kind of dual-purpose policy costs more —about eight times the cost of term insurance for a comparable death benefit.

Cash-value insurance seems to offer some advantages: it is forced savings; it can be fully paid after a number of years; you can borrow against the cash value at relatively low interest rates; and the cash value grows at a tax-deferred rate. Perhaps most advantageous, particularly for the very wealthy, is the fact that life insurance need not become part of your taxable estate.

However, these advantages may not be as glowing as they first appear. For example, you can usually earn more money faster investing it in other ways. Cash-value insurance is sold on the basis of a "policy illustration." Illustrations estimate how much the cash value of your policy will grow and how much interest this money will generate over a period of years. These illustrations are not guaranteed, and, in fact, the interest rates estimated are often far higher than reality.

Moreover, if you borrow against the cash value, your death benefit is reduced by the amount you borrow. If you die while the loan is outstanding, your heirs will receive less than the policy's face value. Also, although you may be borrowing at a relatively modest rate (usually seven to nine percent), bear in mind that you are actually borrowing from yourself. Depending on your situation, it may be more advantageous to borrow from another institution such as a bank or a credit union.

How to Work With an Agent

Most prospective buyers need help in choosing the right insurance policy. Can you count on an insurance agent to help you understand which is the best one for you? Yes—but only if you do your homework first. When you have come to at least a vague understanding of how much coverage you need and can afford, you are ready to ask for help with filling in the details.

Start with an agent (who is a representative of one particular company) or broker (an agent who represents several insurance companies) who has at least one or two clients you know.

Ask the agent how long she has been with the agency she is advocating. Since only 43 percent of all life insurance agents stay at the same agency for more than four years, you will want to establish how long this agent will be available to help you. When you make a major purchase such as life insurance, you obviously want an agent who will be around to service it.

All states require that agents be licensed to sell life insurance. An agent who has studied for the industry credential of Chartered Life Underwriter (CLU) has trained in areas such as insurance contract analysis, personal-risk management, and ethics. Having an agent with such experience may be helpful; however, fewer than five percent of licensed agents are CLU's.

Consider also if you want to buy from a "captive" agent, who sells only one company's products, or from an independent broker. Although captive agents can sometimes offer better prices, they must try to sell you their company's policies even if another firm's might suit you better. Independent brokers may sell for six or eight different insurers. You may pay more in insurance costs for their services, but they can pick the best of what each company has to offer.

Insurance agents sell on commission, and that can work against the consumer. Here is why: the cheapest life insurance is term, which pays agents a commission of about 60 percent of your first-year premium. Cash-value (or whole life) insurance is more expensive for the consumer, and therefore more difficult to sell. But for a cash-value insurance policy, an agent may receive a commission as high as 90 percent of your first-year premium. With that kind of incentive, agents tend to push cash-value policies. If you drop your policy within five years—as about 40 percent of buyers do—"surrender" charges (such as an agent's commission) will absorb most if not all of the money you put in.

HOW AN AGENT HELPS

Nevertheless, an agent can be a big help to you in your search for the right policy. Always ask the agent for a sample policy form to read and request clarification about anything you do not understand. Be sure to ask these questions:

- What is the financial strength of the insurance company? Several major organizations rate insurance companies. Make sure that the company you are considering gets top ratings from at least two of them. (For the names of these organizations, see "Rating the Raters of Insurers," page 333.)
- What assumptions are used to calculate the potential value in the savings component of a cash-value policy? These so-called policy illustrations are not guaranteed. (See also "Illustrations of Dubious Worth," page 328.)

Other Routes for Finding Life Insurance

Calling an insurance agent is not the only way to find the right life insurance policy. Here are some other sources to consider:

✔ *Your employer.* Your employer may already provide some insurance as part of your compensation package. If so, you may have the option of purchasing additional life insurance through your employer. Talk with your director of human resources or your corporate agent.

✔ *Savings-bank life insurance.* If you live or work in Connecticut, Massachusetts, or New York, you can buy term life insurance at many of those states' savings banks.

✔ *Non-agented policies.* Some companies now offer both term and cash-value insurance directly to the public. Their policies have lower fees because no sales commission is involved. For a list of such insurance companies, ask your state insurance commissioner's office.

✔ *NICO.* For sensible and impartial counsel about any aspect of buying insurance, contact the National Insurance Consumer Organization (NICO), a nonprofit, public-interest organization that helps consumers buy insurance wisely. For the address and telephone number of NICO, see RESOURCES, page 493.

- If you are buying a term policy, how often must it be renewed? Can you renew it automatically, or will you have to go through a medical exam again? Under what circumstances?
- Will the premiums of a term policy go up? If so, by how much? And are those figures merely projected or are they guaranteed?
- Is the company licensed in your state? Some states, such as New York, have strict laws governing first-year commissions on life insurance.

If after buying a policy you decide you were pressured or misled into buying it—or even if you simply have second thoughts—you have the right to return it for a full refund within 10 days. Many states, while recognizing the tendency of agents to make an overenthusiastic pitch, hold that nothing an agent tells you before you sign an insurance contract can be legally binding if it is not in writing.

Making Sure Your Policy Keeps Up With You

As your life changes, so should your life insurance. It is important to review your insurance periodically to make sure it reflects your new circumstances. Have you had another child? Have your children all graduated from college? Has your health improved dramatically? Have you been divorced or remarried? These are all milestones that can affect your insurance criteria.

If, for example, you named "my husband" as a beneficiary in the original policy and have since been divorced and remarried, you may want to make it clear that you mean your current spouse, and name him. If you were a smoker and have since given it up, you may be able to get your premiums lowered by as much as one-third. A diabetic who has brought the disease under control, an avid scuba diver who has given up that risky avocation, an alcoholic who has quit drinking—all may be able to show that they have become less of a risk to the insurer, and so get their rates reduced.

If you have a cash-value policy and want to know the effect of rising or falling interest rates on your life insurance investment, you can receive information by sending for an "in-force ledger statement." This is an updated version of the policy illustration you were shown when you first purchased your policy, and it will show exactly how much cash you have built up in the policy. The company's policyholder service department can also draw up ledger statements to show any changes that would

---

occur if interest on your cash value should drop further or move higher.

Thus, there are many reasons why you should check your life insurance policy every year or two to make sure it remains appropriate to your needs. Reading your policy carefully is the only way to be certain what your coverage is and how it might be changed to your advantage.

WHERE TO FIND HELP

Because life insurance is such a complex financial instrument, and because no standardized forms exist for the many different types of life insurance policies, you may need help figuring out what changes you can make to keep your policy timely. If so, try calling the National Insurance Consumer Helpline (800 942-4242), a toll-free consumer information service sponsored by insurance-industry trade associations. Trained staff and licensed agents answer questions and refer your complaints to appropriate sources.

Are You Insurable?

To decide whether to insure you and how much to charge you for it, an insurance company goes through a process called underwriting. An underwriter tries to estimate how much it will cost the company to insure your life by learning as much as possible about your background, your present state of health, and your habits. For example, an underwriter may want to know if you told the truth about your smoking habits or if you have a spotty driving record. Statistics tell the underwriter that these two habits can shorten your life—and thus increase the company's costs for insuring it.

Your application for insurance includes a waiver that allows the insurer to check your background. The higher the amount of insurance you apply for, the more extensive the checking process will be. Usually the waiver states that information can be passed on to the Medical Information Bureau (MIB), a giant clearinghouse of information for the insurance industry.

SEARCHING FOR FLAWS

The MIB is usually the first stop in an underwriter's background check. The bureau, a consortium of about 750 of the largest life insurance companies in the United States and Canada, keeps records on some 15 million people who have medical conditions or other factors that could affect their longevity. The MIB then sells this data to insurance companies, which use it to discover false or incomplete information on insurance applications.

Coming Clean On Your Insurance Application

Much is at stake, for both you and the insurer, when you fill out an application for life insurance. How you answer the questions about your health, previous medical conditions, and lifestyle will affect whether your application is accepted and what rates you will be charged. Giving untrue or incomplete answers—even slightly understating your age, for example—can have serious consequences.

The insurer has two years to find out and correct any misinformation on your application. If you lied or deliberately omitted important information—such as whether or not you smoke—and if you then die within that two-year period, the insurer can deny all or part of your claim. Your survivors will get back the premiums you paid but will not get the substantial sum you wanted them to have.

Your application will probably have a provision authorizing the insurer to check into your background with the Medical Information Bureau (MIB), a computerized medical data bank. Unless you sign this clause, the insurance company probably will not move forward on your application.

Insurers cast a wide net to fish for information about applicants. Insurers hire investigators to get records from doctors, hospitals, financial institutions, medical labs, employers, and the Department of Motor Vehicles. If the underwriter discovers a condition that bears on your health or longevity, he sends a report to the MIB.

What are the chances of your being in the MIB files? The bureau says that out of 10 applicants, it will have a record on only one or two. The MIB also claims that fewer than one percent of consumers who send for their MIB records find them to be inaccurate or incomplete. (The MIB's policy is to eliminate any reports more than seven years old.)

Insurers who uncover a potential medical problem in an MIB search are prohibited by the MIB's rules from making eligibility decisions that are based only on that information. The insurer must then conduct its own independent investigation to confirm the report.

As with credit bureaus, the MIB is required by the federal Fair Credit Reporting Act to either verify or remove informa-

When You Think You Want to Switch Insurance Policies

Whether or not to change life insurers after you have been with a firm for several years is a thorny question. Whatever your reasons for thinking of switching—you are worried about your company's financial stability, for example, or you want a different type of policy—you should proceed with caution, because switching can be costly. Here are some guidelines:

• Consult the agent who sold you your current policy, or another agent from the same company. With their help, you may find a way to modify your present policy to achieve the coverage you want and need.

• Before committing yourself, discuss your plans with at least two insurance agents and let them review each other's advice. That way you can avoid making a bad decision based solely on sales pitches or unrealistic policy projections.

• Be wary of agents who approach you to suggest a switch from your old policy to a new one. First of all, you may have to pay a new sales commission. Agents do much of their most lucrative commission business this way. For cheaper and more objective advice on whether the switch makes sense, pay a nominal fee to the nonprofit National Insurance Consumer Organization (NICO).

• Never cash in your current policy until you get a new one. If your health has deteriorated over the years, you may not pass the medical exam a new insurer is likely to require.

• Insurance experts caution that you will probably take a loss if you switch a whole-life insurance policy that you have held for less than 10 years to a new company. To assess the costs of making the switch, your calculations should include how much you have already paid in, the cash value of the policy, and the insurer's surrender charges. Don't forget that if your cash value is more than the cost of all the premiums you paid in, you will owe income taxes on the difference.

• You can transfer your cash value from your old policy to a new policy by making a 1035 Exchange, named after the tax law that makes this type of transfer tax-free if you transfer the policy directly from one insurance company to the other.

• Switching to cheaper term insurance may well be a sensible move. If you find a lower-priced policy that suits your needs, consider it seriously.

tion that you dispute. To receive a free copy of your file, call or write to the MIB. (For the address and telephone number, see RESOURCES, page 493.)

If Your Insurer Fails

The peace of mind that life insurance is supposed to buy can disappear quickly if your life insurer gets into financial trouble. Between 1989 and 1993, more than 65 life insurance companies in the United States failed. Unfortunately, when that happens, a policyholder has few rights and can face long delays in getting both money and information. Although most of the country's 1,800 life insurance companies are in no danger of going under, every policyholder should understand what can happen if an insurer fails.

One possibility is that another company will buy the failed company's policies. In that case, the insured's death benefit would be protected, since insurers and regulators make paying death benefits in full a top priority. But the new company could raise premiums or lower the interest rates used to build up savings in a cash-value policy. Options to withdraw your cash value may be limited or suspended.

If no other company steps in, a backup system that all 50 states now have, called a guaranty fund, may come to the rescue. Through the fund, state-licensed insurers promise that if one of them fails, the others will put up money to reimburse the failed insurer's customers. These state funds usually have no assets, however; they must collect from other insurers to cover the policyholders of the failed company, a process which can take years. In addition, some guaranty funds have limits to their coverage, typically $100,000 for individual cash-value policies, $300,000 for death benefits, and $300,000 for all claims combined. Many policyholders of failed insurance companies have discovered that the state guaranty funds fell far short of the amounts they expected their policies to deliver.

WHAT IF TROUBLE LOOMS?

If you see trouble looming, you will find no easy solutions. Changing to another company can be time-consuming and expensive. (See "When You Think You Should Switch Insurance Policies," page 332.) One alternative is to take out a loan against your policy, if it is a cash-value policy, and put the money into a safer investment. You will have to pay interest to the insurer, but at least the money will be where you can get it if the company fails.

Rating the Raters of Insurers

How can you be sure your insurance company is financially sound? Consumer experts have long advised that you check with one of the five major organizations that rate the financial health of individual insurers: Standard & Poor's, A.M. Best Co., Moody's, Duff and Phelps, and Weiss Research. (For their addresses and telephone numbers, see RESOURCES, page 493.) While that is still good advice, you should be sure to check with more than one, and to check each year to make sure the company's rating has not slipped.

Here is how the insurance raters operate: Each of the major insurance raters assigns a letter ranking to a company based on its estimate of the firm's financial stability. But the rating services vary in how they interpret financial data the insurers supply to them. One rater gave an A+ to a major insurer just 10 days before the company failed.

Also confusing is the different grading system each rater uses; an A- from one service may not mean the same as A- from another.

In order to make the best-informed choice, stick to insurers that have received a top rating from at least two of the major insurance raters. Also, avoid companies rated less than A+ and triple-A by any of the rating agencies. Even with no guarantees, high marks are still better than low ones.

INVESTING YOUR MONEY

You have worked hard, borrowed wisely, and saved a bit. Now it is time to make that extra money grow. Learn how to protect yourself from the pitfalls of investing.

Investment Basics

Like cash stashed under the mattress, money in the bank is safe—but it earns very little. If you want greater reward from your savings, you will have to invest it elsewhere. The financial world offers a daunting variety of investment prospects, and the law provides a number of consumer safeguards. One of the most basic of these is that any firm or individual who accepts investment funds from the public has an obligation to manage the money responsibly. The law cannot, however, protect you from yourself. Understanding the basic types of financial investments and their degrees of risk will help you avoid mistakes. (Other investment opportunities also abound, ranging from real estate to collectibles; here we will consider the chief financial instruments that are available.)

Financial investments fall into one of two categories: bonds or stocks. The difference between them is the difference between being a lender and being an owner. When you invest in bonds, you are really lending your money to a business or a government. The borrower pays you interest on the money you lend until a specific date, when you expect to get your money back. By investing in stocks, you become an owner of shares in a business. The value of your investment depends on the company's success. You share in the profits of a company in the form of dividends as well as any future increase in the stock price. Stocks are traditionally a riskier investment than bonds, but over time stocks have offered greater monetary rewards.

TYPES OF INVESTMENTS AND THEIR RISKS
Here are brief descriptions of some common investment vehicles, their relative benefits and risks:

U.S. Treasury issues (bonds) raise money for the federal government, and they come in three categories: bonds, notes, and bills. Because the U.S. government backs them, they are the safest possible investment. (Buying shares in a mutual fund investing in government securities is not the same as buying Treasury issues.) "Treasury bonds" are issued with maturity periods of 10 to 30 years, with the minimum purchase price set at $1,000. "Treasury notes" have maturity periods of one to 10 years and are offered in minimum denominations of $5,000 or $1,000, depending on the note's maturity period. "Treasury bills" are issued in three-month, six-month, and one-year maturities, at a minimum price of $10,000.

Treasury bonds and notes provide semiannual interest payments; Treasury bills are sold at a discount, with the interest deducted from the purchase price, so that in effect you get your profit up front. The primary risk associated with "Treasuries" occurs if you sell them before they mature, and even that risk is negligible since, unlike shares of stock, they are never worth less than what was paid for them plus interest.

Series EE bonds (U.S. savings bonds) are high-quality bonds issued by the U.S. government that sell for one-half their face value, which ranges from $50 to $10,000. The maturity period is 30 years, but EE bonds can be cashed in, for their current value (principal plus interest), anytime after six months from the issue date. Federal taxes owed on the interest can be postponed until the bonds are redeemed; they are exempt from state and local taxes. U.S. savings bonds can be bought from banks (in some states) and other financial institutions, or through regular payroll deductions at most major companies.

Series HH bonds (U.S. savings bonds) also are high-quality bonds issued by the U.S. government. They are sold at their full face value and pay interest at a fixed annual rate of six percent. These bonds can be obtained only through the exchange of matured Series EE bonds, and cannot be bought.

Municipal bonds are various kinds of bonds issued through a state, city, or other municipality. Municipal bonds are typically free of federal, state, and local taxes and are generally considered just below U.S. government bonds in terms of safety and quality. You can buy them through brokerage houses.

Corporate bonds are issued by private corporations as a way to raise large sums of money, usually for capital expansion or for diversifying debt. If the corporation is highly rated by agencies such as Standard & Poor's or Moody's, they usually pay slightly more interest than do U.S. government bonds, at relatively low risk. Low-rated corporations offer even higher rates but usually carry higher risk. If interest rates drop, a corporation may call in its bonds and give you the cash amount ("call price") promised when issued.

Annuities are insurance company products that can pay you a guaranteed return annually or at regular intervals. The insurance company invests your money and agrees to pay you back at a rate defined by the annuity contract. (See also "Saving for Retirement," page 357.) Annuities are sold by commercial banks, savings institutions, and other financial service organizations as well as by insurance company agents.

Tips for Fighting Investment Fraud

Americans lose billions of dollars annually to con men who talk them into investing in ventures that are either not as advertised or simply nonexistent. The swindlers mimic the approaches of legitimate firms, but they usually tip their hands in one way or another:

✔ *Large-Profit Expectations.* A swindler might convince you that buying stock in a local cable company will be profitable since cable companies are hot. However, he then exaggerates its value and encourages you to buy more than you should by suggesting the potential profit is far greater than he could possibly guarantee.

✔ *Low Risk.* The con man becomes impatient or angry if you question the risk involved in an investment that he insists is safe. Visionary Cable is so hot, he insists, that your investment risk is virtually nil.

✔ *Urgency.* The swindler pushes you to rush into the investment. Unless you invest in Visionary Cable now, he says, the opportunity to buy at a good price will be gone. If you ask for a prospectus, he ridicules you, saying you will only lose out on a good deal if you take time to do research.

✔ *Confidence.* To secure your trust, the swindler conveys the notion that he is doing you a favor by offering you this investment opportunity, often warning that other people will be interested if you are not.

Stocks represent shares of ownership in a company. Many high-quality stocks pay owners dividends—cash returns on their investments.

Mutual fund money market accounts, although not federally insured like bank money market accounts, are invested in only high-quality, short-term debt such as government Treasury bills, so they are among the safest short-term investments. These funds generally yield higher short-term returns than bank savings or money market accounts and are offered by most major mutual fund companies and by some brokerage firms.

Mutual funds are one of the most popular investment vehicles. Financial instruments sold by banks, such as bank money market accounts and certificates of deposit (CD's), also are popular. (See also "Banking," page 288.)

Buy an annuity cheap, and make your life interesting to yourself and everybody else that watches the speculation.

CHARLES DICKENS
Martin Chuzzlewit

The People's Choice—Mutual Funds

More than one out of every four households in the United States now owns shares in a mutual fund. Mutual funds are investment companies that pool your money with that of thousands of other individuals and invest it in an assortment of stocks, bonds, and other securities.

The numbers and diversity result in a considerable amount of safety, but mutual funds are not guaranteed, and, like the securities in which they invest, the funds will fluctuate in value

---

Three Rules on Risk

The point of investing rather than saving money is to make a bigger profit. But that means taking risks, and in general , the amount of money you can make is relative to the amount of risk you take. Here are some basic ground rules about risk:

• **Never risk money you cannot afford to lose.** For example, if you are retired and depend on Social Security and a pension just to break even, it may be unwise to take risks with whatever extra money you have saved over the years. Or, if you have accumulated a nest egg to pay for a major expense, such as a child's college tuition, you may want to switch that money out of riskier investments, such as stocks, into a federally guaranteed savings account so that you can be sure it is there when the college bills come due.

• **Never invest in anything you don't understand.** In order to invest sensibly, you do not need to understand all the intricacies of the stock market's operation, but you should certainly understand how *your* money is being put to work. If the salesperson cannot explain the terms of the investment (the relative riskiness of a particular stock, for example) to you clearly and briefly, don't buy it.

• **Never exceed your tolerance for risk.** Some people are temperamentally capable of riding the ups and downs of the stock market, while others find themselves unable to sleep at night because they are worrying that their investments might take a dive on the next day's market. Only you can determine how much risk you can handle—but it is the responsibility of your stockbroker to explain clearly how much risk is likely to be involved in a particular transaction.

with changing conditions in the financial markets. For investors accustomed to watching their savings grow, however modestly, in a bank account, this factor can be unsettling.

HOW TO CHOOSE A FUND

With some 5,000 funds to choose from, you may decide you need help. One way to get it is to pay a broker or financial planner an up-front sales commission, or "load," to do the selecting for you. Loads generally range from 4 percent to as high as 8.5 percent of the money you invest. You should be aware of the true cost of the advice you receive. If you invest $1,000 in a fund that charges an 8 percent load, and the fund turns in a 10 percent performance that year, you will indeed earn 10 percent—but it will not be on your full $1,000. You will earn 10 percent on only $920, because the sales load is taken out before your money gets invested.

If you want to act on your own behalf, choose several well-performing "no-load" funds that consistently yield good returns over 10 to 15 years and whose objectives match yours. Most libraries have mutual fund information sources that track thousands of funds, such as Morningstar, Value Line, and *Individual Investor's Guide to No-Load Mutual Funds*, published by the American Association of Individual Investors.

When you have narrowed down the field of funds that match your goals and risk tolerance, call the 800 number for each fund (which can be secured by dialing the 800 number for directory assistance: 800 555-1212) and ask the company to send you its prospectus. A prospectus is a legal document—reviewed by the Securities and Exchange Commission (SEC)—that sets out the fund's objectives, costs, and performance history. It will help you determine which funds will be the most beneficial to own.

COMPARING COSTS

Every fund charges management fees and expenses, and they vary widely from fund to fund. You should look for the funds with the highest returns combined with the most reasonable annual fees and expenses, since those costs can have a major impact on the rate of return on your investment earnings. How do you figure out what the costs are going to be? Some fees, such as the commissions charged by load funds, are obvious, while others are virtually invisible. The only way to be certain of all costs involved in owning a fund is to read the prospectus carefully. The most useful information about costs is summarized in the first few pages. Be sure to watch out for the following fees and hidden expenses:

- **Back-end loads**, also known as redemption fees, are taken

When Banks Sell Mutual Funds

Many people think of banks as rocks of security in a sea of financial uncertainty. But do not take it for granted that your bank is a trustworthy investment adviser.

Since 1993 banks and savings and loan associations have been allowed to sell mutual funds and other securities. But nationwide spot checks made by federal regulators have shown that many bank salespeople consistently fail to tell potential investors that although a checking account in the bank is protected by the Federal Deposit Insurance Corporation (FDIC), the bank's mutual funds are not federally guaranteed.

Salespeople may also neglect to disclose information about the annual operating expenses of funds—which can exceed two percent of your investment—as well as other details about a bank fund's charges and fees.

These are not fraudulent practices. The government so far has not issued mandatory guidelines as to what banks must disclose voluntarily. But to protect yourself, ask for prospectuses for funds you are offered, along with the latest reports from independent rating firms such as Morningstar.

If you do not receive complete answers to all your questions, take your business elsewhere.

Unraveling Mutual Funds

Mutual funds are perhaps the most popular investment instrument on the market today, but they present a mystifying assortment of choices. Before you choose a specific fund to invest in, you should understand the various types that exist within the three main groups of mutual funds: stock funds, bond funds, and money market funds.

STOCK FUNDS

• **Aggressive growth funds.** The portfolio manager seeks above-average returns by taking above-average risks, usually investing in speculative stocks that may rise sharply in value but that generate little or no income from dividends.

• **Growth funds.** With these funds the focus is on firms that have the potential for steady growth in earnings. The degree of risk involved will be roughly comparable to stock market averages; that is, when the market is up, the price per share will be up (although not necessarily proportionally), and vice versa.

• **Growth and income funds.** A stock portfolio balanced between stocks that offer growth in principal and stocks with income greater than stock market averages is the goal of this type of fund.

• **Equity-income funds.** Such funds generally invest about half the portfolio in dividend-paying stocks, which provide the equity. The rest of the portfolio is invested in bonds and convertible bonds that can be switched into stocks, which provide most of the income. High income is a key feature of these funds.

• **Index funds.** Index funds use computer technology to purchase stocks that match an index such as the Standard & Poor's 500 Stock Index. They are designed for consumers who are satisfied with doing as well as the market—not beating it—in good times and bad. The costs of index funds tend to be lower because no research is involved.

• **Small capitalization funds.** "Small cap" funds invest mostly in smaller companies that are more flexible and have the potential to grow faster than many of the larger, more mature corporations. The risks are higher because the companies are fairly new and have no track record, but the rewards, in the right economic climate or with the right young company, can also be high.

• **International stock funds.** International funds invest in firms in foreign countries. The risk involved is hard to figure, because it depends on many factors, including a country's political and economic stability and the fluctuations in foreign currency. Depending on the world area being invested in, international funds can be more volatile than others. One variation, global funds, invests in U.S. securities as well.

BOND FUNDS

• **Corporate bond funds.** Such funds buy and trade bonds of corporations. One type of corporate bond fund buys only investment-grade bonds (based on the judgment of rating companies such as Moody's), thus limiting risk. Another type, high-yield bond funds, also called "junk bonds," specialize in lower-quality bonds that may offer bigger profits because they offer higher interest rates, but also carry much higher risk.

• **Government bond funds.** U.S. government funds offer total protection from bond default, although the value of government bonds will fluctuate with interest rates, as all bonds and bond funds do. They are exempt from state and local income taxes.

• **Municipal bond funds.** When municipalities issue bonds, that investment is free from federal income taxes. There is also a type of state-specific municipal bond fund that holds municipal bonds from only that state, thus avoiding state income taxes, too.

MONEY MARKET FUNDS

• **Money market funds.** A variety of short-term interest-earning securities, such as Treasury bills and bank certificates of deposit, constitute the portfolio of money market funds. They are perfectly liquid, so you can write a check for all or part of your money anytime. Most money market funds limit the minimum check amount you can write. (Bank money market funds also restrict the number of checks you can write per month.)

• **U.S. Government money market funds.** These funds invest only in short-term U.S. Treasury securities. These funds can have a somewhat lower rate of return, but are safe and conservative investments. These are appropriate for the investor who is in a high tax bracket.

• **Tax-exempt money market funds.** The investment is in very short-term instruments that are issued by states or municipalities.

out of the value of your shares when you sell them.

- **Deferred-loads** are fees imposed if you redeem your shares before a specified time, often five years.
- **Dividend-reinvestment fees** are charged by some funds for the service of automatically reinvesting dividends.
- **Management fees** are fees charged by the brokerage for supervision of the fund.
- **12b-1 fees**, named for the pertinent section of an SEC rule, are deducted from a fund's overall assets to cover the costs of advertising and marketing. As of 1994, funds cannot charge a 12b-1 fee of more than 1 percent, and many experts advise looking for funds whose 12b-1 fee is not greater than .25 percent.
- **Expense ratio** is the cost of running a fund expressed as a percentage of the fund's assets. When other factors are equal, the funds with lower expense ratios will outperform higher-cost funds. Many financial experts advise that you look for stock funds whose expense ratio is less than 1 percent and bond funds with expense ratios of less than .75 percent.

MONITORING YOUR FUND

To calculate exactly how much you have made or lost on your mutual fund investment, compare the value of your holdings in the fund today against the dollar amount you originally invested, plus dollars reinvested, if any, minus any loans. First, consult your most recent fund statement to see how many shares you now own. Then, look up the fund's net asset value (sometimes called the "sell" or "bid" price) in the financial section of a major daily newspaper, or, if you are computer-savvy, through one of the popular on-line tracking services. You might also call the fund's 800 number. Multiply the net asset value by the number of shares you own to figure out the present value of your investment. It is important to keep track and to record how much you invest, particularly if you don't buy fund shares at one time.

You and Your Stockbroker

Until the advent of mutual funds, the only way to invest in securities was to buy individual stocks and bonds, which is still done by millions of investors. Stocks, bonds, and certain mutual funds are purchased through a stockbroker, whose basic job is to place orders to buy and sell on the various exchanges where they are traded. A broker, however, is also expected to advise customers on the general state of the market and to make specific investment suggestions. It is here that misunderstandings

1 2 3 ..

HOW TO CHOOSE A STOCKBROKER

A money-smart investor with the time and discipline to research and follow through on investments can do very well without paying for professional investment help. But if you do not have a lot of time or confidence about making your own investment decisions, a stockbroker's assistance can be well worth the commissions you pay. The important thing is to find a trustworthy broker. Here are some guidelines to help you choose wisely:

1. Start by asking for recommendations from friends or associates whose investment objectives are similar to yours —for example, they are also saving for retirement or to send a child to college.

2. Interview several brokers by phone and ask them to send you their résumés. Ask how long they have been in the securities business, how long they have been with their present firm, what kinds of investments they know best, and what most of their clients buy. Look for someone whose experience is relatively extensive and has spanned both a "bull" market and a "bear" market.

3. Check the broker's credentials with the state securities commission to make sure her background and professional credentials match what is on the résumé and to find out whether any of the broker's customers have ever filed complaints.

Warning Signs: Trouble in Your Account

The best way to avoid trouble or misunderstandings with your stockbroker is to communicate often and to monitor your account carefully. Review your monthly statements to ensure that all transactions are listed correctly. Stay alert for signs of trouble, such as:

✔ *Unauthorized trades.* Unless you have given her the authority to trade on your behalf, be sure the broker has not made an investment that you did not discuss. To avoid having to rely on your memory, keep notes on conversations.

✔ *Unsuitable advice.* Weigh the broker's recommendations to be sure you are not being pressured to make investments inconsistent with your objectives.

✔ *Misrepresentation.* Make sure the information your broker gives you about a certain security is consistent with the information in the prospectus describing that stock.

✔ *Churning.* This descriptive word refers to an unethical broker's practice of constantly buying and selling securities for your account solely to generate sales commissions. To determine if a broker is churning, compare your profits from a sale with the commission charge. Was the sale really worthwhile?

with or incompetence on the part of the broker can cause trouble for you, the client. You can minimize such problems by choosing your stockbroker carefully in the first place. If worse comes to worst, there are regulations and legal mechanisms in place to help resolve disputes between you and your broker.

MAKE YOUR GOALS CLEAR

Every investor should understand that the traditional broker, known as a full-service stockbroker, faces an inherent conflict of interest in advising clients because her livelihood depends on the commissions earned by buying and selling. That can be an incentive for brokers to push high-commission financial products, such as limited partnerships, for example, which invest in real estate or gas and oil holdings—and are often highly risky. To protect yourself, make sure your broker understands your long-term investment goals, as well as how much risk you want to take. Confirm in a letter how you and your broker have agreed to handle your account, and have your broker initial it.

Pay special attention also to the account form, which must be filled out by either you or your broker before you can open an account with an investment firm. Among other things, you will be asked questions about your income, net worth, taxes, and past experience with investments. Never exaggerate your income or experience on the account form. Unless a broker knows these things about you, she cannot suggest investments that are appropriate to your situation. If a dispute later arises about an investment you feel was wrong for you—if, for example, your broker puts you into risky junk bonds (bonds with a low investment grade from the rating agencies) when what you needed was something safe and steady for your imminent retirement—you would have compelling evidence in the account form, as well as the letter of agreement, to prove that the broker did not act in your best interest.

For any recommendation your broker makes, ask how it will meet your investment goals. Ask for research material, and read it before you decide. Let your broker know you are keeping dated notes of every conversation. After buying a security, you will receive a confirmation slip and then a monthly statement. Review both to make sure the price and quantity of all transactions are listed correctly.

SETTLING DISPUTES ABOUT YOUR ACCOUNT

If any dispute arises about your account, try to resolve it promptly and in writing. (See also "If Trouble Brews in Your Brokerage Account," page 341.) Let us say your broker did not sell the shares on the day you asked that they be traded, but the next day. First, take the matter to the broker or her manager. If no help is forthcoming, the next step might be arbitration.

When you opened your account with the brokerage firm, you were probably required to sign a form agreeing to submit any disputes to arbitration instead of filing a lawsuit. In arbitration, a panel of one to five people—usually lawyers, accountants, brokers, or business people—reviews the evidence and decides the case. The individual stock exchanges, most commonly the New York Stock Exchange (NYSE) and the National Association of Securities Dealers (NASD), conduct arbitration proceedings. These and other organizations offer consumer guides that explain how to pursue an arbitration claim.

Arbitration is usually a much quicker and less expensive way to resolve a dispute than going into litigation. However, the awards made by an arbitrator are final, which means that you have no right to pursue the matter through the courts should the decision go against you. (Of course, neither does the broker.) Some experts think arbitration may not be fair to consumers; nevertheless, it is in fact a mandatory form of resolution in many states. (For more about arbitration, see YOUR RIGHTS IN ACTION, page 472.)

DISCOUNT BROKERS

Until the brokerage industry was deregulated in 1975, consumers had no alternative to traditional brokers when they made investments. All firms were required to charge the same fixed-rate commission. Today, each firm can determine what

If Trouble Brews in Your Brokerage Account

If you discover an error in your statement, find that your broker bought a stock without asking you, or suffer unexplained losses, you must take action quickly. A delay can weaken the credibility of your claim. Here are steps to take to resolve the problem:

• **Contact your broker.** Often an error may be caused by a computer glitch or miscommunication between you and your broker. Whatever the cause, call your broker immediately. Ask for an explanation of the transaction or for a correction to be made. Follow up with a letter stating clearly what you want the broker to do; for example, "Please sell the 100 shares of XYZ Corporation, and restore my money to my account."

• **Inform the manager.** If the broker's response is unsatisfactory, write a letter to the branch manager outlining your complaint and include a copy of the letter you sent to your broker, along with copies of any records that support your claim. Request a written explanation.

• **Contact your state SEC office.** If a few weeks pass and you receive no response from the brokerage firm, or if the firm rejects your complaint, you still have options. First, write to the consumer protection office of your state's division of securities, often located in the state attorney general's office. Include copies of all your correspondence with the broker and the brokerage firm as well as copies of any records that prove your claim. The state administrator may be able to solve the problem within a few weeks.

• **Go to arbitration.** If these measures bring no success, but you still think you have a case, you may want to consider taking it to arbitration. (See YOUR RIGHTS IN ACTION, page 472.)

Many financial planners offer a free consultation. That is the time to evaluate your candidate and judge whether you will be able to work together. Don't be bashful—after all, it is your money at stake. Here are some direct questions to ask:

1. Are you registered with the Securities and Exchange Commission and your state securities department? The answer should be yes.

2. What types of services do you provide, and what kind of financial products do you recommend?

3. What is your educational and professional background, and what training for financial planning have you had? (See also "Decoding Financial Planning Credentials," page 343.)

4. Will you disclose in advance of the entire presentation any commissions you receive for selling particular products, as well as your general fees?

5. Will you give as references three clients you have counseled for at least two years?

6. Have you been involved in disciplinary actions by state or federal agencies or in arbitration proceedings with a client? The answer should be no.

7. May I see some sample plans you have made for other investors?

commission schedules to use, and this competition in fees has resulted in the rise of discount brokerage firms. Like traditional brokerages, many discount firms do business nationwide and have 800 numbers as well as local offices. They account for approximately 14 percent of all commissions paid by individual investors.

Discount brokerage firms pay their brokers a straight salary, not commissions, and fees are substantially lower than what full-service brokers charge—often 50 to 80 percent less. Discount brokers do not offer investment advice; however, some may provide research reports on securities for an additional fee. If you are willing to do your own research and be responsible for decisions on what securities to buy or sell, your most economical choice would be a discount broker.

To find one, contact the American Association of Individual Investors, a nonprofit organization that provides research and education for investors. For a nominal fee, you can receive its annual nationwide survey of discount brokers and their rates. (For the address and telephone number, see RESOURCES, page 493.)

Do You Need a Financial Planner?

It is a fair question. First of all, financial planning is a relatively new profession, and its standards of ethics and conduct are not well regulated or defined. So the consumer must be both aware and wary: regulators estimate that financial planners have caused consumers to lose some $600 million every two years.

Secondly, many options exist for someone who wants to find her own answers to questions about devising an overall financial strategy. For a nominal fee, for example, the American Association of Retired Persons (AARP) runs a series of workshops called the Women's Financial Information Project in all 50 states. The workshops, open also to men, cover the basics of financial planning. In many states, cooperative extension services have "family resource management specialists," who teach the basics of personal finance.

Still, many investors feel more secure having an individual professional adviser planning the best financial strategies. A good planner is trained to devise a campaign to help you achieve your immediate or future financial goals and can be a great help in piloting you through unfamiliar waters. Just be prepared to do a thorough background check before hiring a planner.

In most states, anyone can be a financial planner—no tests are required. But a planner who charges fees for securities investment advice must register as an investment adviser with the Securities and Exchange Commission, and provide the SEC with a completed Application for Investment Adviser Registration (ADV). Part II of the form is available to clients. The ADV includes information about a planner's education, experience, investment strategies, and potential conflicts of interest. You should request this form from the planner, and if he is unable to produce one, go on to the next candidate. Then be ready to ask pertinent questions. (See also "Questions for a Prospective Planner," page 342.)

A Planner's Risky Advice

PROBLEM
For advice on supplementing a pension from their savings, James and Laura consulted a certified planner at a local brokerage firm. Although the couple requested low-risk investments that would provide steady income, the planner instead put most of their funds into high-risk limited partnerships, telling them they needed the extra income the partnerships would provide. The partnerships failed, and James and Laura were left with less than half their original investment.

ACTION
Because the planner took unsuitable risks for retirees who needed conservative investments, he violated his role as a "fiduciary," a person legally obligated to act in the best interest of a client. James and Laura had a fair claim for restitution. They wrote to the brokerage's branch manager, explaining the situation and emphasizing their lack of knowledge about investing and their reliance on the planner to explain the risks and rewards. The manager, who had had similar though less serious complaints about the broker, arranged for the firm to reimburse James and Laura, and the planner was fired. Had James and Laura not received a satisfactory solution, they could have filed a claim for arbitration with the stock exchange of which their brokerage is a member. They could also have filed a complaint on the planner with the Central Registration Depository, a data bank that tracks brokers.

Most financial planners are compensated through fees, commissions, or a combination of both. A fee-only planner is paid on an hourly or retainer basis, and sometimes charges a fee per job. A commissioned planner is paid through sales that generate commissions. The more financial products you purchase, the more money your planner will make. For that reason, you should be especially wary of stockbrokers and insurance salespeople who call themselves financial consultants or financial planners.

Decoding Financial Planning Credentials

Unlike lawyers and accountants, financial planners are not legally required to have any special training. The credentials listed below are no guarantee of competence in financial planning, but what they do indicates that a person took some pains to learn something about the diverse investment field.

✔ **APFS.** The Accredited Personal Financial Specialist degree is conferred by the American Institute of Certified Public Accountants and can be held only by CPA's. Thus, these planners can claim the advantage of knowing the tax consequences of various financial choices.

✔ **CFP.** The Certified Financial Planner degree is granted by the Denver-based College for Financial Planning to those who have taken a home-study course, passed an examination, and fulfilled an experience requirement. Most of the country's more than 100,000 CFP's work on commission (as opposed to a flat fee) and are employed by security and insurance brokerage firms.

✔ **ChFC.** The Chartered Financial Consultant degree is awarded by the American Society of Chartered Life Underwriters and Chartered Financial Consultants. Planners must complete a 10-section course of study and pass two exams. Most ChFC holders work for insurance companies.

INCOME TAXES

Taxpaying time can be less painful if you understand the rules of the game and know your rights when dealing with the tax collector.

What the IRS Owes You

Most citizens are all too well aware of their annual duty to file a federal income tax return, which reports all taxable income as well as deductions and certain nontaxable income. But not everyone knows that the government also has certain responsibilities toward you, the taxpayer. In 1988 Congress passed the Taxpayers' Bill of Rights, an amendment to the Tax Reform Act of 1986. This federal law imposes behavior standards and limitations on the Internal Revenue Service (IRS), the government agency that collects nearly all federal taxes. The law also sets out your rights in dealing with the IRS, which include:

- **Free help in preparing returns.** You have the right to information about the tax laws and guidance for filling out your tax forms. The IRS offers free publications and walk-in tax help at many IRS offices. It also offers information services available toll-free at (800) 829-1040.
- **Privacy and confidentiality.** You have the right to privacy; in other words, the IRS must keep your personal and financial information confidential.
- **Payment of only the required tax.** You have the right to plan your personal finances so that you will pay the least amount of tax due under the law.
- **Fair collection of tax.** If you disagree with the amount of tax the IRS claims, you have the right to dispute the tax.
- **Representation.** In dealings with the IRS, you have the right to represent yourself, have someone accompany you, or, with IRS approval, have someone represent you in your absence at an audit.

If you are questioned by the IRS, you also have the right to know why the IRS is asking you for information, how it will be used, and what might happen if you do not divulge it. The employees of the IRS are required to explain and protect these taxpayer rights at all times. If you have a complaint about your treatment from the IRS, write to the district director for your area. (For the number, check the U.S. government pages of your telephone directory under "Treasury Department.")

Getting a Helping Hand

Although some taxpayers are undaunted by the chore of filing their own returns, you may be among the many who need both the expertise and reassurance of a professional. Reliance on a tax preparer may be even more necessary if the IRS decides your return needs to be examined and verified, or audited. (See also "How to Survive an Audit," page 348.) No matter who prepares your return, the IRS still holds you responsible for its accuracy. Thus it is vital that you hire someone who is both trustworthy and competent. Tax practitioners fall into four main categories:

■ **Preparers** generally have the least amount of training, and many of them work part time for the major tax preparation firms. If you have an uncomplicated return but do not want to prepare it yourself, a preparer can be the least costly alternative. But although the average tax-return preparer is per-

Types of Audits

Every tax return is scored by an IRS computer program that compares it with the typical return: the more it deviates from the norm, the higher its score. Returns that score too high get marked for further examination, which usually involves one of the three conventional noncriminal audits: correspondence, office, or field. The IRS also makes random audits, as explained below.

• **Correspondence audits.** Audits by mail most often come from the IRS service center. They involve fairly straightforward problems, such as verifying itemized deductions and real estate sales. The IRS will mail you a letter explaining the problem and citing the recalculated tax. You may be asked to pay more, or to complete additional forms. In addition, you may be requested to send copies of receipts or other documentation to substantiate certain statements and figures in your return. Remember, the IRS is capable of human errors, and frequently makes them. Don't be alarmed if you receive a request for substantiation on your return. If you have the evidence to support your figures, the chances are that will be the end of it.

• **Office audits.** You are summoned by a form letter requesting you to call your local IRS district office for an appointment for an audit. At this stage, an agent has gone over your return and has compiled a portfolio of questionable items that he wants to examine more closely. Often the notification letter notes the sections of your return that are under scrutiny, and the letter may also include a list of documents you are requested to take with you to the audit, such as receipts and canceled checks, to substantiate your return.

• **Field audits.** If your return has complex problems, particularly business assessments, an IRS field agent will handle the case. Again, questions will have been generated from the IRS service center and passed on to the field agent for review. The agent will notify you by mail that you are being audited and will inform you of topics being challenged. The field agent will arrange a time to visit you at home or your business. The agent will address a list of items the IRS wants to look at, but the audit is by no means limited to that list; the agent can examine any area of your tax return.

• **Taxpayer Compliance Measurement Program (TCMP).** The IRS selects about 50,000 unfortunate taxpayers at random every three years for this program, designed to develop profiles of "typical" returns for various levels of income in the United States. A TCMP audit is painstakingly thorough and requires you to provide documentation of every line of your tax return.

FINDING HELP FOR YOUR RETURNS

Be sure to get answers to these questions before hiring a tax preparer:

1. Are you available year-round? A preparer who is available only at tax time may be unable to answer questions when you need to ask them. Also, if you hire a preparer who works alone, make sure she has a backup.

2. What is your fee? The charge for completing a tax return ranges from $30 to $400 an hour, depending on the qualifications of the preparer. But the amount you pay should never exceed the value to you of the service in terms of reduced taxes, refunded taxes, or in relation to the time and tax knowledge required.

3. What is your professional education and experience? Determine whether the preparer has a degree in accountancy, is an enrolled agent, or is a CPA. Ask also about his experience.

4. Will you go with me to the IRS if I am audited? Anyone who prepares your return should be willing to go with you to an audit. (Remember, an uncertified preparer cannot legally represent you.) You will probably be charged at a standard hourly rate for this service. Request that the preparer repay you for any IRS charges due to the preparer's error. A reputable CPA will do this—but it would not hurt to get the promise in writing.

mitted to accompany you in responding to an IRS inquiry about your return, she cannot represent you. That means she can explain how your return was prepared, but cannot present substantive legal arguments on your behalf.

- **Enrolled agents** (EA's) must pass a rigorous two-day exam given by the IRS or have at least five years of experience practicing tax accounting with the IRS. They must also take continuing-education courses to retain their designation. The EA certificate enables them to represent you before the IRS if you are audited. The services of an EA are best suited for people who have moderately complex returns but do not need other financial advice through the year. For more information, contact the National Association of Enrolled Agents. (See RESOURCES, page 493.)

- **Certified public accountants** (CPA's) must go through lengthy training and exams to receive the CPA credential. Continuing education is also required. CPA fees can be high —as much as $300 an hour or more in larger firms or for the services of a partner—so consider them only if you have a fairly complex return or when you need advice on other accounting and financial matters beyond your taxes.

- **Tax attorneys** do various types of tax-related work, including tax planning and IRS dispute resolution. Unless you have more than $10,000 at stake in your tax problem, the high fees of a tax attorney will not be practical.

To simplify your preparer's job and to save money, keep your records organized throughout the year. Make sure the figures you supplied to your tax preparer match those on the return. Never sign a completed form without checking it over first. To be extra cautious, you can file your tax return by certified mail. If the return gets lost, you could be charged a late-filing penalty if you owe money. A certified or registered mail receipt is the only proof of filing that is accepted under the U.S. Tax Code; messenger and express delivery receipts are not acceptable. You can also file electronically in some instances. Nevertheless, the IRS will usually accept a reasonable explanation for tardiness.

Penalties and Interest

One of the most frightening aspects of tax filing is the prospect of penalties and fines the IRS can impose for late filing or underpayment of taxes. Suppose you go to the hospital in early April for a serious emergency operation. A few months later you discover that the IRS has branded you a delinquent taxpayer and is not only charging interest on your unpaid income tax but is also demanding a penalty for failing to file on time You know you have to pay your taxes, but what about the penalties and interest that have accrued because you neglected to file on time?

The bad news is that if you owe money, you will probably have to pay interest for late payment—the IRS is usually quite firm about that. The good news is that if the IRS owes you a refund, you will not be charged a penalty; and even if you owe taxes, you may not have to pay the interest. The IRS reduces one-third of the penalties it assesses: it will reduce or abate (eliminate) a penalty if you show that you had a "reasonable cause" for failing to observe the tax law. The IRS Manual suggests the following examples as showing reasonable cause:

- If you or an immediate family member is seriously ill, or dies.
- If you are unavoidably out of the country.
- If your place of business or records are destroyed by fire or other disaster.
- If you could not determine the amount of tax due for reasons beyond your control, such as loss of your 1040 form.
- If your ability to pay was seriously impaired by civil disturbances—the business was looted during a riot.
- If you, despite ordinary business care and prudence, have insufficient funds to pay the taxes.

REQUESTING A PENALTY ABATEMENT

Upon rising from your sickbed, you should immediately file your income taxes. If you anticipate that you will be late filing, you can file for a four-month extension and pay an estimated amount due. (See also "If You Cannot Pay What You Owe," page 351.) If you have received a notice that you are being charged a penalty for late payment, contact the IRS service center that sent the notice and ask for an abatement. You can either write a letter or use IRS Form 843, "Claim for Refund and Request for Abatement." You should include copies of any documents that help prove your claim, such as a doctor's statement and a hospital bill—or, depending upon the reason for your delay, a fire department report, an insurance claim, or the death certificate of a family member. This written proof will help ensure that your request receives serious consideration from the IRS.

You might also enclose payment for the underlying taxes, and be sure to indicate that the payment does not include the penalty. In the lower left-hand corner of your check or money order, write your Social Security number and the tax year for which you are paying. This at least will stop the accrual of interest on the amount you owe. Make several copies of your letter in case the IRS loses your correspondence or ignores it. If you

Should You File Electronically?

In 1994 more than 13 million Americans filed tax returns electronically. For a small fee many banks and tax preparers —dubbed electronic return originators (ERO's) by the IRS —can send your federal return by computer modem straight into the IRS computers. If you pay a little more, some ERO's will also grant you a loan against your refund. To decide if these options are worthwhile for you, consult the checklist below:

✔ *Quicker refunds.* Filing electronically means any refund you are due will arrive in about half the time it normally takes to receive one—usually within two to three weeks.

✔ *Cost.* Depending on where you live, you will pay from $25 to $40 to file electronically; this is in addition to what you pay to have your return prepared.

✔ *Access to loans.* Many ERO's offer "refund anticipation loans" to those expecting a refund. The average fee is $20. This means that if you expect a refund of $1,300—the average refund check for electronic filers—you would in effect pay a hefty (almost 40 percent) interest rate to get your refund in two days instead of two weeks.

get another penalty notice, write another letter and include a copy of your first letter.

UNDOING INTEREST

Interest on overdue tax or a late-filed return is rarely reduced. However, if a tax or penalty is canceled, then interest on the tax or on the penalty should be canceled as well. (The IRS computer is supposed to do this automatically, but check your bills to make sure.) A few other circumstances in which you might get an abatement of interest include:

- The IRS was wrong to charge interest, because you did not owe any tax on which interest could be charged.
- The IRS wrongfully sent you a refund and now wants not only its money back but also interest.
- The interest resulted from the IRS's delay in performing "ministerial acts"—that is, its job.

If you get an IRS notice that wrongfully states you owe more tax, any interest assessed while you resolve this matter should be canceled. If you do owe more money, however, the IRS can charge interest from the moment it requests the money until you pay. As for interest charged on a refund you did not deserve, you are entitled to an interest abatement as long as your actions and return preparation did not cause the refund.

An example of a ministerial act is if the IRS delayed sending you a tax bill after you agreed not to appeal an audit decision but instead to pay the amount decided upon. You are entitled to an abatement of interest on all but the first 30 days of the delay. This is a narrow window, though. Ministerial acts do not cover interest that mounts while you challenge a bill, while the IRS performs an audit, while you are appealing, or while you sue in tax court. To request an abatement of interest, write the IRS service center that sent you the bill and explain why you should not have to pay the interest assessed. If you cannot get the matter resolved there, call the problem resolution officer at your local IRS district office.

How to Survive an Audit

The IRS accepts most tax returns without question. But each year it plucks from the pile slightly more than one out of 100 personal tax returns to be subjected to an audit. The purpose of the dreaded audit is to find out if you reported your income properly, whether the deductions, exemptions, and credits you claimed are allowable, and whether you calculated the tax correctly.

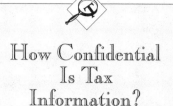

How Confidential Is Tax Information?

The Federal Privacy Act of 1974 ensures that tax files are "confidential." This means that people who prepare your tax return or represent you to the IRS may not divulge any information about your taxes. But how about the IRS itself? Can it give out information about you? Under some circumstances, governed by strict guidelines, it can.

In certain kinds of criminal proceedings and in some cases involving foreign residents, the IRS can release data from its files. But the most common way the IRS shares tax information is through its links to state tax agencies.

Most states that assess income tax do not conduct their own audits of individual taxpayers but rely almost entirely on the IRS investigations. Their computer systems are linked with more than 200 types of IRS files.

This linkage ensures that if you are audited by the IRS, your state automatically finds out—and acts accordingly. For example, if an IRS audit agreement results in an increase in your taxes, you can expect to receive a notice for an increased tax from your state. In many states, you have a defined period of time, such as 60 days, to supply an amended state return.

Tax law gives the IRS wide powers to inspect your papers and financial records during an audit and to ask you and others about your financial affairs. For example, an auditor can issue a summons to get information from your bank, employer, or business associates. And the fact is that the IRS usually finds what it is looking for: six out of seven people who are audited end up owing more taxes. However, it should be noted that the IRS's computerized system for matching income figures reported on your tax return with forms such as 1099's, which confirm those figures, can and does generate errors. Therefore, it is more common for errors to be corrected with a simple exchange of information rather than an office audit.

Nevertheless, can you protect yourself during an audit? The easy answer is to do your utmost to avoid being audited in the first place. (See also "Watch Those Deductions," page 350.) In any case, your first line of defense is to be honest and to keep good financial records. The law places the burden on you to demonstrate that the information on your tax return is correct. Being able to verify the information on your tax return is the key to prevailing in an audit. IRS auditors confirm that the biggest reason taxpayers cannot verify tax-return information is not dishonesty but poor record keeping.

When you receive an audit notice, do three things right away: (1) write down what parts of your return are being questioned; (2) make copies of any documents that support your case; (3) decide whether you need an adviser to help you. The audit notice will say how the IRS wants the information deliv-

🖾

Taxes are what we pay for a civilized society.

OLIVER WENDELL
HOLMES, JR.

Compañía de Tabascos v. *Collector*
1904

🖾

The Problem Resolution Program

What if you cannot get the IRS to resolve a problem? The IRS Problem Resolution Program (PRP) may be able to cut the red tape—but only if you have made strenuous efforts through normal IRS channels. Call (800) 827-1040 to locate the PRP in your area, then see if it can help with:

• **Refunds.** If the problem is that you have not received your refund, the PRP will investigate. However, you must wait at least 90 days after filing your original tax return, and you must have made two inquiries through normal IRS channels before applying to the PRP for help. In other words, you must write two letters to your local IRS office with copies of your return before you can solicit aid from the PRP.

• **Inquiries.** The PRP will assist with an inquiry from you to the IRS, but only after you have posed your question or requested help at least twice through your local IRS office. You must also wait at least 45 days after making your first inquiry, and then have failed to receive an acknowledgment

or a final resolution. If you receive an acknowledgment promising a response by a certain date and then you do not hear anything further from your local IRS office, you may also qualify for PRP assistance.

• **Notices.** Before the PRP will look into a notice from the IRS to you, you must have responded to at least two earlier notices from the IRS by requesting that the tax service correct its information. Your responses should be in writing, and you should include copies of the letters and your tax returns as well as any other appropriate documentation proving that you have paid the taxes due. If you receive a third notice with no reference to your letters, you can call the PRP for help.

ered. The simplest audits are by mail: you send in the requested documentation and the matter is resolved. Most taxpayers can handle such requests without professional assistance.

Much rarer is the field audit, when an IRS agent visits your home or business to sift through records, perhaps to see if your standard of living matches the picture suggested by your return. This is a serious business. Consult a certified public accountant or tax attorney.

Most audits, however, are conducted in an IRS office. You are asked to appear at a specified time (you can request a more convenient date) armed with documents that support your return. Normally, the IRS notifies you in writing and indicates the data desired. However, if the problem is unclear, call to find out, if you can, what the focus of the audit will be. For example, if large deductions for unreimbursed medical expenses triggered the audit, send in copies of canceled checks and medical bills; you may be able to end the audit without making a formal appearance. If you must appear and if someone else prepared your return, you should probably ask him to go with you. Don't forget to ask about his fee.

GOING IT ALONE

If you decide to handle the audit yourself, thoroughly review the return so that you understand how you, or your tax preparer, arrived at its figures. Organize all the records you will need to substantiate your return. The more evidence you present and the more clearly you can present it, the more likely you are to prevail. But take only materials that relate to the areas identified by the IRS so as to limit the scope of the audit. Never volunteer any unasked-for information.

You have the right (granted by the Taxpayers' Bill of Rights) to tape-record your audit interview, but you must declare your intention to do so in writing 10 days before the appointment. In such cases, the IRS will also record the audit for its own protection. Think twice about this gambit, though: it may alienate your IRS auditor, and it might be more important to start your audit on a goodwill basis than to have it on tape.

If you disagree with an auditor's decision, you may want to ask to see her supervisor. Supervisors have more experience than auditors and also have wider authority to make compromises. Often you can make this informal type of appeal immediately. Do so, however, only if the amount of money in question is significant.

If you do not accept the supervisor's finding, the next step is the IRS appeals system. IRS Publication 5, "Appeal Rights and Preparation of Protests for Unagreed Cases," describes the appeal process. Few audited taxpayers appeal their decisions, but the procedure is simple, and your chance of coming

---

Watch Those Deductions

Anything that makes your return stand out increases your chances of an audit. If you take any substantial deduction, such as those listed below, consider attaching relevant documents with an explanatory note. Although this will not stop the IRS computer from flagging your return, the classifier who screens computer-picked returns for potential audits may pass yours over if the additional documents are convincing.

✔ *Casualty losses.* If you claim significant losses due to natural disasters such as earthquake, flood, or fire, make sure you have sales receipts (in the case of jewelry, for instance), repair receipts, insurance reports, and pictures of property damage.

✔ *Cash contributions.* Taking a sizable deduction for cash contributions to charities can be a red flag to the IRS. Since 1994, deductions must be substantiated by a receipt from the charity for amounts of $250 or more. A returned check is not acceptable proof.

✔ *Child care.* Many people pay their child-care providers in cash and cannot substantiate the amounts they have paid. The IRS will not allow a tax credit unless all child-care payments are documented by an employee Social Security number or employer identification number on the IRS form for claiming credit.

out with a better deal is quite good. IRS statistics show that the average appeal results in a 40 percent decrease in the taxes, penalties, and interest imposed by the auditor.

Should you still be at odds with the IRS, your final recourse is the costly and time-consuming one of going to tax court. Before choosing this option, ask the advice of a tax attorney.

If You Cannot Pay What You Owe

The IRS, like any business, would prefer to collect its payments immediately and in full. But in recent years it has become more flexible about taking payments in installments and even forgiving some debts. If you cannot pay all your income taxes, you should still file a return and pay what you can. The penalty for not filing or filing late is quite steep—up to 25 percent of the tax you owe. But for not paying in full, the penalty is only one-half of one percent per month of the tax that you owe. Any amount you can include with your return will reduce the penalty amount.

If you do not have the funds to pay your taxes and cannot take out a loan to make up the full amount, the IRS offers several alternative collection methods:

- You can apply for an extension to pay your taxes by filing Form 1127, the "Application for Extension of Time for Payment of Tax." (This extension is different from the four-month filing extension, which you can get automatically by submitting Form 4868. You pay taxes owed by April 15, but do not have to file the return until August 15.) In 1992, the IRS established an automatic four-month extension that allows you to postpone both filing and paying your federal (but not necessarily your state or local) taxes. The extension must be filed by April 15, stating the amount of tax you expect to owe. The IRS will charge interest and failure-to-pay penalties but will not demand a failure-to-file penalty.
- The same penalty policy also applies to delaying payments when using the two-month additional extension-with-an-excuse alternative, which allows you to extend your filing date to October 15. Winning this extension is not easy (and, again, bear in mind that it may not apply to state tax rulings). You must prove that you neither have nor can borrow the money to pay the taxes and that, if forced to pay, you and your family would suffer "undue hardship." You will also have to provide a list of all your assets and liabilities.
- Another way of paying off the IRS is with an installment plan. When you file your tax return, you also include the

HOW LONG SHOULD YOU KEEP YOUR TAX RETURNS?

To be on the safe side, you should keep all your tax records—bills, receipts, W-2 forms, 1099's—for at least six years. Although your tax return normally cannot be audited more than three years after its original filing date, some important exceptions to this statute of limitations prevail:

1. If you understated your gross income by 25 percent or more on your tax return, the deadline for tax assessment (and possible audit) is six years after the return was first filed.

2. If you are accused of filing a fraudulent return, the three-year limit does not apply, since fraud is a criminal offense. If the government suspects fraud, it can demand your tax returns from any year.

3. The statute of limitations applies only if you have filed a tax return. In any tax year that you do not file, your tax status is always open to assessment by the IRS—until you file a return for that year. Once you file the return, the three-year statute of limitations begins.

4. The three-year statute of limitations applies to refunds as well as audits. Thus, if you discover that you made a mistake on a previous tax return and overpaid your tax, you cannot demand the refund if more than three years have passed from the tax due date or the date filed, whichever is later.

new installment agreement Form 9465, telling the IRS how much you can afford to pay each month and the day of the month you can pay it. Within a month, the IRS notifies you whether the plan has been approved. Then you will have to start your payments within a month—and will still owe the late-payment penalty plus annual interest on the tax.

A third scheme for satisfying the IRS if you cannot pay what you owe is to make an offer to pay what you can. Qualifying for this option—called an "offer-in-compromise"—is tough, but it is worth a try, since in 1994 the IRS accepted almost four times as many candidates as it had before. Your offer must represent what the IRS could collect from you if it seized your property right now. You must also prove that your prospects of acquiring more money are very poor. Because offers-in-compromise negotiations can be complex, you should get professional advice.

The nonfiler program is a long-term effort to improve tax compliance and the whole purpose is to get people back in the system, not to prosecute ordinary people who made a mistake.

SHIRLEY PETERSON
IRS Commissioner
1992–1993

Help for Nonfilers

Technically, you are guilty of a misdemeanor if you fail to file a tax return when you owe taxes. You could be fined up to $25,000 per year and be sent to prison for a year. The IRS has 10 years to collect a tax once it is assessed, but no statute of limitations governs its right to demand an unfiled return. For example, if in 1982 you should have filed a return but did not, you would still owe the IRS a return today—and penalties and interest on the unpaid tax.

In practice, however, the IRS does not prosecute the average nonfiler. The IRS assumes that most nonfilers do so out of ignorance, fear, or an inability to pay. To help bring nonfilers back into the system, the IRS will assist in several ways, but first, a nonfiler must volunteer to file without being notified by the IRS and then file a correct return. If you are missing income records for certain years, the IRS can help you retrieve data such as W-2's and 1099's from its own database. You can also go to your local IRS office to get a form for the year in question and for help in filling it out. Call the IRS toll-free number, (800) 829-1040, for help.

You may fear facing the tax bills when you file an overdue return, but in fact about 40 percent of nonfilers are actually owed a refund. If you file within two years from the time tax was due, you can still claim your refund. If you do face a major tax payment, the IRS has pledged to cooperate in resolving collection problems. Depending on your financial situation, the IRS offers such alternative arrangements as an installment payback plan, a reduced settlement, or an offer-in-compromise. (See also "If You Cannot Pay What You Owe," page 351.)

SOCIAL SECURITY ISSUES

Every payday you contribute to the Social Security fund. When the time comes to get your share, be sure you know what you are entitled to, and how to get it.

Facts About the Benefits

The Social Security Act was passed in 1935 by Congress in the wake of the Great Depression. It was designed as a mandatory social insurance program to provide retirement benefits for working Americans and now provides benefits for survivors, dependents, and some disabled persons as well. Consumers and their employers contribute billions of dollars to the system, and although Social Security was never meant to be a person's only retirement support, it has become a cornerstone of many retirees' guaranteed incomes. You need to know how the system works to get the benefits that are due you.

WHO IS ELIGIBLE?

The program provides income to retirees and spouses, to survivors of workers who die before reaching retirement age, and to some disabled people. You are eligible for Social Security benefits if you have worked under the system for at least 10 years (or 40 quarters, which is the system used the Social Security Administration uses to assess time accrued). Social Security provides for a retirement benefit to be paid to you and your spouse, even if your spouse has not worked outside of the home.

· If both you and your spouse have worked and earned sufficient work credits (quarters) to qualify individually, then each of you will receive your own Social Security benefit. And depending on the amount of benefits payable, a spouse's payment also may be due. The spouse's benefit (at age 65) is 50 percent of the worker's benefit. Here are some examples to explain how this works:

Tom, age 65, is eligible for a $1,000 monthly retirement benefit. His wife Becky, also 65, has never worked outside the home. She will be eligible for a $500 per month wife's benefit. Tom and Becky's total monthly income will be $1,500.

If Becky had worked and earned her own retirement benefit, Social Security would be required to pay her that benefit and supplement it with any spouse's benefits that might be due. For example, if Becky (still due her $500 spousal benefit) is also due a $300 retirement benefit, she would receive the $300

Keeping an Eye on Your Nest Egg

For most workers, Social Security plays an important role in funding retirement-income needs. To plan ahead, you should know what you can expect to receive. The Social Security Administration (SSA) will oblige by sending you a personalized benefit estimate.

To request your Personal Earnings and Benefits Estimate Statement (PEBES), call (800) 772-1213 and ask for Form SSA-7004. If you are age 62 or older, the SSA can provide you with a benefit estimate over the telephone.

After you return the form, the SSA will send you your complete earnings history, along with estimates of the benefits you can expect if you retire at age 62, at full retirement age (which will be somewhere between 65 and 67, depending on your year of birth), and at age 70. As you approach retirement age, you will want to check your Social Security record from time to time to make sure your earnings have been credited correctly. (See also "Setting Your Work Record Straight," page 354.)

Many regional agencies for the aging, churches, and union groups have advocacy programs designed to help with Social Security problems. If you have problems, don't hesitate to go for help.

and in addition would receive a $200 spouse's benefit for a total of $500. Whenever people are due two benefits, they cannot receive more than the higher benefit payable. Tom and Becky's combined monthly benefits, based on Tom's earnings alone, would be $1,500. If Becky's own retirement benefit is $700 per month, she would receive that amount and Tom would receive his $1,000 monthly payment. Their total income would be $1,700 a month, and no spouse's benefit would be payable.

If you are divorced but were married for at least 10 years to an insured worker, you can draw against your former spouse's work record for your "spousal benefit," even if your spouse has remarried. A second spouse also is eligible for benefits even if the first spouse is collecting; in other words, one worker's insurance can supply benefits to two spouses.

RETIREMENT BENEFITS

You can choose to begin receiving benefits as early as age 62 or as late as you want. Currently, Social Security considers 65 a normal retirement age, although this will be moved forward slowly until it reaches age 67 in the year 2027. The later you receive your benefits, the higher the monthly benefit payment will be. For every month you retire before you reach 65, your benefit will be reduced by five-ninths of 1 percent—a 20 percent reduction if you start collecting at age 62. (But remember that if you wait until 65, you are giving up three years' worth of the lower payments.) If you earn income after you begin collecting Social Security, the size of your earnings may reduce

There are people who have money and people who are rich.

Coco Chanel
French Fashion Designer
1883–1971

Setting Your Work Record Straight

Since your Social Security benefits are based on how much you have paid into the system, it is crucial that your work record be accurate. One estimate says that some 9.7 million taxpayers' work records may be wrong. Here are some suggestions for keeping the record straight:

• Make it a habit to check your Personal Earnings and Benefits Estimate Statement (PEBES) regularly (see "Keeping an Eye on Your Nest Egg," page 353), and do not forget to notify your local Social Security office promptly if you change your name (such as when you get married or divorced or if you decide to work professionally under another name) so that you will get credit for your earnings under your new name.

• If you find an error in your work record, locate supporting documents—such as tax returns and W-2 forms—for the periods in question. It does not matter how long ago the mistake was made. Some SSA publications still refer to a three-year statute of limitations that no longer applies.

• Call the Social Security Administration's toll-free number (800 772-1213) or look in the white pages of your telephone directory to find out the location of your nearest SSA office; then call that office to make an appointment. Say you want to submit a "Request for Correction in Earnings Record" and to speak to an administrator in person.

• Take your PEBES and supporting documents to the interview. The SSA will make copies and forward them to SSA headquarters in Baltimore. If your proof is judged sufficient, the error will be corrected. After four months, request another PEBES. Check it carefully to make sure that the error was corrected and that no new problems were created.

your benefits. In other words, you do not have to actually retire in order to collect Social Security benefits, but significant earnings may reduce your benefit amount.

Retirement benefits are not paid out automatically; you must initiate the monthly payment process yourself. You can apply to your local Social Security office in person or by telephone at least three months before you would like your retirement benefits to commence. All follow-up procedures can usually be accomplished through the mail.

SURVIVORS' BENEFITS

The surviving spouse and the minor children of an insured worker can receive benefits when the insured dies, whether or not the worker reached retirement age, but only if he or she had earned sufficient work credits. Social Security pays a lump-sum payment of $255 to a deceased worker's spouse living with him or her at the time of death or to children under 18. It pays monthly survivors' benefits to dependents if they meet the following criteria:

- Widows or widowers receive benefits if they are age 60 or older; are disabled and age 50 or older; or are caring for a child under age 16 or a child who is disabled.
- Children receive benefits if they are unmarried and under 18; under 19 and studying full time in elementary or high school; unmarried and 18 or older but severely disabled, provided the disability started before age 22.
- Parents of an insured worker who depended on their child for at least half of their basic support are eligible.
- If you were divorced from a worker who has died, you may be eligible for survivors' benefits if your marriage lasted at least 10 years.

DISABILITY BENEFITS

You can receive disability benefits under one of two programs administered by the Social Security Administration. If you suffer from a long-term or terminal illness or have a mental or physical disability that keeps you from working or are blind, you may be eligible. Social Security disability benefits are granted to workers or, in some cases, their family members. Supplemental Security Income (SSI) is available regardless of work background, based on financial need. Recipients must have limited income and resources, and states may supplement benefits payments.

HOW MUCH DO YOU RECEIVE?

The amount of your benefit is based on your earnings averaged over your working life, using a formula that places the great-

---

How to Claim Your Benefits

When you apply for Social Security benefits, you will need some of the documents listed below. But do not delay making your claim even if you don't have everything you need; the SSA often can help you get them.

✔ *Social Security number.* You must know your own number; if you are applying for spousal benefits, you will need your spouse's number.

✔ *Proof of your date of birth.* You will need a legal document such as a birth certificate, passport, or driver's license.

✔ *Most recent W-2 forms.* You will need either yours or your spouse's to indicate last employer, last income, and last date of work.

✔ *Schedule C.* If you are self-employed, you will need this schedule from your latest tax return.

✔ *Marriage certificate.* To get spousal benefits, you must have proof of marriage.

✔ *Death certificate.* If you are applying for spousal or child-support benefits from a spouse who has died, you must show proof of death.

✔ *Divorce decree.* If you are claiming benefits from a divorced spouse, you will need your divorce decree.

est emphasis on wages in your years of highest earnings. These benefits currently have an advantage over most kinds of retirement-plan payments because Social Security payments are indexed for inflation.

If You Are Denied Benefits

If the Social Security Administration (SSA) denies you benefits or if you believe it has made an error in the amount it is paying, you have the right to appeal. You must make your request for an appeal in writing within 60 days of the date you received the notice of the decision on your claim. You can do this on a form available from your local SSA office, or you can write your own letter. Be sure to include the date, your name, and your Social Security or claim number. Your case will be reviewed by someone who did not take part in the original decision. Usually you will be notified in writing of the second decision within 30 days.

Divorced and Worried

PROBLEM
Clara, a 63-year-old homemaker, was married to Phil, age 65, for 35 years. They were divorced two years ago, and Phil has since moved to another city and remarried, but he has not retired. Clara, who has never worked outside the home, is not eligible for Social Security benefits in her own right and fears she will not be entitled to any of Phil's benefits, either.

ACTION
As the divorced spouse of a retired worker, Clara is eligible to claim benefits because: (1) her marriage lasted more than 10 years; and (2) she is over age 62. Even though Phil himself has not retired (and even without a court-ordered support agreement), Clara can still draw against Phil's account. Her share will equal 50 percent of Phil's. To initiate her payments, Clara should go to her local Social Security office. If Clara remarries, she will become ineligible for Phil's spousal benefits. (Phil's current wife, incidentally, is also eligible to receive spousal benefits, but only when Phil retires.)

If you disagree with the appeal, you can make a written request for a hearing before an administrative law judge at one of the 200 offices of the Office of Hearings and Appeals of the SSA. If you still are not satisfied after the administrative law judge makes his decision, you can request a review by the Appeals Council based in Falls Church, Virginia. The Appeals Council will decide whether to hear your case or not. If it hears your case and rules against you, your only remaining option is to file suit in federal court.

Taking Bites Out of Your Benefits

The Social Security Administration will tell you what your monthly payments are slated to be after you retire, but your right to that money carries some limitations and responsibilities.

✔ *Earnings decrease benefits.* The SSA docks your benefit payments if after retirement you earn more than a certain amount in wages. This ceiling is higher for those between 65 and 69 years of age than for those between 62 and 64, and after age 70 your earnings have no effect on your benefits. The ceilings, pegged to inflation, change annually. Ask your local Social Security office for the current figures.

✔ *Reporting earning.* If you expect to earn more than the ceiling for your age bracket during the coming year, you should report that to the SSA. Your benefit checks will be decreased accordingly. At tax time you must file your actual earnings for the previous year with the SSA as well as with the IRS. If your estimate was wrong, an adjustment will affect the next year's checks.

✔ *Taxes on benefits.* The law is still in flux, but if your total income after retirement exceeds a certain limit, the government will tax part of your SSA benefits. (This bite out of your benefits is in addition to the SSA's deduction for earnings.) A few states also tax Social Security income.

SAVING FOR RETIREMENT

Guaranteed company pension plans used to be taken for granted, but now more and more people are taking on the job of providing for their retirement years.

How Pension Plans Work

Although employers are under no legal obligation to provide pension plans, more than 50 million American workers are covered by them. A pension is any plan, fund, or program that an employer or union establishes to provide retirement income for its wage earners. (It may be funded entirely by the company, or the employees may contribute as well.) Since pensions are such an important source of retirement income for working Americans, you should learn all you can about the plans and how they work for you.

Every company-sponsored plan is different, but all plans share certain features designed for your protection, most of them mandated by the Employee Retirement Income Security Act of 1974 (ERISA). The plans have defined rights, benefits, and eligibility standards, and they use predetermined formulas to calculate your benefits.

There are two basic types of pension plans: "defined-benefit" and "defined-contribution." A defined-benefit plan pays you a fixed income (usually monthly) at your retirement for the rest of your life. The amount you receive depends on your salary and your years of service. The employer makes all the investment decisions, but regardless of how well or poorly the investments do, you are supposed to receive the full pension. (Note that if your present company does not offer a pension plan, you may have been part of a plan with a former employer that will pay you some benefits. See also "Keeping Tabs on Your Fund When You Change Jobs," page 362.)

About 95 percent of all defined-benefit plans are insured by a government-created corporation, the Pension Benefit Guaranty Corporation (PBGC). Federal law places a cap on the monthly benefit amount guaranteed by the PBGC. In 1994 it was $2,556.82 a month for single workers who retire at age 65, and less for early retirees.

Recently, however, more and more midsize and small employers have been abandoning their defined-benefit pension plans, claiming they cannot afford them. Instead, they are switching to defined-contribution plans such as 401 (k) plans and profit-sharing plans (see also YOUR JOB, page 247). A defined-contribution plan does not promise you specific ben-

KEY QUESTIONS ABOUT YOUR PENSION PLAN

Your retirement may be a long way away, but it is never too soon to learn the details of your pension plan. For answers to these questions consult your firm's "Summary Plan Description," or ask your plan administrator:

1. How are benefits calculated? Find out if bonuses and overtime are counted, and if the payout is based on all earnings or just your peak years.

2. When can I join? Ask how long you have to be employed to start in the plan, and how long after that to benefit fully.

3. Does the promised benefit include Social Security payments? Many defined-benefit plans call for "integrated benefits," which means that your pension checks will be reduced by a certain percentage depending on how much you get from Social Security.

4. What happens if I retire before age 65? If early retirement is allowed, how much will your benefits be reduced?

5. Is the plan insured by the Pension Benefit Guaranty Corporation? Some pension plans are protected by this federal insurance agency; many others are not.

Protection for Women

Because the work force has been comprised mostly of men, pension plans have historically been framed from a male perspective. Women, either spouses or widows, traditionally suffered the most when pension benefits were not available. The 1984 Retirement Equity Act increased protection for women in these ways:

✔ *Maternity-leave protection.* If you have worked long enough to be eligible for your company's pension, you can take up to a year's maternity leave and not trigger a "break in service" that would reduce the size of your pension. (Men can take paternity leave on the same terms.)

✔ *Widow's benefits—before retirement.* You are guaranteed some benefits if your spouse was eligible for a pension but died before retirement.

✔ *Widow's benefits—after retirement.* You do not lose your pension benefits if your retired husband dies. A pension benefit is larger if it is paid out only during the life of the retiree and not to any survivors. Before the 1984 law, many husbands chose to receive the larger payments, which might have left nothing for their widows. Now, unless a spouse agrees otherwise in writing, pensions have to include the benefits for survivors. (The same rights apply to a husband if the wife qualifies for a pension.)

efits at retirement. Instead, your employer may contribute a certain amount to employees' pension investment accounts each year and encourage employees to contribute as well. The amount you receive at retirement depends upon the amounts contributed and on how well the investment account has done over the years. The 401 (k) fund uses a mix of investments and income plans; the employee has the right to choose among varying options. Defined-contribution plans are not backed by government insurance.

BASIC PROVISIONS

Generally, pension plans require that you be 21 and have worked for your company for a certain length of time before you can participate in the plan. Both ERISA and the federal Age Discrimination in Employment Act (ADEA) prohibit companies from excluding workers from a pension plan for being too old, even if they are hired within a few years of the normal retirement age specified in the plan. ERISA also requires your plan administrator to issue various documents that provide complete information about the plan.

The "Summary Plan Description" is a booklet that describes how the plan operates, its eligibility requirements, the method used to calculate your amount of benefits, and how to file a claim. This information must be given to you within 90 days after you become a participant in the plan. The law requires that this summary be updated every five years if important changes in plan rules have been made.

The "Summary Annual Report" is a short document containing information on the investments in your pension plan. If the plan has more than 100 participants, you have the right to request, once a year, a detailed financial report called Form 5500, which your plan must file annually with the government. The form includes an accountant's report, an investment summary, and a statement as to whether enough money has been invested in the fund to pay the benefits that have been promised. If your plan has fewer than 100 members, you have the right to request a full report every three years and an abridged report every year.

If you are married at the time you become a plan member and are at least age 35, you will receive survivor coverage information that explains widows' and widowers' benefits. It will spell out how much the benefit paid while you are alive would be reduced to provide protection to your husband or wife after you die. By law, your spouse automatically receives benefits after your death unless she or he has waived them.

If you make a request in writing for any of this information to your plan administrator, he is required by federal law to respond to you within 30 days.

A Glossary of Pension Terms

Since the first private pension plan in the United States was established in 1875 by the American Express Company, pension plans have grown astoundingly in both number and complexity. Their purpose is to encourage saving for retirement, and to make sure those savings will be there when you need them. Here are some basic terms:

•**Annuity.** A monthly payment made for the lifetime of the retired worker or for the lifetime of the worker's spouse after the death of the worker.

•**Defined-benefit plan.** A type of pension plan that offers a fixed, lifetime income, provided by your employer and based depending on how long you worked for the employer and how much you earned.

•**Defined-contribution plan.** A type of pension plan based on the sums your company and you contribute to it and how well it is invested. These plans include profit-sharing 401 (k) plans and employee stock ownership plans.

•**Employee stock ownership plan (ESOP).** A pension plan that encourages workers to buy their employer's stock, typically at a reduced price. Because the value of your benefit is directly related to the value of your company's stock, ESOP's can be risky. They are not insured by the Pension Benefit Guaranty Corporation (PBGC).

•**Employee Retirement Income Security Act (ERISA).** The 1974 federal act that requires company pension plans to conform to certain rules in order for the employer's contributions to the plan to be tax-deductible. ERISA was amended in 1984 by the Retirement Equity Act (REA), which provides additional protection for spouses of participants and liberalizes ERISA rules on participation and vesting.

•**Forward averaging.** A tax-saving device that lets those whose lump-sum payout benefit is less than a specified amount pay income tax on that benefit as if they had received the money over five or 10 years.

•**401 (k) plan.** A defined-contribution, profit-sharing plan that permits employees to make automatic tax-deferred contributions in investment vehicles provided by the company; 403 (b) is a version for workers in the nonprofit sector. Such plans are named for a section of the Internal Revenue Code that regulates these plans.

•**Guaranteed investment contract (GIC).** A contract between an insurance company and a corporate savings or pension plan that offers a fixed rate of return on the capital invested over the life of the contract, usually one year.

•**Individual retirement account (IRA).** A personal fund that allows for personal income tax deductions on annual $2,000 investments under certain circumstances. In addition, it defers taxes on the money put in and the income it generates until you begin withdrawing your money, which must be after age 59½ to avoid a penalty.

•**IRA rollover.** A technique that allows employees to avoid taxes by transferring a lump-sum payment from a 401 (k) or other profit-sharing plan into an IRA within 60 days of its withdrawal from the original plan.

•**Lump-sum distribution.** The payment of all the money in a worker's retirement account at once, instead of in installments; usually done when the worker leaves a job.

•**Pension Benefit Guaranty Corporation (PBGC).** The federal institution established by ERISA to guarantee private defined-benefit pensions if a company goes bankrupt.

•**Profit-sharing plan.** An agreement by which the company makes annual contributions out of profits to an account for each worker or to a collective account for the workers. This money may be invested in stocks, bonds, or money market securities. The funds are tax-deferred until the employee leaves the firm, or later, depending upon the plan.

•**Qualified plan.** An employer-sponsored retirement plan that meets various requirements of the Internal Revenue Code.

•**Termination.** With reference to a defined-benefit plan, the ending of a pension plan. In a "standard termination," the plan has enough assets to pay off all its obligations; in a "distress termination," the Pension Benefit Guaranty Corporation steps in to guarantee the pension payments.

•**Vesting.** Completion by a participant of a pension plan's "years of service" requirement. Vesting entitles you to a permanent legal right to your pension benefits, whether or not you continue to work for the company.

How to Monitor Your Plan

Warning Signals in Your Pension's Annual Report

Either every year, or every three years, your employer must file a pension report with the IRS, which details your defined-benefit plan's liabilities and assets. Ask your plan administrator for a copy and review it carefully for clues as to how your plan is doing. Scrutinize the following areas, and if you have questions, ask the administrator to explain or call the U.S. Department of Labor's Pension and Welfare Benefits Administration for further information:

✔ **Asset amounts.** Compare the plan's assets over the last one-year, five-year, and 10-year periods. Although every fund will have bad years, a well-managed fund should show at least an eight percent annual growth rate over the last 10 years.

✔ **Types of assets.** All of the pension money should not be placed in one type of investment. The fund should have a variety of investments, such as stocks, bonds, and secure holdings.

✔ **Employer contributions.** Compare employer contribution on the current statement with those for the previous year. A significant drop could mean that the plan has piled up more funds than it needs to achieve its goals—or it could mean that the company has financial problems. If you suspect this, seek financial advice.

You are the best watchdog of your own pension plan. Nearly 2 trillion dollars are invested in hundreds of thousands of company and union pension plans, and government investigators can review fewer than one percent of these plans each year. Fortunately, you have some important rights to help you obtain the information you need to keep watch on your plan yourself.

Start by becoming familiar with the rules that those managing private pensions (defined-benefit plans) must follow. Federal law requires that pension funds be invested prudently. One important provision in the "prudence rule" limits a fund's investment in securities of its own firm to no more than 10 percent of the fund's assets. The law also prohibits loaning *significant* portions of the fund to the corporation. The "Summary Annual Report," which outlines the financial activities of your plan, can give you a sense of how well your pension money has been invested, but you as a worker are fairly well removed from the operation of the fund.

GETTING INVOLVED WITH A 401 (K)

Defined-contribution plans, however, offer their participants more active roles. The fastest-growing type of pension plan, the 401 (k) encourages participants to choose wisely and educate themselves about available options. With the 401 (k) plans, employers may offer a family of several mutual funds for you to choose among for your share of contributions along with guaranteed investment contracts. You agree to put a certain amount of your salary into the plan regularly (your company may add some too); your contribution offers tax-deductible savings whose growth, tax-deferred, depends on the success of the investments chosen. If your plan permits, you may be able to change investment options, and, depending on company policy, borrow against the value of your account.

As a participant in a defined-contribution plan, you should get, and scrutinize, a written performance report from your company at least once a year. If you do not like the plan, you can initiate action by discussing it with the human resources division of the company. Don't expect to move mountains, however. Under voluntary Department of Labor guidelines, firms are not liable for poorly performing investments if their plans satisfy rules about the number and variety of investing options and employees' opportunities to switch investments.

Still, the plan administrator must follow the rules laid down and enforced by the IRS, which monitors the plan's tax aspects, and by the Labor Department, which monitors fund manage-

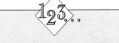

ment and disclosure requirements. If you think the plan's fees are excessive, that its investments are not prudent, or that any of the ERISA requirements have been violated, you should first contact the nearest field office of the U.S. Department of Labor's Pension and Welfare Benefits Administration.

You can get additional advice from several nonprofit consumer groups that publish helpful guides to understanding pension law and your rights. One of these is "Protecting Your Pension Money," available from the Pension Rights Center in Washington, D.C. The American Association of Retired Persons (AARP) also offers several publications on pensions and the rights of participants. (For addresses of these organizations, see RESOURCES, page 493.)

When—and How—to Cash In

At retirement time, and long before then for some, most workers will have to make a decision about how to receive the retirement money from their pension plans. Whether you are actually retiring, have been laid off, or are simply changing jobs, you will need to evaluate your options carefully since some choices can trigger stiff penalties.

For most private pension plans, if you have been at your job long enough to earn the right to a pension, federal law requires that the plan administrator give you your "Individual Benefit Statement" before you leave the job. This statement will tell you how much money you have earned in benefits and, considering the company's years-of-service requirements, what percentage of your accumulated benefits you are actually entitled to receive.

You should review this information carefully before you leave your job. Remember that it may be decades before you actually file a claim for your benefits. If you disagree with or do not understand any statements you receive regarding your pension plan, now is the time to resolve any problems. See your plan administrator—and do it several months before you plan to retire or resign to find out how to claim your benefits.

TAKING IT WITH YOU

When you leave, you may receive some or all of the funds in your pension account as a lump sum. But be warned that if you do not reinvest this payout by transferring the money directly from your former account into an Individual Retirement Account (IRA) or other qualified retirement plan, 20 percent of the money you withdraw may be withheld for federal income taxes. (The government may reimburse you for this 20 percent,

<aside>

APPEALING TO RIGHT A WRONG

As a participant in a private employee benefit plan, your rights are protected by the 1974 Employee Retirement Income Security Act (ERISA). If your claim for benefits is denied or you disagree with the amount coming to you, ERISA requires your plan administrator to notify you in writing within 90 days of the decision and explain the reasons for the decision. Your other rights when appealing are outlined below:

1. You have at least 60 days to file an appeal. Your plan administrator must tell you how to submit your denied claim for a full and fair review.

2. A decision on your appeal generally must be made within 60 days of your filing it. You must be informed of the decision and also of the specific reasons for it.

3. If your appeal is denied, you have the additional right to bring a lawsuit against your pension plan.

4. You cannot be fined, discharged, suspended, or discriminated against for exercising these rights under ERISA. The use of violence or intimidation to interfere with your rights under a pension plan is against the law.

</aside>

but not until you file your annual tax return.)

If you are under age 59½ when you receive the lump sum and fail to reinvest it, you will also have to pay a 10 percent tax penalty in addition to regular income tax. To transfer the money directly, first establish an appropriate retirement account (this could be an IRA or your new employer's plan). Inform your previous employer's benefits department in writing where you want your money transferred.

You can also minimize the taxes owed if you are at least 59½ when you receive the distribution by taking advantage of "five-year forward averaging." With this method, the amount of your pension is taxed as though it were received over a five-year period, and the tax is computed separately from other income. (Ten-year averaging is available to persons who became 50 years of age before January 1, 1986.)

Your retirement money may well be the largest sum of money you will ever have in one place, so if the funds are avail-

KEEPING TABS ON YOUR FUND WHEN YOU CHANGE JOBS

If you change jobs, you may need to find a new home for the money in your 401 (k), profit-sharing, or other defined-contribution retirement plan. (A defined-benefit pension normally remains with your former employer until you apply for benefits.) Your action could trigger penalties and taxes, so be aware of the options below:

If You Decide To:	This Will Happen:
Leave money in a former employer's plan	Your funds will continue to grow tax-deferred. You have the option of moving the money later on to an IRA or a new retirement plan.
Have your employer transfer the money directly into an IRA or other qualified retirement plan	Your money will continue to grow tax-deferred until you withdraw it.
Withdraw the money as a lump sum	Federal law requires that 20 percent be withheld for income taxes from the money you take out. Depending on your tax bracket, you may owe additional taxes at tax time or be due a refund on what was withheld.
Receive a lump-sum cash payment and put the money yourself into an IRA or other qualified plan	Twenty percent of your money will be withheld, but the money may be refunded after your tax return is filed. To avoid tax, you must put the money into an IRA or other qualified plan within 60 days after you take it out. The money will go on growing tax-deferred in the new account.
Begin periodic withdrawals that will continue for at least 10 years	You will owe ordinary income tax on the withdrawals, but no 10 percent penalty — even if you are not 59½. Withholding in this case is voluntary.

able to you, be prudent about managing it. By all means consult a financial professional if necessary, but be as well informed as possible before doing so.

If Your Plan Is Terminated

An employer has the legal right to close down a pension plan if the plan is in serious financial trouble or if the company shows that it cannot afford to continue it. However, the company must disperse funds in the account to everyone who is enrolled. How that is done depends on how the plan is terminated.

In a "standard termination," the plan has enough assets to pay all the pension benefits it owes. Often the plan administrator will transfer the plan money to an insurance company that will then pay your monthly benefits when you retire. If you get a notice informing you that you will be receiving this type of benefit, called an "annuity," be sure that you receive a certificate from the insurance company issuing the annuity. The annuity will be based on credits you have earned as of the date of the plan's termination.

A "distress termination" occurs when the company is in serious financial difficulty. In this case, all or part of your pension may be protected by the Pension Benefit Guaranty Corporation (PBGC), the government's pension insurance program. The PBGC will keep records of plan participants and what they are owed, and will issue the payments from its insurance funds. It will also notify you of your guaranteed benefit and of your right to appeal this decision. But the PBGC covers only certain kinds of pension plans, and even those may not be fully protected. You also should be aware that a pension plan's rules can change over the years. For example, a company may alter the formula for figuring your pension or end special early retirement benefits. Whenever changes occur, your plan administrator must notify you in writing within seven months after the end of the plan's fiscal year.

Self-Directed Plans

Financial experts are unanimous in urging workers who are not part of an employer's pension plan to set up personal retirement plans as soon as they start earning money on their own. Otherwise the retirement years may be bleak indeed.

Even if you are employed by a company with a plan and work part-time for yourself, you are eligible to set up your own

---

ARE YOUR PENSION BENEFITS VULNERABLE?

The federal Pension Benefit Guaranty Corporation (PBGC) was set up to insure workers' pension benefits against the failure of their company's pension plans or the bankruptcy or liquidation of the companies themselves. But the PBGC's protection applies only to the basic benefits of specific kinds of pension plans. This means that significant chunks of your retirement nest egg may be unprotected.

1. First of all, the PBGC insures only defined-benefit pension plans. It does not insure the many defined-contribution plans, such as ESOP's, profit-sharing, or 401 (k) plans, that are now in existence. Even some defined-benefit plans are not covered by the PBGC: e.g., government plans and plans run by religious organizations, and professional offices such as doctors and lawyers, with fewer than 25 employees.

2. Any amount of the monthly benefit from a defined-benefit pension plan that exceeds the PBGC's ceiling is not insured.

3. Extra benefits, such as life and health insurance, severance pay, disability pay, and vacation pay, are not covered.

4. If you earn a high salary, the chances are that part of your pension benefits are going into a supplemental pension plan—one not covered by the PBGC.

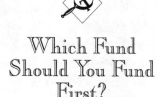

Which Fund Should You Fund First?

Many people have access to more than one type of retirement account. For example, you could have a 401 (k) at work and an IRA for income earned doing freelance work. How should you decide which accounts to contribute to first?

Begin with the plan that returns the most to you. For example, your first contributions should be to an employer-based plan in which your company matches what you put in. That way you double your money, free. Next in line should be any other employer or self-employed plan that enables you to make tax-deductible contributions.

When you have put the maximum allowed into tax deductible plans—or do not have access to any—contribute to an IRA. If you are not eligible for an IRA because you are not earning an income, or have already reached your annual limit on contributions to the IRA, consider an annuity, an investment product sold by life insurance companies.

Annuities, like IRAs, allow your money to grow and compound without being taxed until withdrawal. And you can deposit as much as you want each year into an annuity. On the other hand, you get no tax deduction when you set it up.

retirement plan. Of course, you will have to take the initiative in choosing and starting the plan, but you will have greater flexibility than people in employer-sponsored plans to design one tailored to your needs. Three of the most popular kinds of individual plans are discussed here. Remember that these plans, with their tax incentives, are designed to help you save; if you withdraw your money before you are 59½ years old, you must pay a steep 10 percent penalty plus the taxes due. When you reach age 70½, you must begin to withdraw your funds.

IRA'S, KEOGH'S AND SEP'S

The most common self-directed plan is the Individual Retirement Account (IRA), established with a custodian approved by the IRS, such as a mutual fund, credit union, or bank. You can contribute up to $2,000 of earned income a year. Two-income married couples can contribute up to $4,000 a year. If you do not participate in a qualified retirement plan, IRA contributions are generally tax-deductible

Keogh plans are named after Eugene Keogh, the New York congressman who sponsored the Self-Employed Individuals Tax Retirement Act in 1962, which authorized this form of tax-deferred pension account. Keoghs allow you to put away more of your self-employment income than an IRA—up to a maximum of $30,000 a year, or a certain percentage of your income (15 to 25 percent), depending on which plan you adopt. You can use almost any investment for the account, including stocks and bonds. There are four different types of Keoghs, each with varying rules on contributions, and they can require substantial paperwork to set up and administer. You should seek professional advice in choosing a Keogh, which can be established at banks, brokerage firms, and other financial institutions.

For self-employed individuals without any employees, a Simplified Employee Pension Plan (SEP) is easier to set up and administer than a Keogh. Instead of establishing and maintaining a separate pension plan (required with a Keogh), a SEP lets you deposit tax-deductible money directly into your IRA account. Generally, the amount you may contribute is 13.04 percent of your self-employment income each year, up to a maximum of $22,500. You can decide each year the amount you want to contribute; no minimums apply. Your SEP contributions are tax-deductible to a limit and may allow salary deferral and tax savings.

Before 1993, separate plans such as those described above were each covered by government insurance for $100,000. Now the total insurance you can receive for pension accounts in one bank has shrunk to $100,000. If you have more than this limit in a self-directed account, you may want to spread your funds among several sound banking institutions.

WILLS AND ESTATES

Since death is even more certain than taxes, you and your heirs should take pains to make sure that your worldly goods are distributed the way you want them to be.

Estate Plans Are for You

The phrase "estate planning" sounds like something that goes on behind high gates at the end of a long driveway. But estate plans are not just for the very rich. If you own any more property than a minivan and a pair of running shoes, you should have a plan for making sure that your property will go to those to whom you want it to go as quickly and economically as possible.

An estate plan is simply a legal, written document—or set of documents—that provides for distribution of your estate when you die. Your estate comprises everything you own at the time of your death: house, car, furniture, jewelry, savings accounts, insurance policies, stocks, and bonds. Some of this property, such as insurance policies, will pass automatically to named beneficiaries. Some of it, such as your home, may belong to a person named as the joint owner. But only in a will, the most essential estate-planning document for most people, can you distribute the rest of your assets the way you wish to.

In most circumstances, every adult needs a will. If you have minor children, a will is the only way to name a guardian for them. If you and your spouse should both die "intestate"—without a will—the state courts and social service agencies decide who will raise your children. That in itself is a compelling reason to have a will.

Besides taking charge of your children if you die intestate, the state also decides how to distribute your money and property. State laws on inheritance differ, but states generally will distribute the largest portion of your assets to your surviving legal spouse. Next in line are your children, your parents, and other relatives, starting with those who are closest blood relations. If no heirs are found after a reasonable search, the property "escheats"—passes to the state.

PREPARING A WILL

Whether simple or complex, a will must follow legal forms. There are three types: the formal witnessed will, the "holographic" (handwritten) will, and the "nuncupative" (oral) will. Of these, only the formal witnessed will is valid in all situations. Some states do not even recognize holographic wills, and oral

When Should You Make a New Will?

Once you make a will, it remains valid until you die, change it, or revoke it. In general, you should review your will at least every four years, or in one of following situations:

✔ *Birth of a child.* You may want to appoint a guardian for your child, set up a trust, or otherwise make provisions for your child in the event of your death.

✔ *Change in marital status.* In many states, when you get married, any will you have at the time is automatically revoked and your new spouse legally becomes an heir. If you die without making a new will, the property will be distributed as though there were no will at all—even if you had no changes to make in your original will. On the other hand, in many states, getting divorced does not automatically revoke a will. Thus, a spouse you have divorced may still have a legal claim on your estate.

✔ *A move out of state.* If you move to a different state, you should ask your lawyer to check your will to make sure that the new state laws do not affect your estate adversely.

wills are permitted only in very unusual circumstances—for example, during someone's last illness. The basic requirements for a valid will are not complicated:

■ You must be a legal adult—at least 18 years old in most states.
■ You must be of "sound mind": possessing a general understanding of the property you own and your family .
■ Your will must meet the requirements of your state's will-drafting law.

Most states have similar rules regarding wills. They involve requirements such as dating the will and appointing an executor, the person who sees that the provisions of your will are carried out. You must also sign the will in front of two—and in some states, three—witnesses, who will not receive anything under your will. In most states, if your will is executed properly and notarized upon execution, your witnesses will not need to appear in court when your will is probated after your death. Such a will is known as a "self-proving" will. For safety's sake, some lawyers suggest having one more witness than is required by law so that the will would not be nullified should one witness later be deemed unqualified.

Although you can designate whether or not you want your children to receive an inheritance under your will, in many states you must use the correct language if you want to specifically disinherit a child. If a child is simply omitted, probate

Money begets money.

JOHN RAY
English Proverbs

How to Guard Against Challenges to Your Will

Anyone who might gain from contesting your will may try to do so. The two most common grounds for such a move are that the testator, or will maker, was not of sound mind and that someone used coercion to unduly influence her. Here are some safeguards:

• Use an experienced attorney (ideally one who specializes in estate planning) to draw up your will. Your local bar association can provide you with necessary referrals.

• Use respectable witnesses who can vouch for your mental state when you sign the will. Choose witnesses who are not personal friends so that if the will is challenged, they cannot be charged with bias.

• Videotape the signing and have the will read aloud. This may seem extreme, but especially in cases where a person's health or memory is failing, it is a sensible precaution to record the will being approved by the testator.

• Keep the will clear and unambiguous, and be sure it says exactly what you mean. Do not erase passages, cross out lines, or write new provisions in the margins. Any handwritten alterations could raise suspicions that the changes were made without your knowledge. Be sure you and your witnesses sign or initial each page of the document.

• Consider putting your property into a revocable living trust. You control the living trust during your lifetime; the assets pass to your beneficiaries when you die, avoiding probate entirely. Unlike a will, a trust is private, and courts must be persuaded to make the document public. Only rarely have living trusts been invalidated in court. (See also "When to Trust a Trust," page 371.)

court later might treat it as an oversight. All states, however, prohibit you from disinheriting a spouse, although some may allow you to reestablish such an arrangement with a legal document such as a valid premarital agreement. If you try to disinherit a spouse, the spouse can "elect against" your will after you die, and will probably inherit one-third to one-half of your estate, as though you had died intestate.

Forgiving Debts

PROBLEM
Caroline Leeds, a divorced mother, loaned her son, James, and daughter-in-law, Cathy, $15,000 for a down payment on a house. Caroline was concerned that the couple should not be obligated to her estate for this loan if she should die before the loan was repaid. She decided that she wanted to forgive the debt as a bequest in her will.

SOLUTION
Caroline called her lawyer, and her lawyer advised her to revise her will with a provision that explicitly stated that she forgave whatever remained outstanding on her loan of $15,000 to James and Cathy Leeds. Since Caroline was divorced from James's father when she made the loan, she was free to deal with the debt in her will as she chose. However, if Caroline had made the loan while still married, she might have had the right to forgive only half the debt unless her husband agreed in writing to allow her to forgive his share of the debt as well.

By law, you have the right to draft your own will; forms and kits can be found in stationery, card, and book stores. But using a lawyer to advise you on your will offers several advantages. For example, a lawyer can tell you if there are state inheritance laws that will affect your bequests. She can also suggest the most advantageous ways for you to hold title to your property and can ensure that your will is unambiguous and complies with your state's law. The point is to craft a foolproof document so that when it goes through "probate"—the legal process that proves your will is valid—no one will contest it.

Transferring Property: Other Ways Besides Wills

Making out a proper will and keeping it up to date is by far the most accepted way of making sure that your money and property pass in an orderly way to those you leave behind. Yet wills have some significant drawbacks. The chief one is that assets left in a will must go through probate court (called surrogate court in some states), where your will is authenticated, your assets

Changed Your Mind? Amend Your Will.

Do you have to write a whole new will if you change your mind about whom you want to leave your grandmother's ring to? Probably not. For a relatively small and straightforward change such as that, the traditional procedure is to make a "codicil" to your existing will.

A codicil is a formal legal method for making changes to an already drafted will. A codicil must be prepared, signed, and witnessed with all the formalities of a will. You should sign and date it in the presence of three witnesses, who are told it is your will and who then sign their names. The witnesses do not have to be the same as those for your original will, but you should use them if they are available.

If, on the other hand, you have changed your mind about a lot of things in your will, it is better to make a new one to prevent confusion when the time comes to probate the will. In fact, computers and fast printers have made it so much quicker to prepare a document for witnessing and signing that it is becoming almost as easy to make a whole new will as to write a codicil.

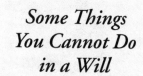

Some Things You Cannot Do in a Will

In general, you can dispose of your property any way you want to in your will. But there are a few things you are not allowed to do in a will. (State laws vary in this area.)

✔ **Disinherit a spouse.** Most states allow a spouse to claim a significant portion of your estate (often one-third) even if you try to disinherit him or her in your will. In community property states, however, where communal property is split equally between the spouses, one spouse has no legal rights to receive any of the other spouse's share unless the will so dictates. In some cases, a will and a valid premarital agreement with the spouse serve to circumvent a spouse's inheritance rights.

✔ **Coerce an heir.** A will cannot try to force a beneficiary into or out of certain types of conduct. For example, a potential gift cannot be made contingent on the heir's choice of a marriage partner or religious conversion.

✔ **Last-minute charity.** Some states do not allow gifts to be willed to charitable or religious organizations if the will was made less than a certain time period—such as 30 days or six months—before the testator dies. If you plan to leave more than half your estate to a charity, consult with a lawyer.

are ascertained, and your debts are paid. After any fees owed to lawyers, appraisers, and accountants are paid, the remaining property is distributed to your heirs.

Although the person named as executor usually must offer the will for probate within 30 days, the average probate proceedings often take a year or more. Probate takes place not only in the state where you live but in every state where you own property. (Although you do not need to file a will in every state, your will should account for all property and reflect the laws in states where you own property.) The legal fees for taking your estate through the probate process can add up to as much as 10 percent of the value of your estate.

For those who want to spare their heirs some of these costly delays, other legal and surprisingly simple strategies are available to help executors avoid the probate process altogether. (Also note that in some states, simple estates can skip the most onerous part of probate. An individual can file independently using form documents and paying small fees. Probate court can often help.) These strategies should not be thought of as substitutes for a will but as supplements to your plan for passing on specific parts of your estate.

- Joint ownership. Joint owners with a right of survivorship, sometimes known as joint tenants, co-own property. When one tenant dies, ownership transfers to the surviving joint tenant (or tenants) without probate.
- Payable on death (POD) accounts. You set up a POD account with a financial institution. When you die, the funds in the account are paid directly to a named beneficiary.
- Life insurance proceeds. Life insurance proceeds normally will avoid probate because you name your beneficiary in the policy instead of in a will.
- Annuities and pension plans. Like life insurance benefits, those paid to your beneficiaries under a pension or profit-sharing plan normally do not go through probate.
- Living trusts. You can set up a living trust so that when you die, all or part of your property will go directly to your named beneficiary. (For more on trusts, see also "When to Trust a Trust," page 371.)

Joint tenancy with a right of survivorship is usually applied to real estate, but any type of property can be owned this way, including bank accounts and cars. You should be aware that you cannot leave your share of a joint-tenancy property to anyone but the other joint tenants. Each joint tenant has rights to ownership. A potential risk of owning a joint-tenancy bank account is that another joint tenant could withdraw your money before you die (although real estate cannot be sold without the

agreement of both or all of the owners). A POD account eliminates that risk, because as long as you live, the beneficiary has
no rights to the money in the account. You also have the option
of closing the account or changing the beneficiary at any time.

Some states have restricted or abolished joint tenancy, and
POD accounts (also known as "informal trusts," "bank trust
accounts," and "Totten trusts") may not be available in community property states—so you should consult a lawyer about
how your state views these strategies for distributing your
property.

GIVING AWAY POWER

Transferring money or assets is the main purpose of estate planning, but good estate planning also involves provisions for
transferring your "power"—that is, authorizing another person to make decisions in your place in case you are unable to
do so. The legal document by which you do this is called a
power of attorney.

There are different types of powers of attorney. Some grant
limited rights, such as allowing another person to pay your bills
while you are traveling abroad. This type expires if you become
mentally disabled, a time when you most need it. But by setting up in advance a document called a "durable power of
attorney," you can authorize someone to make medical and
financial decisions for you if you become incapacitated. Should
you become unable to manage your affairs without having
signed a power of attorney, a judge might appoint someone,
called a conservator or guardian (depending on the state), to
make the decisions for you.

The person who holds this durable power of attorney has
the right to exercise it at any time, even if you are of sound
mind, so choose someone you trust entirely. Or you can ask
your lawyer to set up a "springing" durable power of attorney,
which takes effect only if you become mentally incapacitated.
Whatever kind of power of attorney you set up, it can be
revoked at any time, and it ends when you die.

Estate Taxes—Not Just for Millionaires?

The federal government's estate and gift tax system is
a complicated one. Still, it is less burdensome for
most taxpayers since passage of the Economic
Recovery Tax Act of 1981. Before the act, federal
taxes were levied on all estates worth more than $175,000.
Because an estate that includes nothing more than a house, a
pension, and proceeds from an insurance policy could easily

123...
IF YOU ARE NAMED AN EXECUTOR

An executor is appointed in a will to see that the wishes of the will maker, legally known as the testator, are carried out. If you are named an executor, be prepared to spend a considerable amount of time on the job. For your efforts you may receive a court-appointed fee (a percentage of the estate) that is set by each state. Here is what you are expected to do as executor:

1. Present the will to probate court, and receive legal control of the deceased's property. You may want to hire a lawyer.

2. Open an estate checking account to receive and disburse all funds. File claims for any life insurance and Social Security benefits.

3. File an estate tax return within nine months of the death; pay estate taxes, if any are due; and file a final income tax return on behalf of the deceased.

4. Deal with all personal financial business, such as informing banks, brokerages, and creditors about the death, and attend to all outstanding debts.

5. Make an accounting of the estate's assets to the heirs and distribute the assets as the will directs.

6. Submit an accounting of your activities to the probate court. Petition the court for discharge when your duties have been completed.

pass that minimum, millions of Americans were affected by federal estate taxes.

YOUR TAXABLE ESTATE

The 1981 act, however, raised the amount of your estate that does not get taxed to $600,000. If your estate is clearly worth less than this amount, you will not have to be concerned about federal estate taxes. Be sure to distinguish federal estate taxes from state death (and inheritance) taxes. A number of states levy death taxes on the property of people who lived in or merely owned real estate in that state. If your state has such taxes, it may well have other laws that could affect your estate planning. For example, some states with death taxes require that a deceased person's bank accounts or safe-deposit boxes be "sealed" until a release is obtained from court officials. So when devising your estate plan, consult an attorney about the laws of the states that will have a say about your estate.

In general, all the property you own worth over $600,000 is subject to federal estate taxes. But several important exemptions allow you to transfer substantial amounts of property free of federal estate taxes. Among them are all property left to a spouse and all property left to a qualified tax-exempt charity.

If you think your estate will exceed the federal limit in spite of these exemptions—and so will owe federal taxes—you should prepare a written inventory and evaluation of your property to be sure. Then consult a qualified estate-planning attorney for ways to minimize the taxes on your estate. Estate taxes escalate rapidly as the size of your taxable estate increases.

TAXES ON GIFTS

Most people think of gifts as a personal matter, unrelated to estate planning. However, anytime you give someone a gift worth more than $10,000, gift taxes can become involved. That is because the lifetime federal exemption on estate taxes of $600,000 applies to gifts you make during your lifetime as well as those you bequeath in your will. This is known as the "unified credit" rule. When you give a gift of more than $10,000, the amount over $10,000 gets added to the property you hold at death in calculating your estate-tax liability. (You do not actually pay a gift tax at the time of the gift.) An important exception to the gift-tax rule is that you are allowed to make annual gifts of up to $10,000 each to as many people as you wish without triggering the gift tax. Suppose you are married and have three children and a large estate. You and your spouse could both give each child $10,000 a year, for an annual total of $60,000, without incurring a gift tax.

Any individual gifts of more than $10,000 made during your lifetime, however, count toward the $600,000 estate-tax exemp-

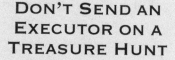

DON'T SEND AN EXECUTOR ON A TREASURE HUNT

Your will provides for the orderly distribution of your assets after you die, but you also have to make sure your heirs and executors know where to find all those worldly goods. You can help by keeping an updated inventory of your assets—and don't forget to tell your executor where you keep the list, which should include:

1. Your Social Security number (and Social Security card).

2. The number and location of all bank accounts and safe-deposit boxes; the location of stock, bond, and mutual fund accounts; and the name and number of insurance policies.

3. The name and address of your lawyer, accountant, broker, and insurance agent.

4. Where your jewelry and other valuables are kept, and the location of any other property you own, such as real estate or a boat.

5. Location of your will and other estate-planning documents, as well as your birth, marriage, and military discharge certificates.

6. Credit card accounts, with account numbers.

7. The details of any outstanding debts that you owe or that are owed you.

tion. So if you make taxable gifts totaling $200,000 during your lifetime, only $400,000 worth of your property can be transferred free of federal estate taxes when you die.

When to Trust a Trust

Trusts, like the concept of estate planning, are often considered to be a trademark of the very rich. But today, people of widely varying incomes find that the versatility of trusts makes them useful estate-planning tools. Although trusts are more complicated and more costly than drafting a will (you or your heirs may have to pay annual fees of one to two percent of the trust's assets to a professional trustee), they offer several advantages.

Broadly, there are two kinds of trusts: the "testamentary trust" and the "living trust." The testamentary trust is set up by a will and takes effect after the will is probated. A living trust, sometimes known as an inter vivos trust, takes effect as soon as

When You Inherit

Between 1994 and the year 2000, an estimated $11 trillion will be passed on to the younger generation by its elders. If you are likely to receive a lump-sum inheritance, large or small, it is smart to figure out ahead of time what you will do with it. To avoid making hasty and costly decisions, take the following steps before spending or investing your inheritance:

• Understand your tax liability. For instance, your inheritance itself is not subject to federal income tax, and estate taxes will usually have been paid off out of the estate before you get it. However, many states have inheritance taxes, and you will owe income tax on any future earnings the inherited money makes.

• Cash your inheritance check and put the money into an interest-earning account immediately—even if you later decide to do something else with it. If you are in the 28 percent income tax bracket or above, you should at least consider putting the money in a tax-exempt money market fund.

• Determine how much of your inheritance you will spend, and in what way. One recommendation: pay off all nondeductible debt first, such as credit card bills.

• Understand the "cost basis" of the property you inherit. The cost basis is the value used to measure the capital gains tax owed when you sell inherited assets. It is fixed at the time of death. Suppose you wish to sell some stocks that you inherited from a parent who bought them at $30 a share and that, at your parent's death, are worth $40 a share. When you finally sell them, they are worth $50 a share. You pay tax only on the difference between the $40 (the "stepped-up cost basis" at the time of the testator's death) and $50. By contrast, the cost basis of assets you are given while the donor is alive is fixed at the asset's purchase price. If your parents give you the $40 stock they bought at $30 a share and you sell it at $50, you pay tax on the difference between $30 and $50 per share.

• Take advantage of the opportunity to set aside an emergency fund for yourself and your family. Financial experts recommend setting aside three months' living expenses as a cushion against an unexpected loss of income or sudden major expenditure.

• If the inheritance is large enough to change the nature of your own estate, get professional advice from an experienced estate-planning attorney to help you review or create your own estate-planning documents.

When You Want to Leave Property to a Minor Child

In general, you have the right to leave property to anyone you want. But the law says that minor children cannot own property outright, free of supervision, beyond a limited amount—in the $2,500 to $5,000 range, depending on the state you live in. So if you want to leave a significant sum to a minor, you may have to appoint a guardian to hold title to the property until the child reaches adulthood under state law, usually age 18.

If the value of the property will be more than $25,000, you should consider a child's trust. This allows you to name a person you can rely on to manage property for your child until he or she reaches an age you have designated (it does not have to be 18). In the meantime, your successor trustee can spend any of that child's trust income or property for the child's health, education, or living needs.

You can set up a child's trust in your will, but using a will means that the property must go through probate before it is turned over to the child's trust. So it is worth considering setting up a child's trust as part of a living trust.

it is established. It is a legal device designed to hold property of an individual, called a grantor, for the sake of one or more beneficiaries. A living trust can be revocable so that the grantor can revoke or change it at any time; or it can be made irrevocable, in which case the grantor cannot change it, regardless of mistakes, altered circumstances, or a simple change of mind.

The trust document will specify a trustee to manage the trust's assets; usually that is the same person who established the trust—that is, the grantor. The trust document will also name a "successor trustee," who takes over after the grantor dies and becomes responsible for distributing the remaining assets to the beneficiaries. If the grantor has young children, the successor trustee can manage their assets until they are whatever age the grantor specifies. In addition, a clause can be written into the trust document that protects an estate plan from attacks by its beneficiaries.

The revocable living trust does not save federal and state estate taxes, but none of the assets in a living trust pass through probate. Instead they go directly to its beneficiaries, bypassing the probate fees, since the title is already in the name of a living entity (the trust) and is not part of the deceased's estate.

WHY BOTHER WITH A TRUST?

Probate costs can be high. Attorneys' and executors' fees vary widely from state to state, as do court costs. In some states the cost of probate is a percentage of the estate's gross value. If you live in one of these states, a living trust is an effective way to sidestep the high probate costs. The nonprofit consumer advocacy group HALT in Washington, D.C., publishes a guide to probate costs in the 50 states. (See also RESOURCES, page 493.)

Another advantage of a living trust is the matter of privacy. Once a will is admitted to probate, anyone can read it at the courthouse. A trust document, on the other hand, remains secret even after the assets are distributed. If you for any reason do not want the world to know about your estate after you have died, the living trust is the answer.

A living trust also enables you to avoid a conservatorship; that is, being placed under a court-appointed guardian should you become unable to manage your own affairs. When setting up the trust, you can provide for a successor trustee to manage your assets if you are incapacitated.

Granted, these benefits come with a price. Trusts, depending on their complexity, can cost from $600 to several thousand dollars to establish. You will also have to go through the process of retitling all your assets that you plan to put into the trust. Finally, a living trust will probably not take care of your whole estate. You will most likely still need a will to deal with any assets that you do not transfer to the trust.

YOUR CAR

Whether you are buying, selling, maintaining, or driving an automobile, knowledge of the law enables you to avoid trouble.

BUYING A NEW CAR ■ BUYING A USED CAR ■ MAINTAINING YOUR CAR ■ INSURING YOUR CAR ■ AUTOMOBILE ACCIDENTS ■ MOTOR VEHICLE LAWS

BUYING A NEW CAR

Homework takes the guesswork out of shopping for new automobile.
Do plenty of research to make sure you get the best deal.

Research, Research, Research

A new car is one of the most expensive items most consumers will ever buy. Knowing your rights as a consumer, doing your homework on car values, and understanding auto-selling techniques will put you in the driver's seat when you go out to shop for a car.

The first step is to determine exactly what kind of car you want to purchase. Are you a single person who commutes to work; a parent who needs plenty of space for kids and gear; or a retiree who values a comfortable automobile? Must your car be practical or can you go for something sporty? Do you want two doors or four? Do you frequently drive long distances, or do you need your car only to run in-town errands?

Next, figure precisely how much you can afford to spend per month on a car. Bear in mind that the cost of a car covers more than simply the price of the vehicle. It also includes insurance, various fees and taxes, operating costs such as gas and oil, and even the price of depreciation. (See also "Calculating the Real Cost of a Car," page 375.) When you arrive at your firm ceiling price, you will be much better able to withstand a salesperson's temptations.

COMPARISON SHOPPING

The third step is to research available choices in the styles you want and the range you can afford. Unbiased information rating new cars and recommending best buys is readily available in a variety of books and journals, such as those recommended in the box at left. You can find these publications in your local bookstore or library.

Compare the cars in your price category for reliability, repair records, cost of maintenance, owner satisfaction, and safety. Note which cars have the most comprehensive warranties and the best fuel economy ratings. Don't forget to take into account the resale value of different models.

You may be able to get the kind of car you want for less if you buy a clone—a similar model sold under another name. For instance, a basic General Motors body may be available with slight modifications as a Pontiac or Oldsmobile. Ford and Mercury share several clones, as do Dodge, Plymouth, and Chrysler.

Generally, a clone has the same auto body as the more expensive car, but perhaps a less powerful engine, fewer mechanical amenities like cruise control, and fewer optional luxuries such as leather seats. However, these clones can provide the basic car you need for hundreds of dollars less.

ALL ABOUT INVOICE PRICES

After you have decided on a model, research the "invoice price" of the car—that is, the amount the dealer actually paid for the basic car. It will also be useful to know the invoice prices for various add-on options such as power steering, air-conditioning, central locking system, and radio. You can get this information from auto-pricing services or auto books and magazines.

If you plan to trade in your old car, find out its cash value by consulting used-car pricing guides such as the *Kelley Blue Book*. Also, get at least one bid from a used-car dealer. If the new-car dealer's trade-in offer is low, it may pay to sell your old car yourself or through a used-car dealer.

Finally, before you venture into a showroom, check out the

Calculating the Real Cost of a Car

Loan or lease payments are only the start of the many factors that go into the cost of driving an automobile. Use this checklist to compare estimated first-year-ownership costs for subcompact, compact, midsize, and large model cars.

- **Financing a loan or lease.** Multiply monthly payments by 12 to calculate the total annual cost of your loan or lease.

- **Depreciation.** The value of a car goes down from the moment it is driven out of the showroom. Depreciation takes into account normal wear and tear as well as the fact that newer models may offer more advanced features. You should figure an average depreciation of 35 percent of the price of the car in the first year.

- **Insurance.** Car buyers are often unaware that sportier and costlier models are more expensive to insure. Calculate the difference in rates before deciding what kind of car you can afford.

- **Registration and license fees.** Most states have annual or biannual fees for auto registration and periodic fees for renewing a driver's license. Divide each total fee by the number of years the fee covers to arrive at an average annual fee.

- **Taxes.** Sales, titling, and property taxes vary by state. The state Motor Vehicle Bureau is the best source for learning what is required locally.

- **Inspection fees.** Most states require an annual inspection, usually done at approved garages, to make sure all parts of the car are in safe working order. Figure the cost of this inspection.

- **Gasoline.** To estimate annual costs, divide the average number of miles you drive each year by the miles per gallon estimate for the auto model, then multiply the number of gallons by the average price per gallon in your area. Example: 12,000 miles divided by 30 miles per gallon = 400 gallons; 400 x $1 per gallon = $400 per year for gasoline.

- **Maintenance and repair.** For the first year, major costs should be covered by the warranty, but there will be ordinary maintenance costs such as oil or filter changes. Ask your service station how much these will cost you.

- **Parking and tolls.** Calculate the amount you spend per week on these expenses, then multiply by 52. The total may surprise you.

- **Total cost.** The total cost is the sum of all of the above. To calculate the cost per mile, divide the total cost by average miles driven.

Repossession— Easier Than You Think

U ntil you have made the last payment on your car, it does not belong to you. In some states, if a borrower fails to make timely payments on a secured loan with the car as collateral, the creditor can repossess the car without going to court—and even without giving notice. Other states require notice of a loan default before repossession.

A creditor cannot, however, commit a "breach of the peace" by using physical force or threats to repossess. For example, removing a car from a closed garage without permission might constitute a breach of the peace in some states.

A creditor may keep a repossessed car as compensation for the debt, or resell it. In some states, if a sale brings in less than is owed on the car, the creditor has the right to sue the borrower for the difference. If the sale brings in more than is owed, the borrower is entitled to the balance.

As a borrower, you also have rights. A repossession may be hasty or in error. If so, contact a lawyer. You may be entitled to "redeem," or buy back, the vehicle by paying the full amount owed on it and the expenses connected with its repossession. Some states also may allow you to "reinstate" the loan by paying the amount you are behind on it together with the creditor's repossession expenses.

latest information on factory rebates, which are discounts and incentives provided by the manufacturer. These deals vary by season, manufacturer, and dealer, but are often advertised in the local media. A legitimate rebate can save you money—as long as it does not tempt you to buy a more expensive car!

Figuring the Financing

With the high prices of even modest automobiles, most car buyers find that they must secure outside financing. The most obvious source of financing is the car dealer, and many dealers offer seemingly sound incentives like no down payment, lower prices, and low interest rates in order to draw buyers. However, just as you must shop intelligently for the car, you should also shop carefully for its financing.

Financing with the dealer is convenient, but the dealer is not a financial institution. He must get the financing from another party, either a bank or the manufacturer, and may add on a small percentage for his service. You may save money by going directly to a bank, savings and loan institution, or credit union. You might even consider taking out a home equity loan, since the interest on such a loan may be tax-deductible and therefore offer that advantage. (See also YOUR MONEY, page 301.)

Research several institutions to compare terms on auto loans; even banks within the same community may offer substantially different terms. Any potential lender is required by law to provide detailed information regarding loans. Therefore, don't hesitate to ask for clarification of any questions from a potential lender, whether a bank or the car dealer.

Compare total payments for your loan for 12-, 24-, 36-, 48-, and 60-month terms. Your monthly payments will be smaller for longer-term loans, but the total amount you pay will be greater because of the added time for which you will pay interest. The extra cost of a longer loan can add up to a significant expense. Thus, it makes sense to take the shortest-term loan that you can afford.

Don't buy credit insurance from a lender if you already have either a life insurance policy or disability insurance. Credit insurance is not required for a loan, and even if you need the protection, you can often purchase it for much less from an insurance broker.

Of course, the cheapest way to buy a car is to pay with cash. If you make regular payments to yourself, the cost of "borrowing from yourself" will be only the interest that money would have earned in your savings account. Usually, this amount is substantially less than the cost of interest on a loan.

Leasing Versus Buying

With car prices rising, leasing has become a popular way to afford a new car. You can lease a car from a leasing company, the leasing division of a car rental firm, or a new-car dealer. Leasing a car, similar to renting, means paying a monthly fee for a set period of time in exchange for its use.

Basically, leasing firms offer two types of contracts. With a "closed-end lease," also known as a fixed-cost lease, you agree to return the car at the end of a specified length of time. You may have a buy-out option, which is the right to buy the car at a price that was set when you entered the lease.

With an "open-end lease," you negotiate a "purchase option," that is, an agreement to buy the car at its "estimated residual value," at the end of the lease. You, the lessee, are responsible for any difference between the "estimated residual value" of the car and its actual value when the lease ends.

Negotiating a Leasing Agreement

A leasing agreement is a legal contract that you will be bound to once you sign. Therefore it is imperative that you are clear about all terms before making a commitment. Ask the dealer to explain all of the terms in detail and pay special attention to the following:

• **Up-front charges.** The lessor, or dealer putting up the auto for lease, must disclose in writing all payments that are due upon delivery of the car. The first month's payment, plus one month's payment as security, is standard.

• **Options.** The contract should specify the options you, the lessee, ordered. You are not required to pay for options you did not request.

• **Taxes and fees.** All taxes and title and license fees must be spelled out, along with the precise penalties for late payments.

• **Capitalized cost reduction.** This is a fancy term for down payment. You will probably be able to negotiate the amount.

• **Warranty.** Ideally, the manufacturer's warranty should cover the entire term of the lease. If it does not, try to negotiate this coverage with the lessor.

• **Mileage limit.** Mileage allowances, or the number of miles provided for under the lease, can range from 10,000 to 18,000 per year. You will be charged for every extra mile.

• **Early termination.** Be clear about the penalties charged if you want to get out of the lease early or if you miss a payment.

• **Gap insurance.** This guarantees the difference between what you, the lessee, collect from the insurance company in case of theft or accident and what you may owe the lessor. Some leases include gap-insurance protection free of charge.

• **Estimated residual value.** This is the value the lessor is anticipating on the car at the end of the lease. The lessor is obligated to disclose this price to the lessee, and it should be included in writing on the lease as well.

• **Purchase option.** Your buy-out price should be written into the contract. On a closed-end lease, it should be the same as the estimated residual value. On an open-end lease, both the estimated residual value and the formula that will be used to determine the final price should be stated.

• **Final costs.** Excess mileage charges, fees for late payment, wear and tear charges, and any other end-of-lease payments must be defined.

If the final resale value is less than the estimated residual value, you owe the lessor the difference. If the resale value is greater than the estimated residual value, you may choose to sell and make a profit. Since the lessee assumes more financial responsibility with an open-end lease, monthly rates are usually lower.

PROS AND CONS OF LEASING

For many drivers, leasing offers several advantages. Since the cost of the lease is based on the car's estimated residual, or depreciated, value, the down payment and monthly payments will be lower than if you were buying a new car. Therefore, you may be able to afford a more luxurious model than if you were buying. Since the typical lease term is from 24 to 48 months, you can always be driving a fairly new car. Leasing may also be a good choice for those who want short-term use of a car.

Finally, if you choose to buy the car at the end of the lease, depending upon the model and the prevailing interest rates, you may have saved thousands of dollars on the car purchase by leasing it first.

On the downside, although you are responsible for all of the costs of car ownership, including insurance, repairs, and maintenance, you do not own the car. You may be charged a hefty fee if you exceed a mileage limit, and you may be subjected to expensive penalties if you terminate the lease early. Some lessors also charge fees to cover wear and tear when the car is returned.

Visiting the Showroom

After you have decided on the makes and models that interest you, how much you can afford to spend, and whether you want to buy or lease, you are ready to visit some showrooms.

On preliminary visits, checking out the cars firsthand and taking test-drives is all you should do. Car salespersons are trained to try to close a sale immediately, but you should resist them. Visit at least three dealers and do not talk price until you have decided exactly which car you want to buy. If you have decided not to finance with the dealer, do not discuss your intentions until after you have settled on a firm price. Dealers may raise their prices if they know they will not be receiving the profitable interest payments from a loan.

STICKER PRICES

Federal law requires dealers to post a sticker on each new vehicle showing the manufacturer's suggested retail price for the base model and for all factory-installed optional equipment.

No-Haggle Shopping

There is good news for buyers who hate haggling: a growing number of auto dealers have done away with high-pressure selling. With the unveiling of their Saturn model in the early 1990's, General Motors was the pioneer in establishing one set price for a specific car model. This policy met with consumer approval even though the car cost might have been higher than what a sharp shopper could have negotiated on her own. Dealers are adapting this approach with "no-dicker stickers," which offer lower prices than factory stickers. These set prices are non-negotiable.

Another option is to hire a broker or buying service to help you out. Some services negotiate with dealers and then order cars directly from the manufacturer for you. Others search local dealerships for the car you want and then negotiate a price. If you want to do the negotiating on your own, some services will send you four or five different quotes on the model you are interested in to give you an idea of what price to expect.

Most services usually charge less than $200, and may be part of a credit union or a discount or automobile club. Your employer may offer services as well, but be wary of brokers that require you to go through a particular lender or dealer.

Car-buying services are also listed in the Yellow Pages under Automobile Brokers or Automobile Purchasing Services.

By law, the dealer's transportation charges and the gas mileage per gallon estimate from the U.S. Environmental Protection Agency must be included on the sticker. Unlike most price tags, the "sticker price" on a new car is usually 10 percent to 15 percent higher than what the dealer actually expects to receive.

Watch out for supplemental stickers marked ADM (additional dealer markup) or ADP (additional dealer profit). These items price expensive dealer-installed extras such as undercoating, and you have the right to refuse to buy any of them.

NEGOTIATING THE PRICE

When negotiating, start from the invoice price that you have learned from your research and work up; don't begin with the sticker price and come down. The best technique is to introduce competition. Draw up a worksheet listing the exact make and model of the car you plan to buy. List each option you want by name and invoice number (which you got from the sticker or your research). Though dealers are anxious to sell the models on hand, you are not obligated to pay for options you don't want just because they are on the floor model. Be prepared to order precisely the car you want from the factory, or to negotiate hard with the dealer for cars on the floor that have options you don't need.

Negotiating a Trade-In

PROBLEM
Richard visited three showrooms and asked for competing bids on a new car. With the invoice price in mind, he negotiated a fair price for the car he wanted, but when he asked about trading in his old car, he was quoted a figure that was $400 less than the used-car guides said his car was worth. The salesman complained that Richard's car had too many miles on it and was not in perfect condition, and therefore was not worth the book value.

ACTION
Because Richard had done his homework he was not taken in by this common ploy used to jack up the overall cost of a car. He knew he had a desirable trade-in model that offered potential profit to the dealer. He also had a quote $200 higher from a used-car dealer across town. As a result, he decided to sell the car on his own for an even better profit.

Tell each dealer that you are getting several bids and will take the best offer. Ask what is the least acceptable amount over the invoice price. Don't settle for a promise to beat any other offer; insist on an exact quote. If the dealer refuses to cooperate, go elsewhere.

A fair price gives the dealer $300 to $500 over the invoice cost, sometimes more on popular models. Often the dealer

Beware of Add-Ons

Dealers try hard to sell expensive extras to new-car buyers. Beware, for many are not worth the money, and you should not pay for any options you do not want. Here are some add-ons to avoid:

✔ *Rustproofing, paint sealant, and fabric protection.* These protect the dealer's profit; most cars are treated by the manufacturer.

✔ *Factory-or dealer-supplied sound systems.* You will get a better buy at a company specializing in car stereos. If you take the dealer's upgraded equipment, be sure that the price of the standard radio is deducted from the cost.

✔ *Extended warranties.* With the protection plans common with most new cars, these are not worth the money.

✔ *Credit insurance.* If you need it, you will get it for less from an insurance broker.

✔ *Advertising fee.* Don't agree to accept this cost. You should not have to pay for the dealer's promotions.

✔ *Options packages.* Often added equipment is sold as a package. This can be an advantage if you want everything; if not, you will save by ordering options individually.

✔ *Dealer preparation.* Before you pay extra to have your car made ready to drive, check the sticker; often the price includes dealer preparation.

makes more because the manufacturer has provided discounts. The only way to know for sure whether or not you are getting a good deal is to check the competition.

Beware if the salesperson who has just offered you a good price leaves to have the deal "approved" by his manager. This is known as "low balling." Having whetted your interest, the manager or another salesperson may tell you that the original salesperson made a mistake and will try to renegotiate—for a higher price, of course. Your best response is to walk out the door. You can be fairly sure that you will get a phone call the next day hoping to get you back in the showroom.

As with financing, do not discuss trading in your old car until you have a firm quote. Having checked competitive rates in advance, you know that you can get financing elsewhere and can sell your old car yourself.

THE PURCHASE AGREEMENT

When the sale is complete, read the purchase agreement carefully. It should specify the make, model, and year of the car, the engine type, and the vehicle identification number, so that you can be sure you get the car you have paid for. Make sure that all of the prices match those quoted by the salesperson and that all of the agreed-upon options are listed. The amount and receipt of the down payment should be noted, and any additional charges should be specified, including relevant taxes, and charges for title and registration.

The purchase order should clearly state the conditions under which a refund of the down payment will be made. If you have accepted dealer financing, insist that the interest rate and monthly payments be specified, as well as your right to cancel and get a refund if the dealer fails to obtain financing on those terms within a specified period of time.

If the contract is for future delivery, it should guarantee full return of the deposit if delivery is not made by a specified date; if you reject the car because it lacks equipment you ordered;or if the car is defective. Be sure an officer of the dealership signs the agreement, because the salesperson's name alone may not be legally binding.

TAKING DELIVERY

Before you drive out of the showroom, make sure your new car is free of scratches or dents, and that all the specified options have been installed. If you asked for air-conditioning, do not drive the car off the lot without it. Have any problems corrected before you leave with the car or, if you cannot wait, make sure the dealer agrees in writing to correct the problem at a later date, and make sure to hold him to his promise.

---

1 2 3 ..

SAVVY CAR-SHOPPERS' CALENDAR

You will have more negotiating power if you shop for a car when dealers are most anxious to sell. Four prime times for best buys are:

1. Late summer and early fall. The end of the model year is peak season for rebates from both dealers and manufacturers who are trying to clear inventory to make way for next year's models.

2. The Christmas season. Business slows down in December, so dealers are very happy to see you just before and after Christmas.

3. Other holidays. Thematic holiday promotions are often held to boost business during other slow holiday periods such as Presidents' Day, Easter, Memorial Day, or the Fourth of July. When you see advertising for these special sales, you know dealers need to sell a lot of cars to offset their promotional costs.

4. The end of the month. When salespeople are striving to meet their sales goals, they are eager to negotiate and may give up some of their commission in order to make a sale.

BUYING A USED CAR

Used cars are thrifty but risky. Before you buy, be sure you know your dealer's or the seller's reputation—and your rights.

Buyer Beware

Many good reasons exist to consider buying a used car, the most obvious being savings. The steepest depreciation on a car is in the first two years of its life. If you find a late-model car in good condition, you may drive away with most of the life of the car ahead of you and pay much less than the cost of a new car.

Although you pay less, you also assume more risk with a used car. Making repairs can be costly. Fortunately, many sources of help are available for used-car buyers.

As with new cars, start with references that rate used-car models by year on the basis of reliability, repair records, and recall history, and that provide pricing guides. (See "Information Sources for Car Buyers," page 374.) Make a list of four or five recommended models that fit your budget.

GOING SHOPPING

With your data in hand, shop around. Try new-car dealers; you may pay more, but they have the widest selection and the greatest accountability for their used cars. Used car dealers may offer better prices, but their stock and follow-up service can be less reliable. Work only with a dealer who has been in business for a long time and check the Better Business Bureau about dealers with whom you are considering doing business.

When car-rental agencies update their fleets, they often sell off their older cars. These cars usually have had regular maintenance, and most come with a warranty. Call a car-rental office to locate the nearest company used-car lot. Auctions also offer bargains, but they also carry risk, since the cars have often been repossessed by lenders and come without guarantees.

Private sellers may be the least expensive source because they have no overhead. However, you may have limited recourse if problems arise once the sale is complete. To survey the options, check local ads. The more ads you see for the model you want, the better your bargaining leverage.

Wherever you find a car that interests you, ask questions like: How many owners has the car had? Who was the last owner? Why is the car being sold? Has it been in any accidents? What is needed to put the car in top condition?

Inspecting a Used Car

Be sure to check these items when you inspect a used car:

✔ *The odometer.* For signs of illegal tampering, check the dashboard for missing screws, and be sure the odometer numbers line up properly.

✔ *Pedals and seats.* Look for signs of age on clutch, brake, and accelerator pedals, and a saggy driver's seat.

✔ *Fenders and trim.* Look for ripples in the metal or patches, indicating rust or body damage.

✔ *Doors and windows.* Look for rust on the bottom of the door; make sure all doors and windows close easily and completely.

✔ *Trunk.* Check inside the trunk for rust. Look under the mat for stains.

✔ *Spare tire.* Make sure the spare is usable and insist on a replacement if it is not.

✔ *Undercoating.* Check for fresh undercoating in the wheel wells or under the carriage, indicating rust.

✔ *Glass and plastic surfaces.* Make sure glass and plastic are intact.

How the Buyers Guide Protects You

Under the rules of the Federal Trade Commission (FTC), dealers are required to post a label called a Buyers Guide in every used car, detailing the mechanical condition of the car and the terms of the car's warranty.

To help prevent mechanical problems, the Buyers Guide includes a checklist of the 14 major systems of an auto and some of the problems that may occur in each. It also advises buyers to have the vehicle looked at by their own mechanics and to get dealer promises in writing.

With regard to warranties, the Buyers Guide must show whether the vehicle is being sold with a full or limited warranty, with only an implied warranty, or "as is" without any guarantee.

State laws concerning warranties vary. Some states do not permit "as is" sales by dealers. All states recognize implied warranties; however, in some states, under an implied warranty, the seller is required to correct major defects that turn up within 30 days. The consumer protection office in your state can provide you with your local laws. In any case, the Buyers Guide must describe the various warranties required in your state and reflect any changes in coverage you have negotiated.

Finally, the Buyers Guide must show the name and telephone number of a person to contact at the dealership if you have any complaints about the operation of the car.

When you find a car you like, test-drive and inspect it carefully in bright daylight. Unscrupulous sellers may have buried body rust or accident damage under layers of paint. Dishonest sellers may also turn back the odometer to make an older vehicle appear more attractive. Follow your own examination with an inspection by a mechanic, with particular attention given to transmission or engine problems. Do not deal with a seller who will not allow you to have the car inspected. If defects are found, they should be corrected by an agreed-upon mechanic, or the price of the car should be reduced.

Making the Deal

The price of a used car is based on its mileage and condition. The bargaining process is similar to new-car negotiations. The best tactic is to ignore the sticker price and make an offer slightly above the listed wholesale price, which you should know from your research. Used-car warranties are negotiable and can vary widely.

Details of the warranty appear on a label known as the Buyers Guide that, by federal law, must be displayed on every used car sold by a dealer. A full warranty means that service will be provided free of charge on the specified parts and systems during the warranty period. A limited warranty usually means that you pay some of the repair costs. The Buyers Guide must detail the percentage of the cost that the dealer will cover, whether you are responsible for a deductible amount, and which parts and systems are covered. If the car you choose has less than a full warranty, try to negotiate. Also, you have the legal right to read the warranty before you buy. Find out from the dealer if he uses a third party to provide repair service; if so, make sure the company is responsible and insured.

Often the dealer will try to sell you a service contract in addition to the warranty. If the contract covers the same repairs offered by the warranty, you do not need it. If it extends beyond the warranty and the potential cost of repairs seems more than the cost of the contract, it may be worthwhile. The service contract should cover towing and the cost of a rental car to be used while your car is being repaired. Be sure to watch for any extra cancellation costs.

When a service contract is offered on a used car, the dealer is required to add the terms of the service contract to the Buyers Guide, which may provide additional rights to the buyer. This additional protection can be particularly valuable if it is available on a car being sold "as is". Although the dealer takes no responsibility for repairs on an "as is" sale, the service contract may cover a the buyer if a serious problem arises.

How to Sell Your Own Car

If your old car is in good condition and you are willing to invest some time, you will get more money for it if you sell it yourself. Since savvy buyers will have researched values, it is important to handle your sale in a professional manner. Here are tips for successful marketing:

• **Set a realistic price.** Find out what the car is worth by checking reference guides, getting quotes from used-car dealers, and looking at ads for similar cars. Decide on the most you can realistically expect to get, and the least you will accept. The actual selling price will probably be between these two figures.

• **Compose an advertisement.** State the year, make, and model, and list desirable equipment, such as air-conditioning or a tape deck. List any strong points such as low mileage or good condition, but if work is needed, say so; if you misrepresent the car, you could face a legal claim if a buyer has problems. Name a price to deter bargain hunters, or say "best offer" to garner the most responses. List only your phone number. Leaving your address out of the ad allows you to screen buyers before they come to your home.

• **Spread the word.** Begin by advertising in less expensive outlets, such as small neighborhood papers. If you do not get enough responses, move up to the local newspaper with the largest circulation. Don't forget free advertising. Put a "For Sale" sign with your telephone number in the car's rear side window. Post an ad on bulletin boards at your office, schools, churches, and shopping centers in the area.

• **Put the car into top shape.** Clean the car inside and out, wax the exterior, repair torn upholstery, and replace worn floor mats. Shine up the chrome, but don't have the car painted; prospects may assume the new coat is covering body work. If you replace worn gas or brake pedals, do it well in advance of when you try to sell the car so that they will not look brand new.

• **Be sure everything works.** Check the air conditioner and heater, the clock, the defroster, the window controls, the windshield wipers and washers, the lights, and the fluid levels for the automatic transmission and brakes. If the tires are worn, either replace them or take the replacement cost into account when you price the car.

• **Have the car serviced and tuned.** Do whatever you can to ensure that it will perform well in a test-drive. Check the battery so that the car will start smoothly. In many states, it is the seller's responsibility to have a current safety-inspection certificate.

• **Have your documents ready.** Your title and registration, warranties, and the owner's manual should be ready for inspection. Maintenance receipts should be available to prove the mileage and service record.

• **Protect yourself.** A serious customer must be allowed to test-drive the car and have it inspected. Go along on the test-drive and allow the prospect to take the car for inspection, but only after leaving a valuable deposit with you, such as the title or registration to his or her car, or a passport. Accept payment only in cash, by certified check, or by money order; never take a personal check.

• **Transfer the title.** State procedures for transferring a title vary. In all states you will be required to fill out an odometer statement, and may be required to sign a statement assigning the title, and to fill out a sales-tax form. The buyer will take these forms to the motor vehicle bureau, get a new registration and license plates, and notify the state that you no longer hold title to the car. Call your motor vehicle bureau for local rules.

• **Pay off any loans.** If your title had a lien on the car from a lender, it is your responsibility to give the purchaser proof of the release of the lien.

• **Remove the license plates.** Unless you are transferring your plates to another car, after the sale is final, turn in the plates to the motor vehicles bureau. Do it before you cancel the insurance or the registration will be suspended, which could cause your driver's license to be suspended. Inform your insurance company of the sale.

• **Create a bill of sale that protects.** The bill of sale is an important legal document that can be used against you in small-claims court if you fail to word it in such a way as to protect yourself. It should state clearly that the car is being sold "as is," with no guarantees. A bill of sale should also state that the seller is the sole legal owner of the car, that the vehicle meets all applicable federal and state safety requirements, and that the emission control equipment is fully operational. It should also state the odometer reading, that the buyer has had the opportunity to drive the car and have it inspected by a mechanic of his choice, and that the seller makes no further claims, either verbally or in writing, as to the condition of the car.

MAINTAINING YOUR CAR

To keep your car in top shape, be sure you understand the basic warranties required by law from the auto manufacturer.

Understanding Your Warranty

Carmakers have a legal responsibility to ensure that the autos they sell have no defects. The so-called warranty is a package of guarantees that spell out their responsibility and define your rights.

The "basic warranty" promises that the manufacturer will make any repair necessary because of defects in materials or manufacture, without charge, for a specified period, which can range from one year or 12,000 miles (whichever comes first) to six years or 60,000 miles.

In addition to the basic warranty, new cars are protected by the "power-train warranty," which covers important parts of the engine, including the transmission, the drive train, and other specified systems. The power-train warranty may last beyond the basic warranty. A separate rust or corrosion warranty is usually included in any sale. Various parts of the emission control system must be warranted by federal law. Most manufacturers include an emission control system warranty on new cars for five years or 50,000 miles.

Parts that are routinely replaced because of normal wear—such as filters, brake pads, fuses, and lubricants like oil and coolant, are not covered, nor are costs for routine maintenance. Tires and batteries come with their own warranties.

To be sure that the manufacturer-provided warranties remain in effect, the driver must follow the maintenance schedule in the instruction manual. The warranties will not cover problems caused by misuse, neglect, or damage from an accident.

FULL AND LIMITED WARRANTIES

The best warranty is a full warranty, which must meet federal standards. It provides free repair within the stated period and permits the owner to elect a refund or replacement if the car contains a defect that cannot be repaired after a reasonable number of attempts. However, most cars come with limited warranties. In either case, you must be clear from the start as to what is covered and for what length of time.

In addition to the manufacturer's warranties, two warranties are guaranteed by law on every dealer-sold car: a "warranty of merchantability," which promises that the car will perform

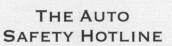

properly, and a "warranty of fitness," which assures that the car can be used for the specific purpose for which it was designed. (See also YOUR CONSUMER RIGHTS, page 404.)

Finally, any claims made to you by a salesperson are "express warranties." If you are misled, you may have a legal case against the seller; make sure you have express claims put into writing so that you have proof of any promises.

THE SERVICE CONTRACT

A service contract, which is offered by the dealer rather than the manufacturer, is sometimes referred to as an "extended warranty." Like the basic warranty, the service contract creates a promise to perform certain repairs or services, but it comes with a price—sometimes a high price. It usually includes a deductible—a specified sum that the car owner must pay toward repairs before free service begins.

Before you agree to a service contract, compare it carefully with the manufacturer's free warranty to make sure that you are not paying for duplicate coverage. Many service contracts will not offer any more protection than the original warranty does. Also note carefully anything that is not included. If the contract specifies only "mechanical breakdowns," you will not be reimbursed for problems caused by normal wear and tear, such as the replacement of brakes.

You should also know whether repairs will be done by the dealer or if you will be sent to other service centers. Find out whether you will be covered if your car breaks down out of town. Are towing charges included? Will parts be replaced with new or reconditioned parts? If you wish to cancel the service, will you be entitled to a full or partial refund?

Cars That Defy Repair

All car owners dread the thought of buying a "lemon," a new car that continually breaks down. If you discover that you bought a lemon and have submitted the car for repair a reasonable number of times, your first recourse is to ask for a refund or replacement from the dealer or manufacturer. If necessary, go straight to the head of the company. If neither dealer nor manufacturer is responsive to your request, you should proceed via your state's "lemon law."

LEMON LAW PROTECTION

Almost all states have enacted "lemon laws" to protect owners of defective automobiles. Laws vary, but the most common definition of a "lemon" is a car that has been back to the shop four times or more for the same problem or that has been out

Jack Brown
1552 Wagar Avenue
Spokane, Washington 19302

August 5, 1995

Mr. Robert J. Thomas, President ❶
Belchfire Motor Company
Detroit, Michigan 11638

Dear Mr. Thomas:

On January 10, I purchased a Belchfire Nebula, serial number JK745839278, from Fairview Auto, an authorized Belchfire dealership at 7 Oak Boulevard in Spokane. I have put 6,200 miles on the car, have fulfilled all the requirements in the warranty, and have enclosed copies of receipts documenting these visits. ❷

I have had repeated problems with the transmission, which locks and prevents the car from being driven. The car has been in the dealer's repair shop four times in the last six months; January 15, February 28, April 15, and July 15. Each time I was told the problem was corrected, and each time it recurred. I have been without the use of my car for over four weeks in the last seven months—a major inconvenience and expense. ❸

I feel this car can never be properly repaired and request that I be given a new car. ❹ I count on you as president to demonstrate the reliability of the Belchfire Motor Company.

If you do not respond favorably to this request, I will have no choice but to invoke my state's "lemon law" and take whatever legal action is necessary. I hope that the company will act responsibly, making further action unnecessary. I look forward to hearing from you within the next 10 business days. ❺

Sincerely,

Squeezing a Lemon

If your attempts to resolve car problems with the dealership are unsuccessful, you may choose to approach the manufacturer with a letter that carefully documents your claim. **1.** Address your letter to the company's top official. **2.** Give the vital statistics concerning the auto, including date of purchase, style of car, serial number, place of purchase, current condition indicated by the number of miles driven, and the fact that you have fulfilled all maintenance requirements in the warranty. **3.** Spell out the problem in detail. State the number of times you have had the car repaired and any contingent problems. **4.** State clearly how you want the problem resolved. **5.** State how and when you will proceed if the problem is not resolved. **6.** Be sure to enclose copies of all bills and invoices, and send the material by certified mail, return receipt requested.

of service for 30 days or more in the first year or first 12,000 miles of ownership. Consult your state attorney general for local lemon law guidelines. In cases where injuries have resulted from a defective car, you should consult an attorney.

When no injuries are involved, consumers can turn to arbitration in order to settle disputes. Owner's manuals usually identify impartial arbitration programs that can be used. For example, Ford and Chrysler have their own arbitration boards, which use outside experts to help decide disputes. General Motors, Honda, and Nissan are among some 15 auto-makers that utilize the Better Business Bureau AUTOLINE. BMW, Mitsubishi, and Saab are among those that recognize the decisions of the Automotive Consumer Action Program (AUTO-CAP), which operates in conjunction with the National Automobile Dealers Association. AUTOCAP operates arbitration programs in more than 25 states, including New York, Florida, and Michigan. State-run arbitration programs, which now operate in 24 states, are also effective. (For addresses and telephone numbers, see RESOURCES, page 493.)

Some arbitration boards require personal appearances, while others take evidence in writing. Either way, to present your case successfully you must have written documentation of your attempts to have the car repaired, and the failure or inability of the dealer or manufacturer to remedy the defects. Keep a careful file with all records, copies of all correspondence with the repair shop, the dealer, and the manufacturer, and a log of all related phone calls.

In most cases, arbitration decisions are binding on the manufacturer, but buyers may pursue further legal action if they feel they have not received fair treatment. Civil suits allow the purchaser to sue the manufacturer or dealer or both for either a replacement vehicle or restitution, and to ask for payment of any attorney's fees and other costs incurred.

Car Repair Without Headaches

While most auto mechanics are trustworthy, some dishonest repairmen will diagnose work far beyond what is actually needed to correct a particular problem. Wise drivers look for a reliable mechanic *before* they need one. Word of mouth from satisfied friends and relatives is usually the best method of finding an honest, reliable, and competent mechanic.

When you visit the shop, look for a current operating license and recent certifications, such as authorization from an approved American Automobile Association (AAA) repair facility or a seal from the National Institute for Automotive

---

HOW AUTO CLUBS HELP MOTORISTS

Auto clubs are worthwhile investments for many motorists. The American Automobile Association is the largest; others include the American Association of Retired Persons Motoring Plan, Amoco Motor Club, Allstate Motor Club, and Mobil Auto Club. Exact offerings vary, but for a yearly membership fee members are usually entitled to the following:

1. Rescue on the road. If you have trouble, clubs will provide necessary help without charge, even for towing.

2. Bed and board. If a trip is interrupted because an auto is disabled, you may receive a refund for meals and lodging.

3. Legal aid. In case of arrest for a traffic violation, members are guaranteed bail in most states, and will be reimbursed for up to $1,500 in legal fees.

4. Travel aids. Maps, guides, discounts on car rentals and hotel rates are benefits.

5. Check cashing. Members can cash personal checks at participating service stations or at local club offices.

6. Personal insurance. Members may receive accidental death and dismemberment coverage in case of travel-related accidents.

7. Convenience. Some clubs provide license plates, registration, and other vehicle documentation services.

Service Excellence (ASE), an organization that certifies professional technicians. Be sure the shop has the modern diagnostic equipment necessary to identify problems in computer-controlled late-model cars.

GETTING THE MOST FROM A MECHANIC

Most disputes over car repairs arise because of poor communication between the repairman and the customer. Prevent misunderstandings or rip-offs by following these guidelines:

- **Put your problems in writing.** Don't expect your mechanic to recall your directives. Write a note listing the problems.
- **Be specific.** Describe where the sound comes from, for example, when it appears, and under what conditions.
- **Get a written estimate.** The estimate should specify work to be done, charges for parts and labor, whether replacement parts will be new or used, and that no work will begin without your approval.
- **Sign only a detailed work order.** The work order should describe the problem and the repairs exactly as they are stated on the estimate. Never sign an open-ended order, or you could be charged for work you did not authorize.
- **Ask for an itemized bill.** Check it against the work order to ensure you have been charged only for work you authorized.
- **Get a written guarantee.** A reputable shop will stand behind its work with a guarantee of 30 to 90 days.
- **Keep records.** Your estimate, work order, and guarantee are contracts. Make sure they are dated, signed, and identify your vehicle and its mileage.
- **Take the car for a test-drive.** Test-drive your car the moment you pick it up. If the problem remains, report it immediately.

IF YOU MUST COMPLAIN

If you are not happy with the work, complain in person to the shop owner or service manager. If the problem is not resolved, write a letter to the service manager explaining why you are displeased and stating what action you will take, such as reporting the shop to the local or state department of consumer affairs. If the problem concerns a new car under warranty, write the general manager or owner of the dealership and include a copy of your first letter. If you still fail to get satisfaction, you may sue the repair shop in small claims court.

You will probably have to pay for your repair in order to take your car out of the shop, since the law usually gives the mechanic a lien on the car until the bill has been paid in full. However, if you paid the garage with a credit card, you may be able to withhold payment to the credit company until the situation is completely rectified.

Beware of Auto Repair Scams

Most mechanics are honest, but occasionally you may run into an unscrupulous person bent on taking advantage of your lack of knowledge of auto repairs. Here are some classic scams:

✔ *New problems.* Your car is in the shop for a new muffler, and the garage calls to say that the oil pump is broken, too. "Discovering" new problems is a common ploy used to con customers into spending more.

✔ *Instant leaks.* Using a concealed can to squirt oil or gasoline on parts, a mechanic may convince you that he has found a leak. Ask to have the part wiped clean so you can see whether the leak reappears as you drive the car.

✔ *Phony parts.* Sneaky shops may charge for a new part, but install a reconditioned used one. Be sure the work order specifies new parts and ask for the box in which they came.

✔ *Illegible work orders.* If you cannot read the work order, you won't know if you are being overcharged. Ask to have your order rewritten clearly.

✔ *Upping the ante.* The mechanic says he will try to save you money with a cheap repair, but if it does not work, a more costly one will be needed. The car goes into the shop, the small repair is never made, and when the problem recurs, you are stuck with the expensive alternative.

INSURING YOUR CAR

Insurance is a necessity for car owners. Learning how to compare companies and choose wisely cuts the cost of owning a car.

How Much Insurance Do You Need?

An auto insurance policy can consist of several types of coverage, including liability, collision, and medical. Each option is priced separately. As a car owner, your goal is to define and obtain the protection you need, and eliminate unnecessary options.

Check your state's insurance laws to see what is required before buying a policy. Liability insurance, which protects other drivers from damage you cause, is required in most states. Each state sets its own minimums. A typical policy provides $25,000 per injury per person, $50,000 per accident, and $10,000 for property damage, commonly expressed as a 25/50/10 policy.

If you are sued for amounts above your policy limit, you will be responsible for the additional amount. Because costs can run high in a serious accident, those who can afford to upgrade their coverage should do so. The protection generally recommended is 100/300/50. An umbrella policy covers liability costs in excess of car and homeowners insurance policies. The extra premium is worthwhile only if you have substantial assets to protect, such as a house.

ADDITIONAL COVERAGE

Collision/comprehensive insurance, usually bought as a package, not only covers the repair of your car after an accident regardless of who is at fault, but also protects you if you drive another person's car, or if someone else drives your car. The comprehensive portion covers theft or damage from causes other than an accident, including fire, flood, and vandalism. If you must rent a car as a result of a theft or accident, the policy may also pay part of the cost. These policies have deductibles that the policyholder must absorb before the insurance company pays. Although collision/comprehensive insurance is optional by law, lenders may insist that it be carried until a car loan is paid off.

Uninsured and underinsured motorist coverage, medical payments insurance, and personal-injury protection are designed to pay for costs of personal injury to you or passen-

Insurance Buyers Guide

Here is a checklist of various auto insurance options:

✔ *Liability.* Covers damage or injury you cause to others and pays for your legal defense.

✔ *Umbrella.* Pays costs beyond the limits of both auto and homeowners policies. Most insurers require you to have both policies with the same company and to buy a minimum amount of coverage.

✔ *Collision.* Covers damage to your car or another car if you are in an accident.

✔ *Comprehensive.* Protects against auto theft or damage not resulting from a collision.

✔ *Uninsured motorist.* Pays costs in case of a collision with a driver who is not insured.

✔ *Personal injury.* Usually optional, but required in some states with no-fault laws; pays for medical costs and income lost if you are unable to work due to an accident. It is more extensive than medical payments insurance.

✔ *Medical payments.* Available in states without no-fault laws; pays for injuries to you or your passengers in an accident, no matter who is at fault.

No-Fault Auto Insurance

Under the traditional insurance system, victims in an auto accident must make a claim to the party who is at fault for medical expenses and for pain and suffering. Often a lawsuit is necessary to gain this compensation. The greatest cost of automobile insurance is the liability portion, which pays the victims and protects the insured party in case of a lawsuit.

No-fault insurance was created specifically to cut down on costly and lengthy lawsuits. It is designed so that drivers are paid up to a certain limit by their *own* insurance companies for damages caused by an accident, no matter who was at fault. Lawsuits are allowed only in extreme cases involving recklessness or severe injury or death, or when the money damages exceed the pre-determined no-fault limit.

More than a dozen states now have some type of no-fault law. In places where the laws are strictly enforced, insurance premiums have gone down substantially.

Some states now give motorists a choice of conventional insurance—in which lawsuits are one option for settling disputes—or no-fault coverage—in which the policyholder gives up the right to sue the other driver in most cases. If you are given this option, and you select no-fault insurance, you may be able to save as much as 25 percent on your auto insurance coverage.

gers in your car. They may or may not be necessary, depending on the coverage you and your passengers may already have through other insurance policies. Before you sign up, read your health-insurance and other insurance policies carefully.

Shopping for the Best Deal

Auto insurance companies base their rates on many factors: a driver's age and driving record, the ages of others who will drive the car, the make of the car, where the driver lives, and how many miles the car is driven regularly. Cars that are less attractive to thieves and cost less to repair will cost less to insure.

In about half the states, rates are determined by "prior approval" by the state insurance commission; little difference in costs exists from one company to another. The grace period for late premium payments before the policy is canceled is also regulated by each state.

Twenty states have an "open competition" system; if you live in one of these states, shopping around for insurance can potentially save hundreds of dollars. Compare rates by checking with two or more agents who represent one insurer; independent agents who represent several companies; and "direct writers," or companies that deal directly with the consumer.

Some state insurance commissions make shopping easier by publishing comparison rate surveys and consumer complaint ratios for companies in the state. Find out whether the state insurance department or local Better Business Bureau has had complaints about an agent or company with which you are considering doing business.

In addition to reasonable rates, be sure to consider reliability, financial stability, and speed in processing claims. To make sure that a company is financially sound, check at least two of the references that evaluate insurance companies for financial stability: A.M. Best Company, Moody's Investor Service, Standard & Poor's Corporation, Weiss Ratings Inc., and Duff & Phelps Credit Rating Company. (For the addresses and telephone numbers for these firms, see RESOURCES, page 493.)

After you determine financial stability, get quotes from three insurers on the same amount of coverage—such as collision/comprehensive rates for a range of deductibles from $50 to $1,000. Make up a chart comparing rates. You will quickly see the best deals.

Here are other ways you can save on auto insurance :

■ **Raise your deductible.** The biggest way to cut your insurance bill is to assume some risk yourself.

- **Buy multiple policies with the same company.** If you use the same insurer for both homeowner's and auto insurance or for insurance for two or more cars, you may be entitled to volume discounts.
- **Limit coverage on older cars.** Consider dropping collision/comprehensive insurance after five years, since the book value that insurance companies will pay if the car is damaged may be less than the cost of insurance.
- **Pay up front.** You will save interest charges if you pay for the policy all at once rather than in installments.
- **Limit teen insurance.** Indicate which car teenagers will drive (and do not allow them to drive another) so that the higher rate for teenage drivers applies only to one car.
- **Take advantage of discounts.** Take advantage of any carrier discounts (see below) for which you qualify.
- **Drive carefully.** Rates go up if you are in an accident or get a ticket for a serious violation, such as speeding.

If you are underinsured or don't have insurance at all, you could be courting disaster if you suffer a loss and have no financial net to catch you.

RALPH NADER
The Frugal Shopper

How to File a Claim

Notify your insurance company immediately after an accident so that an investigation can be made while events are still fresh in everyone's mind. In states with no-fault insurance, each driver is paid by his own insurance company for accident damages, regardless of who was at fault. In other states, when the other driver is at

Discounts on Auto Insurance

Automobile insurance companies have determined factors that lower accident rates, and offer discounts to drivers who take advantage of these findings. Discounts vary from company to company, so comparison shopping pays. Here are ways to cash in on discounts:

• **Install safety devices.** Factory-installed antilock brakes, antitheft devices, automatic seat belts, and passive restraints such as air bags may reduce your premium payments.

• **Take a defensive driving course.** Many states require these courses for learners, teens, and drivers over 55, and some insurance companies give discounts to anyone who takes them.

• **Enroll your teenager in a driver training course.** You may be eligible for a discount if a teenager on your policy takes a driver training course either privately or in school. Students with a "B" or better average may also rate discounts. Notify your insurance company when a child

moves out of your home or goes away to college. Your rates could go down considerably.

• **Join a car pool.** Rates may be cut for those who cut their driving miles. Low-mileage discounts are available for any driver who logs less than the average number of miles per year.

• **Check your claims status.** Insurance companies rate clients according to their claims records. If you fall into a group that has favorable claims records, you may qualify for discounts. Among these categories are drivers over age 50, females who are the sole drivers of their cars, and drivers who have not had a moving violation or an accident in the past two to five years.

Do Rental Cars Need Extra Insurance?

Collision-damage waiver insurance and loss-damage waiver insurance offered by rental car companies are the most expensive kinds of auto insurance you can buy. Moreover, they are protections that most drivers do not need. If you are renting a car within the United States, your own auto insurance policy will most likely protect you when you are driving another car, including one you have rented.

However, be sure to confirm your policy's regulations. Some companies limit the number of rental days they will cover (although you can get around this stipulation by returning one car and renting another) or will not insure car rentals for business purposes.

If you rent frequently for business and your employer does not pick up the cost, you may find it cheaper to extend your personal car insurance to cover business rentals than to pay out high rental premiums.

Another way to be covered, especially if you do not have auto insurance, is to use a credit card that includes collision or theft coverage for rentals charged with the card. Most premium "gold cards," such as those offered by American Express and Diners Club, include this feature.

Bear in mind that credit card insurance is secondary coverage, meaning it pays only what your own insurance policy does not cover. Credit card terms for rental insurance may also be limited.

---

fault, your insurer has the right to sue the other driver's insurance company for compensation. If the company collects, you may receive a refund on your deductible.

Send your insurance company a written account of the accident, and keep a copy. This file will be valuable if you later find yourself in a dispute with the other driver or with your insurance company. Record all expenses you incur as a result of the accident, such as towing, in case they are reimbursable.

If your car has been damaged, the insurer will send an appraiser to inspect it soon after the accident. Appraisers assess the cost of repairing damages and report their findings to an adjuster at the company. The adjuster authorizes a check. It can help to be present when the appraiser arrives. By pointing out features that might be overlooked, you may be able to increase the amount of the settlement.

If the car has been taken to a repair shop, the appraiser usually negotiates directly with the shop. Don't authorize any repairs until the appraiser has done his inspection. Only he can decide what repairs the company will pay for. If the mechanic finds other problems later, he will contact the insurer directly to arrange additional payment.

If you cannot find a shop willing to repair your car for the price the insurance company agreed to pay, notify the company and ask for a higher settlement. Do not accept an inadequate amount or sign away your right to additional claims by cashing a check that says "in full settlement." Get an independent estimate from a reputable repair shop and submit it to the adjuster. If you do not get satisfaction, go to the claims supervisor. If you still cannot reach agreement, the settlement you are offered is unsatisfactory, or your claim is denied, contact the state insurance commission or consult an attorney.

You can seek recourse in the arbitration procedures provided for in some auto insurance policies. To cut down on expensive, lengthy lawsuits, many states have instituted arbitration procedures for cases in which one driver's insurance company files a liability claim against another driver's insurance company. In some states arbitration is mandatory, although the right to a jury trial usually remains if either party is dissatisfied with the decision of the arbitrators.

FAILURE TO REPORT AN ACCIDENT

Many drivers hesitate to report minor "fender benders" for fear of an increase in their insurance premiums. You may well be tempted to settle small accidents directly with the other driver, paying for minor repairs yourself or accepting payment from the driver. However, if the other driver later files a claim against you, your insurer can drop you or refuse to cover you because you failed to report the accident initially.

AUTOMOBILE ACCIDENTS

Accidents can lead to potentially costly lawsuits. Doing the right things after the accident will protect you whether you are suing or being sued.

The Meaning of Negligence

Some automobile accidents are nobody's fault, but most prove to be somebody's fault, and in court that fault is known as "negligence." Legally, negligent driving refers to an individual's omission of any reasonable precaution, concern, or action while driving an automobile. Failing to signal a turn or stop at a red light are examples of negligent driving. When a driver is reckless or drunk and is clearly at fault in an accident, he may even be charged with "gross negligence."

Often both drivers are partially at fault. Suppose you failed to come to a full halt at a stop sign, and a speeding car rushed into the intersection and hit your car. In many states the compensation you or the other driver would receive depends on the degree of fault, or "comparative negligence." There are no set rules to determine degrees of fault; it is up to the jury to decide where the blame lies. In a few states, only the driver considered less at fault can collect damages.

Sometimes the negligence that causes an accident is not the fault of either driver. Road hazards such as potholes, misplaced barriers, or nonfunctioning lights can be to blame, and the city or state highway department may be the guilty party to be sued. If a car malfunctions and causes damage or injury because of faulty parts or improper repairs, the owner and anyone injured may have a legitimate lawsuit against the manufacturer or the repair shop.

PROTECTING YOURSELF LEGALLY

Because the possibility of legal action exists anytime an injured party is not satisfied with the settlement offered by the other driver's insurance company, it is smart to protect yourself from the start by knowing your state's laws and properly responding immediately after an accident.

State regulations require that the police be notified of an accident if anyone is injured or if damage exceeds a specified amount. If you hit a parked car and the owner is not around, you must leave a note with your name and telephone number; some states also require you to notify the police. If the accident involves personal injury, death, or substantial damage, some states require reporting it to the department of motor vehicles within 10 days, or your license may be suspended.

If you are contacted by the attorney of someone you have injured, refer the party to your insurance company. If you give statements directly, you could jeopardize your liability coverage. Your insurer will assign a lawyer to your case, but if the other party is asking for sums higher than your policy coverage, you will probably need your own attorney as well.

If you are hurt in an accident, don't rush to settle claims. Many injuries don't develop fully for months. Some claims must be filed within 100 days, but the statute of limitations in most states is one or two years from the date of the accident.

Keep a careful diary of all doctor visits, hospital stays, and medicines prescribed and retain copies of all your doctor, hospital, and drug bills. Keep track of any work hours lost because of incapacity, days laid up at home, doctor visits, or outpatient treatment. Sometimes several years can pass before a case comes up for trial; your diary will help you remember accurately and your receipts will serve as proof of your expenses.

If You Are in an Accident

Even the most minor "fender benders" can lead to costly lawsuits if you do not handle the situation properly. To protect yourself from a lawsuit following even a minor accident, carefully follow these procedures:

• **Stop.** Failure to stop at the scene of an accident where injuries or property damage occurs can be considered a "hit and run" crime. Always wait until the extent of the damage has been determined.

• **Call the police.** Report the accident as soon as possible. If the accident is serious, wait at the scene until the police arrive, and do not move the car. Get the names and badge numbers of the police officers who come to the scene and the address of the police station where the report will be filed.

• **Seek necessary medical attention.** If anyone is injured, don't try to move him. Cover him with a blanket or coat to help prevent chills or shock; then call an ambulance or emergency care. If you have been injured, even only slightly, see a doctor promptly and get the diagnosis in writing.

• **Get information from the other driver.** Exchange names, addresses, telephone numbers, license plate numbers, driver's license numbers, year and make of car, and names of insurance agents and companies. Don't discuss coverage; let the insurance agents negotiate those details.

• **Do not discuss fault.** You may be upset, injured, and not completely clear about what happened. Anything you say may fog the issues and can be used against you later.

• **Secure witnesses.** Get the names, addresses, and telephone numbers of any witnesses. Ask them to stay until the police arrive. If they refuse, ask them to describe what they saw, write it down, and ask them to sign the statement.

• **Take notes.** Make notes about the road and weather conditions. If possible, take photographs of both cars at the scene of the accident or make a sketch.

• **Notify your insurance agent immediately.** Call your insurance company as soon as possible. You may be violating the terms of your policy if you avoid filing a claim for fear of higher premiums.

• **Get a copy of the police report.** Read it carefully. If you find errors, send a certified letter, return receipt requested, to the police, correcting the information. Ask that your letter be attached to the report.

MOTOR VEHICLE LAWS

Drivers must abide by the rules of the road of their state and town. These regulations protect the rights of other drivers—and your own.

Your License and Registration

Every state has regulations designed to ensure safety for motorists. These laws are devised to assure the public that drivers are competent and vehicles are protected. Speed limits guard against reckless drivers, and parking limitations are intended to ease traffic congestion and open up parking spaces at regular intervals.

DRIVER'S LICENSE REGULATIONS

Before you can drive legally, you must demonstrate your ability and your knowledge of the rules of the road. To apply for a license, you must be a state resident and above the minimum age, which ranges nationally from 15 to 18. Some states issue a junior license or learner's permit to minors younger than the legal age. This license permits them to drive under limited conditions, such as commuting to and from school or with a licensed driver in the car. A safe-driving course—such as the driver education classes offered in many high schools—is required for drivers under 18 in some states.

In addition to a road test, new drivers must pass a written test with questions on local and state laws and regulations. Prospective drivers also must pass a vision test. If you need glasses to see properly, that fact will be noted on your license, and you will be legally obligated to wear them while driving.

Licenses must be renewed periodically. Some states will allow you to complete this transaction by mail, but states with photo identification on the license require you to appear in person to have a new photograph taken. A vision test may be required for a license renewal as well.

If you move to a new state, you usually must apply for a new license within 30 days. Many states automatically accept license transfers from other states without a test, while others require you to take a vision test and a written exam.

AUTO REGISTRATION

Every vehicle must be registered, a process that ensures that owners are identified and certain requirements are met before a car can be driven on public roads. To register, you must show a title to prove that you own the vehicle, present a receipt show-

---

A DRIVER'S DOCUMENTS

To drive legally, you must possess certain documentation. You will be asked to produce these documents if you are involved in an accident, so it is important to keep them safe and current. Here are a few tips regarding documents:

1. You must have a current driver's license, a valid registration, license plates or tags, and in some states, an authorized safety inspection sticker.

2. In most states you must certify that you have the minimum liability insurance required by law. Driving without insurance may result in revocation of your driver's license.

3. Failure to produce legally required documentation could result in a ticket and fine; you may be allowed 24 hours to produce the documents or may be able to appeal the ticket in court.

4. Do not keep your registration in the car or your license in your wallet. Keep your license and registration in a small separate case in a secure jacket pocket or in your purse.

5. Keep your license renewal stub and car title in a safe place at home—not in the car.

What To Do If Your Car Is Towed

You've been on a shopping trip that lasted longer than you expected. You hurry back to the car, concerned that the meter has run out, but the car has disappeared. Perhaps it has been stolen—or towed.

Your car can be towed if you park overtime, park in an illegal space, or if you have ignored parking tickets. State computer systems identify license plate numbers of scofflaws who owe money for past tickets.

When your car is missing, call the police or local parking violations bureau to find out if it has been towed. If so, ask for the location of the pound and the cost of retrieving it. Inquire whether you have outstanding fines since you cannot get your car back until you pay up.

You will have to go to the garage in person and pay a fine, as much as $150, in order to reclaim your car. Be prepared to pay with cash, a certified check, or a money order. You must show your driver's license, registration, and proof of insurance. Act promptly to reclaim your car, or you may be charged a storage fee. After a specified period, anywhere from 20 to 40 days, unclaimed cars are sold at auction.

If your car was damaged in the process of towing, the tow truck company is responsible, but you must file a claim, and it may be hard to prove that the company is at fault. In some cities, cars being seized are videotaped. If the tape shows that damage occurred in towing, the car will be repaired.

ing that sales taxes on the car's purchase have been paid, and in most states, provide written proof that the car is insured. If you buy a car from an individual, you usually pay the sales tax at a motor vehicle bureau when you register the car.

After submitting the necessary documents and paying a registration fee, you are issued license plates and a temporary registration. The permanent registration follows by mail. If you are transferring registration from one car to another, you usually will receive credit for the unused portion of the current registration, and you can move the same license plates to your new car. When you buy from a dealer who is registered with the state's department of motor vehicles, the dealership is authorized to register the car for you and give you a temporary registration and new license plates, if needed.

Most registrations must be renewed every two years. Generally, a reminder arrives in the mail about 30 days before the expiration date, and you pay the new fee and registration by mail. When your registration is renewed, you will receive a tag on your license or a sticker for the windshield showing that the registration is up to date. If you let it lapse, you are likely to be stopped by the police and fined.

MOTOR VEHICLE INSPECTION

To ensure that automobiles on the road are safe to drive, many states require cars to be inspected at an official state-licensed inspection station every 12 to 24 months and whenever ownership changes. Owners must then post a sticker on the windshield showing that the car has passed inspection. Among the features checked in an inspection are brakes, lights, wipers, horn, mirrors, seat belts, steering, and tires. The car may also be checked to see if it meets emission control standards.

Cars bought from a dealer come with a valid inspection sticker. If you do not buy from a dealer, you will receive an inspection extension sticker, usually good for 10 days, when you register the car. You must have the vehicle inspected within that period. If the vehicle fails to pass the test, you must make any needed repairs and have a second inspection. Driving a car without a valid sticker can result in a fine.

Parking Regulations

The most common driving violation is illegal parking, either by using a prohibited space or by staying beyond the time allowed by a meter or sign. You may return a parking ticket by mail with payment of the specified fine, which is equivalent to pleading guilty to the violation, or you may plead not guilty and take the case before a judge or referee. Many areas have a separate court to handle parking tickets, since they are not as serious as other violations.

Though pleading your case is time-consuming, in certain instances you are right to defend yourself. Some valid reasons to contest a ticket are:

- **A defective ticket.** "Defective" means that some required information is missing, such as the nature of the offense, or the description of the car and license.
- **A broken meter.** Usually the back of the summons tells where claims of a defective meter should be sent. An inspection is made to verify that the meter is broken.
- **A disabled car.** If your car could not be moved, you may have a legal defense—but only if you have written proof.

Driving Regulations

More serious than parking tickets are violations incurred while you are behind the wheel, known as "moving violations." These violations may cover a wide range of infractions including speeding, reckless driving, tailgating, failing to obey a stop sign, and driving the wrong way on a one-way street.

If you are stopped by a police officer for one of these violations, you will be given a ticket indicating a fine. As with a parking ticket, in many states you can plead guilty and send in a fine, or choose to take your case to court. The state may require a court appearance if you plead guilty to charges that can result in a license or registration suspension or revocation.

Since single offenses where no injury results usually involve minor fines and no jail time, most states have a separate traffic court to handle them. Generally you do not need an attorney to plead your case, but you will need evidence to support a not-guilty plea, and you may present witnesses to back up your statements. A state prosecutor has the right to cross-examine your witnesses, and, in turn, you may examine any witnesses testifying against you.

You can also plead guilty but with mitigating circumstances, meaning that you are asking the judge to consider the reason for your infraction. If you swerved out of your lane to avoid hitting a deer on the highway, for example, the judge might reduce or even waive your fine.

If you are found guilty, you will be asked to pay court costs in addition to the fine. The judge also has the power to suspend your license. If you do not agree with the decision or penalty given by the judge, you have the right to file an appeal.

A single violation normally will not bring suspension, but

Fight That Traffic Ticket

A traffic ticket on your record can send insurance premiums soaring and can blemish your record for three or more years. So, you should fight tickets whenever you believe you are not guilty. Here's what to do:

✔ *Read your ticket carefully.* Is the information correct? If the policeman made mistakes, the ticket may be invalid.

✔ *Know the law.* Unless the offense is serious, you can defend yourself without a lawyer. Make sure to learn the details of the law you are accused of violating. Ask your local librarian for help with this research.

✔ *Ask for a hearing.* Insist on a formal hearing with the arresting officer present. If he does not show up, your case may be dismissed.

✔ *Question the officer.* If he claims you were speeding, ask what time of day it was, and what weather and road conditions were like. Did he calibrate the radar equipment before checking your speed?

✔ *Bring witnesses.* If you have witnesses to back up your story, bring them to court.

✔ *Appeal the verdict.* If you think the verdict is unfair, you can appeal, although you may want to hire an attorney.

✔ *Call a lawyer.* In serious cases, such as when an accident has occurred or when your license or liberty are at stake, consult a lawyer.

chalking up a number of violations in a short amount of time will. To guard against frequent offenders, most states have a point system for driving violations. Points are charged against a driver's record based on the seriousness of the infraction. A driver going less than 10 miles per hour above the posted speed limit might be given three points; driving 20 to 30 miles per hour over the limit could net six points. High-point infractions other than speeding usually include reckless driving and failure to stop for a school bus.

By law, the information regarding the status of your license is available to your insurance company, and if points mount up, your insurance rates may go up accordingly. If you accumulate too many points within a specified period, such as 18

Sobriety Tests

Two levels of penalties for drunken driving exist in many states. If your driving ability is "impaired by alcohol," your license may be suspended. If you are found "legally intoxicated," your license may be revoked.

Most states follow the guidelines set by the U.S Congress in 1982 determining legal intoxication. Under these rules, if a chemical test shows that your blood has a 10 percent or higher alcohol content, you are judged to be legally intoxicated, and your license can be suspended or revoked.

The most common test for determining intoxication utilizes the Breathalyzer. The driver blows into a tube attached to a machine, which mixes the breath sample with a chemical, resulting in a detailed blood-alcohol reading.

If you are stopped on suspicion of drunken driving, your best response would be to comply with all the police officer's requests. State laws vary about your right to speak to a lawyer before you take a Breathalyzer test.However, most states require you to take a blood or Breathalyzer test if asked, based on the principle of "implied consent," which means that by securing a license to drive on the state's highways, you have agreed to all the state's driving regulations. Refusal to take the test may result in your license being suspended and possibly revoked. In any case, if you are arrested for drunken driving, contact an attorney immediately.

Appearing Reckless

PROBLEM
Ann was driving home late one Saturday night from a party along a busy two-lane highway. The couple in the car in front of Ann were deep in conversation and, as a result, the driver was weaving all over the road. Ann wanted to pass, but she could not see around the other car in order to make sure the oncoming lane was safe. To her chagrin, the police stopped her and accused her of "reckless driving," saying her car, not the car in front of her, was weaving. They also asked her to take a Breathalyzer test, indicating that not only did they think Ann was a reckless driver, they thought she was drunk. Ann was furious—especially since she had deliberately drunk only nonalcoholic beverages at the party because she knew she would be driving herself home.

ACTION
Ann was stopped on suspicion of drunken driving, a potentially serious moving violation. She complied calmly and took a Breathalyzer test, since she knew that in most states the fact that one has a license implied consent to all motor vehicle laws. Of course, the test indicated that Ann had not been drinking. She then explained why it appeared that she was weaving. If she had nevertheless been arrested for reckless driving, she should have taken detailed notes and appealed her ticket in court.

months, you may face a hearing and your license may be suspended or revoked. Conversely, you can clear your record with safer driving. Usually a three-year period with no convictions and no accidents will remove points from your record and may make you eligible for lower rates.

DRINKING, DRUGS, AND DRIVING
The most harmful motor vehicle violations involve driving under the influence of alcohol or drugs. Both substances impair judgment, vision, and reflexes, making it almost impossible to drive safely. Because "driving under the influence" is so potentially dangerous, it is treated in many states as a misdemeanor,

not a traffic violation, and penalties are severe. If you are convicted, your license may be suspended, you may go to jail or be sentenced to do community service, and you are liable for a steep fine. If you repeat the violation, your license may be revoked. In some states, drivers under age 21 will lose their license for one year for even a first offense.

A police officer who spots erratic driving may ask the driver to take a field test, such as walking a straight line, to determine whether reflexes have been impaired. If a driver fails this test, he may be asked to take a medical test to measure the level of alcohol in his bloodstream. This may be done on the spot, using a Breathalyzer, or at a police station or medical facility, where blood, urine, or breath tests can be administered.

If you are arrested for driving under the influence of drugs or alcohol, you have the right to call a lawyer, relative, or friend as soon as possible to arrange for your release from custody. It is best not to make statements to the police or discuss the incident before you have consulted an attorney. Whatever you say can be held against you in court. In cases of drunk driving, the

If Your Driver's License Is Taken Away

A driver's license is a privilege, not a right, and if you fail to obey the law, your license can be suspended for a specified period, or revoked—meaning it will be canceled for a certain period and you will be required to apply to get it back.

SUSPENSION
• In most states causes for suspension include driving under the influence of alcohol or drugs, speeding, reckless driving, driving without liability insurance, refusing to take a blood-alcohol test, leaving the scene of an accident in which someone was injured or killed, or failure to answer a traffic summons, pay a fine, or file an accident report. In states that have a point system for moving violations, accumulating too many points within a specified period can also lead to suspension.

• When a suspension expires, you are free to drive again, although some states impose a fee to have the suspension terminated. In many states, having an accident while you are not insured or refusing to take a blood-alcohol test carries a fine as well as suspension.

REVOCATION
• In most states, your license can be revoked for criminal negligence resulting in death, two convictions for drunken driving involving personal injury, and other extreme situations. Your license may also be revoked if you give false statements on an application for a license or registration.

• You may apply for a new license when the revocation period ends. In some cases, you must pay a fine as well as a fee to reapply. If you have a poor driving record or refuse to meet state requirements, such as to pass a test or take a driving course, your application may be denied.

TRAFFIC COURT
• In many localities, traffic violations other than parking tickets are heard by a special traffic violations court, presided over by an administrative judge. You are considered innocent of the charge against you until proven guilty at the hearing. If you are found guilty, you will pay a fine and surcharge, and may have your license revoked or suspended. At this point you may want to hire a lawyer and take your case before an appeals judge or a specially appointed traffic appeals board.

VIOLATING SUSPENSION OR REVOCATION
• If you drive while your license is suspended or revoked, you can be fined or jailed, or both. Under certain circumstances some states allow you to apply for conditional driving privileges, which permit you to drive in limited situations, such as to commute to and from work each day.

law in many states prohibits your pleading guilty to a lesser traffic violation (called "plea bargaining") unless there is insufficient evidence to support the original charge. If you feel that you have been wrongly charged, your lawyer can present your side of the case in court.

Laws Governing Other Vehicles

Vehicles that share the road with automobiles have their own regulations. Truck drivers must qualify for a special license certifying that they have passed a road test handling a large vehicle. Commercial vehicles also have special registration requirements. For instance, additional lighting and reflectors may be required. Certain highways also have weight restrictions on trucks.

Recreation vehicles (RV's) also must meet state regulations. They must be registered, and must meet certain specifications for electrical, plumbing, heating, fire and life safety established under the American National Standards Institute Recreation Vehicle Standard. Also, many states impose size and weight limitations on vehicles using public highways, and prohibit driving or parking RV's in certain areas (such as large cities) and at particular times.

MOTORCYCLES AND BICYCLES

Motorcycle riders also must pass written and driving tests. In most states they are required to use extra safeguards. Front lights must be on at all times to improve their machine's visibility to other drivers, and motorcyclists may be required to wear helmets. A motorcyclist generally has the right to the full use of a lane, and two cyclists may ride side by side in one, but they may not share a lane with a car and may not drive between lanes. In most states licenses are also required for mopeds; lighter vehicles that travel at lower speeds.

Bicyclists have the right to share most roads except interstate highways, parkways, and expressways. Most state regulations require bicycle riders to travel in the same direction as auto traffic and obey all traffic signs and signals. Bicyclists are advised to ride in designated lanes. Although they need no special license, cyclists must observe safety regulations. In some states, bicycles must be equipped with adequate brakes, a horn or bell, and a visible headlight and taillight. Recently, many states have enacted laws requiring bicyclists to wear helmets.

123...

FACTS ABOUT RECREATION VEHICLES

Recreation vehicles, or RV's, are one of the most popular ways to enjoy an outdoor vacation. To insure your safety make sure you:

1. Check for certification. Before buying an RV, make sure it has a Recreation Vehicle Industry Association (RVIA) seal, certifying its compliance with the safety specifications established by the American National Standards Institute (ANSI) Recreation Vehicles Standard.

2. Double-check conversions. Before buying a conversion vehicle (a van or truck that can be modified for recreational purposes), check that it complies with Federal Motor Vehicle Safety Standards (FMVSS) and the related requirements of ANSI/RVIA.

3. Learn the RV rules of the road. Some RV's are prohibited from the streets of large cities, certain highways or tunnels, and in certain areas during particular seasons. For details contact the RVIA, P.O. Box 2999, Reston, Va. 22090.

4. Rent before you buy. Before you buy an RV, consider renting to see what sort of vehicle you prefer. Check rental regulations carefully. For details, contact the Recreational Vehicle Rental Association (RVRA), 3930 University Drive, Fairfax, Va. 22040.

YOUR CONSUMER RIGHTS

In today's complex marketplace, getting a fair deal can be a challenge. But help is available for consumers who know their rights.

THE WISE CONSUMER ■ CONSUMER CONTRACTS AND WARRANTIES ■ PROBLEMS WITH PURCHASES ■ ADVERTISING AND MARKETING ■ DECEPTIVE SALES PRACTICES ■ BASIC SHOPPERS' RIGHTS ■ BUYING BIG-TICKET ITEMS ■ BUYING ELECTRONIC EQUIPMENT ■ BUYING CLOTHING ■ BUYING FOR CHILDREN ■ SMART SUPERMARKET SHOPPING ■ SHOPPING FOR HEALTH AND BEAUTY PRODUCTS ■ BARGAIN SHOPPING ■ SHOPPING FROM HOME ■ SERVICE PROVIDERS ■ YOUR RIGHTS AS A TRAVELER

THE WISE CONSUMER

As marketing techniques get slicker, consumers become more vulnerable.
Knowing your rights can give you power in the marketplace.

₁₂₃ THE CONSUMERS' BILL OF RIGHTS

The Consumers' Bill of Rights was established to define five necessary consumer guarantees. Today, these guarantees are the basis for all consumer regulations:

1. The right to choose. Consumers have the right to make an intelligent choice among several products and services.

2. The right to information. Consumers have the right to accurate and complete information about all products in order to make a free choice.

3. The right to safety. Consumers have the right to expect that anyone trying to sell them services or products has taken the consumers' health and safety into consideration.

4. The right to be heard. Consumers have the right to register dissatisfaction and have a complaint heard when their interests are badly served.

5. The right to consumer education. Consumers have the right to specific information regarding consumer affairs in order to maximize their power in the marketplace.

Caveat Emptor

Once upon a time, shopping was a simpler matter. Storekeepers were part of the community and knew their customers personally. If you were not happy with your purchase, you knew exactly where to go with your complaint. Of course, unscrupulous people who try to cheat or get away with selling inferior products have always been around, but the motto *caveat emptor* ("Let the buyer beware") is far more relevant today than it used to be.

As buying opportunities have expanded, so have the challenges for the consumer. Local stores that are part of national chains may not maintain company standards. Plastic-wrapped products deny consumers a close look at what they are buying. Electric and electronic appliances are offered in such profusion that consumers may not understand what they are buying. Con artists can operate invisibly from behind telephones, televisions, computers, mail-order scams, and advertisements.

To protect consumers in such a mine-strewn marketplace, Congress has enacted protective measures. It has placed special emphasis on requiring full disclosure by the seller about the products being offered and the financial terms of the sale. To be informed, consumers must be aware of the protections offered by these measures and who enforces them:

- **Federal Trade Commission Act.** Passed in 1914, this act established the Federal Trade Commission (FTC), which is responsible for enforcing most federal consumer-protection laws and regulates harmful, unfair, or deceptive sales practices in commerce. The FTC protects individual consumers' interests by issuing trade rules and guidelines (with the effect of law) to enable companies to avoid practices that it considers harmful or deceptive. On behalf of consumers, the FTC can prosecute companies or industries that violate federal laws through false advertisements or other unfair or deceptive practices.

- **Consumer Product Safety Act.** This 1972 act protects the consumer against unreasonable risk of injury from the ordinary use of consumer products. The Consumer Product Safety Commission can regulate and enforce standards related to dangerous materials or design. Mattresses, children's sleepwear, fireworks, and spray adhesives are some of the products for which it has specified manufacturing standards.

- **Consumer Credit Protection Act.** Passed in 1968, this act includes the all-important Truth-in-Lending Act, which requires anyone extending credit on a purchase to disclose the terms fully, spelling out the total finance charges in dollars and the annual interest percentage rate. It gives the consumer the right to cancel most installment transactions within a specified period. The FTC can prosecute violations of consumer credit laws. (See also YOUR MONEY, page 297.)

- **Uniform Commercial Code (UCC).** Developed in 1952 and revised in 1958 and 1962, the UCC is a comprehensive set of laws (adopted in each state) designed to assure uniformity of understanding and fair dealing between parties with regard to most commercial transactions. For example, the UCC regulates bills of lading, security agreements, banking deposits, investment securities, and certain contract and warranty rights. Real estate dealings, protected under other state and federal laws, are an exception.

- **Magnuson-Moss Warranty Act.** Passed in 1975 and regulated and enforced by the FTC, this act requires disclosure of warranty information to consumers and outlines procedures that permit consumers to make a claim if a product proves defective or if its warranty is breached. (See also "Understanding Warranties," page 407.)

"Consumer product" means any tangible personal property which is distributed in commerce and which is normally used for personal, family, or household purposes.

MAGNUSON-MOSS
WARRANTY ACT
1975

The OCA: What It Is, What It Does

A strong push for consumer protection began in the 1960's with the formation of the Office of Consumer Affairs (OCA), which was soon followed by the establishment of similar offices at state and local levels. Here are some of the ways the OCA helps consumers:

- The Office of Consumer Affairs is a federal agency headed by a special assistant to the president. Its mandate is to guarantee that consumers' rights are heard, and to make certain that consumers' are considered when government policy is being formulated.

- The OCA Federal Consumer Affairs Council is a high-level committee made up of representatives from all major federal agencies. The council is responsible for assuring that consumers' needs are indeed taken into account in all OCA activities.

- Although the OCA does not deal with individual complaints directly, it provides assistance and advice to state and local consumer agencies, congressional staffs, and businesses on how to resolve consumer-related problems effectively.

- One of the functions of the OCA is to encourage consumers, including individuals, businesses, and industries, to act on their own behalf. To this end, the OCA publishes a directory called "The Consumer's Resource Handbook." This publication contains the names, addresses, and telephone numbers of useful contacts, including consumer affairs personnel at corporations, Better Business Bureaus, trade associations, and federal, state, and local agencies. For a free copy of *The Consumer's Resource Handbook,* write to The Consumer Information Center, P.O. Box 100, Pueblo, Colo., 81002, (719) 948-3334.

CONSUMER CONTRACTS AND WARRANTIES

Two basic agreements protect both buyers and sellers.

Bilateral and Unilateral Contracts

The courts make a distinction between two basic types of contracts—bilateral and unilateral. A bilateral contract is created when both parties to the contract make promises. When the fuel-oil company offers to fill your tank with 100 gallons of oil for $1 per gallon and you agree to pay that sum, each side is making a promise. When the agreement is made, the contract is "executory"—it has not been fully performed. When the oil is delivered and you pay the bill, the contract has been "executed," meaning it has been fulfilled by both sides and the transaction is complete.

A unilateral contract involves a promise by one person only. It is conditional on the performance of another. If your health club offers to give you a $100 rebate on your fee for each new member you bring in, the contract does not become binding until you actually sign up a member. You have not promised to recruit members and have no obligation to do so. But the club is required to pay you if you do fulfill the terms of the contract.

Understanding Purchase Contracts

In the simplest terms, a contract means that one party offers to buy some product or service at a certain price, exchange, or some other "consideration," and the other party accepts it, creating an obligation on both parties that is enforceable in a court of law.

Conventionally, we think of contracts as long legal documents, but any agreement—written or verbal—between a seller and a buyer that involves money or some other form of payment is, legally speaking, a "contract." For example, if you redeem a $5-off-on-any-item coupon in a grocery store, you are performing your part of a contract with the grocer who has made the offer; if you offer to pay the teenager next door $10 to mow your lawn and he agrees, that is also a contract.

Once the contract has been made, it can be altered only if both parties agree to any changes. Unless the coupon has expired, the grocery store must honor it. If your neighbor mows your lawn and then demands $15 for his work, you are not legally obligated to pay him that much if he has agreed to work for $10.

The law does not necessarily require that the exchange between the parties be fair or equal, so, except in certain extreme situations, once the agreement has been made, the buyer has little recourse if he discovers that he has overpaid. If you buy a shirt and then see the same shirt for $5 less in the shop next door, the merchant might decide to meet the competition, but he is not legally obligated to do so. (See also "What If You Got a Raw Deal?" page 409.)

These are small, everyday transactions, but the same principle applies to larger, more complex contracts, such as buying a car or a major appliance, renting an apartment, or signing a contract to have a book published.

ENDING A CONTRACT

If one party does not fulfill the stated terms of a contract, the contract has been broken, or "breached." If a major breach of contract occurs, the other party can demand that the contract be canceled or seek other remedies. For example, if a contract specifies that your new dining room table will be delivered by

Thanksgiving and it does not arrive, you may have the right to cancel the agreement and have your down payment returned.

A contract may be declared "void"—indicating that no valid agreement was ever made—if essential terms are missing. For example, a contract may be void if one of the parties is a minor or is incompetent, meaning that he is incapable of understanding what he is signing. A contract may also be deemed void if terms were misrepresented, or if some aspect of the agreement is fraudulent or involves an illegal practice, such as the selling of illegal drugs.

THE IMPACT OF THE UCC

The Uniform Commercial Code (UCC) plays a major role in the definition and expectations of contracts and purchase agreements. When it applies to buying goods, it supersedes the common law of the state. For example, the UCC states that all contracts for the purchase of goods valued at $500 or more must be in writing to be enforceable, unless they are for specially ordered goods that cannot be sold to anyone else; or if the goods already have been accepted by the purchaser. The UCC makes it possible for contracts that are blatantly unfair, or "unconscionable," to be nullified.

Although the UCC states that each party to a contract must act in good faith and in a reasonable manner, it does not define exactly what the term "reasonable" means. "Reasonable" generally refers to what an ordinary person would expect or do in a given situation. In disputes, it is up to a judge to decide whether the terms of the contract seem fair under the particular circumstances.

Even in transactions less than $500, you are always safer if you put your contractual agreement in writing. This does not have to be a formal legal document. A bill of sale or a letter can serve as a contract as long as it clearly states the obligations of all parties and the payment or other consideration involved. Be sure that all oral understandings about a transaction are included in the written document. They are difficult to prove later in a court of law.

The primary concern of laws governing contracts is to protect the "reasonable expectations" that are created in the marketplace between buyers and sellers. The laws governing contracts come from three sources:

- Statutes, or the regulations and laws enacted by Congress and the state legislatures.
- Common law, or the body of rules and regulations that is established by custom.
- Case law, or the law created by the decisions of federal or state courts that interpret the law.

Key Elements of a Contract

A contract can be anything from an oral agreement to a multi-clause, densely worded document. Whatever its form, a contract to be legal must contain several important elements:

✔ *An offer.* This is a promise to do or supply something specific. For example, the baker offers to sell you a loaf of white bread for 89 cents.

✔ *An acceptance.* The contract is made when the offer is accepted. If you think the price is too high and refuse to buy, then there is no sale—and no contract. But if you tell the baker you will take the bread, you are agreeing to his offer.

✔ *A consideration.* The agreed-upon price for the product or service is called the consideration. The contract is completed when each party actually gives or does something in return for something else: The baker gets your money, and you get the loaf of bread. If you shortchange the baker you have breached the contract.

✔ *Duration.* Sometimes a time limit for fulfilling the contract must be stated. If no specific time is spelled out, the law may imply a reasonable time, such as 30 days, for delivery of a household product.

✔ *Nonperformance.* Often, a contract states what action is to be taken if either party does not perform as stipulated.

BILL OF SALE

Date of sale: January 20, 1995

Acme Bike Shop
710 North Avenue
Berea, Ohio 44116
Telephone: 265-8557

Customer: John Newton
51 Lake Drive
Delaware, Ohio 26807
Telephone: 298-3804

Salesperson: Andy Brown

Merchandise ①

Johnstone Mountain Bike, model number 8114, red
Easy-lock padlock

Date of delivery: January 25, 1995 ④

Delivery charge: $50 (Includes assembly)

Total price: $485 ③

Method of payment: Mastercard #299 40 3577

Signature of customer: _____ ② _____ Date _____

WARRANTY: Acme provides no warranty beyond of that provided by the manufacturer. ⑤

ACME BIKE SHOP SALES EXCHANGE AND RETURN POLICY: Merchandise may be returned within 10 days of delivery. If exchanged or returned, the merchandise must be accompanied by this bill of sale. All exchanges are subject to a 10% restocking charge.

A Simple Contractual Agreement

A relatively simple bill of sale is as much a contract as a 20-page agreement between an author and a publisher. As with any contract, it must include: 1. **The offer.** In this case, the offer is a particular bicycle and lock as described under "Merchandise." 2. **The acceptance.** Here the acceptance is confirmed by the customer's signature. 3. **A consideration.** This is the agreed-upon price for the service or product. 4. **Duration.** Even in a bill of sale, a time limit or delivery date can be stated; in this case, the merchandise will be delivered by January 25, 1995. 5. **Performance.** The contract is not complete until each party supplies something. The customer pays the agreed-upon price based on the delivery of the bicycle and lock. If the customer does not receive the bicycle and lock by the date stated, the contract will not be complete.

Understanding Warranties

A warranty may be part of a contract for the sale of a product or service. It is the company's promise to stand behind its products by making repairs or offering replacements if something goes wrong after you bring your purchase home. Just as you compare prices and features of different products, you should also make the warranty an important consideration when you shop.

A warranty may be "express," meaning its terms are explicitly expressed in writing, or "implied," meaning that based on common law, consumers have an implied right to a level of reliability in the product or the service they are buying.

EXPRESS WARRANTIES

Express warranties are written promises from the manufacturer. These warranties commonly come with products such as cars, television sets, and other appliances large and small. While manufacturers are not required to warrant a product, the Magnuson-Moss Warranty Act mandates that companies that do provide warranties for any product over $15 must make a complete and understandable written warranty available to consumers before a purchase is made, thereby providing an important tool in comparison shopping. Although the warranty is often packed in the carton with the product, it must be on hand for you to read before you buy.

The warranty must include the following:

- A description of which parts or components are covered;
- A clear statement of what the warrantor will do in case of a defect or a malfunction, including what items or services the warrantor will pay for and provide;
- A definition of exactly who is covered under the warranty—for example, any owner or only the original buyer;
- A statement of the length of the warranty period and when it comes into effect;
- An explanation of how to obtain service under the warranty.

FULL AND LIMITED WARRANTIES

Under the Magnuson-Moss Warranty Act, written warranties must be classified as "full" or "limited." If the warrantor fails to specify, the warranty is considered full.

A full warranty states that defective products will be repaired or replaced at no cost to the consumer within a certain time after the item is purchased or after the defect is discovered and reported. In some cases the consumer can elect to get a refund or a replacement of a defective product or part if the problem

---

RED FLAGS ON WARRANTIES

Here are some small-print clauses often found in warranties that should be warning signs for consumers:

1. "This warranty is in lieu of any other warranties, express or implied, including any implied warranty of merchantability or fitness." With this, you lose the additional legal protection of implied warranties. Some states prohibit this disclaimer.

2. "No responsibility is assumed for incidental or consequential damages of any kind." This clause limits the consumer's right to sue for personal injury due to product defect. In most states such a warranty is unenforceable.

3. "Defective parts will be repaired or replaced at our option." Baldly, this means that repair or a replacement is at the whim of the manufacturer.

4. "In the event of a claim, mail your product, properly packaged and insured, to the nearest authorized service dealer; any postage, insurance, or shipping charges must be prepaid by the sender." Returning defective products becomes the buyer's problem—and can be an expensive one.

5. "All products must be shipped in their original cartons or in replacements supplied by us." This is a nuisance, but if the warranty is a limited one and the stipulation is spelled out, it is legal.

Extra Protection on Credit Cards

Consumers have an extra source of warranty protection when they buy products with credit cards that extend the original coverage offered by the manufacturer. Terms of this protection vary, so comparing various card offerings may save you money. Here are some terms to consider:

✔ *How long is the warranty coverage?* Some cards offer an extra year of warranty, others double the original period, and some offer protection for the expected service life of the product up to 12 years.

✔ *How do you qualify for coverage?* With some cards, coverage is automatic; others require you to fill out a form within a specified period.

✔ *What products are excluded?* Purchases that may not be covered include those made outside the United States, cars, and items bought for professional use.

✔ *How easy is it to file a claim?* Look for the least complicated procedure. Find out which forms must be filed and whether you need authorization to make a repair.

✔ *What is the dollar limit on repairs?* Find out if the company will cover you for the original purchase price of the item.

✔ *Is there a dollar limit per year?* Many plans have caps on annual purchases.

---

is not resolved after a reasonable number of attempts to fix it. Sometimes this coverage may apply to subsequent owners for the life of the warranty. A full warranty need not cover every product part, but it must spell out exactly what is covered.

Limited warranties may cover only the cost of parts, requiring the customer to pay for labor; or they may cover repairs, but not offer refunds. Customers may have to pay handling or shipping charges when repairs are necessary. The warranty is generally nontransferable. Once again, the written warranty must detail exactly what the seller will and will not guarantee.

IMPLIED WARRANTIES

A consumer is protected against faulty products even when they do not come with written guarantees. Implied warranties are based on the common-law principle that the consumer is entitled to fair value for money spent. One implied warranty is of "merchantability." This implied warranty assures that every product sold is in proper condition and does what it is intended to do. For example, a lawn mower must cut grass.

A second category of implied warranty applies the standard of "fitness for a particular purpose." This comes into play when the consumer relies on a seller's advice that a product can be used for a special purpose. The implied warranty of fitness for a particular purpose assumes that special needs, if made known to the seller, are being met by the product sold. If the seller assures you that the mower you are buying is powerful enough to cut fields of tall weeds, it should be able to do so.

Every product is protected by an implied warranty unless it is specifically marked "as is" or the seller indicates in writing that no implied warranty is given. Some states have now outlawed "as is" sales and exclusions of implied warranties.

WARRANTY VIOLATIONS

The penalties for manufacturing or selling faulty merchandise can be significant. Courts can award monetary payments that go beyond the costs of repairing or replacing the product. Under certain circumstances, courts can also require companies to pay a consumer's attorney fees when the consumer's suit is successful. Consumers can make a claim against the manufacturer for any property damage or personal injuries suffered as a result of the seller's negligence. In addition to filing individual suits, consumers can join together to bring class-action lawsuits against companies that repeatedly violate warranties. (See also YOUR RIGHTS IN ACTION, page 488.)

Returning a registration card is not necessary to validate a warranty unless the manufacturer specifically states that you must do so to be covered. Often warranty cards are simply sales-promotion tools.

PROBLEMS WITH PURCHASES

When you buy any merchandise, you make a contract. If there is something wrong with what you bought, the law will help you make good on the contract.

The Purchase Contract

Most problems encountered by buyers concern overpricing, deceptive advertising, poor service, refunds, and delivery issues. All these problems, on a basic level, are "contractual" problems in that they concern an agreement between the buyer and seller that is protected under the law.

Both a buyer and a seller are protected against "breach of contract," or the breaking of an agreement. For example, as a buyer, unless the contract states otherwise, you have no obligation to pay for goods if they are not delivered. Conversely, you have no right to keep goods you order if you do not pay for them: The seller has a right to sue to collect any money you owe, plus any incidental costs such as interest.

Unless goods have been ordered C.O.D., you have the right to inspect them before paying for them. If you discover that the merchandise is not what you ordered or expected, or is broken or damaged, the seller may make suitable replacements within the time specified for delivery in the contract.

If you discover problems after you accept delivery, as long as you notify the seller within a reasonable time, satisfactory goods must be provided. If suitable merchandise is not delivered within an agreed-upon time period, you may cancel the contract and demand your money back. In some cases, you may have the right to ask for any difference between what you agreed to pay and what it would cost you now to buy similar goods elsewhere, as well as any incidental costs, such as the cost of transporting or storing the rejected merchandise.

In fact, most of the problems commonly encountered in day-to-day purchase agreements are covered by federal or state contract and warranty law.

WHEN YOU NEED A LAWYER

Breach-of-contract suits involving limited sums of money can be tried in small claims or conciliation court. The limit for claims varies by state, usually from $1,000 to $5,000. Most of the time, you do not need a lawyer to present a case in small claims court; in fact, many states do not even allow attorneys in small claims court. If the sum in question is higher than the

What If You Got a Raw Deal?

The Uniform Commercial Code (UCC) rules now in effect in every state offer some solace to a buyer who is grossly overcharged for a product. Contracts that are shockingly unfair or that result from unfair pressure are called "unconscionable." A classic example is a salesman who pressures an unsophisticated or elderly person into buying a product at a price many times higher than its worth.

Sometimes contracts are written with a liquidated-damages clause, which limits how much the buyer can collect in case of a breach of contract. Film-processing firms, for example, claim that if they ruin a roll of film and lose your photos, the processor is responsible only for the cost of the film itself. Liquidated-damages clauses, like clauses limiting the buyer's right to demand damages for personal injury, may themselves be declared unconscionable.

While recourse for unconscionability is available under the UCC rules, going to court is a time-consuming and complex process, and those people who need help the most may be the least equipped to know how to get it. For that reason, the best protection against bad bargains, as always, is to avoid them in the first place.

A SAFETY SHIELD FOR CONSUMERS

In 1972, Congress passed the Consumer Product Safety Act, which empowered a commission to help protect the public against unreasonable risks of injury and death associated with consumer products. The commission has broad authority to research, issue, and enforce safety standards. Here are some of the ways in which the commission carries out its mandate:

1. Obtains the recall or repair of products that fail to comply with mandatory standards or that present substantial hazards to consumers.

2. Bans products for which no feasible standard would adequately protect the public.

3. Regulates and enforces four important federal safety measures: The Flammable Fabrics Act, The Federal Hazardous Substances Act, The Poison Prevention Packaging Act, and The Refrigerator Safety Act.

4. Works with industry to develop voluntary safety standards and requires warnings or instructions for use to appear where appropriate on all consumer products.

5. Conducts research on products that may potentially be hazardous to consumers.

6. Carries out information and education programs, such as issuing safety alerts with regard to particular products.

small claims limit, or if personal injury is involved, your best course is to consult a lawyer.

Make sure to file your claim within a reasonable amount of time following the incident. There is a time limit on filing a breach-of-contract suit. If the UCC governs the transaction, the statute of limitations requires that the suit be started within four years of the breach. States also have time limits for filing cases in small claims court. Check with the court clerk to find out what the statute of limitations is in your state.

ALTERNATIVE DISPUTE RESOLUTION

Consumer complaints involving amounts greater than the small claims court can handle may have to go to a higher court, but whether your problem is small or large you may want to avoid the courts altogether by using alternative dispute resolution (ADR). ADR is an umbrella term that encompasses several ways of resolving disputes: negotiation, mediation, arbitration, and administrative hearings. (For a discussion of ADR, see YOUR RIGHTS IN ACTION, page 472.) What follows is three ways to find an ADR practitioner:

- Consult the Yellow Pages under "Arbitration" or "Mediation" to find the names of possible companies or lawyers who practice ADR.
- Call the Better Business Bureau for directions to a local mediator or arbitrator.
- Write to the American Bar Association Section of Dispute Resolution for the names of ADR practitioners. The address is 1800 M Street NW, Suite 290 South, Washington, D.C., 20036, (202) 331-2200.

Suppose It Doesn't Work?

Products can be considered defective for two reasons: They do not perform as promised, or they are unsafe and cause personal injury. If a product does not perform as the manufacturer promised, you are protected by the warranty. (See also "Understanding Warranties," page 407.) If a product causes personal injury or damage, you can sue the manufacturer or seller for product liability.

Product-liability cases have been brought to court involving almost every kind of defective merchandise, from contact lenses to cars. Cases have also been won against manufacturers of products whose dangers have not been discovered until a much later date, such as the drug DES, which was prescribed for pregnant women in the 1940's and 1950's and proved damaging to their adult daughters decades later.

Product-liability claims can be based on injuries caused by defects in design, faulty manufacturing procedures, inadequate packaging or labeling, inadequate warnings or instructions, or misrepresentation of what the product is able to do. For many years, winning a claim meant proving negligence by the manufacturer in one of these areas—a hard thing to do—but in the 1960's the law began recognizing that manufacturers have a responsibility to customers regarding the products they sell.

STRICT PRODUCT LIABILITY

When strict liability applies, a manufacturer is held responsible for selling any product that is deemed "unreasonably dangerous" and results in injury to the buyer or other foreseeable users. It is no longer necessary to prove the manufacturer was negligent, only that the product was defective, that it was for sale, and, most crucially, that injuries were caused by the defect.

The doctrine of strict product liability puts merchants on their toes as well. If you buy a stove that blows up because of improper design, causing a fire that injures someone, you can

Tried-and-True Tips for Returning

Many consumer complaints fall into predictable categories, and problems with "returns" is a major one. The best advice is to take extra care before you make the original purchase, but if you have bought the goods and want to return them, follow these guidelines:

• **Save receipts for 30 days.** Alternatively, you can use the statement from a credit card if you have charged the purchase. If you do not have the receipt, ask to see the manager when you try to return an item.

• **Save packaging.** Some warranties, especially for appliances and electronic equipment, require that merchandise be returned in its original box.

• **Use a credit card.** Charging gives you more leverage when you need to return. If a store is reluctant to accept a return and you have charged it, you have time to negotiate before you must pay (see also, YOUR MONEY, page 308).

• **Beware of boutiques.** Many small stores have strict return policies. (In many localities, shops are legally required to post their return policy in an obvious place). Often a store will not budge. Make sure you really want the item, or shop in department stores, which have more liberal return rules.

• **Try returning at similar stores.** If you receive a best-selling book or CD as a gift, but you would prefer something else, try taking it to a local book or record shop. A store may take back an item if it has not been opened and if the store stocks it. Or, more likely, it may agree to exchange the item.

• **Save warranties.** Warranties protect consumers for months, and sometimes years. But don't lose hope if your warranty has run out. Manufacturers and retailers take pride in their products and in their clientele. If your new food processor breaks down in six months but was covered only by a 90-day warranty, the manufacturer may still be willing to replace it.

• **Put your complaint in writing.** If, for whatever reason, the store will not accept the return, write a letter to the store and the manufacturer. Address it to the most senior person in the organization and explain the situation. Include copies of receipts and describe the remedy you are seeking. If you do not get the response you want, write to the Better Business Bureau, and copy all concerned.

• **Don't be intimidated.** If you have purchased defective or bad merchandise, you have the right to return it. If you have incurred a loss, consider taking your case to small claims court.

sue not only the manufacturer but the store that sold the item to you and the distributor who supplied the store. They share the responsibility to avoid selling hazardous products, as well as to convey any safety warnings or recall notices.

Generally, with strict liability statutes, you do not need to be the owner or purchaser of a defective item to sue. If you are injured by the flying blade of your neighbor's defective lawn mower, you may have a case against the maker of the mower.

PRODUCT RECALLS

You may be entitled to a refund or a repair of an unsafe product and not even know it. Hundreds of products are recalled each year because either the Consumer Product Safety Commission (CPSC) or the manufacturer has found them defective. When a car is recalled, owners are notified because dealers must keep records of purchases. Large-scale recalls of other products are occasionally reported on the radio and in newspapers, and some states require retailers to post prominent notices of recalls on products they carry.

But if you buy a television set or an infant's car seat, it is not likely that the merchant records enough information about his sales to allow him to notify you personally if the product is recalled. Even if the recall is publicized, you may not happen to see announcements in the media or in the store.

If you have a concern about a product you have purchased and whether it is the subject of a recall, you can call the CPSC hotline at (800) 638-CPSC. The CPSC at any time has listings of as many as 100 current recalls in categories from coffee makers to cribs, major appliances to outdoor furniture.

Complaining Effectively

I f your new toaster will not toast, your new CD player will not play, or your new percolator does not perk, you should not have to resort to a lawsuit to remedy the problem. Too often consumers assume that they will not get satisfaction and do not even voice a complaint. According to the U.S. Office of Consumer Affairs, many buyers do not even try to resolve the problems they have with products, fearing only more frustration. But you can get results if you learn how and where to complain effectively. Here are some basic strategies for asserting your rights when you are wronged:

- **Keep records.** Every time you buy something that costs more than $500, file the bill of sale, receipt or contract, the credit card draft if the item was charged, any canceled payment checks, and all instructions and warranties.

Delivery Woes

When you have ordered something, whether it is a book, a sweater, or a new sofa, you may experience delivery problems. Here are some guidelines to follow:

✔ *Late delivery.* If you order by mail, the FTC requires the company to ship the goods within the time limit promised or within 30 days of receipt of your order. If the company cannot ship your goods on time, it must notify you of the delay, remind you of your right to cancel and receive a refund, and ask if you want to wait. It must supply you with a method of relaying your decision free of charge. If you do not respond, the company can assume that you will wait. If a delivery date is clearly specified on the bill of sale, you can cancel the order and get your money back.

✔ *Canceling a delivery.* If you decide to cancel a mailorder product, the company must refund your money within seven business days of your cancellation. If you purchase by credit card, the company must adjust your statement within one billing cycle after you notify it.

✔ *Delivery of defective merchandise.* If you have ordered something by mail and it arrives damaged, mail it back immediately. If something is delivered, such as a new piece of furniture, make sure you examine it carefully. Don't sign a release stating that you are satisfied unless you are.

- **Start at the source.** Read your warranty carefully and follow the directions on it for seeking redress if the product malfunctions. Usually this means contacting the person who sold you the product or the customer-service manager by telephone or, better yet, in person.
- **Put it in writing.** If the retailer agrees to do what you want but cannot do it on the spot, send a letter confirming your understanding of what action will be taken and when.
- **Go to the top.** If you cannot get action from the store or the retail chain to which it belongs, contact the manufacturer directly. Many manufacturers have toll-free numbers for consumer complaints. Or else write directly to the president of the manufacturing company, and send your letter by certified mail with a return receipt requested.

Taking It To The Top

PROBLEM

Warren bought a lawn mower with a one-year limited warranty covering all parts. After six weeks the mower's blades had loosened, so that it no longer cut properly. The seller tried to repair the mower, but the blades loosened again. When Warren asked for a refund or a new mower, the merchant offered to tighten the blades again, saying he was certain the problem could be corrected. The repair did not hold, and Warren demanded a refund. The dealer refused, claiming the mower must have been misused, since it had worked properly when it was originally sold. Warren wrote to the president of the retail outlet that had sold him the mower, but the president accepted his dealer's assessment.

ACTION

Warren decided to approach the manufacturer of the mower. He addressed his complaint to the company's president, stating that he had chosen this mower because of the manufacturer's excellent reputation. He explained his problem, including a mention that loose blades were a safety hazard that might cause injury. Since apparently the mower could not be repaired to function properly, he asked for a refund or a new mower. The manufacturer realized that not only was the company obligated by an implied warranty—that is, that a lawn mower should cut grass—but that it was important to preserve its corporate reputation. Warren was given a new mower.

- **Ask for help.** When you cannot get cooperation from either the maker or the seller of the product, write or call the Better Business Bureau and the closest consumer-protection agency, either local or state. If your complaint involves a violation of federal, state, or local law, the agency's legal staff will be notified for appropriate action.
- **Go public.** Consumer reporters for local newspapers and television stations perform a valuable service by investigating complaints. The last thing any business wants is to be publicly accused of unfair treatment of its customers.

Using the Better Business Bureau

The Council of Better Business Bureaus (BBB) is a private nonprofit organization that promotes honest advertising and selling practices. From its origins in 1912 as Vigilance Committees, an organization dedicated to correcting advertising abuses, the BBB has grown to nearly 175 bureaus across the United States with more than 11 million consumer contacts each year. Local bureaus are funded by membership dues from the businesses that support their goals.

The BBB collects and reports information to help buyers make informed decisions. If you are thinking of hiring a service or dealing with a store, the BBB files can tell you how long the party has been in business and provide a summary of any complaints received about it.

If you report a problem, in many locations the BBB will first contact the firm involved to try to settle the matter. Some bureaus may offer mediation or arbitration with both parties to try to work out mutually agreeable solutions. The BBB has no official power, but in extreme cases it may refer its file to a law-enforcement agency to evaluate whether further action is warranted.

The BBB depends on consumers to make its files useful. By reporting unethical companies, you will save others from unhappy experiences.

Most BBB services are free, but to cover rising costs, some offices are now using 900 numbers so that the caller pays a nominal fee for the call.

Jane Jones • 2100 Hill Street • Columbus, N.J. 09309

July 14, 1995

Mr. John Harrison
Consumer Relations Director
Speedo Vacuum Cleaner Company
333 Third Street
Littlefield, N.J. 09403

Dear Mr. Harrison,

On May 1, 1995, I purchased a Speedo Vacuum Cleaner Model XYZ from The Floor Store, 212 Main Street, Columbus, N.J. **1** (A copy of the receipt is enclosed.) **2** Unfortunately, I have had problems with both the product and the service I have received.

Specifically, I have the following complaints: **3**

First, the vacuum does not work efficiently to pick up dust or dirt on either bare floors or carpets. Even after I have gone over the same area several times, the dirt remains. The power shuts off by itself when the vacuum has been running for several minutes, then comes back on after 30 to 60 seconds.

Second, when I brought this to the attention of The Floor Store, I was told that because the vacuum was on sale, I could not exchange or return it, which I was not told when I made the purchase. I was also treated rudely by the salesman, Robert Rule, and then by the manager, Alfred Adams.

4 I am requesting that you provide me with a new vacuum cleaner, on condition that if this one proves to be unacceptable, I will receive a refund. I also ask that you investigate the business practices of The Floor Store, as they are poor representatives of your company.

I can be reached during the day at (806) 827-9318 or after six in the evening at (806) 444-2897 **5** May I hear from you before July 31? **6**

Yours truly,

Writing an Effective Complaint Letter

An effective letter of complaint should be polite and free of rancor, but also firm. For best results, include the following points: **1.** Address the letter to someone with sufficient authority to handle the problem; describe the product, then tell when, where, and how you purchased it. **2.** Include a copy of the purchase receipt. **3.** Outline the complaints clearly and concisely, but include all the details. **4.** Make clear the remedy you want, whether it is a new product, a refund, or additional damages; **5.** Tell where you can be reached during business hours. **6.** Set a firm deadline for action. Send the letter by registered mail, return receipt requested.

Advertising and Marketing

The wise consumer knows how to sift through sellers' claims and persuasions.

Advertising's Pros and Cons

At its best, advertising helps inform consumers, makes them aware of convenient new products, and helps them to compare similar products. When products are basically alike, however, advertisers must use subtler means to set their brands apart. Their approaches do not come about by accident. Some of America's brightest minds are devoted to creating advertising intended to create brand awareness and give products an image or a "personality" that will appeal to consumers. To learn which messages are most effective with their target audience, companies spend millions on market research. They often go beyond questionnaires, using electronic testing devices that measure whether viewers' eyes widen when they watch an ad, indicating interest, or whether they wriggle in their chairs, showing that the ad is not capturing their attention.

The result is commercials that may grab attention but may not tell the reader or viewer much about the product. They may show an actor, who looks like a doctor, recommending a cold remedy or may feature a sports hero wearing a particular brand of shoes, implying that you will be in good company if you do the same. Or, they may play on emotions such as fear, showing the wreckage of a burned-out house in order to sell batteries for smoke detectors or pictures of real people touting the safety features of a make of car.

KEEP YOUR WITS ABOUT YOU

Building brand awareness pays off for the manufacturer, but not necessarily for the consumer. Buyers may be willing to pay more for a brand name they recognize, but comparing products on their merits rather than their advertising appeal can save you a lot of money—similar, cheaper products may be just as good as big-name items.

Some misleading advertising claims actually cause consumers to waste money. One product was advertised as being effective against the second-most-common form of baldness. What the ad neglected to say was that the first cause, heredity, is responsible for nearly all baldness in men. Thus only a tiny fraction of people could possibly be helped by the advertised product.

The Soft Sell of Indirect Advertising

Movies and television often subject viewers to hidden advertising. The heroine says a tearful good-bye to her lover at the airport—with the plane and its logo directly behind. Or the hero orders a beer or a soft drink, and the label is clearly on camera.

Although the message is low-key, this indirect technique is a favorite device for building brand awareness. There are companies that specialize in this kind of exposure for products and services.

One of the most popular techniques is the video news release. Whether promoting a new athletic shoe or Dutch tulip bulbs, these highly professional videotapes are made in the format and length commonly used for items on television news broadcasts. They usually contain a legitimate bit of news about the company or product, perhaps a new way of harvesting grapes for wine or a survey showing how many consumers eat cold cereal for breakfast.

Television stations use these slick presentations as free fillers for their news reports—and consumers are never told they are watching a subtle commercial.

Clever demonstrations can also be misleading. Because a razor can peel peach fuzz does not mean it will do as well on a beard. Both federal and state agencies regulate ads that are clearly fraudulent, but it is up to educated consumers to train themselves to be on guard against half-truths and cleverly misleading claims.

Wrapped Up to Sell

Packaging and labeling, like advertising, are used to build brand identity. They are designed so that the buyer will be drawn to a product and to be able to quickly spot it on a shelf crowded with competitors. Extensive marketing studies are done to find out which colors and shapes are most appealing to potential buyers.

Competition has led to many kinds of improved packaging, such as unbreakable plastic bottles, smaller boxes, and more convenient toothpaste dispensers. It has also produced less constructive ploys. Knowing that a product's outward appearance can shape the buyer's perception of what is inside, advertisers put foods in crocks to make them seem homemade or in fancy gold paper to make them seem "deluxe"; of course, the consumer pays for these frills.

Packaging can also be downright deceptive. A large box or container may have less inside than the package implies. Often canned coffee comes in containers that appear to be one-pound cans, when in fact they contain only 12 ounces of coffee. It pays to compare a product's cost per ounce or per pound with the competition's product. Don't assume that a bigger box means more for your money.

Packages frequently bear prominent but vague claims to appeal to consumers. "New and improved" does not mean anything unless improvements are explained. Federal law prohibits false claims and requires specific nutritional data, but some claims though legal can still be misleading. "Lite," for example, can sound great but may be meaningless. Buyers must understand that manufacturers—whether they produce food, cosmetics, or TV's—are wrapping their products to sell.

Sales-Promotion Tactics

Sales promotion—ranging from free samples to coupons to rebates—is another way that sellers encourage people to try their products. A smart shopper will take advantage of promotions on products she can use, and will steer clear of seductive come-ons.

When manufacturers spend millions putting out new products, they often willingly take on the cost of mailing out free samples. They hope that once the product is in your house you will try it—and like it enough to switch from your old brand. Bonuses with purchases are another way to induce you to buy and try. Perfume companies often give a set of free samples with a purchase, or for larger purchases they may offer premiums such as umbrellas or carrying cases.

Packaging can be a sales-promotion tool. By banding three bars of soap together and selling them at a savings over buying each separately, the manufacturer moves more merchandise and may interest more buyers. Packages can also offer premiums that lead to repeat business, such as an offer to exchange a free box of cat food for a proof-of-purchase seal.

RESISTING IN-STORE SEDUCTION

In-store marketing is a direct effort to woo customers. Manufacturers frequently set up booths where a representative offers free samples of their products. Cosmetics companies, for example, often provide free "makeovers" or attractive gifts, such as overnight bags, hoping the results of a professional makeup job or the gifts will please the customer enough to persuade her to buy more of their products.

Savvy supermarket owners are particularly creative with subtle techniques to lower your willpower when you shop. When you walk into a supermarket, you are often greeted by displays that look like specials, but often they are seasonal items, such as picnic supplies in summer, positioned to encourage impulse buying. Or, to draw your attention, a certain product may be on sale, but the rest of the picnic or barbeque needs—paper plates, hamburger buns, or hot dogs—are sold at regular price, or more. The bakery is usually near the front so the aroma hits you immediately, while milk, an essential on most shopping lists, is deliberately placed at the back of the store so that you must pass through all of the aisles and their tempting products.

CATCH YOUR EYE, GET YOUR DOLLAR

Product placement is another ploy. Putting an item at eye level increases sales noticeably, so cheaper items are relegated to the top or bottom shelves. Specials are often displayed at the end of the aisles—but right next to the discounted chips you may find high-priced dips. Magazines, candy, and gum are placed to tempt you while you wait in the checkout line.

Department stores are equally canny about placement of goods. Customers must pass the jewelry counter to get to the clothing; cosmetics are also placed up front to appeal to impulse buyers. Knowing the perils from the start, you may be better able to resist temptation and stick to your shopping list.

Is It Really a Bargain?

Sales are effective promotion tools used by merchants to bring in customers. But a sale may not always be what it seems.

An authentic sale means that the seller is offering stock merchandise for less than the normal price for a limited time only. Seasonal specials such as semiannual "white sales" are a good example of a legitimate sale. Regular sheets and towels are commonly marked down in January and August.

But buyers need to beware of merchants who repeatedly advertise the same items as being on sale. Equally tricky are those who raise prices by putting on higher tags than normal so that they can claim a sale when an item in reality has been "marked down" to the regular price.

A price tag that shows the "suggested retail price" of an item beside the store's substantially lower price may be deceptive as well. The suggested price may be inflated in an attempt to make you feel that you are getting a bargain when you are actually paying the store's full price.

Unscrupulous merchants sometimes keep "going out of business" signs posted in their windows for years, especially in tourist areas where potential customers will not be in town long enough to recognize the classic ploy.

In short, buyers need to be certain that they are getting legitimate savings, not cheap merchandise. Low price alone does not mean a good buy.

DECEPTIVE SALES PRACTICES

An informed consumer is the best defense against fraud in the marketplace.

What Constitutes Fraud

If a seller intentionally deceives you about a product or service and if you suffer a loss as a result, you have been victimized by fraud. Fortunately, a number of laws exist to help you protect yourself against the myriad fraudulent schemes that are constantly being invented—and reinvented—by scam artists everywhere. The Federal Trade Commission (FTC) is the agency empowered to punish businesses that engage in consumer fraud. It has jurisdiction to enforce federal law in cases of false advertising, unfair methods of competition, and unfair or deceptive acts or practices. The FTC does not get involved in resolving claims, however.

Laws enacted at the state and local level are more likely to protect the individual consumer. Most state legislatures have passed laws to protect consumers from fraud and deceptive advertising and sales practices, which may be punishable by fines, imprisonment, or both. These laws may also be concerned with matters that are not expressly covered under federal regulations, such as requiring telephone solicitors to register with the state and post a bond, or making it illegal to falsify an odometer when selling a used car. Such laws often provide recourse for victimized consumers, allowing them to go to court or file a lawsuit.

What to Do About It

You have purchased a freezer from an appliance dealer in your town. The dealer delivers and installs the freezer, but in a week it has broken down and all the food you put in the freezer is ruined. You strongly suspect that the freezer had been used, but the dealer insists he can repair it and refuses to give you an exchange or refund. You begin to realize that you have been the victim of fraud.

A good place to start researching your rights is the National Fraud Information Center Consumer Assistance Service. (You can call the service toll-free at (800) 876-7060, from 8:30 A.M. to 5:30 P.M. Eastern time.) The center can tell you how and where to report the fraud.

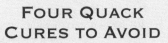

GOING TO COURT

Often the most effective way to deal with a difficult situation is to take the seller to small claims court, possibly on the grounds of violation of your state's deceptive-practices law. (See also YOUR RIGHTS IN ACTION, page 476.) In general, to prove fraud, you must convince the judge or jury that the seller's misrepresentation was intentional; for example, the seller told you that a freezer was new when he knew it was used.

The misrepresentation must be of a "material" fact, or one that is important and relevant. If the freezer had only one basket for loose goods rather than the two you were promised, that probably would not have changed your decision to buy and would not constitute a material fact that would provide grounds for a lawsuit.

In court, you must also prove "reliance"—that is, that you could not have known from your own inspection that the product was not as represented.

DAMAGES

If the seller is found to have committed fraud, victims may be able to collect money for three kinds of damages:

- **Direct damages.** These repay you for what you lost. For example, if you bought a freezer that you believed to be new and able to keep your food frozen and it broke down, you would expect to receive a new freezer or be repaid your costs.
- **Consequential damages.** These cover the cost of foreseeable losses suffered as a result of the fraud, such as frozen foods spoiled by a nonfunctioning freezer.
- **Punitive damages.** These may be added on to direct and consequential damages and are intended to punish the person who has committed the fraud; they can run into thousands of dollars if a judge rules the fraud cruel or excessive. For example, if you purchased a faulty freezer for a nursing home, and the elderly, sick people were forced to go without food, you might be able to collect punitive damages.

Sometimes courts award punitive damages partially as a warning to others not to engage in similar acts. In an Iowa case, a lonely, elderly widow fell victim to a dance studio, purchasing dance lessons totaling over $29,000, including three separate lifetime memberships.

The jury not only ordered the seller to repay her loss but also leveled $40,000 in punitive charges against the studio, to be paid to the victim. When the studio appealed, the Iowa Supreme Court turned it down, stating "courts cannot protect against the folly of bad judgment. We can, however, insist on honesty in selling."

123...

FOUR QUACK CURES TO AVOID

1. **Magic weight loss.** Ads for pills and potions guaranteed to produce rapid weight loss make many claims—that they curb your appetite, or block the absorption of fat or calories, or flush fat out of the body. Some of these products are diuretics that merely rid the body of excess water. Despite "before" and "after" photos of models, none of these products produce permanent weight loss.

2. **Beauty miracles.** "Shed cellulite without exercise." "Make wrinkles disappear." Any quick, painless cure or special formulas available only by mail and from only one supplier are suspect. Ask to see copies of research studies.

3. **Wonder cures.** "Magic bracelet cures arthritis," boasts the ad, with a photo of a woman who claims to have obtained relief from the product. When testimonials or case histories are the only evidence, the buyer should be wary. Be sure to check with your doctor before trying a product that may affect your health.

4. **Nutritionists.** Diploma mills selling certificates for a correspondence course turn out unqualified nutritionists, who may prescribe useless pills for "effortless weight loss" or "fat-burning vitamins." Look for real credentials. Legitimate dieticians have undergraduate or graduate degrees from accredited universities. Registered dieticians have served internships and passed national certification exams.

COMMON SCAMS AND HOW TO AVOID THEM

Frauds are as varied as the con artists who commit them, but they often fall into predictable patterns. Here are some of the most common scams and ways to avoid or remedy them. Always check any questionable offers with the Better Business Bureau, your local consumer protection agency, and the state attorney general's office. Report violations to these agencies and the FTC to save others from dishonest dealers.

The Scam	What It Is	How to Avoid Being Taken
Dishonest advertising	A rug-sale ad claims prices are slashed because the company is going out of business next week. You think you got a bargain but spot the same ad three months later with the same prices.	Don't shop in an unfamiliar store without getting references and doing comparison shopping. When you spot false or misleading advertising, report it. The store is breaking the law.
Mislabeling	The label on the coat says cashmere, but the store owner knows better. It is actually camel hair marked up to an unrealistic price.	When you discover the scam, demand a refund and report the merchant. If you cannot avoid deceptions, at least stop them from happening again.
Bait and switch	The VCR was advertised at a bargain price, but it looks like an outdated model. The salesman says they have had many complaints about it—and recommends a more expensive machine instead.	Bait and switch is a ruse to get customers into the store. When someone tries to pull this all-too-common scam, the best remedy is to leave. Report the store's tactics and do your buying elsewhere.
Inflated appraisals	The jewelry clerk assures you that the ring has a fine one-carat stone, well priced at $1,500. He urges you to have it appraised, even recommends a nearby appraiser—one who will get a bonus for affirming the store's evaluation.	Check jewelers' references carefully in advance. You are at the mercy of their expertise and honesty. Use an appraiser other than one recommended by the store. If you get cheated, you may be able to sue, claiming an unconscionable sale.
Failing to give full disclosure	The art school contract promises weekly painting lessons for $50 per month. It does not say that you have to buy an easel and other materials for $350—far more than an art store would charge.	You can cancel your contract and get a refund, since the agreement you signed did not fully disclose the terms of lessons.
Phony prizes	An official-looking letter or postcard arrives announcing you have won a prize—a diamond, a deluxe vacation, or a food processor. To collect, all you have to do is attend an informational meeting about a new vacation community.	Pass up any "free" offer that requires you to attend a sales presentation. The prize may be worth little—the diamond is a tiny chip, the food processor a hand chopper. And you may be asked to pay a handling charge worth more than the prize.
Sweepstake swindle	"Congratulations," says the official-looking letter. "You have won a consolation prize in the $10 million Pie-in-the-Sky Sweepstakes. The attached voucher for $220 is yours as a consolation winner and may be applied toward your choice of one of the following products..."	You do not have to pay anything to win a legitimate sweepstakes. These letters are simply selling schemes. The products are probably not worth what you will pay even after your $220 credit. Phony sweepstakes offers should be reported to the U.S. Postal Service.
900-telephone numbers	A card promises a prize. Just call a 900-number to find out what you have won. You listen to a long message—and learn that you are only a finalist, not a winner.	Don't make the call. The caller pays for 900- number calls. which can be expensive. If you are curious, write a letter and ask for information on your prize.

The Scam	What It Is	How to Avoid Being Taken
Pyramid sales scheme	The right to distribute a product, such as a line of cosmetics, is offered to four people. Each buyer pays $2,000 and, in turn, may sell four dealerships, making a profit of $6,000. Money is made from selling the dealership, not a product, and finding new prospects gets tougher and tougher as the pyramid grows.	Only the promoter and those who get in at the top of a pyramid make money. The later you enter, the less your chances. Often, you are not told the size of the pyramid when you join, only that you need to find a few other people. Pyramid schemes are illegal. They should be avoided and reported to the authorities.
Art frauds	The gallery owner offers you a "fabulous investment," a signed print by a famous artist like Picasso, costing anywhere from $500 to $10,000. In fact, the prints are counterfeit, reproduced without authorization and bearing a forged signature. "Certificates of authenticity" are probably worthless.	Before buying an important piece of art, check out the gallery's credentials with an expert art appraiser or a museum curator. Make the sale conditional on an appraisal by an expert of your choice. Be sure the sales slip states in writing that you are entitled to your money back, not just an exchange for another print.
Bogus charity	A policeman is killed in the line of duty. The day following the newspaper headlines, you get a call asking for a contribution to his family. The check should be made out to the family friend who is heading the collection.	Never make out check to an individual who is a stranger to you. Ask for the name, address, and telephone number of anyone asking for money by phone. Don't feel pressured to give on the spot. Check out any charity before you give.
Travel scams	The phone call promises you a free vacation—all you have to pay is the airfare. The fare turns out to be much higher, more than twice the price of an economy ticket. The "luxury hotel" is a cheap, run-down resort. You could have bought a better trip for less.	Don't succumb to scam artists who try to tempt you with the idea of a bargain vacation. Strangers are not likely to call out of the blue with a real windfall. Remember the old adage: If it sounds too good to be true, it probably is.
Credit card fraud	The caller says your credit card company has a gift for all cardholders—a $50 credit. She wants to verify your card number. The credit never appears on your bill, but many other unauthorized charges do.	Never give credit card or bank information on the phone unless you have initiated the call. Also, because con artists can get numbers from discarded carbons of sales slips, be sure to destroy the carbons.
Phony IRS audits	The caller says he is conducting an IRS audit and asks for a variety of information, such as social security numbers and information about credit cards and checking accounts. The numbers you give are used to access your accounts.	The IRS always notifies you of any action by mail, and IRS employees must show proper identification. If you are suspicious about a so-called IRS agent, phone the IRS inspection hotline at (800) 366-4484.
Time-share schemes	The salesman shows handsome drawings of a new resort on a Florida beach, and offers you a "time share," a week's vacation at the resort every year, for only $2,000. You pay the money—but the resort is never built.	Never buy until you can inspect an actual building. Never buy without checking fully the builder's track record and his financial stability.
Phony inspector	An inspector in an official-looking uniform comes to the door to say that your home needs immediate repairs to meet city safety standards. He recommends a "reliable" repair service.	Don't let fear tactics make you panic. Get another opinion, and if repairs are actually necessary, get at least three legitimate estimates for the job. Be sure repair firms are licensed.

BASIC SHOPPERS' RIGHTS

Every time you walk into a store to buy something, you are entitled to expect fair treatment and good value.

Are Store Credit Cards a Good Deal?

Many retailers offer their own credit cards, knowing that customers are more likely to buy where they can charge their purchases.

These credit cards offer certain advantages. Because retailers want to encourage return business, store cards are generally easier to get than other credit cards. There is no annual fee and often no purchase limit. Cardholders receive early notice of sales and may be invited to special sales before the general public. It is often easier to return merchandise for store credit than to get a cash refund.

Since they may be easier to get, store cards also can benefit you if you are having trouble establishing credit. If you use your card responsibly, it will give you a credit record that can help you when you apply for other charge cards.

The problem with store cards is that you will probably pay a higher interest rate than to a credit card company if you extend payments beyond 30 days. Many stores charge 18 percent or more. And you may not have the purchase protection or warranty extension that many major credit card companies offer for purchases made with their cards.

Protecting the Consumer

In day-to-day dealings with merchants, shoppers have many rights that are guaranteed by local laws. You are entitled to a safe, clean environment. In most areas, stores must meet sanitary requirements determined by the local department of health. The posting of all store policies concerning returns and refunds is usually enforced by your state's department of consumer affairs. In major cities, a local agency may also issue licenses for businesses of all kinds, and companies that violate the rules risk losing their licenses.

The local department of human rights commonly handles complaints concerning discrimination against buyers due to race—for example, overcharging in certain neighborhoods or refusing service to certain customers. If you have been a victim of discrimination, you may also want to speak to a lawyer.

COMMON SALES PRACTICES

It pays to be informed about sales tax laws. Sales tax varies from state to state and even from city to city within a state. When shopping in an unfamiliar area, ask the amount of the tax. Some states have no sales tax, while others have no clothing tax, which offers big savings on large purchases. It may be worth a shopping excursion if one of these states is close to your home. State rules differ if you have purchases delivered. Some require you to pay tax on any goods shipped in; others charge tax only if the seller also has branches in your state.

When merchandise is marked "as is," it means the seller takes no responsibility for its performance. You may see this marking on damaged sale merchandise, although some states outlaw this practice. If you want to buy something "as is," be sure you do so only after careful inspection.

Receipts are an important part of the sales transaction and should always be kept in case of problems. Receipts should state refund policies clearly.

If a store closes down or goes into bankruptcy with paid-for but undelivered merchandise, government agencies generally cannot help you collect a refund. Your recourse in these cases is filing a claim in bankruptcy court. Full recovery of your money may not be possible.

Perils of Installment Buying

The cost of appliances tempts many consumers to pay on an installment plan. Ads that promise "Only $49 per month" make it seem easy to afford a new dishwasher or air conditioner. But think twice before you sign on the dotted line.

While installment buying is tempting, you are actually taking out a loan from the dealer. Financing with the dealer is convenient—but you may pay dearly for it. High interest can increase the total price of the item anywhere from 50 to 100 percent, far more than if you took out a small bank loan or paid with a lower-interest credit card. Many credit cards also automatically extend your warranty. (See also "Extra Protection on Credit Cards," page 408.)

By law, creditors must disclose the total of all payments required to pay off the amount financed and the annual percentage rate you are being charged. However, some canny merchants manage to hide this total in very small print or in the loan agreement, which you should always read carefully before you sign. Look closely, too, at penalty fees or repossession rights for late payment, and be clear about what happens if you miss payments. (For additional information about credit cards and loans, see also YOUR MONEY, page 297.)

COLLECTION AGENCIES

Sometimes retailers turn their unpaid debts over to collection agencies. The Fair Debt Collection Practices Act (FDCPA), protects you against unethical agencies. For example, without the debtor's consent, the act makes it illegal for a bill collector to telephone or visit before 8 A.M. or after 9 P.M. or to contact a debtor at work. Within five days after the first contact, the collector must send you a written notice stating exactly how much you owe. If you dispute that sum in writing within 30 days, you will be sent verification of the debt.

Always request verification. Because the collector cannot continue trying to collect until he has mailed it, you will be buying a little time if you owe the money and are having temporary difficulty making a payment.

If you notify the collector in writing that you either refuse to pay the debt or that you do not want to be contacted again, the collector must stop communicating with you except to notify you of what further specified actions he will take—such as initiating legal action. If you hire an attorney, the debt collector must deal only with your lawyer. Those who violate the FDCPA can be sued. (For more advice on bill collectors, see YOUR MONEY, page 321.)

"No-Interest" Financing

Many stores have adopted a sales come-on that encourages customers to buy merchandise—usually expensive furniture or appliances—with a store credit card and not pay interest for a period of, say, 90 to 180 days. Consumers sometimes do not realize that unless they pay the bill in full when it comes due, they will have to pay interest on it from the day of purchase, at rates which may be higher than for many bank cards—sometimes as high as 22 percent. Before succumbing to this pitch, check:

✔ *Price.* Shop around to be sure you are getting the best possible price, including interest, for the item in question.

✔ *Due dates.* Find out the exact date when full payment is due, and ask if you must make any installment payments during the interest-free period.

✔ *Interest and Penalties.* Know precisely what the interest rate will be on the bill if you fail to pay it in full by the due date. Also ask if a penalty will be imposed in addition.

✔ *Restrictions.* Ask if other conditions or restrictions are part of the deal.

✔ *Other financial obligations.* Scrutinize the application carefully. The Federal Truth in Lending Act requires that terms of special financing offers be included in advertising, sales contract, or store credit card agreements.

BUYING BIG-TICKET ITEMS

Consumers faced with baffling choices and clamorous advertising need solid information to make smart decisions and avoid buying traps.

The Real Cost of an Appliance

An appliance represents a sizable investment, and the temptation is to look for the best price when you buy. However, the real cost of an appliance over the years depends on how much energy it will consume. An energy-efficient appliance will save money in the long run by cutting down on your electricity or gas bill.

The government has determined that consumers have a right to know the energy cost of an appliance before they buy. Federal law now requires that EnergyGuide labels be placed on all new refrigerators, freezers, water heaters, dishwashers, clothes washers, room and central air conditioners, and heat pumps. (Since all dryers use approximately the same amount of energy, they are not required to carry a label.) The cost information from these EnergyGuides will help you calculate not only the energy cost for one year but how much an appliance will cost over its lifetime.

New federal efficiency standards have also aided the consumer. Refrigerators account for about 20 percent of the home electric bill because they run around the clock, so energy cost is a major factor. Since 1993, refrigerators must meet new federal energy-efficiency standards, using less than 1,000 kilowatt hours per year compared with 1,500 to 2,500 kilowatts on models of 10 or 15 years ago. Some models use as little as 650 kilowatts. These newer units can save as much as $15 per month on utility bills. Similar improvements have also been made on dishwashers.

Delivery and Installation Woes

Having an appliance installed properly is as important as choosing the right one. When you buy an appliance, be sure to find out whether the store will deliver and install it for you, whether there is a charge for this service, and whether the retailer guarantees the work. Ask for a sales contract that specifies delivery terms. Excessive delivery and installation charges can turn a bargain into a bad deal. Ask whether the store has insurance that will

cover any damage that may be done to your home during delivery or installation.

If you buy from a store that does not provide installation, you will most likely have to hire someone to do it. It is equally important to be sure that an independent plumber or electrician has liability insurance. If a problem, such as a plumbing leak, is caused by improper installation, the product warranty may not be valid and turning to the installer is your only recourse. Ask the service provider for the name of his insurance company, call to make sure he is covered, and call the Better Business Bureau to find out if any complaints have been filed on him or his company. (See also YOUR HOME AND COMMUNITY, page 40.)

Headaches arise when purchases do not arrive on the promised date or arrive damaged. You may have the right to cancel the contract if goods are not delivered by the date specified on the bill of sale. You also have the right to refuse delivery if merchandise does not arrive in perfect condition. Therefore, be sure to be at home to inspect goods when they arrive. Insist that the delivery people stay until you have made your inspection. (See also "Delivery Woes," page 412.)

OTHER PROBLEMS WITH APPLIANCES

If you have major problems with a faulty appliance and cannot get satisfaction from the dealer or the manufacturer, contact the Major Appliance Consumer Action Panel (MACAP) at (800) 621-0477. Sponsored by the Home Appliance Manufacturers, the Gas Appliance Manufacturers Association, and the National Retail Merchants Association, this mediation panel, whose members come from outside the appliance industry, will note the details of your problem and then go directly to a top-level executive at the retailer or manufacturer for an explanation or response. If the panel fails to get a response, it will make its own recommendation. MACAP claims that 90 percent of the legitimate complaints it handles are eventually resolved. However, it carefully adds that about half the complaints it receives are deemed to be unjustified.

Appliance Shopping Guidelines

Because appliances come with an ever-widening array of features, finding the best product for your needs at the best price requires research. Fortunately, there are unbiased ratings to guide consumers. Publications such as *Consumer Reports* and the *Consumer Guide* compare and rank almost every type of product for cost, performance, ease of using, and so on. Also included are repair

---

Service Contracts: A Good Buy?

When you buy an appliance, many stores will try to sell you a service contract in addition to the warranty. Often this is a waste of money because it duplicates much of the warranty coverage. Read the warranty carefully to see how long it lasts and exactly what it covers. Is it likely that the appliance will need repairs during the period covered? If so, how much will they cost? You may be better off paying for small repairs than buying a contract you will seldom use. Ask the following questions before purchasing a service contract:

✔ *The Basics.* What is the cost and length of the term offered in the contract, and what services and parts does it cover?

✔ *The Terms.* Is the cost of labor as well as necessary parts included in the contract?

✔ *The Service Provider.* Who provides service if needed, the dealer or an independent repair shop? If it is a repair shop, s it reliable? (Check the Better Business Bureau for any complaints.)

✔ *Transportation.* What are the provisions for getting large appliances to the repair shop? Who pays the cost of transporting a refrigerator, for instance?

✔ *Cancelation.* Do you get anything back if you later decide to cancel the service contract? Is there a penalty of any kind?

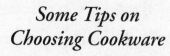
records, an important point for you to consider before you buy.

Still, appliances can put a big dent in your budget, and even after you have done your homework, you should proceed prudently. Here are some suggestions:

- **Recheck your space.** Be sure the appliance will fit into the available space with clearance for ventilation and servicing.
- **Reconsider convenience features.** Will a feature save you enough time or trouble to be worth the extra cost?
- **Compare warranties.** What is the duration of the warranty? Is the coverage full or limited? Is service provided in your home or at a service center? If the appliance needs servicing, who pays for pickup and delivery or shipping?
- **Choose a reliable dealer.** Lower prices may be false savings if the dealer does not stand behind his products.

Buying Furniture and Carpets

When you select furniture, you are creating surroundings that you will live with for many years. The old cliché is true: It pays to buy the best you can afford, since higher-quality products will look better and last longer than poorly made items, saving you money in the long run.

Furniture and rugs are major purchases, and you should plan carefully. Begin by making a floor plan of your room to scale on a piece of graph paper, then make paper cutouts of furniture—sofa, coffee table, chairs, dining room set—using the same scale. Try various arrangements and sizes in the available space. When you decide on dimensions—say, for a new coffee table—that seem right for the room, use them when you shop. Bring a ruler or a tape measure. If you see a piece of furniture you like, write down the measurements and check them out at home before you pull out your wallet.

When you compare prices, include credit terms and delivery charges, which can be substantial. If you find that you like a particular manufacturer, look in the Yellow Pages or in the back pages of home-decorating magazines to see if you can order directly from the manufacturer. Check the manufacturer's prices against those of local retailers to make sure you are getting a fair deal. When shopping for wood furniture, these terms will help you define better pieces:

- **Hardwood** refers to mahogany, walnut, maple, oak, cherry, birch, teak, and other high-quality, long-lasting woods. Less expensive softwoods, such as pine, cedar, and redwood, show dents and scratches more readily.

- **Veneer** means a thin layer of good hardwood has been bonded to a softwood base. Veneer is not as good as a solid wood piece.
- **Bonding** is the composition of several layers of low-quality inexpensive wood, such as plywood, and may be used under veneer in cheaper furniture.
- **Finish** determines the look of the wood. It may be clear, allowing natural color and grain to show through, or tinted to change the color or to resemble another wood.

When choosing upholstered furniture, check for good construction before considering fabric. Lift one end of the frame to see that it does not creak or wobble. Sit down and bounce a bit. If you hear creaks, the springs may be hitting the frame, a sign of cheap construction. Check the upholstery fabric label for cleaning instructions and information on whether it has been treated to resist stains.

CHOOSING CARPETING

Whatever style of carpeting you prefer, the most important factor in carpet quality is the density of the weave. The most expensive carpeting is made of wool, but more carpets today are created from synthetic fibers, many of which are attractive, durable, and economical.

To determine how much carpeting you will need, multiply the length of the room in feet by its width in feet, and divide that figure by nine to get the square yardage. Add 10 percent for room irregularities. To get the price, multiply the square yardage by the per-yard price of the carpeting. When you calculate price, don't forget to include the cost of padding and installation. By the way, don't skimp on the padding. Good padding can add years of wear to your rug or carpet.

DELIVERY PROBLEMS

The problems associated with the delivery of furniture and carpeting are legion. Special orders can arrive months late, wood pieces are delivered with scratches. The new armoire won't fit through your front door. Delivery men are shocked when you ask who will lay the 12-by-15-foot rug. To avoid these problems, make sure you shop at stores that stand behind their merchandise. (If you have doubt about a shop's reliability, check with the Better Business Bureau.) Anticipate delivery and installation, and get solutions in writing. Make sure a specific delivery date appears on the bill and do not accept a delivery until you have inspected it carefully. You should also clarify in advance who installs a rug or puts together an article of furniture as well as who will pay for this service. (See also "Delivery Woes," page 412.)

TIPS FOR BUYING ORIENTAL RUGS

Buying Oriental carpets can be not only a bewildering experience, but a risky one. The "rug world" is full of hucksters ready to take your money and unload a fake or inferior rug on you. If you want to buy an Oriental rug, here are some tips:

1. Do your homework. Don't buy an expensive rug without learning something about rugs. Read a book, go to museums, and ask rug dealers lots of questions. (Most dealers are reputable and enjoy talking about their carpets.)

2. Know carpet quality. Be able to identify the tightest weaves, the best wools, the relative values of various styles, the signs of good color, and other indicators of quality.

3. Avoid shady venues. Oriental rugs are often sold at "Going-Out-of-Business" shops, warehouse outlets, and trunk sales. These rugs are inferior. Don't buy them.

4. Learn how to bargain. As with home or car purchases, rug dealers expect you to make a counteroffer.

5. Understand the market. Just because a rug is an antique does not mean necessarily that it is valuable. Just because it is new does not mean it is worthless.

6. Be wary of auctions. Buyers who bid at legitimate auctions are usually experts. Don't compete against the experts.

Buying Electronic Equipment

Technological change and dealer competition force shoppers to learn before buying.

123..

Discount or Retail—Where to Shop?

Is it better to shop for electronic equipment in a retail specialty store or a discount store? In years past, consumers tended to view discount stores warily and to put their trust in their local retail dealers. Today, the lines are not so clear. Some discount chains hire experienced clerks, have liberal return policies, and offer strong servicing capabilities, while some high-priced retailers cannot afford to permit returns. Here are subjects you should explore wherever you decide to shop:

1. Delivery. Will the store deliver? How long will it take? Is there a delivery charge? What if the delivery is out of state?

2. Installation. Will the store install this equipment? Will you be charged for installation?

3. Returns. Will you be able to return products? Must merchandise be returned unopened or in its original box? Must it be returned within a certain time period?

4. Servicing. Does the store or chain provide servicing? Is servicing factory-guaranteed?

5. Warranty. How long is the warranty? Is it a full, limited, or extended warranty?

Making the Right Choices

When it comes to home entertainment, consumers have more choices than ever before. The selection of television sets, VCR's, stereo equipment, telephones, and computers can be confusing. Unfortunately, the selling climate in some stores makes things even more difficult. Many electronics and camera dealers are extremely competitive in their advertised prices but may give you a hard sell to upgrade to more expensive models once you are in the store. If you do not know what you need, you are an easy mark for a salesman hoping to increase his commission with a bigger sale.

It can be worth paying more if you can find a knowledgeable, reliable merchant who can guide you through the maze of multiplying options and technical terms and can help you to make sensible choices. Or, you can avoid paying for extras you do not need by doing some homework. Analyze how you will use your equipment and which of the available features will be valuable to you. For example, if you use a VCR mostly to show movies and only occasionally for taping, it makes little sense to pay more for a machine that can record many different programs over several weeks. Nor do you need a camera with an expensive set of lenses to take occasional snapshots.

GETTING THE BEST BUY

Once you are sure of the model and features you want, shop hard for the best price, comparing local advertising as well as discount mail-order catalogs and advertising in big-city newspapers. In many cases, electronics prices are negotiable. Some stores advertise that they will beat any price. If you present the competing ad, the merchant must make good on this claim as long as the advertised item is the same model with the same features as the one he stocks.

Repair records should be a serious consideration in deciding which brands to buy; these records can be found in consumer rating guides. Because electronic equipment is usually complicated to repair, good warranties are doubly important, and a dealer who stands behind his products should they not perform can be vital if you have a warranty problem. Choose

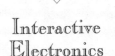

a company that has been around for some time and is likely to stay around.

It is generally true that reputable electronics manufacturers make remarkably similar products in the same price categories. If the TV sets, VCR's, or stereos are of equal quality, the only remaining basis for choice is the convenience of using the various features and controls.

BEWARE OF THE "GRAY MARKET"

"Gray market" merchandise is imported into the United States by someone other than the manufacturer's authorized U.S. outlet. There may not be anything wrong with the goods, but they come without the usual manufacturer's warranty. Sometimes there is an "international" warranty, which offers little help if you need local service. The retailer may tell you that your sales slip is your warranty—meaning that the shop, not the manufacturer, assumes responsibility for repairs—but if the store goes out of business, you are out of luck.

Prices are generally lower on gray-market goods because they have not come through regular channels, but they are a risky way to save, particularly if you are buying an expensive camera or electronic equipment. If you see prices that seem too good to be true, always ask whether the product comes with a U.S. warranty.

Repairing Electronic Gear

The availability of reliable repair service is a key consideration when you choose an electrical-appliance brand, particularly now that so many products are made in other countries, making it impractical to send items back to the manufacturer for repair.

Occasionally, manufacturers operate their own service repair centers. More commonly, they authorize independent repair shops to service their products, using approved test equipment and replacement parts. Technicians in these shops sometimes have had special training by the manufacturer; sometimes they have not. Usually, buyers are required to use an authorized center during the warranty period.

Addresses of authorized service centers are generally included in the warranty, product instructions, or service contact. If not, call the dealer or the manufacturer directly for names. If you have a choice between a product whose manufacturer uses a local repair service and one that requires mailing the product to the manufacturer at your own expense, the product with a local service center is a better choice.

Service-center ads in the Yellow Pages showing the logo or

Interactive Electronics

Interactive technology, which is technology that allows the user to communicate directly with a screen or other piece of equipment, is opening up new ways of seeing, hearing, learning—and buying.

In the past, for example, to order goods advertised on television or to see a pay-per-view movie, you needed to make a phone call. Soon you will be able to make such choices simply by using television controls or touching the screen.

A type of interactive technology that is fast becoming essential in schools, libraries, and homes is the CD-ROM. This is a compact disc—similar to the familiar audio discs—on which have been stored huge amounts of information in a "read-only memory" mode, which means, in brief, that the information on it can be read but not changed.

A CD-ROM disc may contain an entire encyclopedia or dictionary, and the user need only type a few letters or numbers to call up a selection on a screen. Since CD-ROMs have audio as well as video capability, the information you access can have several dimensions. For example, if you look up "Beethoven" on a CD-ROM encyclopedia, you may be able not only to read about the composer but to also see and hear orchestras playing his music.

If you are buying a new computer, it would be smart to get one with a CD-ROM drive, or one with enough expansion room to allow for its addition.

Buying Home-Entertainment Electronics

When you buy audio and visual equipment, it makes sense to select products that can be upgraded to incorporate the latest—or the next—round of improvements. Here are tips and facts to consider when you are buying home-entertainment equipment:

TELEVISION SETS

• **Sound.** Stereo models generally produce good picture and sound quality.

• **Inputs and outputs.** If you want to use a stereo, VCR, cable, laser disc player, or video camera, be sure your TV has video and audio input jacks, an audio output jack, and a coaxial cable jack.

• **Size of screen.** A set with a 19- or 20-inch screen (measured diagonally) is large enough for the family to watch without dominating the room. If you are buying a 35-to 40-inch set, note that the recommended viewing distance (about four times screen height) may be up to 13 feet.

VCR'S

• **Heads.** The most basic videocassette recorder (VCR) has a two-head player and monophonic sound, which will be fine for occasional recording. Four-head models with high-fidelity stereos improve both picture and sound quality. ("Heads" contain sensing devices used in recording.)

• **Other features.** Ease of recording is a key factor in comparing VCR's. Some recorders now have VCR Plus—which is a recording system by which you enter a code found next to the television listings and the VCR is automatically set.

• **Tapes.** Little difference in quality has been found between brand-name or high-grade licensed tapes and ordinary licensed tapes. To be safe, however, don't buy unlicensed tapes; the quality may be poor and they may damage the VCR.

STEREOS

• **Receiver.** This is the heart of the system. Price depends on the power it can deliver to provide sound. The power is expressed in watts; the higher the number, the stronger the signal, and hence the louder the sound without forgoing quality. Twenty to thirty watts per channel is generally adequate, but go higher if you like your music loud or you have a large space.

• **Speakers.** The quality of your speakers determines the quality of your sound. The best speakers deliver both deep bass and high notes clearly and distinctly. However, all speakers combine sounds differently. Listen to several to decide which ones you prefer.

• **Walkabout stereos.** For quality sound with portable radios, compact disks, or tape players, a unit with a snug belt clip is preferable to a shoulder strap, which may bounce around.

• **Compact disc (CD) player.** CD players read music by a laser beam that translates digital information stored on a durable plastic disc. Because nearly every model will provide high-quality sound (subject to the quality of the speakers), the choice between models generally comes down to the features offered, such as a remote control, multi-disc play capability, and programmability.

CAMERAS

• **Lenses.** A 35mm lens provides larger negatives and thus better quality enlargements than 110 models. The greater the versatility of the lens focus, the more expensive the camera. A 35mm to 70mm zoom capability takes quality close-ups and panoramic shots. A 35mm to 105mm lens takes a better-quality distance photo. More expensive cameras can be outfitted with interchangeable lenses, a feature not necessary for a casual photographer.

• **Features.** Cameras today combine many automatic features in increasingly compact models, including auto focus, auto flash, and automatic exposure control and shutter speed. These features enable even beginning photographers to get excellent results.

• **Convenience cameras.** These include Polaroid and disposable cameras. Photo quality may not be as good as with a 35mm camera, but with Polaroids the results are immediate and disposables offer convenience and affordability.

VIDEO CAMERAS

• **Features.** Look for a video camera that has a motorized zoom lens with 6:1 ratio. Preferably, the model should allow for automatic adjustment of the balance of the picture and both automatic and manual adjustment of focus and lens opening. The viewfinder should be designed for use with either automatic or manual adjustment.

• **Size.** Larger models are more cumbersome, but because they rest on the shoulder they are easier to hold steady. Hand-held cameras are more portable, but more difficult to focus..

trademark of an appliance do not necessarily indicate that the service center is authorized by the manufacturer. Even though the repair shop may provide adequate repair service, if you use anything other than an authorized center while the product is under warranty, you will have to pay for service and you may void your warranty.

If you have a serious complaint about a television set, a radio, stereo equipment, or a tape recorder and cannot resolve the problem with the dealer or maker, contact the Electronics Industries Association, which can mediate on your behalf. The EIA can be reached at (202) 457-4900.

Telephone Equipment

Now that telephones are readily available in stores, it makes little sense to pay a monthly rental fee to the telephone company. Federal Communications Commission (FCC) decisions in recent years give you the right to buy and use as many telephones as you wish for your home, and many states allow you to do your own inside wiring and installation of extension hookups or to hire someone other than the telephone company to do it for you. Check the front pages of your telephone directory for local regulations. Special kits and guides are available in retail stores.

A basic telephone is quite inexpensive, but there are great variations in quality. Choose a reputable manufacturer who is likely to be in business to take care of problems, and look for the best warranty, two years rather than one. Choose a phone that seems sturdily constructed, and a brand with service and replacement parts available locally.

Handy cordless telephones use a special radio channel instead of a cord for transmitting sound between the telephone base and the handset. The FCC allows 10 channels in the frequency range used by cordless phones. Phones using only one or two of these channels will not give sound as clear as that of a 10-channel model, which lets you switch among the channels until you find the best static-free connection.

TELEPHONES TO GO

Cellular telephones are more powerful portable phones. Some are called "mobile units" because they can be permanently installed in a car or boat. Others, referred to as "portable models," may be carried around in a pocket, purse, or briefcase. These phones are called "cellular" because geographic areas are divided into "cells" by the telephone company, each with its own mobile-telephone switching office (MTSO). When you dial, your call goes to the nearest MTSO, which routes it into

A Few Facts About Fax Machines

The word *fax* is an abbreviation for "facsimile machine," a device that transmits and reproduces written messages using telephone lines. Fax machines, a virtual necessity for any office, are becoming commonplace in the home as well. Here are some fax features to consider:

✔ *Telephone lines.* If you do not expect to use a fax constantly, you need not install a separate telephone line. Many models can switch from phone to fax with the touch of a button. Others make the switch automatically when the telephone detects a fax signal.

✔ *Paper.* Most home facsimile machines use rolls of heat-sensitive paper, which curls up and may be hard to write on. Machines using plain paper are available at ever lower prices, although their maintenance may be costly.

✔ *Feeder.* An automatic document feeder allows you to stack pages for the machine to send consecutively. This saves you the trouble of feeding each page separately.

✔ *Features.* Many units come with a telephone handset for use as a phone, and some include an answering machine, so that a caller can either leave a message or send a fax. If you are considering one of these combination units, be sure all of the parts do not become unusable if one part fails.

the conventional phone system. As you move from one cell to another, you are switched automatically to the service in the new area.

When you buy a cellular phone, you must also pay an installation fee, an activation fee, a monthly charge, and a usage charge for each minute you use the phone. Often carriers offer free telephones, installation, or activation to encourage people to sign up, because they profit primarily from usage charges, which can be quite high. Be sure to ask about any discounts or special offers when you compare carriers.

One problem that has emerged in relation to cellular phones is the theft of telephone numbers. Electronically skilled criminals are able to intercept the code numbers that identify cellular phones belonging to other users, and then make calls that are billed to those owners. Cellular-phone manufacturers hope to develop foolproof digital precautionary devices, or blocks, to prevent this kind of theft. Meantime, telephone companies are trying to crack down on the cellular phone crooks.

TELEPHONE ANSWERING MACHINES

Tape recorders have been the standard way to record outgoing and incoming messages on home answering machines, but newer digital machines use microchips that record messages in their memory, allowing for faster retrieval and less cumbersome operation. Useful features to look for in answering machines include:

- **Unlimited message and announcement lengths.** This feature allows you to record a lengthy greeting and to record the caller's complete message no matter how long it runs.
- **Time and date stamp.** This allows the machine to record the time when each message comes in.
- **Automatic interrupt.** Machines with this feature stop the recorded message when you pick up the phone—handy if you forget to turn off the machine when you come home or if you like to screen your calls.

Buying Computers

You can save a considerable amount of money buying a new computer if you live without the very latest electronic twists. Technological innovations appear so rapidly and regularly that models considered the latest thing only last year can be had for bargain prices this year. In this sense, buying a computer is like buying a car.

Even so, a computer is a major purchase, and making a selection can be intimidating. Before you shop, it is a good idea to

---

Getting the Best Help With Computer Software

Computer manufacturers' warranties cover only the hardware, and software manufacturers' warranties go into effect only if the software fails to operate at all, which hardly ever happens.

Nevertheless, problems with software are more common than troubles with hardware, usually because of users' lack of expertise. Therefore, before you buy a software program, make sure that the software manufacturer has a toll-free customer-support number available, not just during weekdays and work hours, but also in the evening and on weekends, when you might be using the computer at home.

It is a good idea to ask salespeople, friends, and co-workers about their experiences with various software support lines, since some are more helpful than others. Some manufacturers have a staff of support personnel who will stay on the line with you and give you patient step-by-step instructions for solving your problem. Unfortunately, many software companies are beginning to charge for telephone support, so be sure to ask.

Also don't fail to send back the registration card to qualify for support service, because the computer support person will ask for your reference number before helping you. (This is one way manufacturers discourage people from copying programs instead of buying them.)

read a book for beginners, take a class to learn the basics of what a computer can do for you, and develop a clear understanding of why you believe that you need a computer. If you want simply to "organize your life" or to be "entertained," you may be disappointed.

HARDWARE AND SOFTWARE

The mechanical parts of a computer are known as the "hardware" and include the drive (which is the heart of the computer), the keyboard, and the screen. In order to operate the computer, you also need to become familiar with computer "software." Software is the information and materials (usually stored digitally on computer disks), or "program" that enable the machine to perform specific tasks. There are programs for word processing, making spread sheets, balancing your checkbook, printing labels, playing games, and much more. Learn which programs will be useful to you, since you need to choose a computer with enough power, RAM (random access memory, or storage), and other capabilities in order to to run them. The packaging for each software product should tell you how much hardware memory you need to run it. If it does not, ask the salesperson before you buy.

Be sure that all the hardware inside the computer is under a legitimate warranty. The hard drive, for example, may have a separate warranty if it is not made by the same manufacturer as the rest of the system. An unscrupulous dealer could substitute cheaper parts from the gray market, and you would not know until it was too late. Ask for the registration serial number for the hard drive.

Watch out for come-on ads with unusually low prices, such as ones that say "monitor optional" in tiny print. A computer is useless without a monitor, or screen, which should be figured into all prices. The monitor is already attached to laptop and notebook computers.

VALUE-ADDED RESELLERS

Computer users with specialized needs, such as people with small businesses, may find it worth the slightly higher cost of dealing with a value-added reseller (VAR). The term "reseller" does not refer to the reselling of used equipment; it refers to someone who sells products from one particular producer or brand of computer. VAR's operate from an office rather than a store and will help you choose and set up a personalized system and select the software that meets your needs. They usually offer a support system, which lasts for the length of the warranty. To find a VAR in your area, call the customer service department of the manufacturer of the type of computer you are interested in buying.

Questions to Ask in a Computer Store

When shopping for a computer, you should be able to ask intelligent questions about the hardware you are looking at—and to understand the answers:

✔ *Power.* Ask if the computer has a powerful microprocessor. For example, a Pentium processor is more powerful than a 486. Will the machine you are looking at suit your needs for the next few years?

✔ *Speed.* How fast is the machine? Computer speed is measured in "MHz", or megahertz. A 50-MHz processor is faster than 25-MHz processor.

✔ *Hard-disk storage.* How much overall storage for data is available on the hard disk? It is measured in megabytes. How much will you need for your purposes?

✔ *RAM.* "Random access memory," also measured in megabytes, is the storage space available for running software. The minimum for running most new software is four, and if you want to run CD-ROMs you will need eight.

✔ *Expansion.* How many expansion slots are there? Is there room to add more RAM, more storage space to the hard disk, an internal modem, or a CD-ROM player?

✔ *Service.* Is there a responsive service number? Is there is a fee? If so, how much is it?

BUYING CLOTHING

Be sure you know a store's policy about giving refunds or taking back merchandise, in case you decide you bought the wrong overcoat.

Comparing Stores

Clothing can be bought in many different kinds of stores—from discount outlets to mom-and-pop shops, from large department stores to exclusive boutiques. At times, the same manufacturer's labels might be found in all of those places. But you may also find a substantial difference in the kind of merchandise, the service, and the refund policies even within the same category of store.

Wherever you shop, you have the right to expect courtesy. Look for the store that gives you the best service as well as the best merchandise for your money. Establishments that take pride in their service are liberal about accepting returns, figuring that they will make up the difference in customer satisfaction. They provide comfortable dressing rooms and have adequate personnel to help you find what you are looking for.

If you are willing to give up service to save money, be sure you are actually getting more value for your dollar. A well-known brand name in a discount store does not always mean a bargain. Many manufacturers have several lines and sell their cheaper lines to one outlet, their quality clothing to another. To compare prices realistically, you must also compare the fabric and workmanship that goes into each garment.

In any store, you have the right to know its policy regarding refunds and exchanges before you buy. In many states, the refund policy must be posted. At the very least, it should be explained to you before you pay and should be presented clearly on the sales slip. If it is not, ask the salesperson to put it in writing on your receipt. As a safeguard, save all tags and sales receipts until you have worn and cleaned the garment.

Ways to Save

Canny shoppers can find many ways to save on clothing besides simply keeping an eye on the price tag. First of all, the better a garment is made, the better it will look and the longer it will last, so paying attention to signs of quality construction saves money in the long run. Be sure to read care labels carefully, too, since maintaining clothes that can only be dry-cleaned adds considerably to their overall cost:

- **Take advantage of seasonal sales.** When stores need to make room for the new season's merchandise, the markdowns can be significant. Late summer is the best time to shop for bathing suits or short-sleeved shirts; the biggest price reductions on overcoats come at winter's end.

- **Look for seconds.** Socks, T-shirts, and underwear from major manufacturers are often half price if they have a slight snag or a missewn label that will never be seen.

- **Pay with cash.** If a store accepts credit cards, but you pay with cash, ask for a percentage off the purchase price. Stores pay about 5 percent to credit card companies; some may be willing to pass that savings on to you.

- **Visit clearance centers and once-a-year clearance sales.** Many better department stores have clearance centers or sales where they sell clothing that did not move fast enough in the store. These are not necessarily leftovers—sometimes the buyer simply overordered; sometimes certain sizes did not sell. Clearances may cut prices as much as 75 percent on high-quality merchandise.

- **Never buy something just because it is cheap.** If you feel that a garment does not suit you, or if it does not quite fit, or if it does not match anything else in your wardrobe, the chances are you won't wear it. And clothing that stays in the closet is never a good buy.

All that glitters is not gold.

WILLIAM SHAKESPEARE
The Merchant of Venice

Be Wary Buying Fine Jewelry and Furs

Consumers are at the mercy of merchants when buying jewelry and furs. Only an experienced eye can judge the quality of gems, or gold jewelry, or the authenticity of furs. Your first rule should be to deal only with reputable merchants. In addition, follow the guidelines below:

- **Get an appraiser.** The only way to be absolutely sure you are getting your money's worth on an expensive purchase is by having it evaluated by an independent appraiser. Don't rely on a recommendation by a jeweler or furrier. If the seller is dishonest, chances are he will send you to a dishonest accomplice.

- **Choose a member of the American Society of Appraisers.** Members must have earned degrees from accredited institutions, have five years of experience, meet ethical standards, and have a reaccreditation exam every five years. The organization maintains a directory of certified professionals and their area of expertise. For the name and address of an appraiser in your locality, write or call the American Society of Appraisers (ASA), 535 Herndon Parkway, Suite 150, Herndon, Va., 22070, (703) 478-2228.

- **Get a second opinion.** Even if your appraiser comes well recommended, ask for other references from insurance companies, antique shops, or auction houses that have used her services.

- **If you are misled.** If you discover you have been misled, either by a merchant or an appraiser, you can sue for intentional misrepresentation or fraud. You should file a complaint with the local BBB and department of consumer affairs. In cases involving jewelry, you should also contact the FTC, which regulates the jewelry industry.

BUYING FOR CHILDREN

Safety comes first when shopping for youngsters. Consumers need to check government guidelines and keep up with recalls on toys and equipment.

Car Seats for Different Ages

A child's car seat is one of the most important items you will buy as a parent. Today, car seats are required to conform to federal motor vehicle safety standards, but it is up to the parents to see that the seat is used properly. According to the safety standards, infants under 20 pounds should be belted in the seat in a reclining position, facing the rear of the car. Older children should sit upright and face forward. In most states, use of car seats is mandatory by law.

Another important safety consideration is the harness. It must offer growth adjustments through the shoulder and crotch to accommodate the changing size of the child, from newborn to toddler.

Also take special care to note whether the belt or harness is easy to latch and the straps are easy to adjust. If you have a wriggling, uncooperative baby or toddler to strap in, belts that adjust automatically are a handy convenience.

The most practical car seats convert from recliners to upright seats, and can be used from infancy until a child weighs about 40 pounds. Sometimes the best seats are the most expensive, but safe car seats can be a life-or-death investment.

Buying for Babies

Safety first is always the rule when buying baby equipment. Strict federal regulations apply to manufacturers of cribs, strollers, car seats, high chairs, and other products for infants and small children. Additional voluntary standards have been set by the Juvenile Products Manufacturers Association. When you shop, always look for the seals indicating that a product meets the mandatory federal requirements. Then, do some testing on your own:

- Run your hand over any surface that a baby is likely to touch. Is it rough? Will it become too hot if exposed to the sun?
- Inspect all hinges, springs, and moving parts. Is there anything to catch, scratch, or pinch small fingers or toes?
- Check for stability in any product designed to hold a child. Could a baby unlatch or wiggle out of the seat or harness?
- Strollers should be stable and have solid wheels that maneuver easily, comfortable seats, and secure safety belts.

IS THAT CRIB SAFE?

Because baby cribs used to be a major cause of infant accidents, government safety rules were instituted in the 1970's. They regulate the space between slats and crib height, so that an infant's legs, arms, or head cannot be caught between slats, and an infant will not fall out because the sides are too low.

Still, an occasional unsafe crib may slip by, or you may be getting one secondhand, so you should know what to look for. Slats more than two inches apart can be dangerous. Crib mattresses should be firm and fit tightly, with no spaces where hands or feet could get caught. If two adult fingers can fit between the mattress and the frame, choose another mattress. Avoid decorative knobs or corner posts that could catch a garment and entangle a child climbing out of the crib. Cute panel cutouts are potential traps for small limbs.

RECALLS ON PRODUCTS FOR CHILDREN

The U.S. Consumer Product Safety Commission (CPSC) evaluates, issues recalls, and obtains corrective action on children's products that present potential safety hazards, such as cloth-

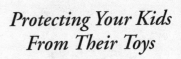

ing, sporting equipment, and juvenile furniture. The Child Safety Protection Act was passed in 1995, requiring manufacturers to label toys that may pose choking hazards. You can learn more about current laws, recalls, product tips, and safety by phoning the toll-free CPSC hotline, (800) 638-CPSC.

Selecting Safe Toys

The CPSC also sets minimum safety standards for toys, and issues hundreds of safety warnings and product recalls every year. Most American manufacturers also adhere to voluntary safety standards developed by the Toy Manufacturers of America, the industry trade association, in conjunction with the CPSC. Even so, products may be sold before problems are discovered, and hospital emergency rooms treat thousands of children each year for toy-related injuries. It remains up to parents to be alert when they select toys. Here are guidelines to help you avoid dangerous toys:

- Watch carefully for toys with small parts that can come off and be swallowed. For example, check for sturdy, securely fastened features on stuffed animals and cloth dolls. Toys with points or sharp edges are also taboo.
- Be sure rubber rattles and teething toys are too large to fit all the way into a baby's mouth, even when compressed.
- Be guided by age recommendations on the labels, which are based on safety considerations as well as age appeal. Toys suitable for older children, like games with small pieces, can be hazardous for younger children.
- Don't give toys with long strings, straps or cords that hang around the neck to infants or very young children. Avoid toys with points or sharp edges.
- Look for the word *nontoxic* on painted toys, *flame retardant* or *flame resistant* on fabrics, and *machine* or *surface washable* on stuffed and cloth toys.
- Electrical toys should have a seal saying "UL approved," indicating inspection by the Underwriters Laboratory.

Bikes, Blades, and Skis

Bicycles, skates, skis, and other sporting equipment can be dangerous if they are not suited to a child's size. Because sports equipment is expensive, the tendency is to buy items that are too large, assuming a child will grow into them. Doing so may force a youngster to deal with equipment he cannot properly control. Bicycle

---

Protecting Your Kids From Their Toys

Government regulation of the toys sold in stores cannot entirely prevent accidents at home. These steps are recommended by the Consumer Product Safety Commission to keep children from injury:

✔ *Avoid strings and cords.* Never hang toys with long strings across cribs or playpens. They are particularly dangerous when infants are learning to pull themselves up.

✔ *Be careful with small objects.* Rattles, squeeze toys, and teethers should be taken out of a crib when a baby is sleeping to prevent choking.

✔ *Teach safety.* When a child is old enough to understand, explain how a toy is to be used and any possible dangers from its misuse.

✔ *Be neat.* Teach children to put their toys away on shelves or in a chest to prevent trips and falls.

✔ *Check toy chests.* Children have been seriously hurt when the lids of their toy chests have fallen on their heads or necks. Add a spring-loaded lid support to avoid accidents.

✔ *Examine toys periodically.* Watch out for sharp edges or points that may have developed. Repair broken toys and throw away the ones that cannot be fixed.

Whether you are buying a bike helmet for a child or an adult, a snug, proper fit is essential to ensure maximum protection. Bicycle helmets are required by law for cyclists in many localities. Check for a good fit by following these guidelines:

1. Size. Buy the smallest size you can use comfortably. Parents sometimes buy "larger" articles for children hoping clothing will last longer. This thinking should never be applied to safety helmets.

2. Helmet pads. Pads should touch your head at the crown, sides, front, and back. When you put the helmet on, try to push it forward, backward, and to the sides. If it moves enough to create a space between your head and the pads, get thicker pads. If it is still loose, choose a smaller size. Also, helmets with sizing pads can be adjusted for better fit.

3. Chin strap. When the chin strap is buckled, the helmet should not move when you shake your head or push the helmet backward or forward. The chin strap should feel tight when you open your mouth.

4. Back strap. This should lie straight and taut, just below the ears. Straps should meet in front just below the jaw and in front of the ears.

seats and handlebars can be adjusted as children grow, but the bicycle frame must be appropriate for you child's size. A bicycle that is too big will be hard to mount and dismount. Never buy a bike without taking the child with you. The handlebars and seat must be adjusted according to the rider's height; toes should be able to reach the ground for balance.

Of the estimated 500,000 annual emergency-room visits related to biking accidents, 80 percent involve head trauma. Proper use of bicycle safety helmets reduces the risk of such injury by 85 percent. Many states and some cities now require children or all riders to wear bike helmets. Look for the seal of approval by the American National Standards Institute (ANSI) or the Snell Memorial Foundation, indicating that the helmet has met or exceeded strict testing standards.

FOR SAFE SKATING

Helmets are equally important for the growing number of children who wear roller skates, sometimes known as Roller Blades. Protective pads for knees and arms are also a necessary safeguard. Boots that are too large will not give proper ankle support, and the skates will be hard to control. Have your child wear athletic socks when you buy skates to be sure the skates allow enough room to fit over the sock. Other in-line skate recommendations include:

- The brake on the rear of the boot should be made of hard rubber. If it is too soft, the child will not be able to control a quick stop. Also make sure it is not too small or too high.
- The frame attaching the wheels to the boot should be strong and rigid. If you can twist it, it could break.
- Choose softer wheels if the skates will be used on the sidewalk. They rebound from shocks and grip the surface better. Hard wheels are suited for indoor rinks.

CHOOSING SKI EQUIPMENT

The proper fit of ski boots is essential for safe skiing. Boots should be tried on with the insulated socks that will be worn on the slopes. Wearing two pairs of socks to fill out the boot is never a safe practice. Skis and poles must also be the proper length. When the skis are held upright, their tips should be no higher than the child's extended arm. Poles must not be too long to plant easily for a turn.

Buying skis and other sports equipment at flea markets and garage sales is an economical way to fit growing children with the correct gear each year. If you buy used equipment, always have it inspected and serviced by a reliable dealer.

SMART SUPERMARKET SHOPPING

You have the right to true measurements, honest labels, and fair guidance.

Laws at Work in the Supermarket

Americans visit supermarkets more often than any other kind of retail establishment. It has been estimated that a shopper spends an average of $30 on a typical trip to the supermarket, and the average weekly grocery bill is around $80. That adds up to a lot of money over the year, and enterprising grocers have stocked their stores in a way to tempt you to spend even more.

Fortunately, dozens of federal and local agencies and federal laws and regulations work to protect consumers. The U.S. Department of Agriculture (USDA) and the Food and Drug Administration (FDA) mandate regulations dealing with the labeling, advertising, production, and content of food. Food labels must indicate the weight inside and all ingredients, in descending order of amount. For example if sugar is the first ingredient listed, you know that the largest percentage (or the primary ingredient) of the food is sugar.

Meat, eggs, and poultry are subject to inspection by the USDA before they are marketed. The National Marine Fisheries Service grades fish products, and the FDA grades milk products, but grading labels are not standardized. The best chickens and milk are Grade A, but the best butter and eggs are Grade AA. Beef is marked prime, choice, or good, in a haphazard system. Ask your butcher or supermarket manager. to explain the different terminologies

LOCAL REGULATIONS

Many state and local regulations require stores to clearly price and label goods. Local offices of weights and measures can be very aggressive in ensuring the accuracy of the weights and measures of many commodities, including food, medicine, and gasoline. Among the most common regulations are these:

- Stores must truthfully describe advertised specials and make them available in a reasonable quantity or offer a rain check if they go out of stock.
- Perishable foods such as eggs, cottage cheese, bread, and cakes must have the last recommended date of sale or of use printed on the package.

Can You Trust the Scanner?

Most large stores have installed electronic scanners at the cash registers. Prices come from a central database that quickly records weekly price changes on thousands of items in each store. Since the advent of scanners, many stores have stopped putting price tags on individual items, and only a few states and cities still have laws that require them to do so. Instead, many stores use shelf tags to give prices.

Scanners can and do make mistakes, usually not in your favor. Often the error is an honest one. The new price of an item on special may not have been entered, and you may be charged the regular price. But dishonest merchants can deliberately overcharge through the scanner if you are not careful.

If a store does not put price stickers on items, jot down prices from the shelves as you put items into your basket. At the checkout, makes sure to watch as items are put through the scanner. Put the items on special at the front; these are the ones most likely to be incorrect. If you spot an incorrect price at the checkout, your store's policy will probably be to correct the error and give you a refund.

- Some areas require stores to reveal to customers when canned, bottled, or frozen items should be removed from the shelf.
- Scales and digital readouts at the checkout counter must be in clear view of the buyer.
- Eggs must be marked with their grade, weight, and size, and the labels on ground meat must say what kind of meat the package contains.

In general, if you find food that is spoiled or short-weighted, take it to the manager at once. If you discover the problem after you get home, take it back to the store. You are entitled to a refund. If you find a recurring problem in a particular store, report the store to the agency responsible for regulating markets: the office of consumer affairs, state or local department of weights and measures, or local department of health.

*The buyer needs a hundred eyes,
the seller not one.*

GEORGE HERBERT

Jacula Prudentum
1651

Understanding Unit Pricing

Unit pricing is intended to help the consumer compare prices by weight or measure—by the pound, ounce, or quart—rather than depending on the size of the container, which may be deceptive. Often unit-pricing labels become confusing because they are placed on the shelf rather than the package, and they are not always lined up beneath the correct product. If you want to

How to Read a Nutrition Label

Nutrition Facts Labels are required on all processed food products to give you the information you need to choose a healthier diet. The labels allow you to compare foods quickly; however, they also require some interpretation. Here are some guidelines:

• **Calories and nutrients.** Calories per serving and serving size are the first references. Also included is the number of calories that come from fat. Next, the amounts of total fat, saturated fat, carbohydrates, protein, sugars, cholesterol, fiber, sodium, vitamins, and minerals are listed. These are expressed as a percentage of the U.S. recommended dietary allowance (RDA) in each serving.

• **Percentages.** The percentages expressed on the chart are based on a 2,000-calorie diet. If you consume more or less, you will be getting a higher or lower percentage of the nutrients from each food. The serving size is key: Check the size of the portions you generally use to see if they match the serving size given on the chart. Serving sizes are standardized, but they may well be smaller than what you would normally eat.

• **Vague terms.** Nutrition labels are subject to regulations that limit diet claims, but terms like "low fat," "fat free," and "light" are permitted. Foods with less than five percent of the 65-gram RDA can be labeled "low fat." To be "97 percent fat-free," a product's fat level may not exceed three grams per serving. No standard definition for "light" has been established, so read the label carefully to be sure the product actually has less fat or fewer calories than similar foods. Finally, check the ingredients listing. You may be surprised to discover that a "low-fat" food is incidentally high in sugar and salt.

accurately compare two products of different weights, bring a small calculator along when you shop. To get each unit price, simply divide the product price by the weight in the package.

Ways to Save in the Supermarket

Y ou can win big savings in the supermarket by becoming a more savvy shopper. For example, always sign up for frequent-shopper programs when they are offered. The card not only entitles you to specials unavailable to the general public, but when your card goes through the scanner, you are often given the week's special prices without having to present coupons.

Stock up when there are sales on nonperishable items such as bottled and canned goods or paper products that can be stored in a closet or basement. Apples, oranges, carrots, potatoes, and onions are generally less expensive when they come already bagged. Use the customers' scale to weigh the bags, and choose the heaviest ones to get the most for your money.

Buy the store's own label instead of brand-name products. Sugar, flour, salt, white vinegar, ammonia, and bleach are identical no matter what name is on the package. Other products vary in taste, but it is always worth your own taste test to decide whether you need to pay more. Store-label ketchup, mayonnaise, sauces, cold cereals, and coffee may be half the price of the name brands. Also worth trying are store-label cat litter, dog food, foil, laundry detergent, and dishwashing liquid.

Don't buy nonfood items in the supermarket. Light bulbs, toothpaste, toiletries, and stationery can usually be found for less elsewhere.

MAKING THE MOST OF COUPONS

A time-tested way to save is using manufacturers' and store coupons. You can save $5 or more on every $100 you spend by taking advantage of coupons found in magazines or with the Sunday newspaper. Some grocery chains have machines in the store that issue coupons instantly for products being promoted. Save even more by using coupons when the item you want is already on special and by watching for periodic double-coupon promotions.

As you shop, look for manufacturers' rebates offered for mailing a form that comes packed with the product. Sometimes these are good for coupons worth the entire price of the item.

A sure technique for regular saving is to pick up a grocery flyer before you shop. Plan your menus regularly around the items that are on sale with or without store coupons, and you will save every week.

Does Your Supermarket Measure Up?

The basic information you need to get the most for your money should be readily available in the supermarket. Check to see how your market compares.

✔ *Scales.* Are scales provided so that you can weigh your fruits and vegetables yourself?

✔ *Prices.* Are unit prices posted under the items they are describing? Can you easily read the name of the product? Are the items themselves marked with price tags?

✔ *Perishables.* Are perishable foods such as milk and juice dated to tell you when they are no longer saleable? Are berries and tomatoes packaged so that you can clearly see the bottom layer?

✔ *Eggs.* Are egg cartons marked with grade and size?

✔ *Meat.* Are meat packages clearly labeled? For example, does the label tell you whether the rib bone is included in the weight of a chicken breast?

✔ *Itemization.* Does the sales receipt itemize as well as spell out your purchases so that you can compare each item with the price charged?

✔ *Rain checks.* Does the supermarket give you another chance when the weekly specials are sold out?

SHOPPING FOR HEALTH AND BEAUTY PRODUCTS

Strict labeling rules help protect buyers of drugs and cosmetics.

Sunglasses in the Spotlight

Sunglasses can cost $6 or $160—so what is the difference? Mostly it is cosmetic. While eye doctors agree that sunglasses can protect the long-term health of your eyes, they stress that mirrored or darker lenses mean little.

The important consideration is whether glasses filter out short-wavelength ultraviolet (UV) radiation, which may damage the eyes. The American Academy of Ophthalmology recommends sunglasses that block at least 99 percent of UV rays. These do not have to be expensive: A recent study found that on average, the best sunglasses for your eyes cost about $1.50 more than the worst. All sunglasses must meet impact standards set by the FDA.

Claims of blocking infrared rays mean little, as research has not shown a close connection between these rays and eye disease. The darkness of the lens has nothing to do with its capacity to block UV light.

Polarized lenses cut reflected glare and are useful for driving, but polarization itself does not affect UV-light absorption. But many polarized lenses are now made so as to be UV blockers as well.

Over-the-Counter Safety

All drugs, whether sold by prescription or off the shelf, can be dangerous. Taken in excess, in the wrong combinations, or under unusual conditions, even the most ordinary medicine can turn deadly. That is why Food and Drug Administration regulations require the labels of over-the-counter drugs to state all ingredients, the recommended dosage, proper storage conditions, the date after which the contents may become spoiled or ineffective, and extensive warnings about any possible side effects.

Manufacturers are legally responsible for any claims about the content of their products and what they can do for or to you. The label can be considered a contract between you and the manufacturer, and if it misstates the facts, you may have a legal claim against the manufacturer.

SAFE SAVINGS

These regulations enable you to safely save on many over-the-counter products, from aspirin to eyedrops, by choosing the store brand over a "name" brand. As long as labels list the same active ingredients in the same amounts, you can feel confident that the products are equally effective. Savings can be dramatic if you choose generic or store brands of nonprescription drugs such as ibuprofen. The same regulations apply to prescription drugs (See also "Generic Prescription Savings," page 443).

Once products are on the shelves, the FDA depends on consumers themselves to sound the alarm on problems that may develop. Any time you suspect that products may be spoiled or unsafe, you should report them immediately to your local consumer-protection agency and to the nearest field office of the FDA. If you suffer an injury from a drug or other product, particularly if there was no clear warning about the danger, you may have a legal claim against the manufacturer or seller. Contact an attorney for advice.

GLASSES OFF THE RACK

Among the items commonly found in drugstores today are reading glasses, sold at a fraction of the cost of prescription glasses. The American Academy of Ophthalmology has found these glasses acceptable and safe for people whose only problem is the loss of focusing ability, a condition known as "presbyopia", which is common after age 40. For more complicated corrections, you should see an eye doctor.

Buying Cosmetics

Under the U.S. Food, Drug, and Cosmetic Act of 1938, cosmetics are defined as any articles other than soap that are applied to the human body for cleansing or beautifying. The long list includes skin-care products, shampoo, deodorants, shaving products, bath oils, baby products—even toothpaste and mouthwashes.

Unlike drugs, cosmetics do not need approval from the FDA. (Since the FDA does not require premarket testing for cosmetics and personal-care products, the government is not responsible for setting standards in animal testing, as is sometimes believed.) However, if a safety problem with a product arises after it has been marketed, the FDA will run tests and, if a defect is found, request that the manufacturer recall the product. In serious cases, it will take legal action against offenders. In recent years, hair straighteners, nail hardeners, and sunscreens have been among the targeted products.

While serious injury from beauty products is rare, allergic reactions and skin irritations do occur, most commonly as a reaction to fragrances or preservatives. Some products are

He who will not economize will have to agonize.

CONFUCIUS

Generic Prescription Savings

Prescription drugs sold under their generic names may cost half as much as those sold under a brand name—the name that was given by the company that held the original patent on the medication. After 17 years, others may produce the drug under a generic name.

• Copying a drug is cheaper than producing it originally because there are no development costs. Thus, the price goes down. The shape and color of a generic pill may be different from those of the brand name, but effectiveness is the same.

• Legislation passed in 1984 requires generic drugs to have the same active ingredients, dosage form, strength, and route of administration (for example, oral or intravenous) as the prescription drugs they are emulating. Inactive ingredients such as coloring agents, fillers, binders, and preservatives must not alter the effectiveness of the drug. To gain FDA approval, the rate at which the drug is absorbed into the body can vary by no more than 20 percent from the brand-name rate. The absorp-

tion rate of critical drugs such as asthma and heart medication can vary by only 10 percent. To be sure your drug is safe, ask the pharmacist to check the "Orange Book," which rates all generic drugs.

• If you remind your doctor that you are concerned about price, she may give you a generic equivalent. If so, ask the pharmacist for the cheapest FDA-approved version.

• In some states, unless the doctor writes "dispense as written" or "brand necessary" on the prescription form, the pharmacist may substitute a generic drug without telling you. Ask questions to be sure of what you are getting. You, not the pharmacist, should benefit from this switch.

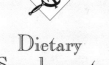

Dietary Supplements and the Law

For years controversy has dogged government's role in the regulation of dietary supplements. By law, a dietary supplement is defined as "any product which contains one or more dietary ingredients such as vitamins, minerals, herbs or other botanicals, amino acids or other ingredients used to supplement the diet."

The arguments concern whether or not these substances should be considered drugs, which the federal Food, Drug, and Cosmetic Act defines as products intended to diagnose, cure, mitigate, treat, or prevent disease. The law requires such substances to undergo lengthy testing before being marketed. The health-food industry resists having supplements called drugs, although many supplements have been marketed with health claims that would put them in the drug category under the FDCA's definition.

In 1994 Congress enacted legislation that treads a middle line between commerce and consumer protection. The Dietary Supplements Health and Education Act (DSHEA) allows dietary supplements to be sold without the extensive testing required for drugs, but forbids manufacturers from making health claims that have not been scientifically proven. Such products must carry the following disclaimer: "This product is not intended to diagnose, treat, cure, or prevent any disease."

labeled "hypoallergenic," implying that they will not cause such reactions. *Hypo* means "less than," and hypoallergenic means only that the manufacturer believes the product is less likely than others to cause an allergic reaction, perhaps because perfume or other problem-causing ingredients have been omitted.

The price of makeup items in department stores can be two or three times what the same items would cost in a drugstore. Comparing labels will tell you if the products have the same main ingredients, but the full formulas will never be identical. Manufacturers guard their formulas as trade secrets. Often the difference in products is purely a matter of packaging—and you can get the same results with products from the drugstore.

The rising awareness of the dangerous effects of too much sun on the skin has produced a flood of sunscreen products, some of which are rated by their "sun-protection factor" (SPF). SPF is rated by the numbers, but don't be fooled by extravagant claims: Research has shown, for example, that an SPF of 45 is no more effective than 30. And be aware that sunscreens do not prevent the serious skin cancer called melanoma.

Health-Food Stores

Be wary of the claims of so-called health-food products that promise everything from cures for the common cold to bulging muscles to eternal youth. Many of the claims are not medically proven. The manufacturers of such products are careful not to make claims in a manner that would get them in trouble with the FDA.

For example, the Nutrition Facts panel required on vitamin packages tells you the U.S. recommended dietary allowance to maintain good health, but makes no reference to the effects of larger doses, such as allergic reactions. Advertising about a product, such as a "muscle-building vitamin" may be misleading, but if the label on the product does not contain false claims there is nothing the FDA can do about it.

Similarly, products sold in health-food stores as "food supplements" are not regulated by the FDA unless they make claims about health or other benefits such as weight loss, which puts them into the drug category and requires manufacturers to prove that they are not harmful. Some diet fads found to be dangerous, such as starch blockers, have been banned.

If you read the label on a liquid diet product carefully, for instance, you will find that it usually protects the manufacturer by stating that the liquid is part of a weight-loss plan. It will often advise you to drink adequate water, eat a sensible diet, and exercise regularly. If you followed this good advice, you could probably lose weight without buying the product.

BARGAIN SHOPPING

Everyone loves a bargain, but before you spend money in stores that promise lower prices, be sure the savings are real.

Outlets, Discount Chains, and Clearance Centers

Stores that promise discounts over standard retail price are tempting, but the words "outlet" and "discount" are not necessarily synonymous with "bargain." They may also mean, simply, "cheap goods." Before you shop the discount stores, check department stores and other traditional retailers for quality and prices so you can recognize true bargains when you find them.

Big savings are possible when department and clothing stores maintain their own clearance centers to move out unsold merchandise. Clearance centers may cut prices as much as 75 percent. Here, as in any discount store, you should examine clothing carefully for flaws or damage and try it on to be sure it is sized correctly.

FACTORY OUTLETS

Factory-owned outlet stores promise savings of 25 to 40 percent off retail. The idea is so popular that giant malls have grown up where dozens of manufacturers sell direct to the consumer. The savings are real, but in many cases the selection and sizes are limited, and you will seldom see the same merchandise that is currently in the stores.

Discontinued patterns and merchandise that did not sell last season are often offered in factory outlets. The best buys are likely to be found in items like sneakers or jeans that do not tend to change with the season.

OVERSTOCKS AND LEFTOVERS

Several retail chains promise discounts on fashions from a variety of makers. Their best values are overstocks, either directly from a manufacturer or from a larger department store. But operations with retail outlets in many cities must often supplement better clothing with cheap merchandise to fill their racks. Labels are often removed, so you cannot be sure whose brand you are buying. Shopping wisely means learning to recognize quality merchandise even when labels are removed. (See also "Quality is in the Details," page 434.)

123...

IS IT A BARGAIN?

Low prices alone do not add up to a bargain on clothing. Ask yourself these questions before you buy:

1. Who made it? Discounters often cut the names from labels so that you cannot identify the manufacturer. But federal law requires all clothing labels to carry a number assigned to each manufacturer. Savvy buyers can use a directory (found in larger libraries) to look up the numbers of their favorite clothing makers and identify their products by the number on the uncut part of the tag.

2. How much alteration does it need? Unfortunately, tailoring may turn a bargain into a major expenditure.

3. Will it need to be dry-cleaned often? Expensive upkeep may negate savings on the initial price.

4. What goes with it? Do you have the right accessories to go with your find?

5. How often will I wear it? Can you wear it a few times each month?. Can you wear it over several seasons of the year, like spring and summer.

6. Does it really fit? If it pulls across the chest or hips, you may never wear it comfortably.

Stores specializing in odd lots of discontinued merchandise other than clothes can also offer substantial savings. You never know what you will find, and you may not see it again, but if you can use what is available, it will probably be a bargain.

ONE-STOP SHOPPING

The fastest growing retailers in the nation are big one-stop marts selling everything from groceries to clothing, home furnishings to auto supplies. Customers at these stores are willing to accept less service and more spartan shopping conditions in return for lower markups.

Compare prices on items like appliances and clothing to be sure the savings are real—and remember that the name brands you see may have been made especially to sell in these chains and may not be the same quality as the same brands sold in other retail stores.

Look-Alike Luggage

PROBLEM
Carolyn saved up for several months to buy some designer luggage. Then just two weeks after she made her big purchase, she was shopping with a friend in a discount store and spotted a set of luggage by the same maker that looked the same as the set she had bought, but for $100 less than she paid. She was furious, and convinced that she had been overcharged.

ACTION
Carolyn's first impulse was to return her more-expensive luggage and berate the manager of the store who had sold it to her. However, her friend suggested that she carefully compare the two sets of luggage before doing anything. So she bought one (returnable) piece of luggage at the discount store and took it home. She discovered that the two sets were not alike. Her more expensive set had larger and sturdier wheels, better zippers, and stronger fabric. Her luggage came with a five-year guarantee, while the cheaper set had a one-year guarantee. Carolyn realized that the same manufacturer made different grades of luggage, providing cheaper products for sale in discount stores. She decided to stay with the quality purchase which would give her longer wear, and returned the cheaper bag.

SUPERSTORES

Huge selections of one category of merchandise—books, toys, home appliances, office supplies—are found in the growing category of "superstores." These stores claim to buy in bulk and pass savings on to the consumer. Often they have a worthwhile weekly special to tempt customers into the store. The surest values are found in stores that offer a standard discount, such as 10 or 20 percent off list price.

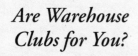

Are Warehouse Clubs for You?

Warehouse clubs are big—in space and in popularity—and depend on selling in large volume for their profits. Typically, goods are marked up only 10 to 15 percent, far less than the markup for regular retail outlets. But here are points to consider before you sign up.

✔ *Annual dues.* You must pay a yearly membership fee, so the clubs offer the best value to those who will shop there often and can take full advantage of the savings.

✔ *No frills.* Warehouse stores really are warehouses, with most goods still packed in their original cartons. You must pick up your own merchandise (even bulky items), wheel it to the cash register, and get it home by yourself.

✔ *Limited selection.* Although the variety of goods includes everything from appliances to toys, tires to groceries, you might find only two china patterns at any given time or only one or two brands of TV sets or toasters.

✔ *Volume sales.* Foods and many other items are available only by the case or the dozen. Big families get the most benefit from such buys.

SHOPPING FROM HOME

By mail, by phone, or from the TV screen, shopping at home is easy and tempting. But before ordering from a distant seller, be sure you know your rights.

Pitfalls of Catalog Shopping

More than 97.7 million busy Americans use catalogs to buy everything from high-tech computers to regional foods, enjoying the tremendous variety of goods available and the ease of shopping from home. Most mail-order merchandisers are reliable. Some 3,600 companies are members of the Direct Marketing Association and abide by industry guidelines and standards. The association mediates between consumers and member retailers in case of disputes.

Still, shopping by mail from an out-of-town retailer offers dangers that you do not encounter when you deal face-to-face with a local storekeeper. Potential problems are magnified if you know nothing about the mail-order company, because there are a few fraudulent ones that tempt customers with misleading ads and other shady ploys. So it is best to do business only with reputable catalog outfits. (You might also try starting out with a small order to test the service.)

The Federal Trade Commission's Mail Order Merchandise Rule requires companies to deliver merchandise within 30 days; otherwise they must make a full refund if asked to. To get this protection, use the mail rather than phoning in your order. Be sure to fill out the order form carefully and make a photocopy for your records.

Shopping From TV

The latest temptations for at-home shoppers are cable-TV networks devoted to shopping. This is already a $2.5 billion business, and it is growing fast. Television gives a better picture than a catalog, and if you like what you see on the screen, you need only dial a toll-free number to place your order.

Some of the jewelry and private-label fashions sold on TV by celebrity vendors are exclusive designs not available elsewhere. But while some items live up to promises of big savings, shopping networks have been accused of inflating list prices to exaggerate the savings. As with any discount shopping, it is wise to compare prices in the stores before you buy.

COMPUTER SHOPPING

Computer owners with a modem and a subscription to an on-line service can order products while sitting in front of a computer screen. Do not give your credit card number out this way unless you are certain the company you are ordering from employs sophisticated encryption software. The nature of on-line communication transmits information to a number of computers, not just the one you are trying to reach. You can never be certain who will have access to your information.

Owners of computers equipped to read CD-ROM disks can combine the visual appeal of television with the ability to browse as you do with a mail-order catalog. CD-ROM shopping services are already available with some two-dozen catalogs on a single disc. Viewers can print out order forms for the goods they have selected. As you would with any catalog, make sure the catalogs are from well-known, reputable companies so that their selections will be safe.

Never buy what you do not want because it is cheap; it will be dear to you.

THOMAS JEFFERSON
1825

Telemarketing

Telemarketing—sales made by telephone—offers great opportunity for scam artists, who can remain unseen behind the telephone. Although some telemarketers represent honest companies, fraudulent operations swindle American consumers out of more than $50 billion each year, according to the National Fraud Information Center

---

Mail-Order Safeguards

Consumers are protected by the FTC's Mail Order Merchandise Rule, sometimes called the "30-day rule." A company must ship an order within the time promised in its ads; or, if no specific time is set, goods must be shipped within 30 days of payment. The 30-day rule also covers:

• **Late orders.** When the shipping date cannot be met, the customer must be notified and given the option of waiting for the merchandise or canceling for a full refund. If the company cannot meet a second shipping date, another notice must be sent. Unless the customer accepts the new date, the order is canceled.

• **Canceled orders.** If an order is canceled, the company is required to give credit on billed charges within one billing cycle or refund a check or money order within seven business days.

• **Telephone orders.** Phone orders charged to a credit card are not covered by the 30-day rule, although the FTC is considering amending the rule.

But orders placed by telephone and paid for by a check sent through the mail are covered.

• **Mail orders.** The 30-day rule applies only when the merchandise ordered by mail has been paid for. If the company has not promised a delivery date, and if you paying for your order with credit extended by the company itself (such as a store credit card), it has 50 days to make your delivery.

• **Fraud.** The U.S. Postal Inspection Service, the law-enforcement arm of the U.S. Postal Service, assists in resolving disputes regarding mail fraud. Consumers who believe they are victims of fraud should contact their local post office and report the problem to the inspector in charge.

(NFIC), with senior citizens as particularly frequent and vulnerable targets. All it takes is rented office space and a bank of telephones for a swindler to be in touch with hundreds of potential victims all over the country.

Con artists usually want to get your credit card number for fraudulent purchases or to use your checking account number for unauthorized withdrawals. With your checking account number they can write a "demand draft" on your account. The draft is processed like a check but does not require your signature. You will not learn of the illegal transactions until you receive your statement.

Dishonest telemarketers have devised dozens of ingenious approaches to separate you from your money. Beware of the following scams:

■ A sales call from a stranger, who might be selling anything from "low-cost" magazine subscriptions (which turn out to be grossly overpriced) to gold mines, to "fabulous" gemstones, to land "bargains" in Florida.

■ A letter or postcard announcing that you have won a prize or a free trip. If you return the postcard with the requested information, you will soon be called by a salesperson ready for the kill.

■ Broadcast and print advertisements that ask you to phone a 900-number for information, such as how to get a major credit card if you have been having trouble getting one. Charges for 900-calls are high and can be excessive if you are kept on the line for an unnecessarily lengthy call, and you may not even get the information you seek.

AVOIDING TROUBLE

The best way to handle unknown telemarketers is to avoid them. Whatever their approach, never give your credit card, checking account, or telephone calling-card numbers over the phone unless you know the person you are talking to or know the company to be reputable. Ask to see all offers in writing, so you can check the details, and be wary if no written information is available.

Be leery of prizes if you have not entered a contest and of all promises of free gifts, especially free trips. Officials at the National Fraud Information Center (NFIC) reported that in 1994, a quarter of the complaints they received involve travel fraud. Don't accept any offer if you have to pay a fee or join a club before you receive the proffered "complimentary" goods or services. Don't respond to any offers that require calling a 900-number. Before you buy anything, check out telemarketing companies with the Better Business Bureau to see if local complaints have been lodged against them.

Use a Credit Card for Home Shopping

Using a credit card for mail or phone orders can be dangerous if you do not know whom you are dealing with. But thanks to the FTC's Fair Credit Billing Act, the card gives you extra protection in case of billing errors or unsatisfactory service. The law lets you withhold payment on the disputed portion of your credit card bill until the dispute is resolved. Here are the rules:

✔ *Good faith.* The buyer must first have made a good-faith attempt to resolve the dispute with the seller.

✔ *Written notice.* The buyer must send written notice of a billing error to the credit card company at the special address indicated on the bill for "billing inquiries." The notice must reach the credit card company within 60 days after the first bill containing the error was mailed to the buyer

✔ *Acknowledgment.* The creditor must acknowledge the letter, in writing, within 30 days after it is received (unless the problem has been resolved). Then the creditor must resolve the dispute within two billing cycles (but not more than 90 days) after receipt of the notice.

✔ *Geography.* In most cases, to qualify under this act you must have bought the item in your home state or within 100 miles of your billing address, and the amount charged must have been more than $50.

If you have difficulty with a telemarketer, the first recourse is to try to resolve the matter with the company. But con artists can be hard to pin down. Often they have only a post-office-box number. You have the right to get the actual business address; the postmaster of the city where the box is located will supply it on request if you explain in writing why you want it. But you may only find that the "business" has moved on to another address using another name and cannot be traced.

If you cannot locate the company or get satisfaction when you do, contact the NFIC at (800) 876-7060 to learn the appropriate authorities in your state. Also file a complaint with the FTC. While the FTC does not intervene in individual cases, the information you provide may help build a case that will lead to legal action.

The American Association of Retired Persons offers a consumer alert describing various schemes and the legal remedies available to seniors if they have been taken. Contact the AARP for information. (See also RESOURCES, page 493.)

Protecting Your Privacy

You have the right to be free from unwanted intrusions in your home. Yet mail-order vendors daily fill America's mailboxes with waves of glossy offerings, universally known as "junk mail," while telemarketers besiege residential phones and fax machines with seductive pitches for everything from rubber boats to retirement plans. By no means all of these offerings are offensive: Mail-order catalogs provide major shopping convenience, and phone callers may suggest useful services. Still, most citizens would happily reduce the volume of uninvited solicitations.

No law prohibits someone from sending you mail (except in special cases such as those involving obscene materials), and nothing you do will staunch the flow overnight, but you can begin by writing letters to all the specific companies that have targeted your mailbox and asking to be removed from their lists. Then write or call the half-dozen or so associations and services that deal nationally with the direct-marketing industry. (See "Stemming the Junk-Mail Flood," at left.) You can also express yourself by marking the check-off boxes that more and more mail marketers, state motor vehicle bureaus, and credit card companies are providing in their mailings.

The law does take a stand when it comes to telephone solicitations. The Telephone Consumer Protection Act requires telemarketers who call your home to put your name on a "do not call" list if you so ask.

Stemming the Junk-Mail Flood

Here are names and addresses of various associations and firms that may help you eliminate some of the intrusive mailings, phone calls, and faxes that come under the general category of junk mail. The Direct Mail Association represents many firms engaged in direct marketing; the other four companies are major list brokers. At your request, all will remove your name from the lists they handle or will ask their clients to do so.

✔ *Mail Preference Service,* part of the Direct Marketing Association, 11 West 42nd St., New York, N.Y.10017, (212) 768-7277.

✔ *Telephone Preference Service,* also part of the Direct Marketing Association.

✔ *R.L. Polk & Co.,* Name Deletion File List Compilation and Development, 6400 Monroe Boulevard, Taylor, Mich., 48180; (800) 873-7655.

✔ *Donnelly Marketing, Inc.,* Data Base Operations, 1235 N Avenue, Nevada, Iowa, 50201; (515) 382-5441.

✔ *Metromail Corporation,* List Maintenance, 949 West Bond, Lincoln, Nebr., 68521; (800) 228-4571.

✔ *Database America,* Compilation Department, 100 Paragon Drive, Montvale, N.J., 07645; (201) 476-2000.

Door-to-Door and Party Sales

In suburban and rural areas, door-to-door salespeople are familiar figures, offering everything from vacuum cleaners to home-freezer plans to cosmetics to vocational-school courses—even home improvements. Another familiar form of person-to-person selling is the at-home party: a friend, or a friend of a friend invites you to a party and tries to get you to buy from a line of cookware, cosmetics, or books.

Many of the products sold this way, of course, are legitimate; but there are also unscrupulous vendors peddling overpriced goods and services. Their sales pitches are hard to resist because the successful door-to-door salesperson has been carefully trained in hard-sell tactics. The more expensive the product or service, the more aggressive the pitch. It is easy to make a hasty decision that you will regret later.

THREE DAYS TO CHANGE YOUR MIND

For that reason, some localities have laws banning door-to-door selling altogether. Where it is allowed, though, both state and FTC regulations protect consumers with a "cooling-off" period. You have three days to change your mind about purchases of $25 or more made at your home.

At the time of sale, the seller must give you notice of your cancellation rights. It must be in writing in the contract or on the receipt. You must also receive two copies of a cancellation form. If you decide to cancel, sign and date one copy of the form and mail or deliver it to the address given before midnight of the third business day after the contract date. Use certified mail so you will receive a receipt proving the date and receipt of the letter. You do not have to explain—under the law, you have the right to change your mind.

COOLING OFF AFTER PARTIES

The same rules apply to party sales. If you have bought something for more than $25 anywhere other than the seller's normal place of business, you must be given cancellation forms, and if you decide to cancel, your money must be refunded. If you are not given cancellation forms, you can write your own cancellation letter, but you should notify the FTC that you were not given the forms.

If you cancel, the seller must return any papers you signed and refund your money within 10 days, and must either pick up items left with you or reimburse you for mailing them back.

The cooling-off rule does not apply to real estate (except timeshares and some vacation properties), insurance, securities, or emergency home repairs. Nor does it cover purchases

---

1 2 3...

DOOR-TO-DOOR SALES PLOYS

The salesperson who calls at your door has been carefully trained to make a sale. Knowing some of the common tactics used will help you to resist the sales pitch:

1. The door opener. Salespersons have many ruses to get past your door. A caller says she is taking a community survey, for example, and adds that your neighbor has suggested your name (which she has just read off your mailbox).

2. The sympathy appeal. Salespersons will tell you how far they have traveled to see you, how badly they need just one more sale to meet a target, or, the oldest ploy of all, that they are working their way through college.

3. The guilt approach. Playing on guilt puts the consumer on the defensive. The book salesman asks, "Can't you put away just this small amount each month for your children's education?" Or a seller of vocational-training courses asks, "Don't you owe it to your family to better your skills?"

4. The price deception. Instead of a total price, you are told only the deceptively low weekly or monthly charge; or the salesperson may offer a very small down payment to induce you to sign up.

5. The long spiel. Carefully rehearsed chatter keeps the seller inside the house long enough to wear down the prospective buyer.

UNORDERED MERCHANDISE

Your mailbox contains a product you never ordered, with a note saying it is yours to try free for 10 days—and a bill. Or you receive a box of greeting cards from a charity asking you for a donation. If this happens to you keep the following points in mind:

1. FTC regulations forbid sending unordered merchandise through the mail unless it is a free sample clearly marked as such, or it is sent by a charitable organization asking for, *but not requiring*, a contribution.

2. Any unordered merchandise sent to an individual is considered a gift. Those who send such merchandise are prohibited from demanding payment.

3. If you receive goods in the mail that you did not order, you have the right to keep or dispose of them in any way you see fit.

4. Bills for unordered merchandise may, constitute mail fraud or misrepresentation or both. The federal mail-fraud statute provides penalties of up to $1,000 and up to five years in prison.

5. If you get bills for merchandise you did not order, or receive items you consider offensive, annoying, or sexual in nature, notify your local postmaster. The Postal Service can take civil action against offenders or refer the case to the U.S. attorney general for criminal action or both.

made at the seller's regular place of business or sales made entirely by mail or phone.

If you have difficulties with a firm belonging to the Direct Selling Association, the association will mediate for you. Write a letter fully describing your problem to Code Administrator, Direct Selling Association, 1666 K Street NW, Suite 1010, Washington, D.C. 20006.

Solving Shop-at-Home Problems

Even the best companies sometimes make mistakes. They send a blue shirt instead of the red one you ordered. An unexpected rush of orders on a popular item may mean it is out of stock when your order arrives. But consumers have rights when ordering by mail or telephone, and those who speak up usually get quick satisfaction from reputable companies who want to maintain good customer relations. Here are some common problems:

- **Wrong merchandise.** A seller may not send you substitute merchandise without your consent. Inspect items you buy by mail as soon as you get them. If goods are not as ordered, the company is responsible for the cost of return postage, whether the substitution was unintentional or accidental.
- **Damaged goods.** It is the sender's responsibility to ensure safe delivery of merchandise to customers. If your order arrives damaged, save the packaging material and contact the company immediately. They will want to take the matter up directly with the shipping company. They should also arrange to have the order returned at their expense and send you a replacement immediately.
- **No delivery.** If a company does not meet the Mail Order Merchandise Rule requiring delivery within 30 days after payment, it must give you a full refund if you ask for it, in the same way you paid for the merchandise (that is., a credit for credit card purchases, a check for payments by check).

DEALING WITH HASSLES

If a mail-order company does not comply with these rules, you can ask for help from the Mail Order Action Line (MOAL). State the problem and enclose copies of a canceled check, money order, or credit card invoice. MOAL will contact the firm and work to resolve the problem within 30 days. The address is: Mail Order Action Line, Direct Marketing Association, 1101 17th Street NW, Washington, D.C. 20036.

SERVICE PROVIDERS

From the telephone company to the dry cleaner, you depend on service providers every day. It is important to know your rights when things go wrong.

Tackling the Public Utilities

Consumers usually have no choice about the companies that provide electricity, gas, or telephone service for their homes, but because these utilities are monopolies, they are closely regulated by a state commission, such as the Public Service Commission (PSC) or the Public Utility Commission (PUC), whose duty is to see that customers receive the services they are paying for.

The commissions set rates, trying to achieve a balance between profit for the company and reasonable cost for the customer. Users have the right to testify when rate increases are being considered. If they come prepared with facts and figures that refute the claims of the utility, they may be able to convince the commission to lower or deny the increase.

State commissions also prevent utility companies from arbitrarily cutting off service without ample notice to the customer. The customer who is behind on his bill must be given a chance to arrange payments. Some states forbid cutting heat service in cold weather even if bills are unpaid. Most gas and electric utilities have plans to even out yearly payments, and some offer free energy audits to help cut energy leaks and costs.

As a utility customer, you have the right to know that your gas and electric meters are working properly and being read accurately. If you think the meter is faulty or a reading was wrong, you can request a field survey to check it. If the company does not comply, go to the state commission for help.

Choosing Service Providers

Unlike the protection offered by law when you buy goods, no uniform codes or statutes govern businesses or individuals who provide services, so when choosing someone to do you a service—whether it is fixing a faucet or shampooing your rugs—dealing with reputable people is key. Here is what to look for:

- **References and reputation.** In addition to getting recommendations from friends and acquaintances, you should feel

Watch Out for 900-Numbers

Telephone numbers starting with *900* are businesses that charge you—often quite a lot—for services that range from astrological predictions to adult entertainment. They have an arrangement with a long-distance carrier who collects fees, takes a handling charge, and remits the rest to the business. The FCC requires all 900-number businesses to disclose their prices in all advertising. Calls costing more than two dollars must clearly identify the company and explain all charges.

To dispute 900-charges, call your phone company. If this does not help, write or call the business within 60 days. The business must acknowledge your complaint in writing within 40 days and either correct the error or explain the reason for not doing so within 90 days or two billing cycles. The company cannot try to collect the debt or report the charge to a credit bureau until an investigation has been completed. Any company that does not comply with these rules forfeits the right to collect.

Many scams have been associated with 900-numbers. If you or a member of your family has been a victim, contact the FCC. (For the address, see RESOURCES, page 493.)

free to ask anyone you are thinking about hiring to provide you with satisfactory references from past customers. The longer an outfit has been in business, the clearer its track record. The local department of consumer affairs can tell you of any complaints against the firm you are considering.

- **Up-to-date licenses and inspection certificates.** Many businesses, such as plumbers, electricians, and home contractors, must be licensed by the city or state. Some states require businesses to post a bond in order to be licensed, guaranteeing funds to remedy consumer damages. Establishments like restaurants, beauty salons, and barbershops must be inspected by the department of health to ensure safe and sanitary conditions. A certificate should be on view.
- **Professional affiliations.** Membership in professional organizations, trade associations, and the Better Business Bureau indicates the willingness of a business or individual to abide by acceptable standards.

Beware of little expenses, for a small leak will sink a great ship.

BENJAMIN FRANKLIN

Recourse for Injuries or Damage

What if a plumber breaks a pipe, causing a flood that damages your furnishings; a beautician burns your scalp; or a carpet cleaner ruins your priceless carpet? Under the law of negligence, consumers may have legal recourse when service providers cause personal injury or property damage.

Choosing a Long-Distance Carrier

Although local telephone service providers are designated by local or state governments, each customer has the right to select a primary long-distance carrier. Competition among carriers is fierce and judging the best deal can be difficult. Here some useful guidelines:

• Check the quality of service of each carrier. Two important factors in comparing companies are quality connections and easy access to an operator when you need one.

• Make sure errors can be corrected easily. With some carriers, errors cannot be claimed until the bill arrives; others have a number you can call to get immediate credit.

• To compare carrier rates, experiment with other carriers besides your primary carrier simply by dialing an access number, known as the "10XXX code," which will connect you to another carrier. By making similar calls at the same time of day using different carriers, you can compare costs

and the quality of the connections. (This is also a backup option if you get a bad or busy connection using your primary carrier.) Here are 10XXX codes for five major long-distance carriers; use the code, followed by 1, the area code, and the telephone number you want to reach (these carriers may not be available in all areas):

MCI	10222
AT&T	10288
Sprint	10333
Allnet	10444
ITT	10488

• Check the cost of using directory assistance. Fees vary among carriers, and if you use the service often, it can make a significant difference.

Negligence is defined as failure to act with an accepted reasonable standard of care. Even if the negligence was unintentional, an individual or business can still responsible for actions that harm others. To win a lawsuit for negligence, you must be able to prove three things (in most states, claims for negligence must be initiated within two years of the negligent act):

- That the negligent person failed to meet his duty or standard of care;
- That the injuries are measurable; that is, you suffered financial or personal harm or both;
- That negligence was the cause of the damage. For example, you must prove that a pipe burst because the plumber botched the job, not because it was a faulty pipe.

BREACH OF CONTRACT

In addition to liability for negligence, home-service providers may be subject to legal action for breach of contract if they do not fulfill their obligations and you suffer a monetary loss as a result. If an electrician does not finish an agreed-upon job and you have to hire someone else at a premium rate to complete it, you could sue him for the additional cost of the work.

While a verbal agreement may be considered a contract, to protect yourself, secure a written contract from a service provider whenever possible. At minimum, include a description of the service to be performed, a proposed completion date, a warranty for any work being done, and a payment schedule. If a service provider has breached a contract with you and you have suffered relatively minimal monetary damages, you may be able to take him to small claims court. (See also YOUR RIGHTS IN ACTION, page 476).

Protection at Home

When you hire someone who will come into your home; such as a cleaning person, a gardener, a plumber, a carpenter, or an electrician, your best protection is to deal only with individuals or companies that are bonded or that have sufficient liability insurance to cover any damage that may occur due to their error. Always ask about their insurance coverage before you sign a contract. When you hire cleaning personnel, babysitters, or handymen without such coverage, you are assuming a risk, since they may not be able to afford to pay for damages, even if you take them to court.

Just as service providers are expected to use care when working in the home, homeowners have the responsibility to pro-

What If You Cancel a Caterer?

Suppose you have hired a caterer, but the wedding is called off, or the guest of honor at your scheduled party becomes ill? If you cancel on short notice, you are breaking a contract, and the caterer could ask for the entire amount agreed upon, claiming that she cannot find another party to fill your date on short notice.

First of all, cancellation policies should be discussed well in advance, including what will happen if a snowstorm, hurricane, or other act of nature forces a cancellation.

Some states and municipalities have laws that limit the amount of damages a caterer may claim in connection with a canceled contract. In one city, for example, if the caterer is able to rebook the date, the cancellation fee cannot exceed five percent of the total contract price or $100, whichever is less, plus any expenses the caterer has already incurred.

To check whether the caterer has rebooked, ask a friend to call requesting the same date and room and have the friend document the conversation. Even if the caterer is unable to rebook, the cancellation fee may not exceed the combined total of lost profit and expenses.

If you find yourself forced to cancel at the last minute, the best course is to try to work out a fair settlement with the caterer. If you cannot come to an agreement, the caterer has the right to take you to court to present her case.

When Care Labels Mislead

The Federal Trade Commission (FTC) requires that manufacturers sew a permanent and easily found care label into each garment. It must list at least one method of safe care for the garment and warn about care that could reasonably be expected to harm the garment or other garments being laundered with it. The tag must be sturdy enough to remain legible throughout the useful life of the garment.

If you follow the manufacturer's instructions and the garment is damaged in washing, your first recourse is to go back to the store where you bought it. If the store will not resolve the problem, ask for the manufacturer's name and address and write directly to the company.

In your letter, provide a full description of the garment and when it was bought. State all the information that is given on the labels and tags, and include a detailed description of what was done to the garment and what happened to it. Estimate how many times the garment has been washed or dry cleaned.

Provide the full name and address of the store where it was purchased. Finally, state what you want done about the problem—for example that you want the garment to be replaced, or your money refunded. Also, send a copy of your complaint letter to the FTC.

vide safe premises for workers. If a workman slips on a broken step or a toy left on a stairway and breaks a leg, you may be sued for negligence—one good reason to maintain adequate liability coverage on your home. (See also YOUR HOME AND COMMUNITY, page 30).

Services Outside the Home

When you use outside services—anything from cleaners to health clubs—you have the advantage of seeing the premises before doing any business. You can judge if a place is dirty or poorly run. Look for licenses and membership in industry service organizations, which shows a desire to maintain standards.

THE DRY CLEANER

Among the most frequent sources of consumer complaints are dry cleaners that lose or damage garments. When the cleaner accepts your clothing, you are creating a type of legal contract known as a "bailment." You put your property in his charge for your mutual benefit—you will get clean clothes and the cleaner will receive money for his work. He is responsible for taking reasonable care of your clothing, and by accepting it, he is implying that it can be safely dry-cleaned.

A Glittering Responsibility

PROBLEM
Andrea bought an expensive sequined dress to wear to a formal New Year's Eve party. When she sent the dress to the cleaner afterwards, it came back ruined, with many of the sequins curled and discolored. She demanded a refund, but the cleaner refused, stating that it was not his fault that the label did not warn about the sequins.

ACTION
The cleaner was a member of the Neighborhood Cleaner's Association, so Andrea asked that the dress be sent to the association's Garment Analysis Laboratory. The NCA found the cleaner at fault because he had steam-pressed the garment despite a warning in a bulletin sent out by the organization, advising that many sequins are heat sensitive and recommending test procedures. A responsible cleaner should first have recognized the potential problem, warned Andrea, and asked for a written release. Then he should have tested the sequins before pressing. Because she still had the receipt proving the dress was brand new, Andrea was able to recover the full price of the garment.

If clothes come back discolored or misshapen after cleaning, they can be sent to a laboratory for analysis to find out whether the dry cleaner is at fault or whether the garment was mislabeled by the manufacturer. The International Fabricare Institute in Silver Springs, Maryland, analyzes garments cleaned by its 6,000-member dry cleaners for a small charge, as does the Garment Analysis Laboratory of the Neighborhood Cleaners Association in New York City, which has 4,000 members in the United States and abroad. Garments are accepted, for a fee, only from member cleaners, retailers, consumer agencies, or the Better Business Bureau.

If a report shows that a garment was not cleaned properly, you should have little difficulty being reimbursed. If the garment was not new, however, you will probably only receive a portion of the purchase price, based on a formula developed by The International Fabricare Institute

If a garment damaged at a dry cleaners was mislabeled or the fabric was shoddy, you may have to take it back to the store where you bought it with a copy of the report and a request for a refund. If the store refuses to accept responsibility, go directory to the manufacturer. Always keep your receipt for purchasing the garment—that is your first line of proof in case of a dispute.

RESTAURANTS

All states have laws requiring restaurants to maintain sanitary conditions and forbidding the serving of contaminated or unwholesome food. If you are served contaminated food, you may be able to sue the restaurant if you suffer harm as a result.

Less hazardous restaurant rip-offs are not always easy to spot. Is it really "100 percent pure butter" or part margarine? Is the "chicken salad" made from less expensive turkey? If you suspect that a restaurant menu is not truthful, the best course is to complain to the local or state restaurant association or health department.

BEAUTY CARE

When you use the services of a beauty salon, you are relying on the experience and expertise of the operators to use safe products and methods. If you are harmed by a chemical process such as a hair dye and you can prove that the operator did not use reasonable care, you can sue for negligence. If the product is faulty, the manufacturer may be liable as well.

You also have rights if the operator does not follow your instructions. If you ask for a trim and come out with a crew cut, or request red hair color and wind up blond, the operator has, in effect, broken a contract. If someone hired to perform a service deliberately disobeys instructions and performs to your detriment against your will, you do not need to pay.

FINANCIAL HAZARDS OF HEALTH CLUBS

Health clubs are blossoming everywhere, but they also are notorious for going out of business, leaving members with worthless contracts. And some offer contracts that need careful scrutiny. Ask these questions before signing up:

1. How long has the club been in business?

2. Is the club bonded to protect members if it should close? If so, for how much?

3. Is the club well maintained and clean? Are there enough facilities? Visit at a busy time to check for overcrowding.

4. What are the qualifications of staff members? Are they trained in physical education?

5. What are the fee arrangements? Some clubs make you sign a loan contract and pay interest on the unpaid balance.

6. Can you get your money back if you get sick?

7. Does a waiver of liability clause say you cannot sue even if the club's negligence causes your injuries? If so, cross it out.

8. What is the shortest membership available? Since 90 percent of health-club members drop out after three months, it pays to start with a short-term commitment.

YOUR RIGHTS AS A TRAVELER

From missing baggage to lost room reservations, traveling can present challenges. Knowing your rights will smooth the way.

Up in the Air

Travel by air has many potential snags, so it is important to know your rights before you arrive at the airport. Airplane tickets are considered legal contracts between the passenger and the carrier, and airlines are required to disclose all terms, including how problems will be handled. Many conditions of the contract are printed on the ticket or the envelope that holds it. Read the small print carefully to learn about check-in deadlines to assure your seat, as well as refund restrictions, liability limitations, lost-luggage procedures, overbooking procedures, claim-filing deadlines, and other relevant information.

Lost airline tickets should be reported immediately, since they can be used by anyone. Since you will need proof of purchase for a refund, using a credit card to buy tickets is helpful. Keeping a record of your ticket number will speed your refund and may enable you to get an on-the-spot replacement ticket.

If you have complaints about the way an airline handles your problems, contact the airline's customer service department. If you do not get satisfaction, your next recourse is the U.S. Department of Transportation, which regulates the airlines.

WAYS TO SAVE MONEY

To get the best airfares, you must be aware of airline pricing procedures. You may be able to save if you are willing to make one change of planes in an airline's hub city rather than flying nonstop. In cities with more than one airport, rates may be less for less popular airports; it always pays to compare.

Planning ahead gets you the best fares. Reservations must be made one, two, or three weeks ahead to qualify for most low fares. Because seats at special fares are limited, the earlier you reserve, the more likely you are to get the dates you want. The cheapest rates are available when the airlines offer sales during slow periods, such as the "off season" when you are traveling to resort areas, or just after a holiday period. Refunds on lower fares are "restricted"; you cannot get your money back. But you should be allowed to change the ticket by paying a service charge. Check the penalties for cancellation or ticket changes before you buy.

Tours and Cruises

Scores of tour operators send parties of travelers on successful jaunts to all corners of the globe, but unfortunately there are those who cancel unfilled trips or, worse, go bankrupt with your money still in the till. To protect yourself, deal only with members of the United States Tour Operators Association, and be sure the operator's membership is current. Members must have been in business at least three years and must post a $1 million bond to protect consumers in case of financial problems. The National Tour Operators Association also offers limited protection—up to $100,000 for a member company that fails.

Read the fine print on the back of tour brochures. Are any fees needed to qualify for the trip; or are strict refund regulations, cancellation policies, insurance charges, or departure taxes part of the deal? If you don't see any of these, ask for detailed information so you are not surprised.

CANCELLATION INSURANCE

If you cancel because of a last-minute emergency, you stand to lose a substantial sum of money, sometimes the entire cost of the trip. So, low-cost trip cancellation insurance is a worthwhile investment anytime you book ahead for an expensive trip. Insurance also includes coverage for any costs that may occur due to travel delays en route.

The great advantage of a hotel is that it's a refuge from home life.

GEORGE BERNARD SHAW
You Never Can Tell

How to Deal With Airlines

Airline passengers cannot do much about weather-related problems, but if you have been bumped from your flight despite holding a confirmed reservation, or if you arrive at a beach resort but your suitcase does not, you are entitled to compensation:

• **If you are bumped.** Airlines are allowed by law to overbook. When too many passengers show up, the airlines can ask for volunteers to take a later flight and offer a free ticket as a reward. If you are bumped involuntarily, the airline must indemnify you on the basis of how late you finally get to your destination. To qualify, however, you must have met the carriers' check-in deadline for the original flight.

• **If you miss a connection.** If the airline's dereliction costs you more than it will pay—if you miss an important connection, for example—you can try to negotiate a higher settlement with the airline. You may also decline a settlement offer, and sue in court for additional compensation.

• **If your luggage is late.** If your bags do not arrive with your flight, airport managers usually are permitted to disburse money for emergency purchases. If you cannot get a cash advance on the spot, you may be able to be reimbursed for necessities after the fact; to collect, submit receipts to the airline.

• **If your luggage is lost.** If a bag is permanently lost, the airlines will reimburse you up to an amount that varies for international and domestic flights. Carriers' settlements are based on the depreciated value of the bag and its contents; so, expect to dicker over the value of your goods. Since they are not covered, always carry jewelry and cameras with you on the airplane.

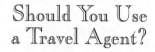

Should You Use a Travel Agent?

A good travel agent can be a great help in planning a trip and handling all your ticket, hotel, and tour reservations. Although changes may be in the offing, currently these services are free: The agent is paid by the airline, hotel, or tour operator.

An agent can also give you the benefit of other clients' experiences with hotels and tours. In case of problems, an agency will usually have more clout than an individual. An agent can be especially helpful when you travel to countries you have never visited before.

A drawback with agents is that they often prefer dealing with clients who pay their commissions. Airlines and hotels may offer bonuses to encourage agents to recommend them. Smaller hotels and airlines with consolidators who offer cheaper fares may not be on the agency's computer. Nor do agents handle many offbeat tours. If you are a thrifty traveler, it can be worth making calls on your own.

Furthermore, like tour companies, travel agencies can be guilty of false advertising or deceptive practices. Use a well-established agency that is a member of the American Society of Travel Agents (ASTA). Pay with a credit card so that the card company can cancel charges for undelivered services. Otherwise, if you find on arrival that a hotel or tour never received payment from your agent, you have no recourse but to pay the charge and try to collect through the courts.

Your Rights in Hotels

Like airlines, hotels sometimes overbook in case of no-shows. If a hotel is full and you have a written confirmation proving that you have a reservation, you are entitled to higher-priced accommodations at no extra charge, if available, or free comparable lodgings at another hotel. If the clerk hesitates, ask for a manager and make it clear that you will take the matter up with local consumer authorities and your travel agent.

If you are sent to an inferior hotel and the first hotel pockets the difference in rates, cancel your credit card payment to the first hotel. Pay the second hotel directly and report this fraud to both the hotel management and to your travel agent.

Innkeeper-liability laws in most states require hotels to provide a safe place to store valuables. Hotels that comply are not liable for theft from guest rooms, and most hotels state clearly that they are responsible only for items put in the safety deposit vault. However, if you are robbed or injured in a hotel and can prove that the hotel was negligent or that security was lax, you still may be able to win a case in court.

Renting a Car on Vacation

Like other reservations, car rentals may not be ready when you need them. Although they sometimes overbook, car rental companies also run into trouble when customers do not bring cars back at the time promised. Always have the reservation number given to you when you reserved the car. It is your proof that you were promised a car. If the class of car you reserved is not available, you are entitled to a larger model at no extra cost.

Always inspect the car before driving away. The agreement you signed promises that you will bring the car back in the condition you received it. If you find dents, scratches, or a missing spare tire, have that noted on your contract or you may be asked to pay for them later.

The rental agency may offer you a collision-damage waiver, which releases you from liability if the car is stolen or damaged. But the chances are that your own auto insurance covers you in a rented car, and your credit card may provide automatic insurance as well. However, the credit card insurance may not include liability insurance—to pay for damages you cause to other cars and people—so be sure you know what kind of coverage you have before you sign or initial any rental agreement. (See also, YOUR CAR, page 389.)

Visas and Vaccinations

Except for travel to Mexico, Canada, and some Caribbean countries, you must have a government-issued passport that identifies you as a U.S. citizen when you leave the country. Some destinations also require a visa, a special stamp placed in the traveler's passport by the nation's embassy or consulate that permits a limited stay in the country.

Passport applications are available at the main post office in each community or at offices of the Passport Agency of the U.S. State Department. To find out whether a visa is required and how to apply for one, call the nearest embassy of the country you plan to visit or write to the Consumer Information Center in Pueblo, Colorado, for the booklet, "Foreign Entry Requirements."(For the address, see RESOURCES, page 493.) Whenever you travel abroad, keep a photocopy of your passport in the bottom of your suitcase for easier replacement in case of loss or theft.

While abroad, you are subject to the laws of the country you are visiting. The U.S. Consulate can step in to see that these laws are fairly applied and may appear on your behalf in court.

HEALTH AND SAFETY CONCERNS

Under the International Health Regulations adopted by the World Health Organization, countries may require proof of immunizations, such as certificates of vaccination against yellow fever, in order to enter. When you travel abroad, it is wise to be sure that such immunizations as tetanus and polio vac-

An International Appendectomy

PROBLEM
Dale was vacationing in France with his wife, Sue, when he was suddenly stricken with appendicitis. Their hotel arranged to get Dale to a hospital, where he had a successful appendectomy. Sue, however, faced problems with all the extra issues that arose out of Dale's emergency. Their American health-insurance policy was not acceptable as payment in a French hospital, and the delay due to Dale's illness meant they were not be able to use their nonrefundable airline tickets to fly home.

ACTION
Fortunately, Dale had a travel health-insurance policy to guard against medical emergencies during his international holiday. The policy, which cost $150, also paid for the couple's nonrefundable air arrangements. Dale also carried a gold credit card that helped out: by calling an assistance-center number collect, Sue got the names of English-speaking doctors and hospitals and help in arranging for transportation.

LESSONS IN HOTEL SAFETY

While hotel thefts are infrequent, they do occur. A few precautions will help ensure your safety:

1. Ask for a room near the elevator. Don't accept rooms at the end of a long corridor.

2. Use the peephole to identify callers before you open the door to your room. If the caller says he is a hotel employee but looks suspicious to you, ask for a name and verify with the front desk before admitting the person.

3. Never put the "Make up my room" sign on the doorknob, announcing that the room is unoccupied. When you leave your room at the end of the day, leave a light on and close the curtains if you will be returning after dark. The "Do not disturb" sign may discourage uninvited visitors, who cannot be sure the room is empty. Leaving the radio or television on is a deterrent, too.

4. Have your keys handy when returning to your room so you don't have to stand in the hallway searching for them.

5. Don't leave money or jewelry where they can be seen by anyone entering the room. Use the room safe provided in some hotels or the safety deposit box at the desk.

6. If you enter an elevator and sense trouble, stand next to the floor-button panel so you can call for help if necessary.

cinations are up-to-date. Preventive medication for malaria is recommended for travel to some areas of South and Central America, Africa, and Asia. Detailed health information can be found in the booklet "Health Information for International Travel," available from the U.S. Government Printing Office, or you can phone the Centers for Disease Control for updated messages about immunization requirements and recommendations for international travel. For their addresses and telephone numbers, see RESOURCES, page 493.

The cautious seldom err.

CONFUCIUS

TO GET COVERED ABROAD

Health insurance secured from an American company is usually not valid outside the United States. However, you can buy overseas health insurance for all except preexisting medical conditions. Ask your insurance broker or your travel agent about these policies. Premium credit cards also may provide a source for medical information for overseas travelers, and the U.S. Embassy in any country can help in case of illness.

To keep travelers posted on safety overseas, free up-to-date information is available from the Office of Overseas Citizens Service. Printed consular information sheets for every country in the world, including the locations of U.S. embassies, are available by mail or fax. These reports detail entry requirements and conditions relating to crime, security, and health, with warnings for countries where conditions are not considered safe for travelers. For the address of the Overseas Citizens Service, see RESOURCES, page 493.

Protecting Your Money While Traveling

Since pickpockets operate in tourist destinations all over the world, it pays to be careful with cash when you travel. The most common safeguard is to carry your money in traveler's checks, which can be easily replaced if stolen and to cash only what you need each day.

• **Use your ATM card.** The advent of international banking networks now means you need to carry less cash when you travel. If your bank belongs to a network, you can use your regular ATM card in major cities throughout the world to access cash from your account. While you pay a transaction fee when you use a bank card abroad, you receive cash in the local currency based on the bank's exchange rate, which is better than the rate that is charged to individuals.

• **Use your credit cards.** Using credit cards to pay for lodging, meals, and purchases gains the same advantaged exchange rate. You can also get cash advances on major credit cards in many places; but unlike getting cash with a bank card in an auto-mated teller machine, you will pay interest on the credit card advance until it is repaid.

• **Change foreign currency.** Change enough foreign currency before you leave home to cover transportation, tipping, and immediate cash needs when you arrive. This eliminates standing in line at airports, where you often find unfavorable, often exorbitant, exchange rates.

• **Limit your cash.** As for the cash you need to have on hand every day, carry it in an inside pocket, zipped or buttoned up. If you use a fanny pack, wear it in front to help foil snatch-and-run thieves, and never walk around with an open purse or shoulder bag.

YOUR RIGHTS IN ACTION

Action brings satisfaction. After learning your rights, you need to know how to exercise them effectively. Here are some guidelines.

PREVENTIVE LAW ■ TAKING ACTION ■ RESPONDING EFFECTIVELY ■ ALTERNATIVES TO COURT ■ GOING TO COURT ■ USING A LAWYER ■ REPRESENTING YOURSELF ■ MAKING YOUR VOICE HEARD

PREVENTIVE LAW

When it comes to safeguarding your rights, an ounce of prevention is worth several pounds of cure.

Protecting Yourself

How many times have you faced a problem and wondered, "How did I get into this mess?" The concept of preventive law, as with preventive medicine, is to take simple measures in advance to forestall potential problems. Of course, not all legal troubles can be avoided, but generally, preventive measures can help keep a bad situation from getting worse.

When you have to make major decisions, whether they relate to health care, schooling, housing, consumer products, or even personal relations, step back and think about them. Arm yourself with facts and information. Get second opinions, not just on medical decisions, but on major purchases and investments.

BE PREPARED

Ask as many questions as you can before entering into an agreement. Don't shy away from a direct query such as: "Have you given me all the facts?" When you are negotiating a major purchase, tell the seller what needs you have. If you make it clear, for example, that you need a riding mower that can cut coarse grass, an "implied warranty of fitness for a particular purpose" may be established, making it more likely that you can hold the seller to that commitment. Be sure that sales pitches or verbal promises are confirmed in writing. Above all, never sign anything you do not understand.

Knowing the relevant laws can be important and helpful. For example, most contracts signed in your home can be canceled within three days. Therefore, if you agree to an insurance policy that you later—within three days—realize you do not want, you can legally cancel the contract.

In some situations, you may want to have a lawyer go over a matter or review documents before you agree to a purchase, contract, or decision. If you face a difficult confrontation, consider taking another person along as a witness. Take notes on all conversations relating to the problem, whether in person or over the telephone.

Before taking action, ask yourself the questions a judge might ask: "Would a reasonable person do the same in this situation?" If the answer is "no," reconsider your decision.

Keeping Records

Your word may be your bond, but when it comes to a legal conflict, your records are your proof. Whether you deal with a situation in a simple one-on-one negotiation or end up going to court, the best chance of securing your rights lies in your ability to prove convincingly that you have the facts, and that they are in your favor.

Get into the habit of maintaining records that are comprehensive, organized, and accessible. You may keep such important documents as insurance policies and military discharge papers in a safety deposit box. Wherever you store your records, you should catalog *all* of them in a master file that is stored in an obvious place so that in an emergency, family members can find important papers quickly.

Maintaining the file will be much easier if you organize it by category. Using a home computer can make the job of creating and updating this essential record much less daunting.

Keeping Track of Your Life

The ever-growing complexities in today's society have created a veritable paper trail of records that you should keep to document your rights. How long you hold on to each document depends on its intended use. And, of course, you need to keep track of where you have put them.

• **Family.** Keep birth certificates and social security numbers for each member, as well as marriage license, adoption, prenuptial, divorce, military service, paternity, and citizenship documents. Keep a signed list of separate property brought into the marriage by each spouse. Have a valid will naming a guardian for children. After a separation or divorce, keep all accounts of child or spousal support payments and child custody conflicts.

• **Home.** While you own your home and, for income tax requirements, five to seven years after you sell it, you should keep your mortgage loan documents, payments, deed, title insurance, escrow account, homeowners insurance policy, renovation contracts and repair receipts, property tax statements, appraisals, and leases with tenants. Renters should keep a copy of their lease, deposit, and letters to the landlord. For insurance purposes keep, at a location away from the home, inventories (including photos and videos) of all personal property, purchase dates, and values.

• **Job.** Keep paycheck stubs until you get a W-2 form from your employer. Retain pension information; your job record for résumés, unemployment insurance, and social security; employee contracts, manuals, and union information.

• **Health.** Keep information on immunizations, allergies, reactions to drugs, blood type, records of disease, health insurance policies, Medicaid/Medicare information, and the names of your doctors. Also create a living will documenting your wishes concerning organ donations and the use of life-saving equipment.

• **Money.** Keep listings of accounts with banks, investment advisers, and financial institutions. File loan documents, credit card agreements, wills , trust arrangements, stock and investment certificates, and pension plan information. Keep checks for tax returns and supporting documents for five years, in case of audit.

• **Car.** Keep purchase and leasing agreements, warranties, repair log, leases, registration, insurance policy, and any accident records.

• **Major purchases.** Keep checks and receipts of major purchases, sales slips, warranties, and a complete file on any problems and complaints.

TAKING ACTION

When your rights are at stake, you need not fold your tent and steal away—but instead of getting mad, get a plan.

Starting Your Problem Log

If you are in an accident or have bought something that does not work, you may have a legal problem. To be prepared for a possible case, start keeping a log that includes:

✔ *History.* Write down everything that has happened relevant to your claim, including any conversations or interactions, with the names of people you called for help. If you need to prove timing or that you were upset (such as in a sexual harassment case), write a letter, include your feelings at the time, address it to yourself, and send it by certified mail. Do not open it until the legal proceeding.

✔ *Physical evidence.* Keep all proof, such as damaged products or all parts (old and new) in a defective repair case.

✔ *Documents.* File original documents, such as contracts or warranties, and keep copies of all letters sent or received.

✔ *Witnesses.* If an accident or incident had witnesses, get their names, phone numbers, addresses, and observations.

✔ *Photographs.* Take photos or a video of anything you can use to illustrate the problem, such as damage to property.

Getting What You Deserve

Problems are like people: No two are exactly alike. Your predicament could be excessive charges for a bounced check, a sagging floor in a new house, or a broken appliance. One way to make many problems easier to cope with is to develop an effective problem-solving strategy. Problems that involve time deadlines, such as being served with court papers and home foreclosures, or serious issues such as injury or job dismissal, require the advice of a lawyer. However, you can solve many consumer issues on your own.

First, write down everything you know about the problem. Next, focus on the solution you are seeking—do you want your money back, the insurance policy changed, or an apology? Find out what protection is already available to you—a contract, an insurance policy, or a warranty that came with a defective product. List anyone who is in a position to help you, such as your bank manager, the building contractor, or the manufacturer. Make note of any limited claim period or deadlines, such as a 60-day limit on appealing property taxes or the duration of a warranty. Try to analyze your problem calmly. Anger, no matter how justifiable, can reduce your chances for success.

CONTACTING THE OTHER PARTY

Now you are ready to contact the other party directly. The initial complaint is often made over the telephone. Use a calm and reasonable tone and keep your complaint brief and straightforward: "I've got a problem, and I'm hoping you can help me." Follow up with a short letter explaining your dispute, which will also serve as evidence of your notification to the other party.

Don't be discouraged if these overtures do not bring satisfaction. Now is the time to enlist the aid of other organizations or persons to help you. Think about what will get the other side's attention: the threat of publicity? government regulations? Then figure out which federal, state, or local agencies may be able to resolve your complaint directly or indirectly by putting pressure on the other side. Keep in mind that while many agencies can order businesses to stop certain practices, they may not resolve individual problems. Still, a letter to the agency may prompt action. For the address and telephone number of the agency, call a regional office of the Federal Information Center, listed in your telephone directory. A free booklet, the *Consumer Resource Handbook*, available from the Consumer Information Center, lists federal and state government agencies and private organizations that help resolve problems. (For this address, see RESOURCES, page 493.)

Although elected officials, such as council members and representatives, may not have an official role in resolving complaints, they often have offices to help people in the community. These offices are variously called ombudsman's offices, citizen's aid offices, or constituent services. Try contacting the mayor's office, your city council or county board representative, as well as your state and federal representatives and senators. Send a duplicate of any correspondence you have with an agency or public official to the party with whom you have the dispute.

Sometimes a letter from an attorney can do wonders. A lawyer's fee for writing a letter may be less than you think, and

---

What Will an Agency Do for You?

Many government agencies deal with consumers' rights—some are listed below—but only a few actually tackle individual complaints. Check the Blue Pages of your phone book for numbers of these agencies, then call to find out if they can help you resolve your specific problem.

• **Office of state attorney general.** The attorney general in most states will investigate and seek recourse on consumer complaints; if an out-of-state business is involved, contact the attorney general in that state.

• **State or local consumer affairs offices.** Most states and some cities have consumer affairs offices that are authorized to investigate consumer complaints by contacting the business and trying to get a solution.

• **State commissions.** Certain industries—including insurance, banking, health, environment, hospitals, and nursing homes—are closely watched by specific state commissions, some of which will investigate consumer complaints. A letter to the commission often prompts a response from the party in question.

• **Human rights and equal employment opportunity commissions (federal, state, and local).** These commissions investigate and act on individual complaints of employment bias. State and local boards may also look into bias relating to housing, public service, or other issues.

• **Consumer Product Safety Commission (CPSC).** This is a federal agency that regulates dangerous products, but does not resolve individual complaints.

• **Federal Trade Commission (FTC).** A federal agency that issues rules and takes action on deceptive advertising, door-to-door sales, warranty claims, and credit practices. In some cases, the FTC may help resolve a problem that affects a large number of people, but otherwise it does not act for individual consumers.

• **Federal Communications Commission (FCC).** This federal agency regulates television and radio, but does not handle individual complaints.

• **Food and Drug Administration (FDA).** This is the federal agency that regulates foods, drugs, and cosmetics; and tests new drugs, and investigates complaints about existing products.It does not seek recourse for individual consumers.

• **U.S. Postal Inspection Service.** This federal agency investigates mail fraud and looks into individual complaints.

pay off more. A letter does not mean a lawsuit, although bringing suit may be your next option if no resolution is found.

Framing a Complaint

The most successful complaint letter does not merely "complain." Instead, it attempts to negotiate a solution. Whether the letter is to the person responsible for the problem or to an outside organization from which you seek help, keep your letter factual and straightforward. Be firm, but reasonable.

Briefly describe the situation. Answer basic questions: who, what, where, when, and how. Instead of casting blame, make neutral statements such as "the bicycle crashed into ...," not "you smashed my greenhouse walls." If a product was involved, give the model and type; when and where you bought it; when and how it stopped working. Finally, if a full account takes more than 15 lines in your letter, include a separate page and state: "The complete history of this problem is attached." Enclose copies of receipts, warranties, or other documents, but keep the originals.

WHAT DO YOU WANT?

The most important part of your letter is the statement of what you want the recipient to do. If you want compensation, the money you seek is referred to as the "damages." Be specific. If a flying ball thrown by a neighbor's child smashed your window, you can seek direct damages for the cost of the broken window and the replacement of rain-soaked furniture.

Make it clear that you expect the recipient of the letter to take action, whether it is to pay for the broken window, correct a safety hazard in an apartment you rent, or finish a contracting job. Describe precisely what you want done, and include dollar amounts if you expect monetary recompense. Before signing off, make a positive statement: "I hope that we can resolve this matter without too much difficulty."

GO TO THE TOP

If you don't get results, send a follow-up letter, stating that you have had no response. Mail this to the highest level person you can locate, such as the president of the company with whom you have a billing dispute, and send it by certified mail, return receipt requested. Keep copies of your letters.

If you need a name or the address of a particular company, consult a corporate directory in your library, or call the company directly. Most large companies have toll-free lines; call (800) 555-1212 for the listing.

123... PLACES TO GET HELP

Avalanches of consumer complaints across the country have resulted in a variety of unofficial agencies (in contrast to government groups) designed to help resolve consumers' problems. When you are planning to take action, consider these:

1. Local Better Business Bureaus (BBB) may attempt to resolve disputes with local businesses.

2. Many local newspapers and television stations run "action" lines for consumers with problems. Some work on general complaints, others look for those that are "news."

3. Trade associations—manufacturers who have banded together to look after the interests of their specific industries, such as electronics, automobiles, or mail-order, may run programs to resolve consumer complaints. Your local library should have directories that list such organizations.

4. Community groups, such as neighborhood centers, senior citizen programs, and nonprofit agencies, may offer help for simple problems.

5. Law schools in a community may have a "clinic" or "hotline" to help consumers.

6. Advocacy organizations, such as tenant and environmental groups, often have good tips and literature to help others deal with problems in those specific areas.

RESPONDING EFFECTIVELY

When problems arise unexpectedly, keep your head—how you respond can make all the difference in securing your rights.

If Someone Sues, Act Fast

Although the judicial system often moves at a snail's pace, some legal actions happen quickly. If you get a "summons" and "complaint"—documents that inform you of a lawsuit against you—you will generally need to respond within 20 to 30 days.

Usually, the summons and complaint are hand-delivered by a process server or sheriff. Sometimes they are left at a residence or published in a paper. For a case in small claims court they may arrive by mail. No matter how you receive them, don't delay in filing your formal response, or "answer."

Except in small claims cases, you should consult with a lawyer immediately. You or your lawyer must file your answer"with the court or with the attorney for the other party, depending on local rules. (In a small claims case a court clerk can advise you.) Failure to file an answer can have dire consequences: A decision or judgment may be taken against you by "default," whether or not right was on your side.

If you cannot meet the deadline for filing, your lawyer must contact the courthouse or the attorney for the party that filed the complaint and formally seek an extension of time. If you miss the deadline, your lawyer can request permission from the court to file a late answer and prevent a default judgment.

If You Are a Crime Victim

Nearly one out of every four American families is victimized each year by crime. The overall statistics are startling: eight million thefts, three million burglaries, and two million crimes of physical violence. When crime hits, victims suffer physical injuries, property loss, and emotional trauma. Knowing your rights can help ease the pain.

Most states have programs to compensate crime victims for losses in certain situations. Eligibility for compensation programs is limited to victims who have reported the crimes to the police promptly, usually within 72 hours to a week, unless the crime involves unusual circumstances. The time limit to file an

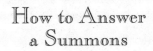

How to Answer a Summons

A process server knocked on your door and handed you a summons and complaint. You are being sued. For all but small claims court, you should contact an attorney right away.

When you are sued in a civil lawsuit, you are the "defendant" and the person suing you is the "plaintiff."

Your lawyer will prepare a legal document known as an "answer." In it, each point in the "complaint" of the plaintiff is "affirmed" or "denied." The document might affirm that your name is correct, but deny that you owe the money claimed by the plaintiff. If you do not deny a point, you are agreeing with it by default.

Although it may appear simple, an answer to a summons may contain complexities, and you need an attorney to ensure that your rights are protected. Your attorney will determine, for example, if you can claim a technical defense, if your answer should include reference to a third party, and other important legal matters.

When you contact an attorney about representing you, make certain that you mention immediately that you have been served with a summons and complaint and that you are facing a deadline.

VICTIM SERVICES

Victim services agencies provide emergency care, counseling, and other services to crime victims. For a referral to a program in your area call the National Victim Center (See RESOURCES, page 493). Here is what victim services offer:

1. District attorneys' offices often have victim and witness aid service centers and social service departments.

2. Crime victim compensation programs help pay for injuries or property losses. If you cannot find one, call directory assistance in your state capital.

3. Elderly crime victims resource centers offer special services for seniors.

4. The Red Cross serves emergency needs of crime victims for housing and food.

5. Traveler's Aid assists people who are victimized by crime while traveling.

6. Hospitals and emergency clinics have social workers or counselors who can aid victims of violent crimes.

7. Shelters offer victims of family violence safety and support services.

8. Crisis prevention hotlines offer tips, guidance, and counseling for victims of rape, domestic abuse, or bias crimes.

application for reimbursement for losses is generally a year. Covered losses can include medical bills, lost wages, funeral costs, counseling services, and transportation expenses not covered by insurance. Most states have maximum limits of payment that range from $10,000 to $50,000.

Taking the Bite Out of Crime

PROBLEM
Returning from a seniors' picnic, Mary and Bud saw their condominium door ajar. From a neighbor's apartment they called the police. Total disarray greeted Bud and Mary when they entered their unit, and they were badly shaken. The TV, VCR, and a pouch with Bud's hearing aid were gone. A window was smashed. The police made a report and took a silver bowl for fingerprinting.

ACTION
Bud and Mary called their son, Fred, who had been burglarized previously. With his video camera, he documented the damage and discovered other missing items, including a camera and credit cards. They canceled the credit cards and made a new list of stolen property. With the list, they went to the police precinct, and asked for copies of the police reports, names of the police officers, and a receipt for the silver bowl. This documentation was needed when they made a homeowners insurance claim. At Fred's suggestion, they also called a crime victim assistance center. A counselor arranged for the broken window to be repaired immediately, as part of a special program for seniors. The counselor also told Bud that, under a state crime victim compensation program, he might be eligible for the replacement cost of his hearing aid, since it was essential personal property.

Crime victims have other rights in the criminal justice system besides compensation. Property taken for evidence must be returned as soon as possible. Get a receipt and send a letter to the prosecutor stating that you want the property returned. If a suspect is arrested and charged with a crime, victims have the right to know the progress of the case, including court dates of hearings or a pending plea bargain. Victims are also entitled to be protected from harassment or intimidation for reporting the crime.

Under federal income tax rules, crime victims may be allowed a deduction for "casualty losses." Only that portion of a loss that exceeds 10 percent of your adjusted gross income can be deducted, and the first $100 is not deductible. (Keep the police report for documentation.)

Victims may also have a civil claim for injuries or loss against a criminal or third party who acted negligently. For example, a college was found liable when a security guard at a dormitory failed to screen a stranger who then assaulted a student. If you have suffered injuries and feel that you have a civil claim, talk to an attorney.

Dealing with Arrest

Getting on the "wrong side of the law" is no joke, and it is particularly important to know your rights if you should be arrested. According to the so-called Miranda decision by the Supreme Court, if you are to be questioned, you must be told by the arresting officer that you have the right to remain silent and to have a lawyer at your side through the entire process.

An officer who takes you into custody does not have to "read you your rights" if you are not going to be questioned about the crime for which you are being arrested. In many cases, particularly minor crimes, you will not be questioned formally by the police. Even if you feel that the arrest is unjustified, do as the officers say. If they are abusive, remember everything that happens to report later. Be aware, though, that a police officer has the right to use reasonable force to make you comply with his orders, and that resisting arrest is a crime.

After you are taken into custody and booked, the criminal justice process is set in motion for a bail hearing, arraignment, and other court proceedings. Prepare to discuss the charges and your options along the way with your lawyer. (If you cannot afford an attorney, you have the right to ask that one be appointed for free.) Until your lawyer speaks to you, say nothing and stay calm. You need give only your name, address, and birth date, and you may decline to discuss anything else.

The law will not bend to the uncertain wishes, imaginations, and wanton tempers of men.

JOHN ADAMS
Argument in the defense
of the British soldiers in the
Boston Massacre
1770

A Child in Custody

You receive a call from a police officer saying that your son has been "picked up" for vandalism and is being held in the "center." You are sure your son would not do anything wrong, but you still need to know what is at stake and what you can do about it.

• Detained minors are held in detention centers separate from adult prisoners. Usually they are not arrested, but are charged with juvenile delinquency based on the commission of an act such as vandalism. However, if a child is charged with a serious crime such as murder or arson, he or she can be arrested like an adult.

• Juveniles are entitled to remain silent and to be represented by an attorney. Parents should tell children not to talk to police if they are detained until a lawyer has been consulted.

• A minor can be released to the custody of a parent, but if charged with a severe crime, he may be held in a detention center until the trial.

• If a child is charged with juvenile delinquency, he will be tried in a non-jury trial in a juvenile court. If the youth is found guilty, the judge may determine him to be a juvenile offender. Or the child may be charged and tried as an adult, and adjudged guilty or innocent.

• If found to be a juvenile offender, a child can be placed under court supervision; ordered to reform school, a detention center, halfway home, or special counseling; or be placed on probation. A minor found guilty as an adult will be sentenced as one.

• Juvenile delinquency records are sealed to the public. Records can eventually be expunged, or cleared from the books.

ALTERNATIVES TO COURT

Going to court is not the only solution for legal confrontations—you can try any one of several alternative proceedings to resolve disputes.

Direct Negotiation

Negotiation is part of daily life. Even much of a lawyer's work involves negotiation, since 90 percent of lawsuits are settled out of court. In direct negotiation, persuasive skills are used to engage another party in an exchange of information and proposed solutions to find a mutually acceptable result.

Good negotiating is an art. To start you need a convincing argument. Gather facts and evidence in advance. If you are asking a neighbor to replace a window smashed by his son's baseball, come to the negotiation with the name of a witness, a photo of the damage, and an estimate of the replacement cost.

Know your bottom line before you begin. This gives you a yardstick to measure counterproposals. You can still consider other alternatives. The neighbor might not have cash, for instance, but offers to paint your garage instead. Is this equal to your bottom line?

Ask for more than you expect, but stay within reason. People anticipate a back-and-forth, as in negotiations for a house, when there are often many offers and counteroffers. If you are asking your absolute limit, say so: "This is my final request and I am unable to change it."

Direct negotiation is not for every situation. If you are in an emotionally charged state, or if you have been the object of physical abuse, do not try to negotiate. It may not serve your purpose to negotiate if you are in a lesser bargaining position in terms of status or power. A cashier at a retail store may not be in a good bargaining position with the president of the firm who has laid off workers. Finally, don't negotiate directly if you know you are not good at it.

Mediating Your Problems

The image of the judge with black robe and gavel is familiar to all. But people are turning to another authority figure to help resolve disputes: a mediator. Mediators do not make decisions. They work with disputing parties to help them reach a voluntary solution.

Mediation involves person-to-person negotiation, but with a disinterested third party present to listen, identify issues, and propose solutions. Since the 1970's, nonprofit mediation programs have opened in more than 200 state and locally sponsored community mediation centers. Call your state or county government to find out what services are available in your area. Private mediation services, listed in the Yellow Pages under "Mediation Services," are available in nearly every city.

WHY MEDIATION?

Mediation can be initiated in several ways. In some cases it may be required by the court, as in child custody decisions in divorce proceedings. (See also YOUR MARRIAGE AND FAMILY, page 135.) A mediation clause might be part of an existing agreement, such as a homeowners association membership. Or, one party in a dispute may take the initiative and consult a mediation service. This claimant fills out a "Consent to Mediation" form that describes the problem. The form is sent to the other party to the dispute, the respondent, who can agree or refuse to participate.

The kinds of problems most susceptible to solution by mediation are landlord-tenant problems, neighbor disputes, family issues such as simple divorces, and certain consumer disputes. The process works best when the parties are on good enough terms that they can come face-to-face without excessive anger, and when both are anxious for a speedy resolution.

Mediators come from all backgrounds, including psychology, law, and business. No single style of mediation prevails, and there is no set of standard rules. Before entering into voluntary mediation, you should know something about the background, training, and approach of the mediator and how sessions are structured, including whether or not your attorney can be present.

GETTING RESULTS

Mediation is oriented toward results, including a compromise solution, rather than vindication. Sessions are set in an office or conference room. To begin, the mediator will give you and the other side an opportunity to present your case, without interruption or objection. The mediator will then lead a discussion, make suggestions, and possibly meet with the parties individually. Rules of evidence do not apply, there is no formal record, and confidentiality is maintained.

Each point to which the parties agree is written down in a document called a "consent agreement" or "memorandum of understanding." The parties are given copies to sign, and it then becomes a contract that the parties are bound to follow.

In some jurisdictions, this understanding can be incorpo-

MAKING MEDIATION WORK

Mediation is a relatively new process, and many people do not know what to expect, even when they agree to use it to solve their particular problem. Although it seems informal, mediation is a serious affair. Keep a clear focus on the purpose and your role in the process.

1. The ultimate goal in mediation is to arrive at a voluntary solution to your problem.

2. Mediation is not concerned with who is right or even what your rights are, but in securing a practical and workable result.

3. The goal of the mediator is to focus on the issues and to get each of you to see the other side.

4. Your goal is to present your case as convincingly as possible, so that the mediator and the other side understand your point of view. No one else can present it for you.

5. In order to be as convincing as possible, bring to the meeting all the evidence that you have to support your argument: photographs, bills, receipts, documents, witnesses, items, and statements.

6. Prepare notes before the session to define the issues, the results you want, and the least you will accept.

7. In the mediation, use your notes to analyze whether proposed solutions are realistic.

Questions to Ask About Arbitration

Before going into arbitration, look carefully at these areas of particular concern: who the arbitrator will be; what rules will apply; and how much it will cost.

Who the arbitrator will be is critical, especially since in binding arbitration the decision is usually final and cannot be appealed. The dispute resolution organization you use should present a short list of suggested arbitrators. You and the other side will then be asked to rank them.

Do as much research as possible. Get the résumés of suggested arbitrators and the types of cases they have decided. Ask for references. Look them up in "who's who" biographies or law directories in the library. Don't select someone about whom you cannot get good information. If necessary, ask for more names to consider, or make your own suggestions.

The rules of the arbitration could shape the outcome. Read the rules as soon as possible. What evidence should you present? Will you need a lawyer? How will the proceeding be handled? Find out if you can observe an arbitration proceeding to get the feel of it.

Expense is another essential ingredient—arbitration can cost more than some court proceedings. How much will it be, and who will pay? Are there ways to limit the costs?

rated in a court decision, for example, in a divorce proceeding; it will then have the effect of a court order. In other cases, the memorandum of understanding relies upon voluntary compliance. If one side refuses to follow it, the other will have to bring a lawsuit based on a breach of contract to enforce it.

You cannot ask the mediator to advise you, so you may want to have your attorney review the agreement before you sign it. Don't sign an agreement if you feel unfairly pressured or do not fully agree to or understand all of its terms.

Arbitration Means Business

Arbitration is a proceeding by which the parties to a dispute, in order to obtain a speedy and somewhat less expensive solution than going to court, voluntarily select arbitrators to settle their problem. In arbitration, a neutral third party, the arbitrator, holds a hearing on a dispute, listens to evidence, and makes a decision. The hearing is not in a court; the arbitrator is not a judge. Arbitration is a substitute for—not a step toward—litigation.

Binding arbitration clauses prevent you from going to court; that is, once an award is made, it cannot be appealed. In the past, these awards were uniformly upheld as valid. Now, however, judges are beginning to question the unfair use of arbitration if it deprives people of their rights.

While a mediator guides the parties to come to their own agreement, an arbitrator or arbitration panel issues an actual determination. Arbitration is often used for commercial cases, involving business, construction, or insurance companies, and arbitration clauses may be a part of employment, appliance, home remodeling, and stock brokerage contracts.

RULES OF ARBITRATION

Arbitration is conducted by dispute resolution organizations, and arbitrators are lawyers or business people selected from a list of names appropriate to the issue under dispute. Dispute centers are often run by private companies, but are also run by state and local governments.

The proceedings in arbitration are less formal than in a trial, but they are more complex than mediation or small claims court. Arbitration is private, and a record of the proceeding is not usually made. At a hearing, one party presents evidence and witnesses, including experts. Then the other side can cross-examine. Depending on the gravity of the problem, both parties may need lawyers to represent them.

After the hearing, the arbitrator sends out a written decision, or award, within one or two weeks. It may order payment or a certain action to be taken. No reasons have to be stated, although the findings may be put on file with the arbitration service. Under both state and federal laws, the decision can be filed with the court and enforced as though it were a court decision or judgment.

Demanding Arbitration

PROBLEM
When the Smiths hired a roofer to put a new roof on their home, they agreed to a clause in the contract stating that "any claim arising from the contract shall be settled by arbitration." Later, with water dripping down the walls and the contractor refusing their calls, the Smiths were concerned.

ACTION
The Smiths decided to take advantage of the arbitration clause and contacted the arbitration service named in the contract. They filled out a Demand for Arbitration form, which was sent to the contractor. The Smiths suggested that the arbitration hearing be held in their home, where the leaks could be inspected, and the contractor agreed. Within 60 days they were sitting face-to-face with the contractor and an arbitrator to present their evidence.

Arbitration is often described as an inexpensive alternative to court—but that depends on the case. A standard arbitration by the nonprofit American Arbitration Association costs a minimum of $300 in administrative fees for a one-day hearing. The costs of arbitration may be low compared to those for a major lawsuit, but still could be 10 times the costs of taking the case to small claims court.

Administrative Hearings

A myriad of regulations by local, state, and federal government agencies touch our lives, and open the way for another type of adjudication process: the administrative hearing. It is not an alternative to going to court as negotiation, mediation, and arbitration are; nor is it a court case. Instead, it is a quasi-judicial proceeding that can be very useful.

If you disagree with a ruling from a government agency—from a property tax assessment to workers compensation to a Medicare claim—you may request a hearing by an agency administrator. The hearing officer will review your case, make a determination about whether the agency decision was correct or fair in your circumstances; and approve any compensation, such as from a Medicare claim.

123
HANDLING AN ADMINISTRATIVE HEARING

When a government agency makes a decision you disagree with, you can seek a review in an administrative hearing. Since it is difficult to successfully appeal the decision made at a hearing (you must prove that you did not get due process or that the agency's regulation does not meet legal standards), it is important to present your case effectively. Here's what to do:

1. Respond promptly. When you receive notice of a government decision that you wish to dispute, you must act in a timely fashion. You usually have 60 days to request an administrative hearing to review the decision.

2. Learn the rules. Ask the agency where to find its rules and decisions; then study those that apply to your case.

3. Collect evidence. Gather documents and other backup material showing why the agency did not apply its rules properly in your case.

4. Know the ropes. Ask for a copy of the hearing process and attend an administrative hearing, if possible, to see how it is conducted.

5. Go to your hearing. You can represent yourself, but you may be wise to hire a lawyer or paralegal to guide you through an agency's complex procedures. You can ask the agency if an attorney is available to you for a minimal fee.

GOING TO COURT

A judge for your dispute may be exactly what you need. For best results, learn your way around the courts.

Appearing in Court

Testifying as a witness, representing yourself, or simply appearing in court can be a nerve-wracking experience. To make the best impression keep these hints in mind:

✔ *Appearance.* Dress as for a business meeting or job interview. Sit upright and speak calmly; project your voice and look at the jury (if there is one) when speaking.

✔ *What to say.* Answer all questions truthfully. Don't elaborate; try to use a simple "yes"or "no". If you do not know an answer, say so.

✔ *Correcting errors.* If you realize you have made a mistake, especially if you are a witness, tell the judge you want to correct something.

✔ *Composure.* Don't get involved in arguments or discussion of objections, and don't be upset by impertinent or snide questions if you are cross-examined.

✔ *Speak for yourself.* If you are representing yourself, give a straightforward account of your version of the events. Describe only what you personally saw, and don't make accusatory statements.

Choosing Small Claims Court

Size says nothing about the aggravation, or the gravity, of a legal problem—losing $100 is as serious to a person of modest means as is the loss of $100,000 to a millionaire. But comparatively smaller claims have one advantage: they can be resolved within the streamlined procedures of small claims courts.

Small claims courts in every state handle cases in which the amount of money sought does not exceed a maximum limit—usually from $1,000 to $5,000. You can initiate a lawsuit by filling out a form stating your claim. Procedures vary by state. The kinds of cases commonly handled include bad checks, return of apartment security deposits, and fender-benders.

Although the process is made easier, small claims court is a still a court, and certain procedures must be followed. In order to file a claim, you must have the exact name and address of the person you are suing—the defendant. The claim must be filed in the state court where the defendant resides, or where a contract under question was made, a product was sold, or an accident involving the defendant occurred. Usually, out-of-state parties cannot be sued in small claims court, unless they do business locally.

The papers—summons and complaints—need to be formally served. In some places, papers can be sent by certified mail; otherwise, a process server must be used to present the papers to the defendant. You can find process servers listed in the Yellow Pages. After receipt, the defendant can make a counterclaim (not just an answer or denial, but an independent suit) against the plaintiff.

TIME TO BE HEARD

Usually within two months, depending upon the jurisdiction, you are granted a hearing before a judge or volunteer attorney; juries are rarely used. Hearings are short (10 to 45 minutes) and formal rules of evidence (such as objecting) are eased, making the situation less threatening. A lawyer usually is not needed and in some states may not be permitted.

Have evidence with you to convince the judge why a decision should be made in your favor. A decision may be made on

LEGAL PROCEEDINGS EXPLAINED

Courts interpret and apply the law to the facts of each case in order to bring about justice. Other proceedings, like mediation and arbitration, are also used to resolve legal matters.Judicial proceedings vary from state to state, but generally those involved with civil cases (non-criminal matters) include:

Types of Proceedings	What They Are/What They Do
Direct Negotiations	An exchange of offers to reach a settlement
Alternative Dispute Resolution (ADR)	Procedures for settling disputes other than litigation
Mediation	A confidential meeting (or meetings) with a neutral third party to obtain a voluntary agreement
Arbitration	A hearing (or hearings) by a neutral arbitrator who will make a binding decision
Administrative hearings	Hear appeals of government agency decisions
Specialized State Courts	Hear cases concerning particular areas of civil law
Small claims courts	Hear simple cases seeking damages, to a state maximum, such as $2,500
Family (or matrimonial) courts	Hear divorce, separation, and child custody cases
Probate or surrogate courts	Hear estate, incompetency, guardianships, and adoption cases
Juvenile courts	Hear juvenile offense, paternity, child neglect, and child support cases
Other local courts	Depending on the state, landlord-tenant, property claims, traffic violations, and lesser criminal cases
General State Courts	Hear lawsuits on civil claims: contracts, injuries, property issues
District or county courts	Trial courts of general jurisdiction that handle larger civil cases of any type
Municipal courts	Trial courts of limited jurisdiction that handle civil cases to a fixed amount, such as $10,000
State Appellate Courts	Hear appeals of decisions made in lower state courts
Specialized Federal Courts	Hear certain areas of law
Claims courts	Hear suits against U.S. government
Bankruptcy courts	Hear corporate and individual bankruptcy cases
Tax courts	Hear appeals of disputes with the IRS
Federal District Courts	Hear claims between citizens of different states seeking damages over $10,000; hear some federal lawsuits
Federal Appellate Courts	Hear appeals of decisions made in lower court
Courts of Appeals	Hear appeals from lower courts and from federal agencies
U.S. Supreme Court	Hears selected federal and state appeals

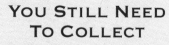

YOU STILL NEED TO COLLECT

Before spending the money to file a claim, consider whether the other side has assets from which you can collect if you win. Very poor people and bankrupt companies do not. If you do go to court and win a judgment, and if the defendant then does not pay, you can take these steps:

1. Go back to court to record the judgment and file what is known as a writ of execution.

2. If the defendant owns property, you may be able to get an order instructing a sheriff to seize it for sale.

3. You could start a garnishment suit to collect from wages that are above the limitations set by law or from a bank account.

4. If assets cannot be found, you can bring the debtor back to court to answer questions about them.

5. You may have to hire a lawyer at this stage. A reasonable cost to cover an attorney's fees can be added to what you are owed.

6. You might be able to engage a collection agency to assist you. A typical fee is half the money collected.

the spot or mailed to you within a week or two. Whether or not you can appeal depends on where you live. In some states, appeals from small claims court are either limited or not permitted. Filing a claim usually costs less than $50. Most states have done their best to make small claims court accessible, providing pamphlets and assistance from a clerk or court adviser.

NOT FOR ALL SITUATIONS

Small claims court is not available for all types of cases. Disputes do not qualify if the remedy sought is not money. A judge in small claims court does not have the authority to order someone to act or to refrain from acting—for example, a judge could not order that a fence be removed or that an abusive spouse be restrained. Cases involving divorce, probate, tax, or claims against the government will not be heard, either.

When You Are Suing

Civil suits that are too large or complicated for small claims court are pursued in state courts of general jurisdiction. Some common names for these courts are district, common pleas, and superior courts (also called Supreme Court in New York State). Federal district courts also hear disputes involving more than $10,000 if they concern citizens of different states.

To sue, you or your lawyer files a complaint that states the basis for the case—the cause of action—and the remedy being sought. For example, you state that you suffered injuries as the result of an auto accident caused by the other party and seek payment for lost wages and medical expenses. Suits with no cause of action or no remedy will be dismissed.

After filing, information about the claim is exchanged, called the discovery phase. In a deposition, witnesses are questioned in private but under oath about what happened. You may be asked to answer written questions, called "interrogatories;" to produce documents that relate to the case; or to submit to a medical examination.

This is the time when settlement proposals are likely to be made. Motions are also made in court to settle sticky or technical legal questions, such as whether or not the time period for suing has expired. At any time during these proceedings and even after the case has gone to trial, it may be settled.

Most lawsuits never get to trial, but are settled out of court. Should your case be one of the small percentage that go to trial, the person who initiated the suit will try to prove the claim by presenting evidence to a judge or jury or both. After the trial, some cases can be appealed to a higher court.

USING A LAWYER

In a complex case or one that is emotionally charged, a lawyer can provide you with vital support, but you should know how to use your attorney wisely.

Do You Need Counsel?

L awyer," "attorney," "counsel," "member of the bar" all mean the same thing: a person who, by law, can represent you in legal matters. Whether you need a lawyer or not depends on three factors: how complicated the matter is, how important it is to you, and whether you need an intermediary.

A case can be complicated because of technical legal procedures, as occurs in lawsuits in federal court, state trial courts (except in small claims court), or binding arbitration. Or it may be made complex because the facts of the case touch many areas, such as a medical problem that involves a hospital, doctors, and a drug manufacturer; or when the parties to the case are numerous, out-of-state, or difficult to identify. One extra complication: If a lawyer is representing the other side, you should probably have one, too.

The importance of a case depends on how much is at stake—in well-being, money, or civil liberties. Any criminal case more serious than a traffic fine ranks on top. Other important situations are cases involving large sums of money or property, such as a home purchase, foreclosure, government benefits, substantial marital assets, large personal-injury claims. The measure of import also may be personal and subjective, as occurs in discrimination or child custody cases.

Whether or not you need an intermediary to speak for you is a personal decision. But if the conflict is emotionally charged, provokes anger, or is threatening, you should get a lawyer

WHAT CAN A LAWYER DO FOR YOU?

Other than yourself, only a lawyer can represent you in legal proceedings. A lawyer is with rare exceptions a graduate of law school who is licensed to practice law in a given state, having passed a bar examination. In most states, a non-lawyer cannot be your advocate because practicing law without a license is usually a crime. In some instances, non-lawyers such as brokers, agents, or bankers, may help you draw up papers. Paralegals who work under the supervision of lawyers may handle minor legal matters, and in a few states, they are allowed to consult directly in limited areas such as divorce or bankruptcy.

In threading this [legal] maze, the lawyer has inherent advantages not merely of specialized training and experience, but of detachment. He is not involved as principal in the problems that he is asked to mediate and advise on, but as an agent, and as such can afford, emotionally and intellectually, to take a broader long-term view of his clients' needs— whether the client be a private corporation, an individual or a government agency—than can the client.

WILLIAM J. BRENNAN, JR.
United States
Supreme Court Justice
1956–1990

Lawyers offer two particular areas of competence. One is familiarity with legal procedure; the other is informed judgment. A good lawyer will listen to your problem, seek out the facts, and do research. The lawyer will advise you on whether you have a legitimate case, or cause of action; enough evidence; a possible remedy; and a favorable position in view of the likely costs and benefits. The final decision is up to you.

Hiring the Right Lawyer

The days when lawyers seldom advertised for clients or when one attorney could handle all your legal business are virtually gone. Television screens, bus displays, radio spots, and newspaper pages bristle with advertisements for lawyers for hire who practice in a wide range of specialties. How do you know which is right for you? Considerations include the individual's availability, specialty, personality, and, of course, price.

In compiling a list of attorneys to choose from, you will need to focus your search. What type of case do you have? Specialties you are likely to find among lawyers include divorce (also known as family or matrimonial law), bankruptcy, tax, workers compensation, personal injury (accidents), criminal, real estate, product liability, probate (wills), discrimination (equal employment)—the list is long because the law has become so complex that lawyers need special expertise. Even a general practitioner probably works in only five or so areas. Lawyers also may specialize in particular types of clients such as older persons, or the disabled.

MAKING CONTACT

When you have put together a list of likely candidates, schedule interviews with several on your list, checking first to see if you will be charged for a preliminary interview. Prepare a short written statement about your problem. Ask if the lawyer has had experience with similar cases, and what steps she recommends taking; how she will keep you informed of progress; and how fees are calculated, including all incidental fees.

Since it is important not only to trust your lawyer but to work together harmoniously, try to get a sense of her personally as well as professionally. Ask a few informal questions, such as how she got into this specialty area.

Initial consultations with a few attorneys will benefit you in the end. You will learn more about your case and how attorneys view it. Because switching lawyers mid-case can be complicated and expensive, it is worth the extra effort to choose one best suited to your needs in the first place.

Where to Find Your Lawyer

Since a tour of the Yellow Pages reveals a wide array of lawyers, how do you choose the right one? Here are some suggestions of where to find a lawyer who best suits you, your legal problem, and your financial situation:

✔ *Recommendations.* Ask friends, colleagues, and professional contacts for referrals to lawyers they have actually worked with.

✔ *Bar associations.* Local or state organizations of attorneys, or bar associations, usually keep a list of recommended attorneys available for referrals.

✔ *Legal advice clinics.* Some bar associations, community centers, or law schools sponsor clinics where volunteer attorneys will meet with a client for a low fee or for free to review a case.

✔ *Legal aid.* People with very little money may qualify for a free or low-cost legal aid lawyer.

✔ *Public defender.* Cases involving poor persons charged with crimes can be assigned to a lawyer serving as a public defender.

✔ *Advertisements.* Lawyers who advertise are usually available to the general public, unlike big firms that serve only business clients.

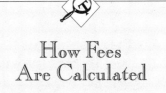

PREPAID LEGAL PLANS

Prepaid legal plans, a newer option in legal services, are offered to members of unions and sometimes through large companies as an employee benefit. You sign up as a member and pay a monthly or yearly fee. In exchange, you get access to a lawyer who will advise you in certain prescribed situations.

Prepaid legal plans are sometimes called legal insurance, but they operate differently from other kinds of insurance. Prepaid legal programs cover the most simple situations for free, but any problems more complex will command an additional fee, which may be discounted.

Services provided in prepaid legal plans vary. Often a plan will pay for telephone consultations, letters from the lawyer to merchants or others, a review of documents such as leases or contracts (sometimes no longer than six pages), and the preparation of a simple will. But read the literature carefully, and note what kinds of legal help you are not going to get. Going to court, for example, is not covered by most plans.

Flat fees may be available for other services, but with limitations. A flat fee, for example, may be offered for a lawyer to handle a divorce—but only if it is uncontested, if there are no children, if there is no attorney on the other side, and there is no property agreement to be negotiated.

Plans also vary in format. In one called "open panel," you select your attorney from a list given to you. In "closed panel," you are assigned an attorney who has been preselected by the administrator of the plan, although you may seek to change attorneys if you are not satisfied. You should know if you can talk to the same lawyer each time you call with questions, or whether lawyers handle calls on a rotating basis.

Be aware that, as for some health insurance, prepaid legal plans will often exclude from coverage problems that began before you joined the plan. Furthermore, if your legal need is immediate, you may not have time to sign up for the prepaid plan and wait for an attorney to be assigned.

A Client's Bill of Rights

Since you rely so heavily on your lawyer for knowledge and advice in legal matters, it is sometimes hard to remember that he works for you. But lawyers are sworn to follow a code of conduct and ethical standards. You should be aware of what they are and how they affect you.

Virtually all that you say to your lawyer is confidential. This principle is known as the attorney-client privilege, which can be broken only in limited circumstances: If you tell your attor-

How Fees Are Calculated

Lawyers' fees vary, depending on the lawyer and type of case. Four types of billing are used: flat fee, hourly rate, contingent fee, and percentage fee. Negotiate first; then secure fees in writing.

A flat fee is a set price charged for a routine matter, such as writing a will or lease, drawing up an uncomplicated divorce, or handling minor criminal offenses in court.

Hourly fees are the most common. You are charged for each hour the lawyer spends on the case, at a stated rate per hour. Rates differ by community and firm; larger firms are generally more expensive.

Contingent fees are often applied when you are seeking an award of money: personal injury, collection, discrimination cases. Except for incidental costs such as filing fees, you do not pay unless you recover money, and then the lawyer takes a percentage.

A percentage fee is based on the value of property involved. In probate cases, for example, the lawyer might charge 7 percent of the estate value.

Be aware that additional expenses, such as filing fees, photocopying costs, depositions, expert witness fees, and travel expenses, may be extra.

You may be asked to pay your lawyer a retainer up front. Some lawyers consider such deposits nonrefundable; so confirm the situation in writing.

In some cases, you can recoup your attorney's fees and ancillary costs from the other side, but there is no guarantee.

123..

THINGS YOU CAN DO TO SAVE LEGAL COSTS

By taking certain steps on your own, you may be able to keep your legal fees and costs from skyrocketing. If you are paying your lawyer an hourly fee, you can save time and money by following these tips:

1. Prepare a chronology of events and a written statement of the problem.

2. Make a detailed inventory and listing of the names, addresses, times, and places that relate to the incident. In accident cases, have the date, time, location, witnesses, description of injuries, names of medical personnel, car registration, and insurance information. In family law cases, have names and birth dates of children, a complete list of personal property and real estate, and a history of your marriage and employment.

3. Organize your documents and make photocopies for your lawyer. To each copy attach an index card that explains what it is, when it was signed, and how it fits into your case.

4. Since lawyers usually charge for their time spent on the phone or in meetings, keep phone calls and office visits focused and concise. Prepare a list of questions or subjects, and stick to the issues.

5. Ask your lawyer if there is anything you can do to keep costs down, such as getting police reports on your own, locating title documents, or researching nonlegal points.

ney about a crime that you are planning to commit, have a dispute over fees; or sue him for malpractice. In some situations, such as criminal cases, documents or evidence that you give your lawyer may be considered "discoverable," which means that the lawyer may be legally bound to turn such evidence over to the district attorney.

You have the right to a full disclosure of the lawyer's fees, and how they are calculated, and what extra expenses might be added on. Your lawyer should represent you zealously, inform you in writing of any conflicts of interest that arise, and tell you if another lawyer is assisting on your case.

Clear communication is one of your key rights. Your phone calls and letters should be returned. You should be regularly informed about the progress of your case and should get copies of all documents, even if you have to pay a fee for them. You should understand the strengths and weaknesses of your case.

Remember that you make the ultimate decisions on the case. Any settlement offers must be explained to you, and you must respond. Finally, you have the right to be treated with common courtesy and consideration.

How To Help Your Lawyer

The path to resolving your legal problem is one that you and your lawyer travel together. Your lawyer cannot succeed without your help. Maintaining a friendly businesslike relationship is essential and, at least in part, is your responsibility.

You will need to educate your lawyer about what happened. Give all the relevant facts and do not hold back, even if something is embarrassing. The information will be far more damaging if it comes out later. Moreover, if your attorney does not have all the facts, he may inadvertently give bad advice or handle the case differently, possibly to your disadvantage. However, this does not mean you should overload your lawyer with meaningless information.

Review documents your lawyer sends to you, and correct errors. Enlighten yourself about the law and court procedures so you will have an idea of what to expect as the case progresses. Be aware that what happened in someone else's case will not necessarily happen in yours. Try to be realistic about outcomes. Keep your lawyer informed of developments that might affect your case or of personal changes—if you change your address, for instance, or your job. If your lawyer asks for a certain piece of information, follow through promptly. Finally, start a written log of contacts with your lawyer and keep files of original documents, legal papers, and correspondence.

Troubles with Your Attorney

As in any other human relationship, problems can arise with your lawyer. If they do, you should speak up calmly and firmly about what is bothering you. Do it right away. The longer you let resentment simmer, the harder it will be to work out a reasonable solution.

Fees represent the most common problem people have with lawyers, and the best cure for this is prevention. Remember, you are entitled to an itemized bill. If you cannot resolve a money problem with your attorney, seek fee arbitration through a bar association.

Another common complaint is that a lawyer is not devoting sufficient time or thought to his client's case. Sometimes your lawyer may not have kept you completely informed of progress, but be aware that many delays may be out of his control. Whatever the problem, if it continues, write your lawyer a letter. Letters usually get lawyers' attention because they know you may be building a case against them. If a significant question about the lawyer's work remains, ask another lawyer to advise you.

If all else fails, remember that you have the right to fire your lawyer. Do so only as a last resort. Unless he did nothing on your behalf or is guilty of malpractice, you will probably have to pay the old lawyer as well as the new one.

The first thing we do, let's kill all the lawyers.

WILLIAM SHAKESPEARE
King Henry VI, Part II

Where to Complain About Your Lawyer

Before a problem with your lawyer gets serious, you should have already talked with him or her about what is bothering you. If you are still not satisfied and have thought the matter through, you have several avenues of recourse. Here are some of your options:

• If the lawyer is in a law firm, you can go to a managing attorney of the firm; if you are part of a prepaid legal plan, you can take your complaint to to the plan administrator.

• If you are not sure that you have a valid complaint, go to the state bar association's attorney disciplinary committee with questions.

• If you think the lawyer's fees are higher than they should be, you can consult a fee arbitration committee of the local or state bar association.

• If the problem is more than a dispute over fees— if a lawyer has stolen money from you or defrauded you, for instance, go the bar association's client security trust fund. If your charge is justified, all or part of your money may be reimbursed. You should also notify the district attorney or the police.

• If you suspect your lawyer has acted unethically, go to the attorney disciplinary board. If his conduct violates state standards, you may want to file a complaint. Your lawyer may then be disciplined, possibly losing the right to practice law, temporarily or permanently.

• You can sue your lawyer for malpractice and seek reimbursement if he has acted negligently and your rights have been damaged. See a lawyer who handles professional liability cases.

REPRESENTING YOURSELF

In some cases, if you are up to the challenge, you can represent yourself in court—but you'll need to do a lot of homework first.

Legal Matters You Can Handle Yourself

By law, even if you are not a lawyer, you are permitted to represent yourself in any legal proceeding. You may automatically handle some routine situations on your own, such as making a purchase or taking out a loan. In small claims court and mediation, you may be called upon to represent yourself because lawyers may be excluded. In certain standardized areas, such as executing a simple will, changing your name, and divorcing when money and children are not in dispute, kits and forms are available that can guide you through the legal thicket, especially if you use them with a bit of caution.

But when disputes enter more elaborate legal arenas or become more complex, even lawyers hire lawyers to represent them. If important rights or large sums of money are at stake, hiring yourself might be more costly in the long run. So, before tackling a legal problem yourself, consider consulting an attorney to get a sense of how legally complex the matter will be. Even if you decide to hire a lawyer, your research will help you better understand the process you are about to undertake.

DUAL ASSIGNMENT

A legal matter has two integral components: substance and procedure. Substance involves the legal subject matter, such as whether you are entitled to a reimbursement of costs under a warranty. Procedure has to do with the legal rules and mechanisms by which you achieve your goal—such as how you state your claim and where you file it.

If you act as your own attorney, you will have to familiarize yourself with both areas. This research involves much effort and can present a challenge even for lawyers. Also, small mistakes can result in great losses; for example, filing the wrong document can result in your forgoing your claim. Judges and clerks are not always sympathetic to the self-helper.

On the other hand, self-representation can have a positive side effect. Whether you win or lose, your efforts may save you hundreds of dollars and result in a feeling of empowerment.

Rules and Regulations

I f you are considering representing yourself, your first step should be to research the rules and procedural questions that relate to your case. Are you within the time period for filing? What is the right court or forum? How do you get the other party into court? What types of evidence will you be permitted to present?

In courtroom litigation, procedure is complex—in fact, lawyers expend much energy trying to solve procedural issues. Federal courts have their own rules, as does each state. In general, there are five types of rules that apply:

- **State statutes and constitutions** define the authority of each court to take certain types of cases; also defined are statutes of limitations, or the time limits for filing each cause of action.
- **Rules of civil procedure** define what civil court papers should look like, and how and when certain actions such as motions (requests for some action made to the judge) and interrogatories (written questions asked by one party in a lawsuit of the other party) are to be completed. These vary for each type of court.
- **Rules of evidence** describe formalities of introducing documents and witnesses in court.
- **Local court rules** deal with the idiosyncrasies of each court, such as whether a certain type of paper should be used.
- **Protocol**, or customs of the court, deal with matters such as how to address the judge, which can be entirely individual. It is your responsibility to be aware of such fine points.

Ask questions, too: How long will the proceeding last? Will you be allowed to call witnesses? If a witness cannot attend, will you be allowed to present a sworn statement, or affidavit?

Try to get documents from a case similar to yours. Court records are available to the public. To find out how to obtain them, call the courthouse where your case is being heard. In an arbitration or administrative hearing, ask if sample documents are on file.

In mediation, arbitration, small claims court, or an administrative hearing, the rules are usually simplified, and you can ask a court clerk or the agency involved, such as the arbitration association, for a copy of them. You may want to attend a similar proceeding before you file. Regardless of the forum you choose, ask questions of the clerk, the bailiff, and lawyers. Understanding the importance of following the rules will make you a stronger advocate on your own behalf.

Where to Get Legal Forms and Information

Here are several resources available to non-lawyers for help in dealing with legal issues or for information:

✔ *Kits and books.* Do-it-yourself materials, including software, for divorce, simple wills, and other similar legal issues are available at bookstores.

✔ *Tele-law.* You can call your state and local bar associations to see if they offer a telephone service with recorded messages that explain common legal questions.

✔ *Legal forms.* Stationery stores carry preprinted documents including wills and leases. Some courts, such as small claims court, also provide preprinted forms.

✔ *Books of "practice forms."* These sample books can be found in law libraries and law school bookstores.

✔ *Law libraries.* Courthouses and law schools often have public law libraries.

✔ *Public case files.* The clerk of courts keeps records of lawsuits open for public review.

✔ *Legal newspapers.* Local legal newspapers carry ads for resources that might be helpful in researching a case.

✔ *Courses.* Seminars are available in some communities for people interested in representing themselves legally.

Strategies for Preparing Your Case

From settlement discussions to arbitration, from small claims court to a jury trial, the key to success in representing yourself is preparation. Since you are going to act as an "attorney pro se," you will have to learn to think like a lawyer. Here are some guidelines, suggestions, and strategies that you can use when representing yourself:

LIST YOUR FACTS
• Using your problem log, documents, or memory, write down a chronology of everything that occurred. In an accident case, include events surrounding the accident, physical injury, medical treatment, property damage, repairs, and contacts with insurers.

• List unknowns—facts that might be known only to the other party or facts that are unknown altogether, such as if a stoplight was working.

STATE WHAT YOU ARE SEEKING
• If you are seeking damages due to injury or property loss, specify the losses you have suffered, such as property damage, physical injury, loss of work. Include the costs involved, such as repair bills, medical expenses, and fines.

• If you want someone to act—to stop making noise or to permit child visitation—-write the desired action clearly in a sentence. Then, state the harm that you will suffer if the action does not occur.

• If you have not incurred injury or property loss or do not seek a definite action, rethink your case. A claim based on hurt feelings or speculation is not legitimate.

• Write down your highest expectation—the most you hope to get, and your bottom line—the least you will accept.

CLARIFY WHO THE OPPOSITION IS
• If an individual or small business is responsible, get the correct name and address. If a corporation is your target, get the name of the company head and the person who can accept the legal papers from the secretary of state. If a government agency is the problem, find out if it is a federal, state, or city agency, and the name of the person in charge .

• Determine if additional individuals might be responsible, such as the owner and insurer of a car as well as the driver involved in the crash.

• For all parties you name in the suit, state what personal assets, insurance, and other remedy they may be able to provide.

AMASS YOUR PROOF
• Compile as much evidence as possible. Every claim must be verified. Organize each contract, letter, receipt, photograph, bill, videotape, drawing, and the like according to the part of your case it supports, and label it.

• Compile a list of witnesses, including full names and addresses, and describe their direct knowledge of the events. Try to get affidavits or sworn written statements from them.

• Look for holes. Seek additional evidence, such as expert witnesses or relevant documents, that will fill in blanks or further verify your position.

ANTICIPATE THE OPPOSITION
• Write down the reasons you think the other side disagrees with your position, and try to anticipate what they will say.

• Write down the evidence that you think the other side may use to support its position; then, list facts that will contradict the other side's point of view.

CHECK THE LAW
• Check out statutes, decisions, and regulations that apply to your claim. Particularly, make sure that you have a legal cause of action. Look for other cases that support your position.

• Check the rules of evidence for your proceeding to determine if your evidence will be permitted, and how it should be submitted.

• List available places for getting satisfaction or recourse, such as small claims court or mediation. List the pros and cons for each option, including the difficulty of presenting evidence in a particular venue, unavailability of the other party, and expense.

OUTLINE YOUR CASE
• Write a one sentence statement that sums up your case and the damages you are seeking. The sentence should read: "This case is about ..., and these are the damages I suffered as a result."

• Make a chart that states your claim, each fact that led to it, each piece of evidence that verifies it, and each legal principle that supports it.

Appearing in Court

Making an appearance in court is the formal term for showing up at a hearing. But the word "appearance" is also appropriate in another way, because personal appearance—your manner of dress and demeanor—is very important in determining how your case is perceived.

In court, wear the type of clothes that you might wear to a business meeting or job interview. Arrive a few minutes early. Even though you may have to wait to be heard, the "calendar call" (a roll call for cases in order of appearance) comes first, and if you are not present, you can be crossed off. If you are late, give your name quietly to the bailiff when you arrive.

REPRESENTING YOURSELF

Have your documents organized and easily accessible. Even in small claims court, you cannot simply show up and tell your story; you must provide documented proof for your case. In major cases, lawyers often prepare a "trial notebook" for themselves, with sections for legal rules, research, evidence, and questions for witnesses.

Whether your appearance is before a judge or a jury, you must show that you are credible, serious-minded, and have done your homework. At all times, be courteous and respectful to the judge, court personnel, and especially to the other side. Speak firmly but without agitation. Stick to the point when you speak, and keep the point short.

If you are the plaintiff, you will be called first. You should know exactly how you are going to present your case. It is not a bad idea to actually memorize one or two sentences to get you going on your opening statement. Then you will call witnesses, testify yourself, and introduce evidence.

TALKING TO THE BENCH

The judge cannot actively help you or the other side. But if you make a reasonable request, the bench might grant it. If the judge rules, for example, that you failed to take proper steps in advance or did not supply necessary information, you might ask for a "continuance" so you will have time to comply. Or if you have forgotten a critical document, you should ask the judge for an "extension" to submit the document later. Or perhaps the bench has just ruled that a piece of your evidence cannot be submitted. You get flustered, and need time to regroup. Address the bench and say: "At this time, your honor, I'd like to request a short recess."

GETTING A COACH

If you decide to represent yourself, you may need help along the way from someone more knowledgeable. A local attorney might be willing to consult with or coach you, although most lawyers who might agree to help will charge a fee and ask that you sign an agreement stating they are not representing you. You might want to use a coach for help with the following:

1. Ask whether you have a valid claim in the early stages of a dispute.

2. Ask for help in preparing certain forms, such as a subpoena or discovery questions.

3. If you have prepared documents such as a contract, release, or rental agreement, ask the lawyer to review them.

4. If you go into a mediation session, meet with your consulting lawyer in advance to outline the points that you want to make and what your bottom line should be.

5. Have a session with the lawyer before you go into court to go over your evidence, testimony, and outline of the case.

6. Have the lawyer go over a settlement or mediation agreement before you sign it.

7. If you can no longer handle your case, ask your consulting lawyer if he or she is willing to represent you or to recommend another lawyer.

MAKING YOUR VOICE HEARD

Some problems seem too big to handle, but you do not have to be alone. Joining forces with others can get action. Many voices make a loud noise.

What to Do if You Receive a Class Action Notice

If you receive a notice in the mail, describing a class action that might affect you, or if you see an advertisement in a magazine concerning a suit, what should you do?

These notices indicate that a group of people has already begun a class action lawsuit, and a court has decided that the group fits certain criteria for a "class," that is, a large group of people with similar claims. A public notice also indicates that a court has "certified" the class, that is, given the group the legal status to conduct their suit. Now, an attempt is being made to notify anyone else who might be in the same situation but who is not part of the original group.

If you think you have a legitimate claim, follow the directions in the notice. At this stage, you have little to lose by investigating further. Usually an address or telephone number will be listed where you can get more information.

At some point you will be asked to submit a proof of your claim, and a court will review it. If you fit into the certified class and the group bringing the lawsuit wins, you should receive a portion of the amount awarded or benefit in some way from its success.

Class Actions Can Help

After analyzing your house payments, you believe that you have been overcharged on a mortgage escrow account. The financial damage is not serious—less than $500—but the bank refuses to cooperate. You know there must be other customers in the same situation.

When many individuals have the same problem, they are sometimes able to join their causes in a "class-action lawsuit." By bringing together several relatively small but similar claims, a group can get the attention of large institutions that might otherwise ignore individual complaints. Class-action lawsuits have been used to pool the claims of groups of 20 to 1,000 people who have been hurt by a particular drug, suffered from pollution, or been excessively penalized for terminating an automobile lease agreement, among other issues.

The requirements for beginning a class action lawsuit are stiff, and specialty lawyers are needed For more information, you can contact the National Consumer Law Center in Boston, Massachusetts (For their address and phone number, see RESOURCES, page 493). Also, State Attorney Generals sometimes represents groups of citizens. In addition to getting a refund for all or part of their losses, participants in a class-action lawsuit often succeed in getting an unfair practice changed. However, such suits can be expensive and time-consuming; corporate opposition can be daunting. Starting a suit should be carefully considered to ensure that the time, energy, and money spent will be worthwhile.

Organizing for Action

A class-action suit involves considerable technical legal machinery, but there are other ways to raise a chorus of voices to get something done: When you encounter an issue that affects a large group of people, getting together to achieve social or political change may be more appropriate than trying to force legal action. By organizing others, you can multiply the resources available and draw more attention to your problem.

In organizing, you use all of the skills of individual problem solving, plus several more. You will need to convince others that what is at stake is important and that their efforts have a possibility of getting results.

There are different types of organizations. A broad-issues organization is an alliance of people with common concerns, such as homeowners or cancer victims. They often have a far-reaching agenda for change or may meet for support and education without a particular focus.

A single-issue group forms around a specific concern, such as parents who are concerned about drunk driving. In this case, the organization MADD, or Mothers Against Drunk Driving, was established to promote awareness of, and find solutions to, the problem. The single-issue coalition, in turn, is developed when different groups are brought together under one umbrella to find redress for a common problem.

Keeping at It to Get Results

PROBLEM
Wally was among several longtime city residents of an urban community who enjoyed a sense of security from having a police precinct headquarters nearby. When a newspaper reported that the police administration wanted to close the old station house and build a new one somewhere else, Wally and his neighbors were sure their community would suffer.

ACTION
Wally got a copy of the new plan, and talked to some experts about the costs and benefits of renovating the old headquarters building as opposed to building a new one. He wrote to the mayor with his findings, describing the neighborhood concerns. To form a coalition of community support, Wally contacted political clubs and religious, business, and community leaders in the area. He made presentations to his block association, passing out copies of the letter he had written. After creating a "Committee to Save the Police Precinct," Wally built an advisory group and designed a letterhead with their names. He circulated petitions at neighborhood fairs, persuaded community organizations to sign resolutions, and made presentations to the city's budget committee. With each contact, he augmented a mailing list. Eventually a community group was so impressed that it offered to serve as a formal sponsor. When a new mayor took office, Wally fired off several letters with the neighborhood's concerns. After several years, his efforts paid off: plans for a new building were shelved, and preparations to renovate the old one began.

Defining the issue is the first step in organizing for action. Research the subject to find out the history of the issue, who has the authority to make the decision that you want, who else has expressed an interest, and how change can be made. Merely complaining is not enough; you need to be specific about the results you seek.

Organizational Tips for Getting Started

Organizational meetings allow you to present your ideas to a wider community. Here are some tips for making such meetings productive:

✔ *Plan a presentation.* Keep it to the point and respect people's time.

✔ *Target a core group.* Try to identify a small group of committed, like-minded people.

✔ *Be pragmatic.* Set specific goals that deal with the primary objective.

✔ *Stick to an agenda.* If other issues arise, postpone them until the meeting's end.

✔ *Take notes.* Record ideas and resolutions, and distribute notes later.

✔ *Mediate.* Assign one group member to lead or monitor the discussions.

✔ *Get names and numbers.* Prepare a sign-in sheet to ensure you will be able to reach volunteers after the meeting.

✔ *Identify special skills.* Find people or parties who can help in specific ways, such as providing particular expertise.

✔ *Locate helpful contacts.* Ask for names of helpful public officials and private executives.

✔ *Set deadlines.* When someone agrees to take on a task, set a date for completion.

USING THE PRESS

Media attention can help you get the action you want. Organized groups have the best chance of getting to the media. Here are some ways to do that:

1. Write letters to the editors of local publications and newspapers, using a short, crisp, informational style.

2. Type one-paragraph announcements of meetings and send them to radio, TV, and newspaper calendar desks.

3. List the contact person and his telephone number on everything you distribute.

4. When a public event is planned, send or fax a press release, no more than two typed pages in length, with pertinent information to media offices.

5. Plan public events in colorful or meaningful locations to encourage television coverage.

6. At public events, have an information kit including one page of background about your group. Keep a list of interesting approaches for story ideas.

7. If the media do not attend an event, call them afterward.

8. Keep a contact sheet of interested media people.

9. Write a 10-second public service announcement and send it to local radio and television stations.

10. Broadcast a video about your issue on your local public access television station.

Early on, create a piece of literature—even if it is a single sheet of paper—that explains the problem. People will know that you are serious. Set a time and place for a meeting of interested people. Post notices in public places and community newspapers. After you give the people who come together some background, brainstorm for ideas toward resolution. Encourage everyone, without criticism, to contribute suggestions for action. Then sort through them, evaluating which are the most likely to be successful.

UTILIZING TEAMWORK

When building an organizational effort, you need teamwork. Through consensus, create a group plan of action that establishes reasonable priorities. Start with the least complex actions first. If problems arise between group members, try to keep the focus on the issue and away from personalities.

If your first steps do not get results, keep going down your action list. There are many group activities that can have a positive impact. Depending on the problem you have or action you want, you can set up community mediation, seek new legislation and lobby for it, plan a protest or march, get signatures on a petition, start a lawsuit, write a local ballot initiative, testify at public hearings, boycott a product, or take your case to the media.

Keeping lines of communication open in a group or among groups is challenging, but critical to the exchange of information and general cohesiveness. Set up a telephone tree in which each member takes responsibility to contact another. Consider using an answering service, creating a mailing list, or using an electronic message system.

Committed leadership will be essential to your organizing efforts. The time involved may well be extensive, but the results can be impressive.

FREEDOM OF INFORMATION

If information is power, the federal Freedom of Information Act (FOIA), is a power tool. In the belief that the government should not operate in secrecy, FOIA and similar state laws have been passed that entitle you to see government documents and records, with certain exceptions.

The government records that you are entitled to see include a broad range of reports, contracts, and policies that could give you insight on issues of local or national concern. Excepted records include many Defense Department documents that have been classified, personnel rules, private business information, bank records, and certain law enforcement records.

You can request to see government files by writing directly to the agency that holds the records. Put "FOIA Request" at the top of the letter. Identify the records as specifically as possible, including all facts you have about the place, time, events, or subject of the records. Since you may be charged a search fee and copying cost, ask to be advised of the expenses in advance. A fee may be waived if your request serves the public interest. Records of court proceedings are public in most cases and can be viewed without a FOIA request.

If your request is denied because the information falls under an exception, you can seek an agency review. A further denial will force you to go to court.

Voting Power

Voting power is a dynamic and, in a democracy, an essential means to getting action. Voting, of course, expresses your approval of particular policies or candidates. If you maximize your voting power, voting can also become a way to get change. Contact candidates while they are running and find out their position on issues of concern to you.

Get involved in campaigns. Help your candidates get petitions signed, raise money, and appeal to other voters. Voting is not limited to government—the political process includes parent-teacher associations, boards of condominiums, and employee committees. Consider running for office yourself.

After an election, keep in touch with candidates. See that they are invited to community events. Volunteer to be a member of a board or committee that is forming. Go to public information meetings.

When you need help with a problem, this groundwork will put you in a good position to approach the officeholder. You might have an idea for new legislation that will solve a problem. You can take a sample to your legislator. You or your legislator can get involved in lobbying, or trying to secure the support of other legislators who will be critical to the success of your project.

Winning at City Hall

You may not be able to "beat city hall," as the old phrase suggests, but by doing your homework, you can win a few battles there. Your local town government may be exactly where you need to go to get action on vital issues. Many essential decisions including those concerning schools, safety, garbage collection, environment, animals, welfare, property, and recreation, are made at the local

Writing an Effective Call for Action

After marshaling local support for a cause or reform that you feel strongly about, you can broaden your influence by writing personal action letters to legislators, corporate leaders, and others in influential positions. Here are some suggestions for writing a letter that can get results:

✔ *Be polite but firm.* Take the time to find the proper salutation for the person you are addressing: "The Honorable Carol Brown" for example, if you are writing your state senator. (Most dictionaries and etiquette books list accepted salutations.) Throughout the letter, maintain a polite tone, but make it clear that you know what you are talking about.

✔ *Be specific.* Tell the leader exactly what action you are seeking. If you are urging acceptance of a piece of legislation, use the bill number. Be brief and to the point.

✔ *Get personal.* Lend credibility to your request by giving details about yourself that explain why the action you seek is important to you. You may be a working mother, for example, urging support of funding for a local after-school center.

✔ *Be persuasive.* Make a clear argument in support of the action.

✔ *Don't be shy.* Ask the person you are addressing to make a specific commitment or response.

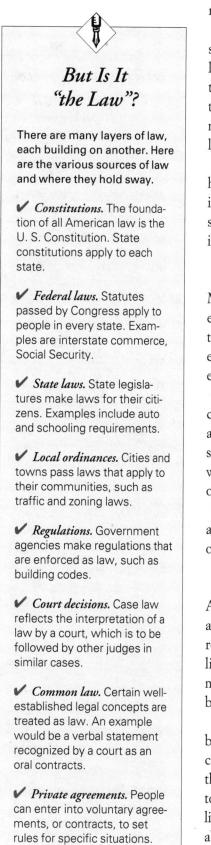

But Is It "the Law"?

There are many layers of law, each building on another. Here are the various sources of law and where they hold sway.

✔ *Constitutions.* The foundation of all American law is the U. S. Constitution. State constitutions apply to each state.

✔ *Federal laws.* Statutes passed by Congress apply to people in every state. Examples are interstate commerce, Social Security.

✔ *State laws.* State legislatures make laws for their citizens. Examples include auto and schooling requirements.

✔ *Local ordinances.* Cities and towns pass laws that apply to their communities, such as traffic and zoning laws.

✔ *Regulations.* Government agencies make regulations that are enforced as law, such as building codes.

✔ *Court decisions.* Case law reflects the interpretation of a law by a court, which is to be followed by other judges in similar cases.

✔ *Common law.* Certain well-established legal concepts are treated as law. An example would be a verbal statement recognized by a court as an oral contracts.

✔ *Private agreements.* People can enter into voluntary agreements, or contracts, to set rules for specific situations.

level. Local public officials such as the mayor and city council members are the elected officials who make those decisions.

To understand your local bureaucracy, and to find the person to help you, you might literally call city hall. Look in your local telephone book for a listing of city departments and call the one that seems to reflect most closely the problem in question. In addition, you might check with non-government organizations, such as the League of Women Voters and your local library, to find references for local agencies and officials.

Try to secure the name of the appropriate local official and his direct telephone number. When you call, if you get no immediate assistance, ask your contact for the name of a person who can help you. If you need to send a request in writing, fax it or deliver it personally to avoid mailroom delay.

HELPING POLITICIANS HELP YOU

Meeting face to face with elected officials is one of the most effective ways to get your message across and to convince them to take action on matters that are important to you. If you can establish a working relationship with a key person on the elected official's staff, it will be very helpful.

If you succeed in scheduling a meeting with the elected official or staff person, get two to five people to go with you. Pick a lead person to introduce the topic with a short prepared presentation. This is a one-sided forum: you have the floor. You will not have it long, so you must be convincing. Have copies of backup materials that you can leave.

If an elected official agrees with you, make yourself available for support by offering to speak at community meetings or to be available to the media for comment.

SUNSHINE AND OPEN-MEETING LAWS

Attending meetings of decision-makers is another way to create an impact. So-called "sunshine laws," in most places, require government agencies to make their decisions in public meetings. The laws entitle you to know when and where meetings by government agencies, boards, and councils are being held, and to attend if you wish to.

The presence of citizens at a meeting—whether a zoning board or a budget meeting—can change its course. Often you can corner bureaucrats or media people and make connections that might otherwise not be likely. In some cases, you can ask to be placed on the agenda to speak. You also can pass around literature that will educate decision-makers and other citizens about your issue. By making the effort to educate people about your concerns, you can stand up for your rights and make a difference in your community.

RESOURCES

General Sources

The following resources may be useful to you in researching and exercising many aspects of your rights. Within each chapter are additional resources relevant to the specific topic being discussed. Write or call the organizations for further information.

Adoptees' Liberty Movement Association (ALMA)
P.O. Box 727
Radio City Station
New York, N.Y. 10101
(212) 581-1568

A national membership organization, ALMA maintains a registry of persons searching for relatives separated by adoption and offers workshops on how to conduct a search.

American Association of Individual Investors
625 N. Michigan Avenue
Suite 1900
Chicago, Ill. 60611
(312) 280-0170

This nonprofit organization helps individuals develop investment philosophies based on their objectives and capabilities. Publishes a newsletter, an annual strategy guide, and a number of other publications.

American Association of Retired Persons (AARP)
601 E Street, NW
Washington, D.C. 20049
(202) 434-2247
(800) 424-3410

This national organization for seniors offers members benefits such as group health plans, travel services, publications, and information on a vast range of topics including eldercare and grandparenting.

American Financial Services Association
919 18th Street, NW
Washington, D.C. 20006
(202) 296-5544
(800) 633-6348

This association assists members with financial services, publishes booklets, and provides seminars on money management.

American Society for Reproductive Medicine
1209 Montgomery Highway
Birmingham, Ala. 35216-2800
(205) 978-5000

A nonprofit organization, the society provides information on reproductive medicine, including a list of clinics practicing in-vitro fertilization according to its standards.

Better Business Bureaus Council of Better Business Bureaus, Inc.
4200 Wilson Boulevard, Suite 800
Arlington, Va. 22203
(703) 276-0100

This national organization maintains a databank of complaints about businesses, and occasionally goes to court on behalf of consumers. Call to complain, or find out if a business has complaints against it.

Centers for Disease Control and Prevention (CDC)
1600 Clifton Road, NE
Atlanta, Ga. 30333
(404) 639-3311
CDC Travelers Hotline
(404) 332-4559

This federal agency provides leadership and direction in the prevention and control of diseases and other health emergencies. The CDC Travelers Hotline gives information about immunization and international health requirements for travelers.

Choice in Dying
200 Varick Street, Room 1001
New York, N.Y. 10014
(800) 989-9455

This national nonprofit organization offers guidance regarding advance directives including living will forms for each state.

Consumer Credit Counseling Services
c/o National Foundation
   for Consumer Credit
8611 Second Avenue, Suite 100
Silver Spring, Md. 20910
(301) 589-5600
National Referral Line
(800) 388-2227

This national organization advises individuals on how to deal with debt. Call for the address of the office nearest you.

Consumer Information Center-Document Distribution Center
P.O. Box 100
Pueblo, Colo. 81002
(719) 948-3334

This center helps federal agencies develop and distribute information of interest to consumers. Call to order The Consumer Resource Handbook, or for a catalog of free government publications.

Consumer Product Safety Commission (CPSC)
5401 Westbard Avenue
Bethesda, Md. 20207
(800) 638-CPSC

This federal agency accepts complaints about unsafe products and provides legal information and consumer tips.

Credit Union National Association
805 15th Street, NW, Suite 300
Washington, D.C. 20005
(800) 356-9655

This trade association represents 92 percent of the credit unions in the country and promotes credit union membership and services.

Department of Veterans Affairs (VA)
810 Vermont Avenue, NW
Washington, D.C. 20420
(800) 827-1000

The VA administers veterans programs and benefits, including educational benefits, home mortgage guarantees, medical care, disability, and burial benefits.

Equal Employment Opportunity Commission (EEOC)
1801 L Street, NW
Washington, D.C. 20507
(800) 669-4000

This federal agency enforces employment regulations related to discrimination.

Federal Communication Commission (FCC)
Public Service Division
1919 M street, NW
Washington, D.C. 20554
(202) 632-7000

The FCC creates and enforces rules on interstate and international communications, including radio and television broadcasts, telephone communications, and computerized transmissions.

Federal Deposit Insurance Corporation (FDIC)
Office of Consumer Affairs
550 17th Street, NW
Washington, D.C. 20429
(800) 934-3342

This government agency provides insurance coverage for bank deposits, and supplies information on deposit insurance, consumer protection matters, and financial data on FDIC-insured institutions.

Federal Information Center
P.O. Box 600-0600
Cumberland, Md. 21501
(301) 722-9098

The Federal Information Center is a national system of telephone numbers that provides referrals, assistance, or answers to questions regarding government-related activities such as applying for a passport, registering a copyright, or locating a federal publication. Check the Blue Pages of your telephone directory for the number of your local office.

Federal Reserve System
Division of Consumer and Community Affairs
20th and C Street, NW
Washington, D.C. 20551
Fraud and Abuse Hotline
(800) 827-3340

The Federal Reserve's consumer division receives complaints and answers questions about financial institutions within the Federal Reserve System.

Federal Trade Commission (FTC)
Public References Branch
Room 130
Pennsylvania Avenue
at 6th Street, NW
Washington, D.C. 20580
(202) 326-2222

This federal agency handles complaints about credit cards, credit bureaus, consumer credit problems, deceptive advertising, and fraudulent marketing practices.

Food and Drug Administration (FDA)
Consumer Complaints Division
5600 Fishers Lane
Rockville, Md. 20857
(301) 443-1240

The FDA answers questions and protects consumers against impure and unsafe foods, drugs, and cosmetics. Call or write to register a complaint or make an inquiry.

Health Care Financing Administration
U.S. Department of Health and Human Services
6325 Security Boulevard
Baltimore, Md. 21207
(800) 772-1213
Medicare Hotline
(800) 638-6833

This federal agency handles complaints about Medicare fraud, provides general Medicare information, and publishes The Medicare Handbook.

Institute of Certified Financial Planners
7600 East Eastman Avenue
Suite 301
Denver, Colo. 80231-4397
(800) 282-7526

This association establishes and maintains professionalism in the field of financial planning and maintains a free referral service of certified planners.

Internal Revenue Service (IRS)
(800) TAX-FORM

Call this number to order tax forms and IRS publications
(800) 829-1040

Call this number for answers to individual tax questions and for the locations of your regional IRS offices.

International Association for Medical Assistance to Travelers (IAMAT)
417 Center Street
Lewiston, N.Y. 14092
(716) 754-4883

A division of the Foundation for the Support of International Medical Training, this association makes 24-hour medical care available to travelers throughout the world and will provide names and numbers of English- and French-speaking physicians overseas.

International Franchise Association
1350 New York Avenue, NW
Suite 900
Washington, D.C. 20005
(800) 543-1038
Fax on Command:
(202) 628-3432

This international association of franchise owners provides information by mail, phone, or fax; educates consumers; and conducts workshops on purchasing, starting, and running a franchise.

Legal Counsel for the Elderly
601 E Street NW
Building A, 4th Floor
Washington, D.C. 20049
(202) 434-2170

This organization provides free legal services to Washington, D.C., residents over age 60, and backup assistance, legal services, and nursing-home advocacy for the elderly across the nation.

Medical Information Bureau (MIB)
P.O. Box 105
Essex Station
Boston, Mass. 02112
(617) 426-3660

A consortium of insurance companies, MIB prevents fraud in medical and life insurance businesses by checking the information that consumers submit when they apply for coverage. Call or write for more information and a free copy of your file.

National Association of Enrolled Agents
200 Orchard Ridge Drive, Suite 302
Gaithersburg, Md. 20878
(301) 212-9608
Fax: (301) 990-1611
24 Hour Referral Line:
(800) 424-4339

This association provides consumers with tax assistance by telephone, referrals from among its 8,300 members, and informs the public of its rights and obligations under tax regulations.

National Adoption Information Clearinghouse
5640 Nicholson Lane, Suite 300
Rockville, Md. 20852
(301) 231-6512

This organization provides information on all aspects of adoption including the adoption of children with special needs, federal and state adoption law, and private and public adoption agencies near you.

National Consumer Law Center
18 Tremont Street, Suite 400
Boston, Mass. 02108-2336
(617) 523-8010
Fax: (617) 523-7398
The center provides references to lawyers and other legal services that specifically handle consumer-related problems and issues.

National Consumer's League
815 15th Street, NW, Suite 928-N
Washington, D.C. 20005
(202) 639-8140
National Fraud Information
   Hotline: (800) 876-7060
This nonprofit organization handles complaints concerning consumer fraud.

National Eldercare Locator
9401 Lee Highway, Suite 402
Fairfax, Va. 22031
(800) 677-1118
This service provides information on assisted living facilities and nursing homes.

**National Employment
Lawyers Association**
600 Harrison Street
San Francisco, Calif. 94107
(415) 227-4655
The association makes referrals of appropriate attorneys to those in need of representation in job-related disputes.

**National Health
Information Centers**
Office of Disease Prevention
and Health Promotion
P.O. Box 1133
Washington, D.C. 20013
(301) 565-4167
(800) 336-4797
The centers put consumers and health professionals in touch with the organizations best able to answer their health questions.

National Hospice Organization
901 North Moore Street, Suite 901
Arlington, Va. 22209
(800) 658-8898
This association provides information about hospice care and gives referrals to local programs.

**National Insurance Consumer
Organization (NICO)**
(800) 942-4242
A nonprofit organization, NICO answers consumers' questions about buying insurance, and provides direction for coping with problems with insurance companies.

National Insurance Crime Bureau
10330 South Roberts Road
Palos Hill, Ill. 60465
(708) 430-2430
(800) TEL-NICB
This nonprofit organization investigates insurance fraud.

National Victim Center
2111 Wilson Boulevard, Suite 300
Arlington, Va. 22201
(703) 276-2880
FAX (703) 276-2889
(800) FYI-CALL
This nonprofit organization provides information on victims' issues, rights, and available programs and services at the local and national level to victims of violent crimes.

Office of Consumer Affairs (OCA)
Department of Commerce
Room 5718
Washington, D.C. 20230
(202) 482-5001
The OCA refers consumer complaints of all types to the proper source for action.

**Occupational Safety and Health
Administration (OSHA)**
U.S. Department of Labor
200 Constitution Avenue, NW
Washington, D.C. 20210
(202) 219-8061
OSHA develops and administers safety and health standards in the workplace, and refers consumer complaints about safety and health to the appropriate office.

**Office of Fair Housing
and Equal Opportunity**
Department of Housing And
Urban Development (HUD)
Room 5100
451 Seventh Street, SW
Washington, D.C . 20410
(202) 708-4252
Housing Discrimination Hotline:
(800) 669-9777
This agency administers and enforces federal civil rights laws related to housing and community development. Call the hotline or your regional office to file a complaint or for information on housing discrimination.

Office of the Inspector General
Department of Health
and Human Services
P.O. Box 23489
Washington, D.C. 20026
HHS-OIG-Hotline:
(800) 368-5779
The Inspector General's office of HHS accepts complaints about fraud within programs of the Department of Health and Human Services.

Office of Overseas Citizens Service
Department of State
2201 C Street, NW
Washington, D.C. 20520-4818
(202) 647-5225
This agency provides emergency help to U.S. citizens abroad and information about health and safety for travelers.

**Office of Thrift Supervision
Consumer Programs**
1700 C Street, NW
Washington, D.C. 20552
(202) 906-6238
(800) 842-6929
This agency handles consumer complaints about savings organizations.

**Pension and Welfare Benefits
Administration**
Department of Labor
200 Constitution Avenue, NW
Washington, D.C. 20210
(202) 219-8233
This division of the Department of Labor manages pension and welfare benefits, answers questions or complaints, and will provide a copy of your employer's Summary Plan Description for your employer-sponsored pension plan.

Pension Rights Center
918 16th Street, NW
Washington, D.C. 20006
(202) 296-3776
A public interest group, the center protects and promotes worker's and retirees' pension rights, publishes booklets about pension laws, and operates a lawyer referral service.

**Small Business Administration
(SBA)**
Washington Office Center
409 Third Street, SW
Washington, D.C. 20024
(800) U-ASK-SBA
The SBA provides publications, videotapes, and counseling on financing and running a small business in the United States.

Social Security Administration
U.S. Department of Health
and Human Services
6401 Security Building
Baltimore, Md. 21235
(800) 772-1213
This agency manages the collection of Social Security taxes and the dispensation of benefits. Call the 800-number or check your local telephone directory for the office nearest you.

U.S. Government Printing Offices

Superintendent of Documents
Washington, D.C. 20402
(202) 512-1800
Fax Watch: (202) 512-1716

This office provides government publications to consumers. Call or fax for a list of the government bookstores across the country, a list of free publications, and information regarding ordering.

Women's Bureau
Work and Family Clearinghouse

U.S. Department of Labor
200 Constitution Avenue, NW
Room S3306
Washington, D.C. 20210
(202) 219-4486

This agency handles complaints or questions involving women in the work force.

Auto Helplines

The following organizations are useful for drivers and car owners.

AARP Motoring Plan Line

(800) 334-3300

This division provides useful travel information for AARP members

American Automobile Association (AAA)

100 AAA Drive
Heathrow, Fla. 32746-5063
(404) 444-7000
(800) 222-4357

A federation of automobile clubs, the AAA provides domestic and foreign travel services, emergency road services, insurance, and information on auto safety and related topics.

AUTOLINE
Division of the Better Business Bureau

(800) 955-5100

This service arbitrates or mediates problems between auto owners and participating auto manufacturers.

Center for Auto Safety

2001 S Street, NW, Suite 410
Washington, D.C. 20009
(202) 328-7700

The center is a nonprofit organization that disseminates auto safety and related information based largely on consumer complaints.

National Highway Traffic Safety Administration (NHTSA)

400 Seventh Street
Washington, D.C. 20590
(202) 366-0123
(800) 424-9393 Safety Hotline

This agency gives information on recalls, child safety seats, crash test results, and how to get NHTSA literature.

Credit Bureaus

The following are the largest credit bureaus in the United States. You may be on file at one or all of them. To get a copy of your report, send the bureau your name, address (and others you have had for the past five years), date of birth, and Social Security number.

Equifax Credit Information Services

Consumer Relations
P.O. Box 740-2411
Atlanta, Ga. 30374-0241
(800) 685-1111

Call to order a credit report. Fees vary.

Trans Union National Disclosure Center

Consumer Relations Department
P.O. Box 119001
Chicago, Ill. 60611
(312) 408-1050

For a copy of your report, send a check made out to "Trans Union Corporation" for $8.

TRW Consumer's Assistance

P.O. Box 2350
Chatsworth, Calif. 91313-2350
(800) 392-1122

TRW provides one free credit report per year.

Insurance Raters

The following organizations rate insurance companies on their claims paying ability. Check your local telephone directory for regional branches.

A.M. Best Company

Ambest Road
Oldwick, N. J. 08858
(900) 555-2378

Consumers will be charged $2.95 to place a call, plus $4.95 per rating.

Duff & Phelps, Inc.

55 East Monroe Street, Suite 3500
Chicago, Ill. 60603
(312) 629-3833

Duff & Phelps ratings are free of charge.

Moody's Investors Service

99 Church Street
New York, N.Y. 10007-2701
(212) 553-0300

Moody's provides up to three ratings per year without charge.

Standard & Poor's Corporation

25 Broadway
New York, N.Y. 10004
(212) 208-8000

Standard & Poor's ratings are free of charge.

Weiss Ratings, Inc.

P.O. Box 109665
Palm Beach Gardens, Fla. 33410
(800) 289-9222

Weiss Ratings charges $15 per rating

Mutual Fund Raters

The following rating organizations analyze and evaluate mutual funds. Write or call for information.

Morningstar

225 West Wacker Drive
Chicago, Ill. 60606
(800) 820-8082

This private organization publishes "Morningstar Mutual Funds" and several other mutual-fund publications, software products, and a newsletter.

Value Line

220 East 42 Street
New York, N.Y. 10017
(212) 907-1500
Fax: (212) 818-9748
(800) 223-0818

This private organization publishes "The Value Line Mutual Fund Survey" and several other investment publications.

INDEX